THE PRESIDENT AND THE PARTIES

THE PRESIDENT AND THE PARTIES

---

*The Transformation of the American
Party System since the New Deal*

SIDNEY M. MILKIS

New York   Oxford
OXFORD UNIVERSITY PRESS
1993

Oxford University Press

Oxford   New York   Toronto
Delhi   Bombay   Calcutta   Madras   Karachi
Kuala Lumpur   Singapore   Hong Kong   Tokyo
Nairobi   Dar es Salaam   Cape Town
Melbourne   Auckland   Madrid

and associated companies in
Berlin   Ibadan

Library of Congress Cataloging-in-Publication Data
Milkis, Sidney.
The president and the parties : the transformation of the
American party system since the New Deal / Sidney M. Milkis.
p. cm.   Includes index.
ISBN 0-19-506620-0
ISBN 0-19-508425-X (pbk)
1. Political parties—United States—History—20th century.
2. Executive power—United States—History—20th century.
3. United States—Politics and government—20th century.
JK2261.M55 1993   324.273'09'04—dc20
92-42965

1   3   5   7   9   8   6   4   2

Printed in the United States of America
on acid-free paper

To my parents,
Howard L. Milkis and Lucille Singer—
with love and gratitude

Preface

The publication of this book marks the completion of a decade of research and writing about the New Deal and its legacy for the presidency and the party system. The project began as an effort to build upon the seminal work on political realignments by V. O. Key and Walter Dean Burnham. I hoped to shed light on the New Deal realignment, which had not received as much attention as I believed it deserved in the party development literature. By the late 1970s, most political scientists and historians focused on what they took to be the decline of party in their work, emphasizing how changes in electoral politics either at the turn of the century or during the late 1960s undermined the role of parties in organizing elections and, more fundamentally, in cultivating the perceptions and habits that connected the public and private orders in the United States. My work was informed by the premise that this work on political parties, as exciting and sophisticated as it was, tended to be incomplete in important ways—that it relegated the party politics of the New Deal to the status of an interregnum, to, as Professor Burnham put it, "a brief, if massive deviation in the long secular decline of political parties."

In contrast, my work on parties started from the premise that the New Deal is properly viewed as the defining moment in setting the tone of twentieth century politics in the United States. A decade of research has not disabused me of that notion. Indeed, I have come to appreciate more fully the work of a number of brilliant and talented historians—most notably, Frank Freidel, Barry Karl, William Leuchtenburg, and Arthur Schlesinger, Jr.—who have found the New Deal period worthy of a lifetime's consideration. I cannot lay claim to the detailed knowledge of this generation of New Deal historians; this book is a study in political science rather than history. As my friend and distinguished colleague Morton Keller once put it to me, "You political scientists seeking to understand history do good work, but you have one serious problem—you have theories!" I plead guilty to this soft impeachment; but I have tried not to slight historical detail in making more general arguments. Indeed, some of my political science colleagues have accused me of taking history *too* seriously. My only hope is that I have written a book that will not frustrate but speak to both historians and political scientists, for I have only begun to address questions that cannot be tackled meaningfully by adhering to conventional disciplinary canons.

My arguments about New Deal party politics are developed in the first part of this volume. I try to make the case that Roosevelt's party leadership and the New Deal mark the culmination of efforts, which begin in the Progressive era, to loosen the grip of partisan politics on the councils of power, with a view to strengthening national administrative capacities and extending the programmatic commitments of the federal government. The American party system was forged on the anvil of Jeffersonian principles and thus wedded to constitutional arrangements such as legislative supremacy and a strict construction of the federal government's authority that were designed to constrain national administrative power. The origins and organizing principles of the American party system established it as a force against the creation of the modern "state." The progressive commitment to building such a state—that is, a national political power with expansive programmatic responsibilities—meant that the party system either had to be weakened or reconstructed.

Theodore Roosevelt and Woodrow Wilson, both of whom sought to use the presidency as the cockpit of national leadership for political and social reform, began to turn away from traditional partisan organizations as vehicles for campaigning and shaping the direction of national policy; their struggles against the constraints of party leadership anticipated the rise of a modern executive who would rely on the executive office and the national bureaucracy rather than the party to fulfill these political and governmental tasks. With the long reign of Franklin Roosevelt, this shift from party to administrative politics became an enduring part of the American political system; he articulated a public philosophy and oversaw institutional changes that ushered in an administrative republic, a polity in which control over programs and policies of the national bureaucracy became a major, if not the most important, prize in modern American politics.

The second part of the book traces the legacy of the Roosevelt "revolution" through the presidency of George Bush, revealing that the pattern of executive leadership established during the 1930s continued to operate irrespective of the president's party and philosophy. Even conservative Republican presidents, such as Richard Nixon and Ronald Reagan, were loath to accept a limited executive role; indeed, they embraced the New Deal concept of presidential power with alacrity, in some cases, with less reserve than their progressive forbears. That Republican presidents have for the most part confronted a situation of divided rule, with the Democrats controlling Congress, has reinforced the need to strengthen executive power as a means to conservative ends. It appears to me, then, that the characterization of the Reagan "revolution" as an engagement to "get government off our backs" is inappropriate. The opposition to liberal form, it seems, ended not in a challenge to the state that Roosevelt built, but in a battle for its services.

The acceptance of a modern concept of presidential power both changed party politics and made them less important in the scheme of things. The elevation of the presidency and administrative agencies to a position of central importance recast parties, so that they were less focused on patronage and local government and more attuned to national politics and programmatic concerns. At the same time, parties were more likely to be defined by presidential politics and governance, thus losing their identity as collective organizations with a past and a future. My sense is that the modern executive became the vital center of a more national and energetic national state, but at the expense of weakening valued representative institutions that helped cultivate a connection between government and society.

The modern executive that arose from the ashes of traditional parties was hardly imperial, as scholars and pundits frequently asserted by the end of Richard Nixon's ill-fated reign. Put simply, "modern" presidents bask in the honors of the more powerful and prominent office that emerged from the New Deal, but find themselves navigating a treacherous and lonely path, subject to a volatile political process that makes popular and enduring achievement unlikely. As the conclusion to this volume argues, the fragile state of modern executive leadership reflects the frayed link between the government and society, a crisis of citizenship that represents the most pressing challenge as America approaches the twenty-first century.

I finished this book in the midst of the 1992 campaign—as I write, a new president, Arkansas Governor Bill Clinton, the first Democrat to win a national election in twelve years, prepares to occupy the White House. The Democrats not only captured the presidency, but managed to retain control of both congressional chambers, ending twelve years of divided party rule in American politics. Soon after the election, one of my most respected colleagues warned me that my decade of labor might be rendered moot by the 1992 election and its aftermath; that Clinton's victory marked a renewal of the Democratic party and promised to ameliorate the institutional estrangement between presidents and parties. In truth, the 1992 election contains both optimistic and pessimistic portents for the modern presidency. Although the Democrats ran an effective campaign and Clinton skillfully, and sometimes boldly, addressed his party's liabilities, the election results showed that fundamental conflicts continue to divide Americans, even as they seem united in their dissatisfaction with the working of their government. Clinton won only forty-three percent of the vote, roughly the same percentage of the total vote failed Democratic candidates had received in the previous three elections; and the strong showing of independent candidate H. Ross Perot, who won nineteen percent of the popular vote (the strongest showing of an independent candidate since Theodore Roosevelt's 1912 Bull Moose campaign) reflected the continuing decline of the electorate's attachment to the two-party system. Perot's campaign, if I can put it so, suggests that the chickens hatched by the New Deal might be coming home to roost.

In a brief postscript I suggest how the 1992 election underscores the changes in American politics described in this book—whether or not it provides an escape from the more worrisome political and constitutional developments wrought by the New Deal is another matter. Resolving the dilemmas of the New Deal political order will not be as easy as my colleague has suggested, however. Were the puzzles created by the New Deal so easily solved, I suspect that the research and writing I have engaged in over the past several years would have been far less exciting and challenging.

In completing this book, I incurred a huge intellectual debt. I am blessed with several gifted and generous colleagues who read the manuscript in various stages and offered thoughtful and honest criticism. The book is far better for their efforts: Harold F. Bass, Donald Brand, Walter Dean Burnham, Marthe Chandler, Robert Faulkner, Fred I. Greenstein, Robert Harmel, James Hollifield, Eileen Mc-Donagh, W. Carey McWilliams, Jerome M. Mileur, James A. Morone, Howard Reiter, Francis Rourke, Theda Skocpol, Abigail Thernstrom, David Truman, John Kenneth White, and Aaron Wildavsky. In addition, I want to thank the anonymous readers who reviewed the manuscript for Oxford University Press, as well as Valerie Aubrey and David Roll for the patient and intelligent editorial assistance they provided in bringing this book to fruition. Stanley George guided the book through the production process with skill and enthusiasm. It is a pleasure, at long last, to offer my gratitude to the Mazer Faculty Fund at Brandeis University, the Institute for Educational Affairs, the National Endowment for the Humanities, and, especially, the John M. Olin Foundation for financial support that made it possible to carry out such an ambitious and prolonged project.

I am also indebted to my graduate students whose interest in my work proved to be an essential and almost daily dose of encouragement. Special thanks are owed to Gina Abshere and Kevin McMahon for their invaluable support in carrying out the research for the book. Daniel Tichenor also helped with the research; and he gave the draft manuscript a thorough reading, offering analytical and editorial commentary that helped get me through the agonizing task of rewriting and cutting the manuscript.

I cannot even begin to thank the special colleagues, friends and family who saw me through this project from start to finish. Thomas Skladony, of the American Enterprise Institute, helped make my frequent research trips to Washington economical, productive, and great fun. Michael Nelson, of Rhodes College, expressed an interest in my work at a critical time, supporting my hope that I was engaged in a worthwhile endeavor; and he offered detailed commentary on the first, unwieldy draft of the manuscript that greatly improved the writing and clarified the arguments of the book. Marc Landy, of Boston College, and R. Shep Melnick, my colleague in the Brandeis Politics Department, carried on a daily, stimulating dialogue with me about the New Deal and its aftermath that often made "days at the office" joyful experiences. Richard A. Harris, of Rutgers University has been putting up with my moods and prolix text since graduate school, yet he has never wavered in his friendship—from our collaboration, which produced two books of which I am proud, I began to understand what happened to the New Deal during the 1960s and 1970s. Martin Levin, director of the Gordon Public Policy Center at Brandeis University, has taught me the true meaning of the word colleague—he provided me with aid and comfort in the form of office space, research support, and a most stimulating environment in which to work. Elaine Hermann typed most of the manuscript; without her skill, perseverance, and sense of humor, the book never would have been finished.

When I arrived at Brandeis University seven years ago, I was not quite prepared for the friendship and counsel of Roy C. Macridis, who both delighted and chastened me with his piquant commentary on my work. Roy died just before the book was finished—his students, colleagues, and friends all miss him terribly.

The tasks involved in seeing this project through would have been unbearably lonely without my family—Carol, and our three children, Lauren, David, and Jonathan. They have been remarkably tolerant of the long hours at the office and the lengthy stays away from home that have been a necessary part of the research for and writing of this book; and after a day of struggling with sources or text, I could always look forward to coming home, where they would quickly show me that my book was not the most important thing in the world. I know they are happier than I that Dad's book is finally finished.

Waltham, Massachusetts   SIDNEY M. MILKIS
December, 1992

Contents

THE PRESIDENT AND THE PARTIES

1

Introduction

On June 24, 1938, Franklin Delano Roosevelt indicated that he intended to participate in the forthcoming Democratic primary elections for Congress. In a national radio address—one of his fabled "fireside chats"—the president told the nation that as "head of the Democratic party, . . . charged with the responsibility of carrying out the definitely liberal declaration of principles set forth in the 1936 Democratic platform," he had "every right" to become involved in the forthcoming primary contests where these principles were at stake between candidates.[1] Roosevelt's message amounted to a public appeal for voters to defeat conservative Democrats, most of them from the southern and border states, who had joined Republicans to defeat or seriously compromise key elements of the administration's program during the 75th Congress, the volatile legislative session that followed the landslide Democratic victory of 1936.

The most dramatic moment of FDR's campaign that summer against recalcitrant Democrats occurred in August when he made a visit to his "other home state" of Georgia. On August 8, Roosevelt endorsed United States Attorney Lawrence Camp for the Senate in a speech at Barnesville, as the conservative incumbent Walter George listened from the same podium. FDR insisted that he felt no personal animosity toward George—he hoped they would "always be good personal friends"—but he was "impelled to make it clear that on most public questions" he and the Georgia Senator did not "speak the same language." The president's "responsibility," Roosevelt told his audience, required that "there be cooperation between members of my own party and myself—cooperation, in other words, within the majority party, between one branch of government, the legislative branch, and the head of the other branch, the Executive." Such cooperation, the President insisted, "was one of the essentials of the party form of government."[2]

Roosevelt's participation in the 1938 primary campaigns, which involved him in one gubernatorial and several congressional contests, represented, as one columnist wrote that October, an unprecedented attempt by a president "to stamp his policies upon his party."[3] Such intervention was not really unprecedented; in

3

particular, William Howard Taft and Woodrow Wilson had made limited efforts to cleanse their parties of recalcitrant members. Yet Roosevelt's campaign took place on an unprecedented scale and, unlike previous efforts, made no attempt to work through the regular party organization. His action was viewed as a shocking departure from the norm: The press labeled it "the purge."

Roosevelt considered the designation of his primary campaign as a "purge" to be a slur on his actions as leader of the Democratic party. Yet it was a slur deeply rooted in historic American views about both the party's place in the political system and the executive's relationship to partisan disputes; indeed, FDR entered the partisan fray belatedly and reluctantly, for as he himself admitted in a radio address to Young Democratic Clubs of America on August 24, 1935, "Whatever his party affiliation might be, the President of the United States, . . . even when addressing the young citizens of his own party, should speak as President of the whole people." Although the Presidency carried with it the leadership of the political party, Roosevelt noted, it also carried with it a far higher obligation, that is, "the duty of analyzing and setting forth national needs and ideals which transcended and cut across all of party affiliation."[4]

When Roosevelt's "purge" campaign ended unsuccessfully, having failed to weaken the position of conservatives in the Democratic party, the New York *Times* columnist Arthur Krock claimed that the president "has demonstrated in the most public way that the American system and tradition are stronger than he is."[5] In fact, however, the controversy that surrounded Roosevelt's attempt to stamp his policies upon his party is best understood as a dramatic example of the difficulty presidents face in reconciling the roles of party leader and chief executive.

The purge campaign and other developments in partisan politics during the 1930s resulted in a worsening of the already difficult relationship between presidents and parties. Roosevelt's party leadership anticipated, in part, the critics of the party system of the late 1940s and 1950s, who advocated a more "responsible" party system composed of national policy-oriented organizations capable of carrying out platforms or proposals presented to the people during the course of an election.[6] FDR and other ardent New Dealers wanted to overcome the state and local orientation of the party system, which was suited to congressional primacy and poorly organized for progressive action on the part of the national government, and to establish a national, executive-oriented party, which would be more suitably organized for the expression of national purposes. Unless such a development took place, Roosevelt argued, the Democratic and Republican parties would be merely "Tweedledum and Tweedledee to each other." The system of party responsibility, he argued, "required that one of its parties be the liberal party and the other be the conservative party."[7]

After the purge campaign, however, Roosevelt concluded that the public good and practical politics demanded that partisan politics be *transcended* rather than *reconstructed*. In fact, his party discipline was directed less at party government than at administrative government. Many of the partisan efforts sought by the New Dealers were directed at legislating procedural reforms that would enhance the capacity and independence of the executive branch in the making of public policy.

The extensive effort to achieve a modernization of public administration between 1936 and 1940 was an important part of this project. Believing that a strong, independent executive had a more secure place in the American tradition than "responsible" party government, Roosevelt aimed at building a more progressive form of government within the presidency rather than through a more permanent link between the executive and legislature. This required extending the personal and nonpartisan responsibility of the president to the detriment of collective and partisan responsibility.

Thus, the Democratic party became during the late 1930s the party to end all parties. Under Roosevelt's leadership, it was dedicated to a program that eventually lessened the importance of the two-party system and established a modern executive as the principal focus of representative government in the United States.[8] This book offers an account of this transformation of American politics, an examination of its legacy, and an interpretation of its meaning.

The Modern Presidency and Party Constraints

The essential incompatibility between the modern presidency and party politics is attributable partly to the origins and organizing principles of party government. In English history, the legitimation of party grew out of an effort to curb and regulate the power of the executive.[9] Similarly, Martin Van Buren's efforts to legitimate party competition in the United States during the 1830s rested on an effort to control presidential ambition.[10]

The defense of parties in the Anglo-American tradition conceived of the legislature, which epitomizes public deliberation and choice (the "force of persuasion"), as the preeminent representative institution. But, as Alexander Hamilton argued in his defense of a unified and energetic executive power, legislatures are apt to move slowly, defy consensus, and fail to recognize, let alone protect the society from, peril. At first glance, then, the executive is not only a more efficient institution than the legislature, but more accountable as well.[11] Still, executive power is most needed at times that render accountability most difficult—when differences of opinion must give way to promptitude of decision and action. The people would need a representative legislature to control a representative executive; moreover, this control of presidential prerogative required party politics. As Wilson Carey McWilliams has noted, presidents can be strong, indeed, best display their personal qualities, "above party." By contrast, "Congress cannot be effective, let alone powerful, without the institution of party. . . . A legislature can rival the executive's claims to public confidence only to the extent that it is accountable, which presumes a principle of *collective* responsibility."[12]

The inherent tension between executive power and party politics is exacerbated in the United States by the structure of government, as well as history and tradition. Parliamentary government elsewhere—most notably in Great Britain but in other Western democracies as well—has provided a link between the executive and legislative party government. The American Constitution, with its division and separation of powers, makes difficult the development of party unity in support of strong executive action; the possibility of linking an energetic executive and party politics is further discouraged in the United States, however, by the *interpretation* of the Constitution that gave rise to the American party system.

Modern party politics in Great Britain and Europe began at the end of the nineteenth century with the effort to reform a state that presumed the existence of strong national controls; in contrast, American political parties matured as the cornerstone of a political order that celebrated democratic individualism and presumed the absence of centralized administrative authority. Both the Democratic and Republican parties were wedded to Jeffersonian principles, dedicated to limiting the role of the national government. Thomas Jefferson, with the invaluable support of James Madison, founded the Democratic–Republican party to rescue the Constitution from a program that would, in their understanding, vitiate popular rule. As Secretary of the Treasury in the Washington administration, Hamilton had proposed an ambitious program, based upon a liberal—"elastic"—interpretation of the national government's powers, that anticipated a significant expansion of executive power. The power of the more democratic and decentralizing institutions—Congress and state governments—were necessarily subordinated in this enterprise. In order to keep power close enough to the people for republican government to prevail, Jefferson and Madison formulated a public philosophy in support of a strict interpretation of the national government's powers. This also became a *party* doctrine, and the principal task of the triumphant Democratic–Republicans after the critical election of 1800 was to dismantle Hamilton's program for a strong executive. The purpose of presidential party leadership in the Jeffersonian mold was to capture the executive office in order to contain and minimize its constitutional potential. As James Piereson has observed in his study of party government in the United States:

> Out of this original clash there developed in America the tension between party politics, on the one hand, and governmental centralization and bureaucracy, on the other. . . . The leaders of the original [Democratic–]Republican party attacked Hamilton's program, and the politics on which it rested, by organizing voters, and by appealing to them on the basis of republican principles, which were inherently decentralizing and hostile to administration, as was the very process of party politics.[13]

The emergence of political parties in the United States, then, grew out of a struggle to curb the power of the executive, especially with respect to expanding national administrative power; accordingly, they have not served as a *link* but as a "wall of separation" between government and society. Jefferson apparently did not expect ongoing party competition to become a permanent part of the American political system. But during the Jacksonian era, Van Buren, supported by a forceful and popular president, defended the party as a legitimate constitutional institution, one that would take its shape from the constitutional principles of Jefferson. It is not surprising, therefore, that the partisan organizations that arose during the Jacksonian era—the Democratic and Whig parties—assumed a form that centered partisan responsibility and practices in the Congress and state governments.[14] American political parties were organized as popular institutions, but they were first organized at a time when popular rule meant the limitation of government power.

The form of party organization that was legitimized during the Jacksonian era endured well into the twentieth century. Even the rise of the Republican party during the 1850s as a result of the slavery controversy, and the subsequent demise of the Whigs, did not alter the essential characteristics of the party system in the United States; and these characteristics—decentralized organization and hostility to administrative centralization—restrained rather than facilitated executive power.[15]

The enduring strength of the party system in the United States can be explained by the fact that its characteristics have embodied the traditional American hostility to administrative centralization. Tocqueville believed that the celebration of equality in democratic society required centralization of authority, but he noticed that certain "peculiar and accidental" causes in the American case, especially the lack of feudal tradition, "diverted" the United States from centralized government. "The American destiny is unusual," he wrote. "[T]hey have taken from the English aristocracy the idea of individual rights and a taste for local freedom, and they have been able to keep both these things because they have no aristocracy to fight."[16] In effect, the strength of party organizations in the United States can be explained by the role they performed as the principal institutional means by which democracy in America was allied to decentralization, an alliance that held until the advent of the New Deal and the modern presidency. Before the New Deal, presidents who sought to exercise executive power expansively or perceived a need for the expansion of the national government's power were thwarted, as Stephen Skowronek has noted, "by the tenacity of this highly mobilized, highly competitive, and locally oriented party democracy."[17]

To be sure, there are conflicting and compensating aspects to the American tradition of party politics. Although based on Jeffersonian principles dedicated to decentralized government, the party system has provided presidents with a stable basis of popular support, and, episodically, during critical partisan realignments, with the opportunity to achieve national reform. The executive, through the partisan electoral process, has become the focal point for the usually separated branches of the Constitution to combine during such times, resulting in sharp departures from the prevailing principles, institutions, and policies of government.[18]

The New Deal realignment was the first to challenge fundamentally the partisan emphasis of previous watershed changes in American politics. Although similar in many ways to previous critical partisan chapters in American history, the momentous political developments of the 1930s marked a fundamental change in the relationship between president and party. Prior to the New Deal, none of the programs to which the electorate had subscribed during a realignment had called for a substantial exercise of executive power. Indeed, the thrust of the first realigning movement, which culminated with the Democratic–Republican victory over the Federalists in the election of 1800, had been explicitly in the opposite direction. Whereas the "Revolution of 1800," as Jefferson called it, gave rise to a party system that dismantled Hamilton's program for a strong executive, the New

Deal realignment centered on an endeavor to deemphasize party politics and to resurrect the Hamilton executive as the steward of the public welfare. Such an enterprise stemmed from an understanding that the development of industrial capitalism had led to a national economy and concentration of private economic power, requiring strong countervailing action by government to ameliorate unacceptable political and economic inequality. As Herbert Croly wrote in *The Promise of American Life,* the task was to give "democratic meaning and purpose to the Hamiltonian tradition and method," and, thereby, "emancipate American democracy from its Jeffersonian bondage." [19]

The assault on the traditional party system and the emergence of the modern executive did not begin during the 1930s. The Progressive era—especially as shaped by the statesmanship of Theodore Roosevelt and Woodrow Wilson—was an important precursor to the New Deal. The New Deal was sufficiently indebted to Progressive theory to share its view of traditional American party politics as decrepit, as all too compatible with decentralizing constitutional mechanisms such as the separation of powers and federalism, thus preventing the development of an executive-centered national state with the capacity to govern the complex social and economic affairs of the twentieth century.[20] FDR was more effective than TR and Wilson, however, in directing this animus against Jeffersonian parties, making a resurrected Hamiltonianism the focal point of a popular and enduring transformation of the political system. Unlike Theodore Roosevelt and Woodrow Wilson, FDR's leadership was the principal ingredient in a full-scale realignment of the political parties, the first in history that placed executive leadership at the heart of its approach to politics and government. After FDR's long tenure, the logic of presidential responsibilities in the new office would lead even conservative Republican Presidents, such as Nixon and Reagan, to wield executive power according to the vision of the presidency celebrated by their progressive predecessors.

The rise of the modern executive and the concomitant decline of the party system during the 1930s was closely associated with the redefinition of the public's understanding of rights. Roosevelt first spoke of the need to modernize elements of the old faith in the Commonwealth Club address, delivered during the 1932 campaign. The theme was that the time had come to recognize "the new terms of the old social contract." It was necessary to rewrite the social contract to take account of a national economy remade by industrial capitalism and the concentration of economic power, a new contract to establish a stronger national state, lest the United States continue to steer "a steady course toward economic oligarchy."

In his Commonwealth address and throughout his presidency, FDR announced that the task of modern government was "to assist the development of an economic declaration of rights, an economic constitutional order." The traditional emphasis in American politics on individual self-reliance should therefore give way to a new understanding of individualism, by which government acted as a regulating and unifying agency, guaranteeing individual men and women protection from the uncertainties of the marketplace.[21] This change in what Walter Lippman referred to as the American public philosophy presupposed either the reconstruction or weakening of the American party system. In particular, the New Deal commitment to building a "modern" state meant that the executive, the leading *national* institution in American politics, would have to be freed from the influence of a party system whose organizational structure and mode of operation curbed the discretionary power of the president and administrative agencies. As Roosevelt put it, "The day of enlightened administration has come."[22] Consequently, the New Deal program included administrative reforms, embodied in the 1939 Executive Reorganization Act, that were conceived with the idea of better equipping the president to make use of his position as leader of the state and nation, not just the party governing the nation.[23] The administrative reform bill institutionalized Roosevelt's extraordinary leadership, ratifying a process whereby public expectations and institutional arrangements established the president as the center of government activity. This development, moreover, signified the decrepitude of the traditional two-party system.

The New Deal Legacy—Party Decline on Transformation

The institutional reforms carried out during the 1930s recast the relationship between political parties and the executive, thus fundamentally redefining the concept of representation in American politics. But this institutional program, designed to transform what New Dealers viewed as a provincial version of popular rule into a progressive democracy, led to two, seemingly contradictory, developments that continue to shape party politics in the United States. On the one hand, the weakening of the traditional party apparatus and the nationalization of the political system during the New Deal established the conditions for the emergence of a more national and programmatic party system. On the other hand, the New Deal resulted in the development of a modern presidency and administrative apparatus that makes party government unnecessary. In the final analysis, party government in the American context requires ongoing cooperation between the President and the members of his party in the Congress. Yet the attainment of a more palpable link between Congress and the President was felt to be manifestly impractical by New Dealers given the structure of the American Constitution and its dedication to the principle, expressed by Madison in *Federalist* 51, "that ambition must be made to counteract ambition."[24] Accordingly, the goal of the New Deal institutional program was to reform and extend the reach of *executive administration,* whereby the president and administrative agencies would be delegated the responsibility to shape public policy, thus making ongoing cooperation within the party councils unnecessary.

To a point, these developments—the rise of national parties and the enhancement of executive administration—are complementary and have given rise to a new executive-centered party system. The New Deal accelerated a development that began during the Progressive era, in which each of the parties, instead of being organized in order to enable its members to consult one another and reach an agreement upon differences of opinion, would be subject to the "benevolent dictatorship" of the president. Yet the emergence of an economic constitutional order and the expansion of administrative power during the New Deal did not remove the prohibitive obstacles in the American political system that stand in the way of establishing party government under dominant presidential leadership. As the failed "purge" campaign revealed, the decentralized character of politics in the United States can be modified only by strong presidential leadership, but a president determined to alter fundamentally the connection between the executive and his party will eventually shatter party unity. Given the fundamental resistance to strong partisanship in the United States, and support for the separation and division of powers, "modern" presidents, subject to the enormous programmatic demands of the post–New Deal era, have been encouraged to rely on plebiscitary politics and unilateral executive action to circumvent the regular procedures of constitutional government, as well as formal partisan channels.[25]

In examining the New Deal institutional legacy, this book has two major objectives. First, it seeks to shed light on the long-term development of the American party system. Most of the work on the history of political parties in the United States, particularly that purporting to explain the long secular decline of parties since the Progressive era, emphasizes how changes in electoral politics either at the turn of the century or during the late 1960s undermined the role of party organizations in American politics. This scholarship focuses on changes occurring in the electoral process, such as the expansion of the direct primary and the advent of "media politics," that have had a direct effect on the decline of partisan loyalties among voters.[26] The analysis of political parties from such a perspective is not so much wrong as incomplete. It does not address the important relationship between the development of governmental institutions and political parties, nor does it examine very carefully the impact of the New Deal, which was a critical historical moment in the development of the American state and, concomitantly, party politics in the United States. Yet an adequate explanation of the present condition of party politics cannot center primarily either on elections or the development of government institutions, but must elucidate the intricate connection between these things.

From the perspective of such an approach, the New Deal, which altered the way government responsibilities were viewed in the United States, becomes an important chapter in the development of political parties, although it is usually ignored as such.[27] Similarly, party reforms such as the direct primary are understood not as the root cause of party decline, but as part of broader changes in principles and institutions that modified the parties' place in the political system. These changes began during the Progressive era but did not become rooted in the working of American politics until the New Deal. As such, the political realignment of the 1930s represents an important bridge, and not simply an interregnum, between the events that led to important changes in the party system at the turn of the century and late 1960s. Indeed, the New Deal marked a watershed in the triumph of progressive democracy, in the commitment to expanding the programmatic responsibilities of the national government. Insofar as this doctrinal change presupposed an increase of administrative authority and efficiency, it proved fatal, given the unique conditions of party politics in the United States, to the traditional two-party system.

Thus, there is a very real sense in which the reconstruction of the executive during the New Deal *caused* the decline of the traditional party system by displacing parties as the principal instrument of popular rule. Furthermore, reforms that weakened the influence of party organizations in the electoral process were concomitant with the reform and expansion of executive authority, a result of the same systemic developments that will be closely examined in the following chapters.[28]

In thinking about the effect the New Deal has had on political parties, it is useful to consider V. O. Key's distinction between "party organization," "party-in-government," and "party-in-the-electorate."[29] The development of the modern presidency clearly weakened party organizations by preempting many of the tasks they performed prior to the New Deal.[30] For example, FDR and subsequent presidents developed their own independent campaign organizations that deprived the regular party apparatus of its responsibility to organize national campaigns. Moreover, modern presidents, especially those like Roosevelt, Johnson, Nixon, and Reagan, who were intent upon ambitious policy reform, crippled party-in-government by developing ways of achieving their policy goals without building coalitions in Congress. Without constant effort to build bridges between the branches, the United States Constitution produces what Hugh Heclo calls "institutional estrangement."[31] Yet the administrative reform carried out during the 1930s, and the concomitant "institutionalization" of the presidency, obviated the need for presidents to overcome this estrangement.

The influence of the institutional legacy of the New Deal on the party-in-the-electorate is far more difficult to discern. The development of the modern presidency and the concentration of policy responsibility in the Executive Department during the New Deal did not affect the electoral influence of political parties directly. Nevertheless, the presidential leadership of Roosevelt set the tone for declining party influence on voters by exalting the *personal* responsibility of the Chief Executive and extensively freeing government action from the influence of partisan politics. Reforms such as the direct primary and campaign finance laws certainly reduced the partisan character of campaigns, but the development of administrative politics further contributed to the decline of parties by making collective partisan appeals less meaningful in the eyes of the voters in the first place. This was particularly likely to happen when programs or benefits were presented as "rights." With the advent of an economic constitutional order, a commitment to limited government gave way to support for programmatic rights, for programs intended to guarantee the social and economic welfare of the individual. The tendency to view programs such as social security as "entitlements" created a veritable "administrative constitution," in which government programs were viewed as tantamount to rights and thus worthy of protection from the vagaries of party politics and elections.[32]

It remains to be seen, however, whether the traditional party apparatus, based upon patronage practices and disciplined organization in Congress at the state and local level, is giving way to a more programmatic party politics, emphasizing national organizations. Indeed, although much of the work on realignments has emphasized party decline, certain developments over the past decade suggest the renewal of party politics. No less distinguished an observer than David Truman, in fact, has argued that the challenge of adapting the national party structures to the governmental and political changes that have taken place over the past 50 years is one that is likely to be met.[33] Working against such a possibility, however, is the emergence of benign administration as the principal tool of governance since the 1930s. In the final analysis, a politics of administration tends not to nationalize and reform parties, but to link interests directly to national governmental institutions, thus making intermediary organizations such as parties less important in the scheme of things.

My second objective in examining the New Deal inheritance is to shed light on some of the most pressing and enduring problems of republican government in the United States. The "emancipation" of the presidency from the constrictive grip of partisan politics has been closely linked to the transformation of the executive office from an institution of modest size and authority into a formidable institution invested with formal and informal powers that often short-circuit the legislative process and judicial oversight. Yet, paradoxically, this more powerful and prominent chief of state has been reduced to virtually complete political isolation, deprived of the stable basis of popular support once provided by political parties. Presidents must now build popular support on the uncertain foundation of public opinion and a diverse, as well as demanding, constellation of interest groups.[34] Thus, the "modern" presidency is characterized by an "extraordinary isolation," to use Woodrow Wilson's phrase, which provides great opportunity for presidents to leave their mark upon the nation, but subjects them to a volatile political process that makes popular and enduring achievement unlikely.

This problem cannot be resolved easily. I do not seek to call the American people back to the "golden age" of parties. Any endeavor to restore parties should be informed by the need to "transcend" party politics in the first place. In effect, American parties, rooted in the political reforms of the nineteenth century, were primary schools of democracy in which Americans learned the art of association, or citizenship, and formed attachments to governing institutions.[35] Yet, inasmuch as they were molded from principles that were inhospitable to a strong executive, parties inhibited the development of a national government capable of undertaking the arduous domestic and international responsibilities that must be assumed by all advanced industrial democracies.

The modern presidency was crafted during the critical political developments of the 1930s to reconcile what was apparently an inherent conflict in the United States between popular rule and the consolidation of national administrative power. The unchecked executive power it has sometimes portended, however, has threatened certain valued traditions of the American political experience such as the separation of powers, federalism, and the celebration of individual autonomy. In this respect, the prominent yet vulnerable status of the "modern" presidency reflects the "uneasy" acceptance of the "modern" state in American politics.[36] The formation of a national, programmatic party system, one that encourages modern presidents and partisan members of Congress to push their causes to the very end of the political process is as likely to aggravate as to strengthen the difficult marriage between American constitutional government and the New Deal order.

Thus, as Barry Karl has written, the "New Deal raises all the most fundamental questions about the character of American government and its relation to governments elsewhere in the world."[37] The battles fought during the 1930s over the question of the appropriate relationship between executive power and popular rule, however, did not so much resolve tensions within the American constitutional order as bring them into bold relief. From this perspective, an examination of the New Deal institutional program and its relationship to past and present patterns of American politics provides the key to a better understanding of the most pressing constitutional problems currently faced by the American people.

Organization of the Book

I will examine three aspects of the relationship between the executive and party politics since the 1930s: (1) the principles and institutional reforms of the New Deal realignment, especially with respect to how this realignment transformed the relationship between the presidency and party politics; (2) the continuing importance of the New Deal legacy in the face of the challenge to programmatic liberalism beginning in the late 1960s; (3) the degree to which current political conditions reflect structural innovations in the constitutional order that were initiated during the 1930s, but extended and radicalized during the 1960s.

Chapter 2 provides an account of how the New Deal realignment built upon the ideas and policies of the Progressive era but reformulated the Progressive program so that it could more readily become the foundation of a full-scale partisan realignment. In effect, New Dealers shared the Progressives' antipathy to party politics and their understanding that a strong and responsible executive required the demise of partisan responsibility. But FDR and the architects of the New Deal more effectively transformed this antipathy into, ironically, a *party* program to which a majority of voters could express their allegiance.

Whereas Chapter 2 attempts to uncover the philosophical and historical roots of New Deal reform, Chapter 3 focuses more centrally on the party politics of the 1930s. The redefinition of the social contract presupposed by FDR's pronouncement of an economic constitutional order brought about major institutional changes, which, at the end of the day, have been more enduring than the extension of social programs that is the most recognized part of the New Deal inheritance. The transformation of the Democratic party into a more national and programmatic organization helped prepare the political landscape for this institutional reform. More than a partisan realignment was at stake, however. By counterpoising New Deal party politics with conventional partisan practices, this chapter reveals how the realignment of the 1930s altered the conditions for partisan transformation by deliberate structural innovation that displaced, once and for all, the Jeffersonian constitutional order.

Chapter 3 examines how the Democratic party was transformed and strengthened as a result of Roosevelt's leadership; Chapters 4, 5, and 6 suggest, however, that the long-term strength of the party formed under the New Deal banner was circumscribed both by the limits on party government in the United States and the way in which New Deal reforms were shaped to accommodate these obstacles to ardent partisanship. Indeed, Chapters 5 and 6 seek to show how the Roosevelt administration sought to impose a program on the Democratic party during the second term—the so-called "Third New Deal"—that would strengthen executive administration at the expense of party politics.

Taken together, the chapters on the New Deal institutional legacy depict a Roosevelt who was highly ambivalent about party leadership. FDR was both very serious and somewhat unsure in his efforts to alter the basis of the American party system. The New Deal represented a shift from "natural" to "programmatic" rights that required either the reform or weakening of the political parties. Paradoxically, both happened as a result of the New Deal. Political parties assumed a more "modern" form during the 1930s, yet were eventually subordinated to the development of a refurbished executive that made the reform of party a moot point. To be sure, this was in part the consequence of deliberate design—the legacy, in fact, of the New Deal Democratic party's institutional program. In the final analysis, however, this paradox reflects the extraordinary, but ambivalent party leadership of FDR: Although he wanted to change the character of the Democratic party, and thereby also influence the American party system, ultimately he concluded that the public good and practical politics demanded that partisanship be deemphasized rather than reformulated.

The remaining chapters of the book examine the significance of the New Deal institutional legacy for subsequent developments in American politics. These chapters will emphasize those presidencies in which the greatest changes occurred in the relationship between the White House and the major political parties. Chapter 7 considers developments in the modern presidency during the two decades after Roosevelt's death. Each of the individuals who occupied the White House during this time—Harry Truman, Dwight Eisenhower, John Kennedy, and Lyndon Johnson—sought to come to terms with the Roosevelt legacy by shaping the expectations and powers of modern presidential leadership to fit their own political objectives. Each in his own fashion upheld the New Deal, and continued the practices of modern executive leadership that tended to separate presidents from their parties. For Lyndon Johnson, however, the New Deal was merely a point of departure—his ambition was not only to equal FDR's record, but to surpass it. Johnson's attempt to reshape the institutions and policies of programmatic liberalism marked the completion and significant extension of the New Deal tradition, while accelerating the long secular decline of the party system.

Chapter 8 examines the political implications of the institutional changes brought by Johnson's reform program. Whereas New Deal reforms began to develop a policy process outside of normal partisan channels, the Johnson administration, as illustrated by its use of "outside" task forces in the development of programmatic initiatives, went much further in developing a policy network that was housed in the executive department and insulated from regular political processes. Eventually, the efforts being made to circumvent traditional partisan channels by the Johnson administration also became prominent in staffing and campaigns, laying the foundation for the decline of parties that became so visible after the 1968 Democratic Convention.

The discussion of the Johnson presidency in Chapter 8 questions the conventional wisdom that the decline of party was *caused* by the party reforms instigated by the Vietnam conflict.[38] Rather, I argue that the events of the tumultuous 1968 Democratic Convention and the party reforms that followed in the wake of those events were preceded and even legitimized by long-standing efforts to free the presidency from traditional partisan influences. In this respect, the expansion of presidential primaries and other changes in nomination politics that were initiated by the so-called McGovern–Fraser reforms *exploited* rather than *caused* the limitations and weaknesses of traditional party organizations.

Johnson rivalled FDR's command of the nation and revitalized the reformative zeal of programmatic liberalism. At the same time, he exposed and widened cracks in the liberal coalition that brought into question for the first time since the 1930s the assumption that it was desirable for a president to dominate the affairs of state. As the liberal order unravelled during the final years of his presidency, therefore, LBJ found himself in near political isolation. In the final analysis, the decline of party made possible the rededication to liberal reform but left the modern presidency without a stable basis of political support.

Chapters 9, 10, and 11 will focus on the "conservative" reaction to liberal reform, examining, especially, the relationship between the modern presidency and party system during the administrations of Richard Nixon and Ronald Reagan. If the New Deal institutional legacy brought about a significant constitutional change, altering fundamentally the character of representation in the American political system, one would expect that the characteristics of the modern presidency would continue to operate irrespective of the executive's party and philosophy.

This final section of the book, focusing on recent events, will explore, first, the prospects for a phoenix to rise from the ashes. The New Deal opened up the possibility for the development of a more national and issue-oriented party system. In particular, the Reagan "revolution" signalled that the Republican party had developed a strong organizational apparatus; indeed, its strength at the national level was unprecedented in American politics. The evolution of the Republican party as a force against administration seemed to complete the development of a "New American Party System."[39] The nomination and election of Reagan, far more ideologically conservative than Nixon, galvanized the commitment of the GOP to such programs as "regulatory relief" and "new federalism," which severely challenged the institutional legacy of liberal reform. These developments contributed greatly to the revitalization of partisan conflict during the 1980s.

Nevertheless, the importance of presidential politics and unilateral executive administration during the Nixon and Reagan years suggests that these administrations essentially continued, rather than fundamentally challenged, the institutional legacy of the New Deal. The discussion of the so-called Reagan "revolution" in Chapter 10 suggests that the strengthening of the Republican party and the revival of partisanship during the 1980s was undercut by the Reagan administration's emphasis, especially during the second term, on administrative practices and actions that essentially continued the New Deal tradition of creating a policy network in the executive department that frequently short-circuited the legislative process and defied shared responsibility among different elements of the party. Chapter 11 reveals that the pursuit of conservative policy objectives through administrative channels continued with the accession of George Bush to the White House. The challenge to liberal policies produced a conservative "administrative presidency," which also retarded the revival of partisan politics.[40]

The aggressive use of the administrative levers of power by Republican presidents after 1968 did not go unanswered. As a program of the Democratic party, the modern presidency depended upon a broad agreement among the Congress, the bureaucracy, and eventually the Courts to expand programmatic rights; energetic administration, therefore, depended upon a consensus that powers should be delegated to the executive. The challenge to programmatic liberalism, however, never extended beyond the presidency, leaving the Congress, as well as most states and localities, under Democratic control. By the time Lyndon Johnson left the White House, support for unilateral executive action had begun to erode. It virtually disappeared under the strain of "divided government" after 1968.

The strategic employment by conservatives of the administrative presidency gave rise to a "reformation" of New Deal administrative politics.[41] Consistent with the tradition of programmatic liberalism, the liberal reform aspirations of the post–New Deal era have been associated with efforts to enhance the administrative capacities of the national government. Yet, unlike the reform pattern of the New Deal and Great Society, the liberalism of this latter period, animated by opposition to conservative Republican executives, is greatly suspicious of, if not hostile to, presidential power. The modern presidency was conceived with the view that it would be an ally of programmatic reform. When this supposition was seemingly violated by the Vietnam War and subsequent developments, reformers set out to protect liberal programs from unfriendly executive administration. Consequently, a new institutional coalition, which includes bureaucratic agencies, courts, interest groups, and congressional subcommittees, was built to house "enlightened administration" and to fetter the administrative presidency.[42]

The Conclusion examines the New Deal institutional legacy for American democracy. Party organization and conflict is certainly not absent from the administrative politics spawned by the New Deal. Indeed, the New Deal—and the erosion of traditional decentralized parties—has made possible a new blending of partisanship and administration—one in which administration has become an instrument for partisan objectives. In effect, political parties are much more focused on government than they once were—especially on national administration. Divided government encouraged the Republicans to organize as the party of administration through the presidency, while the Democrats became the party of administration through the Congress.[43]

The battles that Republicans and Democrats have waged for control of departments and agencies have transcended narrow partisanship, however. As the Presidency of Jimmy Carter revealed, one-party control of the White House and Congress does not assure harmony in the administrative republic. The emergence of Democrats and Republicans as parties of administration marks a new chapter in the longstanding struggle between the executive and legislature for the control of administration. The conflict between the White House and Congress for control of departments and agencies is no longer a squabble for patronage—for spoils that nourish localized campaigns and party organizations. Rather, the Democrats and Republicans practice a form of administrative politics that denies nourishment to the regular party apparatus but feeds instead an executive branch oriented toward ideological and policy disputes.

It is not surprising, therefore, that the "New American Party System" has been associated with a renewed vitality of party organization and party-in-government, but has yet to penetrate the electorate sufficiently to change its basic attitudes and behavior. That is to say, there has not been a restoration of the "party-in-the-electorate." [44] As parties of administration, the Democrats and Republicans have been unable to form vital links with the public. The political legacy of the New Deal currently seems to be a more active and better equipped national state, but one without adequate means of common deliberation and public judgment.

I do not attempt to offer in this book a reform program that might address the troubling aspects of the New Deal legacy. But by highlighting the link between the "administrative state" and party politics, I attempt to suggest a new way of thinking about political parties and their history. In this way, I hope to make a contribution to our understanding about political parties and their role in the American political system.

I

The Presidency and Party Politics
in the New Deal Era

2

The Roots of New Deal Reform

The only book review ever written by Franklin D. Roosevelt, a discussion of Claude Bower's *Jefferson and Hamilton,* appeared in the *New York Post* on December 3, 1925. Its contents revealed that Roosevelt considered the political struggles between these two statesmen from 1790 to 1800 to be of paramount importance not only in understanding American history but also in ascertaining what was to be done in treating the great problems of the twentieth century. It was necessary, Roosevelt wrote, to "apply [the] fundamental differences between the Jeffersonian and Hamiltonian ideals . . . to present day policies of our two great parties." [1]

FDR's fascination with the conflict between Jefferson and Hamilton—his belief that the party battles that consumed them turned on problems that were essentially similar to those of his own day—was hardly unusual. Most progressive reformers during the first three decades of the twentieth century believed that Jefferson and Hamilton stood for two contending theories of government that animated later political controversies in American history and still lay unresolved before them. [2] Many of these reformers, especially those in the Democratic party, looked to a revitalization of Jeffersonian democracy, to a mobilization of popular forces against the special interests they believed were once again perverting republican government in the United States. Just as Jeffersonians believed that Hamilton's program initiatives would tend to restrict the voice of the people and unjustly advantage commercial interests, so these progressive reformers believed that the ascendant Republican party's program of high tariffs and other policies favoring business vitiated popular rule. Thus, Democrats such as Woodrow Wilson and the young Franklin Roosevelt, who served in Wilson's cabinet as Assistant Secretary of the Navy, looked upon the "Revolution of 1800" as a retrospective on the future of American politics. "I wonder if a century and a quarter later, the same contending forces are not again mobilizing," FDR's review of Bower's text concluded. "Hamiltons we have today. Is a Jefferson on the horizon?" [3]

It was not possible, however, simply to resurrect Jeffersonian ideals. In fact, Republican progressive thinkers like Herbert Croly and that political aegis so important to their purposes, Theodore Roosevelt, criticized Wilson for his celebration of the Jeffersonian tradition, which they considered the cardinal vice of American politics. "I have never hesitated to criticize Jefferson; he was infinitely below Hamilton; I think the worship of Jefferson a discredit to my country; and I have . . . small use for the ordinary Jeffersonian," wrote TR in 1906.[4] Although confessing a lack of sympathy for Hamilton's distrust of democracy, TR considered the resurrection of Hamiltonian nationalism and the faith it represented in strong government an essential prerequisite to the reform of American politics.

The differences between Wilson and Theodore Roosevelt on this point were more a matter of emphasis than fundamental philosophical dispute. Wilson's political writings and his two terms as president reveal that he shared the view of "new nationalists" that Jefferson's commitment to limited government was no longer compatible with individual liberty. Like TR and Croly, progressive Democrats believed that the exigencies of modern industrial society, especially the concentration of economic power in the form of huge corporations, or "trusts," required a different understanding of freedom than held by Jefferson. As Wilson wrote in *The New Freedom*, published soon after he was elected president in 1912:

> Without watchful interference, the resolute interference, of the government, there can be no fair play between individuals and such powerful institutions as the trusts. Freedom today is something more than being let alone. The program of government of freedom must in these days be positive, not only negative.[5]

The key for progressive reformers, then, was to mobilize public opinion against the reigning theories and policies of the day, while strengthening the power of the national government, which historically had been considered a threat to popular rule in the United States. Accordingly, FDR recognized during the 1920s as he waited for, indeed, positioned himself, to represent, the new Jefferson, that Jeffersonian ideals would have to be applied to modern problems in such a way that these ideas were respectful of Hamilton's "genius" for sound administrative practices.[6]

Yet there was no easy resolution between democratic aspirations and energetic national government in American politics. Madison and Jefferson carried out the "revolution of 1800" to rescue the Constitution not only from class rule, the "moneyed interest," but from the unfortunate consequences they believed would inevitably follow from expanding the responsibilities and strengthening the institutions of the executive.

Madison emphasized the danger of consolidation in the 1799 Virginia Resolutions, which attacked the Alien and Sedition Acts passed during the Federalist administration of John Adams. A program of nationalization, Madison argued, would result in an ineluctable tendency to delegate authority to the executive as the responsibilities of the central government increased, thereby undermining the constitutional support for popular rule:

> In proportion as the objects of legislative care might be multiplied, would time allowed for each be diminished, and the difficulty of providing uniform and particular regulations for all be increased. From these sources would necessarily ensue a greater latitude to the agency of the department which is always in exis-

tence, and which could best mould regulations of a general nature so as to suit them to the diversity of particular situations. And it is in this latitude, as we supplement the deficiency of the laws, that the degree of Executive prerogative materially exists.[7]

These expressed concerns about delegating responsibility to the executive are remarkably prescient in view of the post–New Deal criticisms directed against what Theodore Lowi and others have called the "administrative state."[8] Unlike modern critics of the administrative state, who look to a reconstituted national power, however, Madison joined Jefferson in an effort to rally public opinion against nationalism itself. In this sense Madison did not view the problem he posed as intractable. But he did believe that political exigencies required significant changes in the governmental order that he had played such a central role in creating.

Whereas Madison originally feared that the security of liberty would be violated by a majority faction bent on a misconceived notion of economic justice, his concern about Hamilton's program focused on the need to discipline public opinion against government consolidation.[9] And whereas the original structure of the separation of powers was designed to check the legislative power, the opposition of Madison and Jefferson to Hamilton's policies led them to support a political program to restrain executive authority and preserve the authority of the more popular institutions. This modification of the "Madisonian Republic" required not only a commitment to states' rights, but also the creation of a political party. Thus Madison, the chief architect of a "Constitution-Against-Parties," to use Richard Hofstadter's term, played a leading role in founding the first majority party on American soil, which, in turn, reformulated significantly his original constitutional design.[10]

The label Jefferson and Madison gave to their party organization, the Democratic–Republican party, signified that it was formed in order to revive the republican character of American government. As Madison put it in his 1791 essay, "A Candid State of the Parties," that party was united by the "doctrine that mankind are capable of governing themselves."[11] Arguably, this revival checked a trend that might have led to "administrative centralization," a development Tocqueville equates with extending the affairs of state into all the particulars of human existence, thus tending only "to enervate the peoples that submit to it." Yet in their zeal to restrain the unfortunate effects of the administrative state, Jefferson and Madison also established a legacy of "governmental centralization," Tocqueville's term for the extension of public authority to "certain interests, such as the enactment of general laws and the nation's relations to foreigners," which are "common to all parts of the nation" and are critical in giving it the requisite vigor "to live, much less prosper."[12] The two-party system that eventually formed in the United States was dedicated to Jeffersonian principles—it provided for a certain unity of government, while at the same time it prevented an increase of administrative authority and efficiency.

In important respects, the great political controversies of the twentieth century tell the story of how the tension between the Jeffersonian and Hamiltonian visions was played out. According to the historian Arthur Schlesinger, Jr., FDR refurbished the Jeffersonian tradition, preparing it to meet the needs of the twentieth century:

> The great achievement of the New Deal was to introduce the United States to the twentieth century. Roosevelt redressed the defects of the Jeffersonian tradition by equipping the liberal party with a philosophy of government intervention—a belief, as he put it, that the government has the definite duty to use all its power and resources to meet new social problems with new social controls.[13]

The New Deal Democratic party, however, was committed to a program of institutional reform that eventually would weaken the two-party system, and substitute for it a refashioned, modern executive as the principal instrument for organizing majorities and intermediating between the popular will and government. Whereas the two-party system was created to protect interests in society against the government, the "modern" presidency and administrative agencies that emerged during the 1930s were molded to use government as an instrument for the attainment of positive public ends.

Thus, FDR represented less a modern-day Jeffersonian, or the embodiment of a marriage between Jefferson and Hamilton, than the triumph of an inverted form of Hamiltonianism. Whereas Hamilton supported an "administrative republic," in which a dominant president would withstand ardent republicanism, New Deal institutional reform sought to transform the president into a force for greater equality at the expense of what was considered excessive individualism.[14] In part, this project to turn Hamilton on his head has indeed brought about a "progressive democracy," which is better equipped to deal with the social and economic responsibilities of a modern industrial society. But this reform came at the cost of undermining valued institutions such as decentralized political parties traditionally relied upon in the American political experience to nurture and make effective popular rule. As Barry Karl has noted, "local government and community control," supported by mechanisms such as federalism and the decentralized structure of American party politics, "remain at the heart of the most intuitive conceptions of American democracy, even though they may also represent bastions of political corruption and locally condoned injustice." Thus, the transfer of the locus of power during the New Deal to the federal government and the concomitant delegation of power to the executive branch threatened the idea of citizenship in the United States.[15]

The tension between the modern executive and popular rule reflects the historical antipathy in American politics to the consolidation of national administrative power. Roosevelt and other New Dealers were not unmindful of this hostility. As FDR wrote to his aide Thomas Corcoran in January, 1941, "Few men have been understanding of the forces of history against which we have contended."[16] That Roosevelt was one of these few helps to explain why an administrative state was finally established in American politics and received its essential organization during the New Deal.

It is interesting and somewhat ironic that the New Deal marks the period during which the administrative state comes into its own, because Franklin Roosevelt is often criticized for his inattention to the institutional problems of administrative management.[17] Such an evaluation of FDR's administrative politics comports with the view of most scholars that the New Deal is essentially pragmatic and experimental.[18] But this portrait of New Deal politics overlooks the rather coherent understanding and program Roosevelt had for reconstituting public administration. As noted, however, formulation of this reform program did not begin in the 1930s. In fact, the New Deal resuscitated a program that had its origins in the Progressive era. The contribution of the New Dealers to this enterprise was to work out a synthesis of contradictory trends evident during the Progressive period, thus facilitating the political triumph of progressive reform under the banner of Democratic liberalism.

Administrative Politics, Party Reform, and the Progressive Tradition

Woodrow Wilson's seminal essay of 1887, "The Study of Administration," marks the first recognition in the United States of public administration as a distinct and separate sphere of government activity.[19] This was not the beginning of the American consciousness about administrative power, of course. Hamilton argued in *Federalist* 70 that "energy in the executive is the leading character in the definition of good government," an essential ingredient of "the steady administration of the law."[20] But, unlike the defense of administrative power Wilson and other Progressive thinkers offered, Hamilton considered administration to have an integral political role. Energetic and expeditious administration was considered by Hamilton to be part and parcel of presidential leadership. He was not averse to the notion of executive institutions and public servants having a certain degree of independence from the president, but there was no thought given to establishing a palpable line between politics and administration—to establishing administrative practices as an independent sphere of action. In contrast, Wilson, in the first instance, did not grant a political character to administration. Rather, the purpose of administration was to devise the most efficient method of putting political programs into effect:

> The field of administration is a field of business. It is removed from the hurry and strife of politics . . . Although politics sets the task of administration, it should not be suffered to manipulate its offices.[21]

The separation of administration from politics presupposes at once a more ambitious and a more mundane task for administration. When subject to the president's "superintendence" as Hamilton proposed, administrative officers would play a leading role in the formulation of political programs. This participation in the hurly-burly of political life would not corrupt public administration, but allow administration, properly formed, to refine and enlarge the working of representative democracy. For Wilson, however, it was critical to place administration beyond political ambition so as to provide it a vantage point to carry out effectively the marching orders that would emerge from the democratic process.

Although such a task would seem to relegate administrators to the part of political eunuchs, Wilson's concept of a separation of politics and administration camouflages his commitment to a very important political role for the bureaucracy—the infusing of liberal democracy with the institutional capability for a significant expansion of public action. Whereas the original purpose of constitutional government was to circumscribe political power, "modern" conditions dictated that constitutional procedures could no longer be the whole of government action. The role of the "science" of administration and its practitioners was to prepare the polity for a situation where, as Wilson put it, "It is getting harder to *run* a constitution than to frame one."[22]

The growing complexity of social activity and the concentration of economic power made it necessary for the government to supervise telegraph and railroad lines and to regulate labor relations, thus making "itself master of masterful corporations." This presupposed the creation of a state that would constantly be "putting its hands to new undertakings," and, consequently, increasingly in need of wise and expert counsel of administrators. In such a critical advisory position, the administrator could not be reduced to the "answering deed" of the political will, but would necessarily have "a will of his own in the choice of means for accomplishing his work." The choice of means for accomplishing the work of the state would become, in fact, the essence of government activity. "The idea of the state and the consequent ideal of its duty are undergoing noteworthy change," wrote Wilson, "and the idea of the state is the conscience of administration. Seeing everyday new things which the state ought to do, the next thing is to see clearly how it ought to do them."[23]

Wilson's commitment to establishing administrators—policy experts—as the "conscience of the state" suggests a theory to supplant rather than refurbish popular government. In fact, he did not desire the replacement of the republican character of constitutional government with the "administrative state." Yet if the "tail was not to wag the dog," it was necessary to reconstitute the working of constitutional government itself. To accomplish such a task, Wilson looked to a fundamental recasting of the presidential office and, concomitantly, the reform of political parties.

The traditional party system, dominated by state and local organizations and patronage practices, was ill suited to the formulation and adoption of comprehensive national programs, which Wilson believed necessarily would have to become part of American politics in the twentieth century. Wilson's criticism of the American party system was linked to constitutional criticism. The party system as it evolved during the nineteenth century supported Jeffersonian principles, emphasizing the primacy of Congress and state legislatures, as well as a strict interpretation of the national government's powers. Although hardly an unreconstructed Hamiltonian, Wilson believed that a more Hamilton-like perspective needed to inform the modernization of American politics. He felt it was necessary to revise Hamilton's concern "that government was not a thing that you could afford to tie up in a nice poise, as if it were to be held at an inactive equilibrium, but a thing which must everyday act with straightforward and unquestionable power, with definite purpose and consistent force, choosing its policies and making good its authority, like a single organism."[24]

In order to achieve this "organic" understanding of government, Wilson proposed major institutional reforms that would establish closer ties between the executive and legislature. In his early writings Wilson proposed that this link would best be formed by centering power in Congress, calling in 1879 for the adoption of the British cabinet system, which concentrated leadership in the executive agency responsible to the legislature—or parliament, as it was called in Britain. This would require a constitutional amendment "to give the heads of the executive departments—the members of the cabinet—seats in Congress, with the privilege of the initiative in legislation and some part in the unbounded privileges now commanded by the standing committees."[25] With power so concentrated in the legislature, the president, who, in Wilson's view, had been rendered virtually useless by developments since the Civil War in any case, would become a mere figurehead, assuming a position similar to that of a monarch in England.

Wilson never abandoned his view that the constitutional system of checks and balances should be replaced by an American version of the parliamentary system, but his perspective on how this task should be accomplished changed dramatically during the early 1900s. He now stressed that the greatest promise for the establishment of more concentrated leadership in the United States lay in the strong assertion of presidential leadership.[26] No doubt Wilson's changed view on the possibility of strong leadership in the presidency was influenced by Theodore Roosevelt, who demonstrated the potential powers of the executive office by his vigorous and independent stewardship of the nation from 1901 to 1909.

Roosevelt had done much to fulfill the promise of the office, but Wilson believed that he did not do enough to exert his leadership of Congress and party. TR's style of leadership inclined him on occasion to appeal "over the heads" of Congress; unlike presidents of the nineteenth century, whose influence on public opinion and Congress was mediated in critical ways by party organization, Roosevelt appealed directly to public opinion by means of his public messages.[27] Moreover, TR held a broad understanding of the president's consitutional powers, frequently acting unilaterally to achieve his policies in defiance of Congress's intent. Thus, he was increasing the contact between the presidency and popular opinion, but at the cost of losing the confidence and good will of Congress. Towards the end of his second term, congressional hostility became a barrier to almost anything he wanted to do.

Wilson agreed with Roosevelt that the president must focus more attention on national problems, but he believed that such leadership would be ineffective or dangerous unless accompanied by a fundamental change in working constitutional arrangements. It was necessary, Wilson argued, to break down the barriers between the president and Congress and to strengthen the president's position as party leader. In this case, constitutional government would be reformed, and its parts would work more in concert, without violating the principles and institutions that protected the nation from an unhealthy aggrandizement of executive power. Furthermore, in the course of unifying the disparate parts of the political system, it was possible for the president to encourage a level of debate in elections and the councils of government that had all too often been lacking from the American political system:

. . . [T]he President represents not so much the party's governing efficiency as its controlling ideals and principles. He is not so much part of its organization as its vital link of connection with the thinking nation. He can dominate his party by being spokesman for the real sentiment and purpose of the country, by giving direction to opinion, by giving the country at once the information and the statements of policy which will enable it to form its judgments alike of parties and men.[28]

Thus, it was necessary to strengthen the role of president as party leader so that the executive as the leader of national opinion could fuse the executive and legislative branches in his own person. Unless political parties were reconstituted as national agents of democracy in this way, they would lose their character as representative institutions. As Wilson wrote:

Party organization is no longer needed for the mere rudimentary tasks of holding the machinery together or giving it the sustenance of some common object, some single cooperative motive. The time is at hand when we can with safety examine the network of party in its detail and change its structure without imperiling its strength. This thing that has served us so well might now master us if we left it irresponsible. We must see that it is made responsible.[29]

After his election to the presidency in 1912, Wilson acted both to perfect the methods of popular leadership already developed by Theodore Roosevelt, and to apply them in a way in which he might establish leadership of Congress and achieve mastery over the Democratic party. Wilson was not completely successful in this endeavor, to be sure. But his two terms in office brought about significant changes in the electoral and governmental institutions of the executive office.

Wilson and Party Reform

Wilson's plan to strengthen the role of president within the party councils led him to examine closely the presidential selection process, and in particular, the party convention system. The nomination of presidential candidates by national conventions, controlled by state and local party organizations, dated back to the Jacksonian era, when this system replaced the congressional caucus, which had left the selection of presidential candidates to the party organizations in the House and Senate. The convention system had the virtue of liberating the president from undue dependence on the Congress, and allowing him to form, through the mechanisms of party organization, a more direct and far-reaching link with the American people. Wilson charged, however, that this method of selecting presidents perpetuated the "archaic" state and local orientation of party politics in the United States and prevented the emergence of a new form of party—one more national and programmatic in its orientation. The existing selection system contributed to leaderless government by producing candidates of limited ability and little stature who were frequently beholden to the "bosses and machines" that controlled the nomination process.[30]

Moved by such an understanding, Wilson became an advocate of the presidential primary. In his first Annual Message to Congress, he urged "the prompt enactment of legislation which will provide for primary elections throughout the country at which the voters of the several parties may choose their nominees for the Presidency without the intervention of nominating conventions."[31]

Wilson's endorsement of a national primary made little headway in Congress. But the progressives did have some success at the state level, and the use of the popular primary as a method for selecting delegates to the national convention gradually increased during Wilson's two terms in office—from the 13 states that held primaries in the election of 1912 to the 21 that did so in 1920. Failing to win approval of a national primary in Congress, the plan of Wilson and progressive reformers was to transform the delegate selection process into what in effect would be a national plebiscite in which the people would choose the nominee. The push for popular presidential primaries slowed after 1920, and the regular party leaders maintained dominant control over the presidential selection process until the 1970s. Yet Wilson's proposal for a national primary served as a blueprint for reformers who fought throughout the twentieth century to weaken the grip of the traditional party apparatus on the presidency.

The Art of Popular and Legislative Leadership

The national primary proposal was but one manifestation of Wilson's concern to increase the authority of the president and to provide the political system with greater capacity for change. He was the first president, Elizabeth Sanders has written, "to recognize the full institutional implications of the distinction between his and his party's electoral constituencies."[32] But rather than attempting to build a "personal coalition" distinct from the coalition embodied by the Democratic party, Wilson sought to exercise his influence to elevate the Democratic party to a higher, more national purpose. This was seen most clearly in his efforts to avow the president's obligation as the voice of the people to bring public opinion to bear upon the Congress.

In contrast to TR, who had viewed popular rhetoric and national speaking tours—or "swings around the circle"—as occasional means for defending specific pieces of legislation, Wilson believed that inspirational leadership of public opinion was the primary responsibility of executive leadership. The high purpose of the modern executive was one of rhetoric rather than administration. Indeed, the president's enhanced role in political life required a diminution of his executive duties. Wilson supported the movement to reform the civil service that emerged at the end of the nineteenth century and acquired considerable influence at the state and national level during the Progressive era. But he viewed the formation of a more "professional" executive branch, one based upon expertise rather than party loyalty, as a development that would free the president from the daily cares of executive administration. With the separation of politics and administration, presidents could safely depend more on a professional administrative apparatus to tend to the details of policy, while they concentrated on the larger matters of state:

> . . . [W]e can safely predict that as the multitude of the president's duties increases, as it must with the growth and widening activities of the nation itself,

the incumbents of the great office will more and more come to feel that they are administering it in its truest purpose and with greatest effect by regarding themselves as less and less executive officers and more and more directors of affairs and leaders of the nation,—men of counsel and of the sort of action that makes for enlightenment.[33]

Wilson's concern to focus presidential leadership on ''enlightenment'' explains in large part why he revived the practice, abandoned by Jefferson, of appearing in person before Congress to deliver the State of the Union Address and other public messages. Jefferson had abandoned the custom (established by George Washington and carried on by John Adams) of appearing before Congress on the grounds that this sort of exercise attached too much ceremony to the executive duties, detracting thereby from the republican character of the presidency. The White House's announcement on April 6, 1913 that Wilson would break this Jeffersonian tradition, and deliver a message on tariff reform in person before the two houses of Congress on April 8, shocked representatives, especially members of the president's own party who revered the Jeffersonian custom. Senator John Sharp Williams of Mississippi, an original Wilson supporter, led the attack against the president appearing before Congress, referring frequently to the proposed speech as the ''speech from the throne.'' In the end, however, the Senate adopted the resolution, already adopted by the House, providing for a joint session to hear the president's address.[34]

Going before Congress was Wilson's way of establishing once and for all the president's role as the true representative of public opinion. Progressive democracy required, he believed, a departure from Jeffersonian methods and traditions, a stronger sense of national purpose, to satisfy the Jeffersonian commitment to equality of opportunity. Appearing in person before legislators, moreover, served Wilson's purpose of breaking down the wall that so long divided the executive from the legislative branch:

> I am very glad to have this opportunity to address the two houses directly and to verify for myself the impression that the President of the United States is a person, not a mere department of government hailing Congress from some isolated island of jealous power, sending messages, not speaking naturally with his own voice—that he is a human being in a common service. After this pleasant experience I shall feel quite normal in all our dealings with one another.[35]

Wilson's precedent-shattering gesture was well received by Congress, and it launched the first successful campaign for tariff reform since the Civil War. More significant, this address was one of several methods the President employed in an effort to give constitutional form to a parliamentary system, or at least an approximation of this system on American soil.

Wilson thus conceived of himself as the responsible leader of his party, as the only leader who could speak for it and the nation. Like the Republicans, the Democrats were sharply divided between conservative and progressive elements. Nevertheless, Wilson decided to work through and with his party in Congress, rather than to govern by a coalition of progressive Democrats and Republicans as he might have done. Wilson considered party debate and organization to be a vital

ingredient of responsible executive leadership, without which the "rhetorical presidency," as Jeffrey Tulis calls it, would degenerate into idle chatter or, even
worse, vicious demagogy.[36] He worked assiduously, therefore, to formulate a
comprehensive policy program and engaged in tireless efforts to establish this plan
as a *party* program. Wilson was even successful in getting the Democrats in the
House to adopt a rule binding members to support the administration's policies.
Similar party discipline was maintained in the traditionally more individual-
istic Senate, where the Democratic caucus declared important legislation such
as the tariff bill party measures and urged the duty of all Democrats to support
them.

As a result, for the first time since Jefferson was president, the executive
formulated a complete legislative program and worked closely with committee
chairmen in giving body to it. Unlike Jefferson, however, who, in deference to
congressional deliberation, maintained a sphinxlike public silence as legislation
was considered, Wilson asserted his personal leadership to focus the attention of
the country on and spur congressional action. And unlike Theodore Roosevelt,
who did not hesitate to work with sympathetic Democrats or appeal over the heads
of Congress when his party leadership opposed him on a crucial matter, Wilson's
public appeals, especially during his first term, were almost always directed at
building popular support for his party and programs against the assaults of private
interests and the Republican opposition.[37]

Wilson's Progressive Critics and the Assault on Parties

Many reformers who exercised influence during the Progressive era believed that
Wilson's program to reform parties was poorly conceived. Indeed, Theodore Roosevelt's "New Nationalism" campaign of 1912 under the Progressive party banner was based on the premise that the two-party system was an intractable barrier
to progressive democracy. The progressive platform devoted an entire section to
an assault on the "old parties," denouncing the Democrats and Republicans as
decrepit and corrupting organizations:

> Instead of instruments to promote the general welfare, they have become the
> tools of corrupt interests which use them impartially to serve their selfish pur-
> poses. . . .
>
> The deliberate betrayal of its trust by the Republican party, the fatal incapac-
> ity of the Democratic party to deal with the new issues of the new time, have
> compelled the people to forge a new instrument of government through which to
> give effect to their will in laws and institutions.[38]

There was little prospect that the National Progressive party campaign or its
program would summon a reformed party system. Rather, the party's call for
more direct government, organized by measures such as the direct primary, as
well as the initiative, referendum, and recall, anticipated the demise of partisanship. As Karl has written, the "Progressive party of 1912 was as much an attack
on the whole concept of political parties as it was an effort to create a single party

whose doctrinal clarity and moral purity would represent the true interest of the nation as a whole."[39]

The most penetrating critic of Wilson's program of party reform was Herbert Croly. Croly and Roosevelt had a close relationship, sharing an antipathy to Wilson's New Freedom, which they believed was "hamstrung by the persistence of a vacuous Jeffersonianism in the President's thought."[40]

Although TR returned to the Republican party after the 1912 campaign, Croly's critique of the American party system continued until the outbreak of World War I. This critique was developed in his important volume, *Progressive Democracy,* published in 1914, and in his numerous articles for *The New Republic,* the intellectually sophisticated journal of progressive thought that he helped found and edit. It is useful to consider Croly's view of party politics in the United States, not only because it profoundly influenced political reforms during the Progressive era, but also because it provides an important bridge between Progressivism and the New Deal.

For Croly, progressive democracy's commitment to expanding the programmatic responsibilities of the national government "particularly need[ed] an increase of administrative authority and efficiency." The American party system, however, was established as an institution to control administrative authority—it "bestowed upon the divided Federal government a certain unity of control, while at the same time it prevented the increased efficiency of the Federal system from being obnoxious to local interests." The consequent weakening of administrative authority, although rooted in the "pioneer" conditions of the nineteenth century, Croly argued, was an essential and incorrigible aspect of the two-party system. "Under American conditions," therefore, "a strong responsible and efficient administration of the law and the public business would be fatal to partisan responsibility."[41]

Wilson believed that it was possible in enhancing the capacities of the state to strengthen parties *and* administration, so that a reformed bureaucracy would "professionally" carry out the programmatic initiatives stemming from a government organized effectively by a majority political party. But Croly argued that the principal instrument of "responsible" party politics, strong presidential leadership, would necessarily be enfeebled by the need to win over fellow partisans in Congress. For that cooperation could only result from the president's acquiescence to patronage and administrative decentralization—the sustaining elements of party politics in the United States that partisans in Congress tenaciously embraced. The essential character of the party system, therefore, could not be dislodged without a transcendence of partisan politics itself. Wilson's notion that the president could facilitate a transformation of the practices that sustained parties, Croly argued, was unrealistic:

> The executive has not the power to make an effective fight against the system, because public opinion on which he depends for his weapons, still fails to understand its real importance. In cleaving to it party leaders in Congress are cleaving to the strongest and most necessary prop of the party system, but by so doing they are making the destruction of that system an indispensible condition of the success of progressive democracy.[42]

Wilson did, in fact, find it very difficult to reconcile his progressivism with the demands of party leader. Indeed, the administrative practices of the Wilson presidency, especially with respect to personnel management, were viewed generally as a betrayal of progressive principles. To the dismay of the President's progressive supporters, traditional patronage practices dominated his appointments to executive departments and agencies. As president-elect, Wilson promised to nominate "progressives and only progressives" to federal posts. "The pity is," his Secretary of Navy, Josephus Daniels, wrote many years later to Franklin D. Roosevelt, "that Wilson appointed some who wouldn't recognize a Progressive principle if he met it in the road." [43]

Wilson's decision to work through the party marked, Arthur Link has written, "one of the early decisive turning points in [his] presidential career." [44] This decision was a major factor in the president's nearly absolute mastery over the Democratic party and the Democratic members of Congress. "The cornerstone of Wilson's entire conception of democratic administration in America was a closer relationship between the President and Congress" noted the President's close associate, Ray Stannard Baker. "He must indeed lead, but they must follow. How was he to bring about the tremendous reforms that he had promised with his own party mutinous behind him? After all there is a political method." [45]

Wilson's "political method," however, weakened the administration of the reform programs enacted into law during his presidency. In addition, Wilson's presidency did little to strengthen the Democratic party's organization or its fundamental commitment to progressive principles. Because Postmaster General Albert Burleson and other Wilson aides who assumed responsibility for patronage practices preferred to control the Democratic party rather than reform it, the result of Wilson's decision to accept standard patronage practices was "the triumph of the professional politician over the idealist in the administration." [46]

Wilson did cause the Democratic party to become a more united, self-confident, and efficient political association than it had been before his ascendence to the White House. But, Croly argued, the Democratic party's support for progressive policies resulted only from the President's "benevolent domination" over it. The enormous power Wilson exercised over his party was "a source, in the long run, of weakness rather than strength." This domination revealed that the party system could not be galvanized to enact a program of reform without a "wise, firm, yet conciliatory man like Wilson." But a statesman of Wilson's talents would "not be born every election," and reforms that attempted to institutionalize executive domination of the party, such as the direct primary, would undermine the shared responsibility among fellow partisans that made party politics a meaningful enterprise. The solution was not to reform a flawed democratic system that was both obsolete and incorrigible, but to democratize the emerging modern state. In the end, the elevation of the presidency above the regular party apparatus by the expansion of direct primaries and other reforms would have that effect:

At the final test the responsibility is his rather than that of his party. The party which submits to such a dictatorship, however benevolent, cannot play its own proper part in a system of partisan government. It will either cease to have any independent life or its independence will eventually assume the form of revolt.[47]

In Croly's understanding of progressive democracy, Wilson was correct in viewing nineteenth century constitutional mechanisms and party politics as impediments to programmatic reform. He was wrong, however, in not facing up to the fact that true reform presupposed not the transformation of party but its demise. The popularity of measures such as the direct primary revealed how centralized and disciplined parties went against the looser genius of American politics. To the extent that government became committed to a democratic program that was essentially social in character, the American people would find intolerable a two-party system that stood between popular will and governmental machinery.[48]

According to Croly, the presidency depended for its primary strength and greatest usefulness as the principal instrument of a national democracy upon its ability to represent and lead public opinion. It was a mistake, therefore, for Wilson to attempt to rule by means of a congressional majority; instead, he should have sought to imitate and embody in constitutional form Roosevelt's method of legislative leadership, which was that of "coercing a reluctant Congress by direct appeals to public opinion." In his defense of the direct primary and other institutional reforms dedicated to the formation of a progressive democracy, as well as in his attention to the creation of a rhetorical presidency, Wilson had contributed significantly to such an enterprise. But his concern to make the responsibility of popular leader compatible with ardent partisanship subordinated the essential and peculiar source of executive strength—an intimate association with public opinion—to the need and desire of cooperating with Congress. Thus, the *New Republic* lamented towards the end of the President's first term, there were really "two Mr. Wilsons, one actively engaged in an essentially constructive task of national reorganization, and the other still clinging to partisan ideas, antipathies and dogmas which pervert the meaning and compromise the success of his greater enterprise."[49]

Wilson's false hope for partisanship also caused him to underestimate the degree to which progressive democracy required "administrative aggrandizement," that is, the development of administrative agencies as the principal instruments of democratic life.[50] Recognizing the necessity of such a development required the legitimization of what amounted to a "fourth department of government." Croly supported expanding and elevating the authority of independent commissions in local and national politics. On the national level, this meant delegating policy responsibility to independent regulatory commissions, such as the Interstate Commerce Commission, which were governed by a bipartisan board whose members served for fixed and overlapping terms. Commissions were thereby not only independent of partisan politics, but of executive influence in the sense that presidents could not remove commissioners at will, as they could with all policy-level officials in executive agencies and departments.

Croly believed it possible to defend such expansion of administrative power because, he argued, regulatory commissions, though the major focus of government action, would not supersede the legislative, judicial, or executive power.

Rather, a commission would simply be "a convenient means of consolidating the divided activities of government for practical social purposes." As independent but subordinate institutions, the administrative commissions would be free "only to do right." Should they abuse their authority, "the bonds [would] tighten upon them."[51]

If Wilson could be accused of not facing up to the aggrandizement of administration that would follow from his progressive principles, then Croly could be charged with underestimating the political difficulties that would arise with the administrative state. Having rejected Wilson's program of party transformation, Croly provides no alternative means to link the political and administrative spheres of government. Without such a link, as Croly himself granted, "the most doubtful and difficult question connected with the administrative organization and a progressive democracy concerns its ability to obtain and keep popular confidence."[52]

The issue of national administrative power was the most important difference dividing Wilson and Croly's candidate, Theodore Roosevelt, in the 1912 campaign. Roosevelt's New Nationalism accepted the evolution of great corporations as inevitable and considered them to be the most efficient units of industrial organization; all that was necessary was to bring them under strict public control through regulation of their activities by a powerful trade commission. A proposal for a commission with broad statutory authority to curb unfair trade practices was an important plank in the Progressive party's platform. The creation of the Interstate Commerce Commission in 1887, and the extension of its power by the Hepburn Act in 1906, had established the national government's supervisory responsibility in transportation policy. What was needed in addition, TR proclaimed during the 1912 campaign, was "the application to all industrial concerns and all cooperating interests engaged in interstate commerce in which there is either monopoly or control of the market of the principles on which we have gone in regulating transportation concerns engaged in such commerce."[53]

The concept of New Freedom expressed Wilson's understanding of Progressivism, one that he believed was rooted in the tradition of the Democratic party. In contrast to Roosevelt's New Nationalism, it called for reform that would free business from the plague of monopoly and special privilege, thus making unnecessary a dangerous centralization of power. "As to monopolies, which Mr. Roosevelt proposes to legalize and welcome," remarked Wilson during the 1912 campaign, "I know that there are so many cars of juggernaut, and do not look forward with pleasure to the time when the juggernauts are licensed and driven by commissioners of the United States."[54] As the leader of the Democratic party, and as one intent upon preserving the Jeffersonian commitment to the political control of administration, Wilson promised remedial measures, such as tariff reform, an overhaul of the banking and currency system, and a vigorous antitrust program, that would "disentangle" the "colossal community of interest" in the United States and restore fair competition to the American economy.[55]

In the final analysis, Wilson's commitment to working within the party system, which impeded the development of a strong national state to direct social and economic matters, reflected his ambivalence about expanding the administrative power of the national government. To be sure, Wilson as president would

move towards positions and policies that were more accepting of national administration. He eventually supported the idea of a regulatory commission with broad
responsibilities for overseeing business practices, resulting in the creation of the
Federal Trade Commission in 1914. But New Freedom Progressives continued to
be highly ambivalent about administrative power. Wilson appointed his important
political advisor, Louis Brandeis, to the Supreme Court. Brandeis was an uncompromising defender of decentralization in political and economic affairs, believing
that the self-governing community had requirements of size, cultural cohesion,
and proximity of the citizen to the instruments of government. Although supportive of progressive policies such as thoroughgoing labor reform, Brandeis sought
to apply New Freedom principles in his approach to the state throughout his long
tenure on the bench. His criticism of the New Deal during the 1930s "rested on
his profound antistatism."[56]

Wilson himself never accepted without reservations Croly's idea of progressivism. Even as he moved towards the acceptance of national administrative power,
an inclination that was strengthened as he reluctantly, albeit surely, advanced the
nation toward participation in World War I, he continued to believe that the formation of the national state and the reorganization of the presidency had to be
mediated in critical ways by party politics.[57] Wilson's disasterous campaign for a
League of Nations exemplified the weakness of this partisan approach.

Party Government and the Demise of Progressive Reform

Wilson's plan for a League of Nations was the most controversial of his Fourteen
Points, a program he formulated in early 1918. He hoped to persuade the Allies
and the Senate to accept these policies, which, in addition to the proposal for the
formation of an international peace-keeping association, advocated lenient terms
for the defeated Axis powers. Yet no sooner had the Fourteen Points been pronounced and peace negotiations started, than Congress, tiring of Wilson's independent course in seeking a settlement, began to challenge the President's conduct
of foreign affairs. Ex-president Theodore Roosevelt, whose nationalism was by
now less reformist than militaristic in orientation, abetted this opposition by urging the Senate to repudiate Wilson's Fourteen points. On October 24, 1918, TR
sent a telegram to Republican leaders: "Let us dictate peace by hammering guns
and not chat about peace to the accompaniment of the clicking typewriters."[58]

Flustered by the efforts of Republican leaders to discredit him with the public
before the November elections, Wilson sought to rally the nation in support of his
war policy. The day after Roosevelt's telegram, he appealed to the voters to return
a Democratic majority to Congress. "If you have approved of my leadership and
wish me to be your unembarrassed spokesman in affairs at home and abroad,"
his announcement to the press read, "I earnestly beg that you will express your-
self unmistakably to that effect by returning a Democratic majority to both the
Senate and the House of Representatives."[59]

The 1918 campaign was a serious error. Wilson was loudly criticized for suggesting the Democrats had a monopoly on loyalty; in doing so he seems to have
overlooked the fact that many Republicans had supported his leadership during

the war, while many Democrats had opposed him. Wilson, in fact, actually began his attempts to secure a sympathetic Congress with interference in the primaries of his own party. He actively sought the defeat of Democrats in five Southern states because they had opposed his policies. The President's intervention, unlike that of FDR in 1938, was for the most part characterized by quiet maneuvering within party councils rather than active campaigning; however, Wilson did write several public letters against congressmen and senators who adamantly opposed the war. He publicly opposed the renomination of Democratic Senators Thomas W. Hardwick of Georgia and James K. Vardaman of Mississippi, for instance, because both voted against the declaration of war and virtually all measures carrying it on. Wilson's intervention succeeded in several important instances in defeating enemies within his own party for renomination.[60] But this purge campaign cast doubt on the President's claim during the general election that the return of a Democratic majority to both houses of the Congress was essential for a successful prosecution of the war.

Moreover, the 1918 campaign, occurring as it did in the midst of an international crisis, seemed an inappropriate occasion for an appeal to party loyalty. So intent was Wilson upon leading through his party in Congress that he was seemingly incapable of nonpartisan statesmanship, even when the occasion so clearly called for him to support those who shared his view regardless of party. The negative response that followed Wilson's message contributed to the Republicans making substantial gains in the November elections and, for the first time since 1911, taking control of both legislative chambers. To be sure, other factors were important in the Republican victory. Workers resented high wartime taxes, consumers were irritated by controls, farmers were discontented with government price ceilings on their crops, and there was the usual opposition strength in midterm elections. The President's tactic, however, provided his critics with ammunition to say, as Roosevelt did soon after the election, that "our allies and our enemies and Mr. Wilson himself should all understand that Mr. Wilson has no authority whatever to speak for the American people at this time. His leadership has just been emphatically repudiated by them."[61]

The results of the 1918 election lessened Wilson's prestige at home and abroad, adding immeasurably to the difficulties he was to have at the Peace Conference—and, especially, with Congress. It was a preface, therefore, to the defeat of the Versailles treaty in the Senate the following year. The defeat of that Treaty, in spite of Wilson's month-long speaking tour of the Western states in support of his peace plan, was dramatic evidence that the presidency, though it had gained considerable influence in the hands of Roosevelt and Wilson, was still limited by the vagaries of public opinion and a powerful, if no longer dominant, Congress.

The final chapter of Wilson's presidency left progressive reformers in despair. The results of the 1920 election, in which the conservative Republican Senator Warren G. Harding, campaigning for a "return to normalcy," won by an overwhelming popular vote, signaled a denunciation not only of Wilson's hope for international cooperation, but for the political and economic aspirations of reformers as well. The Republican party that resumed power in March, 1921, was militantly determined to restore the prerogatives of Congress and the traditional party organization. Its dominance over the next decade ensured that the progressive plan to remake American politics would not again resurface until the national crises of the 1930s and 1940s gave Franklin D. Roosevelt the opportunity to complete the foundation for an alliance between Jeffersonianism and Hamiltonianism.

Franklin D. Roosevelt and the Emergence of Programmatic Liberalism

The New Deal is often viewed as a series of ad hoc responses to the political and economic exigencies created by the Great Depression. This perception of reform during the 1930s is more often than not attributed to the leadership of FDR, who generally has been depicted by historians as a president of extraordinary political gifts, though one lacking a coherent philosophical compass. The most influential proponent of this view is James MacGregor Burns. Burns characterizes FDR as a "broker" leader, whose "shiftiness" and "improvising" detracted from "hard, long range purposeful building of a strong popular movement behind a coherent political program."[62] Yet Franklin D. Roosevelt's presidency was not simply one of broker leadership, nor was his program merely an improvisational response to the crises of the 1930s. In fact, FDR consciously patterned his leadership after that of Woodrow Wilson and Theodore Roosevelt, seeking to reconcile the strengths of these leaders.

Roosevelt and the Progressive Tradition

The important differences between advocates of the New Freedom and The New Nationalism continued to be a source of controversy within the New Deal counsels. For example, Adolf Berle, a member of FDR's celebrated "Brains Trust," sought to direct the New Deal towards the political vision of Herbert Croly and Theodore Roosevelt, presupposing the decline of party and the aggrandizement of administration. Yet Berle's influence on the New Deal was counteracted by influential advisors such as Felix Frankfurter, who was sympathetic to the preoccupation of Wilson and Brandeis with subordinating administrative power to political deliberation and choice. Concomitantly, Berle and Frankfurter disagreed strongly about the appropriate strategy for directing social and economic processes: Whereas Berle promoted government planning that used rather than attacked large economic units, Frankfurter favored an aggressive antitrust policy that would foster a competitive economy and make unnecessary the elevation of "enlightened administration" as the center of American political life.

Although the conflicting political and policy preferences of New Deal advisors were often not conducive to logically consistent government action during the Roosevelt presidency, a rough consensus reigned with respect to fundamental principles. New Dealers drawn from both these progressive strands accepted the need for more positive government intervention in the marketplace to redress the abuses of industrial society while preserving the principles of individualism. Both supported Roosevelt's effort to redefine the liberalism of the Democratic party so that it would become the agent of positive national action. This uneasy consensus on fundamental principles was the basis of Roosevelt's Commonwealth Club Address, delivered during the 1932 campaign, which became "the manifesto of the New Deal."[63]

The San Francisco speech, given at noon on September 23, had its genesis in a Berle memorandum to Roosevelt dated August 15. In it, Berle, although considering Roosevelt's chances to win the election "rather better than even," warned the candidate that the "possibility of defeat had to be reckoned on." Should the campaign go off without any statement of FDR's philosophy of government, Berle wrote, "defeat would probably end your career, as it did the careers of [James] Cox, [John W.] Davis, and even Al Smith." Should Roosevelt come forth, however, with a statement of some "outstanding policy"—something "analogous to Woodrow Wilson's 'new freedom' speech"—his "significance in American public life would continue—as did that of [William Jennings] Bryan and Theodore Roosevelt." The focus for such an address, Berle continued, should be "the idea of individualism." Herbert Hoover claimed that individualism was served by a hands-off approach to social problems, that "government shall keep clear of the entire economic system, confining itself to emergency relief, keeping the peace, and the like." Observing that this laissez-faire doctrine could hardly foster liberty "when nearly seventy percent of American industry is concentrated in the hands of six hundred corporations," Berle offered the outline of a new concept of individual rights. "I can see the opposite view," he noted, "which is a far truer individualism, and might be a policy by which the government acted as a regulating and unifying agency, so that within the framework of this industrial system, individual men and women could survive, have homes, educate their children, and so forth."[64]

Berle's memo testified to the important influence that John Dewey had on the New Deal counsels.[65] Berle's notion to redefine liberalism bore striking resemblance to a six-part series Dewey contributed to the *New Republic* in 1929 and 1930, entitled "Individualism, Old and New," which anticipated many of the ideas of the Commonwealth Club address. These essays drew on Croly's distinction between "pioneer" and "progressive" democracy; however, whereas Croly had called for "the *substitution* of frank social policy for the *individualism of the past*," Dewey advocated a reform program suited to a *new* understanding of *individualism*, one that was appropriate for the modern social and economic stresses of the late 1920s.[66]

Dewey's new concept of individualism represented the distinctly American philosophy of Pragmatism that rose to prominence during the late nineteenth century. Like Croly, Dewey argued that rational planning and public experimentation were the most practical and just means of putting the frail structure of the American constitution on a firmer foundation. But Dewey offered a pragmatic formulation that proved more effective in directing the progressive animus against Jeffersonianism. From Dewey New Dealers discovered the effectual truth about how to get around the American hostility to centralized administration, how to persuade Americans that expansive national power was consistent with their revered traditions. "The great tradition of America is liberal," the philosopher H. M.

Kallen wrote in 1935, "and [Dewey] restates in the language and under the conditions of his times what Jefferson's Declaration of Independence affirmed in the language and under the conditions of his." [67]

It is interesting and important that the essays of "Individualism, Old and New" began appearing in the *New Republic* during a period of relatively high prosperity, and continued after the great stock market crash of October, 1929. The crash seemed to justify Dewey's intense dissatisfaction with laissez-faire liberalism and to clarify the boundaries of the new liberalism he advocated. The Great Depression made painfully clear how the massive industrialization of the late nineteenth and early twentieth centuries, and the concomitant centralization of private power, had created a social and economic milieu of permanent insecurity. "Fear of loss of work, dread of the oncoming of old age, create an anxiety and eat into self-respect in a way that impairs personal dignity," Dewey wrote in "Individualism, Old and New." "Where fears abound, courageous and robust individuality is undermined." [68]

The need to establish a broader security, and thereby revitalize democratic individualism, provided the text for Roosevelt's Commonwealth Club address. Berle's August 15 memorandum and other messages he sent along to the White House apparently persuaded Roosevelt to go forth with plans that he and his advisors had tossed around since the beginning of that month for a speech that would sum up the candidate's political philosophy. Berle was given the task of writing the speech, and the first draft, entitled "American Individualism—Romantic and Realistic," closely paralleled Dewey's analysis of the crisis at hand. Decrying President Hoover for perpetuating the "tiresome and empty" myth that "unfettered economic individualism is the corner stone of our national happiness and the great promise of its future," Berle's draft called for "a real understanding of the role American individualism has played in our national life." "The word individualism," Berle insisted, "has no content when divorced from society." [69]

Roosevelt turned a cold shoulder to this first draft, a rendition that sought to rehash Berle's recently published book on the modern corporation. Roosevelt revealed his interest in the major theme, however, by inserting a passage on individualism in his August 20 speech at Columbus, Ohio. [70] Berle persisted, drafting two more versions of the address. The third was the basic format of the speech that Roosevelt would deliver at the Commonwealth Club during his campaign swing out West in late September. Berle's third draft emphasized politics rather than economics; it enunciated a public philosophy that linked the new concept of individualism, requiring the expansion of national administrative power, to traditional American values. The version of the speech that was actually delivered included some limited, though important, changes made by another Brains Truster, Raymond Moley, and Roosevelt himself on the train out West. [71] More than any other of Roosevelt's speeches, the Commonwealth Club address revealed his understanding of the New Deal and the general direction it should take. [72]

The importance of this address, which was one of several Roosevelt delivered on the campaign swing of Western states, did not go unnoticed. As the *San Francisco Examiner* reported, Roosevelt's speech "outlined his philosophy of the responsibilities of government and the responsibilities of private wealth. It was, in effect, a new economic credo which Roosevelt voiced.'' The New York *Times* noted that the speech was generally well received by the audience of businessmen, although ''the impression was gained that many of the audience failed to appreciate the extent of Governor Roosevelt's liberalism.'' It was clear, however, that FDR had forsaken the usual sort of campaign address at the Commonwealth Club in order ''to set forth his theories of government and politics in frank fashion.''[73]

Historical in tone, Roosevelt's remarks gave an account of the American individual's relations with government from Alexander Hamilton to Woodrow Wilson. It revealed clearly the progressive concern to give new meaning to the Hamiltonian tradition by infusing it with a democratic purpose. Also taken up by the address was the related task of rescuing Jefferson, and his defense of local democracy, from the unchecked right of property with which it had become associated. ''Even Jefferson,'' Roosevelt claimed, ''realized that the exercise of property rights might so interfere with the rights of the individual that the government, without whose assistance the property rights could not exist, must intervene, not to destroy individualism but to protect it.''[74] Individual freedom and possessive individualism were compatible as long as property was principally land, land was widely distributed, and the western frontier provided a ''safety valve'' for those to whom the East did not provide a place. But this stage of American political life—''the day of the individual against the system''—was shattered by the industrial revolution, beginning in the last half of the nineteenth century, ''a history of financial titans, whose methods were not scrutinized with too much care, and also were honored in proportion as they produced the results, irrespective of the means they used.''

For a time, the situation of unlimited and unchecked industrial expansion was acceptable—it resulted in robust economic activity that furthered the national interest. ''The turn of the tide came,'' however, ''with the turn of the century.'' By that time, FDR observed, the closing of the Western frontiers and the growth of industrial combinations to the point ''uncontrolled'' and ''irresponsible units'' within the political system threatened ''the economic freedom of individuals to earn a living.'' With the decline of conditions favoring an expansion of the economic sector, the day of the ''financial titan'' was over. The impetus for the national welfare would now have to shift from the shoulders of the productive private citizen to the government; the guarantee of equal opportunity now required that individual initiative be restrained and directed by the national government:

> Clearly, all this calls for a reappraisal of values. . . . Our task now is not discovery or exploitation of natural resources, or necessarily producing more goods. It is the soberer, less dramatic business of administering resources and plants already in hand, of seeking to reestablish foreign markets for our surplus production, of meeting the problem of under consumption, of adjusting production to consumption, of distributing wealth and products more equitably, of adapting existing economic organizations to the service of the people. The day of enlightened administration has come.[75]

Interestingly, Berle's third draft had said, ''The day of the manager has come.'' The final version of the address, fashioned by Moley and Roosevelt, pronounced the day of "enlightened administration" instead, thus pushing home more clearly than the draft language the extent to which the reform of American democracy seemed to bring with it administrative aggrandizement. The task was not merely to accentuate the role of expertise within public councils, but, as Croly had "foreshadowed," to elevate administrative officials and agencies to a central position in the realization of a progressive democratic policy.[76]

This would be a "long, slow task," however. The Commonwealth Club address was attentive to the uneasy fit between an energetic central government and constitutional principles in the United States. "We now have to rewrite the unchangeable concepts of American government in terms of today," Berle's final draft read. Yet Berle had long been troubled about the relationship between the administrative process and traditional concepts of American democracy. He expressed concern towards the end of Wilson's presidency that the newly created national administrative power was here to stay, but that we were going to have to develop a body of law that would control it. Berle published an essay in 1917 that foretold of the concern within the New Deal councils to modify administrative power gradually into a constitutional democratic government. "Now we have come to a stage where we must not only build anew, but also keep in order the existing structures," he wrote. "Already there has arisen the fear that these public bodies, set to solve given problems, may develop into tyrannous institutions, amenable to no law and subject only to the doubtful safeguards of political action."[77]

It was imperative, therefore, that the New Deal be forged upon a political philosophy in which the new concept of state power would be carefully interwoven with the earlier conceptions of American government. The task of modern government, the Commonwealth Club address announced, was "to assist the development of an economic declaration of rights, an economic constitutional order." Most essentially, this required a serious reconsideration of rights in American politics. Berle's draft of the address spoke of the need to "widen" the principle of the social contract that formed the foundation of constitutional government, so that it went beyond "formal, office holding" power and embraced "economic and business" matters as well. The final version delivered by Roosevelt made clearer the extent to which the New Deal presupposed a fundamental reconsideration of the state's obligations—the traditional emphasis in American politics on individual self-reliance should give way, Roosevelt suggested, to an expansive understanding of rights, characterized by a continuous identification of new problems and the search for methods by which those problems might be solved.[78]

The defense of progressive reform in terms of extending the rights of the Constitution was a critical development in the advent of a positive understanding of government responsibility in the United States. The distinction between progressives and nonprogressives, as most boldly set forth by the New Nationalism campaign of 1912, all too visibly placed reformers in opposition to constitutional government and the self-interested basis of American politics. The national community anticipated by more visionary Progressives such as Herbert Croly was a direct challenge to the Jeffersonian and the Hamiltonian traditions, both of which rejected the concept of a national democracy. Berle's concept (borrowed from John Dewey) of new individualism suggested how personal dignity now required a strengthening of national resolve in the United States. The New Deal concept of reform, however, more deftly linked the Hamiltonian and Jeffersonian traditions by asserting the connection between energetic nationalism and rights, albeit rights that looked well beyond, and were in contradiction with, the purposes of nationalism as defined by Hamiltonian principles. Roosevelt gave legitimacy to progressive principles by imbedding them in the language of constitutionalism and interpreting them as an *expansion* rather than a *subversion* of the natural rights tradition.

The Commonwealth Club address reflected Roosevelt's plan to build upon the work of earlier reformers, combining the New Nationalism commitment to administrative aggrandizement and the New Freedom preoccupation with the individual's rights against the state. Like Progressive thinkers, moreover, Roosevelt emphasized the imperative of strong moral leadership within the White House. "The greatest duty of a statesman is to educate," the conclusion of the speech read, and the task of progressive leaders was to educate the nation "to recognize the new terms of the old social contract." The peroration of Berle's draft stated that the nation would fulfill the new terms of justice in American society, just as it fulfilled "the obligation of apparent Utopia which Jefferson imagined for us in 1776, and which Washington, Jefferson, Madison, and Jackson brought to realization." This suggested both that the Jeffersonian and Jacksonian eras satisfied the terms of the *Declaration* and that the fulfillment of progressive aspirations required looking beyond Jefferson's fertile imagination. Theodore Roosevelt and Woodrow Wilson had begun the construction of a new political order; the task of the New Deal was to consolidate the gains of FDR's progressive predecessors.

In the final form of the address, however, Roosevelt offered a more radical— less time-bound—understanding of the *Declaration*, reiterating the point made earlier in his remarks that the rights pronounced by that document were in continual need of redefinition. In modifying Berle's passage, FDR stressed that the leadership of Jefferson, Roosevelt, and Wilson did not realize, but "sought to bring to realization" the political order that Jefferson pronounced in 1776. This reference to the leadership of the Progressive era as carrying on Jefferson's work, moreover, revealed FDR's intention to realize what the Republican Roosevelt and Wilson had sought but failed to accomplish—a full-scale political realignment.

"More than most presidents," the columnist Anne O'Hare McCormick wrote of FDR in 1936, "he measures himself by his official ancestors."[79] Like Jefferson, Roosevelt intended to be an instrument of historic change, although this would entail redressing the defects of the Jeffersonian political order. By this measure, the success of Theodore Roosevelt and Woodrow Wilson in advancing progressive democracy fell short, as neither of them had presided over a realignment. Only a political change as decisive as the "Revolution of 1800"—one that would make a "return to normalcy" impossible—could make the "apparent Utopia" that Jefferson imagined in 1776 meaningful for the political realities of the twentieth century.

The Role of Leadership and Party in the New Deal

Roosevelt's attempt to reconcile traditional principles of limited government with those of progressive reform resulted in policies, especially during the early days of the New Deal, that seemed excessively compromising and unsystematic to many ardent reformers of the 1930s. Although John Dewey supported Roosevelt's attempt to redefine individualism and liberty in ways that realistically connected them with their social and economic conditions, he feared that the New Deal's pragmatism tended to devolve into unthinking and unprincipled practicality. Dewey advocated the "experimental intelligence" as a method of forging a middle path between bureaucratic absolutism on the one hand, and a laissez-faire economic order on the other. Nevertheless, he cautioned in 1935, with an eye on the early New Deal, that pragmatism, properly understood—the "experimental method"—was "not just messing around nor doing a little of this and a little of that in the hope that things will improve."[80]

According to some scholars, the incoherence of the New Deal resulted from the fact that it drew support from the two competing strands of Progressivism. For example, Ellis Hawley has observed that the National Recovery Administration, the dominant New Deal agency during FDR's first term, suffered from the conflicting counsels of New Nationalists, supportive of regulatory policies that accepted the concentration of economic power, and New Freedom partisans, supportive of vigorous anti-trust action that would make the aggrandizement of national regulatory power unnecessary. "Such conflicting counsels," Hawley writes, "were hardly conducive to logically consistent administration, particularly when they were backed by rival economic pressure groups, subordinated to the demand for action, and set in the midst of the worst depression in American history."[81]

Yet the Commonwealth Club address suggested that the New Deal had a political coherence that transcended its economic contradictions. Indeed, Roosevelt believed that the success of the New Deal required building upon and resolving the competing principles that divided progressives. Similarly, he believed that there were important lessons to be learned from the successes and failures of Theodore Roosevelt and Woodrow Wilson, lessons that had to be applied to the political conditions of the 1930s if the accomplishments of his presidency were to be more enduring than those of his two progressive predecessors.

Roosevelt gave explicit expression to the aspirations of his presidency with respect to TR and Wilson in a revealing correspondence carried on with Ray Stannard Baker, Wilson's close associate and biographer. One of their more interesting exchanges occurred in March, 1935, which Baker initiated by expressing a concern about the New Deal's pragmatic character:

> While the defense and exposition of your policies has often been able and courageous in detail, it has seemed to me to lack the power of a unifying vision. There is such a vision beyond and above the confusing multiplicity of things which you are trying to do. If I did not believe it, if I did not myself feel it and see it, I should no longer support you.[82]

Baker went on to suggest that FDR follow Wilson in appealing "to the profoundest moral and social convictions" in the American people. As the frenzy and motion of the early days of the New Deal passed, he believed, it was necessary to stress, as Wilson had, the rhetorical power of the modern executive office. "I believe that no people in the world respond more readily to great vision, profound moral purposes, than Americans," Baker wrote. "There are resources of conviction and enthusiasm that have only to be tapped by a leadership that can really clarify the fundamental issue behind the confusing and superficial issues, and not afraid [sic] to ask for sacrifice and consecration."[83] The stuff of the campaign address at the Commonwealth Club, Baker thereby implied, must become a routine part of the Roosevelt presidency.[84]

FDR's response to Baker represents a rather penetrating analysis of reform leadership, which belies his reputation as a shallow thinker. This response shows that he sought to combine principled rhetoric and instrumental policy achievement:

> Theodore Roosevelt lacked Woodrow Wilson's appeal to the fundamental and failed to stir, as Wilson did, the truly profound moral and social convictions. Wilson, on the other hand, failed where Theodore Roosevelt succeeded in stirring people to enthusiasm about specific individual events, even though these specific events may have been superficial in comparison with the fundamentals.[85]

This intent to link principles with specific policy achievements reflected FDR's plan to combine the democratic vision of Wilson with the programmatic concerns of Herbert Croly and Theodore Roosevelt. The working out of that combination was resolved not only in a principled defense of social welfare programs, but also in an articulation of a public philosophy that would support the strengthening of the national government's administrative capacities. According to Roosevelt, the linking of principled rhetoric and the particulars of public management was the keystone of responsible democratic leadership:

> You are so absolutely right about the response that this country gives to vision and profound moral purposes that I can only assure you of my hearty concurrence and of my constant desire to make the appeal.
>
> I know at the same time that you will be sympathetic to the point of view that the public psychology and, for that matter, individual psychology, cannot, because of human weakness, be attuned to a constant repetition of the highest note on the scale. . . .[86]

FDR indicated that the time would soon be ripe for a more fervent commitment to principle, and assured Baker that the reform vision expressed during the early days of his administration would be renewed. Anticipating the "militant liberalism" that would inspire the bold programmatic initiatives of late 1935—the so-called "Second New Deal"—and the aggressive reelection campaign of 1936, he ended:

> I am inclined to think that in view of the unfolding of the domestic scene and now of the foreign scene, you are right in your thought that the time is at hand for a new stimulation of united American action. I am proposing that sort of thing before the year is out.[87]

Roosevelt's understanding of presidential leadership as expressed in his correspondence with Baker helps to explain the character of his party leadership and the New Deal realignment. Although a magnificent party leader in many respects, Roosevelt, Burns argues, did not "build a stronger party system at the grass roots, more directly responsive to national direction and more closely oriented around New Deal programs and issues." [88] This failure, Burns and other critics of Roosevelt's party leadership have argued, owed to his "broker" style of leadership, characterized by a philosophical dexterity and command of a variety of political roles, as well as the fact that the New Deal was a series of ad hoc responses to the political and economic exigencies created by the depression. It is true that Roosevelt did not transform the Democratic party into an instrument of militant progressive reform and that he was unwilling to commit himself completely to party leadership. But the pragmatism of FDR was not simply a matter of improvisation. It also reflected his understanding that an excessive reliance on visionary rhetoric and a commitment to a less flexible progressive doctrine would either result in outright rejection by the American people or, as Roosevelt put it to Baker, allow more extreme political actors, such as Huey Long and Father Coughlin, to turn "the eyes of the audience away from the main drama itself." New Deal pragmatism, it would seem, was connected to a rather well-thought-out plan to reshape the working of American democracy.

In the final analysis, a reconstituted party system was not considered the appropriate path to bring about such a change. Unlike Croly, Roosevelt was not willing to abandon the two-party system. He believed that leadership within the traditional two-party framework was necessary to organize public opinion into a governing coalition. For this reason, Roosevelt did not take seriously the efforts of some progressive intellectuals to form a third party. John Dewey took an active part in these efforts, believing that the continuing failure of the two major parties to offer programs that were in touch with the realities of twentieth century American life made necessary the revitalization of the Progressive movement in 1912. In 1929, Dewey helped organize and became the first President of the League for Independent Political Action, which sought to rally progressives around a new party. Paul Douglas, a University of Chicago Professor and member of the League for Independent Political Action, argued in his 1932 volume, *The Coming of a New Party,* that Roosevelt could do nothing with the old parties and that the time was ripe for a new one:

> It is a sobering thought that twenty years ago many Progressives were pinning similar hopes on Woodrow Wilson, who, with all respect to Governor Roosevelt, was a far keener thinker and a more determined fighter. . . .Yet, after eight years, Wilson retired with the Democratic party as cancerous as ever in its composition and as conservative in its policies. If such was the fate of Wilson, how can we hope for better things from Franklin Roosevelt? [89]

Roosevelt considered the project to elect a progressive outside the two-party system quixotic. After all, the fate of Theodore Roosevelt in 1912 was hardly cause for investing progressive hopes in a third-party movement. The progressive's best chance, he averred, was to attempt to succeed where Wilson had failed:

[S]uppose someone with similar ideas, but with more political foresight [than Dewey and Douglas], . . . did get a major party's nomination, and was elected; wasn't that better? In a practical sense—that is, in a sense of making headway toward such objectives—was there any other way in a democracy? . . . The Democratic offering would be less than the radicals would like, but it would be something voters would accept.[90]

Roosevelt understood that the incorrigible character of the party system decried by the third-party movement did not simply reflect its decrepitude. In fact, its institutional decentralization and ideological diversity were symptomatic of obstacles to party government that were deeply ingrained in the United States Constitution. Just as New Dealers chose to circumvent or reappraise fundamental constitutional principles and mechanisms rather than directly assault them, so the Roosevelt administration's party politics avoided a full-scale challenge to traditional partisan practices.

Roosevelt knew, however, that the life of progressive leaders within the old party organizations was hard. Like Croly, he was persuaded that the tradition of party politics in the United States dictated that a strengthening of national administrative power required the eventual decline, if not the demise, of partisan politics. Even as he accepted the Democratic nomination, therefore, he sought to keep his distance from the party. This explains why Roosevelt did not follow Wilson in embracing the role of party leader, but sought instead to unite the progressives of both parties behind the New Deal program. Indeed, at times during his first run for the White House, FDR seemed intent upon resurrecting the New Nationalism campaign of 1912, a campaign that was not simply an attack on the two-party system, but upon the whole concept of partisanship.[91]

Roosevelt's concern to distance himself from conventional party politics was quite evident during the important 1932 Western campaign swing. With the Commonwealth Club address, FDR offered a clear statement of his commitment to progressive principles; on another occasion, he made a nonpartisan appeal to progressive Republicans to support the New Deal. In an overture of great symbolic and practical significance, FDR gave special consideration to the Republican California Senator Hiram Johnson during a campaign stop at Sacramento on September 23. Johnson was the running mate of Theodore Roosevelt in the 1912 break of progressive Republicans away from the GOP "Old Guard," and FDR's words were reminiscent of the Roosevelt–Johnson fight against traditional partisan practices:

There is [a] principle that I am stressing wherever I speak that I know is in line with the fundamental ideas of your State and that is that in this campaign there is going to be less following of party lines than ever before in history.

The people of this country have come to believe that what this country needs is new leadership, and that the battle we are waging is a battle for new leaders; not a mere change of party; not a mere change of the party emblem, not a mere change of names, but a change of principles, a "new deal." . . .

I repeat that in no State is this spirit of nonpartisanship more pronounced than in California. It is written in your law, your primary and election laws. It dominates your thinking, and I may add, it is the great compelling purpose of some of your statesmen.[92]

Roosevelt's expressed support for the "great compelling purpose" of nonpartisanship went beyond short-term political considerations.[93] It reflected the more fundamental consideration that progressive principles were at odds with partisanship itself, that, as Croly had argued, an enlightened administration of the law and public business would be fatal to the two-party system. FDR agreed with Croly and the leaders of the League for Independent Political Action that the traditional party apparatus was for the most part beyond repair, so wedded was it to the decentralizing institutions of American politics. When Ray Stannard Baker wrote to FDR in September, 1936, complaining of the Curley machine in Massachusetts, and expressing the necessity to "clean out the Democratic organization" of that state, Roosevelt's response was one of sympathetic resignation: "There is I fear, much too much in what you say—but what is a poor fellow to do about it: I wish I knew."[94]

Even in his home state of New York, Roosevelt considered hopeless any concerted effort to reform the Democratic organization. Rather than seek to free New York Democracy from the grip of Tammany Hall, with which FDR had a very uneasy relationship, he gave tacit support to militant nonpartisans such as Fiorello LaGuardia, who was elected Mayor of New York City in 1933 on the Fusion Party, an organization dedicated to ridding the city of partisan vices. At the urging of Adolf Berle, a strong La Guardia supporter, FDR stayed neutral in the New York race, even denying support to an anti-Tammany Democrat Joseph V. McKee, whose candidacy on the "Recovery" party ticket was dedicated to reforming, rather than eliminating, party politics in New York. Roosevelt said nothing during the campaign—to the tacit advantage of LaGuardia, upon whom Berle's well-publicized support bestowed the aura of the New Deal. La Guardia won by a quarter of a million votes, and his victory tied the New Deal to local and state forces that eschewed traditional partisanship.

The Roosevelt administration's rejection of party government developed not only from practicality but from principle. As noted, New Dealers did not view the welfare state as a partisan issue but as a constitutional one. The reform program of the 1930s was conceived as an "economic bill of rights," which should be established as much as possible as permanent programs beyond the vagaries of public opinion and elections. This view of New Deal reform, first declared in the 1932 Commonwealth Club speech, was reaffirmed repeatedly throughout the Roosevelt presidency.

FDR himself drafted the 1936 Democratic platform, employing language from the Declaration of Independence to emphasize the need for a redefinition of "the self-evident truths" that formed the foundation of American politics. The fundamental principle of this document, described by Burns as "unusually outspoken and eloquent," was stated clearly at the beginning, preparing the ground for the defense of the administration's specific programs:

We hold this truth to be self-evident—that government in a modern civilization has certain inescapable obligations to its citizens, among which are:

1. Protection of the family and home.

2. Establishment of a democracy of opportunity for all the people

3. Aid to those overtaken by disaster. These obligations, neglected through twelve years of the old leadership, have once more been recognized by American government. Under the new leadership they will never be neglected.[95]

The emphasis on the programmatic character of these obligations was brought home by the section of the platform on social security. "We have built foundations for the security of those who are faced with the hazards of unemployment and old age; for the orphaned, the crippled, and the blind," the document declared about the landmark legislation of 1935. But this legislation was only to be the framework of continuous attention to the intractable problems of industrial society: "On the foundation of the Social Security Act we are determined to erect a structure of economic security for all our people, making sure that this benefit shall keep step with the ever-increasing capacity of America to provide a high standard of living for all its citizens."[96]

With the Democratic triumph of 1936, "the liberal tradition in America," as Louis Hartz calls it, took on a new and more explicitly political meaning. Liberalism in American politics hitherto was associated with Jeffersonian principles, which followed the natural rights tradition of limited government. According to this tradition, associated with the philosophy expressed in Locke's *Second Treatise* and the *Declaration of Independence,* government existed to serve certain inalienable rights, which presupposed a distinction between state and society. Roosevelt was the first statesman to "appropriate" the term *liberalism* and make it part of the common political vocabulary. In doing so, however, he reworked— some claimed perverted—the elements of the old faith into a modern form. Roosevelt pronounced a liberalism that evoked the *Declaration's* concept of rights, but linked this concept to programmatic expansion. Or, as the historian Charles Forcey has written, the new liberalism "turned away from a dream of automatic progress by the free-wheeling exercise of individual rights to a conviction that only the conscious, cooperative use of governmental power can bring reform."[97]

The results of the 1936 election appeared to sanction FDR's interpretation of the Declaration. Roosevelt, of course, won every state but Maine and Vermont. More significant, FDR had won the day on the issue of whether Roosevelt's policies meant greater liberty or tyranny. The New York *Times* reported in February, 1936, "Liberalism and all it stands for is coming forward as an issue in the national campaign. Both New Deal and anti-administration spokesmen declare their devotion to the liberal ideal of freedom and democracy; both assail each other as opponents of true liberalism."[98] The 1936 Republican platform declared that "America was in peril" and dedicated the party to "the preservation of . . . political liberty," which "for the first time" was "threatened by Government itself." The Republican party, with its historical commitment to preserving a large sphere of unrestricted private action, "must become the true liberal party," argued ex-President Hoover. The New Deal, he said, was a "false liberalism" that regimented men and extended bureaucracy.[99] But Roosevelt, joined by supporters such as John Dewey, successfully defended the New Deal in terms of liberalism.

The campaign must have been successful, Ronald Rotunda has written, "for although Hoover continually insisted that he was a liberal, the 1936 election presented the first instances of some Hoover-like liberals who began to admit that they were really conservatives."[100] Roosevelt's great landslide, the magnitude of which was unprecedented in American history, firmly established the New Deal program as the foundation of a new liberal majority and relegated its strident opponents to virtually irrelevant status.

The New Deal never had quite the radical consequences that some of FDR's bolder philosophic pronouncements suggested.[101] The new understanding of rights that Roosevelt made the foundation of New Deal reform was not formally ratified as amendments to the Constitution, nor was it fully codified in statutes and policies. As the chapters that follow reveal, however, these rights became the foundation of political dialogue in the United States, thus redefining the role of the national government. The new social contract heralded by FDR marks the beginning of what has been called the "rights revolution"—a transformation in the governing philosophy of the United States that has brought about major changes in American political institutions.[102]

Roosevelt's reappraisal of values is important in understanding the New Deal, but it is likewise important in understanding FDR's impact on party politics. The achievement of programmatic rights did not demand a new stage of partisanship, but, as Roosevelt argued in his 1937 inaugural address, movement toward a new "era of good feeling."[103] The term *era of good feeling* was first applied to the period between 1812 and 1824, during which the decisive triumph of the Democratic–Republicans over the Federalists had appeared to transform heated party politics into a nonpartisan commitment to Jeffersonian principles. But whereas the decline of party in the earlier "era of good feeling" was forged on constitutional principles dedicated to preserving administrative decentralization, the burden of New Deal reform was to rescue the Constitution from those principles. Moreover, Roosevelt pursued an institutional program during his second term—a "Third New Deal"—that looked to the formation of a national state that would make unnecessary the recrudescence of partisanship.[104]

A Party to End Party Politics

Due to the intractable condition of party politics in the United States and Roosevelt's conceptualization of New Deal program as "rights," which warranted protection from partisan struggles, the "Third New Deal" did not promote party government but fostered instead a program that would help the president and administrative agencies govern in the absence of party government. This program included measures, such as the Court-"packing" plan, the Executive Reorganization Act, and the purge campaign, that would establish a refurbished executive power as the vital center of American politics. Roosevelt did not achieve all that he wanted from this institutional program. Yet, as is generally recognized with respect to the Court-"packing" plan, in spite of losing some battles, he essentially won the war. The result was the gradual demise of a decentralized polity, based on localized parties and court rulings that constrained national administration within a narrow sphere, and the emergence of a presidency-generated administrative politics, dedicated to the enlargement of the power of the federal government. The embellishment of executive administration resulted in a deemphasis on partisan politics both by depriving party leaders of many of their traditional responsibilities and imbedding New Deal programs, considered tantamount to political rights, in a bureaucratic structure that would insulate reform and reformers from party politics and electoral change.

Ironically, this displacement of partisanship required a major partisan effort in the short run in order to generate popular support for an economic constitutional order. To a point, of course, this made partisanship an integral part of New Deal politics. Harking back to Jefferson's project to build the Democratic–Republican party, as a temporary instrument in the struggle to form a constitutional order that would be compatible with popular rule, Roosevelt wrote in *Looking Forward:*

> [Jefferson] has been called a politician because he devoted years to the building of a political party. But his labor was in itself a definite and practical contribution to the unification of all parts of the country in support of common principles. When people carelessly or snobbishly deride political parties, they overlook the fact that the party system of government is one of the greatest methods of unification and of teaching people to think in common terms of our civilization.[105]

It was necessary, therefore, to remake the Democratic party as an instrument to free the councils of government, particularly the president and bureaucracy, from the restraints of traditional party politics and constitutional understandings. In this way the New Deal was not intelligible in terms of the historical dichotomy in the United States between nonpartisan administration and partisan politics. Rather, it made possible a new blending of partisanship and administration, one in which administration would become a vehicle for partisan objectives; for liberal partisanship. The story of how the Democratic party became a party of administration and the implications of that change for representative government in the United States is told in the next four chapters.

3

Whose Party Is It? The Transformation of the Democratic Party

Shortly after FDR submitted his SupremeCourt plan to Congress in 1937, an article entitled "Whose Party Is It?" appeared in the *Saturday Evening Post*. Written by Stanley High, a member of the President's publicity steering committee and speech-writing team during the 1936 campaign, this essay asserted that FDR's triumphant re-election was but a prelude to a forthcoming battle for control of the Democratic Party. The traditional Democratic party, Dr. High observed, dominated by Southern conservatives and Northeastern machine "bosses," had little use for the economic constitutional order that FDR and his close advisors had begun to develop during the first term. The programmatic liberals who were forging the New Deal within the White House and newly created administrative agencies, in turn, had no particular devotion to the Democratic party, save its use as a vehicle to advance programmatic reform. The popularity of Roosevelt and his program as well as the severity of the depression had brought these two "factions" together, a "happy union" that held through the 1936 election, but the union was one of convenience, and was not likely to endure. "The issue, therefore," High wrote, "is to determine whether the Democratic Party is to be the Democratic party as it has always been or whether it is now to become the liberal party." [1]

High's article caused quite a stir on Capitol Hill, and it brought a quick repudiation from the White House, which challenged the editor's description of High as "one of the President's close advisors." A White House announcement issued on February 5 (the day the contents of the article actual broke) said: "The President announced the death of the official spokesman in March, 1933. He now announces the passing of the so-called authoritative spokesman—those who write as one of the president's close advisors." [2]

Tellingly, the "slap down" of High, to use his description, never repudiated the contents of the article itself. In fact, High reports receiving words of contrition from those who were still around the President, notably Thomas Corcoran and Samuel Rosenman. "The thing couldn't have broken on a worse day," Rosenman told High. "FDR was getting his Supreme Court message in shape," he continued. "He knew he'd need the undivided loyalty of all his friends on the Hill. This article—if it had been allowed to stand as something that looked official—would have made the fate of his proposals uncertain."[3]

The controversy surrounding High's essay represents well Roosevelt's ambivalence about his role as the titular leader of the Democratic party. FDR's understanding of the limited place of parties in American politics and his long experience within the party councils had persuaded him both of the necessity to modify the principles and organization of the Democratic party and of the herculean task involved in doing so. Thus, he believed, as High wrote, that he had to wage a campaign against Democratic regulars and assert control over the party. Nevertheless, he was uncertain that the party leaders could be supplanted, and he was reluctant to risk an open assault on the regular party apparatus.[4]

"We Will Break Foolish Traditions. . ."—Roosevelt as Party Leader

During the 1932 campaign, FDR sought an affinity with all elements of party, proclaiming in his acceptance of the nomination, for example, that he supported the rather conservative Democratic platform 100%. But it was suggested in the press that Roosevelt and his close advisors—the members of the so-called "Brains Trust"—were talking about remaking the Democratic party from the very beginning of his presidency.[5] Indeed, Rexford Tugwell revealed years later that he and other close advisors knew that Roosevelt's expressed support for the 1932 Democratic platform was delivered with "tongue in cheek."[6]

Roosevelt's very presence at the 1932 Democratic convention in Chicago reflected his intention to alter traditional partisan practices. In the past, major party nominees had stayed away from the convention, waiting to be notified officially of their nomination. But FDR meant to show his party and the nation that he would not hesitate to break revered traditions that obstructed progress, as he understood it.[7] Conservative Democrats might have been assuaged by FDR's acceptance of the platform and his call for an "immediate program of action" to "abolish useless offices [and] . . . eliminate unnecessary functions of government." But the drama of his trip to Chicago and the overall tone of his speech before the convention gave expression to Roosevelt's unwillingness to carry on business as usual. "I have started out on the tasks that lie ahead by breaking the absurd traditions that the candidate should remain in professed ignorance of what has happened for weeks until he is formally notified of that event many weeks later," Roosevelt told the convention on July 2, 1932. "Let it also be symbolic that in so doing I broke traditions. Let it be from now on the task of our party to break foolish traditions."[8]

Implicit in this call for bold experimentation was a challenge to the dominance of the party organization by leaders in the states and the Congress. The only previous presidential candidate to attend a convention was Theodore Roosevelt, who, having bolted from the Republican party, appeared before the gathering in Chicago that launched the Bull Moose campaign in 1912. TR's personal control of the Progressive party was extraordinary. The Progressive campaign thus fore-told not only of the emergence of a more active and expansive national govern-ment but also of presidential campaigns conducted less by parties then by individ-ual candidates. It fell to FDR to institutionalize the challenge to regular party practices represented by the 1912 Progressive campaign. The closing remarks of his nomination speech, pledging a "New Deal" for the American people, presup-posed a full-scale realignment of the political parties, the first in history that made the executive central to its long-range program. The fact that the Democratic party and representative government in general had been viewed as bulwarks against a strong executive meant that such a realignment could not take place without major changes in, if not a decline of, partisan responsibility.

The Emergence of Ideological Patronage

The need to resolve this long-standing tension between party politics and the re-quirement of efficient and positive governance lay behind Roosevelt's modifica-tion of the partisan practices of previous administrations. Soon after he was elected president, for example, FDR evaluated the personnel policy of Woodrow Wilson with a view to making more progressive appointments than his Democratic predecessor. The President-elect was quite intrigued by a letter he received on December 15, 1932 from Jospheus Daniels, who was Wilson's Secretary of Navy when FDR served as Assistant Secretary, that referred to Wilson's promise prior to his inauguration to "nominate progressives—and only progressives." That promise, made in an article written for *Collier's,* was never kept, Daniels com-plained, as Wilson decided to accept the counsel of his Postmaster General Joseph Burleson to act in a "partisan spirit." [9]

A few days later FDR wrote Wilson's close associate and biographer, Ray Stannard Baker, asking him to authenticate the Wilson quotation Daniels sent him. Baker's reply included the entire piece from *Collier's* and offered an explanation for "Wilson's difficulty in putting his resolution into practice." FDR would have to struggle with the same problems that Wilson did with respect to partisan mat-ters, Baker suggested. He would have to choose between leading a coalition of progressives, who were "divided between the two parties," or attempt, as Wilson did, to employ traditional patronage practices in the hope of enlisting the cooper-ation of his own party in enacting a reform program. "I have been greatly im-pressed," wrote Baker, "with the strong resemblances of the present situation to that which existed in 1913. You are coming into office, just as Wilson did, after years of agitation, with a demand for changes, more or less radical, to meet seri-ous problems which confront the country." [10]

The similarity between Wilson's and his own situation must have been on Roosevelt's mind a few weeks later when he expressed to his Attorney General, Homer Cummings, who presided over the Democratic National Committee during the Wilson years, his desire to avoid Wilson's betrayal of the pledge to appoint reformers to the executive branch. "[FDR] talked about the general rule of pa-tronage as it prevailed during the Wilson administration," Cummings reported in his diary entry for January 15, 1933. "It is his desire to proceed on somewhat different lines, primarily with the view . . . to building up national organization rather than allowing patronage to be used merely to build senatorial and congressional machines."[11]

The administration was careful, however, not to challenge partisan conventions so forcefully as to undermine the party unity forged during the early days of the New Deal. Roosevelt generally tolerated standard patronage practices during his first term; in conformity with long-standing practice, the responsibilities of postmaster general and party chairman were assigned to the president's top political advisor, James Farley, who served as the representative of the regular party apparatus in the Cabinet and coordinated appointments in response to local organizations and Democratic Senators. As the Democrats had been out of power for 12 years, and the country was in the midst of a bitter depression, the administration was besieged by job seekers. "Not since Grover Cleveland's administration," the National Civil Service Reform League warned in 1933, "has the merit system had to face such a serious challenge to its existence as it faces now upon the late change of administration."[12] With a Congress hungrier than usual for patronage, most of the newly created New Deal agencies were exempted from classified service: The result was a public service in which the proportion of offices under the merit system rapidly declined from its previous peak of around 80 percent under President Hoover. By 1936 only about 60 percent of a total federal public service of more than 800,000 was on the classified list, the lowest percentage recorded since Theodore Roosevelt's first term in office more than 30 years before.[13]

The president seldom disapproved congressional exemptions of newly created federal agencies from the cumbersome channels of the classified service. The emergency agencies set up during the early days of the administration had to be staffed quickly; moreover, as these exemptions grew, the appointment power of the president greatly increased. At first, FDR used this power in close consultation with Farley and Democratic leaders to bind together the discordant party he had inherited. The nature of the emergency was the primary force in holding together the Democratic coalition during FDR's first term, but the skill the president and Farley displayed in making appointments certainly contributed to Congress's unusual subservience during the early stages of the New Deal. Given the expansion of federal jobs and projects, Roosevelt was in a better position than was Wilson to reward and punish for support of his social program.[14]

In many respects, then, Roosevelt's use of patronage during his first term represented an intensification of the practices employed by Wilson to bind together the disparate elements of the Democratic party. Like Wilson, Paul Van Riper has written, FDR "found it painfully obvious that control of his party was essential to execute any political program."[15] Nevertheless, Roosevelt believed that an undue dependence on the regular Democratic party would prevent a fundamental alteration of political alignments in the United States. Accordingly, even during the early days of the administration, his support of regular patronage practices was not complete. Instead, he departed from conventional practices to reward certain Republican Progressives and other reformers outside the Democratic party, thus taking the initial steps to develop a national New Deal organization that operated independently of the regular party apparatus. As discussed in the previous chapter,

FDR had expressed support for the "great compelling purpose of nonpartisanship" during the 1932 campaign in his fulsome praise of the Progressive Republican Hiram Johnson. There was more to FDR's departure from conventional partisan practices than appeared in the content of his speeches and symbolic gestures. The New Deal for the unemployed, for example, was in the hands of Harry Hopkins, the head of the Works Progress Administration, and Harold Ickes, the Secretary of Interior and director of the Public Works Administration. Before his appointment, Hopkins had been a social worker in New York City and, at one time, a member of the Socialist party. Ickes, a Theodore Roosevelt Progressive, had long been active in Chicago political causes that sought to emancipate the city from the control of the local Democratic machine.

Recognition of "independent" progressives was not limited to higher administrative posts. In Minnesota, FDR enlisted the support of a reluctant Farley to bypass the local Democratic organization in matters of federal patronage in favor of the Farmer Labor party. Similar alliances were worked out with the LaFollette Progressives in Wisconsin and the Democratic insurgents in Michigan who opposed the regular Democratic organization in that state. The situation in Michigan came to a head in February, 1936, when the Roosevelt administration nominated Arthur F. Lederle to be the U.S. District Judge for the Eastern District of Michigan, although he was not the candidate of the state Democratic organization. There had been several months of controversy over this appointment, reflecting the deep antagonisms between Roosevelt allies and the regular party leadership in the state. Lederle's nomination, which was encouraged by the liberal Republican Senator James Couzens and the Maverick Democrat Frank Murphy, then serving the Roosevelt administration as the Governor General of the Philippines, resulted in the resignation of former Michigan Governor William A. Comstock from the Democratic Party. Accusing Roosevelt and Farley of breaking agreements made in 1932 that Federal patronage should go through regular channels—mainly members of the National Committee and the State organization—Comstock issued a statement that claimed Lederle's appointment furnished "further and final evidence that the national leaders of the Democratic party deliberately disregard the opinions of organized Michigan Democrats in making Federal appointments and desire those who kept the party alive and clean during the dark days be pushed out of the Democratic political picture."[16]

It was Roosevelt's view, of course, that the Democrats party would never escape those dark days without the support of progressive forces, who refused to suffer participation in a coalition with the traditional elements of the party. The support he lent to progressive insurgents in states such as California, Wisconsin, Minnesota, and Michigan was part of a strategy that unfolded gradually during Roosevelt's time in office to establish the President as not only the Democratic leader, but the progressive leader in the country.[17]

The alliances the White House formed with Republican Progressives, insurgent Democrats, and Farmer–Laborites caused Farley considerable discomfort. Although he generally went along with Roosevelt on patronage matters, Farley's advocacy for and close ties to party leaders in Congress and the states caused strain between him and the President. On one occasion, Farley presented a letter to the President from a member of the Minnesota Democratic State Central committee that characterized the Roosevelt administration's attitude toward the regular party apparatus in that state as "pathetic." The Postmaster General's sympathy for this complaint elicited a memorandum from Roosevelt that defended the Administration's support of progressive insurgents in Minnesota and elsewhere in terms that were "as clear as the nose on my face." The trouble with Democratic leaders in Minnesota, FDR wrote, was that they "appeared wholly willing" to occupy third position below the Farmer Labor ticket and the Republican ticket. As in Wisconsin, he continued, "many of them [were] willing to accept the crumbs from the tables of the Republicans and Progressives." By disassociating itself from the "old-line state Central Committee conservative wing" of the Democratic party in Minnesota and Wisconsin, and working in sympathy with the Farmer Labor and Progressive people in those states, the President's memo concluded, the administration "was not opposed by the Farmer Labor crowd in 1932 or in 1936, and the [national Democratic] ticket carried the state of Wisconsin overwhelmingly. Furthermore, the Minnesota Farmer Labor people and liberal Democrats actually supported us in our efforts to stave off the threat of a third ticket." [18]

The Roosevelt administration's circumvention of certain state and municipal machines in making appointments was not only considered good politics, but also indispensable to the transformation of the federal government anticipated by liberal reformers. This transformation, Roosevelt believed, could not take place unless the Democratic party was reoriented to accommodate the new intellectual elite that came storming into Washington after 1932. The necessity for the recruitment of "idea men" from outside the party ranks emphasized the lack of any system for attracting to the national government individuals capable of the intellectual effort and sense of mission that had been considered the principal achievement of the British civil service.[19] Chapter 5 will examine how Roosevelt sought to remedy this situation, in part, by modifying traditional civil service procedures to provide attractive careers for those dedicated to a new role of government in the United States. FDR also sought to instill in American political life a recognition of the value of such individuals to the public service.[20] Unlike Wilson, Roosevelt always doubted that political parties in the United States could be modeled after the British system of party government; nevertheless, the Democratic party had to become a party that was more attuned to a positive role for the national government.

As a result, the recommendations of Farley and organization people were more frequently disregarded after 1936. Beginning in 1938, especially, when Roosevelt's partisan actions became more aggressive, patronage practices consistently circumvented the traditional organization. Concomitantly, White House aides, most notably Thomas Corcoran, became more influential in dispensing patronage.[21]

From a political point of view, this departure from conventional patronage practices resulted, as Van Riper has noted, "in the development of another kind of patronage, a sort of intellectual and ideological patronage rather than the more traditional partisan type."[22] The administration's circumvention of the state party leaders and the national committee in selecting personnel—a practice especially common in staffing new programs—was, in a sense, nonpartisan; however, careful attention was given to the political commitments and associations of job candidates, resulting in a loosely knit, albeit well-defined, group of individuals whose loyalties rested with the New Deal rather then the Democratic party. In looking for a monumental commitment to activist government and individuals who understood but were not part of newly regulated industries, FDR relied to an unprecedented degree on academics and young lawyers. As one of their number wrote at the time, their ascendence in Washington meant that:

> For the first time, short of war, the government had tapped the moral and intellectual energies of the college-bred middle classes. It was a psychic "blood transfusion," which invigorated political administration beyond belief. It frightened the politicians and the bureaucrats and, through the newspapers, amused and puzzled the public.[23]

The development of a new form of patronage during the New Deal was fiercely resented by the individuals who managed the Democratic organization. But the New Dealers had Roosevelt's support, enabling them to gradually impose their will over old-line Democrats. FDR was not averse, in the short run, to working with local leaders who were amenable to liberal policies—at times he cooperated with the likes of Ed Flynn, Frank Kelly, and Frank "Boss" Hague. Clearly, however, his speeches and other political actions were geared towards loosening the grip of local party leaders on the Democratic organization. "Each year that passes," Roosevelt wrote hopefully in 1934, "sees the elimination of more and more local political machines and bosses whose chief function in life has been to feather their own nests. Under a perfect party system of government a bid for public favor should rest solely upon political principles and good administration."[24]

This aspiration for a more principled and programmatic party system led Roosevelt to monitor with considerable interest the La Guardia administration in New York city, which was constantly locked in political combat with regular city Democrats. Against the wishes of Farley and Bronx boss Ed Flynn, who planned to use federal patronage to strengthen the local Democratic organization, Roosevelt encouraged the efforts of the erstwhile Brains Truster Adolf Berle "to navigate" the nonpartisan La Guardia government "into a friendly cooperative basis" with the national administration. Berle, who served the La Guardia administration in the post of Chamberlain, forged ties between New York progressives and the Roosevelt administration that greatly contributed to the financial recovery of the city and, ultimately, to La Guardia's re-election in 1937 on the Republican ticket. "It looks as though the great experiment had come off," Berle wrote Roosevelt on September 1, 1937, "and that we may have demonstrated that you can run a political situation without patronage or the spoils system provided the administration is first-rate and the ideas are progressive and intelligent. I think this will be the first time since Andrew Jackson that the experiment has been successful in any large unit."[25] Patronage was not absent in the La Guardia administration, but it was bestowed to support liberal reform, rather then to nourish a local party organization.

There was no prospect, therefore, that the development of the new type of patronage favored by New Dealers would bring forth "a perfect party system of government." The new patronage—the "ideological patronage" practiced by the Roosevelt administration—was still patronage, and it was often resented, not only by old-line Democrats, but also by progressives who adhered to the British model of a nonpartisan professional civil service. "Taking care of the boys," wrote David Lilienthal, the director of the Tennessee Valley Authority, "is an evil in any guise, whether it is on the basis of personal friendship, business or social ties, or some amateur political notion about an 'elite of brains' (self-selected), a kind of Phi Beta Kappa version of Tammany Hall."[26]

Arguably, however, it was the New Dealers who prevented the Democratic party of the 1930s from simply devolving into a national Tammany Hall. "In spite of all the demand for speed, the complexity of the problem and all the vast sums of money involved," FDR boasted in 1936, "we have had no Teapot Dome."[27] As the journalists Joseph Alsop and Robert Kinter asserted in 1939, without the availability of New Dealers, the story of the Teapot Dome probably would have been repeated, with a new cast and new and richer prizes at stake:

> Fortunately, however, the President was able to use the New Dealers . . . as his administrative technicians. . . . Being men of trained minds, they are well equipped to handle large and novel problems. Being intellectuals of predominantly academic background, they have little of the usual hankering for political success or financial reward. They are, in fact, reasonably disinterested men, chiefly desirous of seeing their ideas become realities, and satisfied with that as their price. Therefore the President has been able to rely on them for the reasonably honest spending of the New Deal's billions and for the reasonably efficient exercise of the New Deal's immense and complex powers.[28]

The New Deal and Congress

The New Dealer's attempt to make the party into a more national organization focused not only on the national committee, which was dominated by state and local party leaders, as a dispenser of spoils, but also on Congress, which registered state and local interests at the national level. In the final analysis, Roosevelt believed that a more principled party politics could only come through the subordination of Congress's position in the development of party policy. As *Fortune* magazine reported in February, 1937, FDR felt that "measures of such scope and complexity that he had in view could be drawn only if they were drawn under the strong hand of centralized control; the New Deal could not be planned and built by debate" within the legislature and traditional party councils.[29]

For this reason, Roosevelt, unlike Woodrow Wilson, did not consult closely with legislative party leaders in the development of his policy program.[30] Although FDR used Farley and Vice President John Nance Garner to maintain close ties with Congress, party leaders complained that they were called into consultation only when it was necessary to have their signatures at the bottom of the page to make the document legal. Moreover, FDR offended Congress by his use of press conferences to announce important decisions to the press and public and to attempt to rally public support before he communicated them to a coordinate branch of government.

Consequently, the Roosevelt administration effected "a startling break from the past," as Van Riper puts it, in the separation of the idea men, associated with the White House, from the political organizers, associated with the regular party organization, in the preparation of legislation for submission to Congress.[31] Traditionally, legislation had been formulated in consultation with, if not in deference to, congressional party leaders and drafted by legislative staff. Especially during the first Hundred Days, however, Congress frequently received its legislation already fully drawn up by the White House staff and usually passed it without substantial change. In an unprecedented fashion, thereby, White House advisors dominated public policy, which was first manifested through the "Brains Trust" and later through the loosely knit organization described as the "New Dealers."

By the end of Roosevelt's first term, Congress, much more than had been the case during the initial 4 years of the Wilson presidency, was "chafing at its subordinate position"; it was looking for an opportunity to rebuke this popular president who threatened to relegate it to the position of a "rubber stamp."[32]

Much of this difference between Roosevelt and Wilson with respect to Congress, of course, went beyond contrasts in personality and character. It also had to do with FDR's greater sense of urgency, given the economic emergency he faced, to get on with his program. In addition, it stemmed from FDR's greater skepticism regarding the place of party in American democracy. Wilson looked to the party as an end in itself, and to its reform as the principal path to elevating democratic life in the United States—he was therefore more willing to risk much in the way of programmatic reform and personal popularity to enhance the importance and extend the practice of party government. FDR, in contrast, saw the party as a limited means to strengthen administration and reconstruct the political economy in the United States. He was, therefore, unwilling to sacrifice very much in the way of social and administrative reform on the altar of party government.

For this reason, again unlike Wilson, Roosevelt made little use of the congressional party caucus. In February, 1934, Democratic Congressman Samuel Pettengill of Indiana wrote Roosevelt's private secretary, Marvin McIntyre, that the American people were so weary of the depression and so anxious to get out of it that "they would welcome strong party discipline in the House." But, at the same time, he asserted that "members should not be placed in the position of acting blindly as rubber stamps to an executive." Instead party policy had to be worked out by the President "*together with* a majority of his House by caucus."[33] Roosevelt found suggestions of this sort interesting, albeit unworkable in the context of American constitutional government. His feelings on the value of party caucuses were expressed when still another plea for common deliberation came from the House in 1937. Fearing that the court-packing plan had deprived the President of his control over the Democratic party, Connecticut Congressman Alfred N. Phillips, Jr., wrote on June 9:

I believe that those sharing the burden of responsibility of Party government should regularly and often be called into caucus and that such caucuses should evolve party policies and choice of party leaders. I do not believe that responsible Party government can long obtain if members of the particular party whose votes are counted upon to pass Party measures are not continually consulted regarding their thoughts as to the shaping of party policies and the bills breathing official life into these policies.[34]

Roosevelt's response amounted to a polite rejection of Congressman Phillips's suggestion. "I have given much thought to your interesting letter of the ninth," he responded. Although there was much in the Congressman's letter with which FDR could agree, the proposal to use the caucus as an instrument of party responsibility foundered on the rock of organization. "Frankly," FDR observed, "it is a question of machinery—how to do it. . . . After all, there are four hundred and thirty-five Congressmen and ninety-six Senators, many of whom have very decided ideas on individual points which they are not at all hesitant to explain at any meeting which might be held."[35]

The Roosevelt administration might have been correct in its view that the measures that formed the backbone of the New Deal would never have been passed had the president followed customary political procedure and confined his consultation to the party leaders and such political laymen as the party leaders would have approved of. FDR's willingness to depart from that procedure, relying instead upon New Deal loyalists regardless of their political affiliation, marked an unprecedented challenge to party responsibility as traditionally understood in American politics. "If Democrats on Capitol Hill have any pride in the New Deal," High asserted, "it is certainly not the pride of authorship. Its authorship goes back to the President himself, and to the assortment of political hybrids with which he was surrounded."[36]

Roosevelt's departure from customary partisan practices in legislation and administration resulted, initially, in a division of labor between the intellectuals and politicians—between policy-making and political policy-selling—within the New Deal councils. By the beginning of the second term, however, this modus operandi had developed into a "split personality," as Alsop and Kintner described it, which afflicted FDR's following.[37] On the one hand, there were the orthodox Democrats, composed of James Farley, most of the representation of the party in both houses of the Congress, and the footsoldiers in the party's state and municipal machines. On the other hand, there were the programmatic liberals, vaguely referred to as "the New Dealers," who wrote the speeches, formulated the program, and administered most of the policies of the New Deal. For a time, Roosevelt refused to acknowledge the party's schizophrenia, fearing that to do so prior to 1936 would damage his re-election prospects. This changed with the celebrated "purge" campaign of 1938, in which FDR intervened in one gubernatorial and several congressional campaigns in a bold effort to replace recalcitrant Democrats with candidates who were "100 percent New Dealers." With the purge campaign, as we will see in Chapter 4, Roosevelt himself publicly recognized his party's split personality and undertook a limited, though dramatic, effort to rebuild the Democratic party in New Deal image.

According to James Farley, Roosevelt's unprecedented effort to stamp his policies upon his party in 1938 was born of an attempt to establish a "personal party," driven by an unhealthy thirst for self-aggrandizement.[38] FDR's actions to establish a New Deal Democratic party, however, must also be understood as part of an effort to alter the protractive character of constitutional government in the United States. "There is no doubt," the columnist Anne O'Hare McCormick wrote in 1938, that Roosevelt "was moved by a sense of urgency," that he was "irked by the slowness of the democratic procedure" in the United States.[39] FDR gave clear expression to this concern in his 1937 inaugural address. "Our pledge was not merely to do a patchwork job with second hand materials. By using the new materials of social justice we have undertaken to erect on the old foundation a more enduring structure for the better use of future generations."[40] This task most essentially required infusing constitutional government with the capacity for action, and Roosevelt believed that such institutional change presupposed the dominance of executive leadership in the formulation and administration of public policy. The extension of presidential power over the party, therefore, was rooted in fundamental constitutional considerations. The advent of a more progressive democracy required the development of not so much a personal party as a presidential party.

Forging the New Deal Democratic Party

Roosevelt's massive partisan effort—this departure from many conventional partisan practices—began a process whereby the party system was eventually transformed from local to national and programmatic party organizations. This change did not occur overnight, but significant developments took place during the 1930s that signalled a shift in the locus of party politics from the state and local level to the nation's capital.

The Special Divisions of the Democratic party

One indication of such change was that the organization of the Democratic National Committee (DNC) was modified to reflect the New Deal's emphasis on enhancing the role of the national government in ameliorating social and economic inequality. Most important, the DNC created or expanded special divisions that cultivated the electoral support of groups or interests that eventually formed the key constituencies of the New Deal coalition. For example, at the urging of Pennsylvania Senator Joseph Guffey, described by Alsop and Kintner as "the first of the liberal bosses," the DNC during Roosevelt's initial term established the first effective Negro division a Democratic committee ever had. The New Deal did not address the race issue directly, but Guffey, encouraged by prominent black political leaders, believed that black voters could be persuaded to give up their traditional loyalties to the Republican party as a result of New Deal economic programs. He was "astonished" to learn that Robert L. Vann, the owner–editor of the *Pittsburgh Courier* (one of the leading national black newspapers) had indicted the Republicans for "indolently draw[ing] checks against the debt of the Civil War, without troubling themselves further with the lot of colored people." Blacks were "beginning to realize their vote was connected to their economic condition," Vann told Guffey in a private meeting. To Guffey's way of thinking, this was an opportunity to be taken advantage of. "At the end of a bright vista he saw millions of negro voters," reported the press, "Republicans no longer, Democrats all."[41]

Guffey persuaded a reluctant James Farley to appoint Vann as the manager in chief of the newly established "Colored Advisory Committee." Vann's efforts on behalf of the Democrats and his ability to swing a number of voters to Roosevelt in 1932 won him praise from party figures like James Farley. His work at Democratic headquarters and elsewhere after the election was instrumental in aiding the dramatic shift in black support for the New Deal between 1932 and 1936.[42] The mobilization of black elites into the Democratic national organization and the efforts by this revamped organization to mobilize black voters was one of several developments during the 1930s that gave rise to a more centralized party apparatus, committed to programmatic reform. From their vantage point within party headquarters, members of the "Colored Voter Division" undertook a determined effort to get patronage for blacks. This task proved difficult, but outside the South, Democratic leaders at every level, the historian Nancy Weiss has written, "found an incentive to woo blacks. Building the Democratic party meant broadening and deepening the party's base; blacks—a constituency that the party had never previously cultivated—were one of the groups that could help to build a powerful new Democratic coalition."[43]

Some of these appointments were traditional patronage that, although of great symbolic and political importance, proved insignificant in the building of the New Deal. For example, at the insistence of Guffey, Roosevelt appointed Vann assistant attorney general as a reward for his effective work during the 1932 campaign. But this position, impressive as it may have been in title, was limited to routine, insignificant tasks. In the fall of 1935, a disappointed and frustrated Vann returned to the *Pittsburgh Courier.*[44]

Nevertheless, black patronage during the 1930s was often of more than symbolic importance. Most significant were the efforts of Robert C. Weaver, who became the first black advisor on Negro affairs in the Roosevelt administration, and Mary McLeod Bethune, director of Negro Affairs in the National Youth Administration, to coordinate regular meetings of black racial advisors in the various departments and agencies. (By 1937, all but five of the New Deal agencies had black advisors on their payrolls.) These individuals, eventually designated the "Black Cabinet," represented a "new breed of black appointees," according to Weaver. "These persons were chosen more for themselves and their ability to define issues relevant to the black community than to pay off political debts."[45] Thus, the unremitting effort to get patronage for Blacks during the 1930s brought individuals to Washington whose commitments were to New Deal reform rather than the party apparatus; as such, black appointments contributed to the redefinition of the Democratic party as a more national and programmatic organization.

Also contributing to this restructuring of the party was the Women's Division of the National Committee, which under the auspices of Molly Dewson emerged as the most politically active and effective special division of the DNC during Roosevelt's presidency. Eleanor Roosevelt convinced the President and James Farley in the spring of 1933 to make the Women's Division a full-time operation, and Dewson, a close personal friend of the Roosevelts and active in the party organization since 1928, soon won the respect of party leaders by demonstrating that the political activism of Democratic women, hitherto denied meaningful participation in the party councils, could contribute to the overall strength of the Democratic party.

Dewson's first objective was patronage, and she proved herself well suited to the task of, as she put it, "wring[ing] as many jobs out of the men for the women who will help the party as I can." Dewson was instrumental in securing the nomination of Frances Perkins as Secretary of Labor, the first woman selected to serve in a President's cabinet, the choice of Ruth Bryan Owen as Minister to Denmark, the first woman sent abroad to represent the United States, and the appointment of Florence Allen to the Circuit Court of Appeals, which was the highest position a woman had obtained in the federal judiciary.[46] These path-breaking appointments were the most visible of the more than one hundred prominent positions that women filled in the New Deal, most of which Dewson played a part in obtaining. Overall, the women's rate of federal employment increased twice as rapidly as men's during the 1930s, a legacy of the Women's Division that Dewson claimed fundamentally changed the status of women in American society.

At the same time, the inclusion of women in Democratic councils contributed to the transformation of the party. Ostensibly Dewson was a practical politician in the traditional mold, who sought to extend the spoils of office to women as a means of building up the Democratic party where it sorely needed it. "I think one of the reasons we get on so well together is that I believe in organization just as you do," Dewson wrote Farley in June 17, 1938. "You have one kind of busy work for the men and I have another for the girls. That is the only difference."[47] Dewson's efforts in directing the Women's Division, however, were not limited to party-building; rather, she used the party as a vehicle to increase the representation of professionally trained social workers, who, she believed, could help pull the country out of the depression. Many of these women, like Dewson herself, had been at the forefront of progressive reform for nearly three decades. The hallmark of their participation in the Democratic party, therefore, was to expect more out of politics than the promise of a job—they wanted the government to act as a positive and constructive force in society. For this reason, the activities of the Women's Division represented a pioneering effort to wed traditional party practices to an issue-oriented style of politics, dedicated to promoting public support for the programs of the New Deal, to mobilize and perpetuate, that is, support for social reform.

The cornerstone of Dewson's plan to promote widespread public understanding of and support for the programs of the New Deal was a scheme she dubbed the "Reporter Plan." Unveiled at Eleanor Roosevelt's press conference of January, 1934, the Reporter Plan encouraged Democratic women to learn how government programs affected their communities, and to spread this information to their friends and neighbors. It marked an ambitious attempt, Susan Ware has noted, to link an issue-oriented approach to politics with the more traditional concern of building an active grass roots organization:

> Every county Democratic organization selected women to serve as Reporters, each one assigned to cover an agency such as the Agricultural Adjustment Administration, the Reconstruction Finance Corporation, or the Civilian Conservation Corps. Fortified with facts, reporters presented their findings before civic groups, clubs, and other organizations, thereby spreading the New Deal message throughout the community.[48]

These assiduous, effective efforts of the Women's Division to get women voters lined up with the New Deal redounded to the benefit of the party, making Dewson and her elaborate organization an indispensible political arm of the Roosevelt administration. Approximately 80% of all Democratic campaign literature distributed in 1936 was produced and distributed by the Women's Division. Its extraordinary efforts in fund raising, publicity, and voter mobilization would result in Democratic women gaining greater influence in formulating platforms at the Democratic national conventions and greater success in receiving patronage jobs. "It was such a big plan that it made me a little dizzy when I inaugurated it in January, 1934," Dewson wrote Farley in 1938. "I wondered if the Women's Division had the drive to make it a real thing, but the plan was psychologically sound and grew lustily with only a little well directed effort continuously applied. Now we have eighty thousand women knowing how to carry it out and doing so."[49]

Relations between Dewson and Farley were not always amiable, however. The Women's Division director emphasized education and policy issues, presupposing attention to governing and commitment to robust organizational activity between elections. This vision of party government occasionally clashed with Farley's more traditional view of the DNC's responsibility. Things came to a head of sorts in April, 1934, when Dewson asked Farley for an increase in her budget, so that, as she put it, "the work of the Women's Division shall be carried on continuously between campaigns at practically the same tempo."[50] Farley denied the request, viewing Dewson's ambitious plans as a violation of sound organizational practices. "Why waste money between campaigns," he argued, "when we are down to the bone."[51] When agreement between Farley and Dewson proved impossible, the matter was taken to FDR. Although siding with Dewson's ambitious and unorthodox plan to involve the party organization in policy issues between elections, the President worked out a compromise consistent with his cautious approach to party reform. He asked Dewson to accept an annual budget of $36,000 instead of the $48,000 she requested. With Roosevelt's support, Dewson was also able to establish her prerogative to control the budget and activities of the Women's Division with limited interference from Farley and the regular party apparatus. This control continued even though Dewson gave up the post of director of the Women's Division to head its Advisory Committee, staffed by women "who were not closely identified with the Democratic organization."[52]

Not only did Dewson work full time without a salary, thereby making up for the budgetary short-fall that resulted from the compromise agreement worked out by FDR, but she also assumed a vantage point to develop an alternative form of organizational activity that reached out to independent voters. After 1934, with the financial and organizational issues settled to Dewson's satisfaction, the Women's Division expanded its activities along the lines anticipated by the Reporter Plan. While embracing the party, therefore, Dewson prodded it to become a more national and programmatic organization, a task greatly aided by Roosevelt.

Arguably the most important link that was forged during the 1930s was between the Democratic party and labor. The 1930s marked a transition in the labor movement from a nonpartisan, voluntarist, and essentially defensive approach to politics, to one of partisanship and aggressive support for the New Deal. Prior to the advent of the New Deal, labor's contributions to national campaigns and party politics had been small and sporadic, largely because of an inability on the part of the more powerful organizations to decide upon any coherent, consistent program of political action. By 1936, however, trade unionists, as well as rank and file workers, had come to view the Democratic party as the preferred vehicle for the promotion of their socioeconomic interests. The integration of labor into the New Deal coalition was complicated by the doctrinal and organizational rift between the American Federation of Labor (A.F.L.) and the newly formed Committee (later Congress) of Industrial Organizations (C.I.O.). Nevertheless, the leading labor organizations were all united behind FDR's re-election campaign of 1936.

This strong labor effort on behalf of Roosevelt was orchestrated by Daniel Tobin, President of the Teamster's Union, who served as chairman of the DNC's Labor Division during all four of Roosevelt's presidential campaigns. Tobin's task was especially difficult in 1936, as only a few months before the election, the A.F.L. executive committee, distressed at the C.I.O.'s aggressive policy of industrial unionism, expelled the ten of its unions that were affiliated with C.I.O. Consequently, Tobin, a Vice President of the A.F.L., was forced to work with a bitterly divided labor movement, a job made more difficult by the fact that leading C.I.O. labor leaders, such as John L. Lewis of the United Mine Workers, Sidney Hillman of the Amalgamated Clothing Workers, George Berry of the Printing Pressman's Union, and David Dubinsky of the International Ladies Garment Workers' Union, set up a separate political organization under the title of the Nonpartisan League. Yet Tobin facilitated a remarkably harmonious labor effort supporting Roosevelt in 1936, and carved out an important role for organized labor within the councils of the Democratic party. The result was that 1936 was a momentous "year of decision," as Samuel Lubell has put it, in which the political allegiances in industrial centers that had grown out of the Civil War were uprooted for good—labor's support of Roosevelt was the key ingredient in a realignment in which the Democrats for the first time since the Civil War became the nation's normal majority party.[53]

With the benefit of hindsight, labor's support for Roosevelt does not seem remarkable. Under the aegis of, first, Section 7(a) of the National Recovery Administration and, later, the Wagner Act, there had been a tremendous growth of labor union membership since 1933. Although some of the more strident labor leaders, especially Lewis, resented what they viewed as FDR's lapses with regard to labor's interests, most trade unionists agreed with Hillman that the rise of a "real labor movement . . . would have been impossible" without the New Deal.[54] Nevertheless, the schism in the labor movement that grew out of the New Deal might very well have prevented a politically effective bond being formed with the Democratic party; the Nonpartisan League, in fact, was viewed by some of its supporters as the launching pad for a labor party that would be, as the Democratic party could not, a genuine party of progressive reform.

Although Roosevelt, with the capable support of Tobin, was able to cement an alliance of the New Deal with what is now called big labor, this alliance was not something that the administration could afford to take for granted. "I do not hesitate to say to you that in the beginning of my work I was somewhat disturbed and worried over the serious division in the Labor Movement," Tobin reported to Farley and the President after the 1936 election. In the beginning the existence of two political shops created considerable confusion because "central Labor Unions, State Branches and the rank and file really did not know whether to follow along under the leadership of the Labor Division of the Democratic National Committee or to become associated with the Nonpartisan Political Party," Tobin related. Nevertheless, the Labor Division head happily informed FDR that a modus operandi had been worked out, thus allowing the insurgent labor leaders to unite with the A.F.L. under the Democratic banner. Although the formation of the Nonpartisan League opened up serious possibilities of an independent third party, unlike third-party ventures of the past, it functioned mainly within and through the Democratic party and made no effort to set up a precinct and county system of its own.[55] "I met with and discussed our policies and laid my cards on the table to every man in labor whether they were in or outside the American Federation of Labor," Tobin's report proudly concluded. "I repeated in meeting after meeting which I addressed that our differences of opinion and policy in the Labor Movement should be set aside for the time being and that all who believed in the progress of the present administration should forget their personal misunderstandings and join hands in one solid mass, to the end that our candidates would be returned to office."[56]

The fact that he was kept close to the throne after 1936, serving as chair of the Democratic party's Labor committee in both 1940 and 1944, and a special presidential assistant between elections, suggests that Tobin's account of his role in coordinating labor support for Roosevelt was more than an exercise of self-promotion. As an important member of the A.F.L., he represented the sort of reserved political posture with which FDR, fearing labor domination of the party, felt comfortable. Yet he was willing to suspend his differences with the more aggressive C.I.O. during campaigns, thus helping to preempt the prospects of a third-party movement. Tobin, then, was the perfect man to aid the President in his objective of making labor a principal, albeit not dominant, constituent of the Democratic party.[57]

The expansion of the Democratic organization to include blacks, women, and labor activists was an important complement to the ideological patronage that brought New Deal intellectuals into the White House as well as various departments and agencies. The individuals whom Roosevelt attached to his personal service—the "New Dealers" such as Harry Hopkins, Thomas Corcoran, and Samuel Rosenman—provided important service in policy and administrative planning; however, although they became heavily involved in politics, they had little political weight. Their place in government owed to Roosevelt alone; their personal following did not extend beyond the youthful lawyers and social scientists serving in administrative agencies who constituted the group's rank and file. Lacking party sensibilities and a genuine concern with the development of grass roots support, the New Dealers could not form the nucleus of a new party structure in the country. To a point, the special divisions formed during FDR's first term promised to compensate for the political shortcomings of the New Deal command. The inclusion of labor, especially, offered the possibility of broad rank and file support for a transformed Democratic party.

The New Deal and Party Finances

Another important element of this incipient transformation was the change in the source of DNC funding after 1932. In 1928, both major parties depended largely upon bankers and manufacturers for their contributions, although the Republicans did receive a slightly larger proportion of their funds from manufacturers than did their rivals. In 1932, although the proportion of the Democratic funds coming from manufacturers dropped appreciably, Roosevelt's promises of a New Deal had no apparent effect upon bankers, who contributed as heavily as in 1928. But the New Deal in action greatly intensified business hostility to the Democratic Party, manifesting itself, as V. O. Key wrote in 1947, in the "pecuniary loyalty of finance and heavy industry to the Republican Party."[58] The Democratic party's loss of big business support was significant for the first time in 1936. For example, bankers and brokers, whose donations made up twenty-four percent of all that the Democrats received in contributions of $1,000 or more in 1932, contributed less than four percent of this part of the fund in 1936. With respect to large individual contributors, moreover, less than one-third of those who gave $1,000 or more 4 years before aided the party in 1936. Significantly, a number of defectors from the Democratic party gave generously to the Republicans. Some of the best known of these were Pierre S. Du Pont, William Randolph Hearst, and William K. Vanderbilt, each of whom contributed $5,000 or more to the Republican National Committee in 1936.

The Democratic party's loss of many traditional funding sources was offset by the financial support of organized labor and the small contributor. Whereas unions for the most part had remained aloof from active participation in the financing of campaigns prior to FDR's first re-election effort, labor organizations poured over three-quarters of a million dollars into the 1936 election; most significant, all the funds aided the candidate of the Democratic party and a substantial part of them (some $200,000) went to the Democratic National Committee.

Responding to these changes in the composition of Democratic campaign funds in 1936, Louise Overacker suggested that "the emergence of labor as an important factor in the financing of the Democratic party would facilitate realignment on 'liberal' and 'conservative' lines and eventually might make possible the birth of a new 'Labor' party under an old name.''[59] The Democrats and Republicans, however, had not divided definitely into the party of "have nots" and "haves," respectively, in 1936. Both made strenuous and successful efforts to increase the number of small contributors in 1936. Moreover, Democrats benefitted from the generous contributions of office holders and Southerners, irrespective of economic interest. The incumbent party also did quite well with professionals, composed for the most part of lawyers, with a sprinkling of physicians, accountants, and authors; 12.7 percent of the Democratic contributions came from this source, compared to 4.4 percent in the case of Republicans.[60]

Nevertheless, the organizational and financial sources of support for the Democrats and Republicans in 1936 revealed that the program of the Roosevelt administration had served to sharpen the division between the parties on economic lines. More significant, the New Deal had effected an important change in the structure of party organization, thus resulting in a more national and programmatic party system. In this way, the New Deal portended more than a cyclical realignment of parties; it suggested the possibility of a party transformation that would end in an alignment of liberals and conservatives that many progressive reformers, beginning with Woodrow Wilson, had long hoped for.

Party Transformation and the 1936 Election

Roosevelt himself took important action in 1936 to ensure that such a metamorphosis would take place. It was not enough to win re-election by a large plurality; in addition, Roosevelt was determined to make use of the campaign and his great personal popularity in order to strengthen the party. With this in mind, FDR sought to effect structural change that would institutionalize the changes in the party during his first term. He also took care to articulate a campaign message that would decidedly associate the 1936 re-election effort with a new understanding of government, thus giving expression to a new public philosophy as a means by which New Deal constituents could form attachments to the revamped Democratic organization.[61]

The most important organizational achievement of the 1936 campaign was the abolition of the two-thirds rule. Adopted in 1832, the two-thirds rule required the support of two-thirds of the convention delegates in order to be nominated as a Democratic presidential or vice presidential candidate. This rule originated in the South, which regarded it as vital hallowed protection against the nomination of candidates unsympathetic to its problems. Although assailed by certain quarters in the party as violative of the democratic principle of majority rule, allowing as it did one-third of the delegates to prevent a decision, it was defended and maintained on the philosophical grounds that democracy owes protection to the minority. The two-thirds rule was also justified, its adherents argued, because it guarded the firmest Democratic section since the Civil War, the South, against the imposition of an unwanted nominee by the less habitually loyal North, East, and West.[62]

The requirement that two-thirds of the convention delegates were necessary to nominate presidential and vice presidential candidates surely violated the vision of a national, programmatic party that Roosevelt had espoused since the 1920s. Yet his assault upon it was cautious once he became involved in presidential politics, lest his efforts at party reform be dismissed as naked self-interest. FDR's supporters mounted a drive to abrogate the rule in 1932, but retreated in the face of a firestorm fueled by the corps of other presidential contenders, who argued that the rules should not be modified in the middle of the contest, and the southern delegations, where Roosevelt had amassed considerable support. The decision not to fight the rule was urged by FDR, himself, and his close advisors, who believed that a full-scale drive to abrogate the two-thirds standard might jeopardize the Governor's standing as the leading contender for the nomination.[63]

There was every reason to have the rule abolished in 1936, however, as Roosevelt entered the convention with great popularity and no real opposition to his renomination. Moreover, Roosevelt's sweep of the country in 1932 left only six states voting Republican, thus strengthening the national presence of the Democrats, and weakening considerably the argument of the South that it deserved special consideration within the party councils. Still, Roosevelt chose to proceed carefully. Fearing Southern protests that might enervate the re-election campaign, the President chose not to exert his influence directly, leaving the visible management of the campaign to alter the Democratic convention rule to Farley.[64] It was widely reported that FDR supported abolition of the two-thirds rule in private conversations, considering it "archaic," but he was far less forthcoming in public pronouncements. His only post-1932 public statement on the rule came in an April 28, 1936 press conference. Asked whether he "join[ed] with Mr. Farley for the abrogation of the two-thirds rule," Roosevelt answered that this was the recommendation of the 1932 convention. When a reporter shot back that "the recommendation was to study it," FDR feigned only mild interest in having the convention eliminate the rule.[65]

Fearing that even this temperate response might arouse opposition, the Administration sought to assure party regulars. That same day, in expressing his conviction that the reform would succeed, Farley told reporters that in putting forth this opinion, he was not presuming to speak for the convention.[66] In fact, however, Farley at Roosevelt's close direction had been working assiduously behind the scenes since late 1935 to change the nomination rules.[67] These efforts centered on encouraging state parties to pass resolutions against the two-thirds rule and stacking the membership of the rules committee, which would report a recommendation regarding the two-thirds rule at the convention to be held in Philadelphia during the summer of 1936. As Farley would reveal many years later:

> We wanted to make certain we had complete control of the committee on rules. So in talking with the leaders of every delegation we tried to get a friendly delegate assigned to that committee. [Each state had one representative on the committee.] We tried to get complete control of the committee and we did. That was a job completely engineered by Mr. Roosevelt. I did it under his direction.[68]

The chairmanship of this committee was assigned to Missouri Senator Bennet C. Clark. This was truly an inspired choice. His father, Champ Clark, former

Speaker of the House, had lost the Democratic nomination to Woodrow Wilson in 1912 because of the two-thirds rule. Although Speaker Clark had a clear majority of the delegates at the Baltimore convention that year, the two-thirds rule and the opposition of William Jennings Bryan prevented his nomination, thus making possible the nomination of Wilson on the forty-sixth ballot. Since the 1912 convention, the deeply conservative Senator Clark, who actually witnessed the events in Baltimore, had fought in the Democratic conventions for the repeal of the two-thirds rule. Roosevelt and Farley gave him his chance to vindicate the injustice to his father.

In the words of his senatorial colleague, James F. Byrnes of South Carolina, Clark pursued his goal "with all the energy of an avenging fury." [69] Clark's determination to abrogate the two-thirds rule, ironically, abetted Roosevelt's plan to weaken the strangle hold the Missouri Senator and other conservative Democrats had over national conventions.

All conservative Democrats were not assuaged by Senator Clark's participation. But after long consideration of this troublesome issue, the rules committee, ably supported by the Roosevelt administration, simply overpowered Southern opposition to a change in the two-thirds rule. Moreover, Clark's committee managed to avoid a fight on the floor of the convention by unanimously adopting a resolution sponsored by Senator Millard Tydings of Maryland, which instructed the Democratic National Committee to work out a new formula of representation in the national conventions based upon the Democratic vote cast in the respective states. Southerners were placated by this compromise, believing that the promise of apportionment reform would maintain the prestige of the solid South by providing it with increased representation at future conventions. [70]

Although most Southern Democrats accepted defeat with good grace, they nevertheless feared that the abolition of the two-thirds rule portended problems in 1940 and beyond. The *New York Times* had published a letter to the editor from a Southern correspondent a few months earlier, for example, suggesting that Roosevelt was paving the way for an unprecedented third-term try. [71] There is no evidence that Roosevelt was thinking about a third term as early as 1936, but according to Stanley High, the President told the publisher Herbert Bayard Swope soon after the 1936 election that although he did not expect to occupy the White House beyond 1940, "he was going to have something to say about the man who was to be there." [72] Surely Roosevelt recognized, as the *Washington Star* had editorialized during the convention rules battle, that it would be easier for New Dealers "to nominate a Democratic candidate of their liking in 1940 under a majority rule." [73] It was just this possibility that deeply troubled the conservative North Carolina Senator Josiah Bailey as he reflected on the developments in Philadelphia. "The abolition of the two-thirds rule will enable the Northern and Western Democrats to control the Party, nominate its candidates and write its platform," he wrote in private correspondence on August 10. "All this will come out in 1940." [74]

Bailey and his conservative colleagues in the Democratic party could not have been comforted by Roosevelt's acceptance speech at the Philadelphia convention. Much has been made of the fact that this address was developed from two separate drafts: one conciliatory message, prepared by Raymond Moley and Thomas Corcoran, and another, written by Samuel Rosenman and Stanley High, that was "a militant, bare-fisted statement of the necessity for economic freedom to supplement the political freedom the people had won in their past." [75] Sensing the time was right for an ardent defense of his program, FDR favored the Rosenman–High draft, but, ever sensitive to the need for reconciling militant public authority with the American antipathy to centralized power, the President did not simply cast aside the milder version, but asked Rosenmen and High to work it into the draft they had prepared. Although their efforts did not produce a smooth, perfectly consistent document, it did somehow capture the complexity of the New Deal. In particular, FDR's acceptance address in Philadelphia of June 27 captured the essence of the New Deal creed, first articulated in the Commonwealth Club address, that progressive reform marked not a departure from, but rather a redefinition of, the self-evident truths that formed the foundation of American politics. As noted in the previous chapter, the 1936 Democratic platform employed language from the Declaration to pronounce a new understanding of individualism that conceived of the state as a guarantor of programmatic rights. FDR's convention address reaffirmed the need for a redefinition of the social contract in terms of a changing and growing social order:

> The brave and clear platform adopted by this Convention, to which I heartily subscribe, sets forth that Government in a modern civilization has certain inescapable obligations to its citizens, among which are the protection of the family and the home, the establishment of a democracy of opportunity, and aid to those overtaken by disaster. [76]

The purpose of the Philadelphia address, however, was not merely to restate the New Deal manifesto. Rather, the task was to arouse New Deal supporters for a militant partisan campaign against the enemies of reform. A statement of New Deal principles as embodied in the platform was not enough, FDR warned, for "the resolute enemy within our gates is ever ready to beat down our words unless in greater courage we will fight for them." Like his cousin Theodore, FDR fashioned himself as a conservative reformer who sought not to oppose private enterprise but to strengthen it by curbing business's most abusive practices and by ameliorating the most extreme conditions of economic inequality. [77] But he was opposed in this effort by an unreconstructed segment of the American business community, represented by groups such as the Liberty League, which was formed in 1934, that denied to the federal government any right to regulate commercial activity. Roosevelt's nomination address castigated his business critics in harsh and provocative terms:

> These economic royalists complain that we seek to overthrow the institutions of America. What they really complain of is that we seek to take away their power. Our allegiance to American institutions requires the overthrow of this kind of power. In vain they seek to hide behind the flag and the Constitution. In their blindness they forget what the flag and the Constitution stand for. Now, as always, they stand for democracy, not tyranny; for freedom, not subjection; and against a dictatorship by mob rule and the overprivileged alike. [78]

The phrase *economic royalists* was Stanley High's. Since December, 1935, he had urged Roosevelt "to redefine the New Deal in those fundamentally American terms in which the Cosmopolitan [sic] Club speech first defined it." In doing so, he suggested comparing the battle for an economic constitutional order with "various American crises—beginning with the Tory record in the revolution and following the Tory thread right on down through our history to the present." How well such a historical comparison would reveal, High enthused, "the New Deal as the real Americanism."[79]

In the Commonwealth Address of 1932, FDR had warned that without reform, the country would come under the grip of "princes of property." But now, in 1936, Roosevelt pressed a more dire message, telling the convention that "privileged princes of these new economic dynasties" had used their political fortunes and legal legerdemain to create a new form of despotism. As a result, the average man once more confronted the problem that faced the Minute Man:

> Against economic tyranny such as this, the American citizen could appeal only to the organized power of Government. . . . The royalists of the economic order have conceded that political freedom was the business of government, but they have maintained that economic slavery was nobody's business. They granted that the Government could protect the citizen in his right to vote, but they denied that Government could do anything to protect the citizen in his right to work and his right to live.
>
> Today, we stand committed to the proposition that freedom is no half-and-half affair. If the average citizen is guaranteed equal opportunity in the polling place, he must have equal opportunity in the market place.[80]

With the inspired help of High, Roosevelt had set the theme of the campaign. It was to be a war upon entrenched privilege. Although it sharpened political conflict along class lines, the message of the 1936 campaign was not really class based. Rather, as Marc Landy has noted, "it was a promise to overthrow a monarchy in the name of the commoners. In a nation where virtually everyone fancies himself a commoner the breadth of the appeal was enormous."[81] More important, FDR provided a means for partisan identification with the New Deal based on a powerful and enduring understanding of rights. In the final analysis, it was the enlistment of New Deal supporters in a war against privilege, in a campaign to reaffirm the social contract, that held the two strands—one militant, the other conciliatory—of FDR's nomination address together. This was not a cause simply for labor and the dispossessed, but a challenge for a generation. For this reason, the stridency that marked most of the speech was not out of step with the more consensual conclusion, most of which came from the Moley–Corcoran draft. Among these final passages, emphasizing "faith, hope, and charity," come the words for which this address would be most remembered: "There is a mysterious cycle in human events. To some generations much is given. Of other generations much is expected. This generation of Americans has a rendezvous with destiny."[82]

The merits of this important public message were recognized far beyond the cheering throngs in Philadelphia's Franklin Field. "Now that I have read the full text," an admiring Felix Frankfurter wrote Roosevelt a few weeks later, "I find in the speech that enduring quality which makes a classic. You have given us something not only to win with, but to win for.''[83]

Frankfurter sensed correctly that the parties had gotten caught up in something big in 1936, and that Roosevelt's convention speech had helped clarify the terms of the fundamental struggle underway. That struggle's conclusion suggested the triumph of the New Deal Democratic organization as a governing party. FDR's victory in 1932 had expressed the public's resentment of Hoover more than its approval of him and the Democrats. But sweeping confirmation of Roosevelt's leadership and of the New Deal program came in 1936, when FDR won 60 percent of the popular vote—the largest plurality ever by a presidential candidate—and carried all but two states. The 1936 election, which also strengthened the Democratic hold on both houses of Congress, marked the Democrats' emergence as the new majority party. In becoming so, the party had undergone an important transformation. The structural and symbolic achievements of Roosevelt's first term had reconstituted the Democrats—hitherto an uneasy coalition of Southern conservatives and Northern bosses dedicated to decentralization—into a national, programmatic party. Yet, as the Roosevelt administration's defensive reaction to High's article ''Whose Party Is It?'' of February 1937 indicated, this transition was hardly complete—it depended upon an uneasy truce between traditional and programmatic liberals that would be sorely tried and eventually broken during Roosevelt's second term. The strains in the New Deal coalition would not undo the important political changes that had occurred since 1932. But after 1937 the Roosevelt administration became embroiled in struggles that raised anew severe doubts about the viability of the Democratic party as a vehicle of progressive reform. Moreover, the nature of these political battles suggested that the ingredients of the New Deal program might provide a recipe for institutional arrangements that would make party politics less important. By 1938, it seemed, the transformation of the Democratic party was a prelude to a less partisan future in the United States.

4

The Limits of Party Government:
The "Conservative Coalition" and the
"Purge" Campaign of 1938

Roosevelt was persuaded that the elections of 1932 and 1936 had led to a definite, albeit inchoate, division of the country into liberal and conservative parties.[1] The completion of this alignment to his satisfaction, however, depended on overcoming the resistance of Southern Democracy to the New Deal. The conflict between the New Deal and conservative Democrats in the South would dominate FDR's party leadership during the second term and throw party alignments, seemingly settled by the dramatic events of 1936, into disorder.

It was the fear of intra-party conflict that led Roosevelt to express concern to the columnist Turner Catledge soon after the election about the virtual obliteration of organized opposition to the administration in Congress. As Catledge suggested, it was more than "mere good sportsmanship" or a "philosophical attitude toward opposition" that caused such regret. Roosevelt's concern about the Republican demise was dominated by the problems he would face within his own party:

> Mr. Roosevelt was no doubt thinking more of the very practical situation that may face him at the next session of Congress, when, without any organized opposition on which he may depend to oppose practically everything he advances, he will be beset by unorganized groups within his own party ranks who may join forces for the measure today and split forces on the other tomorrow, presenting an undefinable and unpredictable collection of shifting blocks, the most annoying opposition with which any leader would have to deal.[2]

Roosevelt's overhauling of the party had opened its ranks to an increasingly pluralistic array of groups and movements, thus making possible the reestablishment of the party's majority status for the first time since the Civil War. But the aspirations of the new Democratic claimants—notably, labor, blacks and women—clashed with most Southern Democrats, who still maintained a strong presence in the party councils.[3] Roosevelt's command of the party, in fact, had not overcome factionalism within the Democratic ranks; instead, the New Deal programs and organizational reforms such as the abolition of the two-thirds rule altered the structure of conflict within the party. Hitherto a multifactional party

75

dominated by sectional interests, the Democrats became after 1936 a bifactional party with durable ideological and policy divisions.[4]

The Emergence of Auxiliary Party Organizations

The difficulty of marrying the progressive and conservative forces resulted in the unconventional organization of Roosevelt's 1936 re-election campaign. The principal problem FDR faced in that campaign was to appeal to activists in the labor movement and other independent progressives who might work for him but refused to do so through the Democratic party. As Stanley High, an erstwhile Republican himself, wrote to the President's secretary, Stephen Early, towards the end of 1935:

> It seems to me that this year—more than most—the result is going to be in the hands of those who think they are voting for something more than party. The opposition is going rapidly at the job of mobilizing all those opposed—not to the Democrats, as such—but to the tendency represented by the present Democratic administration. The sorry thing is that those who ought to be mobilized—regardless of party—on the side of the New Deal tendency are uncertain and sometimes definitely hostile.[5]

Roosevelt apparently agreed with High, for as early as November, 1935, he began urging upon Farley auxiliary organizations and committees that might recruit campaign workers and appeal to voters who were willing to support the New Deal but might not be willing to identify with the Democratic party.[6] The tactical aim of this elaborate structure of subsidiary organizations was to win the support of Republicans, third-party members, maverick Democrats, independents, and political novices. Besides Labor's Nonpartisan League, auxiliary committees promoted by Roosevelt included the Progressive National Committee, headed by Wisconsin Senator Robert LaFollette, Jr., the Good Neighbor League, headed by High, and a committee put together by Molly Dewson of independent and Republican women. By making these organizations an important part of his re-election effort Roosevelt created a new kind of presidential campaign, the basis of which was the "mobilization beyond the regular Democratic party of all elements in the New Deal coalition—liberals, labor, farmers, women, minorities."[7]

These groups made a major contribution to the successful 1936 campaign. Yet the auxiliary organizations that sprang up around the New Deal were significant in a larger sense. These subsidiary organizations had goals of their own beyond the re-election of Franklin Roosevelt; put simply, they represented a new kind of pressure group organized for political campaign action on behalf of candidates for public office.[8]

Such a coalition was deliberately promoted by Roosevelt. The Labor Nonpartisan League, the Good Neighbor League, the Progressive National Committee, and the Women's National Democratic Club remained independent of the regular party apparatus after the 1936 election, acting as important allies to the president in the pursuit of his controversial reform program of the second term, much of which was resisted by regular Democrats in the Congress and national committee.[9] In this way, auxiliary party organizations served Roosevelt in his purpose of transforming the Democratic party into a national and programmatic organization. Yet Roosevelt remained uncertain that the Democratic party could be fully converted into an instrument of New Deal reform. The origins of the party, as well as the structure of the party system in the United States, fostered weak party responsibility and discipline at the national level, thus making it unlikely that a traditional, unconditional marriage could take place between the Democratic party and the "nonpartisan" groups promoted by the Roosevelt administration. Therefore, a more modern, conditional marriage was suitable, based upon limited trust and mutual obligations. As such, the New Deal coalition supported the Democratic party, but subordinated the imperatives of party unity and organization to programmatic liberalism.[10]

Party Responsibility and Presidential Appeal

Roosevelt's promotion of auxiliary party organizations indicates that he viewed himself a leader of a progressive movement, not just the head of the Democratic party. To a point, this transformed the Democrats party; at the same time, it reflected FDR's recognition of the distinction between a Roosevelt constituency and that of his party. The President's more assertive party leadership after the 1936 re-election, including his intervention in the 1938 primary contests, would reveal the prospects and limitations that New Dealers faced in making the Roosevelt and Democratic coalitions compatible. FDR's party leadership during the second term, then, would determine the degree to which the Democratic party could be converted into a disciplined instrument of programmatic liberalism.

President Roosevelt had apparently been discussing the possibility of strengthening the liberal commitment of his party by direct intervention in primary and general election contests since his inauguration. FDR's intimate advisor, Harry Hopkins, especially, had urged such a course on him; in their long talks about undertaking "a realignment fight," as it was referred to in the press, both agreed that it was necessary—"the great question," Joseph Alsop and Robert Kintner reported, "was when to start working for it."[11] Roosevelt took some tentative, behind-the-scenes measures in this direction when he persuaded Illinois Senator James Hamilton Lewis, chair of the Democratic senatorial campaign committee, to provide financial support for liberal Republican candidates against conservative Democrats in the states of California, Minnesota, Wisconsin, and New Mexico in the 1934 congressional elections.[12]

Nevertheless, for a long time Roosevelt refused to participate publicly in a primary contest in a way that directly challenged the conservative members of his party. A cardinal political creed in the United States demanded that presidents keep out of local matters. Underlying this commitment to a decentralized party politics was the constitutional principle of division and separation of powers. Arguably, a president's interference in primary campaigns reflected an unhealthy desire to control Congress, to defeat those members of his party who disagreed with him and secure the election of others who agreed with him, thus undermining the independence of the legislature necessary to uphold American constitutional government. Given the ambiguity built into the constitutional historical role of the presidency, Roosevelt considered it neither desirable nor practical to immerse himself too openly in party politics, and his desire to separate the sheep from the goats was incompatible with an interpretation of the Constitution that long had inhibited Chief Executives from connecting their ambitions too centrally to their party in Congress.

Prior to 1938, therefore, FDR resigned himself to staying out of election contests that might be viewed not only as a direct assault on long-standing partisan practices, but also revered constitutional devices such as federalism and the separation of powers. When Nevada Senator Key Pittman, a loyal supporter and key advisor, asked Roosevelt for help in his 1934 Democratic primary fight, the President replied:

> I wish to goodness I could speak out loud in meetings and tell Nevada that I am one-thousand percent for you! An imposed silence in things like primaries is one of the many penalties of my job.[13]

Roosevelt maintained this "imposed silence" until the summer of 1938, when he finally launched the purge campaign. In 1936, he refused to fight the renomination of the Democratic incumbent Senator from Virginia, Carter Glass, who was the only congressional member of the majority party consistently to oppose the New Deal from the start. Apparently, Roosevelt expected to strengthen his grip on the Democratic party after the 1936 election. "Won't it be fun when this election is over and I'm down here without another election to think about," he told a close group of advisors in the midst of the reelection campaign. "For one thing I'm not going to support any candidates I don't think ought to be elected— regardless of how good Democrats they are."[14] As late as January, 1938, however, in response to pleas from liberal Democrats in Missouri for the President's support in defeating the conservative incumbent Senator Bennet Clark, whose relationship with the administration had cooled considerably since the convention in Philadelphia, FDR still adhered to a "hands-off" policy.[15]

The one exception to FDR's refusal to participate in elections outside his own state of New York prior to 1938 seemed to confirm his unwillingness to get publicly involved in intra-party struggles. This involved the Roosevelt administration's help for the progressive Republican George Norris's 1936 re-election campaign. While Thomas Corcoran worked aggressively, albeit surreptitiously, "to [shake] the bushes all over the East" to raise desperately needed campaign funds, FDR publicly endorsed Norris' candidacy during a visit to Omaha on October 10. "To my rule of nonparticipation in state elections, I have made—and so long as he lives I will continue to make—one magnificently justified exception," the President said of Norris' candidacy. Roosevelt's support for this venerable elder statesmen, whose ardent progressivism had been matched only by his zealous nonpartisanship during a long career in the House and Senate, enabled the President to place the cause of progressive reform above politics. "George Norris' candidacy transcends State and party lines," he argued. "In our national history we have had few elder statesmen who like him have preserved the aspirations of youth as they accumulated the wisdom of years. He is one of the major prophets of America.'' Given the tradition of constitutional government in the United States, presidential involvement in ''local'' matters apparently was justified only when it could be expressed on behalf of a cause considered ''above partisanship.''[16]

Participation in campaigns that were not above partisanship, but directly related to Roosevelt's objective of strengthening Democratic liberalism, was not completely rejected prior to 1938. For example, Roosevelt did quietly intervene to support the liberal Texas congressmen Maury Maverick's 1936 re-election bid. In July 1936, Eleanor Roosevelt wired the president asking him to help Maverick, who was being opposed by Vice President Garner. FDR promptly wired back that he could not play any direct part in a primary campaign, but assured Mrs. Roosevelt that ''the man in question was being helped.''[17] Roosevelt's uncle and close advisor, Frederick Delano, was assigned the task of aiding the progressive congressman, and Maverick was renominated against strong opposition. ''The Administration through the President are going down the line 8000% if not more,'' a grateful Maverick reported to a friend before his victory.[18] But Roosevelt's confidential letter of congratulations revealed his frustration at having to proceed so cautiously against conservatives within his own party:

> Highly privately and extremely confidentially, I am told that I may send you my congratulations. (The etiquette arbiters who own presidents would not let me felicitate my own brother if he won a primary fight.)[19]

The Emergence of the Conservative Coalition

It was really the conservatives within the Democratic party who finally influenced Roosevelt to abandon this caution, who struck the first blow, as it were, when they began to organize aggressively against the New Deal in 1937. The devastation of the Republican party in the 1936 election led conservative Democrats, especially those in the South, to end their uneasy truce with New Dealers—a union of convenience, Stanley High had called it—soon after the start of the 75th Congress and form a coalition with the opposition party.[20] North Carolina Senator Josiah Bailey, who became one of the leaders of this conservative coalition, anticipated such an anti–New Deal alliance in December, 1936, when he wrote to a friend:

> It should be borne in mind, notwithstanding the proportion of [Mr. Roosevelt's] victory, a shift of 10% of the voters from the Democratic side to the Republican side would have elected Mr. Landon. A shift of 10% will bring about conservative policies. This shift can be brought about, but I question whether it can be brought about by the Republican leadership. In this view, it is fortunate that the conservative leadership may now pass to the Democratic side. There are Democrats in the Senate . . . who can put forward the conservative policies and create the background for the contest in 1940.[21]

This much was clear to Bailey; the question remained how to do it. He believed that it was disastrous for conservatives to resist categorically all social welfare reform, considering the alliance formed between the Liberty League and the Republican party especially unfortunate. Like other Southern Democrats, Bailey appreciated the Liberty League's defense of valued American principles such as individual freedom and equality of opportunity. But the elitist character of its chief contributors and officers, and its reluctance to grant the need for any reform of business, served to discredit this group of anti–New Dealers.[22]

Instead, Bailey implied, conservatives could make effective common cause on constitutional issues. Roosevelt's close alliance with labor in the 1936 election portended structural changes in the political economy that would "go to the point of extreme nationalism." The resistance of the Supreme Court to this sort of transformation, moreover, would closely identify labor issues with constitutional principles such as federalism and the separation of powers, thus giving conservatives an opportunity to unite under the unassailable banner of limited consitutional government.[23]

Bailey's expectations or concerns about the New Deal were soon justified. Roosevelt's program for the 75th Congress, announced in the beginning of 1937, called for important extensions of the welfare state, notably proposals to build low-cost housing and to regulate hours and wages, which appealed mainly to the Northern urban wing of the party while alienating Southern and rural representatives. Most important, the president's demand for fundamental structural reforms, as embodied in the pleas to reform the Supreme Court and to reorganize the executive branch of government, touched on constitutional issues that cut across class and region. Whereas Roosevelt's social and economic reforms made conservatives fear a turn against the values of the Constitution, his political proposals affecting the court and executive department greatly accentuated their fears by seeming to attack more directly the practical mechanisms in the Constitution designed to protect limited government. Viewed as a challenge to the separation of powers, these procedural reforms caused the Congress, which had been more tractable than is customary in American politics during Roosevelt's first term, to stiffen its back against presidential domination.

At the center of this opposition to the President was a bipartisan group of conservative senators (Democrats: Bailey of North Carolina; Harry Byrd of Virginia; Edward Burke of Nebraska; Millard Tydings of Maryland; and Royal Copeland of New York; plus Republicans: Arthur Vandenburg of Michigan; and Warren Austin of Vermont) who released a declaration of principles in December, 1937, attacking New Deal reform and extolling a more traditional classical understanding of liberalism. In part, this statement called for a return to normalcy, advocating conservative positions on taxes, labor, and relief. But the conservative coalition's manifesto was not presented as merely a limited disagreement with the New Deal at the level of policy; rather, the connection of conservative policies to the defense of traditional, constitutional democracy suggested that a crisis of regime was at hand. Although Bailey denied publicly that this statement was intended to oppose the President, the conservative declaration, coming on the heels of the controversial Court and Executive Reorganization proposals, implied that the understanding of rights advanced by the New Deal represented a radical departure from the American system of government. "We propose to preserve and rely upon the American system of private enterprise and initiative, and our American form of government," read the conservative coalition's manifesto. "We call upon all Americans to renew their faith in them and press an invincible demand on their behalf."[24]

The constitutional significance of the procedural reforms that dominated FDR's second term will be examined more closely in the next chapter. Whatever the merits of the coalition's critique of this program, however, it was one that proved to be politically effective. It stressed as a major objective "to restore to Congress its proper responsibilities in making laws and enunciating policies for the country," and the publication of this statement of principles in the press signalled the birth of an enduring conservative coalition that would obstruct presidential reform initiatives until the mid-1960s. During the 75th Congress of 1937 and 1938, the conservative coalition scuttled the Court reform bill, the executive reorganization proposal and, for a time, the wages and hours bill. It was soon clear that the battle over this legislation meant that the struggle for control of the Democratic party, predicted with such controversy by Stanley High in early 1937, was now underway. Attorney general Homer Cummings wrote in his diary on August 1, 1937: "It is generally felt that back of all these various fights, including the Supreme Court fight, there lies the question of the nomination of 1940, and the incidental control of party destinies."[25]

By this time, the split within the Democratic ranks had even resulted in a rift between Roosevelt and Vice President Garner, who was playing a leading role in galvanizing opposition to the New Deal. The conflict between FDR and the Vice President was widely reported in the press during the summer of 1937, making the struggle within the councils of the Democratic party the center of national attention. "It's the same old conflict between bourbon Democracy and the agrarian South and the mass democracy of the big industrial cities North and East," Thomas Stokes wrote in the *Nation*. "That they have worked side by side under the New Deal so far is a miracle. The test of strength is fast approaching."[26]

Garner's complicity with FDR's enemies in Congress infuriated the President, apparently persuading him that this test of strength would most likely have to come in the 1938 primary contests. The President told Secretary of the Treasury Henry Morgenthau, Jr., in May, 1937 that he was resolved to act against conservative Democrats:

> He [Roosevelt] said, people like Garner, Senator Bailey, Walsh of Massachusetts, and numerous other conservative Democrats, knowingly or not, are getting prepared for a Conservative Democratic party. They won't go along with any reform measures and are only interested in balancing the budget. . . .
>
> He [Roosevelt] said, I told Jack Garner that it's good for me to get around the country, and, he said, I think I am going to do more of it before the next primaries. He (Roosevelt) said, I wish you could have seen Garner's face. One thing they don't want is for me to get out in the country and fight. He [Roosevelt] said, I gave him the example of Congressman Maverick. . . . Every banker, every public utility man, including Jack Garner, was against Maverick. . . . I sent my uncle, Fred Delano, down there and we elected Maverick with Garner against us. He [Roosevelt] said, I served notice on Garner . . ."[27]

Roosevelt's first action against recalcitrant Democrats came a few months later. In July, 1937, in the fight for Senate majority leader between Alben Barkley of Kentucky and Pat Harrison of Missouri, Roosevelt worked quietly behind the scenes on behalf of Barkley, who was a more consistent supporter of the New Deal. This incident marked the formal parting of ways between FDR and Farley, who refused the President's request to help put pressure on Illinois Senator William Dieterich to get him to vote for Barkley. A disgusted Roosevelt then had Harry Hopkins, whose control of WPA funds could seriously affect the fortunes of Illinois Democrats, contact the head of the Chicago machine, Ed Kelley, to get him to put pressure on the Senator. Dieterich had promised to support Harrison, seconding his nomination for the post, but he now switched to Barkley, a defection that proved crucial—Barkley was elected majority leader by a vote of 38 to 37.[28]

The struggle for the Democratic party became a public issue a month later. In a speech at Roanoke Island, North Carolina, delivered on August 18, Roosevelt expressed the view that his opponents were obstructing the will of the people as expressed in the 1936 election. FDR presented the conservative opponents of the New Deal as a modern representation of the British historian, Lord Macaulay, who had expressed the concern in 1857 that the American constitution was "all sail and no anchor." In a manner reminiscent of his excoriation of New Deal opponents during the 1936 campaign as Tories, the President now depicted those who objected to his program as "American Lord Macaulay's," intent upon placing "supreme power in the hands of a class, numerous indeed, but select; of an educated class, of a class which is, and knows itself to be, deeply interested in the security of property and the maintenance of order." Roosevelt associated himself with a different anchor, "democracy—and more democracy," and proclaimed that the vast majority of Americans supported his assault on privilege.[29]

"If I have read right the President's message at Roanoke Island," Senator Bailey wrote the week after FDR's address, "we have reached a parting of the ways. I gather that the President intends to draw the line and he is really proposing that we shall have here a pure or absolute democracy, and that he intends to drive out of the public life all who do not vote for measures making for this objective."[30] Roosevelt's address, however, depicted his reform program as consistent with the tenets of republican democracy formed by the Constitution; the American political system was based on popular government, even though it contained devices to refine and enlarge the will of the people. The social welfare policy envisioned by programmatic liberalism would not undermine these limits, but reinforce them: "Under it property can be secure, under it abuses can end; under it order can be maintained—and all for the simple, cogent reason that to the average of our citizenship can be brought a life of greater opportunity, of greater security, of greater happiness."[31]

The stage was thus set for a national debate on the constitutional implications of the New Deal. Central to this debate was the question of whether a more national and disciplined version of party politics was compatible with the idea of republican government in the United States. Roosevelt had expressed the hope in his 1934 annual message to Congress that the early political successes of his administration indicated that "a strong and permanent tie between the legislative and executive branches of government was being constructed."[32] Now that Congress, led by members of his own party, had rebelled, thus threatening to restore the more traditional conflictive relationship between the President and Congress, FDR felt that he had no recourse but to seek the public's approval for his constitutional understanding—a purge campaign now was inevitable.

The Purge Campaign of 1938

The battle over the Wages and Hours bill actually triggered the purge campaign. The Democratic platform of 1936 declared minimum wages and maximum hours to be matters "which cannot be adequately handled exclusively by forty-eight different legislatures." A promise was made to seek a solution within the Constitution, but if the Supreme Court continued to void social welfare policy, to work for a constitutional amendment that would make effective government action possible. Encouraged by the results of the election and the changed attitude on the part of the Supreme Court in the Spring of 1937, the Roosevelt administration drafted a bill that Senator Hugo Black of Alabama and William Connelly of Massachusetts introduced on May 24, 1937. With labor strongly in favor of the bill, and with the Administration's prestige behind it, it was generally conceded that the wage-hour legislation would pass the Congress easily. It did pass the Senate on July 31 by a vote of 56 to 28, whereupon it was immediately taken up in the House. "There is no question," wrote New York *Times* columnist Arthur Krock, "that a large majority of the House wants to act favorably on the Wages and Hours Bill."[33]

To the consternation of the Administration and organized labor, however, the bill was blocked in the House Rules Committee—a combination of five Southern Democrats and four Republicans stood against the bill in order to prevent the House members from having a chance to vote upon it. Supporters of wages and hours legislation in the House then looked to party discipline to overcome the obstruction of Southern Democracy; a group of 88 Democratic members signed a petition demanding a party caucus to consider the matter. FDR's conviction that the party caucus was an unwieldy vehicle for formulating and enacting policy could only have been strengthened by what happened next. When the caucus met on August 19, enough Democrats, chiefly from the South, either stayed away or refused to answer to their name when announced, so that no quorum could be called. Although the 157 members who were present "pledged themselves to work unceasingly" for the passage of wages and hours legislation, this meeting, because of a lack of eight votes, failed to become an official caucus. By preventing a formally valid party commitment from taking place, Southern Democrats managed to avoid action on the bill for the first session of the 75th Congress.[34]

The failure to act was denounced by both William Green, head of the A.F.L., and John L. Lewis, chairman of Labor's Nonpartisan League. Lewis was especially vitriolic, accusing the Democratic leadership of being unable to carry out the party's pledges and threatening to end the provisional relationship formed between the C.I.O. and the Democrats during the previous election. "To the leaders of the Democratic party it presents the challenge either to restore sufficient party discipline to permit government to function under their guidance or to confess that their party is not the vehicle by which the people of the country may progress to a solution of their pressing social problems,'' Lewis said in a formal statement issued the day after the ill-fated meeting of House Democrats.[35]

Roosevelt met this challenge. He kept wages and hours legislation as one of the foremost items to be considered through the remainder of the 75th Congress. Then in May, 1938, with the bill once again tied up in the Rules Committee and apparently dead for the last session of the 75th Congress, Democratic representative Mark Wilcox, an opponent of the wages and hours measure and other major New Deal items, came out for the Florida Senate seat of ''100 percent New Dealer'' Claude Pepper. Pepper was one of a handful of young progressive Southerners to whom FDR looked to complete the changes promised by his celebrated re-election victory. An ardent supporter of the wages and hours bill, Senator Pepper announced to his constituents that he was willing to follow the President ''to his death.'' After much soul searching, Roosevelt finally put the Administration's prestige and patronage behind Pepper.

Pepper's resounding victory on May 3, in which he received about 70 percent of the vote, shook the Wages and Hours bill loose from the House Rules Committee, whereupon it easily passed the Congress. Immediately after the Florida primary, a petition to discharge the Rules Committee from further consideration of the bill, and to bring it out on the floor of the House obtained the needed 218 signatures in less than two hours and a half. The Florida primary contest had been watched especially closely by Southern Democrats; the wages and hours bill was thought to be widely unpopular below the Mason–Dixon line, but Pepper's victory seemed to indicate that Roosevelt and his policies were still favored even in the most conservative region of the nation. Twenty-two Southern representatives signed the labor standards bill petition.[36]

The Florida victory encouraged FDR and the New Dealers to hope that intervention in the primaries was an effective means to secure the liberal character of the party. Another test came in the administration's backing of New Deal sympathizer Henry Hess's challenge of incumbent Governor Charles H. Martin of Oregon. Interior Secretary Harold Ickes wrote a public letter endorsing Hess, thus bestowing the imprimatur of the Roosevelt administration. Just 2 weeks before Ickes had responded to a request for help from a Hess supporter with the doubt that there was anything he ''could do with propriety.'' But Pepper's victory and encouragement from Corcoran apparently changed his mind. Ickes's public letter of May 14 to Hess attacked Martin's strong opposition to PWA power projects as evidence ''that he is at heart no New Dealer.''[37]

State Senator Hess's victory over the incumbent Governor, coupled with the Florida triumph, suggested to FDR that the time was propitious for a realignment fight. An ''elimination committee,'' with Harry Hopkins as general supervisor and Corcoran as the day-to-day head of operations, had been formed during the winter months in anticipation of a possible purge campaign. At this point, it began to work in earnest. Now that FDR was finally and firmly committed to the purge, it remained only to explain it to the American people. For that purpose, a fireside chat was prepared by Corcoran and another member of the purge committee, Ben Cohen. But Roosevelt himself dictated the most vital passage of the chat, that drawing a distinction between liberals and conservatives, and proclaiming his intention to liberalize the Democratic party. Liberals, he told the nation on June 24, insisted that "new remedies could be adopted and successfully maintained in this country under our present form of government if we use government as an instrument of cooperation to provide these remedies." This was an ongoing process, FDR continued, that was far from complete. True liberals were opposed, therefore, "to the kind of moratorium on reform which, in effect, is reaction itself."

Whereas liberals used their political office to pursue circumspect, but intrepid progress, FDR argued, conservatives rejected change willy-nilly:

> The . . . conservative school of thought . . . does not recognize the need for government itself to step in and take action to meet these new problems. It believes individual initiative and private philanthropy will solve them—that we ought to repeal many of the things we have done and go back, for instance, to the old gold standard, or stop all this business of old age pensions and unemployment insurance, or repeal the Securities and Exchange Act, or let monopolies thrive unchecked—return, in effect, to the kind of government we had in the twenties.[38]

The critical question in the coming primaries, FDR concluded, was to which of these general schools of thought do the candidates belong. As head of the Democratic party, the President argued, he was charged with the responsibility of carrying out the liberal declaration of principles as set forth in the 1936 platform. He had every right therefore, to speak "in those few instances where there may be a clear issue between Democratic candidates for a Democratic nomination."

Roosevelt's delivery of this declaration of war against Democratic traitors to the New Deal cause formally initiated the purge. Throughout the summer and fall, the President entered the partisan fray, participating in state and local contests in a way that none of his predecessors had dared. As noted in Chapter 2, Woodrow Wilson attempted in 1918 to bring about the defeat of Democratic candidates in five southern states, but Roosevelt intervened on a larger scale—seeking to hurl conservative Democrats from office in a dozen states—and with more vigor than Wilson exercised. Rather than attempt to work through local party organizations as did his Democratic predecessor, FDR chose to make a direct appeal to public opinion.

All the members of the purge committee came from outside the Congress and the National Committee. Besides Hopkins and Corcoran, it consisted of James Roosevelt, son of, and political strategist for, FDR; Joseph Keenan, a Department of Justice official who had been part of the White House political staff during the Court fight and stayed on; David Niles, the top political advisor to Hopkins in the WPA; Secretary Ickes; and Corcoran's close friend and colleague Ben Cohen. This inner New Deal group had no use for Farley, who deeply resented the purge and the "White House crowd," as he called it, that had displaced him as the administration's principal political strategist.[39]

The members of the elimination committee were executives and lawyers in the administration who were essentially without organizational or popular support. "The New Dealers without Roosevelt were a sect, not a majority," the historian Joseph Lash has written of the purge committee. "Roosevelt's majority in the absence of party control was impotent."[40] In the face of this dilemma, the task as defined by Roosevelt was not to overhaul the party organization systematically—the purge team was neither by temperament nor background suited to such a project. Rather FDR sought to put his stamp upon the Democratic party by moving the center of partisan responsibility from the party organization, dominated by sate and local organizations, to the White House, thereby transforming collective responsibility into executive responsibility.

The conditions seemed right for such an appeal in 1938. Columnist Raymond Clapper, in fact, suggested that developments since Wilson's occupation of the White House had made the sort of campaign FDR waged against conservative Democrats inevitable. "It awaited only the appearance of a strong president in a highly controversial setting."[41]

First, there had been the spread of the direct primary during the first three decades of the twentieth century, which provided an opportunity for a direct appeal to the electorate. This reform had begun greatly to weaken the grip of local party organizations on elections. For example, William H. Meier, Democratic County Chairman from Nebraska, wrote Farley in 1938 that his state's direct primary law had "created a situation which has made candidates too independent of the party."[42]

The spread of the direct primary gave the President the opportunity to make a direct appeal to the people over the heads of congressional candidates and local party leaders. Thereby, it provided an attractive vehicle for an attack upon traditional party politics, which Roosevelt saw as an obstacle to his policy goals. Furthermore, radio broadcasting had made the opportunity to appeal directly to large audiences even more enticing. Of course, this was bound to be especially tempting to an extremely popular president with as fine a radio presence as Roosevelt.

Roosevelt's purge campaign, then, marked an important event in the evolution of the "rhetorical presidency," in which presidents would employ oratory to pressure Congress into accepting their programs. Yet, as Herbert Croly had noted about Wilson's "benign dictatorship" of his party, such an emphasis on executive leadership created a serious, if not intractable, dilemma: On the one hand, the decentralized character of American politics can be modified only by strong presidential leadership; on the other hand, a president determined to alter fundamentally the connection between the executive and his party will eventually shatter party unity. In other words, a "purge" might not contribute to the reform of parties, but instead establish the conditions in which partisan responsibility would decline and a more direct and palpable link between the president and public opinion would be created.

Roosevelt was well aware of the dilemma he faced in coming to terms with a sharply divided party and, as he put it, "a thoroughly discombobulated Congress." A close examination of FDR's party leadership during the 75th Congress reveals that his actions could achieve only an ephemeral strengthening of party government. In part this strategy reflects the short-sightedness of the Roosevelt administration's partisan politics. More fundamentally, however, it signifies the limited partisan purposes of the New Dealers in the first place. These purposes were most centrally focused on the South.

The New Deal and the Campaign for a New South

It is not surprising that Roosevelt's selective purge targeted the South as the greatest obstacle to the transformation of the Democratic party into a purposeful liberal organization. As Thomas Stokes wrote after analyzing the important role Southern legislators played in impeding and compromising the wages and hours bill: "Southern Democracy was the ball and chain which hobbled the Party's forward march." [43] For this reason, Roosevelt selected most of the individual targets of the purge from conservative Southern and border states. If the Democratic party was eventually to become a national liberal party, Southern Democracy would have to be defeated.

Roosevelt did not confine his efforts to the South during the 1938 purge attempt, but his most outspoken and unequivocal opposition was directed against traditional Southern Democracy. In particular, he most actively sought to unseat incumbent Senators Walter George from Georgia, "Cotton Ed" Smith from South Carolina and Millard Tydings of Maryland. Although Tydings represented a border state, his political values and practices identified him with the cause of his conservative colleagues from the South.

It has been suggested that Roosevelt erred in attempting to purge candidates from traditionally more conservative states. Charles M. Price and Joseph Boskin, after analyzing polls taken during the 1930s, have argued that Roosevelt faced insurmountable odds because he attempted to oust Senatorial incumbents in areas where he had weak local support. He might better have concentrated, they contend, on Northern industrial states where there was more support for his programs. [44] This argument would seem to be supported by the fact that Roosevelt's one successful purge effort in congressional elections was accomplished against conservative Rules Chairman John J. O'Connor from New York City—which was FDR's only effort in the urban North.

Many Northern New Deal supporters expressed great disappointment during and after the 1938 elections at Roosevelt's relative inattention to areas with substantial numbers of voters who could have readily been converted to the liberal cause. For example, Congressman Herman Kopplemann of Connecticut sought White House support in an effort to unseat conservative incumbent Senator Augustine Lonergan. Corcoran pushed the President to endorse Kopplemann; but, at the suggestion of Connecticut native Homer Cummings, the administration did not intervene, receiving instead a public pledge from the incumbent to support the New Deal and the President in the future. [45] Lonergan was renominated but lost the general election, partly, Kopplemann suggested, because the public resented his repudiation of the President during the 75th Congress. Kopplemann wrote Farley in November 1938, after the general election:

> I don't know how you personally feel about the attempt of the so-called purge but, naturally, that attempt could not have been expected to succeed in tradition-

ally conservative Democratic states. For instance, in Maryland and in Georgia, the people vote the Democratic ticket, but not necessarily the New Deal ticket. Here in Connecticut, for the past seven years, former Republicans have been voting the Democratic ticket because it was the New Deal ticket.

Because of the Administration's relative indifference to the slate of Democratic candidates in Connecticut, Kopplemann argued, the party fared poorly in the 1938 elections.[46]

This Northern strategy, however, might have relegated the Democratic party to being a sectional organization. Roosevelt recognized that writing off the South would lead to the development of a doctrinaire liberal party in the North. This would cause a sectional split that Roosevelt wanted to avoid. The pre–Civil War party was based on a similar assumption, and it was designed to bury slavery as an issue precisely because it could not be managed. Roosevelt was willing to avoid a direct confrontation with the race issue, but he wanted to strengthen the national resolve of the Democratic party on the basis of the issue of economics. Such a national Democratic party could not leave the South alone; it had to be transformed.

Roosevelt initiated his Southern campaign in August, 1938 by endorsing United States Attorney Lawrence Camp in his speech at Barnsville, as Walter George listened from the same podium. Over 50,000 frenzied spectators jam-packed Gordon Institute stadium for FDR's long-awaited visit, ostensibly for the purpose of throwing a switch that would provide power to 357 families along 144 miles of rural power lines. But Roosevelt completely forgot about the switch in the excitement of "one of the most unusual and dramatic moments in American political history."[47]

The President began his talk by arguing that a positive national program of social welfare legislation would be of special benefit to the South, a region that was disproportionately plagued by economic and social problems. The severe hardships of the South were merely a more extreme example of the problems confronted by the whole nation. And since the severity of these difficulties placed them beyond the scope of state action, it was "not an attack on state sovereignty," Roosevelt argued, "to point out that the national aspect of these problems requires action by the federal government in Washington."[48]

Yet effective action by the federal government, Roosevelt told Georgians, could only be achieved by a party of individuals who shared a truly "liberal" political philosophy, who were willing to engage the federal government in attending to the Southern social and economic needs. Such a party might tie the constitutionally independent Executive, Senate, and House of Representatives into a cohesive force for positive government action. The President alone could not bring about such action. The Chief Executive could not take action on national or regional problems, unless they had been "first translated into Acts of Congress passed by the Senate and the House of Representatives of the United States."[49] Congress would not cooperate with the President in this way, of course, unless more effective control of the legislature could be secured by a reorganized—a liberalized—Democratic party. This meant, said Roosevelt:

. . . that if the people of the State of Georgia want definite action in the Congress of the United States, they must send to that Congress Senators and Representatives who are willing to stand up and fight night and day for federal statutes drawn to meet actual needs—not something that serves merely to gloss over the evils of the moment for the time being—but laws with teeth in them which go to the root of the problems, which remove the inequities, raise the standards and, over a period of years, give constant improvement to the conditions of human life in this state.[50]

FDR then referred to his "old friend" Walter George as a "gentleman and a scholar," but declared that the Senator could not in his judgment "be classified as belonging to the liberal school of thought," and he was "impelled to make it clear that on most public questions" he and the conservative Georgian did not "speak the same language." Roosevelt's action against George was motivated by his "responsibility" as President to ensure that the 1936 campaign pledges of the Democratic party were translated into action through cooperation between the Chief Executive and the Congress.

Roosevelt was hopeful that the deep South would support a liberalized Democratic party. FDR and the New Deal, in fact, were very popular in the South during the 1930s. In truth, conservative Democracy in this section of the country was not really an economic conservatism; rather it was firmly established in reaction to the Populist movement at the end of the nineteenth century by the exploitation of the race issue. In a speech at Gainsville, Georgia on March 23, 1938—a speech that in a sense established the ground rules for the purge attempts in the spring and summer—Roosevelt called for an overthrow of what he called the Southern "feudal system." It was this system, he argued, that deprived most Southerners of decent economic conditions.[51] The South could be allied to a new liberal coalition, Roosevelt believed, once the race issue and the reconstruction era were forgotten amid a chorus of demands for economic justice—demands by a majority of whites and blacks.[52]

Such an attitude and a desire on the part of the Administration to focus on economic legislation probably contributed to Roosevelt's lukewarm support of the Anti-lynching bill, which would hold local law enforcement authorities responsible for the lynching of prisoners "escaping" their custody. This legislation had been before the Congress since 1933, but Southern Democrats in the Senate used the filibuster to block its enactment. Walter White, secretary of the NAACP, worked effectively with the Congress to prevent the anti-lynching legislation from being shelved completely, but his fervent entreaties for support from the Roosevelt administration never elicited more than a stance of "benign neutrality" on the part of the president.[53]

After he and Senate majority leader, Alben Barkley, decided to set aside the Anti-lynching bill in early 1938, effectively ending efforts to enact legislation, FDR gave an account of his forbearance to a delegation of black leaders at the White House. Although he favored anti-lynching legislation, his endorsement would permit conservative Southern Democrats who were also opposed to the wages and hours bill and other social welfare measures to "exploit the situation to gain re-election on a campaign of racial prejudice.'' The likely result would be the inflammation of racial tensions, thus further hamstringing the progressive thrusts of the New Deal.[54] It must also have been on Roosevelt's mind that even many ''100 percent New Dealers'' in the South, such as Claude Pepper, did not include blacks in their definition of liberal. Pepper, in fact, helped filibuster to death the anti-lynching measure, going on one day for nearly three hours to forestall its consideration.[55]

This disinclination to attack the race issue may have kept Southern ''progressives'' in the New Deal camp, but did little to assuage the concerns of Southern conservatives. Roosevelt's strong attack on traditional Southern politics—an attack that coincided, not coincidentally, with a report of the National Emergency Council on economic conditions in the South—convinced Southern conservatives that the New Deal would eventually lead to broader black participation.[56] Many Southerners were concerned about the solicitation of the black vote in the North by the Democratic party. They were astute enough to see the possible long-run consequences for politics below the Mason–Dixon line of the efforts by Senator Guffey and others to strengthen the Negro division of the Democratic party during the 1936 campaign. When combined with Roosevelt's attack on the economic conditions of their region, such a campaign strategy portended a class-oriented alignment that would remake Southern democracy. As the unreconstructed rebel Carter Glass wrote to a friend, ''The Southern people may wake up too late to find the negrophiles who are running the Democratic party now will soon precipitate another reconstruction era for us.''[57]

To Southern Democrats, then, it appeared that Roosevelt was intent upon building a new party organization. Senator George was able to excite the fear in many old-time Southerners in Georgia that the purge against him indicated that the advisors around the President, the Corcorans, the Cohens, the Hopkinses— none of whom had any relationship to the regular Democratic organization—were influencing him toward the remodeling of their ancient and honorable party.[58]

The issue of race became especially salient in the South Carolina primary, where ''Cotton Ed'' Smith defeated the New Deal candidate, Governor Olin Johnston. Unlike the naturally reserved George, Smith did not have to be persuaded by his advisors to turn on the full demagogic appeal in his 1938 campaign. Race-baiting and zealous defense of white supremacy, in fact, had been the cornerstone of his long career in the Senate.[59] But the New Deal challenge to Southern politics, *Time* reported, had ''managed to put some life into [Smith's] traditional campaign plank.''[60]

''Cotton Ed's'' defense of traditional Southern Democracy was first displayed before a national audience at the 1936 convention. While Marshall L. Shepard, pastor of the Mt. Olivet Tabernacle Baptist Church in Philadelphia and a member of the Pennsylvania legislature, became the first black minister to deliver an invocation at a national convention session, Senator Smith, followed by a few other South Carolina delegates, left the convention hall. After leaving, Smith told the press that he would not support ''any political organization that looks upon the Negro and caters to him as a political and social equal.''[61] The next day Smith repeated his march from the convention hall to protest another first—when Congressman Arthur W. Mitchell of Illinois delivered one of the speeches seconding Roosevelt's nomination, he became the first black to speak from the floor of the Democratic convention. An exchange between Senator Smith and Reverend Shepard through the press then took place that foreshadowed the purge campaign. "In looking for a party without Negroes," the pastor said of Smith, "it looks like he will have to form his own little party right there in South Carolina." From the Senator came the comment: "I don't have to form my own party. The party already exists. It was born in the red shirt days of the Reconstruction period, when the gentlemen of South Carolina donned red shirts to rid our state of carpetbaggers, scalawags and Negroes."[62]

Smith revived this organization of Red Shirts in 1938 in order to fend off Roosevelt's attempt to purge him. The President sought to make Smith's opposition to the wages and hours legislation the major issue when he traveled to South Carolina during the primary campaign. "I don't believe any family or any man in South Carolina can live on fifty cents a day," he said from the back of his special campaign train before a crowd of 15,000 who had waited for him until nearly midnight at the Greenville, South Carolina station. This comment referred to Smith's opposition to the wages and hours bill, claiming it would unjustly force Southern mill owners to pay the same wage as was paid in New England, where the cost of living was higher—this, the Senator complained, would amount to a "Yankee protective tariff" that would damage Southern manufacturing interests. Textile workers in South Carolina, encouraged by C.I.O. union organizers, grumbled about Smith's remark, now made famous by Roosevelt.

But Smith was able to deflect attention from the national issues to which FDR sought to focus the electorate's attention. His campaign blasted the "interracial C.I.O.," bringing him heavy campaign contributions from mill owners and even the endorsement of President William Green of the rival A.F.L. More important, it shifted the campaign away from Governor Johnston's support of the New Deal, and the President's endorsement of Johnston, to regional concerns that were more favorable to the vitriolic Smith. Telling proudly of his protest marches in Philadelphia 2 years before, he would launch into diatribes that implicitly attacked both the Roosevelt administration's racial tolerance and its desire to impose that view on South Carolina:

> White supremacy, that time-honored tradition, can no more be blotted out of the hearts of South Carolina than can the scars which Sherman's artillery left on the State House at Columbia. . . . Yes, I walked out of the convention in Philadelphia. I'll do it again. I'm not going to be a party to making the Negro a part of this government.[63]

The South Carolina senatorial campaign in 1938, two journalists reported, "brought race hatred to a peak which had not been reached in South Carolina since the palmiest days of Pitchfork Ben Tillman."[64] Smith's race-baiting and his effective attack on FDR's "outside interference" returned him to the Senate with a comfortable majority, the widest margin of all his six races for the Senate. But even after the polls closed, and his victory made known, the Senator did not stop campaigning. *Time* magazine reported that Smith's supporters saluted his re-election by paying homage to the Red Shirts; at one in the morning, Smith donned one of those shirts, worn in memory of General Wade Hampton, who drove the Carpetbaggers back North, and, "like a heavy set Garibaldi led the celebrants to [Hampton's statue] on the State House grounds."[65]

The South Carolina campaign dramatically demonstrated that Roosevelt had failed to focus the primary struggles in the South on national economic issues. Smith was able to deflect attention from these issues by reminding Southerners of the New Dealers' intense pursuit of Black votes in the North and Roosevelt's tacit approval of the anti-lynching bill. Rebel yells did not entirely drown out Roosevelt's promise of greater economic equality; in the textile towns millworkers poured out to vote for Governor Johnston, aroused by President Roosevelt's promise of a better deal for labor. But many mill hands and most propertied people and almost all cotton growers—sharecroppers as well as landlords—trooped to the polls to vote for Smith, many of them influenced by Smith's "white supremacy" speeches.[66]

Although such rhetoric was most prominent in South Carolina, Roosevelt's attack on Southern Democracy aroused similar resentment throughout the region.[67] Roosevelt's sorrowful reaction to Smith's victory revealed that he recognized all too well the failure of the purge to displace racial conflict with concerns for economic justice. "It takes a long, long time," he lamented, "to bring the past up to the present."[68]

The Consequence of New Deal Party Politics

The purge campaign capped Roosevelt's bold and unprecedented bid to challenge conventional party practices. For the most part, however, this challenge to the traditional party apparatus emphasized a direct appeal to public opinion, rather than a full-scale effort to develop an alternative party organization. "Had the so-called New Dealers been more careful of party sensibilities and been more concerned with the development of grass roots support," Paul Van Riper has speculated, "they might have formed, as more traditional politicians sometimes feared, the nucleus of a new party structure in this country."[69] But the Roosevelt administration's attempt to convert the 1938 primaries into a national referendum often fell on deaf ears; the purge campaign, orchestrated by the inexperienced "elimination committee," was no match for well-entrenched incumbents, most of whom had smooth-functioning state organizations.[70]

To be sure, the Roosevelt administration was not indifferent to the organizational side of politics. The White House earnestly, if not always skillfully, enlisted the growing army of federal workers in local and state political activity, including some of the purge campaigns.[71] To conservative pundits such as Albert Jay Nock, this political use of federal employees raised the specter of a "modern Tammany," one that would operate on a national scale, independently of state and local organizations.[72] Press reports of the primary campaigns seemed to support such a contention. After the Florida primary, for example, the *New York Times* reported that the use of relief money and personnel had given the Administration the potential for superior influence in renominating and re-electing its favorites and in punishing independents.[73] The use of relief funds and the Works Progress Administration was especially salient in the Kentucky primary, where Roosevelt sought to help Majority Leader Alben Barkley against a strong challenge from Governor A. B. (Happy) Chandler. Roosevelt's endorsement of Barkley was significant, but equally important was the "Federal machine" that worked feverishly on behalf of the incumbent Senator. After Barkley's victory, *Newsweek* reported:

> Once the New Deal issue and the President's personality had been injected into the fight, the Barkley–Chandler race resolved into a titanic test between the vote getting power of Federal funds—WPA and farm benefits—against the strength of a well-disciplined state machine. The New Deal won: with reports in from most precincts, Barkley lumbered across the finish line 50,000 votes ahead of his rival.
> . . .
> In Kentucky, Senator Barkley had all the blessings the President could bestow, and New Dealers with some justification claimed it as a victory. Yet Barkley had a Federal fund machine . . . more powerful than Chandler's state counterpart.[74]

This federal machine, however, was much more successful in aiding the renomination of pro–New Deal incumbents than it was in "purging" New Deal opponents from the party. With the exception of the congressional primary in New York, which was fought on Roosevelt's home territory, every incumbent legislator who was a target of the purge was able to fight off the challenge of Roosevelt's personality and federal "pap." The enactment of the Hatch Act in 1939, moreover, which will be discussed in more detail in the next chapter, removed the influence of all federal administrative officials who made policies of nationwide application from elections or nominating efforts for President, Vice President, and members of Congress. This legislation short-circuited any effort on the part of Roosevelt and the New Dealers to develop a national party machine based on federal government spending and organization.

It is unlikely, however, that the development of a modern Tammany was the intention of the Roosevelt administration in the first place. FDR probably understood, as E. E. Schattschneider has suggested, that "a powerful national party organization is not merely a magnified local machine consuming a greater quantity of spoils."[75] Still, the Administration made no substantial effort during the second term to develop a national party organization based on principle. Perhaps, as his efforts in 1938 seem to indicate, Roosevelt felt this was not possible in the context of American politics. The New Dealers felt that the President could best mobilize political support by concentrating efforts on directly persuading public opinion. It is not unreasonable that the New Dealers believed this prior to the 1938 primary elections. However, the primary campaign revealed the limitations of the Administration's strategy. That it was attempted at all indicates the ambiguous partisan intentions of the New Dealers in the first place.

Roosevelt wrote in 1941 that he viewed intervention in the primary campaigns as a necessary action to "keep liberalism in the foreground" in the councils of the Democratic Party, "as well as in the legislative and executive branches of government itself." In the President's view there could be no realization of the campaign promises of 1936 without disciplining those Democratic candidates who acted in "repudiation of liberal and progressive government." The toleration of conservative candidates under the banner of the Democratic Party would make the Democratic and Republican Parties "merely Tweedledum and Tweedledee," and elections would become "meaningless when the two major parties have no differences other than their labels."[76]

In part, Roosevelt had a long-term objective that looked beyond any successes or failures in the specific 1938 campaigns. FDR believed that a stronger commitment to disciplined national party organization would have a beneficial effect on American politics; yet he recognized that the American Constitution and the history of party politics in the United States imposed limitations on such an objective. The start of a public dialogue on the character of the American party system might yield definite political results in the future. As Thomas Stokes astutely observed in 1940, Roosevelt "hoped to raise the issue, start a public debate, and provoke the voters themselves to inquire more closely into what the men they elected to office actually did when they got to Washington."[77]

There has been a good deal of controversy among statesmen and scholars regarding the effect of Roosevelt's purge campaign. To some, the 1938 campaign was a success, even though most of the efforts to defeat recalcitrant Democrats failed. Most immediately, the purge got wages and hours legislation enacted into law, along with other parts of Roosevelt's program. It also freed the House Rules Committee from the conservative and smothering grasp of John J. O'Connor.[78] So pleased was the President to cleanse the party of O'Connor, that he insisted that the victory in New York made the entire purge campaign worthwhile. "Harvard lost the schedule but won the Yale game," he happily told the press.[79] Like the successful endorsement of Barkley, the purging of O'Connor was of major importance to Roosevelt in smoothing the path of his bills in Congress.[80]

In addition to these tangible results, it has been argued, the president's intervention in the 1938 primaries revitalized party politics and laid the groundwork for a significantly more liberal Democratic party. To a degree, even in those cases where the purge drive failed, candidates had to make peace with the New Deal program. George, Smith, and Tydings were careful not to attack Roosevelt and the New Deal directly; instead, they sought to turn the attention of the primary voters from economic matters, which favored the President, to racial and sectional conflicts, which highlighted the impropriety of a president interfering in local contests. It may very well be, as Schattschneider and others have pointed out, that had Roosevelt not taken on conservatives within his party in such dramatic fashion, the Democratic party would have reverted to its Jeffersonian traditions.[81]

Notwithstanding these arguments, at least in the short term, the purge was a failure, since it left the anti–New Deal coalition of Republicans and conservative Democrats in a powerful position in Congress. In the dozen states within which the President acted against entrenched incumbents, he was successful in only two of them—New York and Oregon. The triumph over Governor Martin in Oregon, moreover, proved to be a pyrrhic one; the purge left Oregon Democrats in disarray, condemning them to defeat in the general election.[82] As the political scientist E. Pendleton Herring observed in 1940, the success of conservative Democrats in surviving the 1938 primary campaign indicated that "the purge failed both as a disciplinary measure and as a device for clarifying opinion."[83] The divisions within the Democratic party were too deeply rooted to be eliminated through a purge campaign, and as James Farley observed in his memoirs, by violating "a cardinal political creed" of American politics "that the President keep out of local matters," Roosevelt widened and further entrenched the split within the Democratic party between liberal and conservative factions.[84] With the purge campaign, FDR brought into the open the deep and historical divisions that he once sought to obscure. But, having finally moved to answer Stanley High's question—Whose Party Is It?—the president found himself facing a more entrenched conservative bloc. Conservative Democrats had not turned the country against FDR and the New Deal, but they had strengthened their position as a "loyal" opposition, determined to preserve the independence of Congress and local self-determination.

Roosevelt never admitted the 1938 campaign was a failure, and, as we shall see in the next two chapters, he did not completely give up his attempt to wrest control of the Democratic party from its most conservative elements after this effort. Nevertheless, the attempt to make the Democratic party the party of, as he put it, "militant liberalism" was dealt a severe blow by the results of the purge campaign. The purge effort during the 1938 primaries, and its immediate aftermath, demonstrated clearly enough to Roosevelt the great difficulty of establishing a more disciplined and national party system in the United States. The failure of the purge was further reinforced by the general election of 1938, in which the heavy losses sustained by the Democratic party (80 seats in the House and 8 in the Senate, as well as 13 governorships) were partly interpreted as a reaction to Roosevelt's participation in party battles. Farley wrote several party leaders throughout the country after the 1938 election asking for an evaluation of Democratic losses. Many of those who responded, including many from non-Southern states, mentioned unfavorable reaction to the purge. Illinois Congressman James A. Meeks's view was fairly typical among party moguls in Washington and the states. "The so-called effort to purge certain Congressmen and Senators met with unfavorable reaction," he wrote Farley in early 1939. "You readily understand that."[85]

Party chieftains, of course, had opposed the purge campaign from the beginning. But many liberals who supported FDR's assault on the regular Democratic organization and the purge campaign had to agree that the President's intervention in the 1938 primaries had failed. Former Wisconsin Governor Philip LaFollette, one of the several independent progressives who went down to crushing defeat in 1938, wrote in *Nation* soon thereafter, "The results of the so-called purge by President Roosevelt showed that the fight to make the Democratic party liberal is a hopeless one."[86]

Stubbornly, Roosevelt insisted that local issues caused the Democratic decline. He even took heart from the defeat of liberal insurgents in the Midwest. The Wisconsin Progressive party and the Minnesota Farmer–Labor party not only lost gubernatorial re-election campaigns, but also most of their congressional seats. Although unhappy about the Republican gains that resulted from these losses, FDR wrote Josephus Daniels that some good things had occurred: "[W]e have on the positive side eliminated Phil LaFollette and the Farmer–Labor people . . . as a standing third-party threat. They must and will come to us *if* we remain definitely the liberal party.''[87]

Yet Roosevelt never again moved seriously for party realignment. Furthermore, the Democratic party did not become a purely liberal party by the time of Roosevelt's death. To be sure, as Ickes observed, Roosevelt's presidency and the New Deal probably set in motion a "natural evolution" that strengthened the liberal commitment of the Democratic party, one that would work itself out over the long term in spite of the staying power of the traditional party organization.[88] Notwithstanding the defeats of 1938, this evolution would continue; indeed, the probability of its taking place was increased by Roosevelt's third term campaign, which is considered in Chapter 6. Nevertheless, the 1938 primary campaign dramatically defined the limits of party leadership and the prospects for definitive party alignment in the United States. In fact, Roosevelt told Homer Cummings in December, 1938, that his attitude towards recalcitrant Democrats such as Pat Harrison and Burton Wheeler (a progressive, but one who broke with FDR over the "court-packing" plan) had become "all milk and honey."[89] This was not a reconciliation that FDR especially enjoyed nor one to which he was fully committed; yet, apparently, he had reluctantly come to the conclusion that the decentralized character of American party politics recommended conciliation and compromise rather than purges as a salve for intraparty struggles. Moreover, the results of the 1938 campaign had a profound historical impact that went beyond the Roosevelt administration. As Charles Price and Joseph Boskin have concluded:

> Roosevelt's futile bid to unseat the incumbents through the use of primary endorsements has never been attempted by any succeeding President, in view perhaps of the alleged enormity [sic] of the President's failure.[90]

In the final analysis, Roosevelt's program to make the Democratic party a more consistent instrument of liberalism was generally viewed by representatives and the public as an irresponsible attempt to fashion a rubber stamp Congress. The consitutional implications of his actions affected progressives as well as conservatives. Hiram Johnson, to whom Roosevelt directed such lavish attention in 1932, now found himself, due to the "strange mutations of time," as he put it, in league with Southern Democrats against the purge. Reflecting on the President's motivations in attacking Walter George and other Democratic Senators, he wrote to Harry Byrd:

> These [Senators] do not choose to play the part of Charlie McCarthy's, or to give their conscience into the keeping of any one man, and I may remark, parenthetically, that any candidate for the Senate who chooses to do these things is utterly unfit to be a United States Senator and should be consigned to that oblivion which demerits adorn.[91]

Roosevelt's aggressive partisanship, then, revealed the continuing importance of the American "Constitution-against-parties." FDR had "demonstrated in the most public way," New York *Times* columnist Arthur Krock claimed, "that the American system and tradition are still stronger than he is." As such, FDR's public endorsements and New Deal patronage might have hurt the administration's candidates more than they helped. "[I]t is admitted on all sides in Maryland," Krock continued, "that Representative Lewis, an excellent man and not at all the rubber stamp he professed himself to be, would have run a much better race against Senator Tydings if the president had not forcibly intervened. And the cynical Washington belief that lures of Federal projects cannot fail—bridges in Maryland, roads in Georgia, cotton looms in South Carolina—has taken the blow it deserved."[92]

His purge efforts notwithstanding, of course, Roosevelt was always aware of the limitations of the extent to which his purposes could be achieved by party government in the United States. Even before he became president, FDR's role in the Democratic party had combined an ardent desire to remake the Democratic party with a cautiousness bred by rich political experience and the realization that the full power and splendor of his office necessitated rising above partisan politics. This explains FDR's commitment to patronage practices that served programmatic purposes, to the detriment often of party organization. Similarly, Roosevelt's cultivation of auxiliary party organizations such as Labor's Nonpartisan League and the Good Neighbor League reflected his recognition of the full institutional implications of the distinction between his and his party's electoral constituencies. This realization probably limited the purge campaign to a few congressional campaigns and one gubernatorial contest, and prevented a more systematic nationwide attempt to elect New Dealers.

The purge campaign served to strengthen the President's understanding that his principles and policies could not be too centrally tied to the fate of his party. Roosevelt's popularity, both polls and pundits suggested, had been little damaged by the 1938 elections. "There seems little relationship between the standing of New Deal policies and the standing of the Chief sponsor of these policies," wrote one journalist in January, 1939. "There also is scant connection between the President's popularity and that of his party's candidates."[93] These distinctions were surely on the President's mind when he told Farley to read a post mortem of the 1938 election that he received from Iowa. Seeking to explain the Democratic losses there, the author observed that the last election "conclusively established that it was not the Democratic party but the Roosevelt party that carried Iowa in three elections."[94] FDR's interest in this analysis suggests that he was now firmly persuaded of the need to form a direct link between the executive office and the public. In a practical sense, this focused the President's attention on 1940. "One clear implication that may not have been lost upon Roosevelt was that, with his own popularity still at a high level, he could attain New Deal goals in future elections only if he himself headed the ticket," the historian Frank Freidel has written. "His glamour did not rub off on others."[95] FDR's "glamour" did rub off on the institution of the presidency, however; as the next two chapters reveal, this ratified the separation of the executive office and party politics that had been emerging gradually since the beginning of the twentieth century.

5

Administrative Reform and the Displacement of Party Politics: Reflections on the "Third New Deal"

The celebrated journalist William Allen White wrote Felix Frankfurter in October, 1937, "itching" to express his concern that the President tended to mistake the Democratic victory in 1936, which came through the assemblage of a diverse array of factions, as a "personal mandate." Failing to reinforce the unity of his party by the "steel rods of counsel," he warned the President's confidant, FDR threatened the integrity of his party as a collective organization with a past and a future. Two months later, White's message reached the White House through Farley, who received and, in turn, showed the President, an almost identical letter as the one previously sent to Frankfurter. An additional thought was expressed in the letter to Farley, however. In reference to the great differences dividing the "blocks" that added up to Roosevelt's 1936 landslide, White suggested that a separate presidential New Deal coalition might emerge from the inevitable demise of the Democratic organization. "If our beloved leader cannot find the least common multiple between John Lewis and Carter Glass," White wrote on December 28, "he will have to take a mantle and crack the monolith, forget that he had a party, and build his policy with the pieces which fall under his hammer."[1]

In a sense, this is what FDR did in undertaking the purge campaign. Theodore Lowi has described this effort as Roosevelt's attempt "to modernize the Democratic party by transforming it into a truly programmatic national party along European lines of programmatic concerns and membership discipline." When this endeavor ended in a stunning defeat, Lowi argues, "Roosevelt to a large extent abandoned the Democratic party and instead went over the heads of the party and congressional leaders directly to the American people."[2] But, as noted, the purge campaign itself involved overwhelmingly an appeal to public opinion rather than any systematic attempt to work through or reform the regular party apparatus. The purge campaign, therefore, was as much an admission of the limits of party government in the United States as it was an attempt to secure it. When the nonprogrammatic character of the Democratic party became all too clear during the 75th Congress, Roosevelt sought to transfer the allegiance of the American people to his programmatic administration. Had he been successful in doing so, perhaps, the Democratic party might have become a disciplined instrument of programmatic liberalism. More fundamentally, however, FDR's ardent partisanship as displayed during the purge campaign was associated with the objective of forming a more direct link with the public that would better enable him to make use of his position as head of the *whole nation* rather than as merely head of a party governing the nation.[3] Paradoxically, the incipient formation of a more national and programmatic party politics during the New Deal made party politics less important.

In part, this development was an unintended consequence of Roosevelt's use of the direct primary as an instrument of party discipline. Wilson had looked to the primary to elevate the tone of party discourse, but the spread of this progressive institution tended to emphasize campaigns that centered on candidates rather than party principles or platforms. This much was anticipated by Herbert Croly, whose view that primaries would diminish the strength of national parties as representative institutions proved prescient. By regulating the party and forcing it to select its leaders in a certain way, he had observed in 1914, the "state is sacrificing the valuable substance of partisan loyalty and allegiance to the mere mechanism of partisan association." As such, parties would persist—in effect, they would be "legalized"—but at the cost of diminishing the "community of spirit and purpose" that distinguished partisan organizations from ad hoc coalitions or interest groups.[4]

The deleterious influence of the direct primary on the party system was magnified in those states with so-called "open primaries," which permitted voters to cast whatever ballot they pleased on primary day without previous affiliation. Roosevelt strongly opposed such open contests, a view he aired publicly after Senator James P. Pope was defeated by Representative D. Worth Clark in the Idaho senatorial primary of 1938. In that contest some fifteen or twenty thousand Republicans, crossing party lines as permitted by Idaho primary law, were reported to have voted for Clark, a conservative Democrat, thus ensuring Pope's defeat. Consequently, Roosevelt's endorsement of Pope, an enthusiastic supporter of the New Deal, went for naught, prompting the frustrated President to denounce the Idaho results in his August 23 press conference. The crossing of party lines, Roosevelt argued, was a violation of "public morality," a "complete destruction" of the direct primary's objective: "to give the actual voters within a party, in recognition of the party system under which we live, the right to choose their candidates for public office."[5]

Roosevelt's protestations after the Idaho contest notwithstanding, his intervention in the 1938 Congressional contests tended to elevate the importance of the candidate's support of liberal principles over the need to sustain the integrity of party organizations as representative institutions. In Idaho, the President was brought face to face with the contradictory legacy of progressive reform—evident in the disagreement between Woodrow Wilson and Croly, as well as the variety of primary methods adopted in the states—that emancipated critical party decisions from "boss-controlled" conventions, while rendering such deliberations less meaningful (see chapter 2). In this regard, the difference between open and closed primaries was not terribly significant—in both cases parties tended to become convenient labels, thus losing their importance as voluntary associations for the promotion of certain common political and economic objectives. The looming presence of Roosevelt and the radio in the 1938 primary campaigns illustrated the maxim of progressive reform pronounced and celebrated by Croly. "Just in proportion as the official political organization becomes genuinely democratic," he wrote hopefully, "it can disperse with the services of national parties."[6]

Croly's remedy for reform, of course, was not to democratize the American two-party system, which had been sustained at the expense of administrative independence and efficiency, but to democratize government itself. Partisan responsibility, consequently, had to be displaced by executive responsibility before democracy in the United States could be made compatible with a strong and efficient administration of the law.

Roosevelt, to be sure, was not indifferent to such an objective. Throughout his presidency, and especially during the second term, his party leadership was associated with an exalted view of presidential leadership that lessened the significance of party responsibility. The purge campaign was not an isolated initiative unconnected to other measures being pushed at the time. Rather, it was one of several intiatives pursued during Roosevelt's second term that amounted to attacks on power structures viewed as obstacles to the creation of a modern presidency. Two other initiatives were of equal importance: One was the executive reorganization bill, sent to Congress in January, 1937; another was the court-"packing" plan, sent up to the Hill some 3 weeks after the executive reform measure. "The day of enlightened administration has come," FDR had said in the 1932 Commonwealth Club address. With his landslide re-election, Roosevelt felt he could pursue a program dedicated to enlightened government, one that the administration imposed on the Democratic party.

This sequence of events makes clear that FDR launched plans for attaining administrative dominance prior to his attempt to purge the Democratic party of conservative influence. Contrary to conventional understanding, he did not view executive dominance over the political process as a *substitute* for the position of presidential party leadership that had begun to appear unattainable. Rather, Roosevelt wanted to achieve White House control over both the bureaucracy and Democratic party *right from the beginning*—in the belief that both were necessary if his administration was ever to achieve its progressive goals.

Taken together, the institutional reforms of the second term signified the emergence of a "Third New Deal"—a political program that would strengthen the nation's administrative capacities by refurbishing the presidency and freeing it from the constrictive grip of localized parties and laissez-faire court rulings. Once executive administration displaced the "state of courts and parties," the chief executive would be in a position to effect more directly developments in the economy and society.[7]

As the New Deal developed, therefore, it became clear to many observers that it would not yield a European-style party realignment; instead, FDR's style of leadership rendered the concepts of collective responsibility and loyal opposition, as understood in the European context, meaningless. The question of whether the New Deal would lead to a European-style realignment was explicitly considered by *Fortune* magazine in an editorial that appeared in February, 1937. With respect to FDR's leadership and its effect on party politics, *Fortune* observed:

> A useful opposition can function only in a country in which the vital decisions are made in the Legislature. . . . A Republican opposition hoping to recover its lost estate by its success as an opposition party is wasting its time in a legislative body which does not determine the policy of the nation.[8]

The "loyal opposition" theory of Republican policy referred to national chairman John Hamilton's program to revitalize his party as a "responsible" opposition to the New Deal. Hamilton, in fact, traveled to England in 1937 to investigate whether any aspect of the British party system could be adapted to the American political structure, especially with respect to the role and function of the loyal opposition, the out-party. In spite of Hamilton's efforts, however, the opposition to Roosevelt after 1937 emphasized the bipartisan cooperation forged between conservative Democrats and Republicans, reflecting both mutual necessity and the structural setting of party politics in the United States.[9] The strength and efficacy of the anti–New Deal forces, however, were remarkable, attributable in large part to the program of the Roosevelt administration during the second term, which represented a constitutional, and not simply partisan, program to restructure the balance of power in American government. As the strengthening of the presidency was central to that program, congressional Republicans were encouraged to support their conservative Democratic colleagues in a manner that transcended immediate political exigencies.

The Meaning of the "Third New Deal"

The reform program of the second term looked well beyond the Roosevelt administration's practices in the formulation and administration of policy during the first term that strengthened executive responsibility, and diminished, thereby, the role Congress and partisan organizations had previously enjoyed in these government activities. It also involved a comprehensive set of policies that would, in effect, *institutionalize* the restructuring of the balance between executive and legislative power effected by Roosevelt's leadership and the New Deal. The construction of an ascendant executive power was certainly the purpose of the two government reorganization bills—one dealing with the judiciary, the other with the executive department—that dominated the 75th Congress. The enactment of these bills would remake constitutional law and the executive in the New Deal image; henceforth, therefore, what FDR did by improvisation and extraordinary personal popularity would be done deliberately and regularly.

Croly had viewed the development of a more intimate relationship between the president and public opinion, as well as other progressive reforms in support of a more "direct democracy," as a way station on the road to a modern administrative state—progressive democracy, based upon a more fluid and programmatic contract between the people and representatives, presupposed administration aggrandizement. Similarly, Roosevelt's leadership of the Democratic party and the program he sought to impose on it foreshadowed a strengthening of national administrative capacities. The historian Barry Karl, in fact, has viewed FDR's administrative reform efforts between 1937 and 1939 as a systematic effort to establish a modern bureaucratic state in American politics, a project, in other words, to develop the managerial capacity characteristic of modern states elsewhere, but absent in the United States due to the extraordinary antipathy to administrative centralization in this country. The various battles that took place over the courts, executive reorganization, and the Democratic party after FDR's re-election are usually not viewed as part of a systematic effort to remake American politics; rather, the period from 1937 to 1939 is generally portrayed as a time when the reformist aspirations aroused by the electoral outcomes of 1936 were frustrated by the revival of adamant and unreasonable conservatives, as well as the president's ill-advised efforts to punish them. According to Karl, however, "Roosevelt had a plan for his second term, a Third New Deal, if you will, . . . that would have involved a dramatic transformation of American presidential administration." [10]

So characterized, Roosevelt's political program as it unfolded during the second term was a remarkable attempt to legitimize an administrative state on American soil, a serious effort, as Ellis Hawley has put it, to fill the "hollow core" in the American state's bureaucratic apparatus.[11] The centerpiece of the Third New Deal was the Executive Reorganization bill, which would strengthen the administrative power and capacity of the president. Significantly, the bill proposed to create a number of new administrative tools and support staff, not just for Roosevelt, or for a particular president, but for the office as an institution. The Roosevelt administration's efforts to alter the judiciary and party politics were also integral components of administrative reform. The court reform bill would restaff the judiciary with jurists who would not stand in the way of expanding executive administration, and party reform, culminating with the "purge" campaign, would mold an executive-centered party, free of the obstructive power of Southern Democracy. "Had all these initiatives been successful," Hawley surmises, "the period might have become a truly revolutionary one in establishing and legitimizing the kind of institutions that our anti-bureaucratic traditions had long taught us to fear and shun." [12]

Roosevelt's administrative reform program, however, was not so clearly hostile to the Constitution. Arguably, the New Deal sought to put into practice an alternative understanding of the Constitution, albeit one that rejected the constitutional principles and mechanisms that had prevailed since the "Revolution of 1800." The Democratic–Republican party spawned by this realignment was organized to consolidate public opinion against the centralizing and administrative characteristics evident in Hamilton's commercial and financial endeavors. Out of this struggle between the Democratic–Republicans and the Federalists, we have noted, there developed in the United States a profound tension between party politics, on the one hand, and administrative centralization and bureaucracy, on the other. The wedding of parties to a Jeffersonian understanding of the Constitution—a task that was completed by Van Buren and the rise of Jacksonian democracy in the 1830s—signified the triumph of a political philosophy dedicated to the idea that the majority should govern, and that majority rule required the state to be subordinated to society. Similarly, the executive was turned into a party leader, and thus "republicanized," but executive power was severely curtailed by the Jeffersonian doctrine of strict construction of the Constitution.[13]

The New Deal sought to rescue the Constitution and the Democratic party from Jeffersonian principles. With the consolidation of private power in the hands of giant trusts, a constitutional program providing for societal domination of the state was now a recipe for economic oligarchy. Just as Jefferson defined the task of party leadership as rallying public opinion against the state, Roosevelt sought to transfer the American people's allegiance from private interests to public authority. As such, the New Deal Democratic party was organized during the 1930s as a "government party," one based on a program to build a "modern" state, which Roosevelt and his Brains Trust saw as an indispensible element in restoring economic and political democracy to the United States. Such a program did not require for its success the sort of elaborate party apparatus, rooted in the states and localities, that traditionally organized American partisan practices. Rather, the state created by the New Deal Democratic party would organize its supporters through the disbursement of social welfare benefits. This was an inversion, a democratic variant, if you will, of the Hamiltonian enterprise, which would cultivate and maintain the support of commercial interests through the disbursement of bounties, licenses, and tariffs. The Federalists were organized as a government party to wed commercial interests and state power—to develop, in turn, a stable commercial republic. The New Deal Democrats were organized as a government party to wed welfare beneficiaries, broadly understood, and state power against the overwhelming commercial power that had subordinated Jeffersonian principles and institutions to its interest by the end of the nineteenth century.

In the final analysis, the New Deal Democratic party was organized as a party of administration that would make party politics less important in the future. Once a welfare state was formed, social and economic interests would be directly linked to it, thus diminishing the importance of a party to organize public opinion. Party government, therefore, was not required by Roosevelt's program in the long run, nor, given the understanding of rights that underlay the economic constitutional order, was it even congenial to it.

From this perspective, the Third New Deal was not conceived, as Karl and Hawley have argued, as a program to create a "rational," European-style state bureaucratic apparatus, nor did the failure to achieve an administrative state characteristic of modern states elsewhere signify a failure of the program Roosevelt pursued during this period. Unlike Croly, Roosevelt did not believe that progressive democracy necessarily "foreshadowed" administrative aggrandizement that was hostile to the American political tradition. Indeed, he rejected the idea of separating politics and administration advocated by Croly and Wilson during the Progressive era, believing that such a project would deprive the administrative state of the political energy and support required to anchor it within the American political system. That political effectiveness would be derived, in part, by tying the administrative state to the presidency. The recognition by the Founding Fathers of the need for a strong and independent executive was never completely displaced by the formation of the American party system, and the compatibility of formidable presidential leadership with the original constitutional design was a major theme of the Roosevelt administration's "campaign" for government reform. Roosevelt and the architects of administrative reform, for this reason, did not endorse Croly's commitment to the development of a "fourth department of government," which would be the result of delegating policy responsibility to independent regulatory commissions; responsible regulatory policy, they argued, required the subordination of regulatory bodies to an administrative presidency.

Moreover, Roosevelt sought to adapt Hamilton's understanding that a strong executive and administrative apparatus served as a bulwark against tyranny, as a guarantor of rights, to the domestic crisis of the 1930s. The New Deal concept of a modern executive as a defender of programmatic rights was clearly a departure from the Jeffersonian *interpretation* of the Constitution but not necessarily hostile to the Constitution. The Third New Deal is properly understood, then, as an effort to root administrative power within the American political tradition.

Executive Reorganization and the Emergence of an Administrative Constitution

Roosevelt had thought about administrative reform for a long time. He first developed an appreciation of the importance of Executive Department structure while he was Assistant Secretary of the Navy in the Wilson administration. In his testimony before the House Select Committee of the Budget of October 1, 1919, Roosevelt expressed dismay at the inability of the president to formulate and carry out a coordinated public policy. He put much of the blame for this failure on the chaotic organization of the bureaucracy and the lack of administrative personnel available to the president. Responding especially to the lack of presidential authority to hold the various departments and agencies to a comprehensive budget program, Assistant Secretary Roosevelt called for the creation of a budget office, directly under the president, "charged with coordinating the various estimates into one budget and transmitting it to Congress." [14]

This proposal was not adopted by the Congress. The Budget Act of 1921 did significantly enhance the president's authority to oversee the expenditures of the executive departments and agencies, but the effect of this legislation was blunted by the placement of the newly created Budget Bureau in the Treasury Department rather than directly under the supervision of the president himself. This tended to circumscribe the administrative power of the president and to retain the autonomy of executive departments and agencies from the oversight of the White House. Interestingly, the Bureau of the Budget would become a significant part of the administrative reform program Roosevelt proposed in 1937. As Roosevelt had envisioned nearly two decades earlier, the budget office was eventually transferred to the White House, where it would become a principal part of the presidential staff support created in 1939, thus signalling the development of the presidency, hitherto a modest office, into a full-blown institution.

Although Roosevelt recognized the central relationship between presidential power and administrative management as early as 1919, he did very little during his first term to reform the executive branch. This is true despite the fact that Congress passed the Economy Act of 1933, conferring broad reorganization authority upon the president. This act gave Roosevelt during the first 2 years of his administration complete authority to redistribute functions and to reorganize bureaus. But he used this power, further extended to the independent regulatory agencies, very sparingly.

This lack of action is often attributed, correctly, in part, to the need to deal with the emergency at hand. The critical problem of relief and recovery took precedence and shunted reorganization aside. As Lindsay Rogers wrote in 1938, "During an engagement a military commander cannot pause to reform the organization of his army."[15]

Indeed, during the early years, Roosevelt was more intent upon developing a larger welfare state than he was on reorganizing the programs in existence when he assumed the presidency. Only in the latter part of his first term, when he began to turn his attention to irrevocably separating the future course of the political process from the status quo ante, did Roosevelt feel the time was appropriate for thorough administrative reform. The Second New Deal began the process of transmuting the emergency programs of the earlier period into permanent government commitments. But there still was the matter of creating an administrative foundation that would make the programmatic rights embodied in New Deal reforms meaningful.

By 1935, the administration was becoming a bewildering maze of autonomous and semiautonomous regulatory agencies, a state of administrative decentralization and fragmentation that offended Roosevelt's vision of a unified and energetic executive department. Moreover, FDR feared that this uncoordinated government machinery was beginning to represent a political liability, as criticisms of mismanagement and inefficiency were directed at the White House.[16] At the height of the 1936 campaign, Stanley High reports in his diary, the President told his key campaign aides over cocktails, "what fun it could have been if I could have run against Roosevelt [myself]. I don't know whether I could have beaten him, but I'd have given him a close race." The major story in such a campaign, FDR continued, would be "the Democrats can't be trusted with the administration of these fine ideals. I'd have cited chapter and verse on WPA inefficiency (and there's plenty of it). You know the more I think about it, the more I think I could have licked myself."[17]

In a press conference shortly after the election, Roosevelt noted that Landon and the Republicans did not hit on the chief weakness of the New Deal; that he could have made a better attack on himself than did Governor Landon and his backers by bringing attention to the most vulnerable aspect of his first term—administration.[18] Neither the White House's awareness of the administrative problems that plagued the first term nor its desire to tackle these problems, of course, offered any easy solution. The very fact that a "hollow core" existed in the American state's bureaucratic structure, as well as the disinclination of Democrats and Republicans to recognize such a void as a political problem, pointed to the difficulty Roosevelt faced in securing a fundamental departure from traditional administrative practices. The organization of the Executive Department and the establishment of bureaus had heretofore been the responsibility of Congress. Prior to the New Deal, Congress had occasionally recognized the need for greater Presidential control over government machinery, but they vested such powers in the Chief Executive very grudgingly. During World War I, for example, Congress passed the Overman Act that gave the President as part of his own powers the authority to shift bureaus and divisions and to make certain limited organizational changes. Yet such grants of administrative power had always been temporary and carefully circumscribed.

The explosive potential of any effort to restructure federal administration fundamentally suggested to Roosevelt a very careful political strategy. Accordingly, the Administration decided to sell the reorganization plan as a nonpartisan and "scientific" measure merely intended to improve the management of government. This interest in improving the management of government had, Roosevelt argued, a long history—every President since Theodore Roosevelt had shown an interest in providing a "modern, businesslike setup in the administration." [19]

In order to assuage any doubt as to the soundness of his intentions, the President appointed an ostensibly independent and nonpartisan committee of administrative experts to study and report upon the general scheme of organization and the managerial functions of the Chief Executive. The President's Committee on Administrative Management (PCAM) consisted of Louis Brownlow, as chairman, Charles E. Merriam, and Luther Gulick, all of whom had a long-standing interest in facilitating the interaction between scholars of public administration and the federal government. The final report of this committee formed the nucleus of Roosevelt's recommendations to the Congress in early 1937. Thus, from all appearances, Roosevelt's pursuit of good government management was motivated by a nonpartisan and nonpolitical goal.

Of course, this attempt to defuse the controversial nature of administrative reform could not completely obscure from Roosevelt's opponents the fundamental constitutional questions raised by the executive reorganization plan. FDR's assurances that this reform was merely a continuation of the long-standing American concern with sound business practices could not long camouflage the challenge posed by the White House's plans to the influence that Congress and the traditional party organizations had historically exercised over administration. Indeed, Roosevelt's ardent pursuit of comprehensive administrative reform between 1937 and 1939 wrote a new chapter in the long-standing struggle between the executive and legislature for control of administration. The struggle that would ensue between FDR and Congress over the prerogatives of management acquired a special, unprecedented intensity because it occurred just as administration was becoming an important arena of public policy. The expansion of welfare and regulatory programs during Roosevelt's first term meant that the complex responsibilities of government increasingly were set forth in discretionary statutes, each of them little more than a statement of purposes, so that programs would really be shaped by the agencies charged with administering them. Thus, the struggle between the White House and Congress for control of the departments and agencies was no longer simply a squabble for patronage and prestige. The right to shape the direction and character of American public life also was at stake.

Even when there was agreement on the central connection between scientific management and strengthening the president's administrative capacity, there was no guarantee that a consensus could be reached on how executive administration was to be used. The presidency had been central to the work of administrative reform commissions since William Howard Taft occupied the White House.[20] Nevertheless, although previous presidents, including Herbert Hoover, considered administrative management to be essentially an executive task, the aim of executive reorganization prior to the New Deal had generally been viewed as the *reduction* of government programs and expenditures. Roosevelt, however, instructed his Committee on Administrative Management to depart from the traditional emphasis on savings in making its recommendations. As Brownlow reports, FDR told the committee soon after its formation:

> We have got to get over this notion that the purpose of reorganization is economy. I had that out with Al Smith in New York. I pleaded with him not to go to the people with the pledge of economy. But he did, and his first budget after reorganization was way up over the previous budget, though there was some saving in administration salaries. The reason for reorganization is good management.[21]

More accurately, the purpose of revamping the executive in 1937 was to establish the executive office as the centerpiece of a liberal administrative state. As such, Roosevelt's purposes were partisan, although not as traditionally understood in American politics. At the outset, therefore, FDR showed some concern about the commitment of his appointed Committee to his cause. After a lengthy discussion with Merriam in February, 1936, however, he was assured that all three members sympathized wholeheartedly with the New Deal and would respond loyally to the President's concerns.[22] As Karl has noted in his history of the New Deal reorganization movement, Roosevelt welcomed the community of social science as the best center of advice regarding administrative reform, but this advice was directed in such a way by the President that the academic community entered the arena of government divested of its declared commitment to objectivity.[23]

Lindsay Rogers, writing in June, 1938 of the turmoil Roosevelt's administrative reform proposal stirred in Congress and the nation, suggested that this storm might have been avoided had "the President not associated himself so completely with the [controversial] report of his committee."[24] But to distance himself from the Brownlow Committee in this way would have defeated the very purpose of convening it. Roosevelt used the Committee and the prestige of objective scholarly analysis, as Karl put it, to devise a picture of the presidency that was, in effect, a "mirror" in which Roosevelt "could see himself, not the President which Congress saw, or the departments, or the professionals of politics."[25] For this reason, we can gauge Roosevelt's view of administrative reform by analyzing the papers and final report of the Committee on Administrative Management. Careful consideration of the records of the Brownlow Committee is all the more important due to the extensive, albeit not total, practical application of its ideas to the development of the presidency since the 1930s.

Committee on Administrative Management

A distinguishing feature of the Third New Deal, Hawley has noted, "was Roosevelt's close relation for a time to people who would bring top level management to what the New Deal had wrought and would create an up-to-date, efficient, and effective instrument for carrying out the will of the nation."[26] The President's alliance with the likes of Brownlow, Gulick, and Merriam was still another indication of the change brought by the New Deal in the relationship between the presidency and the party system. Roosevelt's plan to reorganize the entire executive branch of the Federal government was no less a challenge to the Democratic party leaders and the state and local machines they commanded than the purge; this program intended, in effect, to seize control over the administrative apparatus, including the patronage system, that had sustained party politics in the United States since the 1830s. We have noted that Wilson shied away from administrative reform in order to gain the loyalty of party leaders in Congress for his legislative program. "Wilson wanted to do what you are doing," Josephus Daniels, Roosevelt's chief in the Navy Department during the Wilson years, wrote the President at the height of the storm over executive reorganization, "but I do not think that he would have taken the bull by the horns and if he had pressed such legislation Congress was not ready for it."[27] Wilson, in fact, Daniels told Roosevelt on another occasion, was further encouraged to govern through his party rather than a bipartisan progressive coalition by the loyalty displayed by the party regulars as compared to the reformers in the Congress. "If you can get them committed to your program," Daniels remembered Wilson as saying, "I'd rather have the regulars, who were not at heart with us at first, to fight for a cause than our progressives who are so enamored of their own particular plan that they break out of the tracks when victory for the cause cannot be won by their methods."[28]

Roosevelt too had suffered from the "capriciousness" of progressives, most notably Burton Wheeler and Hiram Johnson on the court-"packing" plan, and he was not averse to "playing ball" with party regulars who committed to his program. But in the members of the President's Committee on Administrative Management (PCAM), he found steadfast loyalty and a shared vision of presidential government. As the support of many progressives wavered once the programs of the Third New Deal were announced, the succor provided by Brownlow, Merriam, and Gulick elevated their importance within New Deal councils.

They represented the "New Nationalist" side of the Progressive tradition, which celebrated administrative efficiency, executive leadership, and industrial modernization. Although FDR's support of the New Nationalism cause occasionally waivered, it was extraordinary in the context of American politics. For the members of the PCAM, Karl has noted, "The New Deal had proved only one thing for sure: that in American government great leadership could move mountains."[29] They continued to worry about whether the moving of mountains was the best way to govern a modern democracy. But clearly Roosevelt, more than any of his predecessors, was on the right track.

Luther Gulick stated such a sentiment as early as 1933 in an article for *The Annals,* in which he expressed the view—the hope—that the New Deal might "revolutionize the American system of government." Through centralizing power under the political and administrative leadership of the President and by relegating Congress to a general supervisory role in the development of policy, the New Deal, Gulick asserted, would transform the government into the "superholding company of the economic life of America."[30]

In a sense this view of a modernized form of liberal democracy threatened to undermine the responsible role of the legislature in a system of checks and balances. As a co-equal branch of government, the legislature plays a constructive role not by merely accepting or rejecting the whole of executive recommendations but by positively modifying and recommending alternatives to the President's program. Yet in Gulick's view the legislature merely responds positively or negatively to the master plan of policy worked out by the executive, a plan that, in effect, is to be little more than "a declaration of war, so that the essence of the program is in reality in the gradual unfolding of the plan in actual administration."[31] Hence, not only would the legislature be subservient to the executive, because the give and take between executive and legislature in the development of policy would be terminated, but also politics, as traditionally practiced in the United States, would become subservient to administration.

Gulick asserted that such a modernization of American government would come primarily through the development of effective public administration. And more effective public administration could best be achieved by developing an elaborate planning staff as part of the Presidency. Gulick, therefore, felt that the solution to responsible government in the United states lay with administrative rather than party—or political—reform.[32]

Gulick's views anticipated those of PCAM.[33] In 1933, it was only possible to express the hope that the New Deal would involve a constitutional program of administrative reform, but by 1935, as Roosevelt began to consult with Merriam and Brownlow as advisors, his intention to overhaul the machinery of government, and thereby reform American democracy, became clear. Roosevelt formally convened the Brownlow Committee in March, 1936, and consulted often with Brownlow, Gulick, and Merriam during the remainder of that year. Soon after the 1936 election, FDR revealed that he viewed the Committee as a surrogate constitutional convention. The President reflected on such an exalted task for the PCAM during a November, 1936, planning session with Gulick and Brownlow. As Gulick's notes of that meeting read:

> [Roosevelt] said that since the election he had received a great many suggestions that he move for a constitutional convention for the United States and observed that there was no way of keeping such an affair from getting out of hand what with [Father] Coughlin and other crackpots about. "But," he said, "there is more than one way of killing a cat, just as in the job I assigned you."[34]

It is noteworthy that Brownlow omitted this statement from the lengthy discussion of this meeting in his autobiography, *Passion for Anonymity*—it appeared in a manuscript version of the Brownlow autobiography, but was omitted from the published text. Brownlow's editing reflected the view of Roosevelt and his management committee that it was necessary to obscure the constitutional implications of administrative reform; a more straightforward approach, they feared, would result in outright rejection, or allow more extreme political actors—"crackpots"—to take advantage of the fragile political environment created by the domestic crisis of the 1930s. Similarly, in his attempt to weaken the influence of the Court, Roosevelt sought fundamental change with a reorganization bill, rejecting proposals for a formal constitutional amendment.[35]

This was not simply a matter of bringing far-reaching changes in through the back door. FDR was committed to moving the political system from a governmental order based on *constitutionalism* to one emphasizing *public administration*. Or, more accurately, FDR hoped to transmute constitutionalism, so that it was less legalistic and more open to centralized planning.[36] Planning would not be directed at efficiency for its own sake; rather, the goal was to make American democracy more directly responsive to the developing interest in government-provided social services—an interest stimulated by Roosevelt's inspired commitment to programmatic rights.

Roosevelt and the members of the Brownlow Committee were cognizant of the tension between their vision of modern democracy and the historical commitment in the United States to individualism. Riding the crest of overwhelming popular support, however, FDR was hopeful about the prospects of institutionalizing his political advantage. Administrative reform was so close to Roosevelt's heart because he expected the more "efficient" democracy that would evolve from such reform to cultivate amongst the American citizenry an appreciation of government planning and extensive public service. Then the American political process would be pushed inexorably to a more comprehensive government supervision of social and economic conditions. The response of the public to an expanded welfare state, in other words, would lead to the evolution of a programmatic commitment and an administrative apparatus that would be largely insulated from the fluctuations of party politics and elections.

The New Deal was the first realigning endeavor in American political history that made the executive central to its long-range program. The traditional pattern of realignment and the partisan practices that sustained it limited strong presidential leadership to brief periods of reform that tended to reinforce the dominance of the Constitution's decentralizing institutions. The administrative reform program revealed that Roosevelt and the Brownlow Committee members were conscious of the need to counteract the traditional pattern of realignment. As the committee's final report suggested, administrative reform, as a program designed to emancipate the executive from the constictrive grip of party politics, would lay the foundation for a realignment to end all realignments:

> The injustice and oppression intertwined with solid good in our American system will not always yield without a firm display of our national constitutional powers. Our national will must be expressed not merely in a brief, exultant moment of electoral decision, but in persistent, determined, competent day-by-day administration of what the nation has decided to do.[37]

That the Committee expected party politics to become less important is suggested by the instructions of Joseph Harris, the director of the research staff of the President's Committee, to participants in an initial planning session in May, 1936:

> . . . We must consider a planning structure in the light of expansions of functions occurring in collectivist periods like the present and in periods of reaction during contracting phases marked by the dominance of rugged individualistic views. We must assume, however, that these contradictions will always be less in fact than in profession.
>
> We may assume that the nature of the problems of American economic life are such as not to permit any political party for any length of time to abandon most of the collectivist functions which are now being exercised. This is true even though the details of policy programs may differ and even though the old slogans of opposition to the enlargement of governmental activity will survive long after their meaning has been sucked out.[38]

Reminiscent of the views Gulick expressed in his *Annals* piece, Harris' prospectus also made clear that this new planning structure would be built upon an acceptance of massive delegation of policy responsibility to the president and administrative agencies. The Committee was to proceed with the assumption, he wrote, that future government action would "increasingly [be] determined by the administrative branch in the course of elaborating general strategy grants of authority and in the process of filling out the vast areas of administrative discretion."[39]

The New Deal State and the Court-"Packing" Controversy

Critics of contemporary administrative politics—what is usually called the *administrative state*—most notably, Theodore Lowi, view the "rise of delegated power" during the New Deal as setting the stage for "interest group liberalism." By this, Lowi means that the elimination of government based on clear legal standards eventually gave rise to a polity that served the few well organized at the expense of the many without pressure group representation. Lowi grants that "liberal" interest group activity cannot simply be dismissed as a corrupt form of corporate capitalism; it is not quite appropriate to evaluate the administrative state as "socialism for the rich and capitalism for the poor," because many economically disadvantaged profited within the system. This much the New Deal state accomplished. The more accurate characterization is: "socialism for the organized; capitalism for the disorganized."[40]

Roosevelt, however, viewed the delegation of authority to the executive branch as a necessary measure to establish a government responsive to the needs of the majority. He recognized the dangers of delegating too much authority to bureaucratic agencies, but felt that the problem of administrative aggrandizement could be mitigated by executive reorganization that would give the president authority over his domain. The matter of administrative delegation, in fact, was the defining issue of the Supreme Court controversy. Significantly, the two Supreme Court decisions that enraged FDR the most were *Humphrey's Executor v. United States* and *Schechter Poultry Corp v. United States,* both of which imposed constraints on the president's personal authority.[41] These decisions, which were handed down on May 27, 1935, soon known as "Black Monday," threatened to derail the institutional changes that other New Dealers felt were necessary to anchor the economic constitutional order in the American political system. The *Humphrey* case denied the president the right to remove appointees to the independent regulatory commission, a legal power that Roosevelt and his advisors thought had been settled by tradition and affirmed by the 1926 case of *Myers v. U.S.*[42] The *Schechter* ruling was a direct challenge to the modern state New Dealers envisioned. It declared, in a 9–0 vote, that the discretionary authority that Congress had granted to the National Recovery Administration was an unconstitutional delegation of legislative power to the executive. "The unanimity of the Court," Karl has observed, "properly emphasized the singularity of the issue among the many divided opinions of the opposition between the Court and the New Deal."[43] The justices' assault on the New Deal in this decision suggests that FDR's stubborn pursuit of the court-"packing" plan, which continued even after the Court began to change course, might not have been as gratuitous as many accounts of the Supreme Court battle tend to make it.

"It is said," High's diary reads, "that the worst blow the president ever had was the NRA decision."[44] FDR gave voice to this outrage at a news conference on May 31, "holding forth for an hour and twenty-five minutes in a remarkable extemporaneous discourse."[45] Roosevelt analyzed the *Schechter* decision in detail, reading passages from the decision that he considered "more important than any decision since the Dred Scott case."[46] It was bad enough, FDR argued, that the court rejected the National Industrial Recovery Act's delegation of power to the executive, but the judiciary profoundly compounded its constitutional impropriety by denying that the NRA was a proper exercise of the government's commerce power. The matter of delegation of power was not an insurmountable problem—it could be gotten around, the president intimated. But when linked with such a narrow construction of the national government's commerce power, the *Schechter* decision represented an outmoded defense of limited government that would have the consequence of preventing the political system from assuming its essential role in supervising the political economy. The issue raised by the Court's opposition to a national state was not a partisan one, Roosevelt insisted; rather, it raised "a very great nonpartisan issue," to wit, "whether in some way we are going to turn over or restore to . . . the federal government the powers which exist in the national governments of every other nation in the world to enact and administer laws that have a bearing on, and general control over, national economic problems and national social problems." The New Deal had set the United States on the course of joining the community of nations in solving its social and economic crises, claimed the president, but "now it has been thrown right straight in our faces." Then, in words that amounted to a declared war upon the Supreme Court, words that would anticipate the court-"packing" plan and give this press conference an enduring notoriety, Roosevelt concluded his constitutional lecture to the press: "We have been relegated to a horse-and-buggy definition of interstate commerce."[47]

Roosevelt insisted he was not against the Constitution, but rather the Supreme

Court's interpretation of it—the creation of a national state would not be revolutionary, but a "restoration" of sound constitutional principles. The implications of the *Schechter* decision, he believed, would make it impossible to reform constitutional government so that it could deal with the problems created by the concentration of business power and the development of a national economy. FDR's controversial press conference had identified the issues sharply and made inevitable the open struggle with the Court that would occur some 18 months later. The 1937 court-"packing" bill failed in Congress, but Roosevelt would eventually proclaim victory—that he had lost the battle but won the war—for the Court never again struck down another New Deal law. In fact, since 1937, the Supreme Court has not invalidated any significant federal statute to regulate the economy, nor has the Court judged any law to be an unconstitutional delegation of authority to the president.[48] The judicial barriers to national and presidential power for the most part had fallen; the court-"packing" plan, therefore, prepared the constitutional ground for the work of Roosevelt's Committee on Administrative Management.

Lowi has called for the restoration of the Court's ruling on delegated authority, under which, he assures, there is "no reason to fear contraction of modern government toward some nineteenth century ideal." In fact, bringing *Schechter* back to life would reinvigorate statutory law, an essential development for truly responsible and effective government: "the bureaucracy in the service of clear and strong statute is more effective than ever."[49] Like Wilson, Lowi looks in the direction of a revamped party system—that is, national and programmatic party organizations that could secure ongoing cooperation between the president and Congress.[50]

In contrast, Roosevelt and his administrative management committee believed that responsible party government was contrary to American political tradition. Indeed, the PCAM rejected a paper it had commissioned from William Y. Elliot, professor of government at Harvard, which recommended the creation of an American variant of Cabinet government. Dismissing the "oddly persistent notion" of establishing a British-style government on American soil as mischievous, the Brownlow Committee did not have Elliot's paper published among its supporting documents.[51]

The Roosevelt administration viewed presidential government as the most appropriate path to what Lowi calls "the positive state." Whereas party government in the context of American constitutional government presupposes stronger linkages between the executive and legislative, the administrative program of the New Deal would combine executive action and public policy so that the president and executive agencies would be delegated authority to govern, thus making unnecessary the constant cooperation of party members in Congress. Political parties and even a dramatic, albeit temporary, commitment to party government, as the purge campaign revealed, were not irrelevant to the task of strengthening administrative power, to be sure. But the reform of party was almost beside the point.

From Theory to Practice: The Reorganization Bill of 1937

The Third New Deal, especially the administrative reform program, had an ambiguous relationship to democratic government. In part, this program reflected the

Roosevelt administration's objective of strengthening the link between elected representatives—especially the president—and public opinion. Yet FDR was deeply skeptical about the prospects for liberal commitments among the populace to transcend his stay in the White House. The president is said to have told his aides in private that waves of liberalism in the country's history had been of comparatively limited duration. The New Deal was not likely to be different, he warned; popular support for it was unlikely to outlast his administration. In the long run, Roosevelt believed circumstances were working in the New Deal's favor; however, he discerned resistance in the country to extensive centralization of power. Recalling that liberal administrations were often followed by "periods of reaction," he urged those who shared his commitment to creating an economic constitutional order to go as far forward as possible in the least possible time, so that a greater proportion of the New Deal reforms might "survive the inevitable reaction." [52]

This skepticism about the long-term prospects for his program sheds light on Roosevelt's concern—evident in many aspects of the program for institutional reform—to insulate reform and reformers from the vagaries of public opinion and elections. In part, certainly, the concept that New Deal programs were not mere policy, but programmatic rights inclined New Dealers to shelter them somewhat from the rhythms of democratic life. Just as important, however, was the understanding that the political effect of liberal reform would be ephemeral, unless it was sustained by a stable and enduring administrative apparatus.

The ambiguous relationship between administrative reform and democratic politics was revealed by Roosevelt's decision to keep the report of the Committee and the recommendations that would be proposed to Congress a secret until after the 1936 election. [53] Even after his landslide re-election victory apparently signalled a general mandate for his liberal programs, FDR presented his program to Congress and the public in a way that sought to camouflage its constitutional implications. For the most part, however, such a strategy did not work for administrative reform any more than it did for court reform. Indeed, aside from the court reform bill, the executive reorganization proposals became the focus of the most intense political controversy of the Roosevelt presidency.

Roosevelt took his administrative reform plan to the Congress and the people in January, 1937. After presenting his cabinet and the Democratic leaders with a virtual fait accompli on January 8 and 10, respectively, he released his recommendations and a summary of the report to the Congress and the press 2 days later.

In his message to Congress, which was prepared by Luther Gulick, Roosevelt called the committee report "a great document of permanent importance," and he outlined the five-point program recommended by the Committee, asserting that he found it "adequately reasonable and practical." [54] The program included the following major recommendations:

1. Expand the White House staff so that the President may have a sufficient group of able assistants in his own office to keep him in closer and easier touch with the widespread affairs of administrative management, and to

make speedier the clearance of the knowledge needed for executive decision.

2. Strengthen and develop the managerial agencies of the government, particularly those dealing with the budget and efficiency research, with personnel and with planning, as management arms of the Chief Executive.

3. Extend the merit system upward, outward and downward to cover practically all non-policy-determining posts, reorganize the Civil Service system as a part of management under a single, responsible administration, create a citizen board to serve as the watchdog of the merit system, and increase the salaries of key posts throughout the service so that the government may attract and hold in a career service men and women of ability and character.

4. Overhaul the independent agencies, administrations, authorities, boards, and commissions, and place them by Executive Order within one or the other of the following twelve major Executive departments: State, Treasury, War, Justice, Post Office, Navy, Conservation, Agriculture, Commerce, Labor, Social Welfare, and Public Works.

5. Establish accountability of the Executive to the Congress by providing a genuine independent post audit of all fiscal transactions by an Auditor General and restore to the Executive complete responsibility of accounts and current transactions.[55]

Although some of these measures sounded technical and elicited little public interest at first, the sum of these recommendations, if accepted, would have made the Executive Department far more self-sufficient in the development and implementation of policy than ever before. The first two measures would transform the office of the President into the institution of the Presidency. By greatly buttressing the White House support staff, these reforms would make the Executive Department capable of formulating and coordinating comprehensive government policy. Therefore, these measures would provide the tools to make practical the Administration's wish to make the Executive the policy center of a modern welfare state.

The modification of the merit system suggested by the third proposal would in effect freeze New Dealers within the government structure in perpetuity. The expansion of the Civil Service and the centralization of the Civil Service Commission would greatly strengthen the president's hand over government personnel, freeing the Chief Executive from the plethora of patronage claims extended by his party in Congress. The goal of extending the Civil Service is particularly interesting, because, unlike most of the elements of administrative reform that would strengthen any presidency vis-a-vis Congress, this measure would cast an especially New Deal hue over government machinery.

We noted in Chapter 3 that during Roosevelt's first term more than three-fourths of the government employees hired were exempt from the Civil Service. Between June, 1933 and April, 1936 the personnel of the Federal establishment increased form 572,081 to 824,259. Although the competitive classified service gained nearly 43,000 employees in this period, the unclassified service expanded from 116,000 to 325,500. Recruitment of federal personnel outside regular civil service channels resulted in part from FDR's acquiescence to his party's hunger for patronage, which was greater than usual due to the Democrats' long absence from power and the Depression. Especially with respect to the newly created New Deal agencies, however, the Roosevelt administration also began to develop a new form of patronage—a programmatic version—to ensure the recruitment of New Deal loyalists to staff the expanded federal apparatus. Members of the PCAM argued that this circumvention of the Civil Service during the early days of the New Deal was attributable to the inefficiency and mediocrity of the extant merit procedures[56]; there is no doubt, however, that the contradiction between early and later concerns for the merit system was to a great extent politically motivated. Though the Committee argued that the "grand purpose" of administrative reform was to "make democracy work," the proposal to extend merit protection would protect New Deal policies from the uncertainties of popular opinion and election results. Therefore, although the Presidency per se would be strengthened by the Committee's recommendations, this proposal would especially strengthen the hand of presidents sympathetic to the political objectives of the New Deal. Fearing that the New Deal "liberal era" might not outlast his administration, Roosevelt was anxious to ensure that a large proportion of his reforms would survive a turning of the tide. The extension of the merit system to New Deal personnel was one way to perpetuate the policies of his administration.

FDR and the Brownlow Committee did not intend simply to replace one spoils system with another. Rather, the "covering in" of New Deal loyalists, along with the other proposals to reform the merit system, were designed to establish a federal administrative apparatus that would be divorced from traditional partisan considerations, yet embrace the New Deal political order. This was implied in Brownlow's defense during congressional hearings of the administration's proposal to abolish the multimember, bipartisan Civil Service Commission in favor of a single-headed administration, which would be more subject to political control. "A little more than 50 years ago," he told the Joint Committee on Government Organization, "when the Civil Service was introduced into the government of the United States . . . the concept was the negative concept of a protection of the service against excessive evils of the spoils-system. Therefore, a bipartisan board was set up and great advances have been made under that Commission. But the time has come, in the judgment of this committee . . . , when the positive phases of personal management must be considered, not merely the protective phases. . . ."[57]

The meaning of the vague phrase "positive phases of personal management" becomes clearer upon examining the voluminous confidential reports and correspondence that passed between PCAM members. In looking beyond the "protective phases" of civil service, Roosevelt and the architects of administrative reform hoped to cultivate a federal work force dedicated to advancing the cause of New Deal reform. This was the task envisioned by two members of the Brownlow Committee support staff in proposing the formation of a "citizen board" to serve as a watchdog of the merit system. In their report on the reorganization and extension of the merit system of December 4, 1936, Herbert Emmerich and G. L. Belsley wrote:

> It is not only important on the negative side to avoid favoritism, politics, and discrimination in the administration of the civil service laws. From the more constructive angle of supporting progressive programs in the Federal personnel administration, a board of lay advisors properly chosen can be a continual leaven. It can serve to focus the spotlight of public opinion on the human side of government. . . . It can stimulate the initiation of progressive programs in the personnel service and provide a critique which will protect the service form the dangers of bureaucracy and deadly routine.[58]

The executive reorganization bill thus sought to establish an executive-centered administrative apparatus, but one that would not readily suffer the influence of conservative presidents. Even the proposal to reorganize all agencies under 12 departments—which seemingly would strengthen the hand of any executive, conservative or liberal, over government machinery—was not strictly designed to increase presidential power for its own sake. Here the administration envisioned ongoing authority for the president to structure the government machinery as desired. But the essential task was to reorganize the bureaucracy in the New Deal image. It was especially imperative, Roosevelt and the Committee felt, to rein in the dozen independent regulatory commissions, which constituted ''a headless 'fourth branch' of government, a haphazard deposit of irresponsible agencies and uncoordinated powers.''[59] Such a bureaucracy defied any meaningful accountability to the public and precluded the political direction of society envisioned by the New Deal.

Reformers during the Progressive era, especially Herbert Croly, had defended making independent commissions the principal agencies of progressive democracy; as he observed, having executive, legislative, and adjudicative powers, without being or dispensing with the President, Congress, or Judiciary, independent regulatory agencies were ''simply a convenient means of consolidating the divided activities of [constitutional government in the United States] for certain practical social purposes.''[60] Moreover, independent regulatory commissions made possible the separation of politics and administration, thus freeing experts in various policy spheres ''to do right''; as such, administrative tribunals might ''constitute a tentative instrument for the accomplishment of a popular social program.''[61] This view of public administration held sway until the middle of the 1930s, with most regulatory authority being delegated to independent bodies such as the Interstate Commerce Commission and the Federal Trade Commission.

Support for such administrative tribunals was not lacking within New Deal Councils—the prominent New Deal theorist and practitioner, James Landis, for example, criticized the PCAM report's assault on independent administrative agencies as ''apothesizing'' that ''obscur[ed] rather than clafi[ed] thought.'' Like Croly, Landis defended the creation of independent centers of administrative influence as a way to make regulatory power balanced and thus acceptable within the context of American politics.[62] The importance of Landis' view during the 1930s is demonstrated by the organization of several New Deal agencies, most notably the Securities and Exchange Commission, which Landis himself chaired, the National Labor Relations Board, and the Civil Aeronautics Board, as independent commissions.

But Roosevelt's attempt to seize control over the FTC early in his administration revealed that he was never comfortable with such commissions. The *Humphrey* decision that resulted from this campaign no doubt encouraged him to seek a solution to the problem of independent commissions, which he and the Brownlow Committee saw as defying any meaningful accountability to the public and all too susceptible to the influence of interests that would eventually obstruct the development of an economic bill of rights. Roosevelt, in fact, was adamant on this issue. In the meeting with Congressional Democrats on January 10, House Majority Leader Sam Rayburn, also Chairman of the House Committee on Interstate Commerce, asked Roosevelt, "Does this apply to all the regulatory agencies? Is not the Interstate Commerce Commission, which is so popular and so successful, an exception?" The President replied firmly, "There will be no exceptions, not one." Surely this stand implied that Roosevelt was committed to a significant redistribution of administrative power between the president and Congress; as might be expected, FDR's reply to Rayburn was greeted with "shocked silence."[63]

Although the politicization of administration presupposed by the attack on independent regulatory commissions involved strengthening *executive* administration, its most important objective was to legitimize a new and more comprehensive regulatory idea. Just as the plan for reforming the civil service was intended to advance programmatic liberalism, so the proposal to reorganize New Deal agencies into twelve departments sought to form an economic constitutional order, a new relationship between government, business, and society. The plan to reorganize all agencies under twelve departments included the creation of the two new Cabinet positions—Public Works and Social Welfare. To the consternation of conservatives like Virginia Senator Harry F. Byrd, who believed reorganization should be an exercise in government contraction and economy, this proposal would give a permanent status to emergency programs in the Works Progress and Public Works Administrations.[64]

The last recommendation of the Roosevelt Administration was intended to facilitate presidential control over expenditures by eliminating the budgetary influence of Comptroller General John R. McCarl, a Republican appointed in 1921 and a bitter opponent of New Deal spending policies.[65] Nevertheless, this measure had a longer-range purpose than weakening the influence of the obstinate McCarl. The Committee and Roosevelt wanted to establish a fiscal mechanism that would free executive expenditures much more from Congressional oversight than was provided for by the 1921 Budget and Accounting Act, wherein the Comptroller General, as an agent of Congress, was given authority to govern the regulation of expenditures. The Roosevelt Administration argued that this proposal would remedy the violation of separation of powers entailed by the Comptroller's power of preaudit, yet the recommendation to revamp the General Accounting Office, like the administrative reform package as a whole, was aimed at centralizing govern-

ment machinery and expediting government direction of society rather than preserving the separation of powers. This measure envisioned a division of labor
rather than a division of power between Congress and the President that would
facilitate a progressive president's ability to exercise discretion in the distribution
of public funds.

The proposal to secure executive control over fiscal policy was especially significant at this particular juncture of American history. The pursuit of better management coincided with FDR's watershed decision to accept, for all intents and
purposes, full responsibility for the economic health of the country. The fiscal
consequences of this decision were dramatically revealed during the recession of
1937 and 1938. Roosevelt was hardly wild about pump-priming as a way to treat
economic downturns, but he saw no recourse to massive relief spending during
the recession of his second term, one that hit the industrial midwest especially
hard. Concerned that the recession would have a devastating effect on the bur-
geoning labor movement, especially the young United Automobile Workers
Union, leaders of the C.I.O. urged the president to commit his administration to
"compensatory" deficit spending as an ongoing obligation of the federal government. Roosevelt finally relented, confirming a historical departure in budgetary
politics. "For President Roosevelt it was a financial Rubicon," wrote one of
FDR's aides many years later. "He asked the Congress for [a] $5 billion appro-
priation, an astronomical amount for those days abandoning all efforts to balance
the budget."[66]

The $5 billion appropriation was approved by Congress and apparently stabi-
lized the recession. Just as significant, it meant that for the foreseeable future the
federal government would be committed to pump-priming as a mechanism to ensure the financial stability of the nation. This commitment, and the fact that relief
appropriations were relatively free of detailed itemization when compared with
past budgetary practices, made the matter of control over spending, which had
long been a source of conflict between the president and Congress, unprecedently
significant.

The presentation of the PCAM's five-point reform package left Congress
"dazed," according to the *New York Times*. "The Plan," reported Turner Catledge, "was the most daring, and certainly the most far reaching, proposal for
change in the administrative mechanism ever made to the American Congress."
Although Catledge predicted the Bill would pass because of the huge majorities
commanded by the Administration in both Houses, he foresaw an intense battle
emerging, since "no bill of this nature and magnitude," touching as it did "so
many vital spots of individual political organization and Congressional 'sacred
cows,' " had ever "been seriously pressed before."[67]

Few members of the President's entourage doubted that the Bill would pass,
but one New Deal official warned that the president's report, though it had many
merits, did "not take adequate cognizance of the caprices of members of the
House and Senate."[68] This warning proved to be prescient. Not only did Roosevelt and the committee underestimate the "caprices" of Congress but also those
of the American public. The fight over reorganization came after the court battle,
making the political atmosphere ripe for controversy over any increase in Execu-

tive power. Consequently, the Administration's strategy to emphasize the "scientific" and the nonpartisan character of the program began to fail towards the end of 1937. Gulick wrote Roosevelt on September 30, 1937:

> Though the plans were greeted with great enthusiasm from all sides here in New York in January, I now encounter everywhere an undercurrent of opposition from those in positions of great power because they do not want democracy to be truly efficient for fear it will really carry out the promises which have been made to the people.[69]

This opposition built up gradually during late 1937 and early 1938. By March, it posed a serious threat to the executive reorganization bill. Publisher Frank A. Gannett's Committee to Uphold Constitutional Government financed a campaign that distributed 800,000 letters suggesting that administrative reform would make Roosevelt a dictator and urging defeat of the bill. In addition, Father Coughlin delivered an impassioned radio speech just prior to the vote on the legislation in early April, arguing that administrative reform would set up a financial dictatorship, which elicited nearly 200,000 telegrams to Congressional representatives. Ten thousand alone went to Senator Robert Wagner, a staunch New Dealer, albeit one who was suspicious of executive power; Wagner voted against the executive reorganization plan.[70] The campaign against administrative reform reached a climax when, just prior to the vote on the legislation in the House, 150 self-proclaimed and appropriately dressed "Paul Reveres" from Chicago, New York, and New England journeyed to Washington to demonstrate against reorganization in person.[71]

So intense did the campaign against the Reorganization Bill become that in March of 1938, Roosevelt felt compelled to issue a public letter to an unnamed respondent, denying that the Reorganization Bill would make the president a dictator. Charging his opposition with narrow partisan interests, Roosevelt asserted, first, that he had no inclination to be a dictator, and second, that the Reorganization Bill would not allow for such a possibility. Granting that this Bill delegated to the President broad administrative powers, Roosevelt argued that "attempts at detailed reorganization by the Congress itself have failed many times in the past and every responsible member of the House or the Senate is in agreement that detailed reorganization by the Congress is a practicable impossibility." Furthermore, Roosevelt assured, Congress was given authority in the bill to override his executive action by passing a joint resolution.[72]

Of course, the fact that "detailed reorganization" could not easily be carried out by the Congress was an acute problem only for those who wanted to see government become more "efficient" in the meaning of the New Deal. For those who did not favor expediting government regulation of society, the decentralization of administration was not necessarily a problem. Moreover, the delegation of plenary administrative authority to the President, subject only to Congressional veto by joint resolution, would enable Roosevelt to make administrative changes with support of only one-third of the Congress. The Administration fought any attempt to allow an executive directive to be overturned by concurrent resolution, which would not be subject to veto by the president.

In the final analysis, Roosevelt's firm commitment to strong administrative measures reflected his view that the absence, rather than the creation, of a strong, modern executive would breed dictatorship. "A dangerous ambition more often lurks behind the specious mask of zeal for the rights of the people than under the forbidding appearance of zeal for the firmness and efficiency of government," Hamilton warned in *Federalist* 1.[73] Similarly, Roosevelt complained to Frankfurter on April 4 about "the weird doings by the boys in Washington," arguing that the charges of dictatorship lodged against him were misplaced. "The trouble with the people in Washington who keep crying 'wolf, wolf,' " he wrote, "is that some day a wolf might appear from the opposite direction when they least expect it."[74]

Arguably, however, Congress would have been abnegating its constitutional responsibility by forfeiting control of administrative organization just at a time in American political history when administration was becoming the center of government action. FDR did not effectively disabuse legislators of this possibility. Indeed, the fact that Roosevelt thought it necessary to disavow dictatorial ambitions only lent credence to the accusation of the opposition.[75]

Even members of the Administration expressed some concern at the blanket executive power to be conferred to the president, should the Reorganization Bill be passed. Robert Cushman of Cornell University, the member of the Committee's research staff who authored the aspect of the plan devoted to independent regulatory agencies, warned:

> . . . sooner or later it is going to be important for the President to indicate that the proposal made with respect to the Independent Regulatory Commissions is not going to be put into effect suddenly with one clap of thunder. . . .[76]

And Attorney General Homer Cummings warned of the Constitutional questions underlying Title I of the bill that delegated to the president broad powers to reshape the departments and agencies of the executive branch.[77]

This proposal to reform administration, then, touched very centrally on the delicate balance of power between the Congress and the Presidency. This balance had been maintained in part through the shared control of administration, just as it had been through the shared control of legislation. Just as the letter and spirit of the American system of checks and balances had hitherto been maintained by the president's formal and informal role in the legislative process, so had it been buttressed by the legislature's significant role in implementing legislation. As the New Deal seemed to usher in an era where laws were often insubstantial blueprints allowing for extensive administrative discretion, implementation became an even more important ground for political control. In fact, the Roosevelt administration envisioned a government where the line between law-making and administration would grow fuzzier, and the Reorganization Act was intended to prepare the president for an expanded role in the more "streamlined" democracy of post-Depression America. Hence the ardent New Deal opponent, Carter Glass, was not merely giving expression to irrational fear when he wrote in August, 1937,

> As matters are now, Congress is practically a rubber stamp for the Executive, and under the proposed reorganization scheme the President would have no use even for a rubber stamp, he could do his own rubber stamping.[78]

The quiet revolution at which the 1937 reorganization proposal aimed did not take place during the 75th Congress. Although the bill passed the Senate in March, 1938, after a month of debate by a vote of 49–42, it was shadow of the original proposal. For example, in the Senate plan the president's authority to make reorganizations by executive order was limited to 2 years, and the independent regulatory agencies were exempted from authority. And during the subsequent treatment of the bill in the House, the original Administration proposal was watered down even further. In the House version executive orders reorganizing the bureaucracy would not require a joint resolution, which could be vetoed by the President; rather, accountability to the Congress was enhanced by establishing that executive orders were to be submitted to Congress and could be set aside by a concurrent resolution, which is not subject to executive veto.

Even this altered form of the bill did not receive House approval. On April 8, the House voted to recommit the bill by a vote of 204–196. Roosevelt was still intent upon obtaining administrative reform, but in the last days of May, it was decided by Congressional leaders, after a conference with the president, to shelve the Reorganization Bill for the 75th Congress.[79] The failure of administrative reform, following the defeat of the court-"packing" plan, indicated that the president, for a time at least, had lost control of his party.

Executive Reorganization and Party Responsibility

The politics of administrative reform demonstrates the extent to which party responsibility and the creation of the modern presidency became closely associated during the Roosevelt administration. Most obviously, the liberalization of the Democratic party under FDR and the New Deal realignment led to the development of a modern welfare state and, correspondingly, a transition from legislative- to executive-oriented government. In addition, however, the Democratic party was to be used as a means to provide the President with greater control over this newly formed state, so that the executive office could become a more independent policy maker than was hitherto possible in American politics. This was the purpose of the Third New Deal, especially the executive reorganization program. In fact, the administrative reform program became, at FDR's urging, a *party* program; as a result, ironically, a policy directed to making party politics less important became a major focus of party responsibility.[80]

As the *New York Times* reported in August, 1938, this procedural reform took precedence over several other high-priority measures, such as tax and labor legislation: No measure was "closer to the President's heart," and none aroused "more determination to force it through Congress than the Reorganization bill."[81] So strongly did Roosevelt favor this legislation that it became a party-style vote of confidence in the administration. Just before the House voted to recommit the Reorganization Act on April 8, 1938, majority leader Sam Rayburn appealed for party loyalty in support of the president. He asked,

> Is it possible that we want to send a message to the country tonight, even though we have the President in the White House for two years and eight months longer,

that it is a leaderless land? . . . Do we want to send to the people of America tonight the message that Democrats, joining with Republicans, have in effect voted a lack of confidence in that leader and have by their message said that he is no longer the leader of the country?[82]

The president lost this vote of confidence. Nearly one-third—108 of 331—of the Democrats in the House voted to recommit the Reorganization Bill. The focus on such a reform effort was frustrating to many members of the president's party. Administrative reform seemed to incite political controversy, without promising the political rewards of seemingly more tangible welfare programs, such as social security, collective bargaining, minimum wage, and agricultural adjustments. To the applause of the House, Rules Committee Chairman John O'Connor, in a move that ensured the appearance of his name on the "purge" list a few months later, opposed the reorganization bill, expressing dismay that such a controversial but politically unrewarding program was being pushed so hard by the Administration:

> Will someone tell me what a man on First Avenue in my district, out of a job and standing on a street corner, or a little business man on Second Avenue who has not been able to make ends meet, cares whether the Bureau of Fisheries or the Bureau of Plant Diseases is in the Department of Interior or the Department of Agriculture?[83]

But the debate in the Congress over the Reorganization Bill clearly demonstrated that many members of Congress recognized that a good deal was at stake. In the final analysis, Roosevelt's attempt to make administrative reform part of the Democratic program during the 75th Congress failed because the Reorganization Act was perceived by many Democrats as a threat to a responsible Congress. Clearly presidential power had been greatly increased since 1932 due to the dynamism of Roosevelt's leadership and the emergency conditions created by the Depression, and the Reorganization Bill became tied to the question of whether the Executive Department was to be overhauled so as to institutionalize the recent dominance of public policy by the president.

So definitely had administrative reform become a test of the White House's influence that the defeat of the bill was widely interpreted as a vote of no confidence. A *Washington Post* editorial of April 10, 1938, asserted that had such a vote occurred in a parliamentary country, a Cabinet resignation would have followed.[84] Of course, had there been the possibility of a Cabinet resignation, Congress would have passed the Reorganization bill.[85] The institution of separation of powers—the fact that the United States did not have a parliamentary system— enabled Congress to oppose Roosevelt without having to test their resistance before the country directly. Roosevelt, therefore, sought in the purge campaigns to modify the political process so that it would work for a time more like a responsible party government.

In fact, the defeat of this bill in the 75th Congress had an important influence on Roosevelt's decision to undertake his campaign to purge the Democratic party. Following the defeat of the bill in April, Roosevelt received much encouragement to continue the struggle for administrative reform and to punish the deserters of the Democratic party. For example, a few days after the House recommitted the legislation, Congressman David J. Lewis, who was the Administration's candidate in the purge attempt against Maryland incumbent Millard Tydings, wrote Roosevelt:

> The vote of last Friday on the Reorganization Bill settles the question that you and those who have supported the bill in Congress must go to the country.
>
> If it should be decided that I am the one who can best make the fight in Maryland in connection with the Senate, I am willing to do so and to exert all my energy for success.[86]

In June Senator Josh Lee of Oklahoma urged Roosevelt to take action against those who opposed the reorganization program and were running for reelection; interestingly, 2 days later FDR announced his intention to purge the Democratic party of conservatives.[87] Thus, "the campaign for saving liberalism," as Roosevelt called it, had become inextricably linked with administrative power.

In effect, the *raison d'etre* of the Third New Deal, including the purge, was not to persuade Congress to give up its control over the party councils, which were becoming far less significant in the scheme of things; rather, the purpose of the New Deal institutional program was to get Congress to relinquish its control over administration, which inevitably was becoming the center of political life in industrial societies. For this reason, it might be suggested that the institutional program that Roosevelt imposed upon the Democratic party aimed to prepare his party to end all parties; that is to say, Roosevelt's party leadership tended towards the development of a party of administration that would replace party politics with administration.

The failure of the purge campaign weakened considerably, but did not put an end to, this campaign for "enlightened administration." In fact, because the purge and its aftermath confirmed the limits of presidential party leadership, the results of the 1938 elections encouraged the Roosevelt administration to intensify its efforts to establish a modern executive that would be released from the constraints of party politics.

6

The Significance of Partial Success: The Executive Reorganization Act of 1939 and the Creation of the Modern Presidency

The defeat of the administrative reform bill in April 1938 and the failed purge campaign a few months later persuaded Roosevelt that some compromise on the reorganization plan would be necessary. FDR still felt, however, that significant reform could be achieved. He wrote Democratic Congressman Lindsay Warren from North Carolina after the election of 1938, "It is my thought that if we can dress the old House bill up in a new suit of clothes, a lot of people who voted against us before might in the new Congress come back to us." [1]

Such a newly dressed bill became the Reorganization Act of 1939. Sponsored by Lindsay Warren, this bill seemed bland in comparison with the bold program of 1937. For example, whereas the 1937 proposal would have delegated plenary administrative authority to the president, subject only to Congressional veto by joint resolution, an action that in turn could be vetoed by the president, this bill made the president's plans of reorganization subject to veto by concurrent resolution, which was not subject to veto by the Chief Executive. [2] In addition, the 1939 Act exempted twenty-one independent agencies from the President's reorganization power, including the important independent regulatory agencies. Also missing from the bill were controversial measures such as the modernization of the Civil Service System, the renovation of accounting procedures, and the creation of new departments of government. Shorn of many of the controversial proposals of the President's Committee, the Reorganization Bill of 1939 passed with relatively little opposition. On April 3, 1939, President Roosevelt signed the Reorganization Act.

Although the 1939 act was both more limited and vague than the original administrative reform proposal, it was a significant piece of legislation. In fact, it was similar to the final amended version of the 1937 recommendations that the House voted to recommit in April, 1938. "Its passage," one member of the Brownlow Committee support staff would write many years later, "converted the immediate 1938 defeat into a victory over the long term and laid the basis for [an] extraordinary series of administrative management reforms. . . ." [3]

The passage of the administrative reforms of 1939 demonstrated that Roose-

velt, despite generally failing in his attempt to purge conservatives, did retain—
or perhaps attain—enough control of his party to effect important changes in the
Executive branch. That the 1939 act was not an empty shell was indicated by the
serious efforts made to alter the legislation prior to its passage. Although the final
vote on the bill was not close, there were some heated battles over amendments
that came very close to scuttling the bill. Burton Wheeler, for example, a consistent foe of the Third New Deal, proposed an amendment that would have required
both Houses to approve reorganization plans within 60 days, a revision that would
have denied the president the opportunity to make administrative changes through
executive order. A coalition similar to the one that fought the earlier reorganization drive, composed of conservatives as well as liberals who were jealous of
congressional prerogatives in the organization and management of government
machinery, temporarily succeeded. The amendment carried on March 22 by a 45–
44 vote. Supporters of the president, however, managed to force a reconsideration
of the amendment the following day, and the previous action was reversed when
Dennis Chavez of New Mexico changed his vote and Harry Truman flew to Washington from Missouri to join supporters of the bill.[4]

After the defeat of the Wheeler amendment, the more principled opposition to
executive reorganization collapsed and it then passed 63–23. A symbol of the
erosion of opposition was the yes vote of Harry Byrd, who had led resistance to
Roosevelt's reorganization efforts since early 1937.[5] Byrd was appeased by a
"lip-service" amendment pronouncing in favor of economy, which would bind
neither the Congress nor the president to definite cuts in expenditures. That the
most articulate opponent of administrative reform could be reconciled with a measure described by the bill's sponsors as more "apparent than real" showed that
FDR was still a force to be reckoned with.

In a sense, conservative Democrats felt that they had won their war to stay
solvent in the party and restore Congress as a coequal branch of government. As
practical politicians, they were now content to let Roosevelt emerge victorious in
a few minor skirmishes—or battles that seemed small in comparison with the
historic struggles of the 75th Congress. As noted in Chapter 4, moreover, the
"purge," though unsuccessful, did make conservatives think carefully before
crossing Roosevelt after 1938. Given FDR's popularity, the continuation of open
party warfare would prove disastrous in the 1940 election. Thus, North Carolina
Senator Josiah Bailey wrote his friend Julian Miller in early February, 1939, regarding opposition to the president:

> We must restrain him in essential matters, but in non-essential matters, we may
> well afford to let him have his way, lest he go to the radio and tell the people
> their present condition is not due to the failure of his policies, but to the obstruc-
> tive tactics of the Senate and House.[6]

Apparently, once the Wheeler Amendment was voted down, the Reorganization Act of 1939 represented a "non-essential" matter. Only three Democrats in
the Senate voted against the final version of the Reorganization bill—Millard Tydings of Maryland, Peter Gerry of Rhode Island, and William King of Utah. These
Democratic members of the conservative coalition were abandoned by some of

their staunchest colleagues—as noted, Byrd voted for the legislation, and arch opponents of the administration such as Josiah Bailey and Carter Glass abstained. In subsequent years resistance to executive reorganization weakened further, as conservative gradually acquiesced to administrative reform.

Once detached from the court-"packing" plan and the "purge" campaign, executive reorganization did not create the same hullabaloo that it had a year before. The "new suit of clothes" in which the 1939 act was dressed also served to allay congressional anxieties and resistances: The 1939 Executive Reorganization Act did not reorganize anything but gave the president authority to initiate reorganization plans, subject to 60-day legislative veto. Most significant, however, was the fact that Roosevelt concentrated his efforts during the 76th Congress on preparing a suitable institutional loft for the New Deal. For all intents and purposes, he gave up his assault on the Democratic party, focusing instead on preparing the presidency to operate independently of the constraints imposed by the still unreconstructed party system. Woodrow Wilson had argued that the example of British party government indicated that there was no necessary discrepancy between party and administrative reform. Yet the failure of the purge campaign told FDR about all he needed to know with respect to the prospects of forming a "responsible" party system in the United States. In truth, it only strengthened his view that the development of such an institution was extremely unlikely in the United States. By 1939, he was confirmed in the belief that he had tentatively held throughout his presidency—that the concept of an energetic and independent presidency as the fulcrum of progressive change was more easily cast in the American political tradition. From 1939 until the end of his presidency, Roosevelt increasingly turned his attention to rooting such an inverted form of Hamiltonianism in America soil. To be sure, he was not completely successful in this endeavor. But FDR succeeded sufficiently to generate four decades of expansion of the presidency and the welfare state.

The first step in this process came with the issuance of Executive Order 8248 on September 8, 1939 on the basis of authority granted by the 1939 executive reorganization statute. The implementation of the administrative reform law by the so-called Reorganization Plan 1 was an "epoch-making event in the history of American institutions," claimed Gulick, and "perhaps the most important step in the institutionalization of the presidency."[7] One part of the Reorganization Act, the importance of which was not clearly recognized at the time, authorized the president to appoint six administrative assistants. FDR's executive order of September, 1939 established these assistants as personal aides of the president, charged with the task of "gathering, condensing, and summarizing information." Thus, this bill led to the creation of the White House Staff, which has since become the heart of the policy development in the Executive branch. This proposal stemmed from the Committee on Administrative Management's notion that the president "needed help." The Committee's Report suggested that the president needed a White House secretariat composed of men of "high competence, great physical vigor, and a passion for anonymity."[8]

Roosevelt surely benefitted from the creation of the White House Office. Lacking a personal support staff prior to 1939, he was forced to depend upon a shifting group of advisors nominally assigned to other agencies. This was less an organizational problem than it was a political liability for FDR. Two of his most important White House aides, Thomas Corcoran and Ben Cohen, formally assigned to the Reconstruction Finance Corporation and Interior Department, respectively, showed up on the cover of *Time* magazine during the heat of the purge campaign. The visibility and influence of these unofficial White House advisors, as valuable as they were to the president, threatened the legitimacy of FDR's leadership. Corcoran and Cohen were "beyond the rules," *Time* concluded; "they are engaged in making them."[9] The notoriety of Corcoran and Cohen, as Fred Greenstein has observed, "must have contributed to Roosevelt's interest in procedures that would provide the presidency with aides who *were* official but *were not* conspicuous."[10]

Roosevelt appointed James Rowe, Lauchlin Currie, and William McReynolds to the first White House office. Once Roosevelt became accustomed to delegating duties to them, these hard-working and relatively invisible aides became an important instrument of power for the president, providing political and policy support that cut across the more particularistic demands of the various executive departments and agencies.

In subsequent administrations, the tools Roosevelt had developed would become increasingly important, eventually raising fears that the White House secretariat had supplanted the Cabinet. Theoretically, these individuals were not to be interposed between the president and the heads of his departments; they would not be assistant presidents in any sense.[11] Nevertheless, the design of the presidency envisioned by the Brownlow committee anticipated a Chief Executive increasingly independent of his Cabinet and the Congress in the development and implementation of public policy. The Cabinet and Congress were too intertwined with the turmoil of petty politics and party patronage to participate in the "enlightened" administration desired by New Dealers. To manage the affairs of state effectively, the president required a reliable source of information and support in the inevitable tug of war between the president and the executive bureaucracy. This tug of war would develop as the president tried to refashion government machinery for more comprehensive regulation of society in the face of the relatively particularistic demands of the regular Executive departments and Congress. Though the executive assistants were to be no more than the eyes and ears of the president in this attempt to streamline American government, inevitably these surrogate organs would become a force to be reckoned with in the political process.

There was suspicion when this staff was proposed that out of the plan for reorganization would grow a situation in which the regular Cabinet officers would be "short circuited" by the six presidential assistants, who, in time, would find themselves practically administering the government. As one critic of the executive secretariat put it, "give me the opportunity to supply you with information and I'll influence your every action."[12]

Increasing this suspicion was the establishment of the Executive Office of the President by the first plan designed in pursuance of the 1939 Reorganization Act. Just as the White House Office was designed to be a shadow cabinet, the Executive Office of the President was to be the shadow government, the operation of which was to be the job of the White House staff. This office was designed to strengthen and develop the three "management arms" of the president, that is, those dealing with the budget, planning, and personnel.

Following the recommendations of his Committee, Roosevelt proposed to strengthen the president's control over the budget by transferring the Bureau of the Budget out of the Treasury Department to the Executive Office, where it could become the personal tool of the president in coordinating the budgetary process. Roosevelt enlisted the capable Harold D. Smith as its director. With Smith's energetic support, Roosevelt reshaped the Bureau of the Budget into one of the most powerful forces in the administrative branch. Under Smith's leadership, as the *Saturday Evening Post* reported in 1943, "the five branches of the bureau spread far beyond fiscal estimates into a sweeping breadth of function," thus greatly enhancing the president's ability to formulate and carry out a comprehensive domestic program.[13]

To control and develop government planning further, Roosevelt established the National Resources Planning Board (NRPB) within the executive office in 1939. This was created by transferring the independent government establishment, the National Resources Committee, to the Executive Office of the President and consolidating it with the functions of the Federal Employment Stabilization Board, to be transferred from the Commerce Department. The planning board, as Karl has argued, was far more modest than the one originally proposed; in its early versions the proposal was linked to a scheme that would have created a network of regional and local planning authorities responsive to central direction by a national planning board and posing a direct challenge to the whole structure of state and local influence on resource distribution.[14] Karl maintains that the formation of a more modest planning agency, charged with the task of examining "basic and fundamental problems of a long-term nature," rather than the responsibility for directing the actions of a regional system of resource planning boards, was a terrible defeat for Roosevelt. In fact, neither FDR nor the most influential member of the NRPB, Charles Merriam, felt it possible to establish a centralized system of planning in the United States.[15] They did want a planning agency in the White House, to be sure, one that would help emancipate national policy from the inertia and parochialism of Congress and regular partisan channels.[16] As such, the NRPB would play an integral part in a more national and programmatic polity, albeit not as the center of a continental bureaucracy. It was to help flesh out Roosevelt's vision of an economic constitutional order, to serve as a clearing house for the proposals and plans of the activist government envisioned by New Dealers, thus preparing the way for the national government to provide the programmatic rights first declared in the Commonwealth Club address.

One of the most significant of the NRPB reports was its publication on National Resource Development for 1943. This report pronounced a "New Bill of Rights," which delineated in formal terms the programmatic obligations that would constitute an economic constitutional order.[17] "President Roosevelt gave Congress a blueprint of the post-war future yesterday," hailed the *New York Times* when the NRPB report was made public in March, 1943. "More revolutionary in some aspects then Britain's Beveridge report, it guaranteed private or public jobs for every able-bodied person, extending welfare programs to head off booms and depressions, continued wages and price controls, consolidated rail-roads into regional systems, promised housing and assured equal access to edu-cation for all children.''[18] The first installment of this report was given to the president 3 days before the attack on Pearl Harbor abruptly reordered his priori-ties,[19] but with the help of the NRPB, Roosevelt never allowed the attention of the nation to stray too far from plans and proposals for activist government after the war. In this way, the White House planning agency created in pursuance of the 1939 Executive Reorganization Act played a highly important role in the New Deal, although, as Marion Clawson has written, ''more as a stimulator of ideas than a coordinator of government action.''[20]

The significance of the NRPB suggests how the Third New Deal emphasized executive rather than party or legislative responsibility. This proposal for a new era of security was not the product of exhaustive deliberations within the party councils, but a plan worked out within the newly established executive office. Not surprisingly, the activities of the NRPB caused a good deal of consternation both in Congress and the states. Speaker Rayburn asked the President to avoid any social legislation that would be based upon the report because of congressional opposition; so strong did that opposition grow, in fact, that a coalition of Southern Democrats and Republicans spearheaded a successful drive to eliminate the NRPB during the summer of 1943. Roosevelt asked his budget director, Harold Smith, to head off the elimination of his planning agency in Congress, and the president, although preoccupied by the war, made some personal appeals of his own on behalf of the NRBP.[21] But on June 3, Smith reported that the ''Resources Plan-ning Board was dead, no matter what happened.'' The liquidation of the White House planning agency spoke eloquently both to the importance of the changes represented by the NRBP and the degree to which Congress abhorred those changes. It was the high importance of the NRPB, however, that assured its de-mise. As Smith told the president:

> [N]o administrative agency or staff agency on the side of the Administration could issue reports, such as the Resources Board had been issuing, giving the current and prospective future policy, without drawing unto itself the kind of criticism which has arisen—that it is undermining our system of free enterprise, etc., etc. Only the President, the Congress, planning associations outside of the government can discuss these issues publicly and get by with it.[22]

The elimination of the NRPB did not deter Roosevelt from endorsing its plans for the post-war future. He continued to embrace the ideas of the Board's 1943 report, making them the centerpiece of his 1944 State of the Union address, in which he most clearly enunciated the long-term vision of the New Deal. With this ''blast,'' as he put in a letter to Vice President Henry Wallace, Roosevelt became the first American president to call for a war on poverty:

> It is our duty now to begin to lay the plans and determine the strategy for the winning of a lasting peace and the establishment of standard of living higher than ever before known. We cannot be content, no matter how high the general stan-dard of living may be, if some fraction of our people—whether it be one-third, or one-fifth or one-tenth—is ill-fed, ill-clothed, ill-housed and insecure. . . .

> In our day these economic truths have become accepted as self-evident. We have accepted, so to speak, a second Bill of Rights under which a new basis of security and prosperity can be established for all—regardless of station, race, or creed.[23]

Thus, the self-evident truths of the economic constitutional order, as pronounced in the 1936 Democratic platform, did not simply constitute a political strategy to win votes. They were now formally delineated and linked with a program to strengthen national administrative capacities. Among the second bill of rights were the right to a useful and remunerative job, the right to own enough to provide adequate food and clothing and recreation, the right to adequate medical care, the right to a decent home, the right to adequate protection from fears of old age, sickness, accident, and unemployment, and the right to a good education. New Dealers were ambivalent about whether the economic bill of rights should be treated as a formal constitutional program. Chester Bowles, the aggressive head of the Office of Price Administration, voiced such uncertainty in a December, 1943 memo to Roosevelt, urging the president to make these new rights the centerpiece of his State of the Union Address. "[The *Second* Bill of Rights] should not *necessarily* . . . be adopted into the Constitution, although that idea should be studied," he wrote. The most important objective, Bowles concluded, was to articulate "a program which everyone can understand, and will bring to all men in our Armed Forces and to millions of men, women, and children here at home, new hope for the future which lies ahead."[24] These rights never were ratified as constitutional amendments, but, as Bowles anticipated, they became the foundation of political dialogue in the United States. With the advent of the New Deal political order, an understanding of rights dedicated to limited government gradually gave way to a more expansive understanding of rights, requiring a relentless government identification of problems and the search for methods by which these problems might be solved.

The New Deal conception of rights not only became the foundation of political dialogue in the United States, but also a force in reshaping institutions. In the final analysis, the only real security for the economic bill of rights was the fundamental political law as it organized the powers and distributed the functions of government. The modern presidency had contributed to the rise of new tasks for statesmanship; the elevation of these ideas, in turn, helped secure a modern executive that was redesigned to accommodate programmatic ambition. The elimination of the NRPB was only a temporary setback in the development of the modern presidency; the demand for activist government and national planning was sufficiently strong as a result of Roosevelt's influence that the legislative branch, still held captive by localized parties, was soon forced to accept once again executive leadership in public policy. Although Congress certainly retrieved some power in postwar planning after the NRPB was eliminated, Roosevelt transformed many of the board's functions to the Bureau of the Budget, which became the center of positive government planning under the vigorous leadership of Harold Smith.[25] In this position, Smith became an influential advocate of Keynesian policies, helping to convert Roosevelt's tentative commitment to "pump-priming" after April, 1938 into a more systemic fiscal policy.[26] The responsibilities of the budget office, however, went beyond fiscal policy, especially after 1943. With the demise of the NRPB, the Budget Bureau assumed the task of drafting a plan on full employment that was proposed by Roosevelt in his State of the Union Address of 1945. This speech proclaimed the right of employment the "most fundamental" of the "American economic bill of rights," and "one on which the fulfillment of others in large degree depend[ed]."[27]

Because the conservative coalition dominated Congress in 1945, the president's domestic program received little attention. But Roosevelt had developed a blueprint for post-war America that made a return to normalcy unlikely. Moreover, the institutionalization of the presidency helped redefine the purpose of executive leadership. The "task of statesmanship," FDR had said in the Commonwealth Club address, is the "redefinition of rights" upon which the social contract rested "in terms of a changing and growing social order."

The development of the budgetary and planning staff in the reshaped executive office suggested how administrative reform was not conceived as a program to strengthen the presidency for its own sake. Rather, the modern presidency that emerged from the executive Reorganization Act was created to chart the course for and direct the voyage to a more liberal America. This purpose of executive reorganization was also evident in the Roosevelt administration's preparation of the executive office for the third arm of presidential management—personnel.

Roosevelt's ability to exert influence over federal employees was limited by Congress's rejection of the Brownlow Committee's proposal to replace the Civil Service Commission with a single civil service administrator. In what Leonard White called a "neat tactical move," however, FDR gained some of the advantages of a single administrator by asking one of his administrative assistants, McReynolds, to become Liaison Officer for Personnel Management. In his message accompanying Plan I, Roosevelt criticized the Congress for exempting the Civil Service Commission from the provisions of the Reorganization Act; nevertheless, in private correspondence FDR recognized the establishment of a liaison office in the White House as a significant step in improving presidential supervision of the federal bureaucracy.[28]

Roosevelt also made use of executive orders in achieving better supervision of the Civil Service without legislation. By executive order he appointed Directors of Personnel in the departments and agencies, and established the Council of Personnel Administration, through which personnel directors of the various departments and independent agencies would be able to consult with one another and then, as a result of their consultation, to advise the president and Civil Service Commission. Moreover, in order to ensure that the Civil Service was not only better controlled by the president but also imbued with a commitment to programmatic liberalism, Roosevelt issued an executive order in June, 1938 that began the task of "covering in" New Deal loyalists by extending merit protection to some 71,000 employees in New Deal agencies who hitherto had been paid from emergency funds.[29]

The job of extending the merit system upward, outward, and downward could not be completed by executive order, which due to existing legislation only reached a minority of positions then exempt from merit coverage. The completion of this convulsive movement to reshape the civil service was not reached until the passage of the Ramspeck Act of 1940. The Ramspeck Act authorized the extension by the President of the merit system rules to nearly 200,000 positions previously exempted by law, many of them occupied by supporters of the New Deal. Roosevelt took early advantage of this authorization in 1941 and by executive order extended the coverage of the Civil Service Act to the point where about 95 percent of the permanent service was included.[30]

The enactment of this legislation was one of the first New Deal fruits yielded as a result of FDR's decision to break historic precedent and run for a third term. Congress might have been willing to resist a "lame duck," but found it difficult to forestall a popular president during an election year, especially on an issue trumpeted by the Roosevelt administration and the press as an assault on the spoils system. Moreover, the provision in the Ramspeck bill requiring incumbents to pass noncompetitive tests before they received permanent status in the federal public service made it somewhat easier to promote this bill as a nonpolitical bow to good management. The Roosevelt administration received much help on this score by the fact that the bill's sponsor in the House was Robert Ramspeck, a gentlemanly Democrat from Decatur, Georgia, who had devoted much of his career to extending the reach of the Civil Service System over federal personnel.

The "covering in" of the personnel in unclassified offices was not in itself new; it had been a typical feature of the development of the American public services during the closing years of the incumbency of either political party since the beginnings of the civil service system in 1883. But the greater number of offices involved—FDR would blanket in more political appointees than all previous presidents combined since 1900—plus the Roosevelt administration's historic departure from standard patronage practices in its appointments, joined to distinguish New Deal civil service reform from previous politically motivated extensions of the merit system. In effect, the enactment of the Ramspeck bill, occurring simultaneously with Roosevelt's decision to disavow the two-term limit, was a triumph for executive administration, albeit in the form celebrated by New Dealers. It was a landmark of civil service reform in the national government, one that marked a triumph of "enlightened administration" over traditional partisanship.

The politics of the Ramspeck bill underscored the fact that New Deal civil service reform did not simply replace patronage politics with administration, nor did it replace patronage practices with civil service procedures dedicated to "neutral competence." Rather, it transformed the political character of public administration. Previously, the choice was posed as one between politics and spoils on the one hand, and nonpartisan, apolitical administration on the other. The New Deal celebrated an administrative politics that denied nourishment to the regular party apparatus, but fed instead an executive branch oriented towards expanding liberal programs.

Such a project was further advanced by transforming many New Deal emergency programs and agencies into enduring parts of the federal government. In addition to establishing the Executive Office in order to provide the president with direct access to the three principal management arms of the government—fiscal, planning, and personnel—Plan I of the 1939 Reorganization Act also established the Federal Security and Federal Works agencies to institute New Deal reforms more permanently in public welfare. Not authorized to create permanent government departments by the 1939 legislation, Roosevelt created instead two new agencies. In fact, the Federal Security Agency became in everything but words a major department of government, although it was not until the early part of the Eisenhower Administration that it was set up as the Department of Health, Education and Welfare.[31] With the authority granted by the 1939 Act, therefore, Roosevelt in all but fact gave permanent status to the emergency programs of the New Deal. Some of these programs were later eliminated by the Congress, but, as conservatives like Byrd feared, the pursuit of better administration resulted in the recognition of emergency spending as a continuing obligation.

Thus, the 1939 Executive Reorganization Act and the executive orders issued in pursuance of that legislation effected many aspects of the plan proposed by the Brownlow Committee. Roosevelt's successors have carried on their work through essentially the same administrative framework he created.[32] Most significant, the 1939 reforms spurred on the development of the "administrative presidency," which to a much greater extent than previously was possible, could now exercise extensive domestic power autonomously through rule making and implementation. Along with the enhanced rhetorical possibilities that had accrued to the executive, the strengthening of executive administrative restored a version of Hamiltonianism to the American constitution. The absence of detailed specifications in Article II of the Constitution had left the door open for independent presidential action throughout U.S. history. The institutionalization of the presidency, however, forged on the anvil of the new constitutional principles that were legitimized by the New Deal realignment, established a formal organizational apparatus with which administrations could short-circuit the separation of powers, accelerating the shift of authority from Congress, as well as the courts, to the executive. For the time being, the state of "courts and parties" had been displaced by presidential government.

The Third New Deal and the Demise of Party Politics

The Third New Deal gave rise to a modern executive that was equipped to operate without the constraints historically imposed by partisan politics, and almost immediately the institutionalization of the presidency resulted in tension—a struggle—between executive and partisan responsibility. Personnel in the White House Office and the other executive office agencies soon began dealing with interest groups directly, outside regular partisan channels.[33] The New Deal gave rise to political pressures and administrative tools that encouraged the White House to take action independently of partisan considerations. This allowed Roosevelt and his successors to form ties with interests with a greater degree of flexibility than would have been possible within the boundaries of partisanship alone.

One dramatic example of this flexibility was FDR's efforts in the summer of

1941 to stop a march on Washington, scheduled for July 1. The March on Washington Movement was spearheaded by A. Philip Randolph, erstwhile president of the Negro Congress, to secure black opportunities in the armed forces and the national defense industries. As noted, FDR sought to hold the Northern and Southern wings of his party together, maintaining a deafening silence with respect to Civil Rights legislation, refusing even to offer much in the way of support for the anti-lynching bill.[34] The response to the demands of the March on Washington Movement suggested how administrative reform enabled the president to form a direct link with civil rights leaders who had grown impatient with the Democratic party's inattention to discrimination against blacks. With the help of staff in the executive office, such as Wayne Coy of the Office for Emergency Management, Roosevelt worked out a settlement with the leaders of the March committee, thus warding off the scheduled demonstration in Washington.[35] The power of the Roosevelt administration to make partial concessions to black demands was central to the resolution of the crisis: On June 25, 1941, the White House issued an executive order that began with a general statement to the effect that there would be no discrimination in the employment of workers in defense industries or in government because of "race, creed, color, or national origin." Moreover, a President's Committee on Fair Employment Practices (FEPC) was to be set up for the purpose of receiving and investigating complaints of discrimination in violation of the order.[36]

One of the most influential members of the New Deal "Black Cabinet," Mary Bethune, praised Roosevelt's action, especially the formation of the FEPC, as the most "memorable day" since Lincoln signed the Emancipation Proclamation.[37] This reaction was histrionic, more a reflection of Bethune's willingness to accept certain compromises and partial solutions with respect to civil rights initiatives than an accurate characterization of FDR's executive order, which was only a first small step, albeit a healthy one, towards a federal assault on discrimination against blacks. Nevertheless, the response to the March on Washington Movement revealed how the strengthening of national administrative power had begun to free executive power from the constrictive grip of partisan politics; how the emergence of the modern presidency made it less necessary to assimilate "auxiliary" party groups, representing labor, minorities, and women, into the divided councils of the Democratic party. Roosevelt had promoted such auxiliary organizations as the Labor Nonpartisan League, the Democratic Women's Club, and the Good Neighbor League during the 1936 election to recruit campaign workers and appeal to voters who were willing to support the New Deal but were reluctant to affiliate with the Democratic party (see Chapter 4). With the formation of the executive office such subsidiary groups were given a formal role in the development of public policy.

In this way, the National March on Washington Movement, like the Labor Nonpartisan League and the Democratic Women's Club, foretold of "public" interest movements that would make their programmatic demands directly on government institutions. The Executive office, allowing the president to form a political constituency outside partisan channels, often proved to be a more satisfactory forum for lodging policy concerns than a still unreconstructed party system that in its essential characteristics resisted the development of national programmatic commitments.

Tension between executive and party responsibility was also apparent in personnel policy, as the executive office's task to direct the development of a professional welfare state created an institutional barrier between party leaders and the appointment process. Rowe, in particular, whose "misfortune" it was to be liaison between the White House and the Democratic National Committee, fought many battles with James Farley and Ed Flynn, who succeeded Farley as party chair in 1940, over appointments. Rowe was appointed to the White House staff at the recommendation of his close friend Thomas Corcoran, and his position as Special Assistant formalized—indeed legitimized—the New Dealers' circumvention of the regular party apparatus in making appointments. Farley and Flynn continually complained to the president, often through Mrs. Roosevelt, that a "New Deal clique was getting all the appointments." [38]

In October, 1941, Rowe found himself in the awkward position of defending his own appointment as Assistant Attorney General, which Flynn sought to prevent. "I would be particularly insensitive if I did not know there was some friction," Rowe wrote the president about his numerous battles with Flynn. "Such friction is inevitable when one person is passing on the merits and another is passing on political qualifications, unless Flynn has his own man in the White House." The DNC chair did not ask for this much, but he did demand that the White House Office, particularly Rowe and McReynolds, both of whom played important roles in the personnel process, clear all appointments with the DNC. Rowe fought to deny Flynn such authority over personnel, a stance, one suspects, that was not simply the result of his personal interest in keeping the Democratic Chair at bay. "I do not think Flynn should have a veto power on appointments, particularly a personal one such as this," he wrote of his own case. "New Dealers are also Democrats." [39]

By early 1942, Flynn had declared war on the entire "merit system" set up among the White House Office, executive agencies, and the Civil Service Commission. By this time, it was clear that the institutionalization of the presidency and the extension of the merit system upward, outward, and downward was gradually cutting off the party's nourishment. Flynn sought to make use of his close personal bond with President and Mrs. Roosevelt to forestall such a development.

In this endeavor, however, he ran into the presence of Harold Smith, who recognized how the patronage fights between the executive office and the party organization appointments spilled over to the machinery of government. White House control over personnel complemented the creation of support staff in the Executive Office of the President—the overall objective was to enhance executive responsibility in the formulation and carrying out of public policy. With the creation of the NRPB and the renovation of the Bureau of the Budget, a policy network was established outside traditional channels, thus insulating presidential governance from partisan politics. This was an institutional development that Smith, who long had styled himself an enemy of entrenched party machines, relished and fought to protect. Although he possessed a "passion for anonymity,"

Smith was a tough and politically astute administrator who effectively defended institutional development in the executive office against the traditional prerogatives of party leaders and Cabinet officers.[40]

Smith's cause, no doubt, was aided by the war. Unlike Wilson, Roosevelt was not willing to carry on aggressive and open partisanship during a full-scale mobilization against foreign enemies. Nevertheless, the exigencies of the war only reinforced FDR's inclination to distance himself from the regular Democratic party. His commitment to liberal reform, which actually grew bolder during the war, required that he develop an institutional capability and political constituency that was distinct from the Democratic party.

The Hatch Act

The merging of politics and administration took an interesting and significant course as a result of the passage of the Hatch Act of 1939. Until the passage of this bill, the Roosevelt Administration was developing the expanding executive branch into an inchoate national political machine. The Hatch Act, however, which in many respects was passed in reaction to the purge campaigns, made the full development of a presidential political machine less likely.[41] It removed the influence of all federal administrative officials who made policies of nationwide application from elections or nominating efforts for President, Vice President, or members of Congress. The Hatch Act also reduced presidential control over nominating conventions by precluding the participation of most federal administrative officers. At the 1936 Democratic Convention about half of the delegates were federal job holders. With the passage of the Hatch Act, only cabinet officers, Congressmen, and a few top-ranking policy officers of the Roosevelt regime could be delegates in 1940. In effect, therefore, the Hatch Act demolished the national Roosevelt political machine as distinct from the regular Democratic organization.[42] As such, it short-circuited the effort to create a "presidential party."

Not surprisingly, many New Dealers urged the president to veto this legislation, fearing that it would undermine what they viewed as a felicitous union of politics and administration. The task was not to take politics out of administration but to infuse the expanding federal apparatus with the principles and commitment of the New Deal. Charles M. Shreve, Executive Secretary of the Young Democrats of America, argued this point in a letter sent to Roosevelt as the president was considering whether to sign the Hatch Bill. Indicating to Thomas Corcoran, through whom this communication to the president was sent, that "it [was] impossible to exaggerate the importance of this matter," Shreve wrote:

> We cannot encourage public service and enact a law as sweeping as this. Democracy will receive a great setback and the calibre of our public servants will drop drastically, if it becomes law. There is no justification for making political eunuchs of the future statesmen and leaders of our Democracy.
>
> It should suffice to point out that *every* Republican member of the House present for the vote voted *for* the Hatch Bill, together with every avowed Democratic enemy of the New Deal. Many members of both branches of Congress

have admitted to our leaders that they voted for this Bill because they felt it would prevent your controlling the next Democratic National Convention . . . [43]

But the Hatch bill was not so clearly a political defeat for President Roosevelt. FDR never displayed much ambition to create a "modern Tammany"; he was more interested in orienting the Executive Department for the formation of liberal public policy than he was in developing a national political machine, and the insulation of federal officials from party politics was not incompatible with such a task. As the journalists Joseph Alsop and Robert Kintner wrote in 1939, "if men like the New Dealers are to become permanently useful public servants, political eunuchs is precisely what they must be." [44] This explains why, after much consideration, the president, though he fought passage of this legislation, decided to sign the Hatch Bill. Not only would such a veto have split his supporters irretrievably, but it also would have worked against the achievement of Roosevelt's reform program. The liberal and zealously nonpartisan Senator from Nebraska, George Norris, wrote Roosevelt in late July upon getting wind of a possible presidential veto:

> I cannot conceive of your opposition to legislation of this kind. I know that many politicians, in fact most politicians, in both political parties, are bitterly opposed to such a law but I have assumed all the time that you were one hundred percent for it. . . .
>
> I believe this bill is a great step towards the purification of politics and government. . . . To veto it would be the greatest mistake of your career—the full effects of which you could never overcome. [45]

In responding to Norris, 2 days later, FDR did not deny that he was considering a veto of the Hatch bill, but he asked the Senator to reserve judgment about the propriety of his returning the bill to Congress. "Wait until you see what I say about the Hatch Bill," he pleaded. [46] At that moment, the Roosevelt administration was seriously considering a veto message that was drafted by Corcoran and Ben Cohen, with the assistance of the Justice Department. "The Attorney General, Ben, and I have worked out in the attached suggestions for a veto message on the Hatch Bill a line of approach which is outside of any speculation in the newspapers, and which seems to us to offer a real chance to turn the tables," Corcoran wrote FDR on July 30. [47] For the most part, debate on the Hatch Bill pitted traditional partisans against nonpartisan reformers. To intensely partisan New Dealers such as Corcoran, these alternatives represented a "Hobson's choice"; accordingly, the veto message he prepared with Cohen and Attorney General Frank Murphy sought to obviate the debate between partisans and nonpartisans by calling for an alternative bill that would *reform* rather than *transcend* parties.

This message castigated the Hatch bill for not including state and municipal office holders. "So called 'political machines' composed of state and municipal officeholders have given the public no reason to believe that they have a higher regard of the public interest than federal office holders who are members of the national party organizations," read the proposed veto address. "Indeed there is some evidence to the contrary." State and local office holders outnumbered federal workers four to one, the message pointed out, and the decentralized form of party organization in the United States gave these workers in the states and municipalities considerable influence over national elections. The failure to include state and local officials within the Hatch Act, therefore, would make things worse—"the determination of party policies and the conduct of political activities in relation to matters of federal concern will more than ever be subject to the influence and control of state and local machines . . . , whose point of view is local rather than national."

In addition to recommending the extension of the Hatch Act to the states and localities, the draft veto message asked for a revamping of campaign finance, thus asking Congress "to recognize the fact of the party system in American politics." It was not enough to protect federal as well as state and municipal workers from political manipulation, the address insisted; it was just as important "to protect the government from the sordid influence of large private contributors, from interests that hope thereby to obtain concessions and advantages in legislation or administrative action." Consequently, Congress should consider campaign finance reform that might strengthen the national character of the party system. The draft veto message contained a proposal to prohibit all private contributions and to appropriate public funds for the use of political parties, which might "free . . . political parties from the domination or influence of sinister elements and yield unexpected returns in the elevation of the whole tone of our political life."[48]

Had Roosevelt decided to veto this legislation and been able to get an alternative bill along the lines of the draft veto message, the elimination of office holders from the predominant position they held in party councils might have accelerated and strengthened a process, already underway as a result of New Deal reforms, to focus the attention of parties on divergent policies rather than a struggle for office. In the end, however, Roosevelt chose to sign the Hatch Bill on the last day this measure would become law without the president's signature. The message to the Congress that accompanied FDR's signature comported with concerns to overcome partisan politics. Roosevelt asked Congress to extend the act to state and local officials in the future, but he made no mention of restructuring the American party system.[49] The second Hatch Act, passed in 1940, extended these restrictions to state and local workers whose principal employment was in connection with any activity that was financed in whole or in part by the federal government. This concluded a compromise with the Congress that went a long way towards strengthening the nonpartisan character of the New Deal. The complex web of American constitutional government shaped progressive reform in the 1930s so that Roosevelt's great party leadership was in the long run, or at least for a long time, to render party politics remarkably obsolete.

The "Purge" of 1940

The nonpartisan legacy of Roosevelt's leadership was recognized and viewed with favor by George Norris soon after the enactment of the Hatch Act. On August 28, 1939, he sent a letter to Florida Senator Claude Pepper (marked "very confidential"), indicating his intention to support FDR for a third term. Interestingly, this expression of support did not mention the dangerous international situation but stressed instead that "there [seemed] to be no other man of sufficient prominence who [was] capable of carrying on . . . a progressive form of government, of bringing relief to the under-privileged classes of our citizens. . . ." Although generally opposed to a third term, "for fear that a president might build up a personal political machine," Norris noted that FDR had benefitted from and, in turn, extended an important institutional development that protected the presidency and progressive programs from the unfortunate influence of party politics:

> After all, the president we are going to elect in 1940 will be a president of all the people, and not a political party. I would carry this doctrine much farther than President Roosevelt has carried it, although I think it is unquestioned that he has carried the banner farther in advance than any man has carried it, who ever preceded him in this office.[50]

Senator Norris must have been pleased by President Roosevelt's Jackson Day Dinner address a few months later. Ironically, the president chose this party event to herald a less partisan future. Making mention of his reputation for holding "to party ties less tenaciously then most of his predecessors in the Presidency," Roosevelt pleaded guilty. But his admission to "the soft impeachment" had less to do with the impending foreign crisis than with the dawning of an age informed by enlightened administration:

> My answer is that I do believe in party organization, but only in proportion to its proper place in government. I believe party organization—the existence of at least two effectively opposing parties—is a sound and necessary part of our American system; and that, effectively organized nationally and by states and by localities, parties are good instruments for the purpose of presenting and explaining issues, of drumming up interest in elections, and, incidentally, of improving the breed of candidates for public office.
>
> But the future lies with those wise political leaders who realize that the great public is interested more in government than in politics; that the independent vote in this country has been steadily on the increase, at least for the past generation; that vast numbers of people consider themselves normally adherents of one party and still feel perfectly free to vote for one or more candidates of another party, come election day, and, on the other hand, sometimes uphold party principles even when precinct captains decide "to take a walk."[51]

Thus, Roosevelt saw the New Deal as the culmination of the progressive tradition, as understood by Croly. The resurgence of party politics in the 1930s was but a temporary and necessary measure to secure the constitutional and institutional foundations of the administrative state. In part, this realization may be attributable to the disappointing purge campaign, but the pursuit of the Third New Deal, which began prior to that disappointing campaign, suggests that FDR saw the handwriting on the wall before the ill-fated partisan efforts of 1938. As much as anything else, the purge was a desperate attempt to rescue that program, to force it upon the Democratic party. FDR's failure to make his mark indelibly upon the party in that campaign focused his attention on 1940. In order to secure the institutional changes brought by his presidency, Roosevelt probably realized, he would have to run for a third term.

The decision to try for a third term, in fact, was made in the midst of the woeful beating Roosevelt suffered in the 1938 primary elections. "They are already casting lots for the cloak of the Master," Corcoran told Roosevelt that summer. But while Democratic leaders were already discussing FDR's possible successor, the White House was planning his unprecedented try for a third term. Apparently a decision was made by Corcoran and other New Dealers in July, 1938 that the salvation of the New Deal required that Roosevelt run again. No liberal could get the Democratic nomination in 1940, they concluded, except for Roosevelt, and they were determined to draft him. "Accordingly," one of his close associates, Ernest Cuneo, would report many years later, "at a midnight conference with Tommy [Corcoran] at his bare, barracks-like office at Room 1017, in the grimy R.F.C. Building at H and Pennsylvania, it was decided that FDR must be drafted for a third term."[52]

Just as it became apparent that FDR was going to suffer a setback in the purge campaign, therefore, the "elimination committee" was shifting gears, planning for the Democratic convention to be held in Chicago, still 2 years away. The kickoff speech was made by a loyal New Dealer, Governor Frank Murphy of Michigan, in the course of his ill-fated try for re-election. Cuneo flew out to Michigan, where he helped ghost write an address delivered in Traverse City, Michigan on July 26, in which Murphy told 2,000 supporters that it might be necessary for the president to accept a third term. "The New Deal must go on," said the governor, "and we may have to draft the President for four more years of leadership." The speech was duly reported in the *New York Times,* thus initiating the national speculation and suspense about FDR's intentions that both encouraged draft Roosevelt drives in the various states and kept other potential Democratic candidates at bay. The suspense the White House created, Cuneo observed, "was the essence of [FDR's] campaign."[53]

Although he did not personally participate in his aides' efforts to draft him, Roosevelt certainly lent his tacit support. Not once did he make any effort to stop these activities, suggesting that even if he had not determined to run by the summer of 1938, FDR was preparing the way should he decide to do so from that time forward. By early 1940, certainly, several months before the Democratic convention, the president was apprised of, and engaged in, the draft Roosevelt activities. On February 8, 1940, for example, the President wrote his "O.K." on a memo Rowe sent him, seeking approval for the organization of a campaign committee in California by Governor Culbert Olson and Congressman H. Jeremiah Voorhis that would use Roosevelt's name in that state's presidential primary. FDR's approval surprised Rowe, who had told Voorhis that he did not think he could get any sort of commitment from the president. Roosevelt would not consent directly to the use of his name on the ballot, but FDR did give his blessing to Olson's activities on his behalf by assuring the governor that his consent would not be given to any other group in California.[54]

The White House bid for a third term, unlike the purge campaign, was hidden from public view, but it was no less energetic and was perhaps better organized. In important respects, Roosevelt's nomination for a third term in Chicago in July, 1940 reversed the bitter defeats the White House suffered during the 75th Congress and the 1938 primary elections. Despite spirited competition from Farley and Vice President Garner for the nomination, Roosevelt was easily renominated. "For the first time since 1932 Franklin Roosevelt was in absolute command of the party," *Time* magazine reported after the convention. "The purge that had failed in 1938 was being carried through in 1940." [55]

The "purge" of 1940, however, did not secure the liberalism of the Democratic party, not by a long shot. Roosevelt had learned in 1938 that his personal popularity and the strong support in the country for New Deal social welfare policies could not very easily be translated into congressional campaigns; executive responsibility had proven to be an inadequate instrument of party government. That equation had not been changed fundamentally by FDR's precedent-shattering re-election to a third term. Instead, this development ratified the *displacement* of party politics by executive administration. As Cuneo put it, "FDR and Corcoran had pistol-whipped the Democratic party chiefs into nominating him for a third term." [56] As if to underscore the personal nature of his triumph, FDR insisted on having Secretary of Agriculture Henry Wallace as his running-mate. Wallace was a progressive Republican in the George Norris mold; he had not troubled until 1936 to change his registration from Republican to Democrat. No one in the Roosevelt administration more dramatically personified the New Dealers' war on the party system—"as a politician," Corcoran wrote in his memoirs, Wallace "made less sense than the Jolly Green Giant." [57] That the Secretary of Agriculture did not even have the delegation of his home state, Iowa, behind him, testified to his complete disassociation from the party organization. Nevertheless, the Democratic delegates grudgingly ratified the president's choice, sobered by the warning of his surrogates in Chicago that FDR would not run unless Wallace was nominated. It is little wonder, then, that in spite of FDR's nomination and election to a third term as the Democratic standard-bearer, Samuel Lubell's post mortem on the 1940 campaign bespoke of a New Deal—rather than a Democratic—triumph:

> The Republicans do not know what hit them; the Democrats, certainly, as distinguished from the New Dealers, do not know what they hit the Republicans with. The New Deal has aimed at a bloodless revolution.
>
> In 1940 it went a long way toward accomplishing it. [58]

The Administrative Presidency and the "Triumph" of Liberalism

Roosevelt himself gave expression to the New Deal revolution in 1941. In the Introduction to the 1938 volume of his *Public Papers and Addresses,* written in June, 1941, he looked back with satisfaction on the turbulent political battles of 1937 and 1938. "The political struggle of 1938 [the purge] had not been in vain," he rejoiced. "Liberalism in government was still triumphant." [59] The survival of the New Deal, however, had less to do with reform of the Democratic party than it did with the development of the modern presidency. [60] The fight over the Ramspeck bill, the "bloodless revolution" of 1940, and FDR's efforts to deal with the crisis abroad centered on administrative aggrandizement. The Democratic party had changed, perhaps, but only enough to convert it into a party of administration. The New Deal program had the objective of constructing an administrative loft for programmatic liberalism—once built, party politics would give way to a policy-making state. The emergence of that state meant that public deliberation and choice were reduced to, subordinated to, a "second bill of rights" and the delivery of services associated with those rights.

Of course, presidents did not become completely independent of Congress and parties with the creation of the modern executive, nor did they become capable of making policy without extensive Congressional consent. First of all, Congress never surrendered complete control of administration to the president. Most significant, the prodigious body of independent regulatory agencies remained beyond the administrative power of the president. To be sure, the great proliferation of independent agencies that took place during the first four decades of the twentieth century was arrested after 1939, and the Reorganization Act of 1949, as will be discussed, enhanced presidential influence over those already in existence.[61] But the president's limited control over regulatory commissions continued to act as a break on executive power. Since it first rejected the PCAM proposal to bring these bureaus into the regular executive department, Congress has repeatedly refused to give presidents complete control over independent agencies.

Ironically, the rejection of the PCAM's proposal regarding independent regulatory agencies facilitated the Roosevelt administration's long-range policy objectives. Because many of these agencies were created during the New Deal and because Roosevelt had such a long tenure, the continuing independence of the bureaucracy after the 1930s extensively reduced future presidents' ability to reverse or confine New Deal policies. New Deal personnel practices and the enactment of the Ramspeck bill suggest that this inoculation of the agencies against hostile executive administration was, to put it mildly, not entirely accidental. But New Dealers believed that a revamped presidency would generally be an ally of programmatic liberalism. That the continuing independence of the bureaucracy would eventually become a special source of frustration to Republican presidents was an unintended consequence of the defeat of an important part of New Deal administrative reform.

Presidential autonomy was also limited after 1940 by the need to achieve Congressional approval in order to establish most programs in the first place. Although legislation after 1932 was for a time characterized by the delegation of broad legislative authority to the executive, blurring the distinction between legislation and administration, still some influence over Congress had to be maintained in order to better ensure the continuing passage of such broad mandates. The best means of achieving such mandates continued to be the political party. For this reason, even as he sought to disassociate executive power from Congress and party, FDR took some measures to maintain lines of communication between the White House and legislators. After his administration sustained the legislative and primary defeats of 1937 and 1938, regular meetings began between Roosevelt and congressional party leaders in an attempt to inject regular doses of presidential leadership into the legislative process.[62]

Notwithstanding the continuing dependence of the president on Congress and the party, the Third New Deal cleared the way for unprecedented political responsibility and policy development to be centralized in the White House. That FDR was able to accomplish such a task in spite of the formidable opposition that developed to his political designs after 1936 testified both to his extraordinary political gifts and his success in casting the Third New Deal as an adaptation of, rather than a departure from, traditional constitutional government. The New Deal vision of an energetic and independent presidency effectively revived Hamilton's argument in *Federalist* 70, that a strong executive is "a leading character in the definition of good government."[63] A strong presidency, as long as it did not obviously ride roughshod over the Congress and the courts, was quite acceptable within the American political system. And conservatives, too, were inclined to reconcile themselves to such a development, especially once it became clear that a strong conservative movement would need to coalesce in order to counteract the developments instituted into American politics by the New Deal. Perhaps this explains why the Hoover Commission on Organization of the Executive Branch, which reported on administrative reform in 1949, concluded with the same general theory of the presidency and executive administration that the Brownlow Committee had expressed in 1937, although the Hoover Commission reported in an atmosphere of relatively conservative public demands and was headed by a conservative Republican ex-president.[64]

But the modern executive, at least as originally conceived and organized, was expected to manage a liberal state. Just as the nineteenth century state of "courts and parties" was linked to a concept of rights that constrained political choice, so the New Deal state of the modern executive and administrative tribunals was tied to constitutional obligations considered above the "regular" political process. The president was expected to displace the parties as the primary agent of democracy, and administrative agencies would replace the courts as the guarantor of rights. The New Deal faith in administrative discretion explains Roosevelt's veto of the Walter–Logan bill in 1940. This bill would have empowered the courts to review any rule of any administrative agency as to whether it was in accordance with the Constitution and the statute under which it had been issued. In a stern veto message Roosevelt asserted that to so restrict administrative discretion would enable "great interests" with sufficient funds and desire to escape regulation, "to strike at the heart of modern reform." Democracy was better served by *administrative* law replacing court adjudication:

> Whenever a continuing series of controversies exist between a powerful and concentrated interest on the one side and a diversified mass of individuals, each of whose separate interests may be small, on the other side, the only means of containing equality before the law has been to place the controversy in an administrative tribunal.[65]

The evolution of social security illustrates especially well the process by which New Deal reforms were crafted by a merging of programmatic liberalism and administrative reform. Policy was long dominated by the Social Security Board, which was insulated to a remarkable degree from partisan politics, interest group influence, and competition from other administrative agencies. This agency, in turn, was dominated by program advocates who quietly but effectively imbued it with the philosophy of liberalism. The selection and training of personnel was carried out so that clerks, as well as higher-ups, were bound by a strong "client-serving ethic." The commitment to advocacy among program officers within the Social Security Board was largely attributable to its executive leaders' sophisticated circumvention of routine civil service procedures in order to assemble a staff of exceptional competence and "religious" dedication to the cause of reform.[66]

Underlying the success of social security was the notion that it was a program that belonged to the American people as a "right," that it formed the cornerstone of the economic constitutional order espoused by Franklin D. Roosevelt. In fact, Roosevelt committed the government in 1935 to an uncompromising policy of financing social security by payroll tax financing rather than by general revenues, believing that such a policy would make the protection an earned right. To those who complained of the regressive nature of financing social security by a contributory program, Roosevelt stressed the *political* importance of linking welfare programs as closely as possible to the traditional principles and practices of American constitutional government. As he put it to one such critic:

> I guess you're right on the economics, but those taxes were never a problem of economics. They are politics all the way through. We put those payroll contributions there so to give the contributors a legal, moral, and political right to collect their pensions. . . . With those taxes in there, no damn politician can scrap my social security program.[67]

Thus, the New Deal did not simply replace constitutional government with an administrative state; rather, the programmatic rights of the New Deal constituted the beginning of an administrative constitution, which was shielded from the uncertainties of public opinion, political parties, and elections. As Martha Derthick has written about the development of the social security program, its architects "sought to foreclose the options of future generations by committing them irrevocably to a program that promises benefits by right as well as those particular benefits that have been incorporated in an ever expanding law. In that sense they designed social security to be uncontrollable."[68]

In their examination of the American state in historical and comparative perspective, Theda Skocpol and John Ikenberry have argued that the relatively underdeveloped status of the American welfare state when compared to other industrial societies signifies the failure of the New Deal, a failure attributable to a state structure that was "unsupportive of generous, nationally uniform social welfare efforts." That the Social Security Board could "carve out an impregnable, expansionary niche for its preferred programs" is the exception that proves the rule. Social Security was accepted and expanded because it was structured as an "insurance" rather than a "welfare" program, thus making it compatible with the support in American political culture for individual responsibility: "the Social Security Board could venture onto the risky ground of disbursing public benefits to individual citizens—but only where they . . . had earned these by right through their 'contributions.' "[69]

It is misleading, however, to evaluate the New Deal as a failure because it did not bring forth a European-style welfare state.[70] The genius of Roosevelt, we argued in Chapter 2, was to imbed a positive state in American political culture, thereby transforming it without seeming to do so. To be sure, the concept of an economic constitutional order—the view that responsive state action was an extension of individual rights—was not a theory that supported the formation of a highly centralized and autonomous administrative power. Nevertheless, linking national administrative power to rights might have been the only way to transform the governing philosophy of the United States, given the intense commitment of the American people to limited government. As then Senator Hugo Black noted in a letter to Farley on June 19, 1934, the Roosevelt proposal for a program "to bring about a feeling of *social security* . . . is doubtless one of the most far reaching and important documents Congress has ever received." The American public, Black observed, "has little conception of the possibilities of social insurance," and "there are few people in this country who realize that such systems of social insurance have been adopted in most of the civilized countries in the world."[71]

Thus, the commitment to a program of security during the New Deal era envisioned a fundamental change in the American understanding of the national government's responsibility. Although the new concept of rights to which it was hitched limited the power of the New Deal state, the very "uneasiness" of this state allowed it to become part of the American constitution. As such, New Dealers, although they surely did not have everything their own way, were not frustrated reformers. Rather, they were advocates of a zealous practicality that accepted the need to develop the welfare state within the circumscribed parameters of American political culture.

The New Deal, then, laid the foundation for an uneasy state, but one that was to have far-reaching and enduring influence on American society. For a time, the modern presidency would be the center of this new political universe. Since the turn of the century, reformers had viewed a revamped, "modern" presidency as the steward of progressive democracy. The New Deal had gone far in making this dream a reality. It can be said, however, that the institutional legacy of the New Deal gave rise to an administrative Constitution that established an uncertain foundation for strong presidential leadership. On the one hand, the rise of political administration as the center of government activity during the 1930s established the conditions for presidential government. FDR's extraordinary party leadership was institutionalized with the 1939 Executive Reorganization Act, for this statute ratified a process whereby public expectations and institutional arrangements established the presidency as the center of government activity. On the other hand, the administrative presidency was conceived with the expectation that it would be an ally of programmatic liberalism. It is not surprising, therefore, that when this expectation was violated with the rise of a conservative administrative presidency beginning in the 1970s, serious conflict developed between the presidency and bureaucracy. Nor is it surprising that this conflict influenced still another reform of administrative law with the objective of more effectively insulating reform programs from presidential influence.

II

The New Deal Legacy for the Presidency and the Party System

7

Programmatic Liberalism after Roosevelt: Executive Administration and the Transcendence of Partisan Politics

One of the major issues of the 1944 campaign was whether Vice President Wallace would stay on the Democratic ticket. As a strong advocate of the New Deal policies that Roosevelt had stressed in his 1944 State of the Union Address, Wallace had the support of the most ardent New Deal constituencies: Northern urban liberals, blacks, and most of organized labor. Nevertheless, as was the case in 1940, he was almost completely lacking in regular party support. Edward Flynn, who had recently stepped down as party chair, and Robert Hannegan, the current chairman warned FDR in June, a month prior to the Democratic convention, that state delegates—backed by their political leaders and associates—were simply going to refuse to nominate Wallace.[1]

Roosevelt became convinced, therefore, that in order to nominate Wallace as Vice President for a second term he would once again have to "pistol whip" the party regulars as he had in 1940. By the Spring of 1944, however, Roosevelt felt his party, as well as his health, slipping away from him. In March, he lost a dramatic battle with Congress over tax legislation, sending the first veto message of a tax bill ever to be received by Congress. FDR's precedent-shattering veto ended in the defection of majority leader Albert Barkley, who resigned his position rather than support the president's unprecedented "encroach[ment] over the carefully drawn constitutional authority of the Congress to say what kind and how much in taxes should be levied."[2] And the President's veto was easily overridden 299–95 in the House and 72–14 in the Senate.

Although he was not about to give in to party leaders, Roosevelt was clearly alarmed. After flirting with the idea of forming a new liberal coalition with the progressive Republican Wendell Willkie, he reluctantly decided to sacrifice Wallace on the altar of party unity. "I am just not going to go through a convention like 1940 again," he told his aide Samuel Rosenmen. "It will split the party wide open, and it is already split enough between the North and South; it may kill our chances for election this fall, and if it does, it will prolong the war and knock into a cocked hat all the plans we've been making for the future."[3]

Although Roosevelt was willing to abandon Wallace to the party regulars, he had no intention of rewarding them, especially his conservative brethren below the Mason–Dixon line. He spurned the Vice Presidential ambitions of his aide James Byrnes, the former Senator from South Carolina and taunted conservative Democrats with his expressed interest in having on the ticket Supreme Court Justice William Douglas, who was championed vigorously by Thomas Corcoran and his many New Deal allies.[4] In the end, Roosevelt and party leaders settled on Missouri Senator Harry Truman. As a moderate from a border state, Truman was acceptable to the Southern Democrats, and his relationship with the old Pendergast machine gave him an appreciation of old-fashioned organization politics that endeared him to party regulars. At the same time, with a few exceptions like the 1944 tax bill, he normally voted for Roosevelt's New Deal and foreign policy measures. As a Senate insider, he might help heal the rift between the President and his congressional party leaders, and would be a vigorous campaigner. "That was all Roosevelt sought in the weeks before the convention, when his health and optimism had largely returned," historian Frank Friedel has written. "He had not been seeking a likely successor but rather someone who he thought would not cost him votes."[5]

Less then 1 year later Truman would succeed FDR as president. When the Senate session of April 12, 1945 ended at about five o'clock, he was beckoned to the White House. Upon his arrival, Mrs. Roosevelt came up to him, put her arm gently about his shoulder, and said softly, "Harry, the President is dead." After a moment of shock, Truman recovered himself to ask Mrs. Roosevelt: "Is there anything I can do for you?" She replied: "Is there anything we can do for you? For you are the one in trouble now."[6]

Indeed, Truman seemed to be in deep trouble. The country was still at war, the Democratic party remained unreconstructed, and it seemed incomprehensible that anyone, let alone this "little man" from Missouri, as his contemporaries often disdainfully referred to Truman, could replace Roosevelt. Truman was not as diminutive a statesman as his detractors claimed, and he would assume the office of the president in his own right. "Still," the journalist William S. White wrote of his presidency in 1955, "for a time he walked, as completely as did the smallest laborer who had been a 'Roosevelt man,' in the long shadow of the dead president."[7]

The Roosevelt legacy was not an easy one to bear. FDR's long tenure created serious concern about the dangers of concentrating too much power in the White House. Some political leaders stood poised after his death to reverse the constitutional and political changes that had greatly enhanced the powers of the presidency since 1933. But FDR had transformed politics in the United States permanently; he had taught most Americans to expect both that the federal government would remain active in domestic and world affairs and that, within the government, the president would take the lead. As was the case after Wilson's tenure, there was great suspicion of executive power, but in the wake of Roosevelt's reign and the momentous events of the 1930s and 1940s, a "return to normalcy" was unthinkable.

The uncertain status of the modern executive was reflected in the important changes FDR's partisan leadership and the New Deal program had brought in the relationship between the presidency and the party. Roosevelt's legacy had freed the president from the constrictive grip of localized parties. The Democratic party, in particular, had become a more national organization, and, more important, it embraced a program that placed executive administration at the heart of its approach to politics and government. The limits of party reform left the Democrats a divided party, making the prospects for ongoing cooperation within its councils uncertain. But the "Third New Deal" had set in motion an institutional separation of presidential and partisan politics that now made a continuous spirit of cooperation between the president and party leaders in Congress and the states less necessary. The modern executive was less bound than its traditional predecessor, but, at the same time, no longer so steeped in the organizational politics that had historically linked executive power to an extraordinarily diverse and decentralized society.

In this chapter, I examine the relationship between the White House and the party system during the two decades after Roosevelt's death. Those who occupied the White House during this time—Harry Truman, Dwight Eisenhower, John Kennedy, and Lyndon Johnson—wielded executive power according to Roosevelt's vision of modern presidential leadership. They continued the practices that separated presidents from their parties, and contributed to the further decline of the traditional party apparatus. This decline accelerated under the administration of Lyndon Johnson. Johnson's attempt to create a Great Society marked not only the completion and significant extension of the New Deal, but also intensified the effort to transcend partisan politics.

Harry Truman's Party Leadership: Partisan Crusade and the Further Decline of Party

As Truman assumed the office of the President, there were rumors that this supremely practical politician would readily adapt to the more conservative mood the country had lapsed into during the twilight of the war. Samuel Rosenman, who had stayed on as Special Counsel to the President after FDR's death, informed Truman that his "conservative friends," particularly some of his former colleagues on Capitol Hill, believed that he was "going to be quite a shock to those who followed Roosevelt—that the New Deal [was] as good as dead—that [the country] was going back to 'normalcy' and that a good part of the so-called 'Roosevelt nonsense' [was] now over."[8]

As FDR had recognized, however, Truman was essentially a New Dealer; in fact, as William S. White wrote, Truman "felt compulsively and morally bound to a literal pursuit of the policies of his late chief."[9] So much was revealed in the President's 21-point message of September 6, 1945. This address, crafted as a combination of a first inaugural and first State of the Union message, marked the beginning of the "Fair Deal," the point at which Truman felt he finally assumed the office of president in his own right. "This legislative program," he wrote in his memoirs, "was a reminder to the Democratic party, to the country, and to the Congress that progress in government lies along the road to sound reform . . .

and that progressive democracy has to continue to keep pace with changing conditions.''[10]

Truman's concept of sound reform represented an attempt to codify Roosevelt's vision of a complete economic constitutional order. ''The objectives for our domestic economy which we seek in our long range plans were summarized by the late President Franklin D. Roosevelt over a year and a half ago in the form of an economic bill of rights,'' Truman proclaimed. ''Let us make the attainment of those rights the essence of postwar American economic life.'' Repeating the bill of particulars laid out in FDR's 1944 State of the Union message, Truman proposed legislation that would embody the programmatic rights his predecessor had declared. He called for an extension of social security to more workers, an increased minimum wage, national health insurance, urban development, and full employment.[11]

Truman achieved little of his domestic program, however, and the 1946 congressional elections appeared to be a dramatic rejection of the Fair Deal. The Republicans campaigned on the theme that the country had ''had enough'' of Roosevelt–Truman liberalism. When, for the first time in 16 years, the Democrats lost control of Congress, many concluded that the party could not survive the loss of FDR.[12]

But Truman marshalled all the resources that his office had accrued during Roosevelt's tenure to prove otherwise. Faced with the choice of cooperating with an opposition Congress, which, smelling victory in 1948, would cooperate only on its own terms, or of militantly maintaining the autonomy of the executive as representative of all the people, Truman chose the latter. In fact, the President saw some advantage in emphasizing a forceful employment of executive administration in defense of FDR's ''second bill of rights,'' given the deep philosophical and sectional differences that continued to divide his brethren in the Congress. In a letter to Eleanor Roosevelt on November 14, 1946, he observed ''I think we will be in a better position to get more things done for the welfare of the country, or at least to make a record of things recommended for the welfare of the country, than we would have been had we been responsible for a Democratic Congress which was not loyal to the party.''[13]

Truman was far more appreciative of party organization than his predecessor. But the political conditions he faced upon assuming the presidency and the institutional powers FDR's accomplishments made available to him dictated that this most partisan man contribute to the declining significance of party. Ultimately, Truman's reverence for the executive office and his dependence on the powers of that office resulted in a widening of the institutional separation between presidential and party politics. His singular contribution was to extend the New Deal institutional legacy during a period when a Republican-controlled Congress was intent upon dismantling the policies and institutions of programmatic liberalism piece by piece.

Truman and Congress

After the 1946 elections, the Truman White House moved towards implementation of *executive*-oriented reform by undertaking an in-depth exploration of the problems and techniques involved in dealing with an opposition Congress.[14] Perhaps the most important product of the White House inquiry was a paper produced by James Rowe, who had been one of the principal architects of the executive office during the Roosevelt years. Rowe wrote a lengthy memo in December, 1946, which advocated vigorous executive opposition to congressional encroachments upon presidential power and New Deal programs. This document was steeped in sophisticated constitutional and historical analysis, as well as the advice Rowe solicited from "disinterested students of the Federal Government" such as Herbert Emmerich, Charles Merriam, and Louis Brownlow. It is not surprising that the result of this consultation with key alumni of Roosevelt's Committee on Administrative Management was a political strategy informed by "modern" Hamiltonian principles.

Rowe began with a lengthy quote from *Federalist* 71 that contained Hamilton's warning against "executive complaisance to the humors of the legislature." Interestingly, Rowe edited the passage so that it omitted Publius' view that "servile pliancy of the exectuive to a prevailing current in the community" was also a danger; that responsible executive leadership would, on occasion, also require presidents "to withstand the temporary delusion of the people in order to give them time and opportunity for more cool and sedate reflection." What remained was a modified Hamiltonian text that championed the president as the embodiment of popular will and declared the greatest danger in republican government to be the tendency of representative legislatures "to fancy that they are the people themselves," thus betraying "impatience and disgust at the least sign of opposition from any other quarter."[15]

A constitutional system divided by party, Rowe warned, would lead to a realization of the imperious legislative action Hamilton feared. The only possibility of President Truman avoiding such legislative encroachments, he continued, was to reject bipartisan cooperation, which in all likelihood would end in virtual abdication of executive authority, and steel himself for conflict. To prepare himself for this conflict, the memo urged, Truman must follow the formula of executive leadership advocated by the Brownlow Committee and executed with considerable success by Roosevelt. In short, the powers of the executive office had to be used to ally the president with the people against an imperious legislature.

In seeking an alliance with the public against the Republican Congress, Rowe urged an aggressive use of the veto power, the best weapon of a "minority" president in the marshalling of public opinion. It was not enough, however, to withstand the incursions of Congress—even a president in Truman's minority position, Rowe argued, must be prepared to move forward. Truman should follow a strategy, therefore, of proposing ambitious plans for additional programmatic reform, and staffing administrative posts with personnel committed to carrying out the president's program. This plan of action would require that Truman go much further than Roosevelt had in preparing the executive to be a government unto itself:

> The President's real problem is whether he can prevent interference by the Congress in the supervision of purely administrative and executive functions. . . .
> That requires staffing his own office with the kind of person skilled in knowledge of both the executive and legislative branch. These persons must be activated by

a loyalty single to the President and desire for anonymity. It appears to be just as true today as it was in the Roosevelt Administration that "the President is a powerhouse without transmission lines." The President acts but nothing happens. There is too often a short circuit somewhere between the White House and the departments or the departments and Congress. [16]

No one can say how much James Rowe influenced Truman. It is very possible that the president, solemnly committed to FDR's economic constitutional order, would have moved as he did anyway. In its main outlines, however, Rowe's memo, as the historian Alonzo Hamby has written, "amounted to a remarkably accurate forecast of presidential strategy." [17] In the aftermath of the 1946 election, Truman spurned most overtures from the legislature for cooperation or compromise, fighting aggressively against any attempts on the part of the 80th Congress to dismantle the New Deal. He used the veto over 200 times during his presidency, most vigorously in the areas of tax and labor policy. A coalition of conservative Democrats and Republicans, the same sort of coalition that plagued FDR during his troubled second term, sometimes overrode these vetoes. But Truman's forceful actions in the face of overwhelming legislative opposition, as presidential scholar Fred Greenstein has pointed out, "accustomed all but the most conservative national political actors to look at the president as the main framer of the agenda for political debate—even when much of this debate involved castigation of his proposals." [18]

Truman's most significant veto was of the Taft–Hartley bill, passed in 1947, which was widely viewed as an attack on labor unions. [19] On June 20, 1947, the president sent a stinging veto message to Congress to assert that the bill "would reverse the basic direction of our national labor policy"; that same evening he went on radio to declare: "We do not need—and we do not want—legislation which will take fundamental rights away from our working people." [20] The Taft–Hartley veto, although overridden, caused labor to line up solidly behind Truman. The president's action also drew praise from middle-class liberals—"professional liberals," as Truman called them—most of whom still passionately identified themselves with the unions. "[Truman] has given American liberalism the fighting chance that it seemed to have lost with the death of Roosevelt," *The Nation* editorialized. [21]

The Politics of 1948

Shrewdly taking the initiative, Truman turned the 1948 presidential election into a referendum on the Roosevelt era. When Truman caught nearly everyone by surprise by winning a stunning come-from-behind victory over his Republican opponent, New York Governor Thomas Dewey, he stepped at least partially out of FDR's shadow. His successful fight to save the New Deal seemed to be a vindication of the Roosevelt heritage—it revealed that Roosevelt had not simply achieved institutional and programmatic changes during his long reign over the country but a legacy.

The 1948 Democratic victory, which not only kept Truman in the White House but restored the party's hold over both houses of Congress, has generally been viewed as confirming the New Deal as one of several recurring realignments in American history. It was, in the lexicon of American voting studies, a "maintaining election," where the pattern of partisan attachments set during a previous critical historical period persists, and the majority party wins the presidential election.[22] In this respect, Truman's dramatic triumph at the polls owed largely to the partisan achievements of his predecessor.

What is missing from such an analysis of the 1948 election as a cyclical event is the recognition of *secular* changes brought by the New Deal that were making party politics and organizations less important. Arguably, the 1948 campaign confirmed the ascendance of the modern presidency, signalling the emergence of the president, rather than the Congress or the party organizations, as the leading instrument of popular rule. By the same line of reasoning, the 1948 campaign revealed that the liberal movement that triumphed on FDR's watch was embodied in an institutional coalition that existed independently of the Democratic party. The Truman administration, in fact, was well aware of these secular trends, and the campaign strategy and organization behind Truman's re-election both reflected and extended the New Deal institutional heritage.

The plans for the 1948 campaign were conceived by Rowe, who authored still another lengthy memo in September, 1947; Rowe's memo became the basis of a strategy paper prepared a few months later by Clark Clifford, which was presented to, and largely approved by, President Truman. This paper was essentially a rationale for continuing the course recommended by Rowe in his earlier memo on presidential–Congressional relations, which the administration had perceptively adopted by mid-1947; in addition, it was designed to deemphasize the role of party regulars and increase the influence of administration liberals in the president's re-election campaign.

The White House, Rowe argued, should attempt to reinvigorate the party organization wherever possible, but always with the realization of the limits of party in the New Deal political order. They had been supplanted in large measure "by the pressure groups," the memo pointed out, "and the support of those must be wooed since they really control the 1948 election." These independent groups, which organized farmers, blacks, labor, as well as intellectual and social activists, were not simply nonpartisan—farmers, for example, were "traditionally Republican," while organized labor had "become 'traditionally Democratic' under Roosevelt."[23] But they marked a new type of organization; they were auxiliaries of the parties, which subordinated partisan organization to programmatic benefits and causes.

To a point, these organizations had helped to convert independents to Democratic loyalty; more fundamentally, they had promoted an institutional basis for permanent independence among large segments of the electorate. For example, labor support for Roosevelt in 1944 was mobilized by the C.I.O.'s Political Action Committee (PAC). Neither a third party for labor nor an auxiliary of the old professional parties, "it was to function as a full partner in a coalition, mainly with the Roosevelt Democrats, but it would also lend its strength to Progressive Republican candidates for Congress."[24]

The basis of an appeal to these independent voting groups, Rowe argued, would have to be a strongly liberal program—voters no longer could be satisfied, he wrote sardonically, "with a Tammany turkey on Thanksgiving."[25] Liberal reformers themselves constituted one of the important groups whose loyalty the administration had to capture. New Dealers such as FDR's son, James Roosevelt, Harold Ickes, and Adolf Berle had most clearly discerned and, in their official capacities, encouraged a distinction between the Roosevelt coalition and the Democratic party. Truman's ascent to the presidency made many of them feel cut off not only from the party but from government itself. Many progressives were attracted to the movement that formed behind Henry Wallace, who broke from the Truman administration in 1947, and was preparing a third-party campaign. The large bulk of liberals had lost enthusiasm for Wallace by late 1947, finding his criticism of the administration's containment policy unpalatable. But their dismay at the "reactionary domination" exercised by Southerners over the Democratic Party-In-Congress, Rowe claimed, and their hostility to the party's organization leaders, made liberals reluctant to support Truman, who was viewed, unfairly, as a product and captive of traditional partisan politics. Disaffected liberals formed the Americans for Democratic Action in early 1947, which became a haven for most of the Roosevelt New Dealers. It was critical, Rowe urged, for Truman to reach out to such liberal organizations, for although few in number, they were far more important than their numbers entitled them to be:

> The liberal exerts unusual influence because he is articulate. The "right" may have the money, but the "left" has always had the pen. If the intellectual can be induced to back the President, he will do so in the press, on the radio, and in the movies. . . . Since the rise of pressure groups, the men of ideas who can appeal to them on their own ground, in their own words have become an essential ally to the alert candidate in modern American politics.[26]

Rowe concluded that a successful re-election campaign required the creation of electoral machinery in the White House Office that would operate autonomously from the regular party organization. "Some sort of *small* 'working committee' (or 'think' group) should be set up," he wrote, the function of which "would be to coordinate the political program in and out of the Administration." The members of such a committee would be individuals with "understanding of and experience in government," who would be capable of bringing a more programmatic approach to politics. In effect, this would mean a revitalization of a group like Roosevelt's Brain Trust, and the formal extension of its activities to campaigns.

Truman accepted the essential framework of the campaign strategy laid out in Rowe's memo. After Rowe's plan was presented to him in slightly modified form by White House counsel Clark Clifford, the President authorized the establishment of a "Research Division," financed by and nominally part of the Democratic National Committee but actually under Clifford's supervision.[27] This committee was dominated by liberal activists who were prominent in progressive organizations such as the Americans for Democratic Action (ADA), the American Veteran's Committee (AVC), the only veterans organization with a liberal orientation, and the National Association for the Advancement of Colored People (NAACP).

The Research Division was a prominent feature of the campaign, dominating Truman's speech-writing team and helping to coordinate a militantly liberal government program with electoral politics.

In this respect, the President's 1948 State of the Union message marked the effective beginning of his re-election campaign. Largely the work of administration liberals, it went further than Truman's 21-point program in its advocacy of ambitious reform. It not only recommended an extension of the economic bill of rights in areas such as social security, employment, housing, and medical care, but also called for major initiatives in civil rights, which Truman would detail in a 10-point program later that year.[28] Thus, as Rowe recommended, the White House Research Division set the tone for an aggressive liberal campaign that renewed the White House's relationship with progressive and labor leaders.

The direct link the Truman White House forged with liberal activists and "pressure groups" during the 1948 campaign reaffirmed, indeed extended, the establishment of the modern presidency as the center of the New Deal coalition. Truman's long association with the traditional Democratic organization, an association that made him an acceptable alternative to Wallace in 1944, did not prevent him from carrying on the Roosevelt legacy. His literal pursuit of the policies of his chief, his dedication to the economic bill of rights, inclined Truman to forgo old-fashioned organization politics and further define the politics of "enlightened administration." The 1948 campaign and Truman's stunning victory over Dewey was not really a "maintaining election" in the conventional partisan sense. Rather, the first New Deal triumph without Roosevelt strikingly revealed the Democratic party's reliance upon executive administration for its association with liberalism.

Like Roosevelt, Truman recognized the full institutional implications of the distinction between his own and his party's electoral constituencies. Truman's agreement to the formation of a campaign Research Division under the supervision of the White House Office both formalized and expanded upon the separation of presidential and partisan politics that began during the Roosevelt administration. Truman's battles with Congress, moreover, which continued after his re-election, encouraged him to stake out a substantial sphere for independent action in government. Although his veto did not prevent the enactment of the Taft–Hartley Act in 1947, Truman's appointments to, and support for, the National Labor Relations Board provided administrative protection for organized labor under the cloak of a protective Wagner Act.[29] Truman went further than FDR was willing to go, moreover, in tackling civil rights problems by administrative action. Race was the most dangerous fault line threatening the uneasy alliance between Southern and Northern Democrats; even in the 81st Congress, with Democratic majorities controlling both chambers, Truman was to find that it was virtually impossible to improve civil rights through legislative action. The president's decision to move forward on this issue by administrative action strengthened the liberal commitment of the New Deal by emphasizing the executive branch, rather than the Democratic party, as the agent of civil rights reform.

To be sure, Truman was no zealot on the rights of racial minorities. He had not wanted a strong civil rights plank in the 1948 Democratic platform, preferring a proposal that repeated the party's 1944 plank, one that was sufficiently vague to win the acceptance of Southerners. An ADA contingent, led by Andrew J. Biemiller of Wisconsin and Hubert H. Humphrey of Minnesota, fought successfully to strengthen the 1948 platform's civil rights section. This change encouraged liberals, but, as Truman feared, also produced the Southern bolt led by South Carolina Governor Strom Thurmond. Although Truman had been reluctant about civil rights in the party platform, his record on racial relations between 1945 and 1948 was strong enough to encourage an effort by Southern Democrats to veto his nomination; this effort was thwarted when Truman forces fended off Southern efforts to restore the rule, abrogated in 1936, requiring a two-thirds vote for nomination.

Southern opposition to Truman had persisted since December 5, 1946, when the President established by executive order the President's Committee on Civil Rights (PCCR). The PCCR was authorized "to determine whether and in what respect current law enforcement measures and the authority and means possessed by Federal, State, and local governments may be strengthened and approved to safeguard the civil rights of the people."[30] In October, 1947, the Civil Rights Committee delivered its report, which showed that a positive need existed for legislation to secure the rights of American minority groups. The PCCR's recommendations formed the basis of Truman's message to Congress on February 2, 1948, calling for a ten-point civil rights program that would, among other things, provide federal protection against lynching, protect the right to vote, prohibit discrimination in interstate transportation facilities, and establish a Fair Employment Practices Committee to prevent unfair discrimination in employment.[31] When Congress proved unresponsive, Truman acted on his own in the areas in which he had authority as chief executive. Most significant, on July 26, 1948, in the wake of the Southern revolt and in the midst of a heated political campaign, the president issued Executive Order 9981, which decreed that "there shall be equality of treatment and opportunity in the Armed Services without regard to race, color, religion, or national origin." Although the order did not explicitly condemn discrimination, Truman established a committee headed by former Solicitor General Charles Fahey that set the stage for the integration of American military forces.

As the Truman administration came to a close in 1953, of course, much was still left undone to provide even a semblance of educational and economic equality. Truman, in fact, apparently lost some of his enthusiasm for pursuing the civil rights question after his re-election. Rowe and Clifford had persuaded him that he could move aggressively on civil rights in 1947 and 1948 and still hold the party together, but he learned that was not true. Although he lost only 38 electoral votes because of Thurmond's Dixiecrat revolt, he still wished to bring disaffected Southern Democrats back into the party. To do so, Truman was willing to deemphasize civil rights. Like FDR, he hoped to hold the party together, even while deemphasizing its importance, by stressing economic reform.

Nevertheless, Truman's initiatives on civil rights and his willingness to employ executive action to tackle the race issue were significant. Referring to Truman's presidency, the historian John Hope Franklin stated in a 1968 address that "the crucial turning point in viewing the problem of race as a national problem occurred when the executive branch of the federal government began actively to assume a major role.''[32]

The Democratic party built upon Roosevelt policies gave rise to a liberal coalition of autonomous actors. In part, the autonomy of New Deal constituent groups was a result of the limits to party government in the United States. Just as important, however, was the reshaping of executive administration as an instrument of progressive reform, as a more hospitable institutional loft for the political changes represented by the New Deal.

Truman and the Institution of the Modern Presidency

Truman's administration revealed that an executive-centered political coalition could be sustained by a president who lacked the extraordinary political gifts and popularity of Roosevelt. "Truman possessed little or no charisma, struggled with an ego more fragile than most observers have understood, and had extreme distaste for the need to manipulate others," Hamby has written.[33] A poor speaker and awkward in the presence of the press, Truman was very uncomfortable in the limelight of the modern presidency, especially in comparison to the self-command and bonhomie displayed by Roosevelt. Truman's personal and rhetorical shortcomings contributed to his endemically low popularity: His public approval was lower than 50 percent for the larger part of his time in office, including the entire final years of his presidency.[34]

In other respects, however, Truman was a solid heir to the Roosevelt legacy. Although he was all too aware of his personal limitations, Truman understood well and benefitted considerably from the great extension of executive power instigated by his predecessor. He both formalized and expanded the presidency as an institution.

Although FDR devoted enormous political capital and administrative energy in creating the White House Office, his staff support was relatively unstructured, thus reflecting a penchant for improvisation. In 1943, Louis Brownlow had presented Roosevelt with a long report prepared under the auspices of the National Resources Planning Board, proclaiming the necessity for a more effective system of policy development.[35] "I have read [that report] at one page per minute," FDR wrote his Uncle Frederick Delano a few weeks later. "He has not got the answer yet. I don't think anyone has. I am a bumblebee. I am going to keep on bumbling.''[36]

Truman, however, felt the need for more formal—more routinized—relations in the executive branch. Soon after assuming the duties of president, he indicated to budget director Harold Smith that he wanted "to improve the governmental organization and that the improvement would have to start with the White House."[37] Consequently, responsibilities within the White House office became more clearly defined. The president also wanted "to get the whole Executive Office knit together."[38] For this, he relied on the Bureau of the Budget (BOB), which acquired more authority than it had under FDR to coordinate the activities the executive branch. During Truman's tenure, therefore, the BOB acquired the formal responsibility and routine duty to clear and coordinate all legislative requests originating within federal departments, to draft legislation emanating from the White House, and to clear and draft executive orders.[39] As a result, the White House was no longer so clearly "a powerhouse without transmission lines"; as Rowe had recommended, the executive office was organized to provide the president with a stronger and better coordinated staff.[40] This would prove to be of help to Truman not only in managing the affairs of state, but also in planning and carrying out his campaign for re-election.

Congress helped Truman, although for the most part unintentionally, to institutionalize the presidency. Congressional statutes, for example, established the Council for Economic Advisors (CEA) (1946) and the National Security Council (NSC) (1947), to "aid" the president in the formulation of fiscal and foreign policy, respectively, and the legislature appropriated funds for larger staffs to assist him. But Truman acted effectively to "domesticate" these new staff agencies, that is, make them part of the president's team, although the NSC and CEA initially were conceived by many Congressmen as a check on the president's autonomy in fiscal and security matters.

Truman's strengthening of the presidential bureaucracy had surprising help from another quarter—former president Herbert Hoover. As noted in Chapter 6, the Republican-controlled 80th Congress had appointed Hoover to head a commission on the organization of the executive branch. The task of the commission, as GOP leaders in Congress understood it, was to prepare the ground for an assault on New Deal programs and circumscribe the modern executive by reducing the potential for another personalized FDR-type government. Yet though Hoover had spent the previous two decades excoriating the evils of the New Deal, he brought to the commission an appreciation of the expanded capacities of the executive office. It was not the Hoover of the 1930s and 1940s who threw himself into the investigation of executive organization, but the Hoover of the 1920s, who had grappled with the problems of the presidency and executive branch.

Paradoxically, Hoover favored the destruction of many of the modern state's programs while he worked to strengthen its central instrument of governance.[41] After much study, the Hoover commission recommended the executive office be strengthened, not diminished. Its report, in fact, was very similar to the Brownlow report that inspired FDR's administrative reform program. The president needed still more help, the Hoover Commission argued, and even greater influence over the far-flung activities of the enlarged executive branch.[42] These recommendations formed the basis of the 1949 Executive Reorganization Act, which authorized Truman, who enthusiastically embraced the commission's report, to effect important changes in many of the departments and independent commissions.

An especially significant legacy of this legislation was Truman's Reorganization Plan 8, which he issued in 1950. Truman included provisions in the plan that eventually eroded the independent regulatory commissions' autonomy, and, thereby, reduced the effect of the Court's ruling in *Humphrey's Executive v. United States* that the president may not remove a commissioner. The plan provided that the Chairs of the regulatory commissions would be "appointed by the president and serve at his pleasure." The chairs, in turn, were granted considerable authority to appoint and supervise their commission's staff and to oversee the daily business of the commissions. Consequently, presidents were better able to give direction to "independent" regulatory bodies like the National Labor Relations Board than in the past.[43]

Hoover's endorsement of the executive reorganization program suggested that a political consensus was gradually emerging in support of the modern presidency. The Republican party had "historically been against Presidents," as one Truman aide noted, but Hoover's interest in the problems of administrative management apparently presented an opportunity to build bipartisan support for "the kind of Chief Executive office that [would] have enough authority and the right kind of organization to do the most difficult jobs."[44] The controversies that enervated the Truman administration after 1948 would greatly weaken this support, and the 1952 Republican campaign refocused attention on the "evils of executive dictatorship." Still, the growth of presidential powers during FDR's tenure was extensively, if not fully, institutionalized during the Truman years. The modern presidency had both transcended and further undermined partisan responsibility.

Republican Interlude

Like the Hoover Commission, the presidency of Dwight D. Eisenhower fostered the bipartisan acceptance of the modern presidency. Eisenhower, in fact, although the first Republican elected since FDR, seemed at first glance to be a more logical New Deal legatee than Truman. His election in 1952 formally completed the institutional separation of presidential and party coalitions. Eisenhower was no partisan Republican; in fact, many liberals, including James Roosevelt, had tried to draft him to run as a Democrat in 1948. John Gunther, a member of Americans for Democratic Action, assured fellow New Dealers that Eisenhower was a liberal, albeit a reticent one, who could keep the presidency in the Democratic party and resurrect liberal support, which seemed to be flagging. Only Eisenhower's adamant refusal to run put an end to ADA efforts to secure his services in rescuing the Democratic party from the clutches of Southern reactionaries and what seemed like certain defeat in the 1948 campaign.[45]

Eisenhower's decision to run in 1952 represented less a commitment to the Republican party's traditions than it did a desire to preside over a national healing process after the controversy and frenetic activism of the Roosevelt and Truman years. Eisenhower had no intention of dismantling the "Roosevelt Revolution," to be sure, but he came to the White House with a different perception of the presidency from Roosevelt's and with different aspirations. Whereas Harry Truman had fought to preserve the Roosevelt legacy, Eisenhower was "a Roosevelt in reverse," Richard Neustadt wrote in 1960. "Roosevelt was a politician seeking personal power; Eisenhower . . . came to crown a reputation not to make one. He wanted to be arbiter not master. His love was not for power but for duty—and for status."[46]

Eisenhower's "love of duty" initially inclined him to accept the view of many Republicans that balance should be restored in the relationship between the president and Congress. In support of this view, the Republican-controlled 80th Congress had hastily passed the Twenty-Second Amendment in 1947 to impose a two-term limit on the president; this amendment was ratified by the requisite number of states and made part of the Constitution in 1951. As the first Republican president since 1933, Eisenhower did his part, especially during the early days of his presidency, to right the balance between the executive and legislature. Indeed, Eisenhower did not even send forward a legislative program during his first year in office.

Eisenhower's status as a war hero and the popularity he enjoyed with the American people did not free him to reshape the modern executive in his own image, however. Some Americans regarded Eisenhower's constant professions of respect for Congress as refreshing evidence that the hallowed traditions of legislative government were being restored. Others, however, especially the members of the press, looked disdainfully at what one observer called Eisenhower's "civic textbook concept of the three branches of the federal government."[47] After FDR's voracious seizure and joyous exercise of power 20 years earlier, Eisenhower was all too easily characterized as "a man who slipped into the White House by the back door on January 20, 1953, and hasn't yet found his way to the President's desk."[48]

The Hidden Hand

Appearances to the contrary, Eisenhower was not simply a passive figure watching history pass him by. He exercised power with much more relish and shrewdness than his contemporaries surmised. He was a "hidden-hand" president, to use Fred Greenstein's term, exercising power behind the scenes while presenting a public image of detachment from the political machinations of the nation's capital.[49] Eisenhower apparently recognized that the tasks of the "modern" presidency were becoming unmanageable, that under normal circumstances the President was expected to do more than was possible or, from Eisenhower's perspective, desirable. On the one hand, the president was still expected to perform the traditional tasks of the Chief of State, impartially upholding the Constitution and lending dignity to the proceedings of the federal government. On the other hand, since the New Deal, the president was expected to get things done, to exert control over—or, if necessary, circumvent—his party and Congress in pursuit of a program. FDR had bestowed upon presidents the opportunity to act independently of the limiting institutional arrangements formed during the nineteenth century, but Eisenhower believed that the dignity and influence of the office ultimately was lost when the president not only led politically but appeared to lead politically, as had Truman.

Eisenhower's remedy for this dilemma of modern executive leadership was not to abdicate responsibility for policy. Compared to FDR and Truman, Eisenhower was a domestic political conservative with little desire to innovate except in modest incremental ways. Part and parcel of his incrementalism was the belief that the New Deal had become a permanent part of the American political system. When his ardently conservative brother Edgar criticized him for carrying on liberal policies, Eisenhower replied angrily that "should any political party attempt to abolish social security and eliminate labor laws and farm programs, you should not hear of that party again in political history."[50]

Eisenhower's presidency confirmed the positive role of big federal government that had first taken hold under FDR. It further imbedded the institutional changes brought by the New Deal in the day-to-day activities of the federal government. Revisionist scholarship on Eisenhower has revealed clearly that he was not the nonpolitical president he was thought to be. Nonetheless, he did not provide the form of aggressive leadership required to recast either the modern presidency or the Republican party.

Eisenhower's Party Leadership

Paradoxically, this career military man, who lacked a record of party involvement when he deprived "Mr. Republican" Robert A. Taft of the nomination in 1952, was as actively and constructively involved in party affairs as any president after FDR.[51] FDR and Truman fought to impose a program of national reform that looked beyond the sort of limited agreements that could be worked out within their fragmented party. Eisenhower, in contrast, represented "the revolt of the moderates," as Samuel Lubell put it, and thus had surprisingly little difficulty in establishing a comfortable working relationship with the regular party apparatus.[52]

Eisenhower's public nonpartisanship did not veil political activity that was designed to remake the Republican party, but an effort to nurture the traditional Republican apparatus. Paradoxically, by developing a "modern Republicanism" to open the party to supporters of the welfare state, Eisenhower ensured the consolidation of the New Deal legacy. While strengthening the Republican party machinery, this action ratified the advent of an institutional change brought by the New Deal, notably the advent of the modern presidency, that rendered that machinery far less significant.

It is not surprising, then, that Eisenhower's presidency established a more enduring precedent in its creation of a candidate-centered "Citizens for Eisenhower" organization for the 1952 election, which operated independently of the Republican National Committee (RNC), than it did in its eventual support of the regular Republican apparatus. Roosevelt and Truman had undertaken important initiatives to separate their campaigns from the party, making use of White House operatives and "independent" committees. But Eisenhower was the first presidential candidate to form a national organization for the purpose of running a campaign independent of the political party.[53]

Charles F. Willis, Jr., co-founder of "Citizens for Eisenhower," took a position in the White House Office as an assistant to Chief of Staff Sherman Adams. Willis, according to Cornelius Cotter, "kept the RNC under unremitting pressure on the matters of more effective performance of the patronage advisory and clearance role, integration of the Citizens organizations into the regular Republican organization, and an effective campaign role for the Citizens organizations."[54] Willis was not inattentive the needs of party regulars. In patronage matters, for example, he sought to balance the claims of Eisenhower "irregulars"—as the citizen activists were called—with the needs of state party organizations. Eisenhower's strategy for the party was one of quiet infiltration; he would neither ignore nor rebuild the national GOP organization. But the effort to bring the "irregulars" gradually into positions of state and national party leadership was unsuccessful. Throughout the Eisenhower presidency, citizen activists and party regulars coexisted peacefully, albeit not without considerable uneasiness and a certain amount of confusion in both quarters.[55]

Eisenhower's political fortunes had little effect on the GOP. The Republican party never became an organization that Eisenhower felt close to; and the president's studied disregard for partisanship in public only reinforced the growing tendency of the American people to view the White House and party as separate realms. Like FDR, Eisenhower was a shrewd enough politician to recognize that his own popularity and prestige were much greater than his adopted party's and that his own standing would be damaged by open partisanship; moreover, content to govern as a moderate New Dealer, Ike saw little reason to challenge the institutional arrangements Roosevelt and Truman had bequeathed to him that established an independent sphere of presidential action. The voters responded logically: They returned a Democratic Congress in 1956, despite Eisenhower's personal triumph over Adlai Stevenson. For the first time since 1848, a presidential candidate won popular approval while his party failed to secure control over even one legislative chamber.

Soon after the election, Eisenhower acknowledged his failure to make the GOP an instrument of "modern Republicanism." "From my viewpoint," he told reporters, the election of a Democratic-controlled Congress means that "the United States has not been convinced that Modern Republicanism is with us and is going to be the guiding philosophy of the Republican party."[56] Of course political developments since FDR's days in the White House had instructed the American people to consider the attributes of presidential candidates separately from that of their parties. In his 1940 Jackson day speech, Roosevelt had foretold of "the vast number of people" who would "consider themselves normally adherents of one party and still feel perfectly free to vote for one or more candidates of another party." Eisenhower's presidency was a dramatic and somewhat ironic confirmation of this prophecy. The emergence of the New Deal political order meant the traditional party apparatus, established upon state and local organizations, either had to be remade or reduced in influence. Neither the popularity of Eisenhower nor his attention to the details of party leadership altered, in any meaningful way, this situation.

Eisenhower did initiate some changes in the Republican party that were to have important long-term consequences. Most significant, he began the process of strengthening the Republican party in the South. By the 1950s, economic, generational, and political forces had initiated discernable changes that undermined Democracy's dominance of that region. Eisenhower's popularity and interest in party-building capitalized on the erosion of the solid South, thus initiating a revitalization of the long-dormant Southern Republican party. Yet, as Cotter has noted, Eisenhower's success in strengthening the national character of his party had an ironic twist: "The renaissance of the Southern Republican party strengthened the conservative cast of the national party and facilitated the nomination of candidates who promised to turn the nation around."[57]

Eisenhower and the Modern Presidency

The Republican party moved haltingly toward a direct challenge to the New Deal. The party's emergence as a viable opposition force would be preempted continuously by administrative politics and by the tendency of Republican presidents to see the modern presidency as a two-edged sword that could cut in a conservative as well as a liberal direction. This was not Eisenhower's vision of the modern presidency; he was well suited to the task of circumspect management of the liberal state. But in seeking to temper, if not reverse, New Deal policies, Eisenhower's presidency was an important precursor to the conservative embrace of centralized administration.

A case in point was the decision to forego structural changes in modifying labor policy. Organized business was generally dissatisfied with the National Labor Relations Board's application of the Taft–Hartley Act during the Truman years, but business leaders disagreed about how to counteract the agency's sympathetic approach to unions and collective bargaining. One group, composed generally of small manufacturers, felt that its interests would best be served by ending Federal administration of the subjects covered by Taft–Hartley. This approach, which was supported by the Republicans who sat on the House Labor Committee, would allow greater opportunity for state regulation and the adjudication of an abbreviated Federal act by the district courts. On the other side was a faction made up generally of large manufacturers, who preferred a uniform statutory policy and interpretation of a single agency to broader state jurisdiction and decentralized administration of Taft–Hartley through the district courts. In the end, the Eisenhower administration decided to retain the current structural form of labor regulation; it would attempt to alter federal policy towards organized labor and collective bargaining not by abolishing the NLRB but by reshaping it.[58]

The key figure in persuading Eisenhower to adopt an administrative approach was White House Legal Counsel Gerald Morgan, who, before landing in the executive office, had been an opponent of administrative agencies. The president's decision not to seek fundamental structural reform, therefore, surprised and disappointed Samuel McConnell, chairman of the House Labor Committee in the Republican 83rd Congress. "I just couldn't understand it," McConnell later related. "Morgan back in 1947 didn't seem to care for administrative agencies any more than we [Republicans of the Committee] do. Then he wanted to judicialize the Board. Now he's supporting the administrative approach."[59] The presence of a Republican in the White House won Morgan, as well as key business interests, to the administrative approach in 1953. This strategy, in turn, led to a rift between the White House "labor high command" and Republican members of Congress that further inclined Eisenhower to emphasize executive administration in the reformulation of labor policy. This was a significant, if not final, step in the acceptance of the modern presidency by those who were opposed to the general policy thrust of the New Deal. By the end of 1954, the National Association of Manufacturers was able to state:

> Though the language of Taft–Hartley has remained unchanged, its interpretation
> by the Labor Board has not. On numerous and important issues the New Board,
> a majority of whose members have been appointed by President Eisenhower, has
> overturned long established rulings, and given the Act a new, and almost anti-
> labor meaning. Indeed, the Eisenhower appointees seem to have taken office with
> that end consciously in mind. . . .[60]

In truth, the change in policy that governed labor–management relations during the Eisenhower years was modest. Much to the displeasure of anti-union elements of the Republican coalition, Eisenhower chose Guy Farmer, a moderate
conservative, as Chair of the NLRB; Farmer, a well-known and respected attorney
within the labor–management community, directed the agency towards a more
moderate, somewhat less pro-union posture than it expressed during the Roosevelt
and Truman years. As was characteristic of the Eisenhower presidency, however,
there was no effort to repeal the New Deal; rather, there was a case-by-case endeavor to moderate liberal administration.[61]

Eisenhower further routinized the New Deal political order by strengthening
the institution of the presidency. Drawing on his long experience with military
staffs, Eisenhower enlarged and more formally organized the White House Office.
This is not to say that the organization and operations of the Eisenhower White
House were adopted along the lines of a military model, as many Washington
observers concluded erroneously during his time in office. Instead, the enthusiasm
Ike gained for organization in the military predisposed him to entertain seriously
the recommendations of the Brownlow and Hoover Commissions that encouraged
presidents to establish a clearer and more formal line of command between the
White House and the rest of the executive branch.[62] He established a line of
command originating from *The* Assistant to the President, a Chief of Staff who
would report directly to him. Sherman Adams was the first individual to hold this
influential position, zealously freeing the president from the every-day demands
of the White House, thus allowing Eisenhower to concentrate on major policy
decisions.[63]

The designation of an "Assistant to the President," as well as Eisenhower's
creation of a staff secretariat to organize the Cabinet, were political—and not
military—in origin; his effort to provide for more orderly functioning of the presidency simply reflected his admiration for the British Cabinet secretariat.[64] Eisenhower was familiar with the Cabinet secretariat from his experience during World
War II in England; moreover, his interest in making an analogous system work in
American politics echoed the sentiments of the Brownlow Committee. The 1937
PCAM report's prescription to appoint White House special assistants with "a
passion for anonymity" was inspired by its authors' admiration for the Cabinet
secretariat in Whitehall.[65] The Brownlow Committee had rejected the idea of one
individual heading the White House staff, as was the case with the British secretariat, but they were impressed with the orderly functioning brought about by the
Cabinet secretary in England. Roosevelt, seeking creativity and innovation, had
deliberately maintained a measure of disorderliness in his executive office. Eisenhower's political strengths and goals, emphasizing consolidation rather than build-

ing a new political order, inclined him to take the Brownlow Committee's prescription for orderly management more literally.

Yet, like FDR, Ike also understood the importance of retaining the political character of executive administration. He wanted to reshape the militant New Deal cast of the Roosevelt and Truman bureaucracies, but he was no less concerned than his Democratic predecessors to leave an administrative apparatus that reflected his own political objectives. For this Eisenhower could not readily rely on the sort of patronage strategies that FDR had pursued—indeed the covering-in of New Deal loyalists had left the Eisenhower administration with very little patronage. Moreover, Eisenhower wanted to temper rather than expand the programmatic initiatives of the New Deal, and to contract rather than expand, positions in the federal government. The scope of political patronage had "dwindled to a mere shadow," *Time* observed in the summer of 1954.[66]

Eisenhower chose not to initiate a large-scale withdrawal of positions from the competitive service, as had frequently occurred prior to the New Deal when control of the White House was transferred to the party out of power. Eisenhower's management of personnel disappointed the GOP faithful; as the press reported, "the panorama of plenty" they had hoped for when a Republican captured the White House "turned out to be a mirage."[67]

Instead of the patronage grab GOP loyalists hoped for, Eisenhower's management of the bureaucracy strengthened the modern presidency. He carried on the project started by Roosevelt to domesticate the Civil Service Commission. All vestiges of the Liaison Office for Personnel Management in the White House were abolished. Philip Young, former dean of the Graduate School of Business at Columbia and Eisenhower's choice for Chair of the Civil Service Commission, assumed its responsibilities, receiving the new title of Presidential Advisor on Personnel Management. Young was invited to attend Cabinet meetings and to serve as Eisenhower's right-hand man with respect to personnel matters. In fact, Young shared the responsibility for personnel management with Charles Willis, who oversaw the distribution of patronage. But the dual position Young performed seemed to presage a distinct political function for the Civil Service Commission, further blurring the line between the political and permanent services. The restructuring of the relationship of the Civil Service Commission to the presidency assumed greater importance when Eisenhower, with Young's blessing, issued an executive order of March 31, 1953, inaugurating the so-called "Schedule C" positions. As "positions of a confidential or policy determining character," Schedule C appointments would not be subject to merit protection.

Eisenhower's redesigning of the White House's relationship with the Civil Service Commission and his creation of strategic political outposts in the bureaucracy stirred considerable controversy, arousing fears of a spoils raid on the civil service. But this was never Eisenhower's intention; by October 11, 1954, for example, only 1,127 positions had been placed within the "Schedule C" category. Rather, his objective was to enable the White House and its top political executives to bring around them a few people of their own choosing, without going through the strict and often time-consuming merit system procedures.[68] This mix of politics and administration would place an Eisenhower, rather than Republican or traditionally partisan, stamp upon the councils of public administration.

Eisenhower's limited programmatic ambitions notwithstanding, his contributions to the institutionalization of the modern presidency also included the formation of the first White House legislative liaison office. The liaison office was headed by Milton P. Peterson, a retired officer who had handled Eisenhower's congressional relations when Ike served first as chief of staff of the army and then as NATO commander after World War II. Although Eisenhower offered no program to Congress during his first year, pressure from several quarters soon forced him to become more actively involved in legislative matters. Having talked of "restoring the balance," the president soon learned that even a national leader representing a "revolt of the moderates" needed effective representation of his views to Congress. Thus, a presidential program accompanied Eisenhower's January, 1954 State of the Union message, and Eisenhower, with the support of his legislative liaison office, made systematic efforts to have it enacted. Eisenhower became increasingly involved in legislative matters during the course of his presidency, and managed to hold his own with a Congress that, after 1954, was under Democratic control.

As in his management of personnel matters, Eisenhower's leadership of Congress upheld the modern presidency rather than his party. Perhaps the best evidence of this was his successful effort to defeat the Bricker Amendment, which would have curtailed the president's authority to conduct foreign policy. Unlike many members of his party, Eisenhower shared the internationalist aspirations of FDR and Truman. He was contemptuous of those Republicans, led by Senator Taft, who advocated withdrawal to a "fortress America" stance in the world.[69] By the terms of the Bricker amendment, which was sponsored by Taft's Republican colleague from Ohio, John Bricker, executive agreements with other nations would become the law of the land only if they were approved by Congress and did not conflict with state laws. "The idea was, of course," the historian Elmo Richardson has written, "a belated response to Franklin Roosevelt's personal diplomacy."[70] It was this part of the Roosevelt legacy above all, however, that Eisenhower wanted to protect from the conservatives of his party. The President made this clear in a letter of January 25, 1954 to Senate Majority Leader William Knowland:

> Adoption of the amendment in its present form by the Senate would be notice to our friends as well as our enemies abroad that our country intends to withdraw from its leadership in world affairs. The inevitable reaction would be of major proportion. It would impair our hopes and plans for peace and for the successful achievement of the important international matters now under discussion.[71]

In the Senate vote, largely due to the efforts of Eisenhower and his congressional liaison staff, the amendment fell one vote short of the necessary two-thirds for ratification. Only fifteen of forty-seven voting Republican senators supported the president. The close vote on the Bricker Amendment reflected widespread public support for it, thus indicating that many Americans still questioned a chief executive's exercise of initiative in foreign affairs. It was the reluctant modern president "Dwight D. Eisenhower—nobody else," an embittered Senator Bricker claimed nearly two decades after the climatic roll call vote, who preserved the executive's prerogative to make international agreements unilaterally.[72]

The Modern Presidency and the Great Society: Radicalizing the New Deal Political Order

John F. Kennedy had been elected in 1960 to get the country moving again, to pull it out of the complacency that had settled over America in the twilight of the Eisenhower years. A sluggish economy, a simmering civil rights problem, and the Soviet threat abroad had created doubts about the country's future and called it back to the Democratic party, although by a very narrow margin. Running against Vice President Nixon and what he perceived as the lethargy of the Eisenhower years, Kennedy campaigned on a theme of change and premised that campaign on the issue of the presidency itself.

Eisenhower's forbearance with respect to the modern executive's powers, Kennedy argued, might have brought him great popularity, but at the cost of unacceptable stagnation. JFK promised an end to this stagnation. The nation could not afford a Chief Executive in the 1960s, he declared during the campaign, "who is praised primarily for what he did not do, the disasters he prevented, the bills he vetoed—a President wishing his subordinates would produce more missiles or build more schools." We needed instead, Kennedy insisted, "a Chief Executive who is the vital center of action in our whole scheme of government," one who would be "willing and able to summon his national constituency to its finest hour—to alert the people to our dangers and our opportunities—to demand of them the sacrifices that will be necessary."[73]

It is difficult to know what Kennedy would have accomplished had he lived. But his brief tenure in the White House was one of frustration; he came to believe that the nature of the problems he faced were not readily susceptible to the sort of inspirational leadership FDR had provided. "What the federal government had to do today," Kennedy told Justice Felix Frankfurter in 1962, "was far different, more complicated and less understandable to the people than it was at [the time] of FDR." JFK felt that Roosevelt's program directly affected various groups of people—some favorably, some unfavorably—resulting in policy that aroused the public's interest. His problems, in contrast, "were more in the nature of complicated administrative measures, which people found it difficult to understand."[74]

Such a view, one suspects, was partly born of Kennedy's need to grapple with the ineluctable logic of modern executive leadership. It also reflected no doubt the president's exasperation in failing to overcome the "deadlock of democracy" that aroused the ire of James MacGregor Burns and other liberal intellectuals in the early 1960s.[75] In their eyes it must have seemed that executive torpor was the inevitable, if unanticipated, result of the playing out of Roosevelt's institutional program. JFK continued, indeed intensified, the institutional developments begun during the 1930s. His campaign for the presidency and his governing style set significant precedents that increased the power of the White House and further separated its activities from party politics, the cabinet and regular executive departments, and Congress.[76] These developments had given rise to a more powerful and prominent chief executive, but one reduced to virtually complete political isolation. Kennedy did not initiate the changes that isolated the president in this way, but his legacy was a significant personalization of the executive office that greatly accentuated the separation of the presidency from other power centers of American government.

JFK's New Frontier program included proposals for medical aid, support of education and civil rights. But his relations with Congress were extraordinarily difficult. Several measures Kennedy sought, particularly Medicare and aid to education, were stalled during his administration, and two others, tax reduction and civil rights, had not been passed at the time of his death.

Lyndon Johnson seemed at first glance an unlikely figure to grasp the scepter of the fallen president. Prior to his election as Vice President, LBJ had won a substantial reputation as a consummate political operator in the Senate, where as majority leader he exercised enormous influence during the Eisenhower years. It remained to be seen whether this quintessential power broker could successfully adapt his experience and skills to the presidency. Kennedy liberals, most notably the late president's brother, Attorney General Robert Kennedy, doubted Johnson was up to the job—they were bitter, in fact, about this Southern power broker replacing their fallen leader. Johnson sensed, and would come to resent deeply the animus Kennedy liberals felt towards him. But LBJ himself acknowledged that he had to establish his right to govern. As he wrote in his memoirs:

> In spite of more than three decades of public service, I knew I was an unknown quantity to many of my countrymen and to much of the world when I assumed office. I suffered another handicap, since I had come to the presidency not through the collective will of the people but in the wake of tragedy. I had no mandate from the voters.[77]

In spite of the problems Johnson faced, he quickly grasped the reins of power. In fact, he did more than reassure the nation and build confidence in his leadership. LBJ was able to master and amplify the powers and institutions of the modern presidency as no one had since Franklin Roosevelt. The institutions and policies of the New Deal had been accepted, and even extended, since the 1930s. But the stalemate that characterized the relations between the president and Congress since FDR's second term had prevented dramatic breakthroughs in liberal reform, thus threatening to reduce the New Deal political order to administrative ennui. In 1964 under Lyndon Johnson the stalemate ended, as Congress passed a strong Civil Rights bill, a tax-cut measure, and the first installments of LBJ's war on poverty.

This stalemate was broken not only by the 1964 election, which had greatly swelled the Democratic margin in Congress, but by Lyndon Johnson's extraordinary command of the nation. "In the wake of Kennedy's assassination," Jeffrey Tulis has written, "Lyndon Johnson was able to turn the country's grief into a commitment to a moral crusade."[78] This crusade would not stop at completing the policy aspirations of the New Deal. In fact, Johnson wanted a great deal more than that; he was not satisfied to go down in the history books as a successful president in the Roosevelt tradition. In a 1965 interview with LBJ, William Leuchtenburg was startled by the president's strident criticism not only of the Kennedy administration, for which he had barely disguised contempt, but also of Franklin Roosevelt, for whom Johnson had long expressed great reverence. In fact, Johnson's feelings for FDR were as competitive as they were pious; he wanted to be "the greatest of them all, the whole bunch of them."[79]

In the attempt to satisfy his aspirations, Johnson was to have a profound influence of the modern presidency. He continued—even accelerated—developments of the Kennedy era that accentuated the power and independence of the executive; arguably, his administration marked the height of modern presidential leadership. Yet, LBJ's failings also brought into serious question for the first time since the 1930s the assumption by public officials, the press, and the general public that it was desirable for a president to dominate the affairs of state. In effect, the disillusionment that followed his presidency began to unravel the conditions that had given rise to the modern presidency.

Expanding Liberalism and the New Deal

Despite his desire to surpass Roosevelt's accomplishments, Johnson had no wish to depart from the politics in which he was steeped. His ascent to the presidency was thus cause for considerable hopefulness for the militant New Dealers of the 1930s. In April 1964, Thomas Corcoran wrote President Johnson, "The transition to your 'own' administration has long been complete to those who know you; I sensed the end of the 'transition' the day you hung Roosevelt's picture in the Cabinet room."[80] Corcoran thereby gave expression to the view that LBJ's occupation of the White House brought to power someone who, unlike John Kennedy, possessed a deep and abiding commitment to the principles and politics of the New Deal. JFK actually considered the Roosevelt Legacy the stuff of the past, from which he and the Democratic party needed to be emancipated. "[H]e believes that much of the liberalism of the New Deal and the Fair Deal either has become properly entrenched in our way of life, and hence no longer a disputed political issue, or in a few cases has become outmoded or irrelevant," James MacGregor Burns wrote of Kennedy.[81] Johnson, in contrast, both reverentially and competitively, drew inspiration from Roosevelt, whom he resembled as a political leader more than Kennedy ever did.[82]

Significantly, whereas John Kennedy seemed intent upon providing leadership for a generation far removed from the political struggles of the 1930s, LBJ's political career was launched by the heated battles that stirred a constitutional crisis during Roosevelt's second term. Johnson came to Congress in a special 1937 House election, in which he gained the favor of the Roosevelt administration, and managed to distinguish himself from a field of eight other, better known candidates, by running as the most devoted follower of FDR and his program. Johnson revealed his understanding of the Third New Deal, designed to provide an enduring foundation for the modern liberal political order, in several of the speeches given during his run for the House in 1937. One radio address given on

March 18, in fact, strikingly foretold of the task that was to preoccupy, indeed obsess, his own presidency. Remarking on the need to send an eminently qualified and zealously committed New Dealer to the Congress, LBJ noted: "If the administration program were a temporary thing the situation would be different. But it is not for a day or for a year, but for an age. It must be worked out through time, and long after Roosevelt leaves the White House, it will still be developing, expanding. . . . The man who goes into Congress this year, or next year, must be prepared to meet this condition. He must be capable of growing and progressing with it."[83]

In part, LBJ's interest as president in resurrecting the age of Roosevelt led to programmatic commitments that as one journalist wrote in 1965, emphasized "codifying the New Deal vision of a good society."[84] This program entailed expanding the benefits of the economic constitutional order with such programmatic commitments as Medicare, and, even more significant, extension of these benefits to black Americans. LBJ had a self-conscious concern that the Roosevelt he cared about was the one committed to changing the world—but his renowned predecessor had most conspicuously failed to make progress in the area of race relations. According to Johnson's close friend and associate, Horace Busby, coming to terms with the race issue was viewed as the major challenge in completing the work left undone by Roosevelt:

> It's just not true that FDR was a friend of blacks. . . . In 1936, FDR participated in a ceremony unveiling the Robert E. Lee statue in Dallas, Texas. He said that he welcomed the chance to do this, and that Lee was a great Christian gentleman. No president could get away with such a thing today. Johnson acted to fill the gap in the New Deal left as a result of the inattention to racial problems.[85]

When Johnson assumed the presidency, he had substantial reasons for taking a strong civil rights stand. By this time, the Solid South was no more, as Eisenhower and Nixon had won substantial support below the Mason–Dixon line. The best hope for shoring up the national Democratic party was by expanding the black vote. Black voters were suspicious of a Southern president, as were many Northern liberals who had become strongly committed to the civil rights cause after the demonstrations in Birmingham, Alabama and the March on Washington in 1963. Johnson felt the need to prove himself to the growing civil rights movement by carrying out—indeed surpassing—the civil rights program of the Kennedy administration.

Even more, Johnson wanted to make his own historic mark on the presidency. In fact, the Johnson administration, as we will see in the following, would come to view civil rights as only the beginning of a radical departure from the New Deal reform program. If the architects of the Great Society were New Dealers, they wedded themselves to the side of the New Deal that demanded a relentless pursuit of reform.

According to Johnson, the tasks of social liberalism dictated the same focus on "administrative" politics and deemphasis on partisanship that had characterized Roosevelt's presidency. Indeed, Roosevelt's short-lived and ill-fated efforts to guide his party were well remembered by Johnson, whose election to Congress was one of the few victories achieved by New Dealers during the intense battles for the destiny of the Democratic party during 1937 and 1938. His close familiarity with this history led LBJ to expect the cohesion of the Democratic party and the support of Congress after the triumphant 1964 election to be temporary. He understood FDR's troubles with the Democratic party in the late 1930s to be the best example of the generally ephemeral nature of party government in the United States.[86]

President Johnson expressed his understanding of the limits of partisanship in a speech at Johns Hopkins University in October, 1964:

> . . . I believe I speak for you when I say that we believe in parties and we have allegiance to them and their principles, but we believe in our country first. As I said one time in describing my own political philosophy, "I am proud to be a free man first and an American second, a public servant third, and a Democrat fourth, in that order." . . . [T]he truth is clear. Excellence is far too precious in our society to exclude it from our national endeavors on the basis of party alone.[87]

In part, Johnson's nonpartisanship was emblematic of the ambiguous character of party leadership that presidents had expressed throughout American history. More fundamentally, however, it was a logical continuation of the New Deal legacy that gave impetus to institutional changes designed to displace party politics with executive administration. Johnson made this clear during the 1964 presidential campaign in which he was the first Democratic standard-bearer since the 1930s to face a direct challenge to the principles of the New Deal.

The Problem of Consensus

The 1964 campaign brought into bold relief the paradoxical quality of New Deal party politics. It marked, first, an important chapter—though not the final one— in the transformation of the party system from one dominated by local interests and patronage to one more national and programmatic in orientation. At the same time, in the wake of Johnson's landslide victory, the Democratic party was recommitted to being a party of nonpartisan administration. The polarization of the 1964 campaign, which seemed to revitalize partisan conflict, would eventually become a New Deal consensus that would further diminish the role of party in American politics.

Since the New Deal, the Democratic party had been nudged towards a more militant liberal stand by the domination of progressives during presidential election years. The Republican party, however, had not moved towards vigorous opposition, but had been moored near the vital center of the New Deal consensus by the ability of its progressive wing (led by the Lodges, Rockefellers, and Scrantons) to remain in charge during contests for the White House. But in 1964, the GOP congressional conservatives joined with a new breed of right-wing activists that had emerged in the sunbelt, especially in states like California and Arizona, and, with the support of the newly powerful segregationist Southern wing of the party, had managed to shut out the progressive wing of the party.

The Republican nominee, Arizona Senator Barry Goldwater, promised—or portended—the emergence of a party-against-administration that profoundly challenged the New Deal institutional program. His acceptance speech was laced with defenses of property rights while he spoke not a word about programmatic rights, and although proclaiming himself an opponent of discrimination, Senator Goldwater called the recently passed Civil Rights Act unconstitutional, favoring a reliance on the states for the advancement of the constitutional protections owed blacks. This ambiguous position on rights highlighted Goldwater's unbending defense of administrative decentralization. As the Republican candidate told the platform committee, "he did not believe in the contemporary concept of a strong President as chief legislator and chief economist of the Republic." Goldwater's emphasis on states' rights, reported a dazed *New York Times* reporter, "makes the Federal government sound like a foreign power." [88]

There was a sense among many observers in 1964 that Senator Goldwater's candidacy was not simply an unrealistic yearning for the revival of rugged individualism. The Brownlow Committee had designed the modern executive on the premise that no "political party for any length of time could abandon most of the collectivist functions" exercised by New Dealers; this was true, New Dealers felt in the 1930s, even though it was expected that "the old slogans of opposition to governmental activity would survive long after their meaning had been sucked out." As he reflected on the angry polarizing conflict at the GOP convention at the Cow Palace in San Francisco, however, the journalist Anthony Lewis sensed that there might still be some life to the "old slogans." This was more than a passing show, he warned complacent liberals. It reflected a "historic change in the character of the 100-year-old [Republican] party," and it was a change animated by a strong commitment to less encumbered capitalism, assuring that "the shouts of conservative triumph heard at the Cow Palace this week will be echoing through the American political system for years."

Ironically, Lewis tentatively suggested, this challenge to the Roosevelt revolution seemed to be thrown up by the success of the New Deal political order. That success allowed the American working class and lower middle class to partake of the "promise of American life," as Croly called it, to experience the rewards of a reformed free enterprise system. They were the new version of the petite bourgeoisie, however, who were inclined to turn their backs on reform. [89]

Nevertheless, LBJ won over 61 percent of the popular vote, and the largest plurality in history, exceeding FDR's record victory in 1936. Johnson's coattails, moreover, journalist Tom Wicker wrote the day after the election, "proved to be Texas-style in length." The Democrats won thirty-seven new House seats and two in the Senate. [90]

Johnson had his mandate. Just as FDR's resounding re-election in 1936 had secured the liberal banner for his party, so Johnson's overwhelming triumph reaffirmed his illustrious predecessor's redefinition of rights. In fact, from the start, the very premise of Johnson's campaign had been that Goldwater's candidacy was illegitimate, that the Arizona Senator raised issues that had long been settled. This was not a contest between liberals and conservatives, he told the Democratic delegates who gathered in Atlantic City, nor was it a contest between parties. Rather, the cause was reaffirmation of freedom itself: "For more than 30 years, from

Social Security to the war against poverty, we have diligently worked to enlarge the freedom of man, and as a result Americans tonight are freer to live as they want to live, to pursue their ambition, to meet their desires, to raise their families than in any time in our glorious history."[91] The 1964 election results seemed to vindicate LBJ's claim that, for all intents and purposes, FDR's second bill of rights had become part of the American constitution. Goldwater's attempt to resurrect the Republicans as a party-against-administration—and his effort to pose a strident *political* challenge to the Roosevelt legacy—were buried beneath an avalanche of votes for the New Deal consensus.

Johnson viewed his immense victory over Goldwater as an opportunity to strengthen the nation's commitment to programmatic liberalism further. A major task in forging greater national unity was to build a more effective bridge with business. "When people did not like what Roosevelt was doing, he called them economic royalists and money-changers. He said they met their match and would meet their master," LBJ told Leuchtenburg. "It was like people fighting and spitting at one another."[92] To be sure, business was never united in its opposition to the New Deal. Roosevelt received considerable support from business leaders, who for self-interested or principled reasons saw liberal reform as beneficial. But LBJ wanted to overcome any lingering class tension resulting from FDR's assault on those who resented his denunciation of "unconscionable profits." Johnson responded enthusiastically to Henry Ford II's suggestion in August, 1964 that the president "convene [a group of business leaders] from time to time to discuss any business matter in which [he] might have an interest."[93] These "ex parte" contacts were institutionalized and expanded during the campaign. In 1936, Roosevelt had encouraged James Farley to work with independent citizen groups that might organize progressives who were inclined to support FDR but would not associate with the Democratic party. At the suggestion of James Rowe, Harry Truman had continued this practice. Now Rowe, who, along with Thomas Corcoran, had looked after the interests of LBJ after he came to Congress as a militant New Dealer, headed the 1964 campaign. The recruitment of business support, he believed, was the most noteworthy institutional development of that election effort, amplifying the formation of a distinct presidential coalition.[94]

LBJ's ties with business were not formed merely to bring industry and labor together. Johnson sought to strengthen the New Deal consensus as a foundation for additional reform, and business had an important part to play in this plan. Most important, the war on poverty, which was insufficiently funded from the start, was waged only by enlisting business support. The Office of Economic Opportunity, under the entrepreneurial leadership of Sergeant Shriver, worked out agreements with private corporations in 1965 to participate actively in the Job Corps program—these agreements included an $11.5 million contract with Federal Electric Corporation to operate a job training center at Camp Kilmer, New Jersey, and a $13.4 million contract to Litton Industries, Inc., to operate a similar installation in California. These agreements received considerable criticism—Litton and other companies were accused in some quarters of profiting unfairly from this government–business collaboration, "of sermonizing about social change all the way to the bank." But, in general, these agreements seemed to justify LBJ's consensual reform strategy. "Business finally seems to have arrived at the somewhat startling idea of accepting responsibility for alleviating the effects of some of the social change its technological advances have caused," noted the *Reporter* in 1965.[95]

The most serious fault-line beneath the New Deal political order was not class, however, but race. Johnson was determined to do something about civil rights; at the same time, the president and his aides fretted privately that the issue of race might crack up the New Deal coalition, and possibly cost LBJ the 1964 election. Citing "race prejudice" as the most "potent commodity" available to the opposition, Henry H. Wilson, an aide to White House legislative liaison director, Lawrence O'Brien, wrote in July, 1964: "I suggest that it is time someone said to the President what apparently no one has yet said to him—that he could lose this election, and that he could lose it despite having lined up all the press and television networks, all the top labor leaders, all the Negro vote, and perhaps even Lodge and Rockefeller." Wilson believed that the emergence of civil rights as a defining national issue represented a brand new situation in American politics, thus requiring that the president's campaign organization "throw all the rules out the window and play it by ear." When "race prejudice gets going," he warned "organized labor can move right out from under its leadership en masse."[96]

Wilson was not the only aide to express concern about LBJ's election prospects that summer. In fact, Horace Busby prepared a series of lengthy memoranda for LBJ in June and July, with the objective of taking a "hard-nosed look" at the Democratic attitude towards the 1964 campaign. These richly detailed and broadly conceived pieces are interesting not only for the advice they offered on the pending campaign, but also for the long-range view they expressed on the Democratic party, presidential leadership, and liberalism.

The most important matter that Busby urged LBJ to consider was the weakness of the Democratic party as a national party. Only when FDR ran for the presidency did the Democrats command a majority of voters, averaging 55 percent of the vote during his four campaigns. No Democrat since that time, Busby observed, including Truman in 1948, had even approached FDR's percentages. Indeed, the four non-FDR Democratic victories in the twentieth century prior to 1964 (Woodrow Wilson's in 1912 and 1916, Truman's in 1948, and Kennedy's in 1960) averaged only 46.6 percent of the popular vote. Thus, Busby averred, the "Roosevelt Revolution" had failed to secure the status of the Democratic party "as the 'majority party' of the nation in regard to the Presidency." Roosevelt did extend his party's influence so that it controlled more offices at the state and local level—hitherto a regionally based party, resting heavily on the solid South, the Democrats had come to regard their party as stronger "nationally." But this local interest support, Busby concluded, did not translate into Democratic presidential support: "As the local interest party, as the office-holding party—yes, Democrats are in the majority, decisively. As the presidential party, however, Democrats have lost the majority position since the last FDR race."[97]

This development is appropriately viewed as an ironic legacy of FDR's leadership and program—the institutional separation of presidential and party constituencies had left the Democrats weak at the presidential level and dominant, though still unreformed, at the state and local level. And yet, with the emergence of race as a central issue, FDR and his Democratic successors' only recourse in forging a progressive coalition was the presidency. Since FDR's third term and the formation of the Fair Employment Practices Committee, Democratic presidents had relied upon the powers of the executive office to pursue progress on racial matters. Finding themselves the tacit leaders of a party intractably divided between its Southern and Northern blocs, FDR and Truman had formed a direct link with progressives and blacks, thus encouraging an independent political posture among those supporters of reform who viewed the Democrats as the party of local interests, and even of vested interests, to whom genuine progress was an enigma. Thus, FDR had always tried to steer clear of the race issue, and Truman's efforts to make civil rights a central part of New Deal liberalism was frustrated by a recalcitrant Congress. Kennedy, like Truman before him, learned during his presidency that the pursuit of civil rights reform in Congress and the councils of the Democratic party was a futile endeavor that threatened to pull popular support out from under him.

As such, the enactment of the Civil Rights Act in 1964 threatened to weaken Democratic fortunes at the national level further. Roosevelt, Truman and Kennedy had managed to win elections by holding on to the South; yet, as Busby observed in a prescient memo of June 1964, "the resolution of the Civil Rights issues, coming as it has under a Democratic administration, does much more than remove the racial issue—it removes the basic 100-year premise for a Democratic solidity of the southern states."[98] LBJ's extraordinary triumph as legislative leader had strengthened the Democrats as the party of progress only to jeopardize the already difficult task of electing a Democratic president.

The fear that "white backlash"—the new phrase for white resentment of black gains through political action—was a glaring threat to the solidity of the New Deal coalition did not shake Johnson's determination to obtain civil rights progress through legislation and executive action. The enactment of the Civil Rights Act 6 weeks prior to the Democratic gathering in Atlantic City was a testament to Johnson's ability to extend his influence beyond his party and assemble a bipartisan coalition of progressive Democrats and moderate Republicans. LBJ's greatest leadership strength was personal persuasion, a talent he now used to break the long-standing deadlock between the president and Congress on domestic reform. He convinced the moderate Senate Republican leader from Illinois, Everett Dirksen, to support the bill and enlist moderate Republicans in the cause. Dirksen's support was critical to obtain the two-thirds vote necessary for cloture, a Senate resolution closing debate on legislation. Without such an order, Southern Democrats could defeat the bill, even though in a minority, by a filibuster, a strategy that was first employed effectively in 1937 in the struggle over the anti-lynching bill, and one frequently employed thereafter to obstruct civil rights measures.[99]

The Civil Rights legislation represented a dramatic reinvigoration of the president's preeminence as legislative leader. This achievement came as a result of LBJ's willingness to eschew party leadership in his dealings with Congress and place himself at the head of progressives and moderates of both parties.

Liberal Consensus and the Democratic Party

At the same time that he strengthened the Democratic party, Franklin Roosevelt had looked beyond it, seeking to form a direct link with liberal constituencies in a way that made the party less important. The Roosevelt legacy, as our story of the New Deal portrays, was an institutional separation of the presidency and party politics and the displacement of party politics by executive administration. In their own ways, Truman and Eisenhower reaffirmed the basic structure of the modern presidency—and gave further encouragement to the decline of the traditional party apparatus. John Kennedy, seeking to avoid the relative stasis of the Eisenhower years, felt somewhat trapped by this tradition, one that seemed more suited—after FDR—to management rather than the inspirational leadership for which he believed himself so well equipped. But LBJ saw the Roosevelt legacy not as a shackle, but as a source of inspiration to make his own unique mark on American history. LBJ recognized that the principles and institutions of the New Deal, when properly understood, could be a continuing source of progress.

Johnson had learned from FDR that the full splendor of modern executive leadership required looking beyond the boundaries of party politics, even while providing vigorous and assertive party leadership. Truman also understood this part of the Roosevelt legacy, although he acted on it with far more reluctance than Johnson would. As William S. White observed:

> Roosevelt, unlike Truman, thought consistently of the Democratic Party not as a traditional and all-sufficient body, but as a central weapon to which, given determination and luck, he would add other weapons seized from friendly political independents and unwary Republicans. Incessantly, he was trying to expand his base of power beyond his party; and most of the time this is precisely what he did. So, too, with Johnson.[100]

In many important respects, of course, Johnson's party leadership was very different from that of Roosevelt. LBJ's political career was built upon his position as party leader in the Senate, and, consequently, his administration was more intent upon collective responsibility than that of Roosevelt. As Vice President, Johnson pointed out to John Kennedy that FDR's purge campaign was ill-advised, and that in controversial matters such as Civil Rights, the president would be more successful in working with party leaders in the Congress and appealing to the "conscience of the nation" rather than in seeking to punish recalcitrant Democrats.[101] Moreover, when he became president, Johnson built the White House liaison operation, begun in the Eisenhower administration to sell the president's program on the Hill, into an intricate and remarkably successful conduit between the Executive and Congress. Unlike Roosevelt, Johnson pursued his reform program through a process that involved careful consultation with the party leadership in the legislature.[102] Because the Great Society involved not only a continuation but a significant departure from the New Deal, it required, in the short term, a revival of partisan politics. The passage of this ambitious program was made possible by the effective cooperation between the administration and the large Democratic majorities brought to Congress in 1964.

Although Johnson's background and political style were quite different from those of Roosevelt, there were important parallels between the leadership of these two reform presidents. LBJ avoided any sort of purge campaign, but he took strong action to deemphasize the role of the traditional party organization. In fact, according to Rowe, Johnson's neglect of the party machinery exceeded Roosevelt's disregard of the Democratic organization: "He (LBJ) just let it go to hell. He didn't believe in it. I have had arguments with him about it . . . he said, for instance, 'Oh, the Democratic Committee isn't important.' "[103] Whereas the Roosevelt presidency displaced party politics by circumventing the regular party machinery and emphasizing "nonpartisan" executive administration, the Johnson Administration carried out a much more direct assault on the Democratic organization. For example, the Johnson Administration undertook a ruthless attack on the Democratic National Committee beginning in late 1965, slashing its budget to the bone and eliminating the voter registration division. The president also ignored the pleas of several advisors to replace the uninspired leadership of John Bailey as DNC chairman. Instead, he humiliated Bailey, refusing to replace him, while turning control of the scaled-back committee activities over to the top political liaison in the White House, W. Marvin Watson.[104]

As a result of Johnson's disregard for the traditional party apparatus, the "Democratic" triumph of 1964 was short lived. The columnist Meg Greenfield reported in June, 1966 that:

> The President, whose critics have customarily portrayed him as a man obsessed with politics, is now being charged with indifference to the proper political concerns of a party leader. And the party that only eighteen months ago enjoyed electoral triumphs at every level of government is—according to many of its faithful—in a dangerous state of disrepair.[105]

Journalists and scholars have generally explained Johnson's lack of support for the regular party organization by pointing to his political background and personality traits. Some have suggested that Johnson was afraid the DNC might be built into a power center capable of challenging his authority. This fear apparently was tied to LBJ's suspicion that the formal organization, dominated by big city politics, was more sympathetic to the Kennedy wing of the party.[106] Others have claimed that Johnson's "consensus" politics was a product of one-party politics in Texas; for this reason, it has been alleged, LBJ's presidency was based on a far more personal and diverse coalition than were the Roosevelt and Kennedy administrations. According to columnist David Broder, such an unmanageable coalition, including business and labor, black and white, North and South, could not be held together very long.[107]

These explanations, which point to the idiosyncracies of Johnson's leadership style and personal conflicts, are surely not without merit. Roosevelt believed that party leadership should be deemphasized but not abandoned, but Johnson, after 1964, seemed neither to appreciate nor to understand that sort of subtlety. Johnson's political gifts were unmatched in moving the machinery of government to accommodate programmatic change, but he lacked what the political scientist John Roche, who served as an aide to LBJ, calls Roosevelt's "magnificent duplicitous charm," which was necessary to rally enduring political support for those programs. According to Roche, LBJ's failings as a political leader were not only attributable to his Texas heritage, but also to the inappropriateness of his experience as majority leader of the Senate:

> LBJ never really played in the big leagues. Most of his political career was in the Senate, where he could cut deals. LBJ found that those techniques did not work well in the goldfish bowl of the White House. He was an inside operator. . . . He always wanted to know what your bottom line was. He was born without an ideological chromosome.[108]

Yet, if Johnson was not ideological, he surely was, as president, an ardent reformer. And to view his failings as a party leader in such personal terms is to ignore the imperative of policy reform that inspired his Administration. Like Franklin Roosevelt, Lyndon Johnson "had always regarded political parties, strongly rooted in states and localities, capable of holding him accountable, as intruders on the business of government."[109] From the beginning of his presidency, Johnson envisioned the creation of an ambitious program that would leave its mark on history not only in civil rights but in the areas of conservation, education, and urban problems. Johnson's successful battle for the 1964 Civil Rights Act dazzled the liberal members of his party, many of whom had resented his elevation to the presidency. "Many people felt we should rest after the victory of the 1964 Civil Rights Act, take it easy on Congress, and leave some breathing space for the bureaucracy and the nation," Johnson wrote in his memoirs. "But," he added, "there was no time to rest."[110] The racial tensions that erupted in riots during the summer of 1964, and his desire to move the nation well beyond the boundaries of the New Deal towards what he called the Great Society, made LBJ impatient to push on.[111] The results of the 1964 election provided him an opportunity to do so. LBJ was determined to use his temporary advantage to act on a vision that went beyond the liberal tradition of the New Deal.

Johnson had first unveiled his ambitious plans for reform on May 22, 1964, in a speech at the University of Michigan. In those remarks he boldly set the tone for the Great Society, viewing past reform aspirations only as a point of departure:

> The Great Society rests on abundance and liberty for all. It demands an end of poverty and racial justice, to which we are totally committed in our time. But this is just the beginning.
>
> The Great Society is a place where every child can find knowledge to enrich his mind and to enlarge his talents. It is a place where leisure is a welcome chance to build and reflect, not a feared cause of boredom and restlessness. It is a place where the city of man serves not only the needs of the body and the demands of commerce but the desire for beauty and the hunger for community.[112]

This vision of reform gave rise to a program of extraordinary scope, which was put before the 89th Congress when it convened in 1965. With this program, LBJ proposed that the commitments of programmatic liberalism be extended to tasks such as educational opportunity, urban renewal, environmentalism, highway beautification, and consumer protection. As noted earlier, historian William Leuchtenburg was somewhat startled to hear LBJ diminish—sometimes arrogantly—the accomplishments of FDR in a 1965 interview. But there was a method to the president's madness. The day before the interview Johnson received a memo from Bill Moyers, written to "prep" LBJ for his conversation with Professor Leuchtenburg. Moyers informed the president that Leuchtenberg would likely be interested in comparing FDR and LBJ, especially with respect to the programmatic departures represented by the Great Society. "Here I think the thing to do is discuss in a general way the need for turning away from considerations of quantity (except for the poverty ridden 1/5 of the nation) to those of the quality of our lives," Moyers suggested.[113]

This shift from concern with the "quantity" to the "quality" of life in America was the vehicle by which LBJ hoped to become "a national interest leader," to surpass FDR's "bloc-by-bloc politics." Given this context, LBJ's braggadocio was not simply self-aggrandizement, and his consensus politics were more than a national version of cutting a deal on the Senate floor or splitting up the Texas delegation between rival power factions. His actions were rooted in his assessment that American political life was threatened by the indignities, loneliness, and indifference of mass industrial society.

The social movements of the 1960s, LBJ and his aides believed, revealed that America was ready for such a change. "The civil rights revolution demonstrated not only the power and possibility of organized protest, but the unsuspected fragility of resistance to liberating changes," notes Richard Goodwin, who drafted the Ann Arbor speech.[114] Indeed, the civil rights movement established the model for other social movements that grew out of the 1960s—the feminist movement, consumerism, environmentalism. Another social movement for which civil rights politics was paradigmatic, the anti-war movement, would help drive LBJ from office. But in the relatively halcyon early days of LBJ's stewardship, Goodwin, and the president himself, envisioned such social forces as the potential livelihood for a new generation of reform. "Johnson intended to align himself with the cause of blacks and women and consumers," Goodwin claims. "And I saw [their cause] as evidence that the country was ready for leadership committed to social change."[115]

In discussing his preparation of Johnson's landmark Great Society speech, Goodwin credits some of the ideas of the New Left. He reflected on the Port Huron Manifesto, for example, which was issued in 1962 by the newly formed Students for a Democratic Society (SDS). One aspect of that address, in particular, impressed the presidential aide as expressing a yearning that went well beyond the utopian vision of radical fringe groups, and was shared by a great many Americans:

> Some would have us believe that Americans feel contentment amidst prosperity—but might it not better be called a glaze above deeply felt anxieties about their role in the new world? And if these anxieties produce a developed indifference to human affairs, do they not as well produce a yearning to believe there *is* an alternative to the present, that something *can* be done to change circumstances in

the school, the workplaces, the bureaucracies, the government? It is to this latter yearning, at once the spark and agent of change, that we direct our present appeal.[116]

It is not easy to imagine Lyndon Johnson embracing New Left doctrine. But Goodwin avers, not without reason, that such ideas corresponded "to Lyndon Johnson's own impulses, could help to define and fuel the large purposes he wished to pursue."[117] The ideas that animated social movements of the 1960s were not so far afield from certain aspects of the New Deal, parts of the reform impulse of the 1930s that Johnson understood well. Johnson's first government job was to serve as Texas Director of the National Youth Administration (NYA)—one of the few New Deal agencies singled out by the 1943 National Resources Planning Board report for avoiding bureaucratic torpor, and for effectively linking itself to the grass roots aspirations of the people it served. "Those NYA experiences were valuable to me," LBJ wrote in his memoirs, "suggesting some of the solutions we were searching for in the present."[118]

Still, Johnson's bold leadership was tempered by reticence. In the final analysis, the New Deal represented an abiding commitment to "enlightened administration." LBJ prepared to domesticate social causes and movements to presidential government after the election. In doing so, he badly misjudged the difficulty of expanding the liberal coalition to movements that, as Bruce Miroff observes, were in "the process of exploding the usual categories of American group politics."[119] This miscalculation, one suspects, demonstrates just how unreconstructed a New Dealer LBJ was.

Although in some respects the expansion of liberalism during the Johnson presidency suggested that a new philosophy of government had supplanted the principles of the New Deal, the *institutional* legacy of Roosevelt played a critical part in this departure. During FDR's second term, New Deal liberalism was inextricably linked with a program to enhance the administrative capacities of the national government. Such a program was pursued in order to shift the "bias" of constitutional government from the restraint of provincial (partisan) democracy to the energy of progressive (executive-oriented) democracy. This did not overcome the diversity of interests fostered by the original constitutional design, but shifted the locus of interest activity from the more decentralized institutions to the executive branch. The development of political administration dramatically transformed the character of American pluralism: a system of competing particularistic interests, whereby "ambition counteracted ambition," as Madison put it in *Federalist* 51, was subordinated to satisfying the *programmatic* ambitions that were central to the reconstituted executive. Thus, as the Brownlow Commission anticipated, the playing out of administrative reform meant that ambitious policy action was no longer a matter of crisis intervention—or "critical" realignment—but an expected and routine part of everyday American political life.

Until the 1960s, government still restricted its support to genuine constituencies in distress and its tasks to the objective of economic security. With the advent of a liberalism dedicated to enhancing the "quality" as well as the "quantity" of American life, government extended its beneficence to self-styled public-interest groups that represented broader constituencies, and sometimes deliberately rejected anything resembling clientele politics. As the historian Paul Conkin notes about the Great Society: ''. . . more than ever before in American history, an administration moved beyond a response to pressing constituency pressures, beyond crisis-induced legislative action, to a studied, carefully calculated effort to identify problems and to create the needed constituencies to help solve them.'' [120]

The identification of these problems and the creation of these constituencies necessarily brought the Johnson Administration into sharp conflict with the still unreconstructed Democratic party. The Johnson administration's lack of confidence in the Democratic party reinforced its inclination to renew the New Deal pattern of institutional reform. It extended the development started by the Roosevelt Administration to sacrifice partisan politics in order to extend the responsibility of the presidency to wrestle with an ever-expanding number of complex problems. This commitment to executive management presupposed that collective action within the party councils be subordinated to presidential dominance of party deliberations. Chief legislative aide Larry O'Brien counselled Johnson regarding party matters in January, 1964:

> . . . [A]spects of fund distribution should be thoroughly reviewed as we must ensure a stronger presidential role in this area. I should add that this applies to all areas of patronage. You will receive maximum benefit only if it is handled on a completely professional basis under your direction. Any diffusion of this activity will be politically costly and I am sure that applies equally in all areas of party leadership and campaign activity. [121]

The aforementioned virtual dismantlement of the DNC indicates that the Johnson Administration's centralization of functions within the White House that normally were performed by the regular party organization was aimed at marginalizing rather than reforming the American Party system. As Busby says of Johnson's presidential leadership, ''Because of the ambitious reforms that he pushed, it was necessary to move well beyond, to suspend attention to, the party.'' [122] In the next chapter, we will observe how LBJ's disavowal of party leadership not only threatened the party system, but summoned up a challenge to the modern presidency as well.

8

The Twilight of the Modern Presidency: The Troubled Times and Institutional Legacy of Lyndon Johnson

In the initial push towards a Great Society, Lyndon Johnson and the 89th Congress (1965–1966) left an unparalleled record. "No [Congress] since Reconstruction," Theodore White observed, "or perhaps since Roosevelt's 73rd Congress of 1933–34, did more to reorder the nation. . . ."[1] In 1965 alone, Congress passed eighty of the Johnson administration's proposals, while it denied him only three. These measures included such important policy departures as Medicare, Medicaid, the Civil Rights Act of 1965 (pertaining to voting rights), the Elementary and Secondary Education Act, the War on Poverty, the Air Pollution Control Act, and legislation to establish the Department of Transportation and the Department of Housing and Urban Development.

By 1967, Johnson's political consensus had crumbled. A recrudescence of urban riots and the eroding support for the Vietnam War left LBJ trapped politically at home, strategically in Southeast Asia. "The whole situation was unbearable for me," he told his biographer Doris Kearns. "After thirty-seven years of public service," Johnson added, "I deserved something more than being left alone in the middle of the plain, chased by stampedes on every side."[2]

In retrospect, it seems, LBJ had tried to accomplish too much, to assume too many of the problems of governance and for that mistake, he saw his consensus unravel.[3] But according to Harry McPherson, who served as Special Counsel in the Johnson administration between 1964 and 1969, it was not the blindness of LBJ's pride that caused him to stumble and fall; rather, it was a revolt of the generation the president expected to lead that resulted in his undoing:

> Johnson was a manipulator of men when there was a rejection of power politics; he was a believer in institutions at a time when spontaneity was being celebrated; he was a paternalist when parental authority was being rejected; and he came to political maturity during the 1930s, when democracy was threatened by fascism and communism, making him an unbending anti-communist.[4]

Nevertheless, Johnson's presidency also helped to initiate the assault on prevailing institutions during the 1960s and 1970s. For in seeking to surpass the accomplishments of Franklin Roosevelt and the New Deal, LBJ unwittingly encouraged the rise of an administrative politics that extensively circumscribed the power of the presidency. During the 1960s and 1970s, statutes were enacted and federal court rulings were pronounced that greatly reduced the discretionary power of the president and administrative agencies. Furthermore, institutional procedures were designed to foster "participatory democracy," that is, to give "power at the level of immediate impact directly to those people most affected by government policy."[5] The emergence of a new version of programmatic liberalism during the Johnson presidency, inspired by a concern to depart from the New Deal, was the first cause of this fundamental change in the institutional fabric of American politics.

Most significant, the liberalism of the Great Society, holding that the problems of America were more of "the spirit than of the flesh," envisioned moving beyond the New Deal *economic* constitutional order. LBJ had first unveiled his plans for reform in May, 1964 at the University of Michigan. He remained strongly committed to this program, even as he took America into a war in Southeast Asia. In Johnson's 1966 State of the Union address, he declared that the Great Society led the nation along three roads—economic growth, "justice" for all races, and finally "liberation," which would utilize the economic success of the nation, so robust at this stage of the country's history, for the "fulfillment of our lives":

> A great people flower not from wealth and power, but from a society which spurs them to the fullness of their genius. That alone is the Great Society. . . . Yet slowly, painfully, on the edge of victory, has come the knowledge that shared prosperity is not enough. In the midst of abundance modern man walks oppressed by forces which menace and confine the quality of his life, and which individual abundance alone will not overcome.

There followed a list of noneconomic goals: an expansion of health and education programs; the rebuilding of entire sections and neighborhoods in urban areas to establish "a flourishing community where our people can come to live the good life"; a stronger effort to put an end to the "continued poisoning of our rivers and air"; a Highway Safety Act to seek an end to "the destruction of life and property on our highways"; and action to prevent the deception of the American consumer.[6]

With his 1966 State of the Union Address, LBJ forcefully presented himself as more than a power broker, and more, even, than a codifier of the New Deal vision of a good society. Johnson may have lacked FDR's bonhomie and rhetorical ability, but through a relentless pursuit of innovation he had managed to put his own stamp upon the programmatic liberal tradition.

Firmly rooted in FDR's tradition, Lyndon Johnson would seek to uphold, indeed forcefully expand upon, the integrity of the modern presidency. An improved quality of life, he proposed in his 1966 State of the Union message, required that he "take steps to modernize and streamline the executive branch," as well as "the relations between city and state and nation."[7] Yet LBJ's view of the Great Society presupposed a "hunger for community" that suggested the limits of presidential government. Implicit in the philosophy of liberalism that emerged during the 1960s was the view that problems afflicting the well-to-do and poor could not be solved by centralized administration and federal largess alone, but required a more creative intervention of the state that would address the underlying causes of social and political discontent: the decline of community, alienation, and powerlessness. In this sense, the assault on the modern presidency that began towards the end of the Johnson presidency went beyond discontent over the war—it was animated by reform aspirations to which LBJ dedicated himself that sought to advance the human condition well beyond the dominant concerns of the New Deal.

It has often been asserted that the weakening of the party system after 1968 accentuated the decline in the authority and influence of the presidency during the 1960s and 1970s. Most significant, party leaders were virtually stripped of their authority to nominate presidential candidates, displaced by a selection process dominated by primary elections and participatory caucuses. Donald Horowitz has argued that this weakening of political parties left presidents without any reliable basis of popular support: "A president can no longer depend on a large core of committed supporters who will stay with him through thick and thin. Likewise, with the tenuous bonds of common party across the branches loosened further by changes in the presidential nominating process, there is less restraint in Congress on benefitting from a protracted [presidential] crisis."[8]

Nevertheless, presidents in the twentieth century, especially those committed to progressive reform, had found party politics to be more of an obstacle to leadership than an asset. Herbert Croly, it seemed, had spoken truth to power: He had presciently condemned parties in the United States as the cornerstone of an old order that celebrated democratic individualism and presumed the absence of centralized administrative authority. As was the case with the New Deal, the expansion of national administrative capacities during the creation of the Great Society tended to insulate the activities of the White House and public agencies from the party apparatus. Indeed, the extraordinary animus LBJ felt towards partisan politics, and the new, less circumspect phase of liberalism represented by the Great Society, accelerated the declining influence of party leaders. Johnson's assault on the regular party machinery, discussed in Chapter 7, foretold of more serious things to come—the crack-up of the Democratic party over the travails of Vietnam and race at the 1968 Democratic convention and the party reforms that followed in its wake.

Thus, the insurgency that was to challenge the modern presidency and the regular party apparatus was facilitated by long-developing institutional changes that came to a head during the Johnson administration. In fact, the party reforms initiated by the McGovern–Fraser Commission were the culmination of developments that began during the 1930s. The national reform fostered by the New Deal shifted the locus of power away from the traditional party apparatus, as well as the more decentralizing institutions—Congress and State governments. This gave rise to a politics of administration that depended primarily upon a revamped presidency for coherence and energy. The more the emergent "presidential branch of government" preempted the party organization in its limited but significant tasks, the less vital and vigilant that organization became. Such a trend was extended during the creation of the Great Society, ultimately leading to the creation of a fully developed political and policy network outside of the regular political process. In the development of domestic policy, especially, the Johnson administration made a significant push to preempt traditional political channels, and, eventually, efforts in this direction also became prominent in the areas of staffing and campaigns, thus laying the foundation for the disintegration of parties that became so visible after the 1968 Democratic convention. It is ironic that by contributing so much to this development, Lyndon Johnson helped construct the road that eventually enabled insurgents to challenge his presidency successfully.

The Great Society and the Institution of the Presidency

The program development of the Great Society gave new meaning to the idea of a *president's* program. More and more policies began to be invented by the politically appointed policy advocates in the West Wing, who were dedicated to moving quickly on the President's agenda. Concomitantly, career staff in the regular line agencies and the long-time institutional policy analysis professionals in the budget bureau became less influential in legislative program development.

To a point, Johnson's dominance of the political process was an extension of developments that began under Kennedy. Kennedy's promise to "get the country moving again" reflected a desire for policy innovation that was inconsistent with the practice prior to the 1960s of letting domestic proposals emerge methodically through the executive branch agencies, undergoing screening and clarification in the Bureau of the Budget. As a consequence, policy-making initiatives began to shift during JFK's administration from the routines and institutional channels established during the Truman and Eisenhower years. This change originated with Kennedy, but reached fruition under Johnson. Indeed, this personalization of the executive office was not only extended during the Johnson years, but institutionalized. In terms of policy development, one of the most significant innovations of the Johnson administration was the creation of several task forces under the supervision of White House aide Joseph Califano. Califano's work had an enduring effect on the modern presidency—the group of task forces he assembled was the precursor of the Domestic Policy Council, established by Johnson's successor, Richard Nixon, and the domestic policy staffs that have continued to be a feature of later administrations.[9]

In a sense, the task forces represented the Johnson administration's objective of restoring the reformist zeal that had characterized the Roosevelt presidency. They were, in effect, the Great Society's answer to the National Resources Planning Board, which issued reports dedicated to spurring the New Deal towards an expansive concept of the welfare state. In this endeavor, however, the NRPB was used by FDR as much as it stirred him. So it was with Johnson and the task forces. Roosevelt was the first president to welcome the community of social science as the best center of advice regarding programmatic and administrative reform, yet this advice was carefully orchestrated to serve his political objectives. Similarly, LBJ's obsession with the academy often sacrificed its declared commitment to objectivity to the demands of developing the blueprint for the Great Society.

The Great Society task forces were made up of leading academics throughout the country who prepared reports during the Johnson presidency in all areas of public policy, including government organization, education, environmental quality, and urban planning. Several specific proposals that came out of these meetings, such as the Education Task Force's elementary-education proposal, became public policy, forming the heart of the Great Society program. The Johnson Administration took great care to protect the work of these organizations from political pressures, even keeping the task force procedure secret. Moreover, members were told to pay no attention to any political considerations; they were not to worry about whether their recommendations would be acceptable to Congress or to party leaders.[10]

The deemphasis on partisan politics during the creation of the Great Society was also apparent in the personnel policy of the Johnson presidency. For his political talent scout Johnson chose not a political advisor but John Macy, who was also Chairman of the Civil Service Commission. During the Eisenhower years, Philip Young combined the roles of Chair of the Civil Service Commission and Presidential Advisor on Personnel Management. But Young's influence on personnel matters was subordinate to White House aide Charles Willis, who had the difficult task in managing appointments of balancing the claims of the "Citizens for Eisenhower," the party, and the Civil Service Commission. Macy's position was a more powerful one, signifying Johnson's unprecedented interest in subordinating party and, for a time, personal loyalty to the objective of programmatic innovation. Macy did work closely with the White House staff, but, especially during the earlier days of the Administration, he was responsible for making direct recommendations to the president. As the White House staff rather grudgingly admitted, Macy's "wheel ground exceedingly slow but excessively fine."[11] Candidates with impressive credentials and experience were yielded after careful nationwide searches.

The strong commitment to "merit" in the Johnson Administration greatly disturbed certain advisors who were responsible for maintaining LBJ's political support. In particular, Johnson's campaign director in both 1964 and 1968, James Rowe, constantly hounded Macy, without success, to consider more carefully political loyalists. In answer to one of Macy's sympathetic, albeit nonforthcoming, responses to his pleadings, Rowe wrote back:

> I am delighted to learn from your note of September 25th that you are grateful for my words of wisdom and encouragement.
>
>   However that ain't what I want! What I want are some Democrats appointed to something.[12]

Rowe's battles with Macy are noteworthy and ironic, for as a charter member of the White House Office he performed Macy's role for the Roosevelt Administration, upholding the principle of "merit" against the patronage requests of DNC chairman James Farley and his successor, Ed Flynn.[13] Yet Rowe believed Johnson's personnel policy was gratuitously inattentive to political exigencies. As he berated Macy in an April, 1965 memo ". . . perhaps you can train some of those career men to run the political campaign in 1968. (It ain't as easy as you government people appear to think it is.)" Macy never responded, but the president called the next day to defend the policies of his personnel director, and give Rowe "hell" for seeking to interfere in the appointment process.[14]

Paradoxically, in order to compensate for his reputation as an unprincipled horse-trader, Johnson committed himself to what was widely regarded as an excessively principled stewardship of government. In September, 1967, White House aide John Roche wrote LBJ a candid memo, urging that he "obliterate" the memory of the 1964 election. "If you had spent the fall months at the Ranch, relaxing, you would probably had gotten the same vote." The reemergence of racial tension and the expanding commitment in Vietnam ensured that 1968 would be different. "Build an effective national political organization," Roche recommended. "You didn't need one in 1964, but in 1968 organization will be crucial. DNC Chairman John Bailey is out of his depth."[15] Although he appreciated this sort of candor, Johnson made no such effort to strengthen the party, and Bailey was kept on against the advice of Roche and others. "I heard rumors you were a politician," Roche remembers telling Johnson, "but have no evidence of it."[16]

The conflict between the Johnson Administration and the regular party apparatus came to a head in January, 1967 following the Democrats' very poor showing in the 1966 elections. GOP gains were the greatest in 20 years, as Republicans netted forty-seven House seats, three Senate seats, and eight governorships. In the state legislative races, the Republicans more than recovered the heavy losses suffered in 1964—this was, as the highly regarded Chairman of the Republican National Committee Ray Bliss put it, a "victory in depth."[17] Bliss's organizational success contrasted sharply with the meager efforts of the Democratic machinery, which was widely blamed for the party's poor showing. A correspondent for the *Washington Star* reported after the election that Democrats in the nation's capital and across the country were "angered by how little help they got from Washington in terms of money and services." Many traced the problem back to what Johnson had done to the DNC. "The Democratic National Committee is basically a shell," commented Eugene Wyman, a national committee member for California. "In the next two years, the party organization must be rebuilt. If it does not come soon, there may be a general disintegration of Democratic organizations throughout the country." Commenting on the drumbeat of discontent with LBJ's party leadership, Marianne Means wrote in the *Philadelphia Inquirer* on November 16: "A President is not only Chief Executive but leader of his party. The Democratic National Committee and the state organizations are his political arm just as the White House staff and the Cabinet are his administrative arm. But in the past two years President Johnson has sawed off one of these arms."[18]

A few members of the White House staff, most notably John Roche, agreed with this assessment. Roche's concern was strongly supported by a lengthy report on the election prepared by Richard Scanlon, which was passed on to the President by the "born-again" party man, Rowe, on January 6, 1967. "It is clear that the Republicans beat us by out organizing us, getting out their vote," Scanlon's report argued. To be sure, the Democratic losses were aggravated by intraparty fights, especially with respect to the race issue, the only issue on which the party seemed to have lost in the traditionally loyal blue-collar precincts. But there was no need "to panic and retreat from the Great Society," the report claimed. Many Democrats who went down the line for the Johnson administration were sent back to Congress, and many of those who were not generally lost by the smallest of margins. Thus, concluded Scanlon, the 1966 losses could be made up 2 years hence, but only with careful attention to party leadership and nuts and bolts organization. To begin this resurrection, Scanlon recommended that LBJ make a dramatic gesture towards strengthening the place of the party in his administration:

> To revitalize his party, to give it a sense of unity under vigorous leadership, and ultimately to have the best vehicle for getting out the Democratic vote in 1968, *the President, as a first step, must publicly and ostentatiously select a competent man to be the Chairman of the Democratic National Committee—and then he must actually give him some power, a budget and the authority to carry out his task. It is more important that the Chairmen have needed access to the President than that he be famous or particularly articulate.*
>
> What the Democratic party structure must understand is that the Chairman has the ear of the President, and, more important, the *confidence* of the President. This will be visible when the patronage operation begins to make use of the DNC itself and (through the DNC) the Democratic leadership throughout the country.[19]

"This analysis is not brilliant," Rowe opined in an attached letter, "but it is good and I agree with almost all of it."[20] Getting word of the quiet consultation LBJ had begun with his aides on what to do about the Democratic organization, party regulars speculated hopefully about a major overhauling of the DNC. A change in the DNC leadership seemed imminent. An array of Democratic leaders, including Vice President Hubert Humphrey, supported Postmaster General Larry O'Brien, who had so distinguished himself in running LBJ's congressional liaison team, as the perfect man for the job.

As it turned out, of course, expectant party loyalists badly misread LBJ's intentions. He neither dismissed Bailey nor modified the party chairman's marginal position—for the rest of Johnson's presidency Bailey would remain a figurehead, nothing more. Johnson did hold a private meeting with the party chairman at the White House on January 7, and gave him general directives for expanding the committee's operations. But the President and Bailey were not able to satisfy their differences over appointments. Bailey complained that personnel decisions were cleared with the DNC in a purely perfunctory manner; Macy virtually demanded clearance, giving little real choice to party leaders. But Johnson argued that Macy's intransigent position reflected the failure of the party, rooted in the states and localities, "to furnish qualified persons." Bailey understood the Administration's concerns about credentials, but asked for some compromise, citing the state of Connecticut, where patronage appointments were very helpful to the party organization. In the end, LBJ and Bailey agreed to disagree.[21] This confrontation, occurring amidst a fire storm of criticism of the president's party leadership, suggests the degree to which Johnson was willing to deemphasize partisanship in the interest of advancing the "professionalism" of the Great Society.

Johnson's decision to retain Bailey as party chair was never officially announced, but as word got out, the president's forbearance was widely interpreted to mean that the badly needed rehabilitation of the DNC was a remote possibility. Party leaders in Washington and the states correctly surmised that Bailey's retention meant that real control over the party would remain at the White House, with day-to-day problems handled by White House aide W. Marvin Watson. As had been the case since LBJ slashed the committee's operations in 1965, Watson would continue to run the party machinery "out of his back pocket," as John Roche put it, according it little significance in the overall scheme of things.[22] Thus, when Rowe assumed the position as head of Citizens for Johnson–Humphrey, the president's re-election organization, in early 1968, his worst fears about the state of the party had been realized—it was in shambles. The window dressing additions to the DNC staff Johnson had allowed in early 1967 had only alienated the three deputy chairs brought in to bolster its operations. Two of the three, frustrated with the administration's disregard for party matters, had resigned, and one, Billie Sunday Farnum, who headed the important registration division, was rendered inactive by a pitifully inadequate staff and budget.

Clearly, the rupture between the presidency and the party system made it difficult to sustain political enthusiasm and organizational support for the Great Society. Yet Johnson and most of his advisors felt that this deemphasis on partisanship was necessary in order to achieve programmatic reform and coordinate more effectively the increasingly unwieldy activities of government.

As in the case of the New Deal, however, the institutional innovations of the Great Society did not truly eliminate "politics," or separate politics from the activities of the executive department. Rather, the Great Society extended the merging of politics and administration that characterized reform of the Executive Department during the 1930s. In program development and staffing the Johnson Administration attempted to transcend *party politics* in order to strengthen and enlarge the focus of *presidential politics*.

For example, in order to improve his use of the appointment process as a tool of political administration, Johnson issued an executive order on November 17, 1966 to create a new category of positions, called Noncareer Executive Assignments (NEAs). In recognition of their direct involvement in policy making and advocacy, NEAs were exempted from the usual civil service requirements. Johnson, like Eisenhower, established noncareer positions to enhance the responsiveness of the bureaucracy to his directives. The Schedule "C" positions created by Eisenhower typically included high-level posts in agencies, but also reached to a number of lower-level jobs, where the connection to policy seemed remote. As noted in Chapter 7, the Eisenhower initiative was motivated by the modest concern of the first Republican administration in 20 years to enable its top political executives to surround themselves with a few political loyalists. In contrast, the Executive Assignment System LBJ created was focused exclusively on the so-called "super-grades" of the federal service and stimulated by a more ambitious reform objective. The concern was to transform the ranks of the highest civil service by designating a new grade of top civil servants who could be promoted and transferred at the discretion of the president, thus breaking down the rigid rules regarding promotion and job assignment that had traditionally safeguarded civil service employees from executive control.[23]

The NEA established the framework for the Senior Executive System, an elite corps of civil servants created by the 1978 Civil Service Reform Act.[24] The stated promise of the executive assignment system would never be actualized. During the Reagan years, especially, it would be subjected to a political assault reflecting a rejection of the view that there were benefits to be gained by using the knowledge of the civil service. Attention to excellence, in fact, although hardly beside the point, was not the principal part of Johnson's executive order. Creating a new category of positions meant, in effect, a cut-back of the competitive civil service, thus exposing the bureaucracy to greater political control.

To be sure, NEAs gave Johnson a stronger foothold in the agencies. But the criteria his administration used to fill these positions emphasized loyalty to Johnson's program rather than a more narrow personal commitment to the president. The principles to which this program was dedicated, moreover, envisioning an expansive and novel role for government, tended to boost the status and morale of the federal service.

Consequently, Johnson's role as manager of the federal service, which Macy considered unprecedented for a "modern-day Chief Executive," helped to revive the high morale and programmatic commitment that had characterized the bureaucracy during the 1930s.[25] As Bill Moyers noted in a memo to LBJ recommending appointments to the newly created Department of Housing and Urban Development, the goal of the Great Society was to renew "some of the zeal—coupled with sound, tough executive management—of the New Deal days."[26]

The attempt to marry programmatic commitment with technical competence also characterized the work of the Johnson task forces. Each of the outside task forces generated proposals that conformed with Johnson's vision of a Great Society. Moreover, each included both government officials and professors in order to construct what Moyers described as an "umbilical cord" from the campus to Washington. Finally, all task force proposals, as well as staffing decisions, were carefully imbued with the political concerns of the Executive Office and the president, so that Johnson could put forth a reasonably comprehensive program that established his political identity.[27]

The early years of the Johnson administration marked the historical zenith of "presidential government." The White House and the Executive Office of the president had been increasingly active in formulating and carrying out programs since the administration of Franklin Roosevelt. Under Johnson, however, political and policy responsibility centered on the presidency in an unprecedented fashion. Major policy departures were conceived by White House emissaries, expeditiously moved through Congress by the extraordinary legislative skill of the president and his sophisticated legislative liaison team, and administered either by newly created or refurbished executive agencies geared to respond to presidential directives. Finally, Johnson virtually completed efforts that began during the Roosevelt administration to establish a presidential coalition. Johnson drew on political support that, in the final analysis, had little to do with the Democratic party. More than any of his predecessors, including Kennedy, David Broder wrote in 1966, LBJ's leadership and program depended "for its success largely on the skill, negotiating ability, and maneuvering of the president."[28]

Soon, however, Johnson overextended himself. LBJ was a gifted politician, but could not be the kind of leader that was required by the very office he helped to create. LBJ's troubles in managing the "personal" side of presidential leadership were foretold early on by Thomas Corcoran, one of FDR's extraordinary men, who kept a close watch on the skilled Texas politician from the time of his arrival in the House of Representatives. After watching Johnson become Senate majority leader in 1955, and master the upper chamber's centrifugal forces in a way that had not been seen since the heyday of "party government" at the end of the nineteenth century, Corcoran wrote a most prescient letter to the rising star of national politics. Addressed to "Lady Bird and Lyndon," this note of November 10, 1955 anticipated great things for Johnson while offering remarkably clear-sighted observations about his shortcomings. After noting that LBJ's political assets were "unmatchably enormous," Corcoran wrote:

> Lyndon can't keep out of politics because, as Holmes said, "To live is to function: there is no other point in living"; and Lyndon's functioning is politics. But . . . the greater political functioning of Lyndon now is to find a broadening out of his interests in life that relieves his concentration on the infighting of politics and gives his subconscious time to function. His energy has successfully broken him through the gravitational pull that yanks down ordinary politicians who don't "work" every minute. Lyndon's now beyond that pull and he can be confident that his host of admirers know his business as he has taught it to them and they will not let his mundane missions drop. To grow further what he needs now is to find out how to get enough fun so that living comes easier.
>
> That's what FDR found out at a stage when his mastery was infinitely less than Lyndon's. It is good politics as well as good living to play dominoes with your girls, to talk small talk with your wife and neighbors and to enjoy a football game. It makes it easier not to be afraid of you because you are too damned brilliant and too damned efficient.[29]

There was no chance that LBJ could acquire the "duplicitous charm" that came so easily to FDR. He was never able to disguise his gargantuan ambition or camouflage his lust for power. Nor was he able to slough off, as FDR could, what was said and written about him. LBJ's inability to relieve his concentration on the infighting of politics inspired fear rather than adoration. Consequently, he was never comfortable in the White House, never able to display those qualities that modern presidential pundits describe as charisma. It might be argued, of course, that LBJ's failure in this regard could just as easily be viewed as a virtue—as a justifiable unwillingness to partake of those aspects of the modern presidency that threatened the fabric of constitutional government.[30]

Still, Johnson's distaste for and discomfort with democratic politics went beyond a healthy aversion to demagogy. As Corcoran anticipated, he failed to understand and come to terms with the political qualities that were essential to provide the solid benefits of constitutional administration. Walter Lippman once wrote of Herbert Hoover that he was "diffident in the presence of the normal irrationality of democracy.''[31] So it was with Lyndon Johnson, and yet, unlike the reticent Hoover, LBJ did want to excite the nation, to free it from the administrative boredom he and his aides feared the New Deal had become. Johnson felt best able to do so with his laws and policies, but was to learn that he was unable to cultivate a stable basis of popular support for his domestic programs. Thus it was with a genuine sense of regret that he told Walter Cronkite in 1969, during the first of a series of television interviews, that his disadvantage as a leader could be succinctly described as "a general inability to stimulate, inspire and unite all the people of the country, which I think is an essential function of the Presidency.''[32]

In general, LBJ considered the political demands of the presidency—the need to be re-elected, to appeal to political groups, to arouse public support—a distraction from the real tasks of government. Such a view led Johnson to favor less frequent elections, and he urged a four-year term for the House of Representatives and a president elected for a single, six-year term without the possibility of re-election.[33]

The modern presidency had evolved from a concept of executive power that viewed the presidency as both the educator and instrument of public will. Johnson's discomfort with the tasks of popular leadership, however, inclined him to reject the normal tasks of democratic governance in the hope of satisfying programmatic ambitions that might serve the long-term interest of the nation. Yet LBJ's "gargantuan aspirations" magnified the political burdens of the modern executive, as well as his own limitations as a popular leader. In a sense the enormous aspiration and scope of the legislative program enacted under Johnson was a recipe for failure. This necessarily led to hastily packaged programs and unrealistic policy goals. LBJ wanted to be a national leader of reconciliation, and he deserves an honored place in American history for courageously and effectively using the power of the chief executive to fight racial discrimination in voting, education, and vocation. But his campaigns to eradicate poverty and to satisfy the "hunger for community" in America resulted oftentimes in poorly conceived programs that were no match for the intractable problems they were intended to address.

At the end of the day, Johnson's presidency had summoned up a new form of politics that not only aspired to surpass New Deal policies but challenged the very fabric of the New Deal political order. White House aide Hayes Redmon saw the handwriting on the wall as early as the summer of 1966, when LBJ's consensus began to unravel. He wrote a memo on June 9 to his boss, White House Chief of Staff Bill Moyers, conveying the troubling accusations of Fred Dutton, a former White House assistant for John Kennedy, who later would serve as the principal assistant in Robert Kennedy's presidential campaign. "Dutton accused us of being old fashioned and somewhat out of step with the temper of the time," Redmon reported ruefully. For this malady, however, there was no easy solution; it would not be enough to make over LBJ's television persona. Dutton agreed, Redmon's memo concluded, "that it would be 'phony' to attempt to move Lyndon Johnson into the era of the 'politics of existentialism.' ''[34] Indeed, as the "politics of existentialism'' came to life, not only LBJ, but the institution of the modern presidency itself, seemed strikingly antediluvian.

The Modern Presidency Meets the "New" Politics: The Fall of Lyndon Johnson

Ever since Roosevelt's death, the Democratic party had been confronted with the reality that the New Deal realignment had failed to survive in any permanent, meaningful sense. In a partisan sense, at any rate, the New Deal realignment had always been fragile, subordinate to the task of refurbishing the presidency and executive agencies. Thus, New Deal liberalism itself, which had for more than a quarter of a century been tied to the modern executive, seemed jeopardized when Lyndon Johnson, catching nearly every one of his aides and his television audience by surprise, concluded his prepared speech on the evening of March 31, 1968 with the announcement that he would neither seek nor accept the nomination of his party for another term as president. Indeed, as Herbert Parmet has written, ''it does not take much exaggeration to consider [that night] as a landmark for the post–New Deal Democratic Party, as the moment when the old coalition finally yielded to the new fragmentation, when the old politics gave way to the new.''[35]

The "new" politics represented a confluence of the New Deal and the new left. It did not oppose the programmatic and legal achievements of the New Deal, but sought to extend and radicalize them. "This 'new liberalism,' '' Jack Newfield, assistant editor of *The Village Voice* wrote in late 1967, was ''more urban, more activist, more experimental than the old. Decentralist rather than bureaucratic. . . . More geared to the non-working poor than the fat, belching unions. More interested in sympathizing with the unborn revolutions in the Third World, than in containment or NATO.''[36] The new liberalism that left LBJ's presidency in shambles, then, went much deeper than the Vietnam War. It marked the coming to life, in a manner of speaking, of the Great Society and its aspirations to surpass, if not reject, the New Deal constitutional order.

As such, Johnson's abdication marked the failure of his project, first announced at the University of Michigan in 1964, to align himself and the powers of the modern executive with the carriers of the new politics—civil rights activists, consumer and environmental advocates, and those fighting for women's rights. Part of the problem was the backlash Johnson's program caused, depriving him of critical political support not just in the South but in Northern urban areas as well. The pursuit of the Great Society, not surprisingly, had alienated many Southern Democrats, accentuating their long-standing estrangement from the national Democratic party. This disenchantment was voiced dramatically in the 1966 election as three segregationist Democrats—Lester Maddox in Georgia, James Johnson in Arkansas, and George P. Mahoney in Maryland won their party's gubernatorial nomination. In Alabama, moreover, voters ratified a caretaker administration for Lurleen Wallace since her husband, George, was not permitted to succeed himself. George Wallace, dubbed the "prime minister" of Alabama, had by 1966 emerged as a serious threat to consummate the North–South split in the Democratic party, either by entering the 1968 presidential primaries or running as a third-party candidate.

Johnson, as a *Washington Post* editorial reported in October, 1966, "refused to get in a lather" about the momentum of segregationists for several governorships in the South. To be sure, he gave them no succor. But he was not about to try to purge them from the Democratic party. The *Post* endorsed Johnson's forbearance, arguing that a direct fight with the White House would only add fuel to the segregationist challenge to Johnson's civil rights program. "The backwash that defeated President Franklin D. Roosevelt's effort to purge some of the Democrats who were thwarting his program in 1938 has not been forgotten," the editorial concluded.[37]

Certainly, Lyndon Johnson had not forgotten about the purge. As Vice President, he had urged Kennedy to go to the South, as Roosevelt had, in search of political support. But it was no longer possible to sidestep the civil rights issue. "I know one thing," LBJ told Kennedy aide Theodore Sorenson, "that the Negroes are tired of this patient stuff and tired of this piecemeal stuff and what they want more than anything else is not an executive order or legislation, they want a moral commitment that he's [Kennedy's] behind them." That moral commitment, he believed, should not be expressed in an effort to purge recalcitrant Southern Democrats, but in an appeal to their conscience:

> I think the President could do this in North Carolina or some place. I'd invite the congressmen and senators to be on the platform. I wouldn't do like Roosevelt did to Walter George and let him get up and say, "I accept your challenge." I'd have him talk about the contributions that they had made and then I'd say, "Now, we have a problem here. No nation can—a hundred years ago in the Lincoln–Douglas debate, Lincoln said, 'No Nation can long endure half slave and half free.' Now no world can long endure half slave and half free and we've got to do something about it in our own country."[38]

To a remarkable degree during the early days of his presidency, Johnson was able to practice what he preached. The 1964 and 1965 civil rights acts represented LBJ's largest and most enduring achievement—the virtual elimination of legal barriers to black equality; the end to Jim Crow in the South; and the enfranchisement of millions of black Americans. To his usual skill in legislative maneuvering, he found during his fight for civil rights the ability to use the presidency to pique the conscience of the nation. Amidst a crisis in Selma, Alabama that saw civil rights marchers confront an oppressive barrier of state troopers, Johnson spoke with unusual feeling to a joint session of Congress in March, 1965 about the voting rights act. His speech warned that the enactment of the voting rights bill would not end the battle for civil rights; rather, it was but one front in a larger war:

> What happened in Selma is part of a far larger movement which reaches into every section and State of America. It is the effort of American Negroes to secure for themselves the full blessings of American life.

Their cause must be our cause too. Because it is not just Negroes, but really
it is all of us, who must overcome the crippling legacy of bigotry and injustice.
And we shall overcome.[39]

Thus, Johnson had adopted as his own rallying cry a line from an old hymn
that had become the slogan of the civil rights movement. "Much of his audience," Paul Conkin has written in his biography of Johnson, "was in tears, for
he had succeeded in doing what he had asked Kennedy to do in 1963—use the
presidency as a moral platform."[40] LBJ had not won over Southern congressmen,
most of whom slumped in their seats, as the joint session erupted in applause. But
he had triumphed where FDR failed—without embroiling himself in an enervating
purge campaign, he had discredited Southern resistance to liberal reform.

The Democrats had long depended on their Southern base to win national
elections. Yet Johnson had risked this base to achieve his civil rights program.
"He knew very well what the impact would be of an all out Civil Rights program," his aide Harry McPherson related many years later, "that he would be
considered a traitor."[41] Johnson hoped to be forgiven, especially by poor white
Southerners; this was the very purpose of his appeal to conscience. "I can't make
people integrate," he told Richard Goodwin, "but maybe we can make them feel
guilty if they don't. And once it happens, and they find out the jaws of hell don't
open, and fire and brimstone doesn't flood down on them, then maybe they'll see
just how they have been taken advantage of."[42] The elections of November,
1966, however, revealed that the South was not in a forgiving mood, and the
prospect of losing the White House in 1968 made certain members of the administration nervous, if not completely repentant, about Johnson's having alienated
Southern Democrats. A few days after the midterm election, one aide, Ervin Duggan, urged immediate attention to this problem:

Bill Moyers once [said] that Lyndon Johnson's unique mission might be to "free
the white South from itself."
    If President Johnson is to accomplish that, he'd better get busy. Bitterness
and resentment and outright hatred for the President in the South are bad—and
getting worse. If they are to be moderated, if Wallace is to be stopped and the
South saved for the President's party, we should start developing a Southern
strategy now.[43]

Johnson had no stomach for a "Southern strategy" that retreated from civil
rights. The defense of this cause above all was how he intended to make his mark
on history, and Johnson's place in history meant more to him than serving another
term as president. Moreover, the civil rights movement had been far too powerful
and the issues it raised too riveting for a return to relatively "safe" New Deal
issues such as economic security and educational opportunity.

Asked to suggest ideas about "how we can build some strong ground in the
South," Henry Wilson, a member of the legislative liaison team, resorted to an
old remedy. "I think the first steps should be taken along the lines of stressing
the party rather than the President personally," he wrote. "I think that after the
ice is broken, stirring thought back to the relatively uncomfortable environs of the
traditional party, the accommodation of the president can more naturally fol-

low.''[44] Were it not for the earnest tone by which it was offered, one might view this proposal as intended to be ironic. For nearly three decades, liberal presidents had been in conflict, if not at war, with traditional Southern Democracy, and the institutional separation of the modern presidency and the party system had been especially encouraged by the objective of freeing the White House from the ball and chain of Southern obstructionism. Although having no interest in a Roosevelt-style purge campaign, Johnson greatly escalated the tension between the modern presidency and the party machinery. Indeed, his civil rights program was arguably a greater threat to Southern Democracy than was FDR's foray into the 1938 primary campaigns. There was no prospect that LBJ could win back the South under the banner of party loyalty.

In truth, as we have noted, the foundation of the regular party apparatus was in an advanced state of disintegration by 1967, the result of long-developing institutional changes that came to a head during the Johnson years. Democratic organizations in the South were surely not exempt from this development. In fact, the power of the black vote, strengthened so dramatically by the 1965 Voting Rights Act, would soon sound the death knell of traditional Southern Democracy. Billie Farnum, head of the DNC registration division, reported excitedly in early 1968 that ''the registration of Negroes had gone from 20,000 to 250,000'' in Louisiana, with the prospect of registering another 100,000 before the presidential election.[45] This development was repeated throughout the South, severely challenging the foundation of white supremacy upon which the Democratic party below the Mason–Dixon line had been built.

An important sign of change came in 1966, as the fabled Byrd machine in Virginia, the most powerful symbol of resistance to liberal Democracy since the 1930s, was shaken to its cornerstones. Harry Byrd himself retired in 1965, whereupon the governor appointed his son, Harry Byrd, Jr., as his successor. The heir to the dynasty won election in his own right in 1966, but only after surviving a very strong primary challenge by Armisted L. Boothe, who had long been associated with the moderate Democratic faction in the state. The most dramatic signs of change, however, were the defeats of both Congressman Howard Smith and Senator A. Willis Robertson in primary campaigns, thus virtually ending the reign of the Byrd machine over Virginia politics and altering the composition of the state's Democratic party.[46]

The defeat of this formidable obstacle to liberalism would seem to presage the final development, after so many fits and starts, of the Democratic party as a stronger instrument of national reform. To a point, this is what happened. Overshadowing this evolution of party, however, was the further decline of party itself. The extremes on either end were clearly defecting from Johnson and the Democratic party, thus signalling the virtual collapse of the party system. George Wallace and Lester Maddox were of a very different breed from the conservative Democratic obstructionists who confronted Roosevelt. Whereas the likes of Harry Byrd, Sr., Josiah Bailey, and Walter George strongly identified with their states' party organizations and the traditional decentralized national party system, Wallace and Maddox declared war on the two-party system itself. They represented, thereby, a new insurgent version of conservatism, one less rooted in party organization and more devoted to an open, uncompromising opposition to the advance of programmatic liberalism, especially as applied to civil rights. What happened in the 1966 gubernatorial race in California, where former movie star Ronald Reagan handily defeated the incumbent Edmund G. Brown, revealed that this conservative insurgency was not confined to the South.

Johnson and the Civil Rights Movement

This backlash was given further impetus by the emergence of insurgency on the left, which rebelled against the banner of Democracy in the hope of creating a post–New Deal version of liberalism. LBJ had dedicated his presidency to a more activist and experimental form of progressive politics; by 1967, however, liberal insurgency represented the greatest challenge to his presidency.

Towards the end of 1965, the energy and resources committed to the Great Society began to suffer, increasingly threatened by Johnson's preoccupation with the Vietnam war. Black Americans were among the first to sense this change, and civil rights leaders, such as Martin Luther King, Jr., became early and visible participants in the anti-war movement. In late November, Hayes Redmon lamented these efforts of civil rights activists "I am increasingly concerned over the involvement of the civil rights groups with anti-war demonstrators," he wrote in a memo to Moyers. "The anti-Vietnam types are driving the middle class to the right. This is the key group that is slowly being won over to the civil rights cause. Negro leadership involvement with the anti-Vietnam groups will set their progress back substantially." [47]

King was the least of the Administration's problems, however. Much more troublesome was the emergence of a new generation of black leaders dedicated to "black power," a militant, more threatening type of activism. People like Stokley Carmichael, newly elected head of the Student Nonviolent Coordinating Committee (SNCC), and other angry young civil rights leaders such as Floyd McKissick of the Committee on Racial Equality (CORE) were not only dissatisfied with the achievements of the Johnson administration's civil rights program, but were contemptuous of its objective of racial integration. The growing militancy of black America erupted during the summer of 1966 as urban race riots swept across the nation. In the wake of these developments, the moderately conservative middle class, as Redmon feared, grew impatient with reform. Thus, the Administration's string of brilliant triumphs in civil rights was snapped—its 1966 Civil Rights Bill, an open-housing proposal, fell victim to a Senate filibuster. Johnson's leadership of the civil rights movement was a powerful asset to him in 1964; it had become something of a liability by the summer of 1966.

Since Roosevelt, Democratic presidents had considered the White House to be a superior "vantage point" for guiding the campaign for racial progress. Johnson had effectively intervened in civil rights matters during the summer of 1964, the first of the "long hot summers," enlisting the support of most civil rights leaders in forestalling violence in urban areas. At LBJ's request, leaders of the major civil rights organizations held a meeting in New York, where they called for a moratorium on black unrest. In this new crisis McPherson urged Johnson once again to employ the office of the presidency. He suggested that the president call an immediate meeting of civil rights leaders to address the black community's demand for further advances.[48]

Once eager to take steps that would solidify his personal ties with interest groups, this time Johnson hesitated. He referred McPherson's recommendations to Attorney General Nicholas Katzenbach. Katzenbach agreed with McPherson that the racial situation had taken a disturbing turn, but in a memorandum to the White House aide he opposed the suggestion for an immediate meeting between the president and civil rights leaders. Underlying Katzenbach's objection to holding such a meeting was his disagreement with McPherson's characterization of LBJ as a "civil rights leader." To be sure, Johnson was and would continue to be a leader towards racial progress. But to consider Johnson a civil rights leader was to assume falsely that the civil rights movement was constrained by its association with the White House—that it was a loyal part of a presidential coalition. In fact, Katzenbach observed, "one of the principle difficulties of established Negro leadership has been and will continue to be taking positions that are at the same time responsible, practical—and clearly independent of the Administration."[49]

In the end, the president chose not to meet with civil rights leaders. Instead, Johnson followed Katzenbach's advice to send a number of his younger aides to various cities to meet with young black leaders. The Attorney General's suggestion was the origin of ghetto visits that White House aides made throughout 1967; a dozen or so visited troubled black areas in more than twenty cities, including Chicago, Philadelphia, New York, Washington, D.C., and St. Louis. The ghetto visits exemplified how the modern presidency had assumed so many of the important tasks once carried out by parties. Instead of relying on local party leaders for information about their communities, Johnson called on his aides to live in various ghettos for a time, and then report directly to him about the state of black America. Indeed, local party leaders, even Chicago's powerful Richard Daley, were not told of the ghetto visits, lest they take umbrage at someone from the White House rooting about their home territories. At the same time, these visits marked the declining significance of the modern presidency itself as the leading agent of liberal reform. The awkward presence of these Johnson aides—mostly white, mostly from small towns or cities in the Midwest or Southwest—spending a week, sometimes a weekend, in volatile ghetto environments like Harlem and Bedford Stuyvesant was a confession of profound confusion on the part of the White House about racial matters. Aides were not sent out to organize or manipulate or steer, but solely to gain a sense of the ideas, frustrations, and attitudes at the basis of the riots.[50]

Accounts of this program, embodied in the lengthy reports White House aides prepared for the president, confirmed that living conditions in the ghetto were miserable. Moreover, the reports attributed the volatile conditions not to material deprivation alone, but to social alienation as well. Sherwin Markman, whose reports were especially appreciated by Johnson, stressed the "disconnection" ghetto blacks felt with the rest of society as though they "weren't part of the world as we know it.'' That alienation, he sought to persuade LBJ, both explained and perhaps justified the black power movement.[51]

By all accounts, Johnson was deeply moved by these reports. They apparently were pivotal in persuading him to respond to the riots by redoubling efforts to expand civil rights and the war on poverty programs. The Administration continued to propose an open-housing bill, and in the aftermath of King's assassination, one was finally passed in 1968. LBJ also submitted that year and Congress passed the most extensive and most expensive public housing legislation in American history. Finally, Johnson continued to support the war on poverty's Office of Economic Opportunity, even though its sponsorship of Community Action Programs (CAPs) was reportedly having a disruptive influence in many cities and was the target of bitter complaints from local party leaders. The president did not ignore the complaints of local politicians about the CAPs, but, encouraged by the ghetto reports of their valuable work, he never repudiated them and continued to support federal funds for neighborhood organizations.[52]

Johnson's uneasy relationship with the war on poverty provides perhaps the best example of the strengths and limitations of the modern presidency in relationship to the post–New Deal political order. In part, as noted in the previous chapter, the Johnson White House's delegation of administrative responsibility to these local citizen groups, governed by federal guidelines requiring ''maximum feasible participation of residents of the areas and groups served,'' was merely an extension of the modern presidency. Viewing the state and local party organizations as obstacles to good government, to the ''enlightened'' management of social policy, the CAPs were conceived as a local arm of the Office of Economic Opportunity, which was established in the executive office as the principal federal poverty agency, thus enabling the Johnson administration to bypass the entrenched, usually Democratic political machines. Federal guidelines, in fact, stipulated that the community action program had to be conducted by a public or private nonprofit agency (or some combination thereof) other than a political party.[53]

From this perspective, the CAP was evidence of the further displacement of party politics by executive administration. It is important to remember, as Samuel Beer points out, that ''the antipoverty program was not shaped by the demands of pressure groups of the poor—there were none—but by deliberations of government task forces acting largely on the research based theories of two sociologists, Professors Lloyd Ohlin and Richard A. Cloward of the Columbia School of Social Work.''[54] At least in part, then, the communal concerns of the Johnson presidency were closely connected to administrative invention. In the hands of the Johnson administration, moreover, which relied to an unprecedented extent on presidential politics and governance, this invention never fulfilled its stated objective of popular participation. Under the banner of community control, Daniel Patrick Moynihan has suggested, ''the essential decisions about local affairs came increasingly to be made in Washington via the direct CAP–OEO line of communications and funding.''[55] This development was accentuated by Johnson's efforts in 1967, following the recommendations of the Heineman task force on government organization, to tighten management over the CAPs.[56] The following year

George Nicolau, stepping down after running for 18 months the Harlem Community Action Agency (HARYOU-ACT), the largest in the nation, declared himself "a victim of that process which in the space of three short years created and has almost been overwhelmed by its own complexities and its own bureaucracy."[57]

Although centralized administration significantly enervated the participatory aspirations of the war on poverty, the CAP was an important and revealing prelude to the emergence of participatory democracy as the leading principle of the reformers who gained influence with the demise of Johnson's consensus politics. The concern for "community" involvement during the Johnson presidency revealed how an emphasis on the "quality" of life in American society was potentially in tension with the centralization of authority required by an extensive welfare state. Furthermore, the administrative innovation that gave rise to the war on poverty was an attempt to respond to real problems that could not be readily addressed by executive administration. Moynihan has argued that the Johnson administration blundered into the community action program and that the phrase mandating "maximum feasible participation" was a shallow rhetorical bow to the Jeffersonian tradition. Yet, as James Morone has pointed out, Johnson and his aides were not so simple-minded; rather, they were attempting to identify a controversial program with a deeply rooted republican tradition in the United States "by invoking the powerful myths of the American democratic wish."[58] That idea of democracy—abhorring centralized administration—had been severely challenged but not overturned by the New Deal. Johnson, in an admittedly halting way, was seeking to reconcile the New Deal state with the historical antipathy in the United States to bureaucracy. As he wrote in his memoirs with respect to his attraction to the idea of community action: "This plan had the sound of something brand new and even faintly radical. Actually, it was based on one of the oldest ideas of our democracy, as old as the New England town meeting—self-determination at the local level."[59]

Johnson's attraction to the concept of community action went beyond a recognition of the rhetorical power of democratic individualism; it was informed by Johnson's experience as the director of the Texas National Youth Administration (NYA) during the early New Deal years. The National Resources Planning Board's detailed study on "Security, Work and Relief Policies," issued as part of its 1943 report, cited the NYA as one of the few New Deal agencies that did not tend to "divorce the average citizen from participation in the problems involved in public-aid policy and administration."[60] Especially when the NYA was created, the report claimed, it was an outstanding example of a Federal organization that was highly decentralized, with a considerable amount of discretion being left to the State administrators. Even as the agency matured, although there was some increase in centralization of power, it retained a significant commitment to local determination. This character of the NYA was its greatest strength, but also the source of some concern among New Deal cognoscente:

> The present arrangement has made for adaptability of the program to local conditions and community needs and has permitted experimentation in methods and techniques. . . . On the other hand, it has resulted in a marked lack of uniformity in program and methods and techniques and wide diversity of achievement.

This situation would appear to be particularly serious in view of the national significance of the problem of unemployed youth, and the fact that so large a proportion of the young unemployed population is concentrated in areas where both social and economic conditions are likely to inhibit the development of appropriate projects if reliance is so largely placed upon local initiative.[61]

Johnson recognized that the problem of poverty in the 1960s was not the same as that of the Depression, but he considered the NYA experiences valuable to him, suggesting some of the solutions for the Great Society. "I . . . found that when the people had a hand in shaping a project, it was much more successful than any program passed down by decree from a government office," he wrote in his memoirs.[62] Moreover, LBJ and the architects of the Great Society considered "community participation" a critical element of their program to establish a post–New Deal version of the welfare state. They were not oblivious to the political risks involved; however, these risks were taken in the hope of revitalizing, indeed surpassing, the militant side of New Deal liberalism. Interestingly, the evaluations of the task forces charged by the Johnson White House with the responsibility to investigate the administrative problems of the war on poverty are strikingly reminiscent of the NRPB's critique of the NYA. Although creating problems of administrative fragmentation and uneven performance standards, the Task Force Report on Intergovernmental Program Coordination noted in a typical analysis that the decentralized management of the Office of Economic Opportunity should not be condemned out of hand:

Administrative tidiness is not the only test of effective government. In truth, some Federal programs operating from new and revolutionary postulates (e.g., the Community Action Program) may have to measure their success, in part, in terms of what they temporarily disrupt. Furthermore, total program coordination can be brought at too high a price: the imposition of "commissar" sanctions by one agency or one level of government over other agencies, levels, and jurisdictions, and a deadening multiplication of paper work and inter-agency clearance.[63]

Johnson's extraordinary patience with the CAPs, his continuing, albeit certainly not unqualified, support of the war on poverty, in the face of blistering criticism from Congress and local government officials, suggests that he did not disagree with this assessment.[64] As a result, at the same time that he extended the reach of the institution of the modern presidency, he was preparing the ground for its diminished influence. To be sure, he did not appreciate fully the tension between executive management and local self-determination. Nor did he sufficiently appreciate that the civil rights movement was the catalyst for a "new" politics that was inherently suspicious of presidential leadership. It was precisely because the civil rights movement had already built organizations and mobilized community resources that 'maximum feasible participation' was translated so quickly from abstraction to reality," one policy analyst has written.[65] The community action agencies took on the energy and aspirations of the civil rights movement and refocused it, thus giving a new generation of black leaders entree into local and administrative politics. As a 1967 Senate investigation of the war on poverty put it: "The Office of Opportunity policies and programs have produced a cadre

of citizen leadership heretofore neither seen nor heard, in the community arena."
They have brought "to the fore a sizeable cadre, for the first time in the Negro
Community, especially, of young energetic and striving leadership."[66] That
"cadre of striving" leaders, instrumental both in the increasing election of black
mayors in American cities and the growing influence of civil rights groups on
social policy during the late 1960s and 1970s, developed political bases that were
not tied directly to the Democratic party or the White House.

The end of LBJ's confident stewardship of the civil rights issue portended the
rejection of the presidency as the leading instrument of liberal reform. The movement that emerged to protest the Vietnam War was a sign of more than a foreign
policy controversy; that this controversy so overwhelmed LBJ's continuing support for civil rights and the war on poverty, ending in the estrangement of reform
activists from a Democratic president, was a signal of a more profound split in
the liberal order.

Johnson and the Anti-War Movement: Liberalism Unbound

Since the 1936 campaign, Democratic presidents had encouraged liberal activists
to organize independently—to support Democratic presidential campaign and government programs, even as they remained "auxiliaries" to the Democratic party.
With the Vietnam War, liberal activism took on a life of its own.

Allard Lowenstein, a veteran of the civil rights movement, formed the Conference of Concerned Democrats in August 1967, which after failing to enlist
George McGovern and Robert Kennedy to lead a "dump Johnson" movement,
coalesced around the quixotic campaign of Eugene McCarthy. Joseph Rauh, also
active in civil rights causes, enlisted behind McCarthy's insurgent candidacy in
December of 1967, less than 3 months after circulating a memo among his friends
in the Americans for Democratic Action (ADA) insisting that, "No responsible
Democrat will associate himself with an effort to unseat the incumbent President."[67] There were even cracks in labor's generally solid support for the president. In February, 1968, when the governing board of the ADA, then under the
chairmanship of John Kenneth Galbraith, voted to endorse McCarthy's candidacy,
nine unionists, including Walter Reuther, stood by the liberal organization's new
anti-Johnson position.

Reuther's support of the ADA's "dump Johnson" position portended a more
dangerous threat than Eugene McCarthy to LBJ's incumbency, that of Robert
Kennedy, who was slouching towards a candidacy of his own. "Reuther has made
the decision that Bobby [Kennedy] is (to mix metaphors) the wave of the future,"
John Roche had warned Johnson in February, 1967. "And Reuther is busily setting up what amounts to a parallel union movement which—*without technically
breaking with the AFL–CIO*—will disassociate itself from the Administration and
the 'labor establishment.' "[68]

By the beginning of what was to be his re-election year, then, Johnson was
left with the party and union establishment. Because of the Vietnam War, partisans of the post–New Deal liberalism that he had sought to launch, the new generation of liberal activists to whom the early days of his presidency were dedi-

cated, had largely abandoned him. Ironically, it was partly because he was a liberal himself that he had entered the Vietnam War in the first place; he was seeking to continue the internationalism that historically had been associated with reform presidents such as Woodrow Wilson, Franklin Roosevelt, and John Kennedy, who, of course, initiated the U.S. involvement in Vietnam.[69] "History has a peculiar ability to forget what a President does at home and judges him on the size of his impact on the world beyond his shores," Bill Moyers had written in a memo to Johnson back in June of 1965. This "irony of judgment," as Moyers called it, had been good to FDR: "The New Deal's tide was fading out until World War II made Roosevelt a leader of world dimensions." Just as surely, that same irony of judgment would operate on Johnson's place in history. "Some President some day will come along and pass programs topping the Great Society—the country will have greater needs than today and he will have more GNP to use in solving them," Moyers memo concluded. "But no President is likely again to have the chance to redeem Southeast Asia from Red China—or keep the Communists out of the Caribbean—or save the U.N."[70] This memo proved prophetic, albeit with a bitter twist of fate; for in seeking to uphold the liberal internationalism that made FDR a world statesman, LBJ discredited it, encouraging insurgency to the right and left of him. This ended with the Democratic party so badly fragmented that it not only lost the 1968 presidential election, but also undertook a series of reforms that further eroded the link between presidents and their parties.[71]

The fall of Lyndon Johnson, Parmet has observed, "confirmed suspicions that there could hardly be said to be such an organization as the national Democratic party."[72] Of course, there was still a cadre of party professionals in the Congress and the Democratic National Committee, as well as the state and local organizations, and many of them, even when offended by Johnson's style of leadership or his military policy, stuck with the White House to the bitter end. At a DNC meeting in Chicago of January 8, 1968, the much abused party chair, John Bailey, strongly endorsed the president's re-election, and called on his fellow Democrats to disregard the growing insurgency that threatened LBJ's incumbency.[73]

Bailey's support was echoed by party professionals on the hustings, as they fought against a grass roots rebellion aroused by Johnson's Vietnam policies. In the key state of Wisconsin, for example, where McCarthy forces were putting together a strong primary challenge, a White House aide reported that "two elements of strength for the President are emerging: the party leaders and office holders who are loyal to the party and who recognize that the whole party's fate rides with the President" and "organized labor, which probably will stay with national leaders." Given the disaffection of Reuther, the White House must have been pleased to hear from this aide that "the largest local in Wisconsin—the Kenosha U.A.W.—a few days ago voted overwhelmingly against McCarthy's even entering the primary." The report on Wisconsin concluded with one immediate imperative: "strong . . . encouragement to the party people and officials who are standing with the President."[74]

The Johnson White House, however, had never felt comfortable with the regular party machinery, viewing it as an obstacle to the codification of its vision of a good society. The neglect, indeed assault, on the Democratic organization by the Johnson administration now left the president defenseless in his desperate struggle to survive an attack by erstwhile political allies. This irony was not lost on journalist David Broder, who wrote in his column of September 26, 1967: "At the very time when President Johnson is faced within his own party with a precinct level rebellion against his Vietnam policies, his personality or his domestic programs, the incredible niggardliness and neglect by the White House is sapping the Democratic party of its most able national leadership."[75] Thus, the insurgent candidacy of Eugene McCarthy exposed but did not cause the enervation of the regular party apparatus. The foundation for the disintegration of the Democratic party was prepared by long-term developments, to which Johnson himself made an unprecedented contribution.[76]

Some White House aides looked hopefully to organized labor to compensate for the weakened condition of the regular party machinery. The American Federation of Labor and the Congress of Industrial Organizations had merged in 1955, and the AFL–CIO's Committee on Political Education (COPE) had since become the most important Democratic organizational asset. During the unfortunate 1966 congressional election campaign, it had been COPE that had supplied the White House with the organizational muscle that might have been provided by the Democratic National Committee. Reuther's split with the administration over the Vietnam War, moreover, did not reflect the position of most union leadership, which had remained, amid the shattering of the Democratic party, the most loyal supporters of the Johnson presidency.

After the disastrous Tet offensive at the end of January 1968, during which the Vietcong confirmed their military capability despite all the American efforts, AFL–CIO President George Meany moved to discourage any notion that swelling anti-war sentiment would sway labor away from Johnson. The insurgent "dump Johnson campaign," he warned unionists, would only succeed in electing a Republican president, and the stake of labor in keeping a Democrat in the White House was clear. "It was a clear choice between liberalism and conservatism," Meany told a meeting of labor political strategists in February. Comparing LBJ's record favorably with Franklin Roosevelt's, Meany insisted that the outcome of the November elections was crucial for organized labor, and that he planned to throw the full resources of COPE and its $2 million war chest into Johnson's campaign.[77]

The strong support of organized labor, however, was no salvation. The Johnson White House had never really cultivated COPE operatives or attempted to boost their efforts. In fact, Cliff Carter, LBJ's representative at the DNC, openly feuded with Al Barken, COPE's executive director, who privately and publicly attacked the White House in regard to the unsatisfactory operation of the DNC. "I can't help but wonder," Carter lamented in early 1966, whether Barken's criticism of the Johnson administration's disregard of the party "is part of a larger plan to completely break with the White House and enhance Bobby Kennedy's chances in 1968."[78] This fear of a labor conspiracy not only reflected growing White House paranoia about Robert Kennedy, but a striking indifference towards organizational politics. The political operatives of COPE, in fact, had legitimate concerns about the DNC's declining support of political activities that were critical to labor's relationship with the Democratic party. Barken was especially concerned about the decimation of the DNC's voter registration effort. In 1964, COPE worked closely with the Democratic committee on registration drives, and the weakening of the DNC in this area was viewed as a major factor in the losses sustained by the party in 1966, as well as the weak position in which it found itself at the start of a presidential election year.[79]

The Johnson administration's neglect of the party also had its effect on the local level, where the lack of party leadership in the White House allowed friction between labor and party organizations to fester. As the DNC's Billie Farnum reported to the White House from a COPE conference in April, 1967, "This friction exists in most of the states and the reason behind it is the age old problem of running a campaign and how to spend the money. Jealousy stems from the fact that labor organizations are better financed than political parties, and as a result of this personalities get involved causing problems."[80]

Labor's "organizational muscle," therefore, hardly compensated for the disarray in the Democratic party. In important respects, in fact, the efforts of COPE added to the administration's problems, highlighting its indifferent party leadership and excessive dependence on an interest group for organizational succor. Consequently, LBJ entered the presidential election year of 1968 without any effective basis of organizational support.

McCarthy's strong showing in the New Hampshire primary on March 12 confirmed the White House's worst fears about its vulnerability. The Minnesota Senator did not actually win; in fact, Johnson won the primary as a write-in candidate, without appearing on the ballot. The fact remained, however, that a relatively obscure Senator was able to draw 42.2 percent of the vote to the 49.4 percent for the man who was President of the United States. Perhaps most troubling was the failure of the organizational efforts that were made on behalf of LBJ. Labor had worked hard for Johnson, with COPE concentrating on blue-collar workers in the industrial section of Manchester. Despite these efforts, McCarthy received about one-fourth of the vote in labor districts. More surprising, according to public opinion polls taken just before the primary vote, Robert Kennedy, who was not yet a candidate, drew almost as much support from union members as Johnson—to the dismay and surprise of George Meany.[81] On March 16, after weeks of pained vacillation, Kennedy entered the race. McCarthy's New Hampshire performance and Kennedy's entry gave the Dump Johnson movement a momentum that the president's supporters feared could sweep an incumbent president from office. "I think the course we seem to be taking now," wrote Harry McPherson in a memorandum to Johnson on March 18, "will lead either to Kennedy's nomination or Nixon's election, or both."[82]

In the wake of these traumatic events, word came pouring into the White House over the next few weeks of the "McCarthyites" decisively winning the organizational battle with the party regulars and labor troops in state after state. The administration's immediate concerns were with the Wisconsin primary, scheduled for April 2, where an undeclared candidate was forced to run, and appear on the ballot, unless he submitted an affidavit of noncandidacy. Like it or not, therefore, Johnson would face McCarthy head on in that state.

In Wisconsin, as in New Hampshire, Johnson's best hope lay with labor. Because he had publicly assumed the traditional presidential position of being aloof from primaries, LBJ could not campaign himself. Consequently, as Larry O'Brien put it, "the labor effort must be our answer to the [McCarthy] kids in getting out the vote."[83] Yet the Wisconsin organization working for the president was weaker than the one that had failed him in New Hampshire. Moreover, Wisconsin had all the unfortunate problems with respect to the administration that were supposedly absent in New Hampshire: It was not a "hawkish" state; in fact, the traditions of dissent and of pacifism were stronger in Wisconsin than in any other state; and it had an open primary, which would allow Republicans to cross over for McCarthy. "It is my judgment," the state Democratic Chair Richard Cudahy reported on March 19, "that if the Wisconsin Presidential Primary was held today, President Johnson would lose, probably decisively."[84]

Thus, by the time Lyndon Johnson withdrew from the 1968 campaign on March 31, just in time to avoid what looked like certain defeat in Wisconsin, the Democratic party and its labor allies had virtually collapsed around him. Even in the traditionally strong organization states like Connecticut, where John Bailey had long presided over a formidable state Democratic machine, the regulars were having trouble competing with the "children's crusade," as Jim Rowe referred to McCarthy's organization.[85] It is impossible to say whether LBJ could have avoided what happened in 1968 had he followed the advice of those few members of his staff, most notably Roche and Rowe, who had urged him since 1965 to refurbish the Democratic party machinery. Roche made a final plea along these lines in late 1967, using the specter of a Bobby Kennedy campaign, as well as pointed sarcasm, to encourage the president to do something about the forlorn state of the party:

> Nothing could encourage [Kennedy] more than an atomized Democratic party organization—and that is what we have.
>
> With all respect to the individuals involved, Marvin [Watson] can't run the DNC *and* be Appointments Secretary—they are both 25–hour a day jobs.
>
> And Larry [O'Brien] can't do the job on the Hill *and* be Postmaster General *and* watch the political store. Bailey can't decide what color necktie to wear—he has to have a guidance system.
>
> And Bobby feeds this data into his computer as part of the background for escalating his "War of Liberation."
>
> You need a "Farley" not a Bailey. And you need him in a hurry.[86]

It is interesting to consider this advice, sound as it may have been, in historical perspective. Roche's reference to James Farley fails to mention the falling out between that quintessential party man and Franklin Roosevelt. The break between FDR and Farley, of course, came amidst the struggles over the Third New Deal— during the creation of the modern presidency. It was Farley's lack of enthusiasm for certain elements of the Third New Deal, in fact, especially the decline in the status of the traditional party structure it represented, that resulted in his falling out of favor with Roosevelt.

The volatile persona and tempestuous times of Lyndon Johnson made it easy to overlook the logical continuity represented by his presidency. Since FDR's second term that logic had dictated an institutional separation between presidential and party politics. In light of that history, it is easier to understand Johnson's treatment of his party. The "logic" of the modern presidency also sheds light on the disregard for party politics displayed by most of the aides who staffed the executive office. Even as astute a political advisor as McPherson never mentioned the party machinery in the richly detailed memos he wrote during the troubled months of Johnson's demise. The great advantage LBJ had over Kennedy and McCarthy, as well as Republican pretenders to the throne, McPherson wrote in his memo of March 18, was "intelligence, experience, achievement, and the Office of the Presidency."[87]

In truth, no modern president had concerned himself with the health of his national party machinery, and the pursuit of programmatic reform dictated that he should not. A strong party headquarters was very likely to make trouble for a president on patronage and other issues. LBJ's fall from grace might have been hastened by his neglect of party; at the same time, his accomplishments as president were inconceivable within the traditional framework of presidential–party relations.

The origins and development of the modern presidency also help explain why, in the midst of loud protests throughout the country about party neglect, the Johnson administration was putting together a campaign organization in late 1967 and early 1968 that would operate independently of the regular party apparatus. The tendency since Roosevelt had been for presidential candidates to go outside normal partisan channels, using political "amateurs" to round up votes in state primaries and the general election. With Kennedy's triumph in 1960, "citizen's committees," directed by each candidate's personal advisors and strategists, largely took over presidential campaigns; henceforth, coordination and liaison with the party would be of secondary importance. As noted in Chapter 7, Johnson's 1964 election campaign fit this pattern, and the unusual distaste for party politics that characterized his presidency, accelerating the breakdown of state and local Democratic machinery, only encouraged the formation of an unprecedentedly large and complex re-election campaign organization.[88]

As one might have expected, some of the Johnson re-election committee duties would entail tasks that parties had not routinely performed such as issue education. One White House advisor, for example, noted at a planning session of March 5, 1968, "that DNC work was weak in the area of what the situation is state-by-state as to issues"; he suggested, therefore, that the Citizens for Johnson committee "should have coordinators for each state who would look into these matters and provide reports outside the regular political channels which would provide better decision making information available in Washington."[89] In addition, however, before Johnson's withdrawal, the White House was discussing the possibility of organizing and utilizing citizen groups in the various states to "supplant" certain functions ordinarily carried out by party organizations, to wit, "letter writing, the distribution of literature, and local advertising."[90]

James Rowe, who was to head LBJ's 1968 campaign effort, resisted such plans, urging the White House to attend to the "revitalization of the Democratic National Committee to enable it to do the routine jobs it should do."[91] Looking back to Truman's 1948 campaign, and the task force he had proposed to oversee that election effort, Rowe called for a similarly modest Johnson re-election organization: "It should work quietly, it should be small, it should be separated from the Democratic National Committee—*but* be acceptable to the top committee personnel already suffering from shell shock both in Washington and around the country because of its impotent status," he wrote in a planning memorandum of late 1967. "It is *important*, at least in public, that the Committee not be further downgraded."[92]

Johnson did not share Rowe's concern for party renewal. He hoped to follow the pattern of Roosevelt's 1940 campaign, in which FDR enveloped himself in the crises and office of the presidency.[93] The rise of the "new" politics, represented by the McCarthy and Kennedy campaigns on the left and the Wallace challenge on the right, made such a strategy impossible. When this became apparent to Johnson, his only recourse seemed to be a withdrawal from the race, and the turn presidential politics had taken encouraged him to speculate on the value of a one-term presidency, rather than a recrudescence of partisanship.

Party regulars and union leaders usually supported Johnson when push came to shove, but their support was compromised by LBJ's disregard for party politics. Moreover, the support of party professionals and their labor allies was often tempered by their perception that LBJ, no less than McCarthy, represented a severe challenge to their political way of life. Consequently, as White House aide Douglass Cater reported from Massachusetts in November, 1967, McCarthy was mounting a legitimate threat to the president because he "made it clear he was not just mad about Vietnam, but about the President's treatment of Congress and the Democratic party."[94]

Notwithstanding this anger, McCarthy and his supporters were virtually to declare war on the party at the 1968 Democratic convention. But the events that took place in Chicago that August and the reforms that followed in the wake of those events were a logical extension of the modern presidency. Johnson made a singular and partly unintentional contribution to reform, but his role was merely to intensify a long-term pattern of presidential leadership that, at the end of the day, left the White House without a stable basis of political support.

The "New" Politics Ascendent

Soon after LBJ left the White House, one of his presidential assistants, George Reedy, wrote, "we may well be witnessing the first lengthening shadows that will become the twilight of the presidency."[95] This pessimistic view reflected the fact that the evolution of the modern presidency had given rise to an exalted office, but the occupant of that office faced increasingly intractable conditions. There was growing opposition to unilateral use of presidential power; increased public cynicism about the merits of presidential policy proposals; and greater inclinations on the part of the press to challenge presidential assertions and proposals.[96] Yet the declining basis of institutional support for presidents notwithstanding, much was still expected of them—they continued to be at the center of citizens' growing expectations about government responsibilities.

As noted in the previous section, the foundation of the modern presidency was put to a severe challenge by the rise of a new form of politics that was greatly suspicious of, if not hostile to, presidential power. Johnson, of course, had in rhetoric and program sought to "manage" these new political forces; instead, he had been an agent of reform that brought forth a crisis of the liberal order. The two most significant facts of the reforms represented by the Great Society were the aggrandizement of administrative power and, in seeming contrast to that, a deep suspicion of centralized administration. No doubt the reach of "enlightened administration"—the authority vested in the presidency and administrative agencies—became a great deal more intrusive in the 1960s. "Almost any legislation, even welfare measures," writes Johnson's biographer Paul Conkin, "involved new rules, new guidelines, that circumscribed the behavior of some Americans, at times even those who collected subsidies."[97] At the same time, the Great Society's celebration of a "desire for beauty," "hunger for community," and "maximum feasible participation" called for efforts to limit the discretionary power of New Deal institutions. The community action programs, resulting from an odd meld of administrative invention and the rejection of centralized administration, perfectly captured the paradox of Lyndon Johnson's Great Society.

This intriguing and disconcerting paradox—the new liberalism's love–hate relationship with administrative power—defines the crisis of the liberal order. We shall see in Chapter 9 that the efforts to enhance the representative character of government action ultimately did not seek to restrain administrative power but, rather, attempted to reshape it as an agent of democracy. As a result, the policy responsibility of the executive was increased, but Congress, the courts, and "citizen" groups became involved in the details of administration. For a time, however, as the Democrats convened at the 1968 convention, the new liberalism expressed itself in what Samuel Huntington has called a "democratic distemper," as a surge of egalitarianism and participation that seemed to weaken the possibility that anyone in any institution could exercise authority.[98] The Democratic gathering was ravaged by controversy, both within the convention hall and on the streets, where anti-war demonstrators clashed with Chicago police. To be sure, the influence of Johnson and the party regulars was still in evidence. LBJ's heir apparent, Vice President Hubert Humphrey, was nominated without having to contest a primary; the party leaders still controlled most of the convention delegates, and they preferred Humphrey to the anti-war candidate, Eugene McCarthy. Humphrey's most powerful opponent, Robert Kennedy, had been assassinated on the night he won the California primary. Still, in spite of the control of the convention and its apparatus by the "professionals," the 1968 session undertook measures that would eventually lead to the final triumph of progressive reform over the regular party machinery.

One measure put state parties on notice that they would henceforth be admitted only if they "assured" that voters participated fully in party affairs without racial or ethnic discrimination. To monitor the integration efforts, the convention created a special committee on equal rights headed by Governor Richard J. Hughes of New Jersey. The committee on equal rights completed its work just prior to the opening of the Chicago convention, whereupon Governor Hughes assumed the responsibilities of the full Credentials Committee.

This reform was a sequel to the struggle over the seating of the Mississippi delegation at the 1964 Democratic Convention.[99] A Mississippi Freedom Democratic party (MFDP) challenged the "regular" delegation, on grounds that the Democratic party in the state excluded blacks from membership. The conflict confronted Johnson and Democratic party leaders with a dilemma, since they risked antagonizing the civil rights forces if they banned the Freedom party delegation, and much or all of the South if they seated it. To avoid these unpalatable prospects, Johnson, with considerable help from Minnesota Senator Hubert Humphrey, worked assiduously behind the scenes to achieve a compromise. The compromise plan included: the seating of the regular Mississippi delegation, provided its members signed a loyalty oath that pledged them to support the presidential ticket; the symbolic gesture of making MFDP delegates honored guests at the convention, with two of its members seated as special delegates at large; and a prohibition of racial discrimination in delegate selection at the 1968 convention, to be enforced by a special committee to assist state parties in complying with this new expectation.

The MFDP delegates were greatly disappointed by this compromise, criticizing Johnson for his willingness to sacrifice their moral cause on the altar of expediency. But in diffusing the Mississippi controversy Johnson championed a fundamental reform of convention rules that would have enormous long-term consequences for the Democratic party. Previously state parties had sole authority to establish delegate selection procedures. Johnson's response to the conflict over the MFDP established the centralizing principle that henceforth the national party agencies would not only decide how many votes each state delegation got at the national convention but also enforce uniform rules on what kinds of persons could be selected. LBJ, contrary to conventional wisdom, did not propose this compromise merely as a short-term, stop-gap measure to ensure peace at the 1964 convention.[100] Rather, he viewed the new nondiscrimination rule as a justified extension of the national party's power over state delegations that carried on discriminatory practices, one that complemented the 1965 Voting Rights Act.[101]

As became clear at the 1968 Democratic Convention, the rule was no paper tiger. Having found no evidence that the Mississippi Democratic party had "complied either with the spirit or the letter" of the convention call prohibiting racial discrimination, the Credentials Committee voted overwhelmingly to bar the Mississippi regular delegation from its seats. Thereupon, a biracial delegation, including many members of the 1964 Mississippi Freedom party, was seated in its place. The regular Mississippi Democrats, supported by several Southern delegations, as well as Democratic National Committee chairman John Bailey, sought to save their seats with an eleventh-hour offer of another compromise. Bailey's support for a deal apparently resulted from the warnings of other Southern delegations that they would not be able to carry their states for Vice President Humphrey or any other Northerner if the Mississippi regulars were not admitted. But the offers of compromise were turned back, with both Humphrey and McCarthy supporting the claim of the Mississippi insurgents.[102]

The action taken in the Mississippi case was a landmark in party reform. As a *New York Times* editorial observed the next day, it pointed up "the growing power of the national convention as something more than just a meeting of fifty autonomous state parties."[103] The Democrats had given at least one demonstration that the national party had a basic belief in racial equality and that, if an existing state party was not willing to abide by that belief, the convention was prepared to grant official status to a new state party that would live by it. Before the end of the Chicago meeting, the convention gave one more demonstration of this maxim, albeit a more limited one. Pushed by the McCarthy supporters, the convention provided for the sharing of the Georgia vote by rival groups led by black Atlanta state representative Julian Bond and the segregationist forces of Governor Lester G. Maddox, although most of the "regulars" rejected this settlement and walked out.

More than racial discrimination was at issue in the contention over the selection of delegates. At the Democratic convention in Chicago, the carriers of the "new" politics, championing the issue of "participatory democracy," broke through to the surface and demanded immediate recognition of their cause. The struggle between Humphrey and McCarthy served as a catalyst to expand the scope of conflict over disputed delegations. Besides supporting the integration drives in still disputed Southern delegations, the McCarthy forces used the same convention call for full participation to charge unfairness and undemocratic procedure in many other states, including New York, Pennsylvania, Connecticut, Minnesota, and Washington, D.C. With respect to the Northern delegations, the charge was not confined to the question of race, but extended to the entire system of delegate selection, particularly the dominance of party organizations in this process. The central question was whether Humphrey's advantage at the convention was achieved by methods that allowed party professionals in the various states to unfairly impose their choices on the district and state conventions and caucuses.

This charge, of course, was not unprecedented. It was first lodged by Theodore Roosevelt after being denied the Republican nomination of 1912 by party regulars, despite winning most of the presidential primaries. A year later, Woodrow Wilson proposed to Congress a plan to abolish the convention system and replace it with a system of popular primaries. We noted in Chapter 2 that Congress received Wilson's proposal with indifference, but the progressive cause was taken up in the various states, yielding by the 1960s a mixed system of open primaries and party-controlled delegations. Nevertheless, party leaders still controlled two-thirds of the delegates who attended the Republican and Democratic Conventions in 1968. It was this control, achieved through the ability of most state and local party organizations to either directly or indirectly select convention delegations, that formed the basis of the McCarthy challenge to the right of about 1000 delegates and alternates to be seated.[104]

Virtually the same issue came before the Republican convention in 1952 in the contest between Dwight Eisenhower and Senator Robert A. Taft. By losing the procedural argument, Taft lost the nomination, and McCarthy's lieutenants in 1968 had dreams of a similar development. Yet the McCarthy challenge, unlike Eisenhower's, went well beyond a contest between the candidates contending for their party's nomination. Eisenhower's triumph over Taft was an intimation of the future; McCarthy's candidacy was swept up in a confluence of forces that made the 1968 Democratic Convention a watershed in the century-long movement of presidential politics toward a more direct, less party-oriented democracy. Thus, the Minnesota Senator's challenge of those delegates who owed their presence at the convention to state and local party leaders became a cause celebre of a group of party liberals, headed by Iowa Governor Harold E. Hughes, called the Commission on the Democratic Selection of Presidential Nominees. The Hughes commission was set up initially on private initiative, but its report was presented to the 1968 rules committee of the Democratic convention. Denying it had any interest in a specific candidate, the Commission on Democratic Selection of Presidential Nominees contended that the convention system was on trial. "To an extent not matched since the turn of the twentieth century, events in 1968 have called into question the integrity of the convention for nominating presidential candidates," its report read. "Recent developments have put the future of the two party system itself into serious jeopardy." [105]

The McCarthy forces and the band of reformers led by Governor Hughes, well known for his interest in remaking the party system, did not wield enough influence to deny Hubert Humphrey the nomination. McCarthy did not get the seats he wanted; however, the reform principles he espoused with the support of the Hughes Commission were well on the way to becoming official party doctrine. Following the recommendation of the Hughes Commission report, the delegates voted to abolish the unit rule as binding on the delegates for the 1968 convention. For 1972, it would no longer be valid at the precinct level, either. The unit rule bound individual delegates to vote in accordance with the preferences of the majority of the state delegation. As such, it was used by party leaders to strengthen their positions at national conventions; moreover, by using the unit rule on local levels at caucuses that sent delegates to state conventions, party moguls were able to diminish the power of insurgent groups seeking to affect the delegate selection process. [106] Even more significant for the future of the party system were decisions to establish two commissions, one to deal with party structure and delegate selection and another to take up convention rules that would consider structural reform to guide future conventions.

The 1968 convention thus prepared the way for the sweeping changes made between 1969 and 1972 by the national committee and the McGovern–Fraser commission. In 1969, the committee, acting under the mandate from the Chicago convention, established the Commission on Party Structure and Delegate Selection. Under the chairmanship first of Senator George McGovern, who had put himself forward in Chicago as a dovish alternative to Eugene McCarthy, and, after 1971, of Representative Donald Fraser, the commission developed a set of eighteen guidelines governing the state parties' procedures for selecting their delegates to the national conventions. The Hughes Commission report, both its elaborate documentation of the procedures then in use and its recommendations as to what was wrong with them, provided the basis for the guidelines. Their purpose, therefore, especially with respect to the demand for the expansion of the direct primary, comported with the Hughes Commission's praise of "direct democracy." As such, the 1968 Convention's adoption of the Hughes Commission's proposals to guide future conventions sounded the death knell of the traditional party structure. This objective to weaken the prevailing party structure in the name of "meaningful and timely opportunities" for participation, adopted in the form of a mandate by the Chicago convention, was clearly spelled out in the Hughes Commission Report.[107]

The DNC accepted all the guidelines of the McGovern–Fraser Commission and declared in the Call for the 1972 convention that they constituted "the standards that State Democratic Parties, in qualifying and certifying delegates to the 1972 Democratic National Convention, must make all efforts to comply with. And, as Austin Ranney, himself a member of the McGovern–Fraser Commission, has written, "they made it stick."[108] Most states were in full compliance with the guidelines by convention time; those that were not risked not being seated. "Boss control" of the presidential nominating machinery had come to an end.

That Chicago had proven to be the site for the party leadership's "last hurrah" was itself of profound symbolic importance. The Johnson administration chose Chicago as the convention site in recognition of Richard Daley's standing in the Democratic party. Daley was one of the few urban party leaders regarded highly by the president; moreover, his Cook County Democratic organization was widely recognized as one of the few effective local machines still in existence.[109] By 1972, with the party reforms mandated in Chicago fully operational, Daley was no longer welcome at the Democratic convention; the Convention refused to seat the 59 delegates from Cook County because the procedures by which they had been slated violated party rules. Although the Cook County delegates had been elected in accordance with the Illinois primary law, there had been no open access to the process by which the winning delegate slate had been drawn up, a violation of one of the McGovern–Fraser commission's guidelines.

Reflecting on this startling turn of events, John Roche noted several years later: "There is no question that . . . what happened in 1968 was simmering for some time. The fact that a reform delegation could get seated in place of Daley's slate in 1972 was amazing evidence of long-term disintegration. The regular party apparatus was in a state of anomie, a development reflecting broader changes in American politics."[110] Indeed, the very "quietness" of the "revolution" in party rules that took place during the 1970s is evidence in itself that the party system was forlorn by the end of the Johnson era.[111] Similarly, the spread of party reform to the Republican party suggests that the enervation of the party system cannot be attributed to the tumultuous events of the 1968 Democratic convention alone. Although the Democrats changed somewhat more than the Republicans, both parties substantially modified their party rules after 1968. In fact, many of these changes were codified in state laws that affected Republicans almost as much as Democrats. Thus, the changes brought about in presidential politics during the 1970s were facilitated by long-term, system-wide developments that weakened the regular party apparatus. As David Truman has observed, "the McGovern–Fraser reforms certainly could not have been accomplished over the opposition of an alert and vigorous [party] leadership."[112]

Lyndon Johnson's Complex Legacy

Lyndon Johnson was well aware that forces were in place for the collapse of the regular party apparatus by 1968. From 1966 on, his aides virtually bombarded him with memos warning him of the disarray in the Democratic party organization, and LBJ was also informed that reform forces in the states were creating "a new ball game with new rules." These communications indicated that major changes were rapidly taking place in party politics that portended quite clearly what was to happen after the 1968 Democratic Convention. For example, presidential aide Ben Wattenberg informed Johnson in December, 1967 of a growing emphasis on the importance of primaries in various states that was creating a *"Quasi-National Quasi-Referendum"* (Wattenberg's emphasis); "like it or not," he warned, President Johnson would have to face Senator Eugene McCarthy "head on" in states such as Oregon, Wisconsin, Nebraska and New Hampshire.[113]

After the New Hampshire results, it became all too clear to White House aides that the exploitation of a weakened party apparatus by insurgents had created the conditions for someone with as little national prominence as McCarthy to mount a strong challenge to President Johnson that could not easily be fended off by the power of incumbency. In a March 13, 1968 memo, Wattenberg reported that Richard Scammon was impressed with the McCarthy forces in New Hampshire, who reflected the emergence of a new style of politics in the United States:

> Essentially, they ran a European style campaign: canvassing door-to-door throughout the state. This . . . is rare in American campaigns,—usually because of a lack of articulate manpower that could help a candidate.[114]

In the final analysis, this new-style campaign, the roots of which went much deeper than the Vietnam War, did not restore or transform the party, as much as accelerate its long secular demise. The development of the modern presidency helped to ensure such an outcome.

Johnson expressed his own recognition of the decline of party politics in a private meeting he had with Hubert Humphrey on April 3, 1968, a few days after announcing his decision not to run. During the course of that meeting, Johnson, though indicating an intention to remain publicly neutral, wished his Vice President well. Humphrey's major problem, even if he deviated from some of the policies the Administration laid down, "was not with the President," LBJ said, "nor with his staff." Humphrey's "problem was money and organization. This," said LBJ, "the president cannot assure the Vice President because he could not assure it for himself."[115] In part, the lack of organizational support for the Johnson presidency was the result of inadequate statesmanship, and, in part, this lack of organizational support was the price of achieving extensive reforms. Horace Busby notes, "Johnson viewed political parties as an impediment to progress. . . . Parties are little more than figments of people's imagination, a binary system that inhibits political possibilities."[116] Like Roosevelt, Johnson had willingly risked the diminution of political capital in the pursuit of programmatic innovation. "Consciously and subconsciously, [Johnson] reasons that what any man actually does in office is incomparably more important than all the political organizations in the world," the columnist William S. White wrote of Johnson in February, 1968. "More specifically, to influence a single powerful legislative chairman in Congress over a here and now issue is far more vital than any number of huddles with organization politicians standing well outside the arena of decision-making in public affairs."[117]

What Johnson did not recognize, of course, was that by failing to reverse, and even advancing, the decline of party, he was contributing to the rise of a new politics that would eventually turn on him. At the end of the day, he had not presided over the strengthening of the New Deal consensus, but its breaking apart. The Roosevelt Revolution dedicated itself to tangible programmatic rights, thus forging a coalition of blacks, liberal intellectuals and professionals, labor union members, and white ethnic groups that looked to the modern presidency for leadership. The Great Society helped bring to power issue-oriented independents, representing broad causes and movements, who resisted presidential "management," who were less willing to delegate policy responsibility to administrative agencies. The reformers who took control of the party after the Chicago debacle followed the progressive tradition of emphasizing the candidate over the party—of desiring the emancipation of the presidency from the constrictive grip of partisan institutions. But they viewed the modern presidency as the *instrument* rather than the *steward* of social reform. As James Ceaser has noted about the system of reform associated with the McGovern–Fraser Commission:

> [O]ne finds no notion of leadership similar to that of Woodrow Wilson in which the leader possesses a formative influence over public opinion. There is in fact, no attention given to the question of the type of leadership or the type of executive that is desired. The reformers' views on groups and leadership were no doubt influenced by the general ideas current in the late 1960s that group politics was now directed by mass movements.[118]

Johnson, with the encouragement of aides like Richard Goodwin, and even the more circumspect Horace Busby, had come to such a recognition of the demise of broker leadership at the outset of his presidency. By committing itself to this view, the Johnson administration helped to perpetuate and institutionalize it. LBJ, however, was too much of a New Dealer, too dedicated to the presidency, to accept the consequences of "movement" politics. By March, 1968, he had become the hated symbol of the status quo, forced into retirement, lest he contribute further to the destruction of the liberal consensus. "I could not be the rallying force to unite the country and meet the problems [confronted by the nation abroad and at home]," he told Humphrey in their meeting of April 3, "in the face of a contentious campaign and the negative attitude towards him of the youth, negroes, and academics."[119]

LBJ thus saw the mantle of liberal leadership pass to the likes of McCarthy and McGovern, who the Democratic party nominated for president in 1972. In 1972, clearly, the Democratic party was still the party of programmatic rights, but these rights had been extended to broad, less tangible social causes that could not easily be accommodated within the New Deal institutional framework. Richard Goodwin, who left the White House to work for the McCarthy crusade, gave expression to this character of liberalism soon after the 1969 election. Speaking of McCarthy's ability to touch many members of the American middle class, he wrote, "they were not asking to be promised better schools or lower taxes, although they want them. They were looking for some way in which they could regain control and play a real part in the enterprises of society. It was this same nerve that Robert Kennedy touched in two other groups—the blacks and poor whites—when he talked of the need for community control and local power."[120] This search for new answers could be satisfied neither by political parties nor executive administration. It demanded, as we shall observe in Chapter 9, a thorough reshaping of liberalism.

9

The Republican Challenge and the Reshaping of Programmatic Liberalism

In November, 1966, the distinguished English scholar Sir Denis W. Brogan published a post-mortem on the recently concluded American elections that foretold interestingly and unintentionally of the future of American politics. "The results of the American mid-term elections don't constitute a landslide or revolution," he wrote. "But they nevertheless constitute an omen." From abroad, it seemed that the tide of progressivism, ascendent since the Roosevelt revolution, was beginning to ebb. In the name of stability, if not philosophical principle, Brogan's commentary expressed some regret at this—"better the devils that we know," was no doubt the motto of 10 Downing Street, he claimed. Still, there seemed to be more than a concern with continuity in his reflections on the success the election accorded to Richard Nixon (who earned credit for his untiring campaign efforts on behalf of Republican candidates around the country) and Ronald Reagan (who won a stunning victory over the incumbent governor in California). "Even the numerous inhabitants of this sceptr'd isle who deplore the foreign policy of President Johnson and Secretary (of State) Dean Rusk don't think an election that strengthens the position of Mr. (Richard) Nixon and elects to the most populous state of the union's gubernatorial chair a former second-rate film star who was a passionate Goldwaterite in 1964, is likely to be an improvement," he wrote.[1]

Hence, Brogan unwittingly anticipated the emergence of the two figures who would dominate presidential history for the next two decades. The rising stars of Nixon and Reagan, however, did not portend a conservative revolution—or counter-revolution. In the past partisan realignments had been America's surrogate for revolution, but the late 1960s brought disarray rather than realignment to American politics. The most significant New Deal institutional development—the modern presidency—had been founded to secure a less partisan future. The cunning of the New Deal had thus yielded a candidate-centered political process and an executive-centered government that left the voters little reason to express themselves in a partisan manner; consequently, the declining influence of traditional party organizations was reflected not only in administrative politics and the presidential selection process, but in the perceptions and habits of the American people. Institutional changes that deemphasized partisan politics and governance, combining with television's emergence as the most important platform of political action, were "freeing more and more millions of Americans," as Theodore White wrote in 1973, "from unquestioning obedience to past tradition, their union begetting what has been called the age of ticket-splitting."[2]

In fact, the gains the Republicans made in the 1966 election camouflaged considerable voter uncertainty. As the *New York* Times reported soon thereafter, "so many voters split tickets in the election November 8 that it is impossible to categorize them strictly as Democratic or Republican." In twelve of the twenty-two states that elected a Governor and a Senator, a Republican won one race and a Democrat the other. In Rhode Island, Governor John H. Chafee, a Republican, and Senator Claborne Pell, a Democrat, each won re-election by slightly under and slightly more than 2–1, respectively.[3]

Voter indecisiveness was also evident in the 1968 presidential contest. Indeed, the 1968 election marked the beginning of an increased tendency for voters to place the presidency in Republican hands and Congress under the control of Democrats; this pattern of ticket-splitting endured for the better part of two decades. What seemed like an aberration during the Eisenhower years, then, now became a regular characteristic of American politics. When Eisenhower took his second oath of office in 1957, he was the first chief executive in 70 years—since Grover Cleveland in 1885—to confront a Congress of which even one house was controlled by the opposition. With the 1968 election, however, split-ticket voting became both more routine and pronounced. Richard Nixon became the first newly installed president since Zachary Taylor in 1848 to be elected without a majority for his party in either the House or the Senate. Thereafter, the mile and a half of Pennsylvania Avenue from the White House to Congress would rarely be bridged by partisan affiliation.

This condition of divided rule profoundly affected the course of the Nixon administration, exacerbating the problems of modern presidential leadership that had become obvious during the Johnson years. Hardly anyone, least of all those among the outgoing Johnson administration, expected anything but trouble in the post-Johnson years. Johnson aide George Reedy's analysis of the 1968 election, in fact, contained in a November 11 memo to the outgoing president, presented the prospect of an impending constitutional crisis. Expressing thoughts that he would later flesh out in *The Twilight of the Presidency,* Reedy wrote:

> The 1968 election brought into sharp focus a major weakness in the American system of government. The voters, in effect, asked for a coalition government by dividing their ballots very narrowly between the two candidates and by giving control of the executive branch to one party and the legislative branch to the other. Unfortunately, our constitutional system is such that neither our government nor our political parties have the necessary mechanism to form a true coalition.

The advent of the modern presidency made the possibility of forming a modus operandi between Nixon and Congress more difficult. A central tenet of modern executive leadership, one institutionalized by the Third New Deal, was that the president was the master over his own domain. Those who labored with such difficulty to maintain that standard in the Johnson White House did not relish the thought of Democrats now abandoning it—in a statement that would have seemed ludicrous prior to the conversion of the Democratics during the 1930s into a party of administration, Reedy opined that there could be no sharing of power in the executive branch, "for all executive power is concentrated in the hands of one man—the President—and meaningless in the legislative branch because it has no managerial authority." A sharing of policy responsibility between parties, more-over, would not benefit the Democrats, serving only to dilute further its uncertain identity as a national party of reform. As a result, the White House Press Secretary concluded:

> The next four years are going to be extremely difficult. Mr. Nixon's success will require genius of the very highest order. Partisan sniping by the Democratic party could make the American form of government unworkable. On the other hand, efforts to pretend to the existence of a coalition that cannot truly exist will only lead to the disintegration of the Democratic party and make it impossible to have a truly viable nation.[4]

It goes without saying that Johnson and his aides did not think Nixon had the requisite political "genius." Still, they were hopeful that he could use the powers of the presidential office to create a "government of national unity."[5] Reedy suggested to Johnson that he advise the new president that his problem in establishing national unity would not really lie with "the Democratic party per se." Professional politicians were accustomed to the realities of partisanship, and Democrats were not going to rip the country to pieces because they did not receive a large share of executive offices. But many liberals felt differently, Reedy knew, especially economic and social groups who feared there would be no place for them in Nixon's concept of "enlightened administration"—the blue-collar worker, blacks, intellectuals, and students. Unless these groups were given far more consideration than one could realistically expect in the organization and policies of the Nixon regime, Reedy knew, they "might well react bitterly."[6]

Nixon's election, and the challenge to liberalism it represented, revealed far more clearly than Eisenhower's how the New Deal expansion of administrative power had created an uncertain foundation for strong presidential leadership. Roosevelt's administrative reorganization program, carried out in pursuance of the 1939 Executive Reorganization Act, established the presidency as the center of government activity. Yet the administrative presidency was conceived with the expectation that it would be an ally of progressive reform. This ambiguous legacy of programmatic liberalism meant that Congress was not the only quarter from which Nixon could expect opposition; it was likely that he would face bitter resistance from liberal activists and their allies in the bureaucracy as well.

Because the country had only elected one other Republican since the onset of FDR's pathbreaking presidency 36 years earlier, Nixon faced a bureaucracy that had a large number of Democratic holdovers. Many of those holdovers were protected by civil service procedures, which had been extended "upward, outward, and downward" since the New Deal, encompassing most of the federal service.

Moreover, the personnel policies pursued by Democratic administrations since the 1930s did not aim to replace party patronage with "neutral competence." Instead, as noted in previous chapters, the New Deal initiated, and the Great Society extended, another kind of patronage—an intellectual and ideological patronage—that infused the bureaucracy with an entrenched programmatic liberal commitment. Eisenhower had faced pockets of bureaucratic resistance; however, the magnitude of such opposition, even with the availability of Schedule C and Noncareer Executive Assignment positions, was much more threatening to a more conservative Republican president who did not control either house of Congress.

In his memoirs Nixon explained in colorful terms how one of the most important tasks of his administration was to place its stamp on the federal bureaucracy as quickly and firmly as possible:

> I urged the new Cabinet members to move quickly to replace holdover bureaucrats with people who believed in what we were trying to do. I warned them that if we did not act quickly, they would become captives of the bureaucracy they were trying to change. I said . . . "We can't depend on people who believe in another philosophy of government to give us their undivided loyalty or their best work. . . . If we don't get rid of those people, they will either sabotage us from within, or they will just sit back on their well-paid asses and wait for the next election to bring back their old bosses."[7]

Although the thrust of this hostile statement is directed at the career civil servants, the Nixon administration also became increasingly wary of some of its own appointees. Especially galling to the Nixon White House was the way Cabinet and sub-Cabinet appointments to departments and agencies responsible for social services—most notably, HUD, HEW, and OEO—were coopted by their civil servants, who managed to enlist them as allies against the administration's policies. John Erlichman, who eventually became Nixon's domestic policy advisor, remarked at a press briefing late in 1972 that after the administration officials were appointed and had their pictures taken with the president, "We only see them at the annual White House Christmas party; they go off and marry the natives."[8]

Nixon's belief that the bureaucracy was intent upon thwarting his program was not the result merely, as his detractors charged, of his chronic tendency to distrust the motives and goodwill of other actors. He quite accurately perceived the domestic program bureaucracy as ideologically hostile to his legislative goals and program cuts. This hostility was not simply a matter of politics or partisanship, narrowly understood; rather, it was rooted in the New Deal conception of welfare and social programs as tantamount to rights, thus deserving institutional cover from the management of a hostile executive. Noting the striking differences between Nixon's views and those of the civil servants who administered his program, the political scientists Joel Aberbach and Bert Rockman have written, "The setting for the Nixon administration was one which makes the quip that 'even paranoids may have real enemies' seem appropriate, although the very aggressive behavior of the administration made a difficult situation much worse than it need have been."[9]

Nixon and the Liberal "State"

The tension between Nixon and the bureaucracy suggests a significant change in the character of programmatic liberalism. Since the New Deal it had been posed as a challenge to the dominant strand of laissez-faire liberalism in American politics; as such, it was wedded to institutional arrangements—a refurbished executive and empowered social groups—that circumvented, and eventually challenged, the normal pluralistic pattern of American politics. In 1936 the philosopher John Dewey called for modern liberalism to "become radical in the sense that, instead of using social power to ameliorate the evil consequences of the existing system, it shall use power to change the system." It is in this sense that the Great Society marked a departure from the New Deal and in doing so radicalized the programmatic liberal tradition. Yet by the end of the Johnson era, liberalism seemed a beleaguered establishment as much as a reform movement. In Nixon's presidency it seemed to have spawned an administration intent upon what Nixon speech writer Pat Buchanan called a "counter-revolution." [10]

Faced with what they too frequently perceived as the chaos of the liberal order, members of the Johnson White House began to urge a strategy of consolidation upon the president in late 1967. Johnson aide John Roche, inspired by William Blake's biography of the great conservative statesman Benjamin Disraeli, suggested in a memorandum of July 6 that LBJ needed to recognize that Americans in the late 1960s were like the British people of 1874, who threw out the reigning Liberal party and voted in the Conservatives, making Disraeli Prime Minister. "Disraeli, who was a brilliant, intuitive politician, explained it simply: 'Englishmen are tired of being improved,' " Roche wrote. That Americans were tired of "being improved" was obvious; the question was what Johnson could do about it. "This presents some real problems," Roche concluded. "As Harry [McPherson] puts it, we have to utilize 'conservative' tactics to protect the substance of liberalism—liberalism as enacted over the past three years has to become the status quo." [11]

This sort of advice comported with LBJ's political intuition and had a powerful effect on him. He frequently mentioned to his aides as the end of 1967 approached that politics went in cycles and that the kind of leadership he had provided was no longer suitable. Yet the prospect of playing a Disraeli-like role as the zeal of Great Society reform played itself out had no appeal for Johnson. According to White House aide James Gaither, the president's belief that this would be necessary was an important factor in his withdrawal from the 1968 campaign. "I think the President felt, and he did mention this the prior December, . . . that the next President, if he were Lyndon Johnson or someone like him, would find it a terribly frustrating job to have because he would be defending everything that he had done. . . ." [12]

Playing the role of Disraeli to the Great Society, however, was precisely what Richard Nixon had in mind for his presidency. At the beginning of Nixon's administration, his aide Daniel Patrick Moynihan, who had also served in the Johnson administration, gave him a copy of the same book that inspired Roche's memorandum to LBJ, Blake's *Disraeli*. Moynihan's gift made a deep impact on the new president. Nixon wrote in his memoirs that he read it twice, and he apparently thought about what he read with considerable frequency. A quotation from Blake's biography appears in the files of Robert Haldeman, Nixon's chief of staff, which warrants careful consideration:

> Where Disraeli excelled was in the art of presentation. He was an impresario and an actor manager. He was a superb parliamentarian, one of the half dozen greatest in our history. He knew how much depends upon impression, style, colour; and how small a part is played in politics by logic, cool reason, calm appraisal of alternatives. This is why politicians appreciate him. They realize that a large part of political life in a parliamentary democracy consists not so much in doing things yourself as in imparting the right tone to things that others do for you or to things that are going to happen anyway.[13]

In pondering this passage one is reminded of Nixon's attempt, especially during his first term, to manage rather than depart from, or undo, the New Deal and Great Society. Nixon was no Eisenhower, certainly, but his time in office reflected as much as Eisenhower's a recognition of the inevitability of programmatic liberalism. Just as Eisenhower accepted New Deal labor reform as irrevocable, seeking only to administer the National Labor Relations Board more moderately than his Democratic predecessors, Nixon believed that it was unrealistic to attempt the sort of counter-revolution aides like Patrick Buchanan countenanced. This explains why Nixon's Secretary of Labor, George Schultz, was able to win him over to a quite liberal Civil Rights plan, the so-called Philadelphia Plan for the construction industry. The Philadelphia plan required quotas, called "targets," for hiring minorities of those trade unions working under federal contracts.

It was during the Johnson presidency that civil rights policy shifted from a color blind to an affirmative action orientation. Only during the Nixon administration, however, did affirmative action become unambiguously the established, bipartisan policy of the United States government. From the earliest days of Nixon's administration, high officials in the departments of Labor, Justice, and Health, Education, and Welfare pushed hard for affirmative action, not only by means of contract compliance, which could only work in the private or nonfederal sector, but also by means of Executive Order 11478, which provided Affirmative Action for the federal civil service.[14]

That the Nixon administration made affirmative action national policy seemed strange in view of the president's legendary and fierce opposition to bureaucracy. From the perspective of the conservative principles he had long espoused, affirmative action appeared to be the quintessential anti-individualistic or fully bureaucratized social policy. Yet, as Nixon's attraction to Disraeli suggested, there was nothing doctrinaire about his conservatism. In the final analysis, Nixon believed that it was imprudent to oppose affirmative action, in practice, even though he denounced quotas, emphatically, as late as his Labor Day Address of 1972.[15]

It is interesting and noteworthy that Nixon's response to the recalcitrance of the bureaucracy was not to eliminate affirmative action programs, which he could ostensibly accomplish with the stroke of a pen; instead, he sought to "impart the right tone to it." He seemed to believe, as one scholar has written, "that during his presidency there was no critical point of genuine choice on Affirmative Action."[16] Of Nixon and his relationship to the liberal order it can be said as Blake wrote of Disraeli: "He did not care which way he travelled providing he was in the driver's seat."[17]

Indeed, Nixon most clearly distinguished himself from Eisenhower by his more zealous attempt to direct the course of the liberal state spawned by the New Deal and Great Society. Eisenhower accepted the responsibilities of the modern executive, and increasingly so as he came to realize that even a conservative president who wanted to delimit, and not expand, the boundaries of government responsibility had to exert strong leadership. But Eisenhower was a reluctant modern president who did not actively seek to expand the powers of the executive office or challenge the policies of the Democratic party. His "hidden hand" approach to leadership emphasized flexible accommodation to the New Deal and respect for, if not deference to, the other power centers of American government. Nixon, however, aggressively sought to expand presidential prerogatives. He, too, accommodated himself to programmatic liberalism, yet made a much more aggressive administrative effort than his Republican predecessor had to reshape it. Unlike Eisenhower, Nixon assumed office at time when the New Deal approach to the modern welfare state was being seriously questioned, even by liberals—this situation, he believed, presented an opportunity for significantly changing domestic policy. Arguably, Nixon's enthusiastic embrace of the modern presidency, his bold effort to recast the liberal order in a way that seemed appropriate to the late 1960s, fit more securely within the New Deal tradition than Eisenhower's more cautious approach to the affairs of state. But this effort to consolidate liberal reform occurred at a time when programmatic activists were becoming increasingly suspicious of the modern presidency. Thus, even had the White House been occupied by a more trustworthy figure, the possibility of forming any sort of "national unity" government was in all likelihood a chimera.

New Federalism

In truth, Nixon's years in the White House represented both a consolidation and challenge to the New Deal order. "Expansion of government programs in all areas . . . moved with surprising ease from the Johnson administration into the Nixon administration," Barry Karl has written. Yet Nixon envisioned and partly achieved a New Federalism that took seriously for the first time since the 1930s a plan eventually to devolve administration of these programs to the local and state governments. As a result, Karl continues, "the equation—familiar since the New Deal days—of expanded federal programs and a strong presidency with liberalism, the opposite with conservatism, no longer applied, for Nixon as much as Johnson wanted to centralize control of the bureaucracy in the White House."[18]

Thus, Nixon's presidency entailed a more decisive effort than Eisenhower's to use the presidency as a lever of conservative public policy. His administration was the first to look to the possibility that the modern presidency could be characterized as a two-edged sword, which could cut in a conservative as well as a liberal direction. For the first time since Theodore Roosevelt, a Republican president enthusiastically embraced a broad understanding of executive authority. But whereas TR was the first chief executive to envision and embody a transformation of the presidency into a veritable cockpit of national leadership for social reform, Nixon sought to recast the executive office as the center of growing doubts about such reform. It was this skepticism above all that gave rise to Nixon's New Federalism.

The New Federalism program was announced in a nationally televised speech of August 8, 1969. "My purpose tonight," said the president, "is to present a new set of reforms—a new and drastically different approach to the way in which government cares for those in need, and to the way responsibilities are shared between the State and the Federal Government." [19] Nixon's program was "drastically different" only in the sense that it represented the first challenge to the presumption underlying the creation and expansion of programmatic liberalism that societal problems were most effectively managed at the national level. The thrust of "new federalism," in fact, was to sort out rather than radically decentralize the administration of national policy. For example, Nixon believed that welfare required uniform standards and should, like social security, be brought under the jurisdiction of the national government, whereas manpower training required a more flexible approach and should be devolved to the states. Similarly, Nixon believed environmental regulation required national administration.

With respect to economic security and "quality of life" issues, Nixon was sensitive to matters of equity and efficiency that underlay the New Deal constitutional order. Moreover, the deference to decentralization Nixon displayed in conceiving of a New Federalism, reflected in proposals to return the administration of federal manpower programs to the states and local governments and to create a system of revenue sharing, seemed similar to the views that liberals had been expressing during the 1960s with respect to community and self-determination. But the New Federalism opposed reliance on the kinds of community agencies that had been established in the Great Society era. As noted in Chapter 8, the community action program that was the centerpiece of the war on poverty tended to disrupt and undermine the traditional fabric of federalism; its purpose was to provide for creative national intervention that circumvented the authority of state and local governments. The task of New Federalism, in contrast, was to reduce, not embellish, the federal presence in those policy areas where the Nixon administration perceived that conditions and needs varied among communities and where local decision-making was especially important—education, social services for the poor, manpower training, hospitals, urban and rural community development, and law enforcement. [20]

The difference between community action during the Great Society and the Nixon administration's New Federalism, therefore, was not merely a matter of semantics. The community action program represented a celebration of participatory democracy that was indifferent, if not avowedly hostile, to the administrative decentralization that was the foundation of American federalism. New Federalism, although hardly the stuff of a counter-revolution, reflected a growing concern that liberal innovation had taken a mischievous turn in the 1960s that portended a serious constitutional crisis. Even the moderates in the Nixon administration, such as Richard Nathan and Daniel Patrick Moynihan, tended to view maximum feasible participation as a bureaucratic invention, resulting in special "side games" for social activists. In the end, as Nixon argued in his 1971 State of the Union message, federal sponsorship of community action detracted from, rather than enhanced, republican government:

> The idea that a bureaucratic elite in Washington knows best what is best for people everywhere and that you cannot trust local governments is really a contention that you cannot trust people to govern themselves. The notion is completely foreign to the American experience.[21]

Such a message, of course, made conflict between the bureaucracy and the Nixon administration inevitable, as the thrust of Nixon's brand of New Federalism was to weaken the executive departments and agencies. Even where his plans called for national responsibility, the emphasis would be on uniform standards (an income rather than a service strategy for the poor, for example) that would reduce the discretion of administrative agencies to manage public policy. In this struggle for the administrative levers of power the bureaucracy received considerable succor from Congress, the courts, and public interest groups; as we shall see, deprived of the presidency, activists began to forge a new institutional coalition to house liberalism.

The opposition from Congress, civil servants, and, oftentimes, even his own Cabinet appointments embittered Nixon and strengthened his resolve to run the government out of the White House. Although philosophically committed to returning some social power to the private sector and local communities, Nixon felt that the federal government and its social interests—the liberal "establishment"— had grown so powerful that only a very strong president could "reverse the flow of power from the states and communities to Washington."[22] Accordingly, his commitment to decentralization went hand in hand with a program of administrative reform that would help him accomplish his policy goals by executive fiat.

Leonard Garment, a member of the Nixon White House legal staff, observed that "the central paradox of the Nixon administration was that in order to reduce *federal* power, it was first necessary to increase *presidential* power." Or, as Nixon himself described this paradox, "Bringing power to the White House was necessary to dish it out."[23]

In the end, Nixon's project to marshall the powers of the modern presidency in the service of New Federalism failed. A sharp electoral realignment that produced Republican Congresses and a dramatic change in court rulings might have cut off the political leverage of the bureaucracy, and eventually resulted in a substantial devolution of federal power. Such a realignment would have required extraordinary party leadership, however, and Nixon's administrative presidency contributed to the further decline, rather than the restoration, of party politics.

The displacement of party politics by executive administration during the 1930s created the conditions for the end of parties, unless or until an anti-administration party would spring up. It has thus been in defense of programs such as New Federalism that the Republican party has presented itself most effectively as an organized opposition to the New Deal and a potential instrument of political realignment. But the Republican party, enervated by an undue emphasis on presidential politics and governance, has slouched towards providing such loyal opposition to the New Deal.

Nixon's Administrative Presidency and the Republican Party

Just as the presidency of Dwight Eisenhower ratified the existence of the modern executive, the administration of Richard Nixon reinforced and dramatically exposed that institution's deleterious influence on the party system. More particularly, Nixon's presidency contributed to the development that began with the New Deal, whereby the party system became more national and programmatic at the same time that partisan politics became less important in linking the White House to Congress, state and local governments, and the electorate. With Nixon, one might say, the Republicans replaced the Democrats as the party of executive administration, only to be sacrificed, as the Democratic party had been, to the modern presidency to which it had been dedicated. This occurred as Nixon's overwhelming emphasis on executive administration eventually displaced early efforts during the Nixon presidency that apparently were designed to transform the character of the Republican party.

According to Louis Koenig, Nixon was "one of a handful of Presidents who strove to restructure his party by enlisting sufficient numbers of adherents to transform it from a minority party into a majority party of future decades."[24] In 1970, for example, he participated actively in Senate campaigns to ensure the election of Republican challengers, such as William Brock of Tennessee and J. Glenn Beall, Jr., of Maryland, who would increase support for his program in Congress. The most important event of this 1970 campaign, as far as the Republican party was concerned, was the "purge" of the New York Republican Senator Charles Goodell, who opposed the Administration on many important issues, in favor of the Conservative Party candidate James Buckley, who pledged unqualified support for Nixon's policies.[25]

The victories of Buckley, Brock, and Beall aroused fear among liberal Republicans that Nixon might complete the reshaping of the party that began with Goldwater's nomination in 1964. Howard Reiter, a member of the National Governing Board of the progressive GOP auxiliary, the Ripon Society, wrote in January 18, 1971, that "the irony of the 1970 elections was that, while they occasioned a general failure of conservative Republicanism at the polls, they may have produced the party takeover that Goldwater urged."[26] Most significant was the purging of Goodell, who had been appointed by Governor Rockefeller to fill the seat left empty by Robert Kennedy's assassination. Goodell had fought Nixon on a number of policies that the president counted personally: the anti-ballistic missile system; his nominations of Clement Haynsworth and G. Harold Carswell to the Supreme Court; and, most important, the Vietnam War. With White House approval, Vice President Spiro Agnew referred to Goodell during the course of the campaign as a "radical liberal who has left his party."[27] The next day, GOP National Chairman Rogers Morton endorsed Goodell, whereupon the Vice President dismissed him as a "mere party functionary." This comment widened the already serious breach between the pragmatic politicians in the National Committee and conservatives in the White House, notably Charles Colson and Murray Chotiner, who worked against Goodell's re-election.[28]

In the wake of these internecine party battles, Nixon, who hitherto had negotiated a centrist course in rhetoric and policy, seemed to lend his support to the more ideological of his supporters. The president made a special stop at Westchester County airport to speak kindly of Buckley, stating, "I appreciate the fact that he's for me."[29] Although the president stopped short of an open endorsement of Buckley, his tacit opposition to Goodell prompted the defeated incumbent Senator to declare after the election that he hoped the Nixon administration "would back off from this temptation to purge" liberal senators with whom it disagreed.[30]

Since Roosevelt's futile bid to unseat incumbents through the use of primary endorsements, Nixon was the first president to contemplate a purge of his party. The purging of Goodell hardly constituted evidence that the immensity of FDR's failure was now irrelevant or forgotten. Nixon's intervention stopped short of an open declaration of support or opposition. Moreover, this action, limited as it was, alienated several important Republican senators from the Nixon administration. Many conservative as well as liberal Republicans in the Senate criticized the President's purge campaign and actively supported Goodell's candidacy. During the election, no fewer than 20 of his colleagues, including GOP leader Hugh Scott, came to the aid of Goodell. Their gestures ranged from statements delivered on the Senate floor in praise of their beleaguered colleague to campaign tours in the Empire State.[31] It is questionable whether gaining Buckley's support in the Senate outweighed the negative reaction among the Republican regulars caused by the martyrdom of Goodell. At a press conference of December 10, the president was asked "in light of what has generally been considered the purge of Senator Goodell of New York, is it likely you and the administration will support third-party candidates in other States against Republican nominees who may disagree with some major points of your policies?" Nixon's response was emphatic—"Under no circumstances."[32]

Like Roosevelt, Nixon had found the extraordinary isolation of the presidency to be a limited partisan weapon. Notwithstanding the successful purging of Goodell, and the victories of a few other Republicans favored by the White House, the overall results of the 1970 election were disappointing. The Republicans gained only two seats in the Senate, which remained in Democratic hands, and Republicans lost nine seats in the House. These losses were "small only when one fails to consider that Nixon was the first modern president to begin his presidency with the opposition in control of Congress."[33] The fact that the Nixon White House's assault on Goodell aggravated many Republican legislators, including the GOP Senate leadership, did nothing to ameliorate the president's troubled relations with Congress. Faced with these unsatisfactory results and with few legislative achievements during the first 2 years of his presidency, Nixon came to rely on presidential politics and executive action in seeking to carry out his program.

Nixon's administrative presidency developed in two stages. The first phase entailed an expansion and reorganization of the Executive Office of the President, which would preempt or cow into submission the regular party apparatus and program bureaucracies. As a result, the White House Office doubled in size, swelling from a staff of 292 under Johnson to 583 members by the end of Nixon's first term. For example, an organization was formed under the control of Robert Haldeman and Attorney General John Mitchell—the Committee to Reelect the President (CREEP)—which assumed full responsibility for Nixon's 1972 campaign. The development of the president's re-election strategy was the culmination of the administration's assault on the Republican machinery that was closely patterned after, and in fact surpassed, Johnson's attack on the officialdom of the Democratic party.

Following the 1968 election, Ray Bliss, who had rebuilt and modernized the Republican organization after the Goldwater debacle, was fired, and his replacement, Rogers Morton, had experienced difficult relations with the White House in seeking to maintain the integrity of the party machinery. These relations, as noted, became embittered during the 1970 elections, and the White House moved in during the latter stages of the campaign, effectively replacing the committee staff as the central organizer of the effort. After the 1970 election, Morton moved to the Interior Department and was succeeded by Senator Robert Dole of Kansas. "The Morton tenure," Clifford Brown, Jr., has written, "was a sort of transition between Bliss's attempt to rebuild the party and Dole's subsequent anguished performance totally subservient to the interest of the White House."[34] As the presidential election of 1972 grew nearer, the creation of CREEP further eclipsed the national committee staff, and it was given a series of perfunctory roles during the re-election campaign.[35] Furthermore, the strategy of CREEP in the 1972 campaign conceived by Mitchell, H. R. Haldeman and Clark MacGregor, who headed the reelection staff, was to keep Nixon's efforts totally separated from congressional races.[36]

The attempt by the Nixon White House to establish a political constituency that would be separated institutionally from the Republican party complemented its efforts to govern the nation from the White House. Nixon's efforts to enact New Federalism, reshape the Court, and continue a strong American presence in world affairs with the support of a narrow bipartisan coalition in Congress were continually frustrated. Nixon gave voice to this frustration in his memoirs. Referring to his inability to gain congressional acceptance of the plan to give money directly to the poor, without intercession by liberal social workers—the so-called "income strategy"—he wrote: "[O]ur bold attempt to reform the federal welfare system—the Family Assistance Plan—illustrated the problem of the Senate's tendency to fracture into special interest groups. As George Schultz later summed it up. 'He who walks in the middle of the road gets hit by both sides.' "[37]

To strengthen his position as the tribune of the national interest, to establish government power independent of the fragmentation to which the American polity was prone, Nixon abandoned the legislative strategy that he had pursued during the first 2 years of his presidency. He now shifted to a strategy that achieved his objectives through administrative action. As a former member of the Nixon administration, Richard Nathan, has noted: "Nixon came to the conclusion sometime in 1971 that in many areas of government, particularly domestic affairs, *operations is policy*. Many day-to-day management tasks for domestic programs—

for example, regulation writing, grant approval, and budget apportionment—are substantive and therefore involve policy.''[38]

The first phase of Nixon's administrative program was to create a White House counter-bureaucracy that could take on the liberal opposition. White House assistant John Erlichman headed a newly formed Domestic Council, which dominated the domestic policy process. Furthermore, the Bureau of the Budget was reorganized and expanded to strengthen the president's influence on domestic affairs. On July 1, 1970, by executive order, it was transformed into the Office of Management and Budget (OMB), signifying an added cadre of presidentially appointed assistant directors for policy who stand between the OMB director and the bureau's civil servants. Consequently, the budget office attained additional policy responsibility and became more responsive to the president. The budget bureau had been an important part of the executive office since being moved from Treasury in 1939, but the OMB became a more visible and conservative actor after 1970. Whereas budget directors since 1939 had played a central role in coordinating liberal programs and instituting Keynesian policies, henceforth they would increasingly be assigned the task of fashioning a more circumspect, if not hostile, approach to programmatic liberalism.

The aggrandizement of presidential power during the Nixon years was reinforced by foreign policy considerations. While Johnson intended to make his mark upon history in domestic affairs, Nixon's ambitions lay principally in the realm of foreign policy. Oftentimes, it seemed, Nixon merely wanted to restore enough stability to domestic matters so affairs at home could be subordinated to international concerns, which he considered of far greater significance. As the 1972 election approached, he encouraged Ehrlichman to concern himself more with "selling" the administration's domestic program than its substance. Making tough decisions in the domestic realm, even if justified, was inappropriate if politically expensive, because the consequences of mischievous programs were not so profound. Political wounds in foreign affairs, in contrast, as Nixon risked in his controversial decision to send troops to Cambodia, could not be avoided for the sake of popular approbation. To reject the Cambodian operation, he noted, would have been easy to sell, but "would have left the United States with no credible foreign policy position not only in Southeast Asia but in any other part of the world." In the final analysis, such a foreign policy failure had to be avoided at all costs: "Mistakes in domestic policy can be rectified. Very seldom is that the case where a major foreign policy mistake is made."[39]

Nixon's thoughts on foreign policy meant that he could not simply concentrate power in the White House to reduce federal power. In the realm of foreign affairs, Nixon wished to strengthen and make creative use of the state, to leave a legacy of enduring national resolve in world affairs. It was this ambition that made it impossible for Nixon to take the easy way out in Vietnam. "I am not going to end up like LBJ," he once remarked, "holed up in the White House afraid to show my face on the street. I'm going to stop that war. Fast."[40] Nevertheless, his foreign policy required that the Administration find a way to withdraw American troops without abandoning South Vietnam, to obtain "peace with honor," which became the guiding slogan of the Nixon administration's Vietnam policy.[41]

Nixon's desire to play a major role on the stage of world events and prevent the nation's loss of resolve as a result of the Vietnam War not only reinforced, but made more rigid and controversial, his aggressive use of presidential power. Similarly, Nixon's foreign policy required that he make new use of, rather than dismantle, the administrative power forged on the liberal order. Consequently, Henry Kissinger created the first complete White House–dominated system for management of international affairs. Since Kennedy there had been a tendency for the National Security Council (NSC) to assume many of the functions of the State Department. But Nixon and Kissinger built an NSC staff of unprecedented size and power. So marginal was the Department of State in Nixon's foreign policy making that Secretary of State William Rogers was not even informed in advance of the administration's most dramatic foreign affairs departure—the opening to China.[42]

The swelling of the executive office, representing the first phase of Nixon's administrative presidency, did not bring about the desired control over public policy. In domestic affairs, especially, recalcitrant bureaucrats and their allies in Congress managed to resist effectively Nixon's efforts to seize control of the administrative levers of power. Two weeks before the 1972 election, former president Dwight Eisenhower wrote Nixon to express his hope for a big victory, big enough to give Nixon ''a strong, clear mandate'' and a Republican Congress. Eisenhower noted that a huge electoral victory could help Nixon ''change the ingrained power structure of the federal government (the heritage of the years of Democratic rule), placing more responsibility at state and local levels.''[43] Nixon did win a victory of massive proportions—his popular majority (60.7 percent) was exceeded in modern history only by those awarded to Johnson in 1964 and Roosevelt in 1936. But, befitting his extraordinary emphasis on an embellished and autonomous presidency, Nixon won a landslide victory that did not redound to the benefit of his party. The Republican party failed to make inroads in either the Congress or the state legislatures.

Still lacking the support he needed from Congress to become an effective legislative leader, Nixon expanded further the administrative presidency. This second phase of Nixon's program of administrative reform began with his decision that the counter-bureaucracy operating out of the White House was an inefficient means for managing the executive branch. With the president's approval, Haldeman and Ehrlichman began to lay plans for gaining direct White House control over the entire bureaucracy. Their aim, according to Haldeman, was to strike, ''for the first time, at the lower levels where the government is really run.''[44]

Thus, early in his second term, Nixon undertook a reorganization intended to rebuild the bureaucracy in his own image. ''I regretted that during the first term we had done a very poor job in the most basic business of every new administration of either party: we had failed to fill all the key posts in the departments and agencies with people who were loyal to the President and his programs,'' Nixon wrote in his memoirs. ''I was determined that we should not fail in this area again, and on the morning after my re-election I called for the resignation of every non-career employee in the executive branch.''[45] Undertaking massive personnel changes, the Nixon administration sought to move its proven loyalists into the regular program departments and agencies and to consolidate leadership of the bureaucracy through a "supercabinet" of four reliable secretaries who would implement his policies.

Nixon's plan to carry out a sweeping reorganization of the executive branch was first announced in his 1971 State of the Union Address. State, Treasury, Defense, and Justice would remain, he announced, but the other eight major departments would be consolidated into four: Human Resources, Community Development, Natural Resources, and Economic Development. "Under this plan, rather than dividing up our departments by narrow subjects, we would organize them around the great purposes of government," he argued.[46] The super-department scheme never had a chance to fulfill the promise envisioned by Nixon, because Congress, which since 1939 had grudgingly accepted the notion that the presidency could be empowered to govern the state by managing it, was no longer prepared to sanction this tenet of modern executive leadership: None of the bills to create the "super-departments" ever left congressional committee. Fourteen months later, however, emboldened by his landslide re-election, Nixon attempted to institute through administrative arrangements what he earlier sought in the super-department legislation. The president declared that the Cabinet would no longer be composed of equals, designating several members to be responsible for larger segments of domestic policy and administration. A supersecretary was also designated for foreign affairs, Henry Kissinger, who while retaining his position as assistant to the president for national security affairs, assumed the position of Secretary of State, thus becoming fully responsible, in a formal as well as informal sense, for foreign policy.[47]

Nixon's attempt to expand the reach of presidential power, and, by doing so, to achieve political and policy objectives autonomously, has been widely viewed as a usurpation of power that foreshadowed the Watergate scandal, which would end in his resignation from office. It was, to be sure, both the improprieties of the White House re-election operation, particularly the attempt to bug the Democratic National Committee offices and the subsequent attempt to cover up that break-in, that gave rise to the Watergate revelations.

But Nixon's version of the administrative presidency was not entirely new; in important respects, of course, it was a logical extension of practices carried out by previous Democratic presidents, such as Franklin Roosevelt and Lyndon Johnson, who were intent upon bringing about significant programmatic change. The complete autonomy of the Committee to Re-elect the President from the regular Republican organization in the 1972 campaign was but the final stage of a long process of White House preemption of the national committee's political responsibilities. And the administrative reform program pursued after Nixon's reelection, in which executive authority was concentrated in the hands of White House operatives and four Cabinet "supersecretaries," was the culmination of a long-standing tradition of the modern presidency to reconstitute the executive department into a more centralized and independent instrument of government.

Toward the end of the Johnson presidency, as noted in Chapter 8, the White House was in the process of forming a presidential re-election committee that would have little connection with, and, in fact, assume many routine tasks of, the national committee. Before LBJ left the White House, moreover, the administration gave attention to the need to consolidate further the president's power over the executive department. The second Johnson task force on government organization—the Heineman task force—made many recommendations in 1967 that formed the basis of the Nixon administrative reform program. It called for the formation of a policy coordinating staff in the executive along the lines of the Domestic Council that Nixon formed; a reorganization of the budget bureau with a view of widening its responsibilities, so as to transform the BOB "from intelligent reaction to departmental demands to active, independent leadership in program development that supports and is responsive to the president and his perspective"; and the regrouping of executive departments and agencies into a smaller number of "superdepartments" that would be "far more useful and much more responsive to, and representative of, Presidential perspectives and objectives than the scores of parochial department and agency heads who now share the line responsibilities of the executive branch." The evidence is that LBJ favored the Heineman task force's central recommendations and planned to implement some of them after his re-election in 1968; of course, Johnson's retirement came sooner than expected.[48] But the Ash Council, named for its director, Roy Ash, drew extensively from the Heineman report in formulating an administrative reform program for President Nixon.[49]

Thus, just as Roosevelt's presidency anticipated the Great Society, Johnson's presidency anticipated the administrative presidency of Richard Nixon. Ironically, the strategy of pursuing policy goals through administrative capacities that had been created for the most part by Democratic presidents was considered especially suitable by a minority Republican president embattled with a hostile Congress and bureaucracy. Nixon, therefore, surpassed previous modern presidents in viewing the party system as an obstacle to effective governance.

This view was informed apparently by Nixon's belief in the decisive triumph of the New Deal, a belief no doubt encouraged by the disappointing results of the 1970 campaign. The institutional legacy of the New Deal made it unlikely that a stable majority could be won to support a conservative party in the United States. The triumph of the New Deal signified a deterioration of party and the rise of an administrative politics that envisioned an unmediated, nonpartisan tie between government and the American people. Consequently, it was not a "Republican majority" but an "American" majority, necessitating the creation of a direct link between the president and the people, that would appeal to detachable non-Republicans.[50] The New Deal and Great Society established a government dominated by executive management of social and economic problems; the hope of conservatives, therefore, was to develop administrative practices informed by conservative principles. When asked in March, 1971, how he intended to put the Republican party back where it was before 1932, the permanent majority party, Nixon indicated clearly that he considered the development of a coalition upon a White House rather than a partisan program to be more practicable:

> That probably will not happen . . . to either the Republican or Democratic party.
> . . . [We] will never have a time again, in my opinion, in this country when

you are going to have polarization of Democrats versus Republicans. I think you are going to have Independents controlling basically the balance of power. . . .What I think will happen is that both parties will vie for building the new coalition, starting with their hard core of hearty supporters and then moving into that group of Independents trying to get a field of Independent voters and also moving over into the other party and picking up a considerable number of them.[51]

The immense proportions of the victory in 1972 did not fundamentally change Nixon's view of the New Deal legacy and how it defined his task. To be sure, Nixon was less committed to liberal policies the second term. But his administration's more conservative and pessimistic position on domestic issues after 1972 was not tied to a plan to strengthen the Republican party; instead, Nixon intensified his efforts to strengthen executive administration during the second term, thus undermining his avowed commitment to New Federalism and short-circuiting the emergence of the Republican party as a party against administration.

Of course, the Nixon White House might have believed that the capture of the bureaucracy was central to the eventual formation of a new Republican majority. Just as some members of the Brownlow Committee viewed administrative reform as the foundation for a more national and programmatic Democratic party, there were members of the Nixon White House who considered the program to remake the bureaucracy as the basis of a "modern" Republicanism. White House aide Patrick Buchanan urged upon Nixon soon after the President's re-election an ideological form of patronage that would recast *both* the bureaucracy and the Republican party: "Beyond the purging of the disloyal and recalcitrant and the infusing of new blood, there is an over-riding need for this Nixon administration to create a new 'cadre' of Republican governmental professionals who can survive this Administration and be prepared to take over future ones," he wrote in a memo of November 10. This ideological form of administrative politics, and not attention to good management, would ensure Nixon his place in history as the Republican Roosevelt:

Our primary objective in the second term should be making of the President, the Republican FDR, founder and first magistrate of the political dynasty, to dominate American politics long after the President has retired from office. . . . If the President is not to enter the history books as a second political Eisenhower— a Republican regent between Democratic magistrates—then we have to begin to make permanent the New Majority that returned the President to office. That new majority essentially consists of the Republican base nationally, the Nixon South, the ethnic, blue collar, Catholic, working class Americans of the North, Midwest and West.[52]

Nixon was deeply interested in Buchanan's analysis. He asked Haldeman to discuss with Buchanan the contents of his memorandum, but to do so quietly— without copying and distributing it to other aides—lest "anything get out to the press on matters of this nature."[53] Clearly, Buchanan's memo conformed with the president's own thoughts on the election, for he acted quickly on some of its recommendations. Nixon instructed the White House staff to develop a personnel selection process that would not only put Nixon loyalists in charge of the bureaucracy, but reward individuals who could be the foot soldiers of a new majority party. This sudden attention to the minutiae of party building greatly disrupted the carefully laid plans that Haldeman and Frederick Malek, who was in charge of developing a "talent bank" of personnel to fill administrative posts in the departments for the second term, had been formulating since the summer of 1972. As Malek recalled:

> The President decided that the election had shown that a "New Majority" had formed in the United States, and that this New Majority should be represented throughout his administration in the second term. These had not been the criteria we had used for selecting people to fill positions in the second Nixon administration. We had not given consideration to geography or ethnic balance or anything like that. Being Italian or being Irish or being southern or being a member of a trade union or being a veteran had not been among the priorities we had used.[54]

This sudden fix on coalition politics hardly represents a careful plan to forge a new Republican majority. It is interesting mainly in revealing Nixon's reconsideration of the New Deal legacy, one less obsessed with the decline of party and more hopeful about the strengthening of the Republican party to promote conservative values. It is tempting, and not entirely inappropriate, to interpret the Nixon administration's adoption of a realignment strategy as an action of considerable long-term significance, as the beginning of a plan of action that would severely threaten the liberal order by the late 1970s. In the short term, however, it led to disarray rather than concerted party building within the Nixon White House.

Nixon's new-found concern to nurture a new majority had a similar effect on the regular party apparatus. In early 1973, Nixon had concluded, according to the press, that "the 1972 [re-election] strategy developed by [the White House] was totally flawed." According to one of his aides, Nixon had come to recognize that "this strategy, which kept the President's campaign strictly separated from others, resulted in a landslide for him but the election of another Democratic Congress."[55] This revelation apparently left the president determined to attend more closely to party matters in his second term. Nixon's resolve was strengthened no doubt by his not having to worry any longer about his own electoral fortunes, thus obviating the need to retain an independent political organization. Just as significant, Nixon was now more inclined to equate his place in history with the fortunes of his party. George Bush, who replaced the beleaguered Robert Dole as party chair after the 1972 campaign, was brought in to rebuild and recoup the party machinery, and he was given assurances by the White House that he would have a free hand in reorganizing the party and redefining its role.[56]

Nevertheless, the Nixon administration's commitment to party revitalization as well as its relationship to the regular party machinery remained tenuous during the second term. There was concern among party regulars, and even some members of the White House, that Nixon might "enforce ideological purity on the Republican party from the top down."[57] Nixon's dedication to any form of ideological purity was never very evident, but there is no doubt about his desire to direct the course of events, and his commitment to a strengthening of the GOP presupposed presidential dominance of the party councils. Indeed, even after 1972, the view that presidential politics and governance, not partisanship, were central to the task of forging a new conservative movement continued to pervade the White House. Soon after Nixon's re-election, the White House planned to impose Charles Colson as General Counsel of the RNC on the new party chair, George Bush, to ensure presidential supervision, if not control, over any efforts to rebuild and recoup the Republican machinery. The Nixon administration eventually decided against this plan, but not because such a move would compromise the vitality of the party. Rather, the White House concluded that Colson was too valuable to waste on party politics. "The idea of you functioning as RNC Counsel is not a good one after all," Haldeman informed Colson in a memorandum of November 22, 1972. ". . . [Y]our concentration should be on the New Majority, not the National Committee."[58]

In the final analysis, Nixon, like the modern presidents who preceded him, subordinated the tasks of party leadership to executive administration. Neither his temperament nor his concept of leadership was well suited to forming a partisan alternative to the New Deal, to forging a new Republican majority. He did not want to remake the political system as much as he wanted to bestow his own concept of management upon programmatic liberalism. This, and the difficult political circumstances he faced, inclined Nixon to embrace enthusiastically, rather than challenge, the New Deal institutional framework. Especially in matters touching foreign policy and defense, Nixon insisted on the need for broad presidential discretion. Nixon appreciated Buchanan's analytical construct of the 1972 election as the beginning of a New Majority; however, the president's own reflections on his landslide, expressed in response to his speechwriter's post mortem, stressed that it was his "very tough decisions" on Vietnam and China, which incurred the wrath of the left and right, respectively, that won the day.[59] Nixon's commitment to tackling the challenging foreign policy problems the nation faced, and his view that world affairs far surpassed domestic matters in importance, strengthened his dedication to the administrative aggrandizement.

The concern expressed in the White House after the 1972 election about the importance of party politics, and the need to rededicate the purpose of administrative power in the service of building a new Republican majority, is an important preface to the revitalization of the Republican party a decade later. The development of the modern presidency had been associated from the start, albeit indirectly, with the transformation of the American party system, pushing it closer in style and organization to the party systems of Europe. By more boldly associating the Republican party with the expansion of administrative power, Nixon further advanced what Irving Louis Horowitz called in 1974 "the Europeanization of American Politics." As Horowitz wrote, McGovern's nomination by the Democratic party and the Nixon administration's reaction to it meant that "coming into the 1970s, the competing philosophies of the two parties could be summarized as follows: for the Republicans, the main purpose of citizenship is service to the state; for the Democrats, the main concern of the state is service to its citizens."[60]

In the Nixon administration, however, the attention paid to philosophical or ideological questions was limited; the concern displayed for political realignment emphasized making the president the founder and first magistrate of a political dynasty. Political parties were not irrelevant to this task of conservative state building, to be sure. But the reform of the party was only considered in the service of molding a more conservative form of executive administration.

In many respects, the "conservative" administrative presidency was ill conceived. The centralization of responsibility within the presidency was carried out to build a more "liberal" America. As a program of the Democratic party, the modern presidency depended upon broad agreement among the Congress, the bureaucracy, and eventually the courts to expand the welfare state; a formidable politics of executive administration depended, then, upon a consensus committed to delegating powers to the executive department. Once such a system was in place, a conservative pursuit of better management as intended by Nixon needed to be more intense and calculated than those of liberal presidents, a necessity that would have made his attempt to change the American political landscape very problematical, even without the ignominy brought by the Watergate activities. By the time Johnson left the White House, the political environment for presidents was becoming increasingly intractable. Because of Watergate, Nixon's presidency had the effect of strengthening the opposition to unilateral use of presidential power, while further attenuating the bonds that linked presidents to the party system. The evolution of the modern presidency had left it in complete political isolation.

The Reshaping of Liberalism

The political isolation of the modern executive would continue during the Ford and Carter years, so much so that by the end of the 1970s statesmen and scholars were lamenting the demise of the presidency as well as the party system. The political control once provided by political parties for facilitating consensus and redirecting policy seemed to be a thing of the past. The modern presidency, which was developed to alleviate the need for parties in the political process, now seemed burdened by an overload of responsibilities and a lack of organizational support. Although in the past critical realignments had restored the vigor of democratic politics in the United States and provided the opportunity for extraordinary presidential leadership, American government now seemed stricken by a "dealignment," by a disintegration of partisan attachments in the electorate that seemingly defied the renewal of popular consensus in the American polity.[61]

These developments were partly brought on by the national reaction to controversies that in a span of 6 years saw two consecutive presidents win overwhelming popular approval at the polls only to be unceremoniously forced from office. Having witnessed the indiscretions of the Johnson and Nixon years, the New Deal historian Arthur Schlesinger, Jr., hitherto one of the most eloquent long-standing defenders of strong presidential leadership, wrote in his influential 1973 volume, *The Imperial Presidency,* "In the last years presidential primacy, so indispensable to the political order, has turned into presidential supremacy. The constitutional presidency—as events so apparently disparate as the Indochina War and Watergate affair showed—has become the imperial presidency and threatens to be the revolutionary presidency.''[62]

Schlesinger's concern should not be dismissed merely as the lament of a disappointed liberal. The modern presidency had created constitutional problems that transcended partisanship, ideological differences, and policy disagreement. The ugly events of Watergate, moreover, were not simply the result of Nixon's character flaws; in part, they grew out of his determination to uphold the modern presidency in the face of growing doubts about its legitimacy. As Peri Arnold has written with respect to Nixon's attempt to seize control of the executive branch:

> President Nixon's use of reorganization was consistent with a tradition of administrative reform. But he made it too apparent that reorganization was about political power. By association with the political embarrassments of his administration, Nixon had made reorganization planning itself a suspicious enterprise. . . . The 1970s opened the question that had seemed closed since the Brownlow Report; can the presidency be empowered to govern the state by managing it?[63]

In truth, that question had been reopened in the late 1960s with the emergence of the "new" politics. The embarrassments of Vietnam and Watergate had only accentuated and added legitimacy to liberal reformers' growing suspicion of the presidency. Their successful efforts to reshape liberalism in the wake of the controversy and scandal that plagued the White House during the Johnson and Nixon years brought institutional changes that, for a time, not only restrained but severely impaired the presidency. "Probably no development of the 1960s and 1970s has greater import for the future of American politics," Samuel Huntington wrote in 1976, "than the decline in the authority, status, influence, and effectiveness of the presidency."[64] But the reforms of the 1960s and 1970s were not, as Huntington has asserted, simply an antinomian attack on the New Deal political organization.[65] Rather, the "new" politics of the late 1960s evolved, even matured, into a new stage of liberalism that sought to strengthen, rather than dismantle, the New Deal constitutional order. The immediate objective of the liberalism that emerged in the 1970s was to provide an institutional loft for "programmatic rights" that could withstand Republican control of the White House. But this latter stage of liberalism involved more than conserving the New Deal constitutional order. Informed by the reform aspirations of the 1960s, the liberalism of the 1970s sought to make administrative power compatible with "participatory democracy." Johnson's presidency, dedicated to a new, more experimental liberal politics, was the first cause of this concern to enhance the representative character of New Deal institutions. But in seeking to surpass the accomplishments of Franklin Roosevelt and the New Deal, LBJ unwittingly encouraged the rise of a liberal politics that extensively circumscribed the administrative power of the president.

Thus, the reforms of the late 1960s and 1970s collectively brought about a significant departure from the institutional legacy of the New Deal and Great Society. Consistent with the tradition of programmatic liberalism, the reforms of the late 1960s and 1970s were associated with efforts to enhance national administrative power as a means of expanding the programmatic responsibilities of the national government. But, unlike the reform pattern of the New Deal and Great

Society, the liberalism of this later period, incited by the disappointments of the Johnson and Nixon administrations, was greatly suspicious of, if not hostile to, presidential power. We have noted that the modern presidency was conceived with the view that it would be an ally of programmatic reform. When this supposition was seemingly violated by the Vietnam War and subsequent developments, reformers set out to protect liberal programs from unfriendly executive administration. The recent surge of liberal reform resulted in not only the McGovern–Fraser reforms, which administered further damage to the traditional party apparatus, but also a plethora of laws and administrative mechanisms that imbedded liberal programs in an institutional network designed to be independent of the president's influence.

The new institutional coalition that displaced the modern presidency as the steward of public welfare—composed of public interest (or citizen) groups, bureaucratic agencies, the courts, and congressional subcommittees—further insulated liberal programs and program advocates from the conventional operations of American politics. The efforts during the 1960s and 1970s to enhance the representative character of government action ultimately did not seek to restrain administrative power but, rather, attempted to recast it as an agent of democracy. As a result, the policy responsibility of the executive was increased, but Congress, the courts, and public interest groups became involved in the details of administration. The legacy of the most recent variant of liberal reform, therefore, did not lead to a wholesale attack on administrative authority, but to the formation of an "institutional partnership" designed to make public administration as "enlightened" as the New Deal was supposed to have been.[66]

The Modern Presidency and the "New" Congress

As noted in Chapter 5, Roosevelt's Third New Deal, his attempt to strengthen executive administration, involved efforts to domesticate Congress and the Courts. He succeeded in the latter, in spite of the failed court-"packing" plan. After 1937, the Supreme did not invalidate any significant federal statute to regulate the economy, nor did the Court judge any law to be an unconstitutional delegation of authority to the president. The "Constitutional Revolution of 1937" was consolidated with FDR's appointment of seven new members to the Court between 1937 and 1941. But the attempt to overcome Southern democracy in the Congress—FDR's celebrated purge campaign—failed, thus inviting programmatic liberals to strengthen the presidency and executive agencies as a bulwark against a refractory legislative body.

During the Eisenhower administration, the Warren Court demonstrated that at times it could outpace and, to a point, even force the reluctant hand of the president in advancing liberal programs. This suggested to ardent New Dealers that their goals could now be served more readily through judicial activism than through the Court's deference to the other branches. Two Supreme Court Justices, William Douglas and Felix Frankfurter—both of whom could make claims upon the proper understanding of the New Deal legacy—were adversaries on the point of the judiciary's role in the liberal order. The liberal activism of Douglas eventually triumphed over the institutional norms defended by New Dealer Frankfurter. White House opposition to programmatic liberalism, which intensified during the Nixon years, encouraged reformers to look elsewhere for the initiation of new programs and the promotion of racial and economic equality.[67]

Although liberals were not encouraged to look to Congress until the end of the Johnson presidency, change started in 1958 with the significant gains Democrats made outside the South that year in congressional elections. Liberals, in fact, now made up a majority of the House Democratic party. Frustrated by the advantage that the seniority rule continued to accord conservatives from the noncompetitive South in obtaining the powerful committee chairs, liberal Democrats created the House Democratic Study Group (DSG) in 1958. This group of liberals within the House Democratic caucus focused their efforts on lessening the power of the conservative committee chairs and spreading that power more widely among all Democrats, particularly the liberal majority.[68]

Nevertheless, the conservative coalition—the alliance forged between Southern Democrats and Republicans during Roosevelt's second term—continued to thwart liberal legislation through the Kennedy presidency. Johnson's mastery of legislative matters enabled him to overcome the opposition of the Southern Democrats in the enactment of the 1964 Civil Rights Act, and the landslide victory he achieved soon thereafter brought enough Northern liberal Democrats into Congress to wrest power in the House and Senate from the "conservative coalition." With the passage of the 1965 Voting Rights Act, moreover, Johnson ensured the transformation of Southern Democracy that eluded his illustrious predecessor. The weakening of the conservative coalition and the concomitant rise of the DSG combined to cause the transformation of the legislative branch, culminating in the procedural changes of the early 1970s that dramatically altered the congressional power structure.

The reconstructed Congress was not content to protect programmatic liberalism from an indifferent or hostile presidency. Rather, it pursued an ambitious liberal agenda that sought dramatically to extend the boundaries of programmatic rights. The problem of hunger, for example, was "discovered" in America just as LBJ was cutting back on the War on Poverty to make room in his budget for the military build-up in Vietnam. This was no accident—it was the result of efforts by a few Senators, notably Robert Kennedy, George McGovern, and Joseph Clark, and their allies in the labor movement (especially Walter Reuther), foundations (such as the Ford and Field Foundations), newly formed "citizen" groups, and media to make the problem of hunger more apparent to the American people, and thus to revitalize the flagging War on Poverty. As a result, the politics of food stamps changed suddenly and dramatically towards the end of the Johnson era.

This coterie of food stamp reformers, dedicated to the creation of a right to a "nutritionally adequate diet," had previously seen the president and the Department of Agriculture as their primary allies in the fight against the conservative coalition in Congress. They now turned on Lyndon Johnson and Secretary of Agriculture Orville Freeman—a member in good standing of the Minnesota Farm Labor Party—whom they accused of being callously cautious. The liberal reform strategy focusing on executive administration became what R. Shep Melnick calls "a boisterous 'outside' strategy." Liberal Democrats in Congress, using the Senate Select Committee on Human Needs as a forum, worked with the press and a small but skilled group of "hunger lobbyists" to force Johnson's hand and to write legislation requiring program expansion. Food stamps—both its programs and politics—would henceforth become the province of a new form of liberal politics, centered in a new set of institutional arrangements.[69]

The hunger issue was an important prelude to a reform endeavor that reshaped liberalism during the 1970s. When the right to a "nutritionally adequate diet" first emerged in 1967, it was tied to a broader attack on LBJ, who was falling out of favor with liberals active in the civil rights and anti-war movements. Mc-Govern, Kennedy, and Reuther were not only important actors in the "dump Johnson" movement but part of the "new politics" Democratic faction that was intent upon moving liberalism well beyond the New Deal economic constitutional order. As noted in Chapter 8, the expansion of the liberal agenda included a commitment to new issues such as community control and "participatory democracy" that led new liberal activists to challenge New Deal institutions. Once Nixon sat in the White House, partisan politics sharpened the reformers attacks on the executive branch. Although his administration proposed and implemented the largest expansion in food stamp history, it was constantly the object of attack by food stamp advocates. Before long, however, the enemy had become not just the Nixon administration in particular, but the "modern presidency" in general.[70]

In the final analysis, Nixon's downfall grew out of his bitter relations with Congress. The sequence of events that defined the Watergate affair was the principal cause of Nixon's having the unhappy distinction to be the first president in American history to resign his office. Nixon's impeachment was assured by the Supreme Court action in *United States v. Nixon,* which rejected the president's sweeping claims of executive privilege and forced release of tapes that showed the president had known all along of the coverup.[71] But the willingness of Congress to take the extraordinary step of removing a president was in part a response to Nixon's repeated attempts to circumvent the legislature.[72] Certainly, Congress' resolve was strengthened by the ideological and partisan struggles that marked the relations between the president and Congress. These struggles revealed how the emergence of the conservative administrative presidency had in a sense not challenged the administrative state but inaugurated a battle for its services. The New Deal represented the transfer of considerable decision-making power on a number of major issues from the electoral arena to administrative agencies, and the augmentation of executive power was carried out with the hope of strengthening the president's administrative capacities in the service of programmatic rights. With the Nixon presidency, the revitalization of the Republican party as a party against administration was sacrificed to executive prerogative, thus accentuating the importance of administrative politics to the further detriment of parties and elections.

Nixon's challenge to the liberal "establishment" relied on what Benjamin Ginsberg and Martin Shefter call "institutional combat," a form of political warfare befitting an era of party decline and electoral stalement. With the advent of divided government, they have written, "the Democrats and Republicans continue to contest elections. But rather than pin all its hopes on defeating its foes in the electoral arena, each party has begun to strengthen the institutions it commands and to use them to weaken its foe's governmental and political base."[73] Thus, the playing out of the New Deal legacy, and the opposition it spawned, was gradually developing into a form of party politics centered on government rather than the electorate. Furthermore, this partisan and institutional combat revolved around the task of controlling the administrative levers of power, thus further eroding and making unlikely the renewal of partisan attachments in the electorate. Indeed, the Liberal response to Watergate emphasized the need to tame rather than win back the administrative presidency. Above all, this domestication of the president's administrative power required circumscribing executive prerogative in foreign affairs. The Nixon administration's primary defense of its aggressive expansion of executive powers was that these actions were motivated by concern for the country's future during wartime. Nixon even justified the firing of the special prosecutor Archibald Cox, who issued a subpoena that would force the president to release tapes of White House conversations related to the Watergate investigation, on the ground that acquiescence to Cox's aggressive investigation would make the president appear weak in the eyes of Soviet leader Leonid Brezhnev and other foreign leaders.[74]

Thus, the protection of—and hope of extending further—programmatic liberalism depended upon imposing strong restraints on the executive's initiative in foreign policy. The legislation passed during the 1970s designed to accomplish this task, such as the War Powers Resolution of 1973, should be viewed only in part as an attempt to revive Congress' constitutional prerogatives; just as surely, such measures were intended to facilitate an ambitious expansion of welfare and regulatory programs. Similarly, the passage of the Budget Control Act of 1974, which was designed to give Congress control over the executive budget, was intended to protect social reform from the sort of fiscal assault on social welfare programs Nixon sought to carry out after his 1972 re-election.

These laws in and of themselves would only have a marginal effect on presidential power. But their enactment was associated with a determination of the "new" Congress to reestablish itself as an equal partner, indeed, the dominant force in the governance of the nation. It was this determination that gave rise to the procedural reforms of the early 1970s that remade the legislative power structure—the result was a decentralized yet aggressive legislature that was well equipped to participate in the details of administration. The most important reforms were those that increased the number, power, autonomy, and staff of congressional subcommittees. A decentralized institution since the rebellion against Speaker Joseph Cannon during the Progressive era, Congress became even more so; in effect, the power of standing committees devolved to subcommittees. But this time, the legislative rebellion was carried out by insurgents whose target was as much the president as their more stolid and conservative adversaries in Congress. Thus, the rise of subcommittee government resulted in a severe challenge to the modern president's preeminence in legislative and administrative matters. As Melnick has written about this structural reform:

> Using subcommittee resources, members initiated new programs and revised old
> ones, challenging the president for the title of "chief legislator." No longer

would Congress respond to calls for action by passing vague legislation telling the executive to do something. Now Congress was writing detailed statutes which not infrequently deviated from the president's program. Subcommittees were also using oversight hearings to make sure that administrators paid heed not just to the letter of legislation, but to its spirit as well.[75]

It is important to recognize, however, that the reform assault on the modern presidency was not simply a pragmatic adjustment of institutional arrangements to ensure a more strident and consistent commitment to programmatic liberalism. In fact, the restraints imposed on presidential power during the late 1960s and 1970s reflected a strong suspicion of administrative power that was not open to public participation. In important respects, such a suspicion was a logical outgrowth of the reform vision of the Great Society. Lyndon Johnson was a presidentialist—the thrust of his institutional approach was to strengthen the managerial tools of the presidency with a view to enhancing the programmatic vision and energy of executive agencies. Yet the Great Society emphasized services and breaking the culture and cycle of poverty rather than income maintenance or even public works programs, and this approach to the poor suggested the limits of "presidential government." Consequently, the task of government as defined by the War on Poverty was not simply to deliver "the goods" to the needy, but to develop approaches to poverty that would teach the unfortunate how to organize and play a role in developing welfare programs.

Such programs became less attractive to Johnson once the political activity that was supported moved beyond his sphere of influence. The Nixon administration, as noted in the previous section, had little use for the federal sponsorship of participatory democracy, and eliminated the community action program. Yet the concept of participatory democracy and its influence on federal policy endured.

During the 1970s, the concern for participatory democracy ripened into a "procedural right," whereby Congress created elaborate, detailed procedures designed to help various groups procure benefits from various levels of government as well as from the private sector.[76] Just as the Community Action Program represented more than a substitute for substantive benefits during the Johnson era, so the support for procedural niceties in statutes enacted during the 1970s was not simply intended by Congress to be an ersatz government benefit, nor were congressionally created procedural rights merely a method for avoiding issues on which legislators received conflicting pressures. There was a strong anti-bureaucratic, anti-institutional ethos in the "new" Congress; in fact, those legislators who had revolted against the seniority system claimed to support "participatory democracy" within Congress. Republican control of the presidency made liberal Democratic legislators even more enthusiastic about guaranteeing public interest groups and "average" citizens, most of whom were adversaries of Nixon's New Federalism, an active role in the administration of government programs. Consequently, by one count, there were approximately 226 citizen participation programs mandated by federal statutes by 1977, and the courts were vigilant in making sure that state and federal agencies adhered to the letter and spirit of these participation requirements.[77]

Although the efforts to make the shaping of federal programs more inclusive were rarely a response to public demands and have not involved a large number of citizens in the actual running of federal programs, a genuine commitment emerged by the late 1960s to a norm of participation that transcended concerns to check the abuses of presidential power. As a result, the assault on the prerogatives of the modern presidency was associated with institutional changes that expanded the national government's administrative power but tied the use of such power to procedural safeguards designed to reconcile the administrative state and participatory democracy.

Public Participation and the Reform of Administrative Politics

The effort to enhance the representative character of the administrative state was most closely associated with the expansion of regulatory programs during the late 1960s and 1970s. Most significant, ambitious new undertakings were launched in the area of "social" regulation, leading to the creation of new administrative agencies and the redirection of certain existing ones to address issues such as employment discrimination against minorities and women, environmentalism, consumer protection, health, and safety. The rise of social regulation began with the 1964 Civil Rights Act, which created the first of the new social regulatory agencies: the federal Equal Employment Opportunity Commission, charged with administering Title VII (concerned primarily with employment discrimination) of the landmark civil rights statute. During the late 1960s and 1970s, a vast array of new federal laws and new federal agencies were enacted that looked well beyond civil rights, thus giving concrete expression to the "quality of life" concerns that most clearly distinguished the New Deal and Great Society.[78]

In part, the "new" social regulation constituted a change in the political economy that required unprecedented centralization of the national government's administrative power. Business found the new social regulation especially disturbing, since it empowered executive agencies to intrude into broad problem areas with detailed prescriptions for the manufacture and sale of products. As Bernard Falk of the National Electrical Manufacturers' Association noted about the expansion of the government's regulatory role in the 1970's, "In the past going back ten or fifteen years, you didn't have a consumer movement. The manufacturer controlled the make-up of his own product, and Washington could be ignored. Now we all have a new partner, the federal government."[79]

Yet, paradoxically, this government intrusion went hand in hand with changes in administrative law that reflected strong suspicion of administrative power. As such, the institutional initiatives that were linked with the social reforms of the 1970s were motivated by concerns to recast the concept of citizenship in American politics to conform with the emergence of the administrative state. These changes reflected the view, first articulated by the carriers of the new politics during the 1960s, that the New Deal, while bringing certain valued reforms, had devolved into an impersonal, bureaucratic, centralized form of governance that was dehumanizing American society. Moreover, reformers during the late 1960s and 1970s believed that the procedures by which decisions were made in the administrative state were controlled by large business interests that were inattentive to public values—the prominent social problems that dominated the political agenda of the 1970s, such as the despoliation of the environment and the manipulation of consumers, were depicted by reformers as a by-product of the capture of the public sector by corporate interests.

As noted in Chapter 1, hostility to administrative power has a long tradition in the United States. Although the New Deal eroded the American "bias" against the national government's supervision of society, the deeply ingrained distrust of administrative power continued to be a powerful influence on political life in the United States. This distrust was fueled by the fact that the expansion of administrative power in American politics after the 1930s came at the expense of the more decentralizing institutions, such as Congress, political parties, and local governments, which traditionally were the primary agents of popular rule.

The apparent tension between the administrative state and democratic citizenship created a real dilemma within the American political system. On the one hand, local government and community control remain at the heart of the American idea of democracy. On the other hand, since the New Deal, Americans had come to accept as just and inevitable the development of a strong national state, deemed necessary to provide for economic security, protect freedom from foreign threats, limit the power of corporations, and guarantee equal protection of the law.

The public interest advocates who had such a strong influence on public policy during the 1970s were committed to expanding the programmatic responsibilities of the national government, and, therefore, were not predisposed to reduce the prerogatives of executive departments and agencies per se. Consequently, the task in large part was to establish new agencies, such as the Environmental Protection Agency, and refurbish existing ones, such as the Federal Trade Commission, thereby creating new centers of administrative power that would not become as inefficient and unresponsive as regulatory agencies typically had in the past. Consequently, as Ralph Nader urged, regulatory bodies were not to be delegated responsibility to act for the public, but to be governed instead by administrative mechanisms providing liberal provision for public participation, "so that agency lethargy or inefficiency could be checked by interested citizen activity."[80] The achievement of civil rights, consumer, and environmental regulations was deemed worthless so long as the administrative process was not opened up to direct citizen action.

This commitment to public participation required an ongoing presence of public interest groups in administrative decision making. Hence, the culmination of liberalism was associated not with the renewal of party politics, but with the rise of public interest groups tailored to facilitate the direct participation of citizen activists in the administrative process.

In this respect, many regulatory reform groups differ little from the organizations that became part of the New Deal coalition. A critical aspect of the New Deal realignment was Roosevelt's encouragement of certain constituent groups that could not easily be married to the Democratic party to organize as "auxiliaries." Consequently, labor and civil rights groups formed political institutions that often worked with but did not formally become part of the party. This represented a new form of presidential coalition that both converted independents to Democratic allegiance and made conventional, partisan participation less important. But public interest activists, lacking the well-defined popular support labor unions and civil rights groups could draw upon, largely abstained from partisan strategies of grass roots mobilization and electoral alliance as a means of developing effective political influence. Although conceding that the goal of expanding popular electoral participation may be valuable in itself, public interest liberals have found such a strategy largely irrelevant in the face of the New Deal institutional legacy— unrelated to the task of rendering either the bureaucratic state or corporate elites accountable to the public.[81]

The attempt to marry administration and democracy had, and continues to have, a tremendous influence on American politics. As Samuel Beer notes, "it would be difficult today to find a program involving regulation or delivery of services in such fields as health, education, welfare, and the environment that does not provide for 'community input.' "[82] The objective of expanding this participation in administrative channels was largely indifferent to electoral realignment, which would not get to the heart of the matter; rather, the purpose was to bring about a fundamental realignment of administrative power. As one public interest reformer succinctly put it, "To take office is not to take power."[83]

An instructive example of the reformation of executive department during the 1970s is provided by the metamorphosis of the Federal Trade Commission (FTC).[84] The FTC, first established in 1914, was authorized to protect the consumer with the passage of the Wheeler–Lea Act in 1938. Yet, until the 1970s, this authority was mainly latent potential; the FTC's amiable relations with business and bureaucratic torpor rendered the Commission notoriously inactive. Beginning in 1969, however, the FTC underwent dramatic change that transformed an agency once known to its critics as "the little old lady of Pennsylvania Avenue" into an aggressive consumer advocate. The remarkable aspect of this change is how independent it was of presidential influence. The presidency was not without influence on the FTC in the 1970s; Nixon and Carter, in particular, appointed Commissioners who upgraded the agency's organization and personnel, as well as encouraged its pursuit of ambitious consumer protection. But the transition at the FTC would have been far less dramatic were it not for a loosely organized but influential coalition of consumer advocates among Senate and House members, a talented and programmatically ambitious Congressional staff, an aggressive core of investigative and advocacy journalists, and an elaborate network of consumer public interest groups.[85] In the absence of such a coalition, which constantly prodded the Commission and brought episodic but heated public pressure upon it, it is unlikely that the agency would have followed the aggressive course that it did.

The efforts of this coalition culminated in the mid-1970s. Particularly important was the passage of the Magnuson–Moss Act in 1975, which authorized the FTC to engage in industry-wide rule making. The Commission had in a few cases issued trade regulation rules prior to Magnuson–Moss, and the 1971 regulation requiring octane ratings to be posted on gasoline pumps led to the first judicial recognition of the FTC's asserted rule-making authority.[86] Yet Congress' passage of this legislation in 1975 eliminated lingering doubt about the legitimacy of this authority, and, more important, expressed Congress' support for the Commission to exercise what amounted to wide-ranging legislative power. With this authority firmly established by Congressional action, the FTC became, as one former staff member put it, "the fourth most powerful body in Washington," capable of altering the structure of industry.[87]

This power, however, was accompanied by a number of procedural obligations that, in effect, restricted the administrative discretion given to the FTC. These provisions, characteristic of legislation passed during the 1970s, required the Commission to conform to procedural safeguards such as publicizing proposed rules, stating with particularity the reason for the proposed rule, and allowing interested persons to submit written data, views, and arguments, all of which were to be made public.

The procedural obligations established by the Magnuson–Moss Act were a response to, as a 1969 American Bar Association report on the FTC had put it, "Commissioners [having] been criticized for making themselves available to those representing respondents or potential respondents on an *ex parte,* off-the-record basis."[88] Accordingly, public procedures were crafted to allay the possibility of the agency's "capture" by the targets of its activities, as well as to facilitate the participation of public interest groups in the rule-making process.

The goal of enhancing the participation of public interest advocates was addressed specifically in Magnuson–Moss with the establishment of an "intervenor funding program." These funds overwhelmingly went to public interest groups supportive of the ambitious pro-consumer policies that were increasingly pursued by the FTC after the enactment of Magnuson–Moss. The list of grants made under the public intervenor program read very much like an honor role of staunch consumer advocates, including Americans for Democratic Action ($177,000 in grants to participate in five separate rule-making proceedings), Action for Children's Television ($84,614 to participate in a children's advertisement proceeding), and the Consumers Union ($132,257 to participate in four separate rule-making proceedings.)[89] It is rather ironic that these "public" participation funds were concentrated among a relatively few organizations and law firms that came to comprise a specialized "pro-consumer FTC bar." Yet consumer activists claimed that the failure to foster genuine "grass roots" participation was symptomatic of the great difficulty involved in striking a balance between the technical competence demanded by the administrative state and "participatory" democracy. Those groups that were part of the privileged "public" asserted that without the continuity of representation achieved by a few organizations receiving federal support to participate in several regulatory proceedings, the consumer activists could not achieve equality with business and trade group respondents.[90]

The attempt to reconcile the administrative state and participatory democracy through funding a rather limited universe of "public" interest groups was troublesome; the development of the judiciary during the 1960s and 1970s as a critical channel for public participation in administrative rule-making procedures was no less problematic. The Judiciary did not intervene in the details of FTC proceedings because this agency, which was first created during the Progressive era, is an independent regulatory commission, and is thus entitled to act as a court of equity in defining and enforcing public values.[91] Yet many other agencies, particularly those created at the height of the "participatory revolution," were subjected to extensive judicial oversight that played a significant part in expanding regulatory activities in the areas of civil rights, environmentalism, public health, and safety. This expansion went hand in hand with the courts' recognition of elaborate procedural rights for groups directly affected by government programs, as well as for organizations claiming to speak for the "public."

The alliance between citizen action and the judiciary is a strange one, since the courts are organized within the American constitutional framework to be extensively independent of the public views. We noted in Chapter 6 that FDR's veto of the 1940 Walter–Logan bill, which would have involved the courts in virtually every agency proceeding, did not merely reflect the judiciary's cool view of regulatory controls over the private sector as compared to the executive branch; Roosevelt's veto also represented the view that the advent of *administrative* law, and judicial deference to the president and executive agencies (the preeminence of *executive* administration), promised a more flexible and energetic response to public problems. The Administrative Procedures Act (APA), enacted in 1946, was, in effect, the Roosevelt administration's answer to the restrictive Walter–Logan legislation. Although the APA imposed some constraints on administrative procedures, it left agencies considerable autonomy from judicial and legislative interference.[92]

The statutes passed by Congress during the 1960s and 1970s were often couched in terms of entitlements rather than bureaucratic obligations, thereby inviting the federal judiciary to become a forceful and consistent presence in administrative politics. A landmark statute in the establishment of programmatic rights was the 1964 Civil Rights Act.[93] This legislation did more than offer a long-delayed response to *Brown vs. Board of Education. Brown* had brought to life the dormant Equal Protection Clause of the Fourteenth Amendment by ruling that de jure segregation is a form of racial discrimination. But the act went beyond the formal Constitution in extending the nondiscrimination principle to private as well as public establishments: Title II forbade discrimination in hotels, restaurants, and stores; Title VII, as noted, prevented employers from engaging in discriminatory practices; and Title VII expanded the nondiscrimination principle further by banning discrimination on the basis of gender. Reflecting on John Kennedy's reference to his civil rights bill as "constitutional policy," Alexander Bickel observed that the notion of "constitutional policy" was novel, a hybrid of the previously distinct categories of "constitutional law" and "public policy."[94]

We noted in Chapter 8 that the enactment of the Civil Rights Act of 1964 signaled a dramatic reinvigoration of the president's preeminence as legislative leader. Equally important in the long run was that the act enlisted the president and several executive agencies in the ongoing effort to ban racial discrimination. It empowered the federal bureaucracy—especially the Department of Justice, the Department of Health, Education and Welfare, and the newly formed Equal Employment Opportunity Commission—to assist the courts by creating parallel enforcement mechanisms for civil rights. These proved to be effective. For example, within 4 years the executive branch under Johnson accomplished more desegregation in the Southern schools than the courts had in 14. This cooperation between the executive branch and the judiciary in enforcing the nondiscrimination doctrine, however, created the constitutional groundwork for the cementing of an agency–court partnership that would eventually dramatically constrain the administrative power of the modern presidency.[95]

The importance of the Civil Rights Act lies not just in its own extensive reach, but also in the model it established for further legislation. The formulation of a new version of liberalism during the Great Society led to the great expansion of policy entitlements, adding to them, along with the right to be free of discrimination and the so-called "collective" rights associated with consumer and environmental protection, the right of those affected by government programs (and those representing the "Public") to participate in the administration of these programs. As public participation—the aforementioned procedural rights—became a central tenet of programmatic liberalism, the courts became vigilant in making sure that federal agencies adhered to the newly recognized procedural requirements. These developments resulted in a de facto, if not de jure, amendment of the Administrative Procedures Act. In the 1960s and 1970s, as Martin Shapiro has observed, the courts greatly reduced the scope in the APA for executive branch initiative and agency expertise: "They invented a host of procedural requirements that turned rulemaking into a multi-party paper trial. They also imposed a rulemaking record requirement that allowed courts to review minutely every aspect of that trial. . . .The courts . . . did these things to reduce the independence and discretionary scope of a mistrusted bureaucracy and to subordinate it to more control by the regulated, the beneficiaries of regulation, and the public at large."[96]

The statutory provisions relating to procedural rights reinforced the courts' extensive efforts beginning in the late 1960s to expand participation of those claiming to speak for the poor, racial minorities, consumers, and environmentalists. In particular, lawsuits in the 1960s and 1970s helped to establish the standing of citizen groups to sue federal agencies for law enforcement. Moreover, many statutes, especially environmental laws, lent Congress' support to this development by granting automatic standing to sue and establishing liberal provisions for class actions. Consequently, the lawsuit, once considered the province of the privileged, became the principal tool during the 1970s of opening up the administrative process. "[C]ourts have changed the focus of judicial review (in the course of expanding and transforming traditional procedural devices)," Richard Stewart has written, "so that its dominant purpose is no longer the prevention of unauthorized intrusions on private autonomy, but the assurance of fair representation for all affected interests in the exercise of legislative power delegated to agencies."[97] As with intervenor funding, however, it was "public" interest groups, rather than the public, that benefitted directly from this development.

Citizen Action and the Crisis of the Liberal Order

Although the public interest movement did gain substantial influence on the policy process by building elaborate organizational networks and making effective use of the media, this influence was never really solidified into an enduring political coalition. The emphasis of public interest groups on single issue advocacy and use of the media was characteristic of what James Q. Wilson refers to as "entre-preneurial politics," that is to say, consumer and environmental policy was dom-inated by a small number of Washington-based activists, who served as "vicarious representatives" of diffuse and poorly organized interests.[98] Entrepreneurial poli-tics was especially important in the area of social regulation. In a sense, this was necessary, for environmental, consumer, and health laws and regulations con-ferred general benefits on the public at a cost to small, albeit well-organized, segments of society. Since the incentive to organize is relatively weak for benefi-ciaries but strong for opponents of such policies, it is perhaps necessary for public interest advocates to position themselves in the regulatory process as the represen-tatives of the public interest. Nevertheless, the defense of "collective" rights puts environmental and consumer activists in a precarious position: Because as defend-ers of general rather than specific concerns, they are often without strong political allies.

The public interest movement, then, while capable of eliciting popular support by dramatizing corporate abuse and defending unassailable values such as clean air and consumer rights, was, in fact, built upon a fragile institutional foundation. This institutional structure was well suited to harnessing symbolic political cam-paigns into regulatory programs, yet incapable of establishing deeply rooted polit-ical affiliations among the American public. In this sense, as the consumer advo-cate and former Chairman of the Federal Trade Commission, Michael Pertschuk, notes, public interest advocacy was less a fundamental departure from the New Deal than a decrepit version of liberalism, which was all too tenuously linked with the American public:

> [I]t might be said that we [public interest advocates] represented the late New Deal liberal tradition. . . . We were disproportionately Ivy Leaguers, do-gooders, knee-jerk liberals, occupied with alleviating the hardships of others, fueled by faith in the capacity of government to represent the people against "private greed," so long as the government was peopled or stimulated by us. We defended ourselves against charges of elitism with the strong evidence that the principles we stood for and the causes we enlisted in enjoyed popular, if sometimes passive support. But if we were "for the people," for the most part we were not comfortably "of the people."[99]

This aspect of the public interest movement was reinforced by its emphasis on administrative politics. The push for social regulation was motivated by the view that the bureaucracy created by the New Deal was unrepresentative. Yet, in the end, the advent of social regulation did not challenge the New Deal emphasis on public administration, nor did it lead to a fundamental reconsideration of the pro-gressive tradition in American twentieth century politics that lead to the displace-ment of the regular political process by executive administration. Rather, the pub-lic interest movement embraced administrative politics while seeking to make it more accessible to direct political action. Consequently, contemporary liberal pol-itics expressed a deep distrust of public administration, yet contributed greatly to administrative aggrandizement.

This ironic development entailed not only continuing the New Deal emphasis on the executive branch, but also the recruitment of courts into administrative activity and the design of legislation to foster vigorous regulatory enforcement that necessarily fixed the business of government more on administration. Indeed, the role of the courts and the Congress in the "new" American political system has constituted less a challenge to administrative government—and the revival of legislation and adjudication per se—than it has involved the legislative and judicial branches in the "details of administration." [100] The heavy reliance of Congress on mechanisms such as the legislative veto, which allows Congress to pass judgment on administrative regulations, and oversight committee hearings suggests that the role of the legislature has been altered dramatically with the advent of an administrative state. [101]

By the same token, the Judiciary's decreasing reliance on constitutional decisions in its rulings affecting the political economy and its emphasis on interpreting statutes to determine the programmatic responsibilities of executive agencies is symptomatic of its post–New Deal role as the "managing partner of the administrative state." [102] The controversial activism of the 1960s and 1970s did not result in the courts becoming the primary expositors of the law as they were in the nineteenth century. Rather, they review "law" made by administrative agencies with a view to its consistency with programmatic rights. [103]

Thus, whereas the reformers of the late 1960s and 1970s rejected the New Deal institutional forms—emphasizing the president as the primary instrument of progressive government—as undemocratic, they devolved public authority to a less visible coalition of bureaucratic agencies, courts, Congressional subcommittees, and public interest groups, that defied meaningful public discourse and broad-based coalitions. Public interest groups did generate large rosters of committed supporters through direct mail solicitations. But these appeals to the public asked not so much for citizens' votes, time, energy, or ideas as for small contributions to fund campaigns waged by legal experts. Consequently, as Hugh Heclo has pointed out, with the most recent liberal innovations, American society has further "politicized itself" and at the same time "depoliticized government leadership." [104]

In important respects the roots of this problem can be attributed to the origins of programmatic liberalism. From its inception during the 1930s, modern liberalism was defined as a "second bill of rights," and, as such, worthy of protection from the regular political process, party politics, and the vagaries of public opinion. Consequently, as noted, New Deal administrative reform only in part was dedicated to strengthening the presidency. Its aim in fact was to establish a polity dedicated to programmatic rights that both presupposed a fundamental reconsideration of the purposes of American politics and laid the foundation for an administrative constitution, which gave institutional effect to this reformulated social contract. The reformers of the 1960s and 1970s extended the institutional basis of the administrative state and greatly expanded the scope of programmatic rights. The focus on rights favored social policy that was enforced uniformly at the national level and shielded from the uncertainties of the regular political process, including the influence of public opinion and elections. Thus, the link between individual rights and public policy has facilitated the acceptance of reform, but in the end eroded the fabric of republican government. Just as the New Deal's focus on "rights" established a tenuous foundation for the steward of the economic constitutional order—the modern presidency—so the public interest movement's commitment to extending rights circumscribed the participatory revolution of the late 1960s and 1970s. Consequently, "procedural rights," designed to enhance the representation of the public in administrative politics, were limited to a rather small circle of program advocates.

The reforms of the late 1960s and 1970s, then, should perhaps be viewed as a natural extension of the philosophy at the heart of programmatic liberalism. That theory of governance required extensive and continuous administration of society—it entailed an expansive understanding of rights, characterized by a relentless identification of new problems and the search for methods by which those problems might be solved. Although Roosevelt's commitment to "rational" planning was limited, he accepted and gave force to a new form of liberalism based on the understanding that the traditional emphasis in American politics on individual self-reliance was inadequate. As he noted in the Commonwealth Club address about the social contract established by the *Declaration,* "The task of statesmanship has always been the re-definition of these rights in terms of a changing and growing social order. New conditions impose new requirements upon Government and those who conduct Government." [105]

Beginning with the Great Society, however, this task of "circumspect but intrepid social progress" underwent an important change that deepened the administrative character of modern liberal politics. The pursuit of "quality of life" issues resulted in an indifference to, if not a rejection of, the self-interested basis of American politics. Whereas the New Deal emphasis on economic security essentially accepted commercial values as an inherent part of American life, the expressed aims of the Great Society explicitly rejected a view of the individual as most essentially defined by acquisitive desires.

The Johnson Administration's indictment of material self-interest was for the most part restrained; for all his commitment to reform, Lyndon Johnson was a cautious leader. But such restraint was less evident in the rhetoric and political actions of citizen activists, who expressed a far less compromising commitment to addressing problems of the "spirit rather than the flesh." As Ralph Nader wrote in 1971:

> This year the gross national product of the United States will exceed one trillion dollars, while the economy will fail to meet a great many urgent human needs. . . . Indeed, the quality of life is deteriorating in so many ways that the traditional statistical measurements of the "standard of living" according to personal income, housing, ownership of cars and appliances, etc., have come to sound increasingly phony. [106]

It is easy to dismiss such a concern to deflect attention from material progress as mere rhetoric. But the moral principles that animated programmatic liberalism during the 1960s and 1970s resulted in a dramatic transformation of the American political economy. This transformation starkly demonstrated the potential power of the "uneasy" state—indeed, it seemed to mark a fundamental reformation of American politics. The American Constitutional framework established conditions whereby "ambition would counteract ambition," thus fostering a system of mutual constraints among a diversity of interests. The New Deal altered this free play of self-interest in significant ways, particularly in shifting the locus of decision-making to the executive, but the institutional reforms of post–New Deal liberalism extensively displaced the pluralistic character of American politics. The regulatory system that emerged during the 1970s established an institutional framework that frequently subordinated particularistic political ambitions to the programmatic ambitions of reformers, though these programs were usually constructed within discrete issue areas.

The moral basis of post–New Deal liberalism helps to explain its paradoxical relationship to democratic politics. If the frenetic materialism and conspicuous consumption of American society could merely be attributed to the machinations of corporate capitalism, then direct and widespread citizen action might be consistent with the strident criticism of public interest advocates. To the degree that relentless materialism was deeply imbedded in the American way of life, however, "citizen" advocacy was in tension with a commitment to democratic politics. Widespread support could readily be obtained for many of the specific goals of social regulation, yet the principles underlying these specific programs were largely unacceptable in the context of American politics, and, when unchecked, capable of creating a strong backlash against the consumer and environmental movements. To be sure, these movements were not anti-capitalist—there was no vision that conveyed an urgency to eliminate private property or redistribute wealth. In fact, the advocates of social regulation defended values, such as clean air and product safety, that cut across traditional class conflicts, explaining in large part their success in achieving broad, if not deeply rooted, support among the American people. Yet the emphasis on "quality of life" issues, the warning about resource limitations, and the criticism of consumer preference that characterize much public interest advocacy indirectly rejects the foundation of a society dedicated to the pursuit of material satisfaction.

Thus, in seeking to depart from the New Deal's emphasis on economic security, contemporary social reformers were alienated from the values and institutions that earlier progressives accepted as an inherent part of American life. American political culture is not simply materialistic; the concerns for democratic citizenship and the criticisms of big business that characterized the reform activists of the late 1960s and 1970s have a long tradition in American politics.[107] But the public was not willing to reject the materialism that many citizen advocates found unacceptable. Reflecting on the demise of the national Democratic party in the wake of intrepid liberal activism, Harry McPherson, an important and thoughtful member of the Johnson White House, observed in a 1985 interview:

> Johnson's Great Society legislation may have been the death of the party due to its very success. LBJ achieved the agenda of the Democratic party which had been developing for some 50 years. With this achievement accomplished, the party platforms of the Democratic party have been starved of real meat. We are the activist–government party, and we've achieved just about all that the public

wanted activist government to do. So we may be out of substantive gas: perhaps the time has come to declare victory and retire to the farm.[108]

The activists who were summoned by the Great Society's trumpet did not view the prospect of "retirement" with such equanimity. It is not surprising, then, that the reformers of the late 1960s and 1970s focused on administrative and legal channels that were far removed from the more democratic institutions in American politics. In part this institutional strategy was linked to the vision of liberal reform as an extension of rights, warranting protection from the regular political process. The focus on programmatic rights was reinforced, however, as the vision of liberalism was extended to "quality of life" issues. Administrative tribunals and the courts were certainly more appropriate forums than the more political institutions for efforts to remake so substantially the character of the American political system. It is ironic and tragic that the resulting triumph of administrative politics, designed to strengthen citizen action, signified a distressing deterioration of representative democracy.

The Legacy of Liberal Reform

Throughout American history, critical partisan realignments, characterized by pervasive shifts in party support and major departures in public policy, refreshed democratic politics and restored the vigor of public authority in the United States. The strengthening of public authority, so that the nation's resolve could be expressed less episodically, was the great contribution of the New Deal realignment. This realignment reinforced the fragile sense of national community in the United States, and did so, seemingly, without undermining the personal independence of democratic individualism. It enhanced administrative capacities while avoiding, as Tocqueville called them, "the puerilities of administrative tyranny." [109]

Nevertheless, the link between administrative power and individual rights forged by the New Deal began a process whereby the more democratic and decentralizing institutions that facilitated deliberation and choice in the political process were displaced by executive administration. While the expansion of programmatic commitments may have been modest in the United States compared to other advanced industrial societies, the conceptualization of these programs as rights promoted the expansion of national administrative authority at the expense of Congress, State governments, and especially political parties. Thus, in the United States, administrative centralization has been limited, but virtually all government activity is dominated by the politics of administration.[110]

The reforms of the 1960s and 1970s continued, even increased, the dominance of political administration in the councils of American government. The expansion of the "administrative constitution" during this latter period limited the administrative power of the president, but involved Congress, the courts, and public interest groups in the details of administration. In the final analysis, the institutional developments of the 1960s and 1970s not only fixed the business of government more on administration but also accelerated the decline of political parties.

Thus, the triumph of the New Deal Democratic party gave rise to an administrative politics that created the conditions for a realignment to end all realignments. A party against administration might make party politics newly important, but the Republican party's challenge to the institutional legacy of liberal reform, embodied in Nixon's New Federalism, was confounded by an administrative reform program that only shifted more political decision-making and conflict to the administrative realm. In the wake of this development, the modern president was relegated to the role of modulating the liberal state; the executive was no longer in command of it. Nixon, Ford, and even the Democrat, Jimmy Carter, sought to put a lid on "uncontrollable" spending and to moderate the activities of the many regulatory agencies that were refurbished and created by the newly resurgent Congress. Most dramatic were the battles between Republican presidents and the Democratic Congress over spending and deficit levels. But conflict between the president and Congress, especially with respect to budgetary matters, had become institutionalized since 1974. Carter, although he was less conservative than his Republican predecessors, tried to hold budget costs down, especially as inflationary pressure mounted during the latter part of his term. He was no more successful than Nixon or Ford, however, in getting the liberal Congress to respond to his call for fiscal restraint.

The most important development of the administrative presidency during the 1970s was Nixon's reorganization of the budget bureau. Just as the subcommittee became the soul of Congress during the 1970s, so the Office of Management and Budget had become the nerve center of the administrative presidency.[111] Not only did the enlarged OMB review spending requests and legislative proposals, as it had prior to the 1970s, but proposed agency rules as well. The reshaping of liberalism established a loose coalition of bureaucratic agencies, congressional subcommittees and staff, courts, and public advocacy groups that considerably eroded the discretion of presidents and executive officers to shape public policy. These channels posed a direct threat to presidential governance. Moreover, the explosion of regulation and the recasting of administrative institutions coincided with, and to a degree contributed to, increasing public doubt about the expansion of government. Beginning in the early 1970s, therefore, presidents were compelled to undertake the unenviable task of controlling the expanding and increasingly disparate activities of the bureaucracy.[112]

But after Nixon's fall, Ford and Carter were unable to regain control of the president's domain. The OMB became an important competitor in the administrative process during their presidencies; it did not dominate it. Consequently, federal administrators found themselves whipsawed between the competing demands of subcommittees and the lieutenants of the president in the executive office. The end of the Carter years seemed to mark the triumph of the new institutional partnership that had been built to house liberalism while creating considerable doubt about the viability of the Democratic party as an instrument of government.

Carter's ostensible purpose was to move his party to the center and thus prepare it to compete more effectively at a time when the New Deal and Great Society appeared to be losing support in the country. He said often and earnestly that he intended to cut waste, run things efficiently, and balance the budget. But

Carter's presidency marked the culmination of the institutional separation between the presidency and the party. His 1976 campaign demonstrated how the new rules that governed the nomination process made it possible for an outsider to win his party's nomination; moreover, Carter's election demonstrated the striking decline of the regular party organization that reformers since Woodrow Wilson had decried as a stain on the American political process. Reagan's ferocious challenge to President Ford in the Republican primaries that same presidential election year strongly suggested such a development. Carter's election confirmed it.

Carter's presidency revealed the enduring and troublesome legacy of programmatic liberalism. To Carter and his supporters, any consideration of electoral or party politics in the administration's counsels was unseemly. Whereas Roosevelt and Johnson took these political concerns into account and then calculated how to circumvent them, Carter was an anti-party outsider whose devotion to "enlightened administration" made his isolation profound. By the late 1970s, transcending party politics was no longer part of a calculated agenda—it was now assumed, indeed, almost a sacred truth. Carter's "trusteeship politics," as Charles Jones calls it, presupposing the absence of party considerations, underscores the extent to which the New Deal and Great Society had marginalized the party system.[113]

Significantly, one of Carter's most important policy achievements was the enactment of the Civil Service Reform Act of 1978. This legislation created a new Senior Executive Service, one that was less specialized and more expansive than the corps of senior civil servants Lyndon Johnson established in 1967. Carter's civil service reform also established the Office of Personal Management, a single-headed administration, which replaced the bipartisan Civil Service Commission. In seeing this bill through Congress, Carter codified changes in executive management of the civil service that FDR had initiated as part of the Third New Deal and subsequent presidents had advanced in seeking to strengthen the institutions of the modern executive office. This was an impressive achievement—Roosevelt's attempt to include a provision in the 1937 executive reorganization act that would substitute a single-headed personnel agency for the Civil Service Commission was perhaps the major reason why Congress attacked his administrative reform proposal as a "dictator bill." That Roosevelt and subsequent presidents had moved in this general direction through executive orders does not diminish the importance of Carter's accomplishment in getting Congress to legislate a restructuring of the federal government's personnel system. Nor does the fact that Carter proved unable to direct the personnel system to his own managerial taste belittle the contribution his civil service reform made to the administrative presidency.

Carter's presidency, therefore, represented the celebration of the "extraordinary isolation" of the presidency, as Wilson called it, and the secular decline of parties that followed from the disassociation between executive leadership and party politics. At the same time, Carter's unsteady command of the nation revealed that the splendid isolation of the presidency spawned by the New Deal and Great Society was at best a mixed blessing. Presidents and legislators had become independent entrepreneurs, establishing their own constituencies. As a result, they were less likely to view each other as partners in a shared endeavor, dedicated to promoting a party program. "I learned the hard way," Carter noted in his memoirs, "that there was no party loyalty or discipline when a complicated or controversial issue was at stake—none. Each legislator had to be wooed and won individually. It was every member for himself, and the devil take the hindmost!" [114]

Carter never did anything to ameliorate this disarray; in fact he greatly contributed to it. His relationship to his party was usually aloof, occasionally accommodating, but never purposeful. One Carter aide analyzed the problems the president had in seeking to transcend the exigencies of political leadership:

> I always had the sense of a man who was an engineer, who truly believed that if he knew enough about the details of a subject, he could make a decision that was in the public interest rather than in the interest of particular groups. Therefore, you needed a lot of information; therefore, you needed substance; therefore, don't bother me about politics.
>
> But then suddenly, he would be forcibly jerked back from this position . . . into a sort of purely political context in which a decision had to be made and I don't think that was ever resolved. I don't think it was ever integrated. I had the feeling of moving between the two [substance and politics] but never of pulling it together. [115]

The disassociation between "substance and politics" contributed to Carter's image as a weak president. In matters of public policy, the White House staff reflected the president's desire to be fiercely independent and a scourge to traditional Democratic approaches. But his appointees to the Cabinet were liberal Washington insiders, such as Joseph Califano (Health, Education, and Welfare) and Patricia Roberts Harris (Housing and Urban Development), thus setting the stage for enervating conflict between the White House and executive departments. Furthermore, acting oftentimes on the recommendations of Ralph Nader, Carter appointed aggressive public-interest advocates to many regulatory agencies, such as Pertschuk (FTC) and Joan Claybrook (National Highway, Safety and Transportation Administration), who proceeded to convert strong commitments to social regulation into government policy. The collective impression that Carter's appointees gave was one of an irresolute leader who was eager to accommodate all sides.

Carter never seemed to be in control of events, but this weakness was not merely attributable to his personal inadequacies. As Erwin Hargrove has suggested, Carter's political demise can largely be explained by his times. Carter was president at a time of transition, after a Democratic period of reform and achievement and before a Republican resurgence. "The Ford and Carter presidencies belong together in this respect," Hargrove concludes, "both providing few possibilities for heroic leadership." [116] Liberals in Congress, prodded by their institutional partners in public interest groups, the courts, and administrative agencies, had imposed severe constraints on the executive since the end of Nixon's reign, reflecting a profound suspicion of the modern presidency. Not surprisingly, they provided a limited audience for decisive leadership that challenged the prevailing pattern of liberal policy demands.

Tellingly, Carter's irresolute effort to move his party towards a new combination of liberal centrism anticipated many of the themes of the Reagan "revolution'' that would force him from office. In the final analysis, Carter's unhappy isolation was emblematic of the extent to which programmatic liberalism had both enervated and sundered the Democratic party, rendering effective Democratic presidential leadership an elusive, if not unattainable, prospect.

By the end of the 1970s, programmatic liberalism had reversed the relationship between government and administration once observed by Tocqueville: The American political system now faced centralized administration and governmental fragmentation.[117] With administrative centralization, there had been a decentralization of Congress, devolving policy responsibility to subcommittees and subcommittee staffs, as well as other institutions, such as the Congressional Budget Office, that supported the altered—more administrative—character of the national legislature. Fragmentation of governing institutions was greatly accentuated by the active involvement of the judiciary in administrative politics, an involvement facilitated by the principles of programmatic liberalism and the increased tendency of Congress during the 1970s to couch statutes in terms of entitlements rather than bureaucratic obligations. The involvement of Congress and the Judiciary in administrative politics ostensibly checked the development of a coherent administrative state. But the fragmentation of government actually facilitated an expansion of regulations directing the course of many matters in the society and economy. There is no inherent contradiction, then, between administrative centralization and governmental decentralization; on the contrary, in the American case there is a logical connection between these developments.[118]

Nor is there any incompatibility between the celebration of "direct democracy" represented by the McGovern–Fraser reforms, and the expansion of administrative power. Progressive reforms such as the direct primary, the participatory caucus, and the initiative and referendum were designed to overthrow the party system, which bestowed upon the divided federal government a certain unity of control, while at the same time it restrained programmatic ambition and prevented the development of a stable and energetic administration of social policy. By the same token, the triumph of progressive democracy would put the American people directly in touch with the councils of power, thus strengthening the demand for government succor and allow, indeed require, administrative agencies to play their proper role in the realization of progressive democratic policy.

This administrative aggrandizement did not establish the sort of national state that Progressive reformers like Croly hoped for—one that would establish regulations and welfare programs that could be an expression of national unity and commitment. The combination of government fragmentation and administrative centralization that occurred in the United States was reflective of the debasement of American pluralism rather than its replacement by a Hegelian-like instrument of national will. Indeed, the hallmark of administrative politics in the United States is the virtual absence of a state that can impose its will on the economy and society. In this respect, administrative centralization to the degree it has occurred in the United States has, in fact, simultaneously transformed and taken its shape from the American Constitution. Arguably, the mixture of legislative, executive, and judicial powers that characterized American administrative politics at the end of the 1970s represented a perverse institutional arrangement that deprived the branches of government of their particular virtues, but this perversion did not lead to the formation of an autonomous state that was able to direct all the details of American life. The limits of administrative centralization in the American context were revealed clearly enough by the fact that strong opposition to the enlargement of government (read administrative) activity continued to have force in American politics, especially during times of frenetic government activism. Indeed, the Great Society was widely perceived as "excessive statism," giving rise to a political movement that would pose hard challenges to liberal reforms.[119]

Still, the expansion of administrative power tended to undermine the republican character of the Constitution. For most of the twentieth century, the party system had been either abondoned or attacked in favor of forming a progressive democracy based upon a reconstituted executive power. In Croly's words, the progressive task was to expand and remake administrative power so as to give "meaning and purpose to the Hamiltonian tradition and method." Yet, this presupposed that there could be a democratic variant of Hamiltonian nationalism, that it was possible to turn Hamilton on his head. Even reconstituted administrative processes, however, may not be hospitable to public deliberation. Perhaps this explains why the continual efforts to enhance the representative character of the bureaucracy were self-defeating; why the culmination of these efforts during the 1970s provided participatory opportunities for only a small circle of program advocates, while undermining the electoral process. The decline of turnout in elections, the emergence of the "plebiscitary Presidency," and the vitiation of the legislative process that characterized these years were in a very real sense associated with the expansion and reshaping of administrative power, and, as such, a testament to the fact that the noble experiment to turn Hamilton on his head had gone badly awry.

10

The New Deal Legacy and the
Reagan "Revolution"

The resurgence of Congress and other developments during the 1970s seemed not only to curb the worst abuses of the modern presidency but to undermine its authority. Hence, the view that presidential power had become excessive began to be displaced by the notion that presidential power had become distressingly anemic. This view was propounded by Gerald Ford, who understandably felt the reaction against presidential "imperialism" had gotten out of hand. "Some people used to complain about what they called an imperial presidency," he wrote in 1980, "but now the pendulum has swung too far in the opposite direction. We have not an imperial presidency but an imperiled presidency."[1]

Like Ford, Jimmy Carter faced serious competition for his party's nomination at the end of his presidency. Although he did manage to fend off a serious challenge from Massachusetts Senator Edward Kennedy for the Democratic nomination, he entered the 1980 campaign as damaged goods. His defeat at the hands of Ronald Reagan in the general election marked the first time an elected leader had been defeated since Herbert Hoover. The unhappy bond that linked Carter and Hoover, and the impressive manner in which Reagan assumed command of the country, ignited considerable speculation that the 1980 election, like that of 1932, marked a realignment in American politics. Indeed, in many respects, Reagan seemed to represent the forceful challenge to the New Deal that ardent conservatives had long awaited. Much more than Nixon, he presented himself in word and policy as the founder and first magistrate of a conservative political dynasty—as the Republican FDR.

Certainly, Reagan did not express ambition, as had his controversial Republican predecessor, to play Disraeli to liberal policies. Nixon was a relatively conservative man who posed challenges to the policies of the New Deal and Great Society. But generally, especially during the first term, he accommodated himself to liberalism, seeking only to curb its excesses. In contrast, Reagan had been an outspoken conservative for many years. During the Johnson presidency, for example, he was one of the few governors to challenge the centralizing thrust of programmatic liberalism.[2] Such long-standing dedication to conservative principles led some pundits quickly to dub Reagan's landslide victory in 1980 "the Reagan Revolution."

In fact, the results of the 1980 election were somewhat ambiguous. In a three-man race between Reagan, Carter, and an independent candidate John Anderson, Reagan won an overwhelming landslide in the electoral college, claiming forty-four states and 489 electoral votes. Yet he won only 51 percent of the popular vote, a mere 2 percent increase over Gerald Ford's total in 1976. Nor were the results of the congressional races decisive. For the first time since 1953–1955, the Republicans held the majority of the Senate seats, and several liberal senators—including George McGovern—were defeated. Nevertheless, although the GOP did manage to pick up thirty-three seats in the House, the Democrats retained control of the lower chamber. Thus, Reagan faced political conditions that were considerably more favorable than those Nixon and Ford were forced to deal with, but there was no unambiguous realignment.

Indeed, the 1970s raised doubts about whether the changes brought by the New Deal and Great Society had left room for another realignment in American politics. The institutional legacy of liberal reforms had the effect of expanding national administrative power, but at the cost of fragmenting the institutions of government and "dealigning" the electorate. In the face of the changes brought by the New Deal, and the inability or unwillingness of previous Republican presidents to reverse these changes, the prospects for realignment in 1980 were dim.

Still, Reagan was able successfully to represent his ambiguous victory as a national mandate and bring about important policy changes during the first term of his presidency. Unlike Carter and Ford, he was renominated without opposition and re-elected handily. From the beginning of his first term until the damaging revelations of the Iran–Contra scandal in 1986, Reagan and his associates conveyed the impression that strong, effective, popular leadership had restored the presidency to prominence in the political system. Even after the embarrassing disclosures of the Iran–Contra affair, Reagan managed to move forward, maintaining control of the government's agenda, if not its policies. To a surprising degree his stay in the White House demonstrated the capacity of a fixed purpose to substitute for a dominant political party that might serve as an institutional vessel to carry the ideas of the Reagan "revolution." Indeed, Reagan's firm adherence to conservative principles contributed significantly to the emergence of a new kind of Republican party, one more national and programmatic in its orientation than the traditional GOP.

Reagan's success in translating his ideological purposes to concrete achievements owed to considerable rhetorical gifts and the effective mustering of the institutional powers available to the modern presidency. As a result, as we shall see, the Reagan administration marked both a restoration of the modern presidency and a revitalization of partisan politics. But the politics of the 1980s did not ameliorate the crisis of the liberal order. On the contrary, the rise of conservatism suggested by the results of the 1980 and 1984 elections and the policies of the Reagan administration actually extended in important respects the *institutional* inheritance of liberal reforms. The Reagan "revolution" did not really challenge the aggrandizement of administrative power; rather, it surpassed the Nixon administration in attempting to extend the benefits of the national polity to those who wished to make new uses of, rather than limit, the state.

The Reagan Presidency and the Revival of Party Politics

Reagan represented a different breed of Republican than Nixon. Nixon never articulated a philosophy of government that galvanized the Republicans as a vital opposition to the Liberal tradition. Under his command, the GOP was treated as an obstacle to presidential politics and administration, as an organization that threatened the objective of making the government responsive to him personally. Reagan, in contrast, embodied a historical link with the effort made in 1964 to refashion the Republicans as an anti–New Deal party, as a party against administration. In fact, Reagan's words were but variations on the same theme he had been enunciating since he gave a nationwide television address on behalf of Barry Goldwater on October 27, 1964. "The Speech," as his speech writers referred to it, consisted of a single, abstract idea, universal in application: the idea that centrally administered government tended to weaken a free people's character. By acting "outside its legitimate function," a central state perverted the concept of rights in the United States—"natural unalienable rights" were presumed to be a "dispensation of government," thus stripping people of their self-reliance and their capacity for self-government. "The real destroyer of liberties of the people," Reagan warned, "is he who spreads among them bounties, donations, and benefits." [3]

After the confusing array of solutions offered to treat the social and economic maladies of the nation during the Carter years, Reagan's message, rooted in fundamental principles of government, focused the nation's attention on the need to steer a different course. His inaugural address was the first in almost 50 years to make an appeal for limited government, thus defining clearly his intention to preside over a redirection of public policy for the country:

> In this present crisis, government is not the solution to our problem; government is the problem. From time to time we've been tempted to believe that society has become too complex to be managed by self-rule, that government by an elite group is superior to government for, by, and of the people. Well, if no one among us is capable of governing himself, then who among us has the capacity to govern someone else? [4]

Thus, Reagan's rhetoric challenged the foundation principles of the New Deal. Yet this challenge to the Roosevelt legacy was issued in terms that paid homage to Franklin Roosevelt. Whereas Democrats since Kennedy had been searching for a message and policies that looked beyond the New Deal, Reagan made an extraordinary effort to associate himself with FDR. In 1980, for example, he made frequent references to Roosevelt in his speech accepting the Republican nomination. So strong was Reagan's claim of kinship with FDR at the Detroit convention that the day after his acceptance speech, the *New York Times* lead editorial had an eye-catching title: "Franklin Delano Reagan." [5]

In quoting FDR in Detroit, Reagan had not really "moved toward the center," as the *Times* editorial had claimed; rather, as William Leuchtenburg discerned, "Reagan had not modified his views but exploited Roosevelt for conservative ends."[6]

Reagan's identification with Roosevelt reflected his desire to lead as FDR had led, to exploit fully the powers of the executive office in getting the United States to move toward a new rendezvous with destiny. Richard Nixon had seen the possibility of the modern presidency being used to take the country away from the New Deal, but not to the same degree as Reagan saw it. As for policy, Reagan's agenda was less reminiscent of Nixon than an earlier, less pragmatic defender of limited government—Calvin Coolidge. Coolidge's leadership had "a major effect on Reagan as a teenager and his ideas greatly influenced those that governed the Reagan presidency," a speech writer in the Reagan White House noted. "Coolidge was, of course, a champion of individualism, free enterprise and traditional values." Reagan's public addresses, like Coolidge's, conveyed the president's commitment to limited government in moral terms, as a righteous cause that served mankind at home and abroad.[7]

The effort of the Reagan administration to state the governing philosophy of his administration in such exalted terms was most clearly reflected in Reagan's speech on March 8, 1983 to the National Association of Evangelicals in Orlando, Florida. This speech became known as the "evil empire" speech, but it was not simply an effort to liken the Soviet Union to the dark forces depicted in a popular movie. Rather, it represented an effort to state the principles of the Reagan "revolution" in moral and religious terms. After expressing his disdain for communism as another "sad, bizarre chapter in human history," Reagan concluded:

> I believe . . . the source of our strength in the quest for human freedom is not material, but spiritual. And because it knows no limitation, it must terrify and ultimately triumph over those who would enslave their fellow man. For in the words of Isaiah: "He giveth power to the faint; and to them that have no might He increased strength. . . . But they that wait upon the Lord shall renew their strength; they shall mount up with wings as eagles; they shall run and not be weary. . . ."
>
> Yes, change your world. One of the Founding Fathers, Thomas Paine, said, "We have it within our power to begin the world over again." We can do it, doing together what no one church could do by itself.[8]

To his political opponents, Reagan's rhetoric was a cynical manipulation of the public that disguised a mean-spirited public philosophy. But Reagan's words and what he stood for stirred something deeply rooted in American politics. With his nomination in 1980, the Republican party was not turned into an instrument of personal power as it was during the Nixon years; instead, Reagan's nomination and ascent to the presidency signalled the conversion of the GOP into a vehicle to advance Reagan's conservative principles. Some party workers believed the Reagan administration emphasized rhetoric at the cost of inattention to the nuts and bolts of the party building, but other professionals appreciated the exalted purpose Reagan's leadership envisioned for the GOP. As the Research Director of the Republican National Committee marveled in the summer of 1986:

The Reagan revolution is not an ephemeral phenomenon, and continuity depends on more than rhetoric. It depends on broad principles and the support of these principles by a strong party organization. In respect to this long-term vision and the understanding of what it takes to make it practical, Reagan is very much of a philosopher–king.[9]

This rhapsodic characterization of President Reagan by a grateful party worker reflected no doubt the dramatic shift in partisan loyalties that Reagan's leadership seemed to inspire. Prior to his presidency, polls were showing a substantial Democratic advantage in expressed partisan preference—more than a twenty-point advantage in 1980. Yet this long-standing advantage gave way after Reagan's re-election when all the major polling organizations found the Republicans nearing parity with the Democrats.[10] From the beginning of his Administration, Reagan envisioned and worked for a realignment that would begin a new era in American politics. The 1984 presidential election, in which the Republican ticket won the electoral votes of all but one state, Minnesota, and Washington, D.C., and the demonstrated shift in partisan loyalties that followed that landslide convinced many Republican faithful and the president, himself, that things were indeed moving in that direction. In a speech to the Conservative Political Action Conference in March 1985, Reagan heralded the end of the long period that FDR and the New Deal had held sway over the country, relegating the "Right" to a "diffuse and scattered" existence. "It has spent its intellectual capital," he said of Liaberalism, and "it did its deeds."[11]

These deeds, according to Reagan, had vitiated the American constitutional order. Liberalism had undermined the American commitment to limited and balanced government, encroaching on individual freedom and violating the integrity of federalism. The task, then, was not to "conserve," but to restore the principles and mechanisms of the American Republic. Thus, the "New Beginning" Reagan called for in his first Inaugural Address presupposed, in fact, a "second American revolution," which was the theme of Reagan's 1985 State of the Union address:

The time has come to proceed toward a great new challenge—a Second American Revolution of hope and opportunity; a revolution that will carry us to new heights of progress by pushing back frontiers of knowledge and space; a revolution of spirit that taps the soul of America, enabling us to summon greater strength than we have ever known; and, a revolution that carries beyond our shores the golden promise of human freedom in a world of peace. . . . Nearly 50 years of Government living beyond its means has brought us to a time of reckoning. Ours is but a moment in history. But one moment of courage, idealism and bipartisan unity can change American history forever.[12]

In this endeavor to resurrect the American Revolution, Reagan benefitted from and in turn helped to galvanize the renewal of party politics. Partisanship, to be sure, might seem inappropriate for a "bipartisan"—constitutional—program. Yet throughout American history fundamental periods of reform—"America's surrogate for revolution"—have been associated with partisanship. We have claimed that the triumph of administrative politics meant that deliberation and authorization—activities that promote the differences of opinion and the jarring of parties that had marked previous critical realignments—were greatly reduced in importance. But some developments during the Reagan presidency suggested that a phoenix may yet emerge from the ashes. In important respects, political parties had an unprecedently formidable presence in the political system during the 1980s. In effect, the erosion of old-style partisan politics opened up the possibility for the development of a more national and issue-oriented party system, providing the foundation for the cultivation of stronger ties between presidents and their parties.

The Republican party in particular developed a formidable organizational apparatus, which displayed unprecedented strength at the national level. The refurbishing of the GOP organizational apparatus owed largely to the efforts of William Brock, who during his tenure as chairman of the Republican National Committee from 1976 through the 1980 campaign set out to rejuvenate and ultimately to revolutionize the national party. After 1976, the Republican National Committee and the other two national Republican campaign bodies, the National Republican Senatorial and Congressional (House) Committees, greatly expanded their efforts to raise funds and provide services at the national level for GOP candidates. Moreover, these efforts carried the national party into activities, such as the publication of public policy journals and the distribution of comprehensive briefing books for candidates, that demonstrated its interest in generating programmatic proposals that might be politically useful. The Democrats lagged behind in party-building efforts, but the electoral losses suffered in the 1980 elections encouraged them to modernize the national party machinery, openly imitating some of the devices employed by the Republicans.[13] As a result, the traditional party apparatus, based upon patronage and state and local organizations, gave way to a more programmatic party politics based on the national organization. These developments led some to suggest that there was not simply a revitalization but a reconstruction of political parties as more formidable organizations.[14] Arguably, a party system had finally evolved that was compatible with the national polity forged on the anvil of the New Deal.

The evolution of the Republican party as a force against administration seemed to complete the development of a "New American Party System." The nomination and election of Reagan, a far more ideological conservative than Nixon, galvanized the commitment of the GOP to programs such as "regulatory relief" and "new federalism" that severely challenged the institutional legacy of the New Deal. The Reagan administration represented the first concerted and far-reaching commitment to devolve substantial policy and revenue responsibility to the states since the advent of the modern presidency; moreover, the administration's regulatory program marked the first effort since FDR significantly to reduce government intervention in the economy.[15] Had such a trend continued, the circumvention of the regular political process by administrative action could very well have been displaced by the sort of full-scale debate about political questions usually associated with political realignments in American history.

It is also significant that the Reagan administration made a concerted effort to strengthen the Republican party.[16] This is especially noteworthy, because it represented a sharp departure from previous modern presidents who harbored ambitions for significant policy reform. But whereas the national party organization suffered at the hands of presidents such as Roosevelt, Johnson, and Nixon, all of whom considered it an obstacle to their intentions, a case can be made that Reagan was remarkably concerned with nurturing party responsibility and organization. This loyalty to party had actually long been characteristic of Reagan—when he ran for governor of California, for example, Reagan took the unprecedented step of persuading the entire ticket of Republican candidates for state office to run as a team. This inclination to run a cooperative partisan campaign was displayed in Reagan's run for the presidency as well, when, at the start of the 1980 general election campaign, he posed on the steps of the Capitol with scores of Republican candidates for Congress to symbolize an inclusive party effort.[17]

Recent presidents have tended to be especially inattentive to the needs of their party once elected, and the Reagan administration was seemingly indifferent to party building during its first 2 years. William Brock left the RNC in 1981 to head the Office of the United States Trade Representative, and his successor, Richard Richards, did not show the same enthusiasm for strengthening and expanding the party's organizational base. But a decision apparently was made after the 1982 Congressional elections, in which the Republicans fared poorly in House contests, to strengthen the party machinery. In order to enhance cooperation between the White House, the national committee, and the Congressional campaign organizations, Reagan in January 1983 chose his close personal friend, Nevada Senator Paul Laxalt, to fill a newly created position, General Chairman of the GOP. Senator Laxalt's close associate Frank Fahrenkopf, former Chairman of the Nevada Republican party, replaced the ineffective Richard Richards in the traditional post of the RNC chair. The White House, with Senator Laxalt's support, then actively intervened to replace the head of the Republican Senatorial Committee, Senator Robert Packwood of Oregon, a frequent critic of President Reagan, with a more reliable political ally, Senator Richard Lugar of Indiana.[18]

These developments enabled the Reagan Administration to improve the coordination of campaign efforts and policy development within the party without undermining the GOP's organizational strength. In fact, national party activities continued to expand under the capable guidance of Fahrenkopf, who in 1983 launched an ambitious 8-year plan to strengthen the GOP at the local level. In carrying out these activities, party professionals received almost complete cooperation from the president.[19] Reagan surprised even his own political director with his "total readiness" to shoulder such partisan responsibilities as making numerous fundraising appearances for the GOP and its candidates. Apparently after spending the first 50 years of his life with the opposition, Reagan brought the enthusiasm of a convert to party activities.[20] William Brock, who has observed the relationship of every president since Eisenhower with the party, noted in 1987:

> . . . Reagan has been in many respects an ardent party leader. Of the six presidents I have known, he has worked the hardest to strengthen the party. The difference between Reagan and Carter is especially stark: Carter was against the party, and as president, he never did anything to nurture it. Carter believed that

he had become president on his own; but Reagan grew to appreciate the party—he recognized that his success was due to a lot of people in the party who worked hard and made a difference.[21]

Reagan's motivation and political skill to support his party might have been an exception, yet his successor, George Bush, had close ties to the party regulars. Moreover, the "institutionalization" of the national committees and the strengthening of the campaign committees in Congress over the past decade have created the foundation for a national party organization that is no longer so exclusively focused on presidential politics.[22] The new character of the national party is revealed by the fact that Brock was able to retain his position as RNC chairman during the 1980 presidential campaign, although the previously established practice was for the presidential nominee to replace the Chairman with his own choice.[23] Reagan, despite pressures from his own supporters, including his campaign manager, Paul Laxalt, decided to retain Brock rather than risk a major intra-party feud. In the final analysis, Brock's ability to avoid a purge owed largely to his commanding substantial political support as a result of his success in rebuilding the party machinery; indeed, the broad scale of the activities carried out by the revitalized GOP apparatus enabled an astute chairman to build a political constituency of his own. Consequently, when Chairman Brock refused to comply with the request of Reagan's emissary that he step down, the presidential nominee really had little alternative but to retain the incumbent chairman. The ability of the moderate Brock to withstand the challenge of Reagan's more conservative loyalists was, Brock argues, "a tribute to the party's own self-worth," acquired from three-and-a-half years of successful redevelopment. "I felt my determination to stand up for the independence of the party organization was justified by the 1980 campaign, especially by the gains we made in local elections," Brock reflected a few years later.[24]

Although far behind the Republican party in its professional development, the Democratic party apparently acquired a degree of independence from presidential candidates and the presidency as well. In many respects, DNC Chairman Charles Manatt's role after the 1980 election was comparable to the earlier role of RNC chairman William Brock. And, like Brock in 1980, Manatt remained as chairman during the presidential campaign at the end of his 4 years in office, even though the party presidential nominee, Walter Mondale, wanted to follow the older custom of replacing him. As Leon Epstein noted, "at least a degree of institutionalization is thereby suggested in the Democratic as in the Republican case."[25]

The institutionalization of national party organizations has increased the distance between the regular party apparatus and the presidency in one sense, but it also makes possible a strengthened alliance. The rise of national parties has been associated more with issues and sophisticated fundraising techniques than patronage; as such, the reconstructed party system poses less of an obstacle than did the traditional party apparatus to the programmatic ambitions of the president. For example, leading members of the modern party organization are far more supportive than were traditional party operatives of the exigencies of governance that prevent presidents from adhering strictly to partisanship. As William Greener, former Deputy Chief of Staff for Political Operations at the Republican National Committee put it:

> [I]t is unreasonable to expect a President to be a partisan in all respects. Maybe twenty years ago complete partisanship made sense. But the scope of what government undertakes now is much greater. You could not strictly speaking use the party as a spoils system.[26]

The emergence of the Republicans as a more national and programmatic party was strongly supported by an activist core of conservative congressman who sought to sharpen and air their party's ideological differences with the Democrats. Led by Georgia Representative Newt Gingrich, the Conservative Opportunity Society (COS), composed of about a dozen lawmakers who committed themselves to attend weekly meetings on strategy and tactics, had the long-term objective of securing a Republican majority in the House of Representatives. But Gingrich and his supporters believed that the GOP could not win control of the lower chamber until the Republicans were unified behind a comprehensive conservative program dedicated to tax cuts, aggressive anti-communism, and incentives, embodied in policies such as the development of inner-city enterprise zones, to spur economic growth. Just as important, however, was the interest of the COS in reforming procedural rules in the House—believing that public opinion was on their side, ardent conservative legislators intended, as Gingrich put it, "to make the House a forum of debate on the issues."[27] To accomplish this task, COS members sought to mobilize their House colleagues in a campaign directed against subcommittee government. This push for change in the legislative process strengthened the Republican opposition to the liberal institutional legacy by attacking the arrangements that encouraged Congress's involvement in the details of administration. As one charter member of the COS explained:

> The idea of the COS was to move the House from one to another series of activities. The feeling was that we had to have a new process—a retraining for members of Congress. Most significantly, it was necessary to force issues on the floor of the House, to keep them from being buried in the committee system, so that members of Congress would be forced to make decisions about controversial issues. . . . [I]f we were going to be the majority party, we had to operate that way. We thought we could change the country, but this place [the House] is designed to ensure that doesn't happen.[28]

Neither the Reagan administration nor the COS was able to break the strong grip of the Democrats on the House of Representatives. Indeed, Reagan's landslide re-election had little impact on the partisan alignment of Congress. The 1984 elections gave House Republicans a gain of just 14 seats. The additional seats did not compensate for the losses suffered in the 1982 midterm campaign, leaving the Republicans well short of the 24 seats they needed to match the 192 seats they held after the 1980 election; the Democrats held a 253–182 House majority for the 99th Congress. Republicans suffered a net loss of two Senate seats, reducing their majority in that body to 53–47.

Some members of the Republican party, including some conservatives, considered the push for a national Republican party united behind the COS's vision for America and dedicated to its methods a poorly conceived strategy for capturing the House. "What is needed now—and what the NRCC [National Republican Congressional Committee] is moving toward—is a serious effort to pick up that necessary majority by concentrating on the individual concerns of 435 different constituencies," argued Oklahoma Congressman Mickey Edwards soon after the 1984 election. "That is a very different approach from the guerilla activities urged by some, who think ferment and turmoil will create new strength." [29] Edwards' concerns were echoed by many Senate Republicans and party professionals who considered an ideological partisan strategy that did not attend to the diversity and complexity of American society detrimental. Thus, serious disagreements between ardent conservatives intent upon forging a unified national party and those who favored a more incrementalist approach to party building divided Republican councils during the Reagan presidency.

Notwithstanding these disagreements, by 1984, the Republican party had become a solidly right-of-center party, made over in Ronald Reagan's image. Reagan had not completed the realignment many conservatives hoped for in the early days of the administration, but he had significantly advanced the party transformation represented by Barry Goldwater's 1964 presidential campaign. Whereas Goldwater's nomination signified a conservative shift in the Republican party, Reagan took the realignment one step further by making the Republican party and program an electoral success. And Reagan's brethren in the COS, although frustrated in their objective of capturing the House, managed to prod their GOP colleagues, and sometimes even the president, to act more assertively, thus abetting the transformation of the Republican party. [30]

The experience of the Reagan Administration suggests how the relationship between the president and the "new American party system" can be mutually beneficial. Republican party strength provided Reagan with the support of a formidable institution, solidifying his personal popularity and building support for his programs in Congress. As a result, the Reagan presidency was able to overcome the paralysis that seemed to afflict American government by the end of the 1970s, even though the Republicans never attained control of the House of Representatives. In turn, Reagan's popularity served the party by strengthening its fundraising efforts and promoting a shift in voters' party loyalties, placing the Republicans by 1985 in a position of virtual parity with the Democrats for the first time since the 1940s. It may be, then, that the 1980s marked the watershed both for a new political era and for a renewed link between presidents and the party system. Furthermore, the cooperation between Reagan and the Republican party was not simply attributable to the president's extraordinary commitment to his party, but also to structural changes that could have an enduring influence.

Significantly, the Democratic party had become a more national and programmatic party as well, with an ideological center of gravity that was decidedly left of center. The playing out of the New Deal and Great Society, and the Republican response, had sharply reduced the presence of traditional Southern Democracy in Congress, thus emancipating the party from the ball and chain that hobbled its liberal march. In the 75th Congress that balked at FDR's court-"packing" plan, there were 120 House seats in the 13 Southern states (the old Confederacy, plus Kentucky and Oklahoma). A full 117 of those 120 were in Democratic hands. On their own, Southern Democrats possessed more than half the votes needed to carry a majority of the House on any question. By the end of the Reagan era, those same states had 124 seats. But only 85 of them were Democratic; more than a quarter had migrated to the GOP side of the aisle. Moreover, the 1965 Voting Rights Act had substantially increased the number of black voters in the South, thereby transforming the voting behavior of those Southern representatives who remained on the Democratic side of the aisle. As *Congressional Quarterly*'s Alan Ehrenhalt wrote in 1987:

> . . . [I]n the vast majority of districts across the South, a Democratic incumbent knows two things: Blacks will provide the basis of his support against any Republican, and they can cause him trouble in a Democratic primary if they turn against him. For both reasons, the black community and its wishes have to be listened to. It was the sign of the times in 1983 when Southern Democrats voted 78–12 in favor of the holiday honoring the Rev. Martin Luther King Jr. [31]

Despite the recent changes in the party system, any celebration of a dawn of a new era of disciplined party government is premature. The Democratic party's recapture of the Senate in the 1986 elections and the devastation brought by the Iran–contra arms scandal soon thereafter derailed the resurgence of the Republican party that once was perceived by many as signalling a new era in American politics. To be sure, the results of the 1986 elections and the Iran–Contra affair could be explained in part by the "natural" rhythms of the electoral cycle and "localized," if massive, mismanagement of policy, neither of which would necessarily thwart the future surge of the Republican party. But these events had a profound and enduring influence, for they reflected the fact that the Reagan Administration was insufficiently attentive to the problematic political and constitutional effects of liberal reform. Moreover, the troubles Reagan confronted during the last 2 years of his presidency suggest that imposing obstacles will continue to block a fundamental revival of the American party system. We will take these matters up in the next section.

The "New" Party System and Presidential Prerogative

The relationship between the presidency and the party always has been difficult, but the advent of the modern presidency greatly aggravated this relationship. Put simply, the institutional legacy of the New Deal transformed the presidency and the executive agencies into a "surrogate political process," which deprived the parties of a limited but very important role in elections and governance. [32] As this development unfolded, it did not so clearly redound to the benefit of presidents. The transformation of the executive during the twentieth century established the president, rather than the party, as the leading instrument of popular rule. With this development, presidents became more powerful, yet constantly faced the danger of having popular support evaporate. The modern president claims to promote equality and tame private interests while embodying the will of "the people." Yet the party system, though it restrained executive action in many respects, provided an elaborate mechanism by which presidents maintained a vital link with the American people. Wilson Carey McWilliams is on solid ground when he claims political parties played a crucial part in "relating the private order to the public life of the United States."[33] As such, the modern presidency, and the enhanced rhetorical and administrative possibilities of that office, strengthened the national purpose, but also contributed to the long secular decline of the party system and thus to the desiccation of American citizenship.

Since the turn of the century, especially since the New Deal, presidents have faced a serious dilemma. On the one hand, the traditional party system has made the presidency accountable to local government and community control, which remains at the heart of the most intuitive conceptions of democracy in the United States. On the other hand, that party system, emphasizing organization at the state and local level and nourished by patronage, has been viewed as an impediment to the development of a strong national state, which has been deemed necessary to protect freedom from foreign threats, limit the power of corporations, and guarantee the equal protection of the law. The modern presidency was crafted as a means to reconcile the seemingly inherent conflict between popular rule and the consolidation of national administrative capacities, but the unchecked executive power it has occasionally portended threatens certain valued traditions of the American political experience such as the separation of powers, federalism, and an emphasis on the private life. The vulnerability of the modern presidency stems most essentially from the fact that these traditions remain an important, if somewhat weakened, part of the American democratic experience.

Perhaps national parties will bridge more effectively the traditions of republican government in the United States and the exigencies of state power. The Reagan presidency demonstrated that ardent leadership of the reconstructed party in American politics could be an effective instrument for working with, rather than circumventing, Congress, and persuading, rather than manipulating, public opinion. The rise of more national and programmatic parties deprives partisanship in the United States of some of the tolerance that heretofore has made party loyalty so compatible with the pluralistic tradition in American politics. It may be, however, as A. James Reichley notes, "that a politics tied more clearly to principles and ideals is more appropriate to the current stage of our national life."[34]

Still, the revival of partisanship has not gone far enough to warrant consideration as a "new American party system." The restoration of the party to an important place in American politics continues to be retarded by the nomination process, a legacy of the McGovern–Fraser reforms. These reforms established the conditions for a candidate-centered system of presidential selection that discourages close cooperation between presidential candidates and their fellow partisans during the course of the general election campaign.

There have been important efforts to "reform the reforms," and the decline of party due to its loss of control over the nomination process has been ameliorated by the strengthening of the financial capacity and organizational functions of the national and Congressional committees. Yet the process of selecting presidential candidates by a series of state primaries and caucuses is so permeable that it may be virtually impossible to sustain any substantial spirit of partisan unity. This problem is made more acute by the election campaign finance laws, passed during the 1970s, which provide public funds directly to candidates. According to former RNC chairman Frank Fahrenkopf, the present system of public funding, which distributes matching funds to any candidate who can raise $5000 in each of 20 states in contributions of $250 or less, makes it too easy for candidates who are not legitimate contenders for the nomination to run, thus reducing the serious business of presidential selection to a virtual free-for-all.[35]

During the 1980s, the modern nominating process created especially difficult problems for Democrats, who were more divided than Republicans on most issues and were therefore less able to develop a strategically unified national party organization.[36] The fragility of the Democratic party-building efforts was revealed all too clearly during the 1988 campaign. The 1988 Convention Rules Committee was controlled by Massachusetts Governor Michael Dukakis, who was eager to placate his chief rival for the nomination, Jesse Jackson. The committee agreed to changes in the nomination rules for 1992 that subordinated the interests of the party to short-term tactical considerations of the leading candidates. These changes—one tied the selection of the Democratic delegates more closely to each candidates share of the primary or caucus vote, and another reduced sharply the number of "superdelegates" (party and elected officials with guaranteed seats as uncommitted delegates) at the 1992 convention—were a retreat from efforts made by Democratic officials to strengthen the role of party leaders in the nominating process. Representative David Price, D-N.C., a leader in the effort to reform the reforms, observed with dismay: "It's a familiar path we see. Candidates meet their short-term needs but sell out the long-term interests of the party."[37]

The problem of nurturing partisan community is also aggravated by the fact that the revitalization of parties has thus far primarily taken effect as a result of Washington activism and "high-tech" campaigning, which, according to some critics, has yet to reach beyond the Capital Beltway.[38] This is an especially salient problem for the Republican party, which has had far more success in presidential campaigns than it has had at the state and local level. Loren Smith, who served as chief counsel for the 1980 Reagan campaign, expressed skepticism about the thesis that the "parties are back":

> For all the talk about the revival of parties there has been very little consideration of what this means. Are parties more effective in screening the nomination of candidates, providing services to them, acting as a link between candidates and voters? While it is true that the national party organization, especially, in the case of the Republican party, has become a source of services to candidates, the party remains weak at the state and local level, no longer serving, as it once did, as a link between candidates and the people. There may be a revival of parties in some respects, but it is not clear this means very much to the American people.[39]

The Republican party was not indifferent to this problem. William Brock, in fact, notes that the refurbishing of the GOP party machinery was carried out with the intention of strengthening its organization at the state and local level. The national organization was rebuilt to enhance the party's ability to present a more coherent message—to offer a clearer vision of the Republican party's themes and values. The coordinated effort to commit the Republicans to tax cuts that resulted in the GOP gathering on the steps of the Capitol during the 1980 campaign was an effort, as Brock put it, "to demonstrate that a party rather than an individual, or a bunch of disassociated individuals, could make a difference." But, at the same time, the strengthening of the national organization was carried out with the understanding that in American politics a party could not be "strong without a state and local base." Accordingly, a considerable part of the enhanced fund-raising capacity of the Republican National Committee was channeled into party building at the state and local level.[40]

This project to strengthen the Republicans at the community level was especially important to Fahrenkopf, who headed the Nevada state party for 8 years prior to assuming the duties as RNC chair in 1983. His aforementioned 8-year plan was designed to strengthen the party at the grass roots by redirecting the resources of the RNC to county and township organizations, with the intention of refurbishing all of the some 3,000 local Republican bodies, many of which were found to be moribund in 1983. This program was particularly notable in that Fahrenkopf worked out an unprecedented agreement with Republican state party chairmen that would allow the national party committee for the first time "to interface" directly with county and township organizations. According to Fahrenkopf, therefore, the thesis proposed by several scholars concerning the rise of a national party was wrong; rather, he insisted, "just the opposite is happening, we have turned that theory on its head."[41]

Nevertheless, this effort to strengthen state and local party organizations, which, on a smaller scale, had also been attempted by Democrats, did not succeed. Few practicing politicians, and few observers close to actual political life, believed by the end of the 1980s that the long-term decline of state and local parties had been reversed or even stabilized. Indeed, Joseph Gaylord, former Executive Director of the Republican Congressional Committee, expressed concern in 1986 that the conditions required to resuscitate a grass roots party politics may no longer exist:

> There is significant change in the direction of [national consolidation] caused in large part by the breakdown of political geography—traditional geographic units no longer make any difference. The county party is insignificant, because the insulation of town and city politics has broken down. At the local level political parties per se are not terribly relevant. . . . Advances in technology have contributed to such a change, for example, the use of direct mail. [And] the number of volunteers is down because our society has changed—more two income families, for instance; and the personal involvement in local politics has declined.[42]

Thus, though the strengthening of state and local organizations may be necessary for the renewal of parties to become rooted in the perceptions and habits of the American people, the conditions for carrying out such a task may no longer exist.

Although the "natural conditions" to sustain local political associations might have declined, effective efforts are being made "artificially" to create vital party organizations at the state and local level.[43] The success of such an endeavor is still in doubt, but it is premature to dismiss the reconstructed party system as merely a "beltway" phenomenon. If the party-building efforts of the Republican and Democratic organizations continue, a national party may yet be formed that will reach beyond the Washington community and ameliorate the challenges posed by the emergence of administrative politics.[44]

In the final analysis, the major obstacle to party renewal is not likely to be the lack of flexibility in the new party system, but the failure of party transformation to remedy sufficiently what ardent programmatic reformers have long considered the deficiencies of American constitutional government. The disparate character of American political institutions provides a precarious context for the cultivation of comprehensive party programs. It is unlikely that the emergence of stronger national parties will fundamentally alter the limits of party government in the American constitution, a fact that will continue to encourage modern presidents, particularly those intent upon ambitious policy reform, to emphasize popular appeal and administrative action rather than "collective responsibility." The Reagan White House, intent upon a "conservative" revolution, fought to impose a program of reform that necessarily looked beyond the limited agreements that could be worked out in the fragmented processes that structure American party politics. It is not surprising, therefore, that the Reagan presidency frequently pursued its program by acts of administrative discretion that short-circuited the legislative process and weakened the prospects for policy to emerge as an endeavor shared between different elements of the party.

In the case of Nicaragua, for example, the Reagan administration elected to build an alternative intelligence apparatus, attached to the National Security Council. This apparatus enabled the White House to conduct covert operations (such as aid to the Contras) that the Congress had refused to approve, and activities (such as weapon sales to Iran) that Congress certainly would not have sanctioned. The attempt to circumvent limits on the freedom of action in such areas as Central America and Iran exposed the administration to severe political risks and resulted eventually in a damaging scandal. In two successive revelations, the nation learned in late November, 1986 that, with the president's approval, the United States had sold weapons to Iran and that, allegedly without the president's knowledge, some of the proceeds had been diverted by National Security Council officials to assist the Contras.

Public reaction to the Iran–Contra scandal was dramatic—following these revelations Reagan's approval rating fell from 67 percent to 46 percent in one month. The Iran arms sales, undertaken apparently to secure the release of seven U.S. hostages held by terrorists in Beruit, Lebanon, although not illegal, ran directly counter to the administration's own policies on terrorism and military support to Iran, and the diversion of funds to the Contras, although consistent with the Administration's policy in Central America, was in view of the Boland Amendment, a 1985 congressional ban on aid to the Contras, widely regarded as illegal. Hence, as James Ceaser has observed, "President Reagan could be ridiculed for allowing the United States to be duped by the Ayatollah at the same time the administration could be vilified for a zealous anticommunism that led to a 'secret government' outside normal constitutional channels.''[45]

The report of the president's appointed review board, the Tower Commission, soundly criticized Reagan's management style and lent official sanction to the charge that Reagan was out of touch with the affairs of state, a mere figurehead completely at the mercy of his staff. But the Iran–Contra affair was not simply the result of a president being asleep on his watch. Rather, it revealed the Reagan administration's determination to carry out its foreign policy without the interference of the bureaucracy and Congress. Although the president might not have known about the diversion of funds from the Iranian arms sales to the Contras, this activity was not especially surprising, given the so-called "Reagan Doctrine," which entailed a commitment to support selected insurrections against Marxist-governed states at the periphery, such as Nicaragua, Angola, and Afghanistan. As the minority report of the congressional committees investigating the Iran–contra affair granted, "President Reagan gave his subordinates strong, clear and consistent guidance about the basic thrust of the policies he wanted them to pursue toward Nicaragua. There is some question and dispute about *precisely* the level at which he chose to follow the operational details. There is no doubt, however, . . . [that] the President set the U.S. policy toward Nicaragua, with few if any ambiguities, and then left subordinates more or less free to implement it.''[46]

Many, if not most, members of the president's party supported the administration's efforts to aid the Contras. Although expressing doubts about the wisdom and legality of the diversion of funds from Iran to the Contras, the Republican Senators and Representatives who signed the minority report of the select committees charged with investigating the Iran–Contra scandal endorsed the thrust of Reagan's policies and actions with respect to Central America. "Our *only* regret," read the report, "is that the administration was not open enough with Congress about what it was doing." The long-term prospects for building political support for its policies, these GOP legislators averred, would have been enhanced by taking on congressional opposition directly. The president simply should have vetoed the Boland amendment, they insisted, even though it was a specific rider within a long-continuing appropriations resolution. To take on the issue openly in this way would have given the president the opportunity to challenge Congress on the merits before the nation.[47]

A close examination of policy-making during the Reagan years provides other examples of the Administration resorting to unilateral executive action when it anticipated or was confronted with resistance within the party councils. From the start, in fact, the Reagan White House pursued programmatic change by utilizing the tactics of "institutional combat" that characterized the Nixon years.[48] Not only was policy centered in the White House Office and Executive Office of the President, but much care was taken to plant White House loyalists in the departments and agencies—persons who could be relied on to ride herd on civil servants and carry forth the president's program. As Bert A. Rockman has observed, "it was the Nixon presidency, particularly in its aborted second term, that became celebrated for its deployment of [the administrative presidency]," but "the Reagan Presidency intended to perfect the strategy and to do it from the beginning."[49]

Especially in the area of social regulation, "regulatory relief"—the Reagan administration's attempt to weaken environmental, consumer, and civil rights regulation—came not through legislative change but through administrative inaction, delay, and repeal. President Reagan's Executive Orders 12,291 and 12,498 mandated a comprehensive review of proposed agency regulations and centralized that review process in the Office of Management and Budget (OMB). Reagan also appointed a Presidential Task Force on Regulatory Relief, headed by Vice President Bush, to apply cost–benefit analysis to existing rules. This review included a consideration of so-called midnight regulations of the Carter administration, on which the president imposed a 60-day freeze on January 29, 1981.

These actions demonstrated quite clearly the extent to which emphasis was placed on employing administrative regulatory relief. We observed in Chapter 9 that during the 1970s, presidents established elaborate administrative mechanisms to gain control of the far-flung activities spawned by social regulation. But the Reagan administration's regulatory oversight program represented a marked departure from past policy. This program's commitment to centralize review processes and to clamp down on the expansion of regulatory authority far surpassed that of previous administrations. Whereas previous attempts to review regulations distributed authority among several executive branch offices and departments, such as the Council of Wage and Price Stability and the Regulatory Analysis and Review Group, which was formed by the Carter administration, the Reagan program was carried out exclusively within the Office of Information and Regulatory Affairs of the OMB. Moreover, for the first time cost–benefit analysis was made mandatory, except where prohibited by law, thus ensuring that the Reagan administration's review program would have a much greater impact than that of previous administrations on the regulatory activities of line departments and agencies.[50]

In this light, the Iran–Contra scandal was not simply an aberration but an extreme example of the prevailing pattern of policy-making throughout the Reagan presidency when it faced resistance from Congress. In fact, the Reagan presidency was the most administratively ambitious since the advent of the modern presidency. Reagan surpassed Nixon in employing and strengthening the administrative levers of power developed in the pursuit of liberal reform for conservative objectives.

In doing so, the Reagan White House made effective use of the Civil Service Reform Act, which was passed under the Carter administration as a device to make the bureaucracy more responsive to political leadership (see Chapter 9).[51] This act replaced the bipartisan Civil Service Commission with the Office of Personnel Management (OPM), an agency headed by political appointees, and subjected some 1500 Schedule C positions and 700 senior executive service appointments to explicit control by a presidential administration through demotion, transfer, or removal. The Carter administration had made some use of this law to enhance its influence over the bureaucracy, but the Reagan White House made much more ambitious use of its provisions. Reagan's choice to direct the OPM, Donald J. Devine, vigorously reduced the distance between politics and administration, taking aggressive steps to ensure "a response to what elected officials want."[52] In effect, Devine transformed the role of the OPM from an oversight agency to a political arm of the Administration, thus permitting an unchecked circumvention of civil service protection. The erosion of the status of the senior civil service was especially devastating. The Senior Executive Service was envisioned by the authors of the 1978 reform bill as a buffer between political appointees and program specialists; yet few program specialists were insulated under Reagan, and the politicization of the OPM by Devine undermined any prospects for a corps of neutral and competent civil servants to be established at the top of the federal bureaucracy.[53]

Of course, the attempt by a president to control the bureaucracy was nothing new, nor were previous efforts to exert political control over the civil service limited to Republican administrations seeking to contain liberal programmatic ambitions. Yet, whereas presidents such as Roosevelt and Johnson had employed civil service reform as an instrument of programmatic policy, the Reagan administration's use of personnel tactics marked an unprecedented challenge to long-standing political arrangements that favored program advocates. It is one thing to provide an opportunity for political intervention to generate more creative and energetic policy, and quite another to use this opportunity to put a harness on federal departments and agencies. The former intention gave impetus to the 1978 Civil Service Reform law; the latter suggests how the Reagan personnel program represented an unintended and ironic legacy of civil service reform.

The importance of presidential politics and executive administration in the Reagan presidency may actually have weakened the prospects for a Republican realignment. The journalist Sidney Blumenthal has argued that Reagan "did not reinvent the Republican party so much as transcend it. His primary political instrument was the conservative movement, which inhabited the party out of convenience."[54] This observation is only partly true, for President Reagan's commitment to strengthening his party was sincere and, in many respects, effective. Nevertheless, the Reagan administration's devotion to certain conservative ideological tenets led to a reliance on unilateral executive action and conservative citizen groups that ultimately compromised the president's support for the Republican party. To some extent, at least, Republican leaders were justified in blaming Reagan's emphasis on White House politics and policy for the failure to convert his personal popularity into Republican control of the government. William Brock's lament of 1987 was echoed by many GOP officials during the twilight of the Reagan years:

> Too many of those around [the president] seem to have a sense of party that begins and ends in the Oval Office. The White House really does not have an appreciation of the party's institutions and its professional cadres. Too many really don't understand what it means to link the White House to a party in a way that creates an alliance between the presidency, the House, and the Senate, or between the national party and officials at the state and local level.[55]

In this respect, the failure of the American people to heed the president's plea during the 1986 House and Senate campaigns to elect Republican majorities was, in part, an understandable response to Reagan's inattention to the deliberations necessary to make collective, and not simply presidential, responsibility meaningful. The loss of eight seats and a majority in the Senate was widely viewed by

Republican partisans as a disaster that need not have happened. It was not unusual for the party in control of the White House to lose ground in midterm elections— Eisenhower, Johnson, and Nixon, for example, saw their parties sustain serious congressional defeats at similar junctures of their administrations. But the popularity Reagan enjoyed after 6 years in power and the economic prosperity the country was then experiencing might have worked against the tide of history. As Ehrenhalt wrote soon after the election, "All the other midterm Senate debacles of modern times occurred against the backdrop of serious problems in the country—a national recession in 1958, the Vietnam War in 1966, the Watergate scandal in 1974. No such problem existed for the Republicans this year."[56]

Reagan, to be sure, displayed his characteristic support for his party during the campaign, taking part in fundraisers for the GOP and campaigning for Republican candidates; moreover, the political shop in the White House worked closely with the Republican National Committee, as well as the House and Senate campaign committees. But a conscious decision was made within the White House to avoid a highly charged partisan campaign in 1986, a determination that was imposed upon the vaunted Republican national machine.[57] The deliberate choice to work closely with the GOP campaign organizations and candidates while avoiding a thematic partisan campaign was an unwitting betrayal of the party the president hoped to elevate to majority status, Minnesota Representative Vin Weber of the COS argued, compounding the flawed strategy of Reagan's re-election effort:

> The campaign was not run as a national partisan campaign, highlighting the philosophical differences between Republicans and Democrats. Instead the focus was on state and local issues and the same feel good, empty rhetoric that dominated the 1984 race.[58]

Reagan's speech for Senator James T. Broyhill in North Carolina was a fairly typical example. It did not offer any broad themes that might have projected the GOP as a governing party, but presented the president and Broyhill as part of a team that modulated the excesses of the liberal establishment. "Will you choose the Democratic leaders who in 1980 weakened our nation and nearly brought our economy to its knees," the president asked, "who raised your taxes and have announced their plans to do so again, and who opposed efforts to build a defense to protect us from attack by nuclear ballistic missiles? Or will you choose to give the cleanup crew of 1980 a chance to finish the job?" In characterizing himself as part of a "cleanup crew," Reagan failed to give the voters a sustaining reason to support his party.[59]

Reagan's failure to head a partisan realignment did not necessarily point to the absence of fundamental and enduring policy change. The Progressive era, for example, entailed major shifts in public policy that were not directly attributable to a partisan realignment. Moreover, leading characteristics of the political landscape fashioned by liberal reform—the expansion of the nation's regulatory apparatus, the decline of parties, the growth of the media, and the enhancement of ideas and ideology in the day-to-day affairs of state—might increase the prospects for a major policy realignment to occur without fundamental partisan change. Indeed, there were major departures from the New Deal during the 1960s and

1970s in the absence of fundamental partisan change. The reforms of the 1960s and 1970s, however, were the product of widespread legislative and institutional reform. In this sense, the interesting question about the Reagan "Revolution" may not be whether a partisan realignment has occurred, but whether the evolution of an administrative constitution has advanced so far that a policy realignment can occur independently of both partisan swings *and major legislative change.*

A realignment of this sort would signify a remarkable triumph of the modern presidency. Yet even without the devastating influence of the Iran–Contra affair, such a triumph would have been unlikely, for though forceful and centralized political administration may appear to be a logical and necessary response to the legacy of liberal reform, it is unlikely to nurture the substantial change in public values and institutions required to bring about a fundamental departure in the prevailing patterns of governance. Even Reagan's most impressive legislative achievement was marked by the absence of serious public deliberation and choice. The budgetary and tax reforms achieved during 1981 brought a dramatic departure in fiscal policy: over $35 million in domestic cuts, a multi-year package that projected a reduction of nearly $750 billion in tax cuts, and a 3-year 27% increase in defense spending. But this legislative breakthrough was achieved by employing some of the same tactics that were used during the Great Society to undermine the normal patterns of American politics. In doing so, Reagan was able to use the Congressional Budget and Impoundment Control Act, which was enacted to strengthen Congress's role in fiscal policy, to impose his will on the legislature.

Reagan's OMB director, David Stockman, had figured out a way to subvert a provision in that act, the "reconciliation" process, which Congress had devised to coordinate its budgetary activities more effectively. Using the reconciliation process, the respective House and Senate Budget Committees could package every proposed budget cut made by authorizing committees into a single bill. The House Appropriations Committee belatedly described in a 1982 report how this approach could play into the hands of the president:

> It is much easier for the Executive Branch to gain support for its program when it is packaged in one bill rather than pursuing each and every authorization and appropriation measure to ensure compliance with the Executive's program. This device tends to aid the Executive Branch in gaining additional control over budget matters and to circumvent the will of Congress.[60]

The driving force for a program of change was the political support aroused by Reagan during the 1980 campaign and the early days of his presidency, but the reconciliation process represented a critical action-forcing mechanism that overcame the natural inertia of Congress. "The constitutional prerogatives of the legislative branch would have to be, in effect, suspended," Stockman explained. "Enacting the Reagan administration's economic program meant rubber stamp approval, nothing less. The world's so-called greatest deliberative body would have to be reduced to the status of a ministerial arm of the White House."[61]

The important budgetary changes called for by the Administration were enacted before the end of the first session of the 97th Congress, but the Reagan fiscal program was based on flawed and false promises. As Jeffrey Tulis has written, "Like Lyndon Johnson's, this public policy was prepared hastily in the executive branch, and like the War on Poverty, the nation's legislature played no substantive role in planning the program. In short there was no public deliberation."[62] As a result, the questionable premises of Reagan's budgetary reforms went unchallenged. The justification for such large tax cuts, which far exceeded the reduction in domestic spending and came at the same time that defense spending was being increased, was the supply-side economic theory that high levels of taxation were stifling economic productivity. Economists such as Arthur Laffer and Paul Craig Roberts argued that a large tax cut would provide such a stimulus to productivity that tax revenues would actually increase and allow the budget to be balanced in 1984 despite unprecedented levels of defense spending and growth in major entitlement programs, such as social security, that were not effected by the 1981 reconciliation act. Inflation rates would also fall, thus bringing down interest rates, because the expectations of investors would be changed. Money saved from the tax breaks would not be consumed by tax payers, but would be saved and invested in productive activities. "We anticipate," the administration claimed, "that savings rates will increase, perhaps to historically high levels."[63] Yet, as Stockman admitted at the time, "None of us really understand what's going on with these numbers."[64] The Administration later became saddled, contrary to supply-side projections, with the largest national debt in United States history.

This was an ironic and troubling legacy for a fiscal conservative. Yet many pundits argued the fiscal conundrum of the Reagan era had aborted the liberal state. The Reagan revolution had significantly altered the facts, if not the values, of government action. For the budget deficit and overhaul of the tax system had, in effect, "defunded" the welfare state, thus leaving the Democratic party, historically the party of domestic reform and largess, in a serious bind. As former Vice President Walter Mondale, the Democratic party's ill-fated nominee in 1984, lamented:

> Reagan has practiced the politics of subtraction. He knows the public wants to spend money on old folks, protecting the environment and aiding education. And he's figured out the only way to stop it is to deny the revenues. No matter how powerful the argument the Democrats make for the use of government to serve some purpose, the answer must be no.[65]

Nevertheless, the failure of the Reagan administration to bring forth either a party realignment or a fundamental reshaping of the institutional arrangements that sheltered liberal programs both circumscribed and left unresolved the achievements of the Reagan era. The president himself granted as much in one of his last important public speeches, delivered on December 13, 1988, before administration officials. In these farewell remarks, Reagan blamed the disappointments of his tenure, the greatest of which he counted the failure to balance the federal budget, on an "iron triangle," composed of "parts of Congress, the media, and special interest groups." This unholy trinity had not only made it impossible for him to carry out a comprehensive program of domestic reform, but had weakened the presidency in order to retain control over the federal government:

> When I came to office, I found in the Presidency a weakened institution. I found
> a Congress that was trying to transform our government into a quasi-
> parliamentary system. And I found in Washington a colony—that through the
> iron triangle—was attempting to rule the Nation according to its interests and
> desires more than the Nation's. I've used the President's ability to frame the
> broadest outlines of debate to compensate for some of the weakening of the of-
> fice. . . . But we have not restored the constitutional balance, at least not fully,
> and I believe it must be restored.[66]

As President Reagan admitted, the modern presidency of the 1980s did not,
as it had during the early days of the Johnson administration, command the political system. Instead, it was challenged forcefully by a "modern" Congress that
had developed considerable tools of its own during the 1970s to exert influence
on domestic and foreign policy. For example, members of Congress, acting in
partnership with the courts, bureaucratic agencies, interest groups, and the press,
were able to fend off the Reagan administration's challenge to New Deal entitlements and circumscribe its program of regulatory relief for corporations and other
private institutions. Executive agencies were important actors in this institutional
partnership, but they were sustained, and sometimes harassed, by the political
support mobilized by programmatic advocates in public interest groups, Congress
and the courts.

The influence of the media in the post–New Deal institutional coalition suggests how Reagan's plans were not thwarted behind closed doors but within the
"participatory" mechanisms that evolved from the reforms of the late 1960s and
1970s. To be sure, as Chapter 9 argues, there were troubling political and constitutional consequences associated with those reforms, but they have effectively
established many liberal programs as rights, which elicit broad, if somewhat soft,
support from the American people. Thus, Reagan's interest in rolling back the
social welfare obligations of the national government came up against the post–
New Deal understanding of rights that conceptualized programs such as social
security, aid to education, Medicare and Medicaid, and even the less popular Aid
to Families with Dependent Children (AFDC) as entitlements, thereby deserving
a status beyond the control of public opinion, elections, and political parties.

Similarly, the social regulatory initiatives of the post–New Deal era associated
with civil rights, consumer protection, and environmental hazards were generally
accorded status in the media and elsewhere as programmatic rights. Moreover,
reforms that were enacted in the late 1960s and 1970s in the area of social regulation were usually linked with administrative procedures that established a formidable barrier between the presidency and public policy. Many of these recast
institutional channels that formed the heart of the administrative constitution were
created by statutes and cannot be transformed by executive actions alone. The
institutional framework that was the product of the reforms of the 1960s and 1970s
represents a form of post–New Deal administrative politics, which are based upon
legal requirement rather than presidential and bureaucratic discretion. The limits
of the administrative presidency—even during the term of an incumbent with substantial political gifts and a clear agenda—were demonstrated rather dramatically

by the ability of Congress and the courts to resist effectively Reagan's program of regulatory relief.[67]

In the view of the Reagan administration, its frustrated efforts to remake American politics owed largely to a few zealous bureaucrats and citizen activists running amok through the polity. They were aided in their efforts, the president charged, by the media, which displayed excessive sympathy for the arguments of Congress and the programmatic interests. That Reagan and many members of the executive office viewed programmatic liberalism as part of a triangular conspiracy both weakened and misplaced efforts to achieve a conservative revolution. It led to an emphasis on presidential politics and executive administration that, in the end, relegated the Reagan presidency to the task of managing—even reinforcing—the state apparatus it was committed to dismantling.

11

Divided Government and the Administrative Constitution

At the end of day, Ronald Reagan had not transformed Washington. Rather, he had only managed to strengthen the Republican beachhead in the nation's capitol, solidifying his party's long-standing dominance of the presidency and providing better opportunities for conservative interests to become part of the Washington "colony." Concomitantly, Reagan's two terms had witnessed a revitalization of the struggle between the executive and legislature; indeed, his program had become a foundation for more fundamental philosophical and policy differences between the branches. In part, the keen, often bitter competition for control of government by the president and Congress during the Reagan years testifies to the extraordinary staying power of the Constitution. Two centuries after the Founding Fathers agreed upon the vague outline of Article II of the Constitution, the presidency continues to resemble its blueprint in a number of ways. It is an office of great potential, particularly in the "modern" era, but this potential depends upon the concurrence of power in a political system of checks and balances that makes most unlikely the transformation of presidential leadership into presidential imperialism.

Yet the 1980s also continued a development in American politics of rather recent vintage. Prior to the 1960s, institutional arrangements provided for bounded conflict between the branches of government. Party politics, especially when crystallized by national emergencies and strong presidential leadership, enabled the president, the Congress, and even the courts to work in harness, to govern. The creation of the modern presidency was viewed by its supporters as a means of strengthening, and to a degree replacing, the traditional party system, and thus as a vehicle for infusing the councils of power with national and programmatic concerns that were relevant to the twentieth century. The modern executive, however, eventually was pulled into the vortex of a bitter struggle over the administrative levers of power that had accrued to it. Amidst this struggle was born a modern Congress that was intent upon asserting its own influence on the administrative state. The new party system that formed around these institutions did not combine but divided in an unprecedented manner these separate realms. The result was not

284

institutional competition, which the framers anticipated and celebrated, but institutional combat, which threatened to defy policy responsibility.

The period of divided government that emerged in 1968 was marked not just by differences between the president and Congress over policy, but by each branch's efforts to weaken the other. The efforts of Republicans to compensate for their inability to control Congress by seeking to enhance the powers of the executive and to circumvent legislative restrictions on presidential conduct were matched by Democratic initiatives to burden the executive with smothering legislative oversight by congressional committees as well as through the imposition of statutory limitations on executive power. A major, if not the main, forum for partisan conflict during the Reagan years, for example, was a sequence of revelations and investigations in which the Democrats and Republicans sought to discredit each other. This is suggested by the tenfold increase between the early 1970s and mid-1980s in the number of indictments brought by federal prosecutors against national, state, and local officials, including more than a dozen members of Congress, several federal judges, and a substantial number of high-ranking executive officials. As Morris Fiorina has written, "divided government encourages a full airing of any and all misdeeds, real and imagined." Thus, in the 1980s, disgrace and imprisonment joined electoral defeat as a risk of political combat in the United States, at least for some office holders.[1]

This development gave startling testimony to the displacement of representative government by a raw and disruptive administrative politics, to the enervation of representative government by the tendency to push policy decisions off to administrative agencies and the courts. The polity of the 1980s, in which ideological polarization and divided rule exacerbated the normal conflict resulting from the separation of powers, has been taken by advocates of responsible party government as proof of their case and cause for pressing it once again.[2] Taking account of the renaissance of the responsible party school, the historians James Sterling Young and Russell L. Riley have written, "In the last decade of the 20th century, as in the first, prominent political scientists are calling for a new policy of governance in America. In 1990, as in 1950, a committee of luminaries in Washington and academia are publicizing the need for a responsible two party system in order to save the republic from deadlock and decline."[3]

The call for major Constitutional surgery was not limited to pundits, nor was it confined to self-styled progressives. Just as many liberals felt stymied by checks and balances during the first three decades of the twentieth century, especially in the way constitutional government was molded in this era by an activist judiciary, so conservatives often felt unfairly restricted in their efforts to reconstruct the American political landscape by a refractory legislature and obstreperous courts while Ronald Reagan sat in the White House. As a disillusioned member of the Conservative Opportunity Society conceded privately in 1987:

> It may be that we cannot truly have a partisan debate in this country without major constitutional change—i.e., establishing a parliamentary system. I have come to support that sort of change. In our present form of government, people do not see the value of voting—what their vote means. It is the perception of a lot of people that voting does not matter that causes low turnout in this country.

Basically, people are smart about things, and their political inaction reflects the fact that politics simply does not matter.[4]

It is unlikely, however, that constitutional reform that would facilitate party government will come to be viewed widely as an antidote to the situation abhorred by the Congressman. Resistance to a British-style party government is not merely built into the Constitution and laws. As Young and Riley conclude, "it seems to be deeply rooted in a political culture that gives preference to a different way of governing."[5] In the United States, in fact, aspirations for reform since the New Deal have been expressed in demands for new rights, thus continually reducing the political space that once allowed for the sort of public dialogue that linked the American voter to parties.

Conservative Rights and Party Government

The emphasis on administrative reform and the conceptualization of liberal programs as rights by New Dealers reflected their view that the normal patterns of American politics were too readily accessible to particularistic interests. Interestingly, the twilight of the Reagan years brought us full circle. In his Independence Day address during the bicentennial celebration of the Constitution, President Reagan, in language remarkably reminiscent of Franklin Roosevelt's, called for an "economic bill of rights," which would, through a balanced-budget amendment and other fiscal reforms, force government "to live within its means." Included among these rights were four economic freedoms based upon Reagan's professed dedication to limited government: the freedom to work; the freedom to enjoy the fruits of one's labors; the freedom to own and control one's property; and the freedom to participate in the free market.[6] Whereas Franklin Roosevelt's "economic declaration of rights" presupposed public responsibility to guarantee social and economic security, Ronald Reagan's economic constitutional order intended to make permanent a restrictive fiscal policy that would fully revive the commitment in the United States to pursue, with minimal public supervision, private material satisfaction.

Nevertheless, the Reagan pronouncement of rights, although ostensibly a clarion call to renew the understanding of economic freedoms that preceded the New Deal, is symptomatic of the same disregard for the American political process that animated many programmatic liberals. According to former Reagan aide Martin Anderson, who first broached the idea for an economic bill of rights in a policy memorandum to candidate Reagan of August, 1979, "the animating idea for this proposal was it was no longer possible to solve the deficit problem without a constitutional change—it was necessary to go over the normal political process." The Founding Fathers did not envision the present situation, Anderson claimed, "one where fiscal policy is dominated by powerful interest groups that feed off the public sector."[7] Ultimately, this is a view that reinforces the New Deal tradition of transcending rather than shoring up the institutions that promote the differences of opinion and the jarring of parties that are essential to republican government.

The struggle over the proper definition of "new" rights camouflaged and added moral outrage to the administrative combat that characterized presidential–congressional relations during the Reagan years. It is not surprising that this struggle for the Constitution led to an unprecedented battle to control the judiciary, which had become a critical agent in overseeing the competition between the president and Congress for mastery over the administrative state. The culmination of Reagan's effort to remake the Judiciary came with the nomination of Federal Appeals Court Judge Robert Bork to the highest court in 1987. In a resounding defeat for the Reagan administration, Bork became the twenty-sixth Supreme Court nominee in history—but only the fourth in the twentieth century—to fail to be confirmed by the Senate. No previous nominee had been worked over the way Bork was in his nearly 30 hours of testimony, and the opposition to his nomination (58–42) was the widest margin of rejection in history. In spite of Bork's defeat, the 8 years of Reagan judicial appointments left a major impact on the judiciary, but Congress' resistance to his appointment and other Reagan nominees to lower federal tribunals left uncertain the future direction of the courts. In any case, nothing as decisive as the 1937 constitutional revolution took place during the 1980s.[8] In fact, the importance the Reagan administration accorded judicial politics testified to its failure to bring about the sort of realignment that occurred during the 1930s. As one conservative scholar lamented soon after the Bork debacle:

> The Reagan administration has not tried to hide the fact that it hoped to leave its longest-lasting legacy through the process of judicial appointments. This is little more than a tacit admission that it has been unable to change the political landscape through the electoral process. Its failure to do so—and its failure in a sense even to attempt to do so, which has given some the impression that the Republican party is grown accustomed to, if not fond of its minority status—has in turn proved extremely costly in the waning years of the Reagan presidency. The President's inability to get confirmation of his leading nominees to the Supreme Court is but one case in point.[9]

Bork's rejection and other nomination battles during the Reagan presidency testified to a new level of conflict over judicial rulings in an era of divided government. This conflict was not limited to appointments. Congress was not hesitant to reverse judicial rulings it did not like, in spite of efforts by the White House to uphold the judiciary's retreat on certain social policies. For example, Congress overturned the Supreme Court's 1984 decision in *Grove City College v. Bell,* which narrowed the reach of Title IX of the 1972 Education Act Amendments. Reagan vetoed this civil rights restoration bill; however, Congress overrode his veto, with no Democratic Senator and only 10 members of the House opposition voting to sustain the president's action.[10] The ongoing dispute between Democratic legislators and the Republican White House about judicial rulings and appointments testified to the limits of the Reagan legacy with respect to the courts.

The fact that this dispute had less to do with setting the boundaries of an expansive national administrative power than it did with defining its objectives lent a special urgency to the politics of the judiciary. It has been argued that recent developments have resuscitated the tradition of limited government, and the Reagan administration presented itself as committed to renewing the principles of the framers. Yet, the economic freedoms pronounced by the president during the bicentennial celebration were not really facilitative of restoring a sense of limits and balance to the political system. As discussed in the previous chapter, the emphasis Reagan placed upon executive action in the pursuit of his policies put the advocates of limited government who served him in the uncomfortable position of carrying out a program to reduce the burden of government regulation through what amounted to unprecedented administrative aggrandizement. "Regulatory relief," therefore, led not to institutional reform that imposed restraint on government action, but to an important confirmation of a substantial government presence in overseeing social and economic activity.

Moreover, there were many members of the "new" right, with whom the Reagan administration frequently expressed common cause, who would prefer not to limit but to make new uses of the state. Accordingly, the Administration became committed to programmatic innovations in defense and foreign policy that required the expanding, rather than the rolling back, of the national government's responsibilities. Furthermore, the moral imperatives of the modern conservative movement, which President Reagan identified as that movement's most fundamental calling, are animated by a missionary zeal that seems to want to abolish, rather than restore, the distinction between state and society. The supporters of this movement often confuse persuasion with conversion in a way that belies an understanding of the appropriate relationship between the individual and community in a free secular society. As such, the arguments brought to bear by moral conservatives to defend prayer in school suggest a mixing of church and state—an ambition for social control—that would hardly challenge the political and constitutional failings of the administrative state.

It may be significant, therefore, and not simply attributable to clumsiness, that conservatives have adopted the language of rights used by liberals (in referring, for example, to "the rights of the unborn") in the abortion dispute.[11] The use of such language makes unlikely a restoration of the boundary between individual rights and affirmative government action. For instance, in early 1988, the Department of Health and Human Services issued a regulation declaring that a program that received federal funds "may not provide counseling concerning uses of abortion as a method of family planning." The Reagan administration was eventually forced to suspend its efforts to prevent federally financed family planning clinics from helping women to obtain abortions, when a federal district judge in Boston issued a nationwide injunction permanently prohibiting enforcement of the restriction.[12] Whatever one thinks of the action taken by the Reagan administration in this case, it reflects support among many conservatives for the discretionary use of administrative power that hardly challenges the institutional legacy of liberal reform.

Thus, a conservative Republican administration, while promising to bring about a "new federalism" and "regulatory relief," was stalled in these tasks by the conception that a strong national state was needed to resurrect a free enterprise system, oppose communism, and nurture "traditional" values. In this respect, the challenge to liberal reform might end not in a challenge to the administrative state but in a battle for its services. Should this be the case, the Reagan legacy would be an extension of the administrative constitution brought by the New Deal. The "Reagan Revolution" extended the support for this regime by demonstrating, or earnestly striving to demonstrate, that collectivism could serve the purposes of those who were opposed to the liberal welfare state. In the wake of this development, neither the current Democrats nor the Republicans respect principles that might provide the foundation for a revival of those political institutions, such as political parties and local governments, that nurture an active and competent citizenry. Rather, the current political debates tend to take place within bureaucratic agencies and courts in such a way that enervates representative democracy.

The Accession of George Bush

The results of the 1988 election did not seem to offer a way out of the constitutional conundrum created by divided government. Indeed, it appeared to yield a intensification of this puzzling and worrisome condition. On the one hand, the elevation of Vice President Bush to the White House was a triumph for Ronald Reagan. The campaign took its shape from the Reagan legacy. In the final analysis, Bush's victory by a substantial margin (54 percent for Bush and 46 percent for his opponent, Massachusetts Governor Michael Dukakis, in the popular vote) attested to his ability to focus the election on the achievements of the Reagan administration. Bush won the support of almost 80 percent of the voters who approved of Reagan's performance as president.[13] The force of Reagan's legacy was revealed not only in the success of the campaign that apparently approved the political changes he instituted, but also in the person of his immediate successor, as Bush was the first Vice President to succeed as president by election since Martin Van Buren in 1837. Like Andrew Jackson, Reagan had proved to be unusually helpful to his Vice President, both in his popularity and his actions.[14]

On the other hand, the 1988 election results did not so much herald the ratification of the Reagan Revolution as it sanctioned the continuation of the ideological and institutional combat that characterized the last 2 years of the Reagan presidency. In fact, the 1988 election is best understood as an extreme manifestation of the underlying pattern that characterized American politics for the better part of two decades: Republican domination in the White House, Democratic ascendancy almost everywhere else. Never before had a president been elected—by a landslide no less—while the other party gained ground in the House, the Senate, the state governorships, and the state legislatures.[15] Never before had the voters given the newly elected president fewer fellow partisans in Congress than they gave Bush. Never, in short, had the American system of "separated institutions sharing power" been characterized by such partisan segmentation.

Thus, the Reagan Revolution had left the United States in a state of striking and unprecedented ambiguity with respect to its governing institutions. By many indications, moreover, it left the American people in a funk. Unlike previous realignments, the split verdict of the 1980s did not result in a surge of democratic participation. Instead, the 1988 campaign signalled a new low point in the deterioration of American electoral institutions that was now more than two decades old. Less than one-half of the eligible electorate bothered to vote in 1988, the lowest turnout in a presidential contest since 1924. In fact, in the non-Southern states, where three-quarters of the American people live, the 1988 turnout was the lowest in some 164 years—the most dismal showing since the United States became a mass-based democracy during the early part of the nineteenth century.[16]

Few believed as Bush took the oath of office on January 20, 1989, that the post-Reagan years promised anything but problems. Surprisingly, Bush's first year in office belied these forebodings. He pursued a more pragmatic and conciliatory approach with Congress and the Washington community that initially met with widespread approval from citizens grown weary of the ideological and institutional confrontation of the Reagan years. As Kenneth Duberstein, who was Reagan's chief of staff, observed:

> If Reagan's was a "defining" presidency that in bold strokes and grand ideas set the tone of the present political order, Bush's promises to be a "refining" administration that in pastel colors and day to day steps will consolidate the gains of the Reagan years. Bush's task, although less dramatic, is every bit as important.[17]

Duberstein's view was endorsed by many other Republicans during the early days of the Bush presidency. Even the ardent conservative Newt Gingrich, who was elected minority whip at the beginning of the 101st Congress (1989–1990), was optimistic about the Bush presidency:

> I do not think [Bush] needs to be another Ronald Reagan. Reagan laid the foundation for a new paradigm in American politics. George Bush is well-suited to institutionalizing the gains made over the last eight years. It takes different types of statesmen to build a regime, on the one hand, and to implement it, on the other hand. I think Bush can serve and benefit from Reagan, just as James Madison served and benefitted from Thomas Jefferson.[18]

Bush's inaugural address expressed his own understanding of his place in history. Although he stressed continuity with the Reagan administration, the new president called on the people to make "kinder the face of the nation and gentler the face of the world." The federal government's attention, the new president implied, must be directed to the real and seemingly intractable problems that Reagan had neglected: homelessness, urban decay, and environmental degradation. Bush also urged that the harsh ideological and partisan conflict that had characterized divided government during the past two decades give way to a new spirit of cooperation:

> We've seen the hard looks and the hard statements in which not each other's ideas are challenged, but each other's motives. And our great parties have too often been far apart and untrusting of each other.
>
> A new breeze is blowing—and the old bipartisanship must be made new again.[19]

Bush's conciliatory approach to governance partly reflected the obvious—that he had a more eclectic vision of Republicanism than his predecessor. Just as significant, however, were the continuing obstacles to the restoration of partisanship in the presidency. Facing a Democratic Congress and lacking his predecessor's rhetorical ability to appeal directly to the electorate, Bush had little choice but to reach across party lines to accomplish his goals. This "kinder, gentler" approach to Congress was often reciprocated during his first year. After intensive negotiations, Bush managed to reach agreements with Congress on two of the most troubling issues he faced upon taking office—aid to the Contra rebels in Nicaragua and the crisis of the savings and loan industry. The president won high marks from many legislators for his give-and-take approach to domestic and foreign policy, as well as for the personal attention he paid to the political needs of Democrats and Republicans alike. But several Republicans, especially the party's more conservative members, grew restless at Bush's disinclination to lead in a partisan style. Jeffrey A. Eisenach, who advised the 1988 presidential campaign of Delaware Governor Pierre S. DuPont, expressed the widespread fear of conservatives that the Republican party would not gain control of Congress in the 1990s should Bush "submerge the difference between the parties so it's impossible to create a set of issues to distinguish Republicans and Democrats."[20]

In many ways, however, Bush's conciliatory approach camouflaged an aggressive partisanship aimed at extending the political effects of the Reagan revolution beyond the presidency. Having served as a Republican county chair in Texas during the 1960s and as chair of the RNC during the Watergate scandal (the first president to have served as national party chair), Bush, more than any other recent president, came to the White House with a zeal for his partisan duties. He not only continued the Reagan practice of campaigning for fellow Republicans and of raising funds for the regular party apparatus, but he also gave his party's national organization an unprecedentedly high profile in the era of the modern presidency. Significantly, Bush placed his principal political adviser, Lee Atwater, not in the White House (the usual custom of modern presidents), but in the national party chair.[21]

Atwater, with Bush's approval, did not confine himself to the customary role of party chair to preside over the party's institutions. Instead, he sought to transform the RNC into an aggressive political organization that would highlight the differences between Republicans and Democrats on economic, social, and foreign policy issues at every level of the political system. As such, Atwater's aggressive partisanship provided balance to a presidency that otherwise favored consultation and compromise over confrontation.

Whereas political strategy during the Reagan years was conceived by assertive and influential presidential aides within the oval office, the Bush White House political shop was run by a second-ranked aide, former Atwater associate James Wray. Wray attended to Bush's long-term schedule and routinely reviewed administration appointments, while leaving the party's "big-picture" strategy to Atwater. Atwater talked with Bush three or four times a week, in addition to several conversations a day with White House Chief of Staff John Sununu, to coordinate operations and to mobilize the resources of the national party on behalf of the president's political program.[22]

In early 1990, the head of the research division of the RNC prepared a memo for Atwater that hailed the felicitous union between the White House and the party. Citing statistics suggesting how Bush's popularity had redounded to the benefit of Republicans with respect to the public's expressed partisan loyalties, he wrote, "After a year of the Bush presidency and after nine years of Republican leadership in the White House, the Republican party is stronger than its been since the 1940s and is poised to assume majority status." As noted in Chapter 10, gains in Republican identification also occurred in 1981 and 1985 following Reagan's victories. But what was different about 1989, the memo reported, was that "the gains following the presidential election still exist[ed] more than a year after the election." This was the first sustained period that the two parties had been at virtual parity since 1946, the year that Republicans last won control of both houses of Congress in a mid-term election. One of the most promising trends in party identification for Republicans was the enormous shift to the Republican party among young voters: The 1989 *Times*/CBS polls showed that among Americans 18–29 years old, 51% identified themselves as Republicans, while only 40% identified themselves as Democrats.[23]

Yet the Bush administration's efforts to consolidate and extend the GOP gains of the Reagan years were not successful. In the final analysis, the failure of this project can be explained by the absence of consensus in American politics, by fundamental substantive disagreements between liberals and conservatives that defied Bush's efforts to forge a more inclusive Republican party. By the Fall of 1991, a serious intraparty struggle had emerged over the 1991 budget. Seeking to work out a compromise with the Democratic leadership, Bush accepted a fiscal package that included excise tax hikes on gasoline and home heating oil. In turn, the Democratic leadership agreed to domestic spending cuts that came out of Medicare, requiring sharply higher payments by the elderly. The deal satisfied no one and left liberal Democrats and conservative Republicans furious. Especially strong resistance arose in the House, where the Democratic opposition abhorred the big Medicare cuts and the regressive nature of the new taxes; Republicans in the lower chamber, led by Gingrich, felt betrayed by Bush's willingness to abandon his celebrated campaign pledge to oppose new taxes.[24]

At the urging of Democratic and Republican supporters of the tax agreement, Bush went on television to attempt to sell the package to the American people. This was the president's first attempt to mobilize public opinion to pressure Congress; it ended in dismal failure. Despite Bush's rhetorical appeal and feverish administration lobbying efforts, a majority of House Republicans followed Gingrich in opposing the compromise, dooming it to defeat. The subsequent budget agreement that passed both the House and the Senate included a hike in the tax rate on high-income taxpayers, a proposal that Bush had bitterly opposed—it passed with the support of Democratic majorities but most Republicans in Congress voted against the final agreement. Bush's extraordinary personal popularity, as measured by public opinion polls, did not prevent a devastating intraparty feud that appeared to leave him in political isolation.

Bush's problems were compounded by the loss of Atwater, who had collapsed in early March while delivering a speech. Physicians soon diagnosed a brain tumor, and Atwater, although he continued to occupy the party chair, had to abandon his political responsibilities. This left the party headquarters without effective leadership for almost a year, before Bush, after receiving several rejections, finally tapped his Secretary of Agriculture Clayton Yeutter, to replace Atwater.[25] Atwater's absence returned the center of political strategy to the West Wing of the White House, leaving Bush's Chief of Staff John Sununu as Bush's political advisor.[26] Lacking his predecessor's close personal relationship with the president, Yeutter was not in a position to challenge the preeminence of the White House staff in the conduct of political operations. Reflecting on the low morale at party headquarters in the wake of its declining importance, a former member of the Research Division wrote, "RNC is a sad place. . . . Few people there care about issues. The only 'policy'-oriented material coming out of the First Street [RNC] bureaucracy consists of brief pamphlets that are nothing more than rewrites of White House press releases. Working there was the most frustrating political experience I've ever had. . . ."[27]

The bitter feud over the 1991 budget and the loss of Atwater left the Republican party in a state of disarray during the 1990 mid-term election campaign. Bush's efforts on behalf of his fellow partisans was spurned by some, who could not forgive the president for reneging on his "no new tax" pledge. For conservatives this was not simply bad policy, but violation of a sacred trust.

Conservatives believed that Bush not only deserted a sacred pledge, but the party's best hope of becoming a majority in the House and the Senate. The budget agreement debacle obscured the differences between the parties, thus undercutting Republican congressional candidates' chances to campaign in 1990 on what they considered their party's most fundamental and effective issue. In late October, Bush became embroiled in a feud with the co-chair of the Republican Congressional Campaign Committee, Ed Rollins, who circulated a memo urging House GOP candidates not to hesitate to distance their campaigns from the president.[28] This spectacle embarrassed the White House, which pressured Rollins to resign in early 1991. But the damage had been done—Republicans had not only lost their philosophical compass, but further ground in the House and Senate. The Democrats added one seat in the Senate, strengthening their majority to 56 to 44, and they added 8 seats to their already lopsided advantage in the House, yielding an advantage of 268 to 167.

The losses were mild by historical standards; indeed, some Republicans argued that by losing only 8 seats in the House and 1 in the Senate, their party fared rather well for a mid-term campaign, in which the president's party almost always loses seats. But this argument ignored the fact that the GOP was starting from a very low base in the legislature and that it suffered very disappointing defeats in the Florida and Texas gubernatorial races. These states were considered pivotal areas in the Republicans' long-sought goal of taking control of the House, which they believed hinged on the party's success in capturing governorships and state legislatures. This would not only benefit the party in recruiting and supporting the campaigns of candidates for Congress, but in getting a better deal in the redistricting process that would take place after 1990. The redistricting process was the target of the "1991 Plan," discussed in Chapter 10, named for the year in which work on congressional redistricting would begin. To the dismay of GOP strategists, Ann Richard's victory in Texas and Lawton Chiles's in Florida gave Democrats total political control of the redistricting process in two states that together will gain 7 new House seats after the decennial reapportionment.

Many Republicans, therefore, admitted privately that the 1990 election was a tremendous disappointment, that all their efforts since the late 1970s to recruit candidates and build up county organizations by the 1990 campaign had gone for naught. The 1991 Plan, one of its principal architects bemoaned, had not succeeded in strengthening party organization at the precinct and county level. Indeed, "the Bush RNC had allowed grass roots party building to atrophy." This inattention to local party organizations combined with Bush's betrayal of his promise on taxes led to a "disaster" for the party in 1990. The results of that election suggested that the quest for Republican control of Congress would have to be put off for another decade.[29]

The Renewal of Institutional Confrontation

The closer ties that Reagan and Bush tried to forge between the modern presidency and the Republican party did not alter the unprecedented partisan and electoral divisions that characterized the era of "split level" realignment. Furthermore, the persistence of divided government itself retarded the restoration of partisanship to the presidency. Presidents were encouraged to concentrate power in the White House and executive office—to pursue action through the exercise of prerogative power—while Congress sought to circumscribe this power with detailed legislation and aggressive oversight of presidential activities.

This was not merely a matter of strategy; it reflected raw and disruptive conflict over the meaning of rights in American politics. Issues such as race, gender, and abortion rocked the country during the 1980s and into the 1990s because they were associated with an understanding of rights that abhorred constitutional restrictions on centralized power. The programmatic rights embraced by modern liberals and conservatives do not protect individual autonomy against collective action, but require an aggressive use of national power that seems to threaten, if not violate, the original bill of rights. Amid such a new variant of factionalism, conservative support for the rights of the unborn and their conception of Contra rebels in Nicaragua as the "moral equivalent of the Founding Fathers," as Reagan put it, cannot be dismissed as mere rhetoric, for such words convey the solemn commitment of conservatives to use the centralized power built on liberal principles and programs to further their own constitutional objectives. "Our goal is not to join the Washington establishment," the Heritage Foundation's Edward Feulner has proclaimed. "It is to create a new establishment that will supplant the old."[30]

During the early days of his presidency, George Bush showed little interest in participating in the remaking of what his predecessor called the "Washington colony." He seemed content to join the old, to reach out to Democrats in Congress, and to restore the badly frayed consensus of American politics. But he gave no reasonable defense for this pragmatism; indeed, the defiant sound bites and images of his campaign, as well as the hard-edged partisanship of his party chair, Lee Atwater, promised a continuation of the divisiveness of the previous 8 years. The echo of those words and the memory of the stricken Atwater would undercut his efforts to reach a budget agreement in 1990. Once he abandoned his anti-tax pledge and lost his top political strategist to illness, Bush's presidency floated adrift—his search for agreement with Congress in the absence of any clear principles threatened the modern presidency with the same sort of isolation and weakness that characterized the Carter years.

Bush's standing was not even helped by an international development that seemed to mark the triumph of American principles abroad—the death of Communism in Europe. During the last half of 1989 and into 1990, Communist rule collapsed in one Eastern European country after another, and democratic institutions seemed on the verge of ascendancy. Ronald Reagan's words and policies had done much to set the stage for the collapse of the "Evil Empire," yet victory abroad left America without a compelling mission in world affairs and intensified demands for renewed attention to intractable problems at home. Moreover, the Cold War had provided the Republican party with a unifying purpose that ameliorated the tension between the different strands of conservativism that composed the Reagan coalition; the apparent death of communism left the Republican party less united, more prone to the fractiousness that had long plagued the Democrats. Hitherto praised for his more moderate conservative orientation, Bush's cautiousness now seemed to be a liability—he seemed but a spectator as a remarkable drama played itself out abroad and a restlessness with ideological and institutional estrangement grew more pronounced at home.

Bush's command and popularity were restored, for a time, with the emergence of a crisis in the Persian Gulf. Iraq's invasion of Kuwait in August 1990, created a situation that stirred the president's deepest commitments and allowed him to display considerable skills of crisis leadership. Bush showed a deft and steady hand in diplomacy and military strategy, and the United States–led allied forces rapidly triumphed over Saddam Hussein's troops, forcing Iraq to withdraw from Kuwait. Amid a national celebration that seemed to dispel the agonizing memory of Vietnam, Bush's popularity reached an historic peak, with 89 percent of the American public approving of his performance as president.[31]

Nevertheless, the patriotic fervor aroused by the Gulf War hid fundamental differences over foreign policy that foreshadowed a recrudescence of institutional combat. A January 12, 1991 vote authorizing Bush to use United States troops against Iraq revealed a deeply divided Congress, which voted largely along party lines. Not since the War of 1812 had the Congress so narrowly approved the use of military action: while Republicans lined up solidly behind Bush (by 42–2 votes in the Senate and by 165–3 in the House), Democrats voted against authorizing military action by surprisingly large margins (45–10 in the Senate and by 179–86 in the House). After the vote, Democrats closed ranks behind Bush as the nation prepared for war, but a broader dispute over constitutional powers lingered in a reference to the War Powers act, the statute passed in the wake of the Vietnam controversy that granted Congress specific statutory power for using force. Although Bush came to the conclusion that the deep divisions in the Congress and the country over the use of force in the Persian Gulf required him to seek Congress's approval, he reasserted the claim of every president since the War Powers Resolution was passed that it was unconstitutional. The administration's pronouncements that it would welcome congressional support for the Persian Gulf war were followed by a statement, released after Congress passed the Solarz–Michel resolution, that explicitly denied that the president needed congressional authorization to implement the UN resolution authorizing force against Iraq. Viewing this conflict between Bush and Congress as symptomatic of the excesses of what he describes as a "National Security Constitution," Richard Pious criticized the administration's disavowal of the War Powers act as the most recent example of "presidents . . . playing a shell game, claiming to act according to law yet dispensing with statutory law at their convenience in national security matters."[32]

In fact, the "national security constitution" is but one element, albeit an extremely important one, of a broader, more profound transformation of the fundamental law, one that has yielded an administrative constitution, in which partisan conflict centers on battles to control the bureaucracy and the courts. This constitutional change had survived, indeed undermined, Bush's kinder and gentler version of conservatism. Consequently, the Gulf War did not establish the conditions for the restoration of consensus but set the stage for bitter conflicts in domestic affairs that rivaled the ideological and institutional clashes of the Reagan years.

The most bitter of these fights occurred over Bush's second nomination to the Supreme Court, Clarence Thomas, a black appellate judge and the former chairman of the Equal Employment Opportunity Commission (EEOC). Thomas had been one of the more thoughtful and independent administrators of the Reagan administration, and his call for the country to recapture the significance of the Declaration of Independence as "the center of the frame formed by the Constitution" offered an opportunity for a national dialogue over the appropriate understanding of "natural rights."[33] Unlike many participants in the Reagan "revolution," Thomas seemed actually to support an understanding of rights based on a commitment to limited government—his record at the EEOC and on the bench revealed that his commitment to a more traditional understanding of rights was not a rhetorical fillip, but informed his day-to-day activities in government.

The promise for a public debate over the principles involved in Thomas' nomination foundered on the rock of divided government. Mindful of the fate that befell the outspoken Bork, the White House counseled Thomas to dismiss his voluminous writings and speeches as "philosophical musings." Thomas and the Senate Judiciary Committee engaged in an unsatisfying but polite game of "cat and mouse" that ended with a split vote along party lines.[34] Still, his nomination seemed assured by the full Senate. Then 2 days before the scheduled vote, University of Oklahoma law professor Anita Hill, following a leak to the media of her confidential complaint to the Judiciary Committee, went public with allegations that Thomas had sexually harassed her when she worked for him at the Department of Education and the EEOC. The Senate did finally vote 52–48 to confirm Thomas, a verdict that reflected the same sort of bitter partisan opposition that characterized the Bork hearings. Thomas was spared Bork's fate by the support he received from 11 Democrats, mostly Southerners, whose votes for him were encouraged by the strong support the judge, a Georgia native, had amongst Southern blacks.

While the White House celebrated a victory that seemed to secure a dominant conservative majority on the Court, the fierce battle between the branches left the nation in a state of profound unease. This was the closest Supreme Court vote in more than a century. And, as one journalist reported, "the hearings [that investigated Hill's charges on national television] marked one of the wildest spectacles in modern congressional history, a subject for satire and scorn that rocked the Senate."[35]

The rift between the White House and Congress was not completely beyond repair. Indeed, soon thereafter, Bush and Congress reached agreement on a civil rights bill that appeared to limit in important ways the transformation of the judiciary that Thomas' confirmation secured. The Civil Rights Act of 1991 nullified nine Supreme Court rulings, five of them from 1989, thus restoring legal standards that placed the burden of proof in anti-discrimination lawsuits on employers. Most significant, the legislation restored the standard established by the Supreme Court's 1971 ruling in *Griggs v. Duke Power Company,* which held employers responsible for justifying employment practices that were seemingly fair but had an "adverse impact" on women and minorities. A 1989 ruling, *Wards Cove Packing Co. v. Atonio,* had shifted the burden, saying workers had to show that companies had no legitimate need for the challenged practices. The new legislation instructed the courts to follow the standard of *Griggs* and related rulings prior to *Ward's Cove.*[36]

The enactment of the Civil Rights bill ended 2 years of acrimonious partisan debate on the civil rights legislation. Bush had vetoed a similar bill in 1990, arguing that it would lead to quotas for minorities and women in hiring practices. A key to the compromise in the new bill that assured Bush's support was an open-ended provision on how employers may justify the discriminatory effects of seemingly fair hiring practices, such as tests and academic requirements, essentially leaving it to the courts to decide what constitutes a "business necessity."[37] Beleaguered moderates of both parties hoped the agreement, coming on the heels of the explosive Thomas hearings, would avert a confrontation between the Bush administration and the Congress that threatened to intensify tension over civil rights issues.

Bush's signing of the Civil Rights legislation, and his willingness to accept other sweeping regulatory measures related to the environment, consumer protection, and discrimination against the disabled, showed him to be more moderate than his predecessor.[38] But the bizarre denouement of the civil rights bill revealed how Bush, no less than Reagan, was prepared to augment national administrative power to control the reach and cost of social regulation. As was the case in the Reagan era, the Bush administration's efforts to lessen the impact of environmental, consumer, civil rights, and health regulations have not come through legislative change but through administrative action, delay, and repeal.

A draft signing statement, prepared under the direction of White House Counsel, C. Boyden Gray, contained remarks that ordered the heads of all federal departments to review immediately their equal opportunity programs and eliminate many affirmative action practices. "Any regulation, rule, enforcement practice or other aspect of these programs that mandates, encourages or otherwise involves the use of quotas, preferences, set-asides or other similar devices on the bases of race, color, religion, sex or national origin," the draft read, "is to be terminated as soon as legally possible." [39] When this remark ignited protests in Congress, including a threat from the respected Republican Senator John Danforth of Missouri that he would not attend the signing ceremony, the draft was changed. Still, Bush's final speech proclaimed that documents introduced by Minority Leader Robert Dole, which offered a narrow understanding of the statute, would "be treated as authoritative interpretive guidance by all officials in the executive branch with respect to the law of disparate impact as well as other matters covered in the documents." [40]

Bush's willingness to abandon the statement directing the government to end affirmative action appeased moderate Republicans, but failed to head off a boycott of the signing ceremony by Democratic lawmakers. Representative Don Edwards of California, whose committee oversaw the legislation in the House, complained that the message of the White House was, "Let's not put a damper on today's festivities. We'll lower the boom tomorrow." [41] Before Bush's signature on the civil rights bill could dry, therefore, the much acclaimed compromise that led to the enactment of this legislation dissolved in administrative combat.

It soon became clear that this administrative conflict would not be confined to civil rights. As the 1992 election approached amid a serious recession, the Bush administration turned its attention to "liberating the economy" from the regulatory explosion that was pending as a result of the legislative mandates enacted during his first term. A President's Council on Competitiveness, founded in June 1990 and headed by Vice President Dan Quayle, assumed increasing importance in executive deliberations, putting regulatory agencies on notice that the White House expected them to justify the cost of existing and proposed regulations. Furthermore, Bush imposed a 90–day moratorium on regulations as part of his 1992 State of the Union Address, with which the administration sought to set the tone of its re-election campaign. The president's proposal promised to revitalize the Office of Information and Regulatory Affairs within the Office of Management and Budget. This agency, the focal point of the battle between the White House and Congress over federal agencies during the Reagan years [see Chapter 10], had been a casualty of the Bush administration's more tolerant attitude towards social regulation. But that attitude was apparently being displaced in the White House by a growing anti-regulatory fervor. "The impact of the President's proposal sends a chilling message to agencies that the President is waging a war on his agencies," the public interest group OMB Watch lamented. "It is almost as if the President is choosing to run in this year's election as an outsider campaigning against the bureaucracy." [42]

By all appearances, the Bush administration planned to run against Congress as well. And some Republican leaders in Congress were hopeful that the White House would duplicate Harry Truman's feat in 1948, when the beleaguered heir to the Roosevelt Revolution ran a spirited campaign against a Republican Congress that resulted in a personal and party triumph. Interestingly, Minority Whip Gingrich and his aides closely examined and drew inspiration from the memo authored by James Rowe in 1947 (discussed in Chapter 7), which laid out the political strategy for that campaign. Unlike the situation in 1948, Gingrich granted, the country had not yet adopted a new public philosophy—Reagan failed to accomplish in 1984 what Roosevelt had in 1936. But a campaign that "combined the positive vision of FDR's re-election campaign and the partisan assault of Truman's 1948 effort" promised to bring about the long-awaited Republican realignment.[43]

Such a development had little chance for success. In the final analysis, the ratification of the Roosevelt Revolution signalled by the 1948 election secured an understanding of rights and institutional arrangements that subordinated *party* politics to *presidential* politics and the tasks of "enlightened administration." The Reagan and Bush administrations had not abandoned this project but sought to redirect it—this both responded to and reinforced the intractable state of divided government that had organized American politics for the better part of 20 years. The administrative presidency, which Reagan brought to fruition and Bush finally embraced, was supported by a modern conservative movement whose advocates wanted to expand rather than restrict administrative power.

Bush's position on the abortion issue revealed the degree to which even a more pragmatic conservative was willing to accept centralized administration. In 1990, Bush had joined Atwater in an effort to extend the GOP's appeal to the pro-choice constituency by asserting that the party "was a big enough tent" to hold differing views on abortion.[44] But the interest that Bush showed in steering his party towards a more tolerant position on this explosive issue faded as his administration proceeded with plans formulated in the Reagan administration to bar employees of federally financed family planning clinics from providing basic medical information about abortion. As noted, the Reagan administration had been thwarted in this policy by the lower courts, delaying the regulations for 3 years. But in late May, 1991 the Supreme Court upheld the so-called "gag rule" in *Rust v. Sullivan,* and the Bush administration prepared to carry it out. Congress quickly passed legislation that would stop the administration from enforcing rules barring abortion counseling in federally funded family planning clinics; however, the House failed by a dozen votes to override Bush's veto of the legislation.[45]

Thus, partisan politics was hardly absent as the 1992 election neared. Yet parties focused much of their effort on administrative struggles that detracted from efforts to build electoral majorities. The legacy of the New Deal, it seemed, was not the end of party politics but the transformation of Democrats and Republicans into parties of administration.

12

Conclusion: Whither the Administrative Republic?

Towards the late 1970s, political analysts kept a death watch over the American party system. Reforms and the mass media had deprived political parties of their limited but significant influence in American politics, scholars lamented, and there was little prospect of recovery. By the mid-1980s, there were some interesting signs of party renewal, but, as the previous two chapters suggest, the national parties that emerged from the ruins of traditional state and local organizations failed to reach beyond the Washington Beltway and influence the perceptions and habits of the American people.

Advocates of party government, of a more "responsible" party system, consider the decline of party an opportunity to build a new kind of party, one that could assemble and register the will of programmatic and disciplined majorities. Indeed, many political scientists question whether the decline of party is a symptom of fundamental flaws in the American Constitution and the philosophy that informed its creation. According to Walter Dean Burnham, the forlorn state of parties points overwhelmingly to the conclusion that the American polity had entered the most profound turning point in its history. In his seminal 1970 volume, *Critical Elections and the Mainsprings of American Politics,* Burnham argued that the task confronting the United States today is no less than the "construction of instrumentalities of domestic sovereignty to limit individual freedom in the name of collective necessity." This would require "an entirely new structure of parties and of mass behavior, one in which political parties would be instrumentalities of democratic collective purpose." But, Burnham concluded, "this in turn seems inconceivable without a preexisting revolution in social values." [1]

The decline of parties, however, is not the result of ineluctable constitutional forces. It is rather a partisan project, one sponsored by the Democratic party and built on the foundation of the New Deal realignment. Nearly every reform of the past half-century that has weakened the existing parties in the electoral process— more primaries, public financing of campaigns, quotas for constituent groups in the national conventions, and the elimination of patronage—has been sponsored by the Democratic party, and within that party by its most liberal wing. [2] Furthermore, reforms that weakened the influence of party organizations in the electoral process were concomitant with the reform and expansion of executive administration, a result of the same doctrinal change reflected in the shift from classical to progammatic liberalism. The development of administrative politics further contributed to the decline of parties by exalting the *personal* responsibility of the president, thus making *collective* partisan appeals less meaningful in the eyes of the voters. This is particularly likely to happen when programs or benefits are viewed as "rights." Because it conceives of specific programs as entitlements, programmatic liberalism gave rise to a veritable "administrative constitution," in which policies are deemed worthy of protection from the uncertainties of party competition and the electoral process.

It might be said, therefore, that the New Deal preempted the constitutional transformation anticipated by the advocates of "responsible" party government. It did so by sponsoring institutional changes that chartered an alternative path to a more national and programmatic government. This path, the New Dealers believed, was more compatible with the principles and history of American constitutional government. One of the principal architects of the New Deal institutional program, Charles Merriam, had observed in 1931 that he did not expect to see the development of a British-style party government in the United States. "There is little probability of a modification of the Constitution either by amendment or custom in such a fashion as to permit the adoption of a parliamentary system," he surmised, "in view of the fact that the trend is strongly in the direction of Presidential government, with constant strengthening of executive power."[3]

Merriam's commentary was not simply prescient. As a member of the Brownlow Committee, he would play an important part in consolidating the trends he observed. That contribution, however, was made possible by a dramatic, though short-lived, commitment to party responsiblity. With the Third New Deal (see Chapter 5), Roosevelt imposed the task defined by the Brownlow Committee on the Democratic party; by doing so, he strengthened partisanship in the short term and carried out a great experiment on the character of the American party system. But this test of responsible party goverment transformed the Democratic party into a way station on the road to administrative government—that is, a more centralized and bureaucratic form of democracy that focused on the presidency and executive agencies for the formulation, the enactment, and the execution of public policy. Consequently, this development diminished the role of traditional party politics, Congress, and the state legislatures.

There were limits to this change, to be sure. Congress, the courts, and the states remained central to the structure and activities of the New Deal political order. The news of Roosevelt's death in April, 1945 caused most Americans to weep, openly and unashamedly, for the passing of a mighty leader. "Even so," Barry Karl has written, "they hoped they would never need such heroic presidential leadership again."[4] Soon thereafter the people would initiate and approve a constitutional amendment limiting future presidents to two terms. There would be no more Roosevelts.

Karl contends that the New Deal did not displace the anti-bureaucratic tradition in the United States, which continued to play an important role in American politics.[5] It is true that Roosevelt himself was ambivalent about this tradition. He certainly never intended to establish a centralized bureaucratic apparatus characteristic of modern states elsewhere. But he did strive to strengthen national administrative power, albeit in a form that would be sui generis American.

The New Dealers' celebration of a second bill of rights was not merely a rhetorical fillip, nor was it simply a clever manipulation of a traditional formula of justice. Rather, it revealed the New Dealers' commitment to strengthen those parts of the Constitution that would allow for an alliance between rights and administration, to resurrect Hamiltonian nationalism as the steward of security. In forging such an alliance, Roosevelt did not abolish the obstacles to the creation of an autonomous "state"; he unintentionally created new ones that would continue to thwart statist ambitions. But he transformed American attitudes towards the role of the national government and gave rise to an executive that would nurture this new public philosophy. Roosevelt and his successors embraced administrative power as the principal means to their objectives. This invariably gave administrative officials and agencies a central part in the realization of economic and social policy.

After the Third New Deal, the presidency was no longer simply an office but an institution. As a result, as Robert Eden has written, "what Roosevelt did by improvisation could henceforth be done deliberately and regularly."[6] It is customary today to make much of Harry Truman's energetic stewardship of the nation. For example, a 1981 survey of historians judged Truman to be "near great," putting him in the same company with Theodore Roosevelt, Woodrow Wilson, and Andrew Jackson. "Often dismissed by his contemporaries as a 'little man' because his deficiencies were more apparent than his strengths," Alonzo Hamby has argued, "he actually was one of the more important twentieth century presidents."[7] As Chapter 7 reveals, however, Truman's effective presidency is inconceivable without Roosevelt. Indeed, after Roosevelt's long tenure, the new understanding of presidential responsibilities would lead even conservative presidents such as Nixon and Reagan to wield executive power according to FDR's vision of the office.

As the party of administration, the Democrats established the conditions for the end of parties unless a party sprang up that was anti-administration. No such party has arisen in American politics, although the Republican party has flirted with that role. As programmatic liberalism began to lose support, the Republican party under Richard Nixon and especially Ronald Reagan embraced programs such as New Federalism and Regulatory Relief that challenged the institutional legacy of the New Deal. As noted in chapter 10, this bolder conservative posture coincided with the construction of a formidable national party apparatus, one that provided Republican candidates and office holders with valuable finanacial and organizational support.

Nevertheless, the emphasis they placed on presidential politics and unilateral executive action suggest that Nixon and Reagan essentially continued the institutional legacy of the New Deal. Thus, Republican presidents, intent upon transforming the liberal political order, have conceived of the modern presidency as a two-edged sword, which could cut in a conservative as well as a liberal direction.

The pursuit of conservative policy objectives through administrative action continued with the elevation of George Bush to the White House. Indeed, the institutional legacy of the New Deal encouraged such a development—given that the New Deal was based on a party strategy to replace traditional partisan politics with administration, it is not surprising that the challenge to liberal policies produced a conservative administrative presidency, which also retarded the revival of partisan politics.

That the national protest against programmatic liberalism centered on presidential campaigns reinforced the need to strengthen executive power as a means to conservative ends. Ironically, the attempt to bring about changes in public policy with administrative tools that were created, for the most part, during Democratic administrations has been thought useful by Republican presidents facing a hostile Congress and bureaucracy intent upon preserving the programs of those administrations. Conservative presidents have thus deepened the commitment in the political system to executive administration, by demonstrating (or attempting to demonstrate) that centralized power can serve the purposes of those who oppose the welfare state.

The conservative administrative presidency, of course, did not go unchallenged. The modern presidency was conceived as an ally of programmatic reform. When this supposition was seemingly violated by Vietnam and subsequent developments, reformers set out to protect liberal programs from unfriendly executives. The result, as described in Chapter 9, was a "reformation" of New Deal administrative politics, which brought Congress and the courts into the details of administration. The new liberal institutional coalition forged during the 1970s, composed of Congressional committees and staff, courts, public interest groups, and administrative agencies, spawned "issue networks" that were insulated from close presidential control in a number of policy areas.[8] As a result, Nixon and Reagan confronted many of the same problems in dealing with a fragmented executive branch that presidents faced when seeking to exert influence over a decentralized party system.

Indeed, the New Deal and the opposition it aroused gave rise to a form of conflict that has made consensus newly problematic in American politics. This follows from the singular character of the realignment of the 1930s. The developments of the 1930s marked a secular change that made unlikely still another rendezvous with America's political destiny, unlikely in the form, that is, that had characterized all previous realignments in American history. All previous realignments had involved a return to first principles, a remolding of the American liberal consensus in a manner demanded by social and economic developments. Although these realignments involved wrenching change, and in one case a civil war, they occurred within parameters established by the dominant liberal tradition in America. "Americans are constantly modifying or repealing some of their laws," Tocqueville wrote, "but they are far from showing any revolutionary passions."[9]

That Americans love change but are afraid of revolution tells us much about the regular pattern of realignments in American history, about episodes of frantic, albeit infrequent, change, bounded by what the historian Marvin Myers has called "venturous conservatism." With all the agitation of the Jacksonian realignment,

Myers observed, conflict in the 1830s occurred within parameters set by a consensus in the United States dedicated to private property, limited government, and administrative decentralization.[10] Even the Civil War, a regime crisis of the first order, failed to signal a departure from the political conditions that sustained this consensus; instead, it marked a heroic effort to eliminate the major stain on the American Constitution. More than anything else, slavery kept the American people from being true to themselves, to the principles embodied in the Declaration. As the remarkable return to routine party politics at the end of the nineteenth century suggests, the Civil War realignment did not challenge the liberal consensus, but only made it a bit more consistent with what Lincoln referred to as a "fair race of life."[11] This consensus was refashioned by acquiescing to "Jim Crow," by retreating from efforts to enforce the Fourteenth and Fifteenth Amendments. The unsavory bargain struck by Democrats and Republicans to settle the controversial 1876 presidential contest between Rutherford B. Hayes and Samuel Tilden, which ended the politics of Reconstruction, was the most dramatic example of how passions in America could be whipped into motion by moral conflict and then arrested by fears of centralized power. The retreat of Republicans and Democrats from the purposive, ideological politics of the Civil War could not have been more complete.[12]

It is only in the twentieth century, with the emergence of the Progressive movement, that a fundamental challenge to this consensus is offered. Samuel Huntington views the Progressive era as a realignment, one that proves that critical political change does not depend upon the agent of party.[13] What Huntington misses, however, is that the Progressive era marks an initial stage of change that would emancipate American government from political parties and the restrictive character of the realignments they provided for. The progressive political program, as discussed in Part I, was institutionalized, or made an enduring part of the American constitution, during the New Deal—as such, the central thrust of the New Deal realignment was to open the American political experience to possibilities outside the parameters set by the dominant strand of liberalism in the United States. John Dewey observed during the 1936 campaign that the New Deal pointed towards the displacement of the dominant "laissez-faire" liberal stream in the United States by a "humanitarian" one, which emphasized the qualitative and communitarian, rather than simply the materialistic needs of the individual. Although these two schools of liberalism had in common an emphasis on individualism and respect for democratic procedures, they represented competing streams of thought that unprecedentedly rent the consensus that historically had defined political life in the United States.

This split was widened by the way the New Deal redefined the collective aspirations of "humanitarian" liberalism. This form of liberalism, drawing on the thoughts of Rousseau and the evangelical zeal of religious movements had a long-standing, if subordinate, place in American political life; however, whereas nineteenth century "humanitarian" liberalism expressed itself most actively in personal and voluntary effort, it turned to government agencies in the twentieth. To be sure, some expressions of the humanitarian movement prior to the Progressive era, such as abolitionism, were not averse to employing government agencies, but progressivism brought forth a more pronounced programmatic liberal commitment, one that was defined by appeals for government action and centralized administration. "The whole movement toward what is known as social legislation with its slogans of social justice derives from this source and involves more and more appeal to government action," Dewey observed. As a result, an inner split in liberalism that was there from the beginning grew wider: "Any attempt to define liberalism in terms of one or the other of its two strains [laissez-faire and humanitarian] will be vehemently denied by those attached to the other strain." [14]

This rending of the liberal consensus was the root cause of divided government, a new and intractably fragmented political order that appeared to represent the "end of realignment." [15] Until the 1960s, the effect of the "Roosevelt Revolution" was circumscribed, limited to the enactment of programs dedicated to economic security. With the advent of the 1960s, however, as Chapters 7 and 8 describe, the New Deal was extended and radicalized in a way that accentuated the tensions in the American polity that emerged with the attempt to broaden the American understanding of liberalism. The "natural" reaction to this—the Reagan "revolution"—is most appropriately viewed as the completion rather than the decline of the New Deal political order, a completion, that is, of a transformation from a consensual political order to one that is more fundamentally divided by competing strands of liberal thought.

The absence of realignment has not meant the end of party conflict. In fact, the New Deal—and the erosion of traditional decentralized parties—has made possible a new blending of partisanship and administration, one in which administration has become a vehicle for partisan objectives. Parties have shifted much of their effort from the building of constituencies to the administration of public policy; as such, party politics have come to focus on the management of the economy and society and its attendant problems. Moreover, the concept of rights has become increasingly associated with the expansion of national administrative power—even conservatives in the abortion dispute demand governmental intervention to protect the rights of the unborn. The expansion of rights has further shifted partisan politics away from parties as associations that organize political sentiments as an electoral majority. When rights dominate policy discourse, majority sentiments are commonly viewed as the problem and not the solution. Consequently, as the dispute between Democratic legislators and the Republican White House over judicial appointments and rulings has demonstrated, the Supreme Court threatens to displace elections as the principal focus of partisan politics. Because administration is so central to current political debates and conflicts, both parties are essentially parties of administration. As the polity settled into a persistant pattern of divided government, the Republicans became the party of administration through the executive branch, while the Democrats became the party of administration through the Congress. [16]

The American people, one suspects, were rather mystified by this development, and comforted only in part that divided government muted somewhat the ideological polarization and administrative aggrandizement that characterizes modern party politics in the United States. An ever smaller proportion of the electorate voted, and those who did expressed a striking ambiguity. The indecision at the polls and the concomitant perpetuation of divided government reflected the fact that more was at stake in American politics than at any other time in our history, with the notable exception of the Civil War. The commitment to limited government that prevailed until the New Deal tended to reduce the stakes of political conflict, to confine our political battles to "safe" issues. Yet the emergence of activist government after the 1930s attenuated the constitutional boundaries that once contained political conflict in the United States, and the Reagan "revolution" further eroded the wall that separated politics and society. The checks that divided government imposed on the extreme tendencies of the Democrats and Republicans provided some protection against the abuses of centralized administration, but this security did not come without its costs. As the extraordinary budgetary evasions and jarring nomination fights of the past decade revealed, the dark side of split-level government is that it tends to obscure political responsibility and to mire government in petty, virulent clashes that undermine respect for American political institutions.

The question that must be faced as the American polity approaches the twenty-first century is whether the conflicts and institutional arrangements that now divide the realm in the United States can responsibly engage the people—thus leading to public deliberation and choice over the appropriate understanding of their rights. The burden of this book has been to suggest that such a possibility will require a serious reconsideration of the New Deal legacy, and that a reconsideration of our inheritance of liberal reform should begin with the assumption that responsible political leadership presupposes a reasonably active and competent citizenry.

The revitalization of civic attachments imposes on leaders above all an obligation to recognize the limits and appropriate use of administrative power. Political parties were first formed and defended in the United States to contain and minimize the executive's constitutional potential, especially its potential to consolidate and centralize administrative power. As Secretary of the Treasury, Hamilton pursued a program, based on an elastic interpretation of the national government's powers, that required a dominant executive in the formation and administration of public policy. In effect, Jefferson and Madison chose to defend a strict interpretation of the national government's powers because Hamilton's nationalist aspirations would invariably give rise to an administrative power that would undermine popular rule. Jefferson and Madison became committed to a program of political decentralization in the 1790s, then, that renewed the conflicts that had divided the Federalist and Antifederalists and, consequently, gave birth to the American party system. By the 1830s, political parties had become a integral part of the "living" Constitution, and national administrative power was constrained not only by the decentralized organizational structure of these parties but also by the fundamental doctrine of government to which they adhered—namely, to limit the activities of the national government.

Progressive reformers understood that the development of a more purposeful national government meant loosening the hold of traditional parties on the loyalties and voting habits of citizens. But they failed to appreciate the purpose these parties served as effective channels of democratic participation. Representative democracy is essentially fostered by public speech, by political discussion that most effectively occurs in the legislature and local community. Civic involvement is enervated by a political process dominated by executive action, which can strengthen and lead, but not replace, the decentralizing institutions as the home of representative government. The benefit of a strong executive, as Hamilton noted in *The Federalist,* No. 70, is "promptitude of decision," which does not allow for the "differences of opinion and the jarring of parties" that promote popular rule.[17] Consequently, the advent of progressive democracy strengthened the national purpose, but deliberation and legislative authorization, activities that are the essence of popular rule, were displaced as the center of government activity. The involvement of the Congress and the courts in the details of administration since the 1970s has tended to relinquish the energy and responsibility of the executive formed on the foundation of the New Deal realignment for a fragmented administrative politics that further insulates the affairs of state from the understanding and control of the rank and file citizenry.

With the decline of the traditional party system, there has arisen a politics of entitlement that belittles efforts of Democrats and Republicans alike to define a collective purpose with a past and a future. Instead, this yields a partisanship joined to a form of administrative politics that relegates electoral conflict to the intractable demands of policy advocates. Indeed, a partisanship that emphasizes national administration in support of programmatic rights has little chance to reach beyond the Washington Beltway and win the loyalty of the American people. This development does not mean, necessarily, that the Democrats and Republicans consider elections unimportant and have despaired of extending their influence through them. It does suggest that, as parties of administration, the Democrats and Republicans are hobbled in their efforts to form vital links with the public. This is the novel and pressing challenge for those who would take the idea of party renewal seriously.

Their task is not to restore traditional political parties or a strict construction of the Constitution, but to find a place for political associations in the political system wrought by the New Deal. This will require reasserting the balance between rights and obligations, as well as the the central and local governments. The vitality of the American Constitution has come from its flexiblity, from its extraordinary capacity to endure, even as it has, as Jefferson put it, "belonged to the living." [18] Critical elections have enabled each generation to claim its right to redefine the Constitution's principles and reorganize its institutions. The New Deal continued this unending task to ensure that each generation of Americans could affirm its attachment to the fundamental law. The burden of this generation is to recapture the understanding of democracy that has made such momentous deliberation and choice so central to the pursuit of America's political destiny.

Postscript on the 1992 Election

The events leading up to the 1992 election promised nothing but a worsening of the troubling political and constitutional legacy of the New Deal. Lacking his predecessor's personal popularity and conservative convictions, Bush's term in office badly exposed the weaknesses of the Republican party. More fundamentally, his unhappy stay in the White House was a painful reminder of the modern executive's isolation, subjecting the president to a volatile political process that could rapidly undercut popular support. As late as the Fall of 1991, Bush was basking in the triumphs of the Gulf and Cold Wars, his popularity rating at an historic high of about 90 per cent; a little more than a year latter, aggravated by a sluggish economy and institutional estrangement, the American people rejected him—as Bush, himself, put it (seeking to identify with the fall of Winston Churchill that followed the triumphant end of World War II), "he had been given the order of the boot." His defeat at the hands of the Democratic candidate, Arkansas Governor Bill Clinton, seemed to presage the end of the Reagan Revolution, at least in the kinder, gentler form that Bush represented. Bush's losing share of the popular vote, 37.7 per cent, was the worst defeat of an incumbent since William Howard Taft in 1912.

Like Taft, whose re-election effort was plagued by the presence in the race of former Republican president Theodore Roosevelt, Bush was beset by a strong third candidate—Texas billionaire H. Ross Perot. In fact, Perot's nineteen per cent of the popular vote posed the most serious electoral challenge to the two-party system since TR's 1912 Progressive Party campaign. The comparison between TR and Perot was both telling and disturbing. Roosevelt, of course, was a former president, whose considerable stature and skill dominated the Progressive Party. His campaign thus foretold not only of the emergence of an active and expansive national government but also of presidential campaigns conducted less by parties than by individual candidates.

Perot's campaign suggests just how far presidential politics had been emancipated from the constraints of party. As this book reveals, the New Deal rooted the progressive program in the American political system. It set off a new dynamic whereby executive administration, coupled with the greater personal responsibility of the president, enhanced by FDR's political leadership and the emergence of the mass media, diminished the role of collective responsibility in American politics in many ways. As such, the New Deal, which is often seen as an episode that revived partisan politics, was less a partisan program than an exercise in extending nonpartisan, "enlightened" administration. Similarly, the New Deal Democratic party can be viewed as a party to end all parties, thus preparing the ground for a Perot-like candidacy.

Perot's campaign, dominated by thirty-minute and hour-long commercials and appearances on talk shows, set a new standard for direct, plebiscitary appeal that may sound the death knell of the party campaign. Disdaining the importunities of those interested in party renewal that he form a third party, Perot launched his campaign without the bother of a nominating convention—his supporters were summoned on "Larry King Live."[1] Just as significant, the broad appeal of Perot's call for better planning as a solution to the nation's economic and political ills testifies to the resonance of simple-minded notions of "enlightened administration" in American politics—and to the threat that this politics of instant gratification poses to constitutional forms. With polls showing Perot leading both Bush and Clinton into the early part of the summer, the progressive idea of "Direct Government" seemed destined to play a more important and frivolous part in American political life.[2]

In the end, however, the American people invested their hope for constructive change more cautiously, in the possibility that Bill Clinton embodied a new form of Democratic politics that could cure the ailments brought on by the ideological and institutional combat of the past two decades. This hope was abetted by the Democrats' ability to take surprising advantage of Bush's misfortune. Mindful of how intractable fractiousness had denied them control of the presidency for twelve years, the Democrats ran a rather effective campaign that not only captured the White House, but left them in control of both Congressional chambers. To be sure, Clinton's share of the popular vote was hardly a "mandate" (his forty-three percent of the vote was roughly the same percentage of the total vote failed Democratic candidates had received in the previous three elections). But Clinton's support, although not deep, was impressively broad—he won an electoral college landslide, sweeping thirty-two states, many of them states the Democrats had not captured since 1964 (California, with 59 electoral votes, led a list of 9 states voting Democratic for the first time in 28 years). In addition, over one-hundred new members joined the House and Senate, many of them, even some Republicans, committed to working cooperatively with the new president. For twelve years, due to the voter's striking ambiguity about the parties, the government had been caught in the cross-fire between the Republican White House and a Democratic Congress; but an exit poll revealed that sixty-two per cent of the voters now preferred to have the President and Congress controlled by the same party, expressing the hope that the ideological polarization and institutional combat they perceived with divided partisan realms would now come to an end.[3] This hope, one suspects, was partly responsible for the largest voter turnout, 55 percent of the eligible electorate, in twenty years.

A plurality of the voters who sought an end to divided government voted for the Democratic party; and the amount of straight party ticket voting was unusually high in the context of the past two decades: for example, 89 per cent of Clinton backers voted for a Democratic House candidate.[4] This support for the Democrats hardly represented a revitalization of programmatic liberalism. Rather, Clinton won the election because he successfully presented himself as a "New Democrat"; as an "agent of change" who offered the hope of an alternative to liberalism and conservatism, to which the American voters in their indecision at the polls and, often, their absence from them, had responded with "a plague on both your houses."

To be sure, the economy was important. But the recession, while serious, was not bad enough in and of itself to defeat Bush (unemployment, inflation, and interest rates were all lower than the recession of the early 1980s, which the Reagan administration weathered). The severity of the recession was amplified by the fear that the structural foundation of the economy was crumbling; that productivity gains, net investment rates, and overall growth, all had lagged for two decades. As a result, Clinton was able to make the case that the United States faced a long-term economic crisis, one that undermined its citizens' hopes for the future.

Yet there were deeper than economic discontents expressed in the 1992 election. The political system itself was under attack, reinforcing the fear that the promise of American life was fading.[5] At the core of this political discontent was the people's perception (certainly more than half true) that there was a crisis of leadership in the country; that neither liberals nor conservatives offered the hope of restoring the vitality of the political system.

Unreconstructed conservatives claim that Bush could have won had he been more resolute, more like his predecessor in his opposition to taxes and government regulation. We observed in Chapter 11 that breaking the "no new taxes pledge" did Bush great harm; yet Ronald Reagan's star had faded considerably by the end of Bush's first term—by then it seemed that the Reagan "revolution" had gone badly off course, worsening rather than healing the fundamental philosophical and institutional conflicts that emerged during the 1960s. Like the Democratic party, the Republican party had become a loft for powerful interest groups, whose demands upon government threatened to dismantle the cornerstone of American constitutional government—the celebration of the personal dignity of the democratic individual. They pursued an unconstrained economic market, but, in the name of "family values," were prepared to impose national administrative solutions upon the cultural and sexual sphere. The spectacle of Patrick Buchanan, who challenged President Bush in the Republican primaries, speaking at the GOP National Convention in Houston before a prime-time television audience, while Ronald Reagan waited off-stage until after 11 P.M. EST, was striking evidence of just how powerful new right groups had become in the party. With the end of the Cold War, it seemed, the new right had set out in search of enemies at home—gays, feminists, even single and working mothers. Buchanan likened his party's quarrels with liberalism to a "religious war," a dark tale that testified to the decrepitude of the Reagan "revolution." It was no longer viewed as a solution to the nation's problems; it now seemed to be a symptom of them.

Bush might have won, however, had the Democrats offered a more conventional Democrat—someone such as Senator Thomas Harkin of Iowa, civil rights leader Jessie Jackson, or even the gifted, but strangely diffident, Mario Cuomo, the Governor of New York. By large margins, voters queried in exit polls rejected the traditional Democratic solution of "tax and spend." When asked whether they would rather have "government provide more services but cost more in taxes" or "government cost less in taxes but provide fewer services," by 54–38 per cent voters opted for less government and less taxes.[6] The greatest obstacle to a Democratic victory in 1992 was that a majority of Americans had a lingering concern that the solution to the economic and political crises in the United States was to fulfill the failed promise of the Reagan "revolution"—to get government off the backs of the American people. Even so, this commitment to limited government went against the tide of new demands for government succor in matters of economic security and health.

Clinton dedicated his campaign to principles and policies that "transcended," he claimed, the exhausted left-right debate that had immobilized the nation for two decades. Significantly, Clinton heralded "a new social contract," "a new covenant"; one that would seek to constrain demands for rights summoned by the Roosevelt Revolution in the name of responsibility and community. Clinton thereby pledged to take the American people to school, as Roosevelt had, while dedicating his party to the new concept of justice he espoused. The "sacred principles" of the "New Covenant" were first pronounced in a speech at Georgetown University on October 23, 1991. Making reference to Roosevelt's Commonwealth Club address in the final months of the 1932 campaign, in which FDR outlined the "economic constitutional order," Clinton said that the hopes of his generation rested on the possibility of securing a new rendezvous with America's political destiny—"forming a New Covenant of change that will honor middle-class values, restore the public trust, create a new sense of community, and make America work again."[7] The essence of Clinton's message was that the rights revolution had gone too far; the objective of the New Covenant was to correct the tendency of Americans to celebrate individual rights and demand government entitlements, without any sense of reciprocity, of mutual obligation they owe to each other and their country.

Clinton's commitment to educational opportunity best exemplified the objective of restoring a balance between rights and responsibility; its central feature, the formation of a national service corps, was emblematic of the core New Covenant principle—national community. A trust fund would be set up out of which any American could borrow money for a college education, so long as they paid it back either as a small percentage of their income or with a couple of years of national service as teachers, police officers, child care workers—or other activity designated as work that "our country desperately needs." With respect to this policy and others—welfare, regulation of business, and family—the Clinton presidency sought to revive the progressive tradition by combining its commitment to guarantee economic and social welfare with more respectful attention to the reciprocal obligations of the citizen.[8]

In this book we have looked for clues to America's political crisis—the expansion of national administrative power, the decline of party, the diminution of civic values—in the New Deal's support for programmatic rights, which expanded entitlements at the expense of civic associations and practices.[9] Vital parties require some compromise between a deep and abiding commitment to rights and a due attention to common deliberation and choice—some decisions must be left to a national party majority. Yet Roosevelt's party politics rested on a new understanding of rights that was not congenial to such partisan responsibility. The "economic constitutional order," he heralded, presupposing the codification of an "economic bill of rights," conceived of New Deal programs, such as social security, as permanent entitlements—and, thereby, beyond the vagaries of public opinion, elections, and parties. FDR's commitment to "enlightened administration," embodied in the Third New Deal, followed logically from this premise (see Chapters 5 and 6).

Clinton's campaign promised to correct and renew the progressive tradition as shaped by the New Deal; but a Clinton administration is unlikely to set the tone for a departure from the existing ills of American politics, unless the president and his advisors recognize the origins of our discontent. Even as he challenged the explosion of rights and hidebound bureaucracy that arose form the New Deal realignment, Clinton's unabashed celebration of activist government threatened to accentuate, rather than correct, some of the most troubling characteristics of the Roosevelt "revolution." Although his call to balance rights and responsibility seemed to resonate with the American people, Clinton's dedication to a renewal of community was muffled by the promise to form new middle class entitlements—his campaign called for an expansion of government support for health care, job training, and, as noted, a college education. Neither the popularity of these programmatic promises nor the necessity of the national government doing something about health care, corporate mismanagement, and educational opportunity, should blind us to how the creation of new rights tends to undermine the fragile sense of citizenship in American politics. In the face of this powerful centrifugal pull, the reciprocity expected of those beneficiaries of college loans seems unlikely to nurture a sense of national community; indeed, the option of paying one's country back through a small percentage of one's income, thus avoiding national service, greatly dilutes the idea of national community.

The diffident, sometimes apologetic stance that Clinton displayed in the face of traditional liberal causes was partly strategic. The wing of the party he represents, which includes the members of the Democratic Leadership Council, is a significant but still minority wing; only the weakness of liberal groups and the emphasis on candidate-centered campaigns in presidential politics made Clinton's nomination and election possible. The majority of liberal interest group activists and Democratic members of Congress still prefer entitlements to obligations, regulations to responsibility. To actualize the new mission of progressivism he espouses, President Clinton will at some point have to confront the dominant groups in his party, a battle that may leave him as isolated as was his Democratic predecessor, Jimmy Carter.

Clinton's disinclination to engage his party forcefully, however, is not simply a matter of strategy, but of conviction. Clinton is not a *moderate* Democrat—he is a progressive who displays an uncommon faith in what government can do. There is a danger, thereby, that the noble commitments to responsibility and community could deteriorate into a new form of enlightened administration, a new bill of entitlements, dedicated to making welfare beneficiaries more moral, young people more civic minded, and corporations more socially conscious. Such a turn would not only amplify the administrative republic but exact a terrible political cost, banishing the Democrats to the political wilderness from which they have only just begun to emerge. The next four years will tell whether President Clinton offers leadership that moves the nation toward political renewal or presides over a recrudescence of the Democratic commitment to the aggrandizement of administrative power.

Notes

Chapter 1

1. Franklin D. Roosevelt, *Public Papers and Addresses,* ed. Samuel J. Rosenman, 13 volumes (New York: Random House, 1938–50), **7:**397–400.

2. Ibid., **7:**469.

3. Raymond Clapper, "Roosevelt Tries the Primaries," *Current History,* October, 1938, 16.

4. Roosevelt, *Public Papers and Addresses,* **4:**337.

5. New York *Times,* September 18, 1938, **4:**3.

6. Roosevelt's party leadership probably influenced the report of the American Political Science Association (APSA) Committee on Political Parties, which advocated and gave prominence to the doctrine of party responsibility. See APSA Committee on Political Parties, *Toward A More Responsible Two Party System* (New York: Rinehart, 1950), V, 22–25. An influential member of the committee, E. E. Schattschneider, considered Roosevelt's attempt to reform the Democratic party "one of the greatest experimental tests of the nature of the American party system ever made." See E. E. Schattschneider, *Party Government* (New York: Holt, Rinehart and Winston, 1942), 163–69.

7. Roosevelt, *Public Papers and Addresses,* **7:**xxviii–xxxii.

8. For an overview on the development of the modern presidency, see Fred I. Greenstein (ed.) *Leadership in the Modern Presidency* (Cambridge, MA: Harvard University Press, 1988).

9. Harvey C. Mansfield, Jr., *Statesmanship and Party Government* (Chicago: University of Chicago Press, 1965). Mansfield observes that Edmund Burke "conceived the respectability of party because he was willing to accept the less exact principle in exchange for a lessened reliance on statesmen; for great statesmen are unreliable, at least in the sense that they may not always be available" (17–18).

10. James Ceaser, *Presidential Selection: Theory and Development* (Princeton, New Jersey: Princeton University Press, 1979).

11. Alexander Hamilton, James Madison, and John Jay, *The Federalist Papers* (New York: New American Library, 1961), Number 70, 423–31.

12. Wilson Carey McWilliams, "The Anti-Federalists, Representation and Party," *Northwestern University Law Review,* Volume 84, Number 1 (Fall, 1989), 35. For the original constitutional design of the executive, the Founders looked to the concept of "Patriot King" [emphasis in original] provided a half-century earlier by the British author and statesman Lord Bolingbroke. Such an ideal executive stood above the "merely" political conflicts of parties and ruled benevolently in the public interest. See Ralph Ketcham, *Presidents Above Party* (Chapel Hill, North Carolina: University of North Carolina Press, 1984).

13. James Piereson, "Party Government," *The Political Science Reviewer,* **12** (Fall, 1982), 51–52.

14. According to the Whig opposition, the legacy of Jackson's presidency was the dangerous expansion of executive prerogatives. Jackson's aggressive use of the veto and appointment power during the bank controversy, they argued, demonstrated that the Chief Executive now possessed power that dwarfed the influence of Congress as well as the Judiciary, thus undermining the separation of powers. Yet the extension of executive powers during Jackson's presidency did not simply expand unilateral executive action. This extension depended upon the emergence of the president as popular leader that was mediated in critical ways by party organization. And party organization, which took its form from the convention system and patronage, had a decided state and local orientation.

The powers of the presidency were not only limited by the decentralized character of the party system but by the doctrine of the Democratic party that was organized to advance Jacksonian principles. This doctrine, as evidenced by Jackson's veto of the bank bill, was dedicated to limiting the role of the national government. Jackson defended the principle of union against the extreme states' rights claim of South Carolina in the nullification controversy; generally, however, he was a strong advocate of the rights of the state governments and opposed expanding the responsibilities of the national government and executive. Thus, as Alexis de Tocqueville wrote about the executive of the 1830s, "General Jackson's power is constantly increasing, but that of the president grows less. The federal government is strong in his hands; it will pass to his successor enfeebled." Alexis de Tocqueville, *Democracy in America,* J. P. Mayer, ed. (New York: New American Library, 1969) 395; see also Sidney M. Milkis and Michael Nelson, *The American Presidency: Origins and Development, 1787–1990* (Washington, D.C.: Congressional Quarterly, 1990), Chapter 5.

15. Milkis and Nelson, *The American Presidency,* Chapter 7. The Republicans, like the Democrats, traced their origins to the Jeffersonian era, claiming that as the party opposed to the expansion of slavery in the territories they, and not the Democrats, represented the "republican" principles that defined that era. The restoration of a strong executive as the vital center of a new national program was unanticipated. Most of what Lincoln accomplished in consolidating the executive power during the Civil War, in fact, surprised most of his Republican colleagues in the Congress, who acted forcefully to weaken the presidency after his assassination.

16. Tocqueville, *Democracy in America,* 676.

17. Stephen Skowronek, *Building A New American State: The Expansion of National Administrative Capacities, 1877–1920,* (Cambridge: Cambridge University Press, 1982) 40.

18. The two seminal presentations of critical realignment theory are V. O. Key, Jr., "A Theory of Critical Elections," *Journal of Politics* **17** (February, 1955): 3–18; and Walter Dean Burnham, *Critical Elections and the Mainsprings of American Politics* (New York: W. W. Norton, 1970). Occurring at critical junctures of American history—1800,

1828, 1860, 1896, and 1932—realignments have resulted in dramatic shifts in voter affiliation, major changes in public policy, and the forging of a new public philosophy. See also
Harry Jaffa, "A Phoenix From the Ashes: The Death of James Madison's Constitution
(killed by James Madison) and the Birth of Party Government." Paper delivered at the
1977 Annual Meeting of the American Political Science Association, September, Washington, D.C.

19. Herbert Croly, *The Promise of American Life* (New York: G. P. Dutton, 1963,
original work published in 1909, by the MacMillan Co.), 169.

20. See, for example, Woodrow Wilson, *Constitutional Government in the United
States* (New York: Columbia University Press, 1908), especially Chapters 3 and 8; and
Herbert Croly, *Progressive Democracy* (New York: The MacMillan Co., 1914).

21. Roosevelt, *Public Papers and Addresses,* **1:**752.

22. Ibid., 752.

23. Morton Frisch, *Franklin D. Roosevelt: The Contribution of the New Deal to American Political Thought and Practice* (Boston: St. Wayne, 1975), 79.

24. Hamilton, Madison, and Jay, *The Federalist Papers,* 322.

25. Jeffrey K. Tulis, *The Rhetorical Presidency,* (Princeton, New Jersey: Princeton
University Press, 1987). Tulis argues that the emergence of the president as a leader of
public opinion during the twentieth century constitutes the emergence of the "second Constitution." The tendency of the second constitution to make extraordinary executive power
routine, Tulis notes, undermines the logic of the original constitutional framework. While
Tulis sees the Progressive era as critical to this development, Theodore Lowi links the
emergence of a "personal president" and "second republic" to the New deal era. See
Lowi, *The Personal President: Power Invested, Promise Unfulfilled* (Ithaca and London:
Cornell University Press, 1985). This book suggests that the key to understanding modern
presidential leadership is found in the displacement of *party* politics by *administrative* politics, a development that has not always put a premium on active and continuous presidential leadership of public opinion. See Chapter 2.

26. For example, see Burnham, *Critical Elections and the Mainsprings of American
Politics*; and Everitt Carll Ladd, *Transformations of the American Party System* (with
Charles D. Hadley), 2nd edition (New York: W. W. Norton, 1978).

27. Thus, the prevailing view of the New Deal realignment as "a brief, if massive,
deviation in the long secular decline of the party system" may be misleading. See Burnham, *Critical Elections...,* 132–33. The New Deal is properly viewed as contributing to,
rather than simply interrupting, the long secular decline of the party system.

28. The value of such a systemic perspective is clearly demonstrated by the excellent
work on presidential selection and governance authored by James Ceaser and Jeffrey Tulis,
respectively. See Tulis, *The Rhetorical Presidency* and Ceaser, *Presidential Selection...*

29. V. O. Key, Jr., *Politics, Parties, and Pressure Groups,* 5th edition (New York:
Thomas Y. Crowell Company, 1964).

30. Lester Seligman, "The Presidential Office and the President as Party Leader (with
a postscript on the Kennedy–Nixon Era)," in Jeff Fishel, ed., *Parties and Elections in an
Anti-Party Age* (Bloomington, Indiana: Indiana University Press, 1978); Harold F. Bass,
"The President and the National Party Organization," in *Presidents and Their Parties:
Leadership or Neglect?* (New York: Praeger Publishers, 1984); and Lowi, *The Personal
President . . . ,* Chapters 3 and 4.

31. Hugh Heclo, "One Executive Branch or Many," in *Both Ends of the Avenue,* ed. Anthony King (Washington, D.C.: American Enterprise Institute, 1983), 38–42.

32. E. Donald Elliot has suggested that the expansion of administrative power over the past century has created a "Constitution of the Administrative State," but that this expansion has not been accomplished by formally amending the Constitution. This "quasi-constitutional evolution," as Elliot notes, "is not a mere additive change to the structure of government. Inevitably it has transformed the nature and functions of existing institutions as well." See his "INS V. Chadha: The Administrative Constitution, the Constitution, and the Legislative Veto," *Supreme Court Review* (1983), 167.

33. David Truman, "Party Reform, Party Atrophy, and Constitutional Change: Some Reflections," *Political Science Quarterly,* **99** (4) (Winter, 1984–1985): 637–655.

34. Lester G. Seligman and Carey R. Covington, *The Coalitional Presidency* (Chicago, Illinois: The Dorsey Press, 1989).

35. Even when political parties were relatively indifferent to broad moral questions and dedicated to the personal ambitions of their members, Tocqueville found them to be valuable political associations in which individuals learned the art of cooperation and became citizens. See Tocqueville, *Democracy in America,* 189–95, 509–13, 520–24; see also Wilson Carey McWilliams, "Parties as Civic Associations," in *Party Renewal in America,* Gerald M. Pomper, ed. (New York: Praeger, 1980).

36. Barry Karl, *The Uneasy State* (Chicago, Illinois: University of Chicago Press, 1983).

37. Ibid., 231.

38. For example, see Nelson W. Polsby, *Consequences of Party Reform* (New York: Oxford University Press, 1983); and Byron E. Shafer, *Quiet Revolution: The Struggle for the Democratic Party and the Shaping of Post-Reform Politics* (New York: Russell Sage Foundation, 1983). For a critique of this approach, see Stephen A. Salmore and Barbara G. Salmore, "Candidate-Centered Parties: Politics Without Intermediaries." In *Remaking American Politics,* Richard A. Harris and Sidney M. Milkis, eds. (Boulder, Colorado: Westview Press, 1989).

39. As noted in Chapter 10, these developments have led some scholars and public figures to suggest that there was not only a revitalization but a reconstruction of political parties during the 1980s. See, for example, Joseph A. Schlesinger, "The New American Party System," *American Political Science Review* **79** (December, 1985): 1152–69.

40. Richard Nathan, *The Administrative Presidency* (New York: John Wiley, 1983).

41. Richard B. Stewart, "The Reformation of Administrative Law," *Harvard Law Review* **88** (June 1975): 1669–813.

42. R. Shep Melnick, "The Courts, Congress, and Programmatic Rights," in Harris and Milkis, *Remaking American Politics.*

43. Robert Eden, "Partisanship and Constitutional Revolution: The Founders' View is Newly Problematic," in *Constitutionalism in Perspective: The United States Constitution in Twentieth Century Politics,* ed. Sarah Baumgartner Thurow (Lanham, New York, and London: University Press of America, 1988).

44. For a discussion of the American electorate during the 1980s and the prospects for party renewal, see Walter Dean Burnham, "Elections as Democratic Institutions," in *Elections in America,* ed. Kay Lehman Schlozman (Boston: Allen and Unwin, 1987), 58–60; and Martin P. Wattenberg, *The Decline of American Political Parties, 1952–1984* (Cam-

bridge, MA: Harvard University Press, 1986). Benjamin Ginsberg and Martin Shefter argue that since the New Deal, and especially since the advent of "divided government" during the late 1960s, there has been a shift from an electorally to an institutionally centered party politics in the United States. As a result, party politics entails "institutional combat" between the Republican executive and Democratic legislature, tending to insulate decision-making processes and restricting political participation. See their *Politics by Other Means: The Declining Importance of Elections in America* (New York: Basic Books, 1990).

Chapter 2

1. Franklin D. Roosevelt, "Is There A Jefferson On The Horizon?" in *The Roosevelt Reader: Selected Speeches, Messages, Press Conferences, and Letters of Franklin D. Roosevelt*, ed. Basil Rauch (New York: Rinehart and Co., 1957), 44. Originally published in *New York Evening World*, December 3, 1925.

2. The term *progressive* is understood broadly to refer to types of reformers who dominated both the Progressive era and the New Deal.

3. Roosevelt, "Is There A Jefferson on the Horizon?" 47.

4. Roosevelt to Frederick Scott Oliver, August 9, 1906. *The Letters of Theodore Roosevelt*, Elting E. Morrison, ed. (Cambridge: Harvard University Press, 1952), 351; see also Charles Forcey, *The Crossroads of Liberalism* (New York: Oxford University Press, 1961), 128.

5. Woodrow Wilson, *The New Freedom* (New York and Garden City: Doubleday, Page and Co., 1913), 284.

6. Roosevelt, "Is There A Jefferson on The Horizon?" 45.

7. Gaillard Hunt, ed. *The Writings of James Madison* (New York: G. P. Putnam's, 1906), Vol. 6, 358.

8. Theodore Lowi, *The End of Liberalism: The Second Republic of the United States,* 2nd edition (New York: W. W. Norton, 1979). The meaning of "administrative state" is rather obscure in the literature, but generally it refers to the empowering of bureaucratic agencies, staffed by unelected officials, to carry out important government functions. For an unusually careful discussion of the meaning of the administrative state, see John A. Rohr, *To Run a Constitution: The Legitimacy of the Administrative State* (Lawrence, Kansas: University Press of Kansas, 1986), XI, 217 no. 11.

9. At the time the Constitutuion was written, Madison feared that raw and disruptive party conflict would weaken constitutional safeguards, the division and separation of powers, designed to prevent a popular and oppressive majority from "sacrific[ing] to its ruling passion or interest both the public good and the rights of other citizens." Should a strong faction manage to secure control of the three branches of government, constitutional sobriety might all too easily be lost with the uncompromising pursuit of a party program. Alexander Hamilton, James Madison, and John Jay, *The Federalist Papers* (New York: New American Library, 1961), Number 10, 80.

10. Richard Hofstadter, *The Idea of A Party System* (Berkeley: University of California Press, 1969), 40–121; see also James Ceaser, *Presidential Selection: Theory and Development* (Princeton, New Jersey: Princeton University Press, 1979), 88–122.

11. Hunt, *The Writings of James Madison*, Vol. 6, 118.

12. Alexis de Tocqueville, *Democracy in America*, ed. J. P. Mayer (New York: Doubleday, 1969), 87–99.

13. Arthur Schlesinger, Jr., "Broad Accomplishments of the New Deal," in *The New Deal: Revolution or Evolution?*, ed. Edwin C. Rozwene (Boston: D. C. Heath, 1949), 100.

14. The term *administrative republic* comes from Harvey Flaumenhaft, "Hamilton's Administrative Republic and the American Presidency." In *The Presidency in the Constitutional Order*, eds. Joseph M. Bessette and Jeffrey Tulis (Baton Rouge, Louisiana: Louisiana State University Press, 1981).

15. Barry Karl, *The Uneasy State: The United States From 1915 to 1945* (Chicago: The University of Chicago Press, 1983), 236, 238.

16. Franklin D. Roosevelt to Thomas G. Corcoran, January 20, 1941, *Harold Ickes Papers*, Box 160, Folder: "Thomas G. Corcoran, 1941–1943." Library of Congress, Manuscript Division, Washington, D.C.

17. For example, see Hugh Heclo, "The Executive Office of the President," in *Modern Presidents and the Presidency*, ed. Marc Landy (Lexington, Massachusetts: D.C. Heath, 1985).

18. The most influential presentation of this view of the New Deal is James MacGregor Burns, *Roosevelt: The Lion and the Fox, 1882–1940* (New York: Harcourt, Brace and World, 1956), especially 183–208.

19. Woodrow Wilson, "The Study of Administration," *Political Science Quarterly* 2 (June, 1887): 187–222.

20. Alexander Hamilton, James Madison, and John Jay, *The Federalist Papers* (New York: The New American Library, 1961), 423.

21. Wilson, "The Study of Administration," 209–10.

22. Ibid., 200 (Wilson's emphasis).

23. Ibid., 201.

24. Woodrow Wilson, *Constitutional Government in the United States* (New York: Columbia University Press, 1908), 199.

25. Woodrow Wilson, "Cabinet Government in the United States," *International Review* 7 (August, 1879), 150–1.

26. Wilson's mature thought on presidential leadership and constitutional change is expressed in his *Constitutional Government in the United States*.

27. On TR's importance in the development of modern executive leadership, see Jeffrey Tulis, *The Rhetorical Presidency* (Princeton, New Jersey: Princeton University Press, 1987), 95–116.

28. Wilson, *Constitutional Government in the United States*, 68.

29. Ibid., 220.

30. For an excellent discussion of Wilson's thoughts and influence on party reform, see Ceaser, *Presidential Selection: Theory and Development*, 170–212.

31. Woodrow Wilson, "First Annual Message," December 2, 1913. *In The State of the Union Messages*, ed. Fred L. Israel (New York: Chelsea House, 1966), 2548. Theodore Roosevelt was moved to endorse the national primary after being denied the Republican nomination in 1912, resulting in his third party campaign under the banner of the newly formed Progressive party that year.

32. Elizabeth Sanders, "The Institutional Conditions of An Instrumentalist Presidency: Contrasting Threads of Reform in American Political Development." Paper presented at the Annual Meeting of the American Political Science Association, Atlanta, Georgia, August, 1989.

33. Wilson, *Constitutional Government in the United States*, 81.

34. New York *Times*, April 8, 1913, 1.

35. Woodrow Wilson, *The Papers of Woodrow Wilson*, ed. Arthur S. Link (Princeton: Princeton University Press, 1966–1985), Vol. 27, 269–70.

36. Tulis, *The Rhetorical Presidency*. Tulis' very important discussion of Wilson is insufficiently attentive to the importance that party organization played in Wilson's administration. As Link has noted, Wilson disappointed many Progressives by his willingness to subordinate leadership of public opinion to the task of forming strong bonds with his party and its congressional leadership. See Link, "Woodrow Wilson and the Democratic Party," *Review of Politics* **18** (April, 1956): 146–56; see also the discussion of Herbert Croly's criticism of Wilson's relationship to the Democratic party in this chapter.

37. Arthur Link, *Woodrow Wilson and the Progressive Era, 1910–1917* (New York: Harper and Row, 1954), 35; and Link, *Wilson and the New Freedom* (Princeton: Princeton University Press, 1956), 152.

38. "Progressive Platform," printed in *History of American Presidential Elections*, eds. Arthur Schlesinger, Jr., and Fred Israel, (New York: Chelsea House, 1971), 2186.

39. Karl, *The Uneasy State*, 234–35.

40. Forcey, *The Crossroads of Liberalism*, 302.

41. Croly, *Progressive Democracy*, 346–47.

42. Ibid., 348.

43. Josephus Daniels to Franklin D. Roosevelt, December 15, 1932, *Ray Stannard Baker Collection*, Franklin D. Roosevelt File, Firestone Library, Princeton University.

44. Link, *Wilson and the New Freedom*, 159.

45. Ray Stannard Baker, *Woodrow Wilson: Life and Letters* (London: William Heineman, 1932), Vol. 4, 47.

46. Link, *Wilson and the New Freedom*, 160.

47. Croly, *Progressive Democracy*, 346.

48. As an editorial that appeared in the November 14, 1914 issue of the *New Republic* read, "By means of executive leadership, expert administrative independence and direct legislation, [progressivism] will gradually create a new governmental machinery which will be born with the impulse to destroy the two-party system, and will itself be thoroughly and flexibly representative of the underlying purposes and needs of a more social democracy." 52. "The Future of the Two Party System," *The New Republic*, November 14, 1914, 10–11.

49. "Partisan Democracy as a Dogma," *The New Republic*, October 7, 1916, 234–35.

50. "Unregenerate Democracy," *New Republic*, February 5, 1916, 17–18; Croly, *Progressive Democracy*, 350.

51. Ibid., 365.

52. Ibid., 371.

53. Theodore Roosevelt, "A Confession of Faith," address before the national convention of the Progressive Party, Chicago, August 6, 1912, *The Works of Theodore Roosevelt* (New York: Scribner's, 1926), Vol. 18, 279.

54. Wilson, as quoted in Link, *Woodrow Wilson and the Progressive Era,* 21.

55. Woodrow Wilson, "Monopoly, Or Opportunity," in Wilson, *The New Freedom,* 188.

56. Barry Karl, "The Constitution and Central Planning: The Third New Deal Revisited," in *The Supreme Court Review, 1988,* eds. Philip B. Kurland, Gerhard Kasper, and Dennis J. Hutchinson (Chicago and London: The University of Chicago Press, 1989), 197.

57. Consequently, although Wilson did commit his administration to the creation of a Federal Trade Commission, he followed standard patronage practices in staffing it. George Rublee, the former member of the Progressive Party who successfully urged the idea of a regulatory commission on Wilson, lamented the President's appointment of mere "politicians" to the FTC: "I was shocked by these appointments. It seemed to me totally inconsistent with what the President seemed to understand so well, when we were discussing the idea of the Commission. But that was the Commission. It really had no chance to do its job with that kind of membership. It was hopeless, really." In "The Reminiscences of George Rublee," Columbia University Oral History Project, Part 1, 125.

58. TR as quoted in Sidney Warren, *The President as World Leader* (Philadelphia: J. B. Lippincott, 1964), 107.

59. Wilson, *Papers,* Vol. 51, 381.

60. *New York Times,* August 12, 1918, 9; September 8, 1918, Section 3, 1. Wilson's willingness to work through regular party channels in challenging recalcitrant Democrats led to one embarrassing incident. This involved the President's intervention in a Texas contest for the House. Wilson's telegram of July 24, 1918 said, in reference to Democratic Congressman James Luther Slayden, "no one can claim he has given support to the Administration," thus giving tacit support to the incumbent representative's primary opponent Carlos Bee. When Wilson's telegram was made public on July 25, Slayden, then campaigning in Texas, immediately announced his withdrawal from the primary contest, thus ending a congressional career of 22 years. Wilson was later embarrassed to learn that his Postmaster General, Albert Burleson, had gotten him involved in a contest to aid Burleson's brother-in-law, a San Antonio lawyer, Bee, who was nominated and elected to the House. Burleson had drafted the telegram and sent it to the White House for Wilson to sign, thinking that the President was unlikely to do so. To Burleson's surprise and Wilson's eventual embarrassment, the President, who relied heavily upon his Postmaster General in managing party affairs, signed the telegram. See Wilson, *Papers,* Vol. 49, 209, 407–8.

61. TR as quoted in Warren, *The President As World Leader,* 108.

62. Burns, *The Lion and the Fox,* 375–80.

63. Jordan A. Schwarz, *Liberal: Adolf A. Berle and the Vision of the American Era* (New York: The Free Press, 1987), 79.

64. Adolf Berle, "Memorandum to Governor Franklin D. Roosevelt," August 15, 1932, *The Adolf A. Berle Papers,* Box 15, Franklin Delano Roosevelt Library, Hyde Park, New York. The discussion of the Commonwealth Club address owes much to the help and insights offered by my colleague and friend Robert Eden. Professor Eden generously shared materials with me that he uncovered in his own research on the speech, and he taught me a great deal about FDR's statesmanship in our long discussions on the New Deal.

65. The historian Kenneth S. Davis has observed that the "Dewey impact upon the

overall mind" of the New Deal was "substantial." See Davis, FDR: *The New Deal Years, 1933–1937* (New York: Random House, 1986). Rexford Tugwell testified to this influence on FDR's Brains Trust: ". . .[M]y generation owed to Dewey liberation from old concepts, if it was wanted. He encouraged my turn away from classicism in economics and politics and my admission of the future as the chief influence on the present. This was a complete reversal, of course; pragmatism meant something more than judging things or institutions by working tests. It meant the future could be brought into focus; judged in advance as a working hypothesis, and altered before it was reached. This was and is the essence of planning. I found a comprehensive justification for much of my own work in Dewey. I felt myself deeply in his debt." Tugwell, *To the Lesser Heights of Morningside* (Philadelphia: University of Pennsylvania Press, 1982), 157.

66. John Dewey, "Individualism, Old and New," Reprinted in *John Dewey: The Later Works, 1925–1953*, ed. Jo Ann Boydston, (Carbondale and Edwardville: Southern Illnois University Press, 1984), Vol. 5, 41–123.

67. H. M. Kallen, "Salvation By Intelligence," a review of Dewey's *Liberalism and Social Action. Saturday Review*, December 14, 1935, 7.

68. Dewey, "Individualism, Old and New," 68.

69. "American Individualism—Romantic and Realistic," *Adolf Berle Papers*, Box 17, Folder: "Speech Draft: Individualism." Rexford Tugwell attributes this first draft to two economic advisors of the Harvard Business School, John Dalton and Robert K. Strauss. See Tugwell, *In Search of Roosevelt* (Cambridge, MA: Harvard University Press), 178. Dalton and Strauss did play an important part in the "new individualism" project, and they may, in fact, have written the first draft of the Commonwealth Club address. But the ideas in this draft closely parallel Berle's and, in fact, are almost entirely a rehash of the book he coauthored with Gardner Means on the American political economy. See Adolf A. Berle and Gardiner C. Means, *The Modern Corporation and Private Property* (New York: The MacMillan Co., 1932).

70. Franklin D. Roosevelt, *Public Papers and Addresses*, ed. Samuel I. Rosenman, 13 volumes (New York: Random House, 1938–1950), Vol. 1, 680–84. Berle's book, *The Modern Corporation and Private Property*, was coauthored with Gardiner Means. See Note 69.

71. The second draft is attached to the first. *Adolf Berle Papers*, Box 17, Folder: "Speech Draft: Individualism." Berle's final draft, written with an assist from his wife Beatrice, is also in his papers, Box 18, folder: "Commonwealth Club." The final version is printed in Roosevelt, *Public Papers and Addresses*, Vol. 1, 742–56.

72. On the genesis of the Commonwealth Club address, see Raymond Moley, *After Seven Years* (New York and London: Harper and Brothers, 1939), 58, no. 6; Rexford G. Tugwell, *In Search of Roosevelt*, 172–80; Schwarz, *Liberal: Adolf A. Berle and the Vision of an American Era*, 78–79; Beatrice Bishop Berle and Travis Beal Jacobs, *Navigating the Rapids, 1918–1971: From the Papers of Adolf A. Berle* (New York: Harcourt Brace Jovanovich, 1973), 57–59, 61–70. There is some dispute about the origins of the Commonwealth speech, especially with respect to FDR's contribution. Moley reports that Roosevelt worked on the speech, while Tugwell denies that Berle's draft "had the same sort of consideration and revision that all the others had had." My examination of the files at the FDR Library and the events surrounding the Commonwealth address suggests that Moley had it right; that is, Berle's draft was crafted for and edited by Roosevelt. This is perhaps best revealed by a comparison of the Commonwealth address and the 1936 Democratic platform, which FDR drafted. The similarity of these documents belies Tugwell's notion

that FDR was a passive agent in the genesis of the 1932 speech. On the 1936 Democratic platform, see the discussion to follow.

73. *San Francisco Examiner,* September 24, 1932, 9; *New York Times,* September 24, 1932, 7.

74. Roosevelt, *Public Papers and Addresses,* Vol. 1, 746. This view of Jefferson was based on a document, which Gilbert Chinard originally attributed to him in his study *Thomas Jefferson: The Apostle of Americanism,* purporting that the people had two sets of rights, those of "personal competency" and those involved in acquiring and possessing property. With the first, by which Jefferson meant the right of free thinking, the freedom of forming and expressing opinions, and freedom of personal living, the government was not to interfere; the right of property, however, was not so sacrosanct. As it turned out, Chinard had falsely attributed this document to Jefferson and had erroneously put the time of its writing as 1776. In fact, as Chinard noted in a later edition of his study, "it came from the pen of Thomas Paine and was probably written ten years later." See Chinard, *Thomas Jefferson: The Apostle of Americanism* (Boston: Little, Brown, 1948), 2nd edition, 80–85.

75. Roosevelt, *Public Papers and Addresses,* 1:751–52.

76. This change in wording was consistent with the themes Berle's draft meant to convey. Indeed, the substitution of "enlightened administration" for "manager" was probably prompted by Berle's September 19 wire to Moley, alerting the President's party that the speech had been airmailed that day. In outlining the address, Berle's telegram read: "Fundamental issue today adaption old principles to new and probably permanent change in economic conditions which can only be done by *enlightened* government." Telegram, Adolf Berle to Raymond Moley, September 19, 1932, *Adolf Berle Papers,* Box 15 (my emphasis).

77. Adolf A. Berle, "The Expansion of American Administrative Law," *Harvard Law Review* 30 (1916–1917), 430; see also Karl, "Constitution and Central Planning: The Third New Deal Revisited," 194.

78. The new understanding of rights required a rethinking of the meaning of the Declaration of Independence: "Under [the Declaration] rulers were accorded power, and the people consented to that power on consideration that they be accorded certain rights. The task of statesmanship has always been the redefinition of these rights in terms of a changing and growing social order. New conditions impose new requirements upon government and those who conduct government." Roosevelt, *Public Papers and Addresses,* 1:753.

79. Anne O'Hare McCormick, "Next Four Years." *New York Times Magazine,* November 8, 1936, 26.

80. John Dewey, "The Future of Liberalism." *The Journal of Philosophy* 32 (9) (April 25, 1935), 228; see also Kenneth S. Davis, *FDR: The New Deal Years, 1933–1937* (New York: Random House, 1986), 232–33; and Donald Brand, *Corporatism and The Rule of Law: A Study of the National Recovery Administration* (Ithaca and London: Cornell University Press, 1989), 53.

81. Ellis W. Hawley, *The New Deal and the Problem of Monopoly: A Study in Economic Ambivalence* (Princeton: Princeton University Press, 1966), 51. For a critical review of Hawley's position, see Brand, *Corporatism and the Rule of Law,* 66–79.

82. Baker to FDR, March 6, 1935, *President's Personal File,* 1820, Franklin D. Roosevelt Library.

83. Ibid.

84. Baker's letter to FDR of April 10, 1935 praised the President's of March 20, which will be discussed, for its "penetrating comparison between the methods of Woodrow Wilson and Theodore Roosevelt." Baker also reaffirmed his call to Roosevelt for a "rebirth of vision," favorably citing a passage from the President's book *Looking Forward,* published in 1933, which was taken verbatim from the Commonwealth Club address. Baker to FDR, April 10, 1935, *President's Personal File* 1820; Franklin D. Roosevelt, *Looking Forward* (New York: The John Day Company, 1933), 14.

85. FDR to Baker, March 20, 1935, *President's Personal File,* 2332.

86. Ibid.

87. The term *Second New Deal* has been applied by historians to the veritable storm of executive-directed legislative action, which began in the first week of June, 1935. As far as I know, however, no one has yet pointed to direct evidence that FDR was planning such action well before the summer of 1935, and that this plan was tied to a broader understanding of democratic leadership. For a critical view of James MacGregor Burns's thesis that the Second New Deal was the result of Roosevelt stumbling leftward in an unsystematic response to the attack of business upon the New Deal, see Brand, *Corporation and the Rule of Law,* 281–89.

88. Burns, *Roosevelt: The Lion and the Fox,* 378.

89. Paul H. Douglas, *The Coming of A New Party* (New York and London: McGraw–Hill, 1932), 168–70.

90. FDR's comment on the League for Independent Political Action is cited in Rexford G. Tugwell, *The Brains Trust* (New York: The Viking Press, 1968), 161. It was elicited by Tugwell, who had brought Douglas's book to Roosevelt's attention during one of the New York Governor's sessions with his Brains Trust. Tugwell was especially interested in FDR's reaction to the passage about the Governor's presidential candidacy. Implicitly, of course, FDR rejected Douglas's unfavorable comparison between Wilson and himself.

91. Dewey too hoped that party politics would eventually give way to more "impartial" inquiry and policy. As he wrote in *Liberalism and Social Action,* "The idea that the conflict of parties will, by means of public discussion, bring out necessary public truths . . . has nothing in common with the procedure of organized cooperative inquiry which has won the triumphs of science in the field of physical nature." Dewey, *Liberalism and Social Action* (New York: G. P. Putnam's Sons, 1935), 71.

92. A full report of FDR's overture to Hirman Johnson and the text of his speech at Sacramento appears in the *New York Times,* September 23, 1932, **1,** 10; see also Robert Barry, "Hiram Johnson's Plea for toilers, Farmers Praised," *San Francisco Examiner,* September 23, 1932, **1,** 7.

93. To be sure, as head of the minority Democratic Party, FDR's hopes of winning the 1932 campaign and effectively governing after the election depended upon Republican disaffection. In California, for example, Republicans had a registration advantage over Democrats of some 460,000 voters.

94. Baker to FDR, September 26, 1936, and FDR to Baker, September 30, 1936, *President's Personal File,* 2332.

95. "Democratic Platform of 1936." In *National Party Platforms,* ed. Donald Bruce Johnson (Urbana, Chicago, and London: University of Illinois Press, 1978), 360. For evidence of FDR's dominant role in drafting the platform see the materials of the *President's Secretary File,* 143, Folder: "Democratic Platform." Upon reading FDR's draft, his aide Stanley High wrote enthusiastically, "Apropos of the Platform memorandum which you

showed me yesterday afternoon, . . . I think the use of the phrase 'We hold this truth to be self-evident' is great.'' High, Memorandum for the President, June 18, 1936, *President's Secretary File,* 143, Folder: "Democratic Platform.'' On Roosevelt's domination of the proceedings of the 1936 Democratic convention, see Burns, *Roosevelt: The Lion and the Fox,* 271–78.

96. "Democratic Platform of 1936,'' 360.

97. Louis Hartz, *The Liberal Tradition in America* (San Diego, New York, and London: Harcourt Brace Jovanovich, 1954); Samuel Beer, "In Search of A New Public Philosophy,'' in *The New American Political System,* ed. Anthony King (Washington, D.C.: American Enterprise Institute, 1979); James Ceaser "The Theory of Governance of the Reagan Administration,'' in *The Reagan Presidency and the Governing of America,* eds. Lester M. Salamon and Michael S. Lund (Washington, D.C.: American Enterprise Institute, 1981); and Forcey, *The Crossroads of Liberalism,* XIV.

98. *New York Times Magazine,* February 23, 1936, **3.**

99. "Republican Platform for 1936.'' In Johnson, *National Party Platforms,* 365. It was Hoover, rather than the Republican presidential nominee, Alfred Landon, Governor of Kansas, who formulated the Republican case against the New Deal. Landon, who had bolted the party in 1912 to support the Bull Moosers, represented a much less fundamental challenge to New Deal principles and policies. Ronald D. Rotunda, "The Liberal Label: Roosevelt's Capture of A Symbol,'' in *Public Policy,* eds. John D. Montgomery and Albert O. Hirschman (Cambridge: Harvard University Press), Vol. 17 (1968), 399.

100. John Dewey, "A Liberal Speaks Out,'' *New York Times Magazine,* February 23, 1936, **3,** 24; and Rotunda, "The Liberal Label: Roosevelt's Capture of A Symbol,'' 398–401.

101. The election of Roosevelt and the coming of the New Deal did not change Dewey's conviction that a new party was needed. Without the "formation of a strong united radical new party,'' he believed, liberal reform would always be a "half-way house'' in the nation's endeavor to build a more just and democratic social order. Advocating a socially controlled and planned economy like that supported by the more radical parties in England and the continent, Dewey voted for the Socialist candidate, Norman Thomas, in the presidential elections of 1936 and 1940. See George Dykluizen, *The Life and Mind of John Dewey* (Carbondale and Edwardsville: Southern Illinois University Press, 1973), 253–54.

102. As R. Shep Melnick has observed: "The 'rights revolution' refers to the tendency to define nearly every public issue in terms of legally protected rights of individuals. Rights of the handicapped, rights of workers, rights of students, rights of racial minorities, rights of women, rights of consumers, the right to a hearing, the right to know—they have become the stock and trade of political discourse.'' See his "The Courts, Congress, and Programmatic Rights,'' in *Remaking American Politics,* eds. Richard A. Harris and Sidney M. Milkis, (Boulder, Colorado: Westview Press, 1989), 188.

103. Roosevelt, *Public Papers and Addresses,* **6:**3.

104. The term *Third New Deal* has been coined by Karl to represent the period from 1937 to 1939 when Roosevelt pursued measures that intended to establish a rational system of administrative government, thus representing a revolutionary attempt to create and legitimate the kind of institutions that the anti-bureaucratic tradition in the United States had long taught Americans to fear and shun. See Karl, *The Uneasy State,* 149–81; and Karl, "Constitution and Central Planning: The Third New Deal Revisited.'' I have found evi-

dence in the file of the Franklin D. Roosevelt Library that the label *Third New Deal* was applied to Roosevelt's institutional measures of the second term as early as August, 1937. See Alexander Sachs to Foxy and Co., August 17, 1937, *Alexander Sachs Papers,* Box 107, Folder: "Government, General—Philosophies." I agree with Karl that the Third New Deal represents a radical and far-reaching challenge to the American concept of democracy. But I do not believe that FDR sought to create a rational, European style state bureaucratic apparatus, nor do I think the accomplishments of the second term fell as short as Karl seems to believe. In this program, as with his reform aspirations generally, FDR intended to fashion a form of administrative politics that was sui-generis American. Roosevelt wanted to remake American politics, but by circumventing, rather than challenging directly, its fundamental principles. For more on this point, see Chapter 5.

105. Roosevelt, *Looking Forward,* 11.

Chapter 3

1. Stanley High, "Whose Party Is It?" *Saturday Evening Post,* February 6, 1937, 10–11, 34, 37.

2. *New York Times,* February 5, 1937, 1.

3. Diary Notations, February 9, 1937, *Stanley High Papers,* Franklin D. Roosevelt Library, Hyde Park, New York.

4. Roosevelt's experiences with the Democratic party during the 1920s were significant in shaping the ambivalence he felt with respect to party leadership. He witnessed the tragic end of Wilson's presidency as a member of that administration's cabinet, and as a prominent figure in the party councils during the 1920s, he had the misfortune to observe closely the consequences that followed from Wilson's failure to reform the Democratic party. Roosevelt was the party's vice-presidential candidate in 1920, a disastrous defeat for the Democrats that signalled the restoration of Repblican dominance over the country and a "return to normalcy." Four years later, FDR's "Happy Warrior" speech, placing Al Smith's name in nomination, was the only bright spot of a disastrous convention, in which a deadlock between Smith and California's William Gibbs McAdoo dragged on for 103 ballots before a compromise candidate, John W. Davis, was finally nominated.

The experiences of the Democratic party during the 1920s, Roosevelt believed, were dramatic evidence that the party needed to be thoroughly renovated. The initial results to strengthen the party were not encouraging, however. FDR's short-lived campaign to reorganize the Democratic part as a national instrument of progressive reform after the 1924 election summoned up the continuing internal discord over the principles of the party, dissention that sustained the Democratic commitment to organizationl decentralization. Having failed to overcome these centrifugal tendencies, FDR despaired of the prospects for party renewal. "We have no leaders in a national sense at all," he concluded; it was an "unspeakable groping about in the darkness." James McGregor Burns, *Roosevelt: The Lion and the Fox, 1882–1940* (New York: Harcourt, Brace and World, 1956), 95. Roosevelt's party-building efforts did not go for naught, however. They helped build a network of support for his successful campaigns for governor and president. See Sean Savage, *Roosevelt: The Party Leader, 1932–1945* (Lexington: University Press of Kentucky, 1991), especially Chapter 1.

5. See, for example, Joseph Alsop and Robert Kintner, "We Shall Make America Over," *Saturday Evening Post,* November 19, 1938, 91.

6. Rexford Tugwell, *The Brains Trust* (New York: The Viking Press, 1968), 261.

7. FDR also wanted to demonstrate dramatically that his physical disability (the po-liomyelitis he contracted the year after the 1920 campaign) would not hinder him as a candidate or as a president. The difficult flight FDR experienced in the small plane he hired to take him to Chicago added to the drama of his precedent-shattering appearance before the Democratic delegates. "The Convention rose enthusiastically to the voyager of the skies," marvelled one reporter, "and accepted his method of travel and the fact that he endured the rigors so well as a proof of his venturesome spirit and fine physical equipment for the office of the President of the United States." *New York Times,* July 3, 1932, 1.

8. Franklin D. Roosevelt, *Public Papers and Addresses,* 13 volumes (New York: Random House, 1938–1950), Vol. 1, 647–48.

9. Josephus Daniels to FDR, December 15, 1932, Ray Stannard Baker Collection, Franklin D. Roosevelt File, Princeton University Library. This letter and Wilson's patronage practices are discussed in Chapter 2.

10. FDR to Baker, December 21, 1932; and Baker to FDR, December 28, 1932, President's Personal File, Franklin D. Roosevelt Library.

11. Personal and Political Diary of Homer Cummings, January 5, 1933, Box 234, Number 2, p. 90, *Homer Cummings Papers* (#9973), Manuscripts Department, University of Virginia Library, Charlottesville, Virginia.

12. Cited in Paul Van Riper, *History of the United States Civil Service* (Evanston, Illinois: Row, Peterson, 1958), 318.

13. Ibid., 320.

14. The materials in Farley's papers, located in the manuscript division of the Library of Congress, note with barely concealed delight the interest of Roosevelt and his advisors in patronage practices. Even Eleanor Roosevelt, long credited with elevating the moral tone and social conscience of the Administration, involved herself in the details of federal pap. "Have we a Democratic postmaster appointed at Newbury, South Carolina?" she inquired of Farley in August, 1934. "A distant cousin has turned up." An attached memo, written by Farley, noted dryly that "Mrs. Roosevelt was not bashful about asking to have a relative placed in the position." Farley to Eleanor Roosevelt, and attached memorandum, August 28, 1934, Folder: Eleanor Roosevelt, 1934–1936, *James Farley Papers,* Manuscripts Division, Library of Congress. In actuality, as noted in Chapter 6, Mrs. Roosevelt's support of and interest in patronage went beyond family ties. During the second term, she would become an important representative to the President for DNC chairs Farley and Ed Flynn in their struggles to wrest control of the appoinment process from the newly created executive office.

15. Riper, *History of the United States Civil Service,* 320.

16. *New York Times,* February 25, 1936, 2; see also, Memorandum: FDR to Farley, February 14, 1936, and attached; and Marvin McIntyre to James Farley, February 25, 1936, and attached, *Farley Papers,* Box 35, Folder: 1936, January to March. Roosevelt persuaded Murphy to enter the 1936 Democratic gubernatorial primary against the regular organization candidate Lieutenant Governor George W. Welsh. Murphy defeated Welsh by a two to one margin in the primary, and won the general election by a close margin as a result of the Roosevelt landslide. Lacking much in the way of organization support, Murphy would fail in his re-election bid of 1938, but his short tenure as governor was important—through his sympathetic attitude towards unions and the sit-down strikes of 1937, which became a national issue during his tenure, Murphy played an instrumental part

in the victory that the C.I.O. finally won over the auto industry. Moreover, Murphy played a helpful part in associating the New Deal with pro-labor policies, thus vitally contributing to the long-term political strength of the national Democratic party. See John H. Fenton, *Midwest Politics* (New York: Holt, Rinehart and Winston, 1966), Chapter 2.

17. Responding to Raymond Moley's letter of September 26, 1933, averring the need for FDR to look beyond the traditional basis of Democratic support, Ickes wrote, "You give expression to a very firm belief that I have all along entertained, namely, that there be an amalgamation of the Republican–Progressives with the Democratic party, if the latter is to continue as a majority party in the years immediately ahead of us. So firmly am I convinced of this that I cannot understand the political short-sightedness of certain Democratic leaders who resent any recognition of the Republican–Progressives." Harold Ickes to Raymond Moley, October 2, 1933, *Harold Ickes Papers,* Box 227, Folder: Political (3), Manuscript Division, Library of Congress.

18. Memorandum, FDR to Farley, April 24, 1939, *Farley Papers,* Box 36, Folder: 1939, January to June. For an excellent treatment of the Farmer–Labor Party and the New Deal, see Richard M. Valelly, *Radicalism in the States: The Minnesota Farmer–Labor Party and the American Political Economy* (Chicago and London: University of Chicago Press, 1989).

19. Van Riper, *History of the United States Civil Service,* 329.

20. "I think they're much more sensible about politics than we are," FDR is reported to have observed about the British system of government. "Clear down the line, there's a respectability attached to politics in Great Britain that isn't found here." Diary Notations, *Stanley High Papers,* October 28, 1936, Franklin D. Roosevelt Library, Hyde Park, New York.

21. As Ed Flynn, who became Democratic chairman in 1940, wrote in his memoirs with respect to the growing tension between Roosevelt and Farley, "Under the leadership of Corcoran, [the so-called New Dealers] became more and more pressing in their urging of appointments. In an sense, this short-circuited the National Committee over which Farley presided. As a result, many of the appointments in Washington went to men who were supporters of the President and believed in what he was trying to do, but who were not Democrats in many instances, and in all instances were not organization Democrats." Edward J. Flynn, *You're the Boss* (New York: Viking Press, 1947), 153.

22. Van Riper, *History of the United States Civil Service,* 327.

23. John Franklin Carter, *1940* (New York: The Viking Press, 1940), 31–32.

24. Franklin D. Roosevelt, *On Our Way* (New York: The John Day Company, 1934), 248; see also, Van Riper, *History of the United States Civil Service,* 328–29.

25. Berle to FDR, September 2, 1937, Box 10, Folder: Franklin D. Roosevelt, *Adolf Berle Papers,* Roosevelt Library; see also Jordan A. Schwarz, *Liberal: Adolf A. Berle and the Vision of An American Era* (New York: The Free Press, 1937), 91–103. Berle and La Guardia were instrumental in forming the American Labor Party (ALP) in 1936, thereby giving Roosevelt two places on the New York ballot that year and, more important, providing a political home for progressives who believed that party lines had no place in progressive government. La Guardia and Berle used the political vehicle they helped create in 1936 virtually to compel the Republicans to renominate La Guardia for mayor. La Guardia was put on the GOP ticket after Berle got the ALP leaders to agree not to endorse any Republican if the Republicans did not renominate La Guardia. With ALP aid, La Guardia handily defeated the Democratic candidate.

26. David Lilienthal, *TVA: Democracy on the March* (New York: Harper and Row, 1953), 179.

27. Roosevelt, *Public Papers and Addresses,* Vol. 5, 184.

28. Joseph Alsop and Robert Kintner, *Men Around the President* (New York: Doubleday, Doran, 1939), 10.

29. "His Excellency's Loyal Opposition," *Fortune,* February 1937, 70.

30. For a primary account of Roosevelt's treatment of Congress that compares his party leadership to Woodrow Wilson's, see Lindsay Rogers, "Reorganization: Post-Mortem Notes," *Political Science Quarterly,* Vol. 53 (June, 1938): 161–72.

31. Van Riper, *History of the United States Civil Service,* 325.

32. Rogers, "Reorganization: Post-Mortem Notes," 170.

33. Pettengill to McIntyre, February 24, 1934, President's Official File 299 (Democratic Party), *Roosevelt Papers* (Pettengill's emphasis).

34. Phillips to FDR, June 9, 1937, President's Personal File 2666, *Roosevelt Papers.*

35. FDR to Phillips, June 16, 1937, ibid.

36. High, "Whose Party Is It?," 34.

37. Alsop and Kintner, *Men Around the President,* 5–11.

38. James A. Farley, *Jim Farley's Story* (New York: McGraw–Hill, 1948), 146–47.

39. Anne O'Hare McCormick, "As He Sees Himself," *New York Times Magazine,* October 16, 1938, 3.

40. Roosevelt, *Public Papers and Addresses,* Vol. 6, 2.

41. Joseph Alsop and Robert Kintner, "The Guffey—Biography of a Boss," *Saturday Evening Post,* March 26, 1938, 5–7, 98–102; and Nancy J. Weiss, *Fairwell to the Party of Lincoln: Black Politics in the Age of FDR* (Princeton, New Jersey: Princeton University Press, 1983), 14–15.

42. John B. Kirby, *Black Americans in the Roosevelt Era: Liberalism and Race* (Knoxville: The University of Tennessee Press, 1980), 132–39.

43. Weiss, *Fairwell to the Party of Lincoln,* 95.

44. Ibid., 43–44.

45. Robert C. Weaver and Charlotte Morton Hubbard, "The Black Cabinet," in *The Making of the New Deal: The Insiders Speak,* ed. Katie Louchheim (Cambridge: Harvard University Press, 1983), 262.

46. Dewson, as cited in Susan Ware, *Partner and I: Molly Dewson, Feminism, and New Deal Politics* (New Haven: Yale University Press, 1987), 184; Ware provides a thorough treatment of Dewson's party activities in chapters 11–13.

47. Dewson to Farley, June 17, 1938, *Molly Dewson Papers,* Box 2, Folder: James A. Farley, Franklin D. Roosevelt Library.

48. Ware, *Partner and I,* 198.

49. Dewson to Farley, June 17, 1938, *Dewson Papers,* Box 2, Folder: James A. Farley.

50. Dewson to FDR, December 15, 1934, *Dewson Papers,* Box 4, Folder: Franklin D. Roosevelt.

51. Farley as cited in Ware, *Parner and I,* 200.

52. Dewson to FDR, December 15, 1934, *Dewson Papers,* Box 4, Folder: Franklin D. Roosevelt.

53. Samuel Lubell, *The Future of American Politics,* 3rd edition (New York: Harper and Row, 1965), 56–57.

54. Hillman as cited in Mathew Josephson, *Sidney Hillman: Statesman of American Labor* (Garden City, New York: Doubleday, 1952), 398.

55. Ibid., 399.

56. Tobin to FDR, and attached report to James Farley, December 30, 1936, President's Personal File 1180, *Roosevelt Papers;* see also Tobin to Marvin McIntyre, November 9, 1936, and attached editorial for the December issue of the Teamsters and Chauffers Journal, President's Personal File 4046, *Roosevelt Papers.*

57. Tobin's "balanced" view of Labor's role in partisan politics was revealed in his union activities as well. For example, at a Teamster's Convention of September 9, 1935, he successfully led the fight to defeat a resolution that would have prevented the Executive Board of the Teamsters from making contributions to partisan political campaigns. While defending the principal that American Labor get more involved in partisan politics, however, he was careful to point out, "Don't misunderstand me, I am. not in favor now of the establishment of a Labor Party, but it may come to that. I have been opposed to it in every convention and gathering for the last thirty five years." "Report of the Committee on Resolutions," President's Personal File 1189, *Roosevelt Papers.*

58. V. O. Key, Jr., *Politics, Parties, and Pressure Groups* (New York: Thomas Y. Crowell, 1948), 464.

59. Louise Overacker, "Labor's Poltical Contributions," *Political Science Quarterly* **54** (1) (1939), 59. The figures listed in the text come from this article by Overacker and another by the same author, which provides a detailed analysis of the campaign funds of 1936; see Overacker, "Campaign Funds in the Presidential Election of 1936," *American Political Science Review* **31** (June, 1937): 473–98.

60. Overacker, "Campaign Funds in the Presidential Election of 1936," 488–89. Thomas Ferguson argues that Roosevelt and the Democratic party developed ties with financiers and industry, especially capital-intensive firms, that favored free trade policies and were not opposed to, if not strongly in favor of, moderate labor reform. See, for example, Ferguson, "Industrial Conflict and Coming of the New Deal: The Triumph of Multinational Liberalism in America," *The Rise and Fall of the New Deal Order,* eds. Steve Fraser and Gary Gerstle, (Princeton, New Jersey: Princeton University Press, 1989). Ferguson's work is interesting evidence that business was hardly unified in its opposition to the New Deal. It is less persuasive in its argument, or implication, that this "new historic bloc" of capital-intensive industries, investment banks, and internationally oriented commerical banks dominated—or formed the "center"—of the New Deal coaltion. Considerable evidence points to the ability of the Roosevelt administration to put the Democratic party upon a broad foundation of campaign finance during the 1930s, with the largest gains made among labor and small contributors. Interestingly, one of the most prominent actors in recruiting business support for the New Deal, the Massachusetts retail merchant Edward A. Filene, had a difficult time gaining any sort of audience with the President during the 1936 campaign. "May I say that I have been sending you a number of things within the past few weeks, all of which have a definite bearing on helping the re-election of the President, which re-election I consider by far the most important matter before us all today," Filene wrote FDR's secretary, Marvin McIntyre in May, 1936. "In return for these I have received the same stereotype form letter signed by you, which makes me fear that what I am

sending you does not appeal to you as being important enough to reach the President—at least in a way that will lead him to take the time to look these matters over." McIntyre's response was polite but hardly repentent. "I have shown this last letter of yours to me to the President," he wrote on June 2, "and he asks me to . . . express his appreciation for your continued interest and worth-while contributions." Filene to McIntyre, May 25, 1936; and McIntyre to Filene, June 2, 1936. President's Personal File 2116, *Roosevelt Papers.*

61. For an enlightening discussion of Roosevelt's 1936 campaign along the lines considered here, see Marc Landy, "Party Leadership and Party Realignment: Forging the New Deal Democratic Party." Paper presented at the Annual Meeting of the American Political Science Association, Washington, D.C., August 31, 1984.

62. A lengthy primary account of the debate over the two-thirds rule as it took shape during the 1930s is provided by Frank Clarkin, "Two-Thirds Rule Facing Abolition," *New York Times,* January 5, 1936, Section IV, 10.

63. For a report of the 1932 events, see Farley, *Behind the Ballots,* 116–24. The following discussion of the two-thirds rule controversy has been informed by the excellent account of this battle provided by Hal Bass, "Presidential Party Leadership and Party Reform: Franklin D. Roosevelt and the Abrogation of the Two-Thirds Rule." Paper presented at the 1985 Annual Meeting of the Southern Political Science Association, November 7–9, Nashville, Tennessee.

64. *New York Times,* January 19, 1936.

65. The transcript of the press conference reads as follows:
The President: I think it was recommended. I have forgotten the exact language.
Question: You think it will be abrogated?
The President: Oh, I think so. I don't know why we should be tied up as we have in the past. We all have recollections of 1924, 1920, and so on. They do not help in a political party.
Press Conference #290, April 28, 1936, vol. 7, 221, Franklin D. Roosevelt Library.

66. *New York Times,* April 29, 1936, 2.

67. Farley to FDR, December 5, 1935, President's Secretary File 87 (Post Office), *Roosevelt Papers.*

68. "Two Political 'Pros' Analyze Their Art," *New York Times Magazine,* August 10, 1958, 28.

69. James F. Byrnes, *All In One Lifetime* (New York: Harper and Brothers, 1958), 95.

70. *New York Times,* June 26, 1936, **1,** 14. As Bass has observed, "even this change worked to exacerbate the deteriorating status of southern influence within the party. Rising Democratic vote totals outside the south combined with waning southern electoral support for the party ticket diminished the proportion of convention delegates coming from Dixie." Bass, "Presidential Party Leadership and Party Reform . . . ," 24.

71. *New York Times,* May 12, 1936, 22.

72. Diary Notations, January 1, 1937. *Stanley High Papers.*

73. *Washington Star* editorial, printed in *New York Times,* May 3, 1936, Section IV, 8.

74. Bailey to R. R. King, August 10, 1936, *Josiah Bailey Papers,* Senatorial Series, Political National Papers, Box 475, Manuscript Department, William R. Perkins Library, Duke University, Durham, North Carolina.

75. This is Rosenman's description. See Rosenman, *Working With Roosevelt* (New York: Harper, 1952), 105.

76. Roosevelt, *Public Papers and Addresses,* Vol. 5, 234.

77. As Roosevelt wrote in a letter to Felix Franfurter in early 1937: "The return of prosperity might blunt our senses but under it all I am certain that the maintenance of constitutional government in this nation still depends upon action—but it is the same old story of those who have property to fail to realize that I am the best friend the profit system ever had, even though I add my denunciation of unconscionable profits." Roosevelt to Frankfurter, February 9, 1937, *Felix Frankfurter Papers,* Microfilm Reel 60, Manuscript Department, Library of Congress, Washington, D.C.

78. Roosevelt, *Public Papers and Addresses,* Vol. 5, 234.

79. Memorandum, Stanley High to Stephen Early, December 22, 1935, *Farley Papers,* Box 35, Folder: Franklin D. Roosevelt, 1935 (October to December). Obviously, High meant to refer to the Commonwealth Club address, the New Deal manifesto pronounced during the 1932 campaign. This speech and its connection to the 1936 campaign are discussed at length in Chapter 2.

80. Roosevelt, *Public Papers and Addresses,* Vol. 5, 234.

81. Landy, "Party Leadership and Party Realignment," 15.

82. Roosevelt, *Public Papers and Addresses,* Vol. 5, 235.

83. Frankfurter to FDR, July 11, 1936, *Frankfurter Papers,* Microfilm Reel 60.

Chapter 4

1. Anne O'Hare McCormick, "Next Four Years," *New York Times Magazine,* November 8, 1936, 26.

2. Turner Catledge, "Huge Majority Means Threat of Bloc Tactics," *New York Times Magazine,* November 8, 1936, 4.

3. The "solid South" enabled Democrats from below the Mason–Dixon line to benfit disproportionately from the seniority rule—many Southerners as a result held key congressional committee positions. Moreover, the South was important to party finances, owing to the effectiveness of Farley's organization there. In 1936, more than 37% of all Democratic contributions of $100 or more came from the South. See Louise Overacker, "Campaign Funds in the Presidential Election of 1936," *American Political Science Review* **31** (1937), 496.

4. Ralph M. Goldman, *Search For Consensus: The Story of the Democratic Party* (Philadelphia, PA: Temple University Press, 1979), 326.

5. High to Early, December 22, 1935, *James Farley Papers,* Box 35, Folder: Franklin D. Roosevelt, 1935 (Oct. to Dec.), Manuscript Division, Library of Congress.

6. On November 20, Franklin Brooks, the Ohio state chair of the Republicans for Roosevelt League, wrote the President urging the formation of "a national organization known as the Roosevelt Republicans headed by prominent Republicans in every State of the Union working for a Roosevelt Republican Committee in Washington." Six days later, FDR wrote a memo to Farley stating "I honestly believe there is a good deal of value in this idea of organizing 'Roosevelt Republicans' in every community. Will you talk to me about it?" Brooks to FDR, November 20, 1935; and FDR to Farley, November 26, 1935, *James Farley Papers,* Box 34, Folder: Franklin D. Roosevelt, 1934.

7. Arthur Schlesinger, Jr., *The Age of Roosevelt: The Politics of Upheaval* (Boston: Houghton, Mifflin, 1960), 592.

8. Donald R. McCoy, "The Good Neighbor League and the Presidential Campaign of 1936," *Western Political Quarterly* **13** (December, 1960): 1011–21. The Good Neighbor League argued the case for the New Deal to religious groups, especially those with close ties to the black community.

9. The activities of Women's National Democratic Club were organized by Emma Guffey Miller. It served Miller's objective of challenging Molly Dewson's leadership of the Women's Division, which she considered too timid in its support of women's issues and controversal New Deal measures. See Susan Ware, *Partner and I: Molly Dewson, Feminism, and New Deal Politics* (New Haven: Yale University Press, 1987), 230–32; and Ware, *Beyond Suffrage: Women in the New Deal* (Cambridge: Harvard Universrity Press, 1981), 77, 79–80.

10. This analogy was suggested to me by Professor Richard Harris of Rutgers University.

11. Joseph Alsop and Robert Kintner, *Men Around the President* (New York: Doubleday, Moran and Company, 1939), 183.

12. See Lewis's letter to North Carolina Senator Josiah Bailey of July 13, 1934, which reveals the President's interest in supporting Republican Progressives against more conservative Democratic candidates. Lewis to Bailey, July 13, 1934, *Josiah Bailey Papers,* Senatorial Series, Political National Papers, Box 474, William R. Perkins Library, Duke University, Durham, North Carolina. See also Lewis' letter to FDR's secretary, Stephen Early, indicating his intention to go along with the President. Lewis to Early, October 10, 1934, *Official File* 300 (Democratic National Committee), *Franklin D. Roosevelt Papers,* Franklin D. Roosevelt Library, Hyde Park, New York.

13. FDR to Pittman, August 25, 1934, President's Personal File 65, *Roosevelt Papers.*

14. Stanley High, Diary Notations, October 28, 1936, *Stanley High Papers,* Roosevelt Library.

15. A. L. Meir to FDR, January 22, 1938, President's Personal File 4658, *Roosevelt Papers.*

16. Roosevelt, *Public Papers and Addresses,* Vol. 5, 331–32. For evidence of Corcoran's efforts to raise money for Norris, see Corcoran to John Robertson (Secretary to Senator Norris), August 15, 1936; and Corcoran to Blackwell Smith, October 15, 1936, *Thomas Corcoran Papers,* Box 247, Folder: George W. Norris, Manuscript Division, Library of Congress.

17. Eleanor Roosevelt to Franklin D. Roosevelt, July 17, 1936; and Franklin D. Roosevelt to Eleanor Roosevelt, July 19, 1936, President's Personal File 2, *Roosevelt Papers.*

18. Maverick to Robert Allen, July 6, 1936, cited in Stuart L. Weiss, "Maury Maverick and the Liberal Bloc," *Journal of American History* **57** (1970–1971), 890.

19. FDR to Maverick, August 5, 1936, President's Personal File 3446, *Roosevelt Papers.*

20. For a solid historical account of the conservative coalition, see James Patterson, *Congressional Conservativism and the New Deal* (Lexington: University of Kentucky Press, 1967).

21. Bailey to J. E. S. Thorpe, November 13, 1936, *Bailey Papers,* Box 475, Folder: 1936 (Oct. to Dec.).

22. Bailey wrote, "You cannot win a battle in America with such organizations as the Liberty League justifying Mr. Roosevelt's proclamation that he was doing battle with economic royalists," ibid. The Liberty League was not completely composed of rich industrialists; for example, it included Al Smith among its ranks. But, although its uncompromising support for individualism and industrial America might have elicited greater response in good times, during a time of severe economic collapse the defense of economic freedom sounded hollow. For a primary report on Smith's role in the Liberty League, see *New York Times*, January 26, 1937, Section 1, 37. An analysis of the philosophy of the League and its place in the American political tradition is given in Frederick Rudolf, "The American Liberty League, 1934–1940," *American Historical Review* (October, 1950): 19–33.

23. Bailey to Thorpe, November 13, 1936, as cited in no. 21.

24. *New York Times*, December 16, 1937, 1.

25. Personal and Political Diary of Homer Cummings, August 1, 1937, Box 235, Number 9, 119, *Homer Cummings Papers* (#9973), Manuscript Department, Alderman Library, University of Virginia, Charlottesville, Virginia.

26. Thomas Stokes, "Garner Turns on FDR," *Nation*, June 10, 1937, 723; see also Robert S. Allen, "The New Deal Fights For Its Life," *Nation*, July 10, 1937, 35–36, which depicts Garner as "burying the knife deep in the programs of the New Deal."

27. Henry Morgenthau, Jr., Diaries, May 17, 1937, Vol. 68, 235, Roosevelt Library.

28. For an account of the majority leader fight, see James Farley, *Jim Farley's Story* (New York: McGraw–Hill, 1948), 91–92; James F. Byrnes, *All in One Lifetime* (New York: Harper and Brothers, 1958), 98–100; and Homer Cummings Diary, July 21, 1937, Box 237, Number 7, 97.

29. Roosevelt, *The Public Papers and Addresses of Franklin D. Roosevelt*, 13 volumes (New York: Macmillan, 1938–1950), Vol. 6, 331.

30. Bailey to S. Clay Williams, August 25, 1937, *Bailey Papers*, Box 475, Folder: 1937, August through December.

31. Roosevelt, *Public Papers and Addresses*, Vol. 6, 333.

32. Roosevelt, *Public Papers and Addresses*, Vol. 3, 14.

33. *New York Times*, August 18, 1937, as cited in Paul H. Douglas and Joseph Hackman, "The Fair Labor Standards Act of 1938," *Political Science Quarterly* **43** (4) (1938), 507.

34. *New York Times*, August 20, 1937, 9.

35. *New York Times*, August 21, 1937, 1, 4.

36. Paul H. Douglas and Joseph Hackman, "The Fair Labor Standards Act of 1938," 512.

37. Richard L. Neuberger to Harold Ickes, April 24, 1938; Ickes to Neuberger, April 29, 1938; and Ickes to Hess, May 14, 1938, *Harold Ickes Papers*, Box 231, Folder: Political (33). A draft of Ickes's letter was found in Corcoran's papers, suggesting that he, and perhaps Benjamin Cohen, had collaborated with the Secretary of Interior in formulating an endorsement for State Senator Hess; see Ickes to Hess, draft letter (no date), *Corcoran Papers*, Box 201, Folder: Harold L. Ickes.

38. Roosevelt, *Public Papers and Addresses*, Vol. 7, 398–99.

39. Farley, *Jim Farley's Story*, 120–50.

40. Joseph Lash, *The Dealers and the Dreamers: A New Look at the New Deal* (New

York: Doubleday, 1988), 353. Former NRA director, General Hugh Johnson dubbed the members of the purge committee "White House Janizaries." Janizaries were soldiers (at first mostly castrated personal slaves, later conscripts and sons of subject Christians) of the Turkish Sultans from the fourteenth to the nineteenth Centuries, who became so potent that, when they revolted in 1826, thousands of them had to be killed, the rest dispersed, their organization abolished. By this appellation, Johnson meant to imply, not without cause, that the purge committee was composed of an inner circle of political eunuchs who were seeking to affect party politics. *Time,* September 12, 1938, 22.

41. Raymond Clapper, "Roosevelt Tries the Primaries," *Current History,* October, 1938, 17.

42. William H. Meier to James Farley, December 23, 1938, Official File 300 (Democratic National Committee), *Roosevelt Papers.*

43. Thomas Stokes, *Chip Off My Shoulder* (Princeton, New Jersey: Princeton University Press, 1940), 503.

44. Charles M. Price and Joseph Boskin, "The Roosevelt Purge: A Reappraisal," *Journal of Politics* **28** (3) (August, 1966): 660–70.

45. On the Connecticut situation, see Cummings to FDR, September 20, 1938, *Cummings Papers,* Box 170; and Arch McNeil to FDR, August 12, 1938, Official File 300 (Democratic National Committee), *Roosevelt Papers*; Ickes to FDR, September 5, 1938, and attached letter from Thomas B. McDermott, *Ickes Papers,* Box 232, Folder: Political (35); and Corcoran to Ickes, June 26, 1938, *Corcoran Papers,* Box 201, Folder: Harold L. Ickes. In addition, Homer Cummings's diary entries have considerable information on the Roosevelt administration's deliberations about what course to take in Connecticut; see especially the entries between July 18 and September 6, 1938, Personal and Political Diary of Homer Cummings, Number 8, 105–19.

46. Koppleman to Farley, November 29, 1938, President's Official File 300 (Democratic National Committee), *Roosevelt Papers.*

47. Alan Michie and Frank Ryhlick, *Dixie Demagogues* (New York: Vanguard Press, 1939), 193.

48. Roosevelt, *Public Papers and Addresses,* Vol. 7, 466.

49. Ibid., 466.

50. Ibid., 466–67.

51. Roosevelt, *Public Papers and Addresses,* Vol. 7, 164–69.

52. When asked whether he thought the solid South would stay Democratic very long, FDR replied: "I think the South is going to remain Democratic, but I think it is going to be a more intelligent form of democracy than has kept the South, for other reasons, in the democratic column all these years. It will be intelligent thinking and, in my judgment, because the South is learning, it is going to be a liberal democracy." *Complete Presidential Press Conferences of Franklin D. Roosevelt* (New York: Da Capo Press, 1972), April 21, 1938, Number 452-B, Volume 11, 338–40.

53. Memorandum, Walter White to FDR, January 2, 1936, *Corcoran Papers,* Box 257, Folder: Negro Matters, 1936–1939; *Time,* September 9, 1938, 12.

54. FDR as cited in Nancy Weiss, *Farewell to the Party of Lincoln: Black Politics in the Age of FDR* (Princeton, New Jersey: Princeton University Press, 1983), 14–15.

55. Claude Dewson Pepper and Hays Gorey, *Pepper: Eyewitness to a Century* (San Diego, California: Harcourt, Brace Jovanovich, 1987), 65.

56. On the same day that FDR endorsed Lawrence Camp in Barnesville, he spoke explicitly about Southern conditions and the prospects for a new South at the University of Georgia. "The South was building a new school of thought," the President said, "a group principally recruited from young men and women who understood the economy of the South was vitally and inexorably linked with the Nation, and that the national good was equally dependent on the improvememnt of the welfare of the South." Roosevelt, *Public Papers and Addresses,* Vol. 7, 472. Ten days prior to this dramatic tour of Georgia, Corcoran assured FDR that "the report of the National Emergency Council on Southern economic conditions will be released on Monday, so that it will be in the Southern newspapers before you speak at Athens." Memorandum, Corcoran to FDR, August 1, 1938, *Corcoran Papers,* Box 210, Folder: Franklin D. Roosevelt, 1938–1939.

57. Glass to Jack Dionne, October 17, 1938, *Carter Glass Papers,* Accession Number 2913, Box 383, University of Virginia Library. Senator Josiah Bailey of North Carolina, who had fretted over the possibility of a New Deal assault on the South since the two-thirds rule was abolished, warned James Farley that the purge would destroy the Democratic party below the Mason–Dixon Line. "[T]here will always be a white man's party in the South and I am hoping the Democratic party will always be the white man's party of the South," he wrote. "Should the Democratic party fail to take this course, you may rest assured that a white man's party will arise in the South and take this course and it would prevail." Bailey to Farley, October 3, 1938, *Bailey Papers,* Box 476.

58. *New York Times,* September 16, 1938, 8.

59. Michie and Ryhlick, *Dixie Demagogues,* 266.

60. *Time,* September, 19, 1938, 12.

61. *New York Times,* June 25, 1936, 12.

62. *New York Times,* June 26, 1936, 12.

63. Smith as cited in Michie and Ryhlick, *Dixie Demagogues,* 280–81.

64. Ibid., 277.

65. *Time,* September 12, 1938, 26.

66. Ibid.

67. As one irate Georgian wrote in a letter to FDR's secretary Marvin McIntyre: ". . . the rebel yell is sounding again from the Sea Islands to the Alabama line. Edith Moses to McIntyre, no date (Georgia folder, 1938), President's Official File 300 (Democratic National Committee), *Roosevelt Papers.*

68. *Time,* September 12, 1938, 21.

69. Paul Van Riper, *History of the United States Civil Service* (Evanston, IL: Row, Peterson, 1958), 327.

70. Frank Freidel, *Franklin D. Roosevelt: A Rendezvous With Destiny* (Boston: Little, Brown, 1990), 287.

71. On the use of federal employees in the 1938 primaries, see Special Committee to Investigate Senatorial Campaign Expenditures and the Use of Governmental Funds of 1938, *Investigation of Senatorial Campaign Expenditures,* Senate Report, 76th Congress, 1st Session, number 10288; see also John Edward Hopper, *The Purge: Franklin D. Roosevelt and the 1938 Democratic Nominations,* unpublished Ph.D. thesis, University of Chicago, 1966, 107.

72. Albert Jay Nock, "WPA, the Modern Tammany," *American Mercury* **65** (179) (October, 1938): 215–19.

73. *New York Times,* May 8, 1938, Section 4, 2.

74. *Newsweek,* August 15, 1938, 9–10.

75. Schattschneider, *Party Government,* 167.

76. Roosevelt, *Public Papers and Addresses,* Vol. 7, xxviii, xxxii.

77. Stokes, *Chip Off My Shoulder,* 503.

78. O'Connor was one of the few Northern Democrats to oppose the abrogation of the two-thirds rule; see *New York Times,* June 26, 1936, 1. His alliance with Southern conservatives continued during the tempestuous 75th Congress. On the role he played in blocking the wage-hours legislation, see Stokes, *Chip Off My Shoulder,* 504–5.

79. *Time,* October 3, 1938, 9.

80. Freidel, *Franklin D. Roosevelt: Rendevous With Destiny,* 286.

81. Schattschneider, *Party Government,* 163–69; see also Hopper, *The Purge: Franklin D. Roosevelt and the 1938 Democratic Nominations,* 220–21.

82. On the Oregon events, see the exchange of letters between Ickes and the Managing Editor of the *Journal,* a Portland newspaper. Donald J. Sterling to Ickes, December 2, 1938; and Ickes to Sterling, December 7, 1938, *Ickes Papers,* Box 232, Folder: Political (35).

83. E. Pendleton Herring, *The Politics of Democracy* (New York: W. W. Norton, 1940), 222.

84. Farley, *Jim Farley's Story,* 146.

85. Meeks to Farley, February 9, 1939, President's Official File 300 (Democratic National Committee), *Roosevelt Papers.*

86. Philip F. LaFollette, Elmer Bensen, and Frank Murphy, "Why We Lost," *The Nation,* December 3, 1938, 587.

87. FDR to Daniels, November 14, 1938, reprinted in *FDR: His Personal Letters, 1928–1948,* 2 volumes (New York: Duell, Sloan, and Pearce, 1950), Vol. 2, 827 (Roosevelt's emphasis).

88. Ickes to Michael L. Igoe, n.d., *Ickes Papers,* Box 227, Folder: Political (4).

89. Personal and Political Diary of Homer Cummings, December 30, 1938, Box 235, Number 8, 270. No doubt Roosevelt's moderation towards his Democratic foes was partly the result of the threatening foreign situation. I would suggest, however, that especially after the purge Roosevelt considered aggressive partisanship to be as unfortunate a strategy in domestic matters as it was in managing foreign policy.

90. Price and Boskin, "The Roosevelt Purge," 662.

91. Hiram Johnson to Harry Byrd, July 12, 1938; and Johnson to Byrd, August 13, 1938, Scrapbook #24, *Harry Flood Byrd, Sr. Papers,* Manuscript Department, Alderman Library, University of Virginia, Charlottesville, Virginia.

92. *New York Times,* September 18, 1938, Section 4, 3.

93. Richard L. Neuberger, *Forum,* January, 1939, 11.

94. Memorandum, FDR to Farley, with attached letter, December 10, 1938, *Farley Papers,* Box 35, Folder: Franklin D. Roosevelt (September–December).

95. Freidel, *Franklin D. Roosevelt: A Rendevous With Destiny,* 288.

Chapter 5

1. W. A. White to Frankfurter, October 11, 1937, Microfilm Reel 60, *Felix Frankfurter Papers,* Manuscript Division, Library of Congress, Washington, D.C.; and White to Farley, December 28, 1937, *James Farley Papers,* Box 35, Folder: Roosevelt, Franklin D., 1938—January–April, Manuscript Division, Library of Congress. After getting White's permission to show the letter to the President, Farley forwarded the letter to FDR with an attached note on January 14, 1938. Ibid.

2. Theodore J. Lowi, "The Roosevelt Revolution and the New American State," in *Comparative Theory and Political Experience: Mario Einaud and the Liberal Tradition,* eds., Peter J. Katzanstein, Theodore Lowi, and Sidney Tarrow (Ithaca and London: Cornell University Press, 1990), 203.

3. Morton Frisch, *Franklin D. Roosevelt: The Contribution of the New Deal to American Political Thought and Practice* (Boston: St. Wayne, 1979), 79.

4. Herbert Croly, *Progressive Democracy* (New York: Macmillan, 1912), 342–43.

5. *Complete Presidential Press Conferences of Franklin D. Roosevelt* (New York: Da Capo Press, 1972), #478, Vol. 12, 35; *New York Times,* August 28, 1938, Section 4, p. 1. Soon after his primary defeat, Senator Pope conferred with Roosevelt at Hyde Park, where the possibility of his taking the field as an independent—possibly on the Progressive ticket—was discussed. This consultation, which included members of the "elimination committee," was a source of embarrassment to James Farley, who, as Democratic national chairman, had already pledged Clark the cooperation of the party organization. In the end, Pope decided to accept the primary verdict. "Since I participated in the primary," he announced to the press on August 31, "I can best serve our people and the cause of liberal government by abiding by the results." It was intimated in the press, though no official word was issued, that Roosevelt influenced Pope's decision by choosing not to press the issue beyond a protest of the Idaho primary results. To go further and support Pope as a third-party candidate would have raised the stakes of the purge to a point of risk the President was not willing to accept—the result of such an action, as the *Times* reported, "would be not only to carry further his "purge' of conservative Democrats but possibly to jeopardize the leadership of the party as represented by the National Committee." See *New York Times,* August 22, 1938, 3; August 25, 1938, 1; August 28, 1938, F1; and August 31, 1938, 6. Moreover, Roosevelt was no doubt influenced by Farley's warning that an independent Pope candidacy would merely give the Republicans a victory in Idaho's senatorial race and, perhaps, in other state and local contests. See "Farley's Thumbs Down," *Newsweek,* September 12, 1938, 7.

6. Croly, *Progressive Democracy,* 343.

7. The concept of a state of "courts and parties" comes from Stephen Skowronek. The foundation of this decentralized state was the political party, which was the carrier of a local-oriented popular democracy that impeded the creation of more centralized, stable, and functionally specific institutional connections between state and society. The federal judiciary molded this political character of the nineteenth century state into formal legal tradition: "With constitutional laissez-faire, the Court sought to sharpen the boundaries between the public and private spheres, to provide clear and predictable standards for gauging the scope of acceptable state action, and to affirm with certainty of fundamental law the prerogative of property owners in the market place." Skowroneck, *Building A New American State: The Expansion of National Administrative Capacities, 1877–1920* (New York: Cambridge University Press, 1982), 41.

8. "His Excellency's Loyal Opposition," *Fortune,* February, 1937, 70–71.

9. Joseph Boskin, "Politics of An Opposition Party: The Republican Party of the New Deal Period, 1936–1940." Unpublished Ph.D. dissertation, University of Minnesota, 1960; and Ronald Bridges, "The Republican Program Committee," *The Public Opinion Quarterly* 3 (April, 1939): 299–306.

10. Barry D. Karl, "Constitution and Central Planning: The Third New Deal Revisited." In *The Supreme Court Review,* eds., Philip B. Kurland, Gerhard Casper, and Daniel Hutchinson (Chicago and London: The University of Chicago Press, 1989) 187–88. See also Theda Skopcol and John Ikenberry, "The Political Formation of the American Welfare State in Historical and Comparative Perspective," *Comparative Social Research* 6 (1983): 87–148. For a very insightful review of the historiography and events of Roosevelt's second term, see Ellis W. Hawley, "The New Deal State and the Anti-Bureaucratic Tradition." In *The New Deal and Its Legacy: Critique and Reappraisal,* ed., Robert Eden (Westport, Connecticut: Greenwood Press, 1989).

11. Hawley, "The New Deal State and the Antibureaucratic Tradition," 87. Interestingly, the "Third New Deal" is not only a concept of historiography, but one proposed by a primary observer. In August, 1937, Alexander Sachs, the Director of Economics and Investment Research of the Lehman Corporation, coined the phrase in a lengthy critique of an anonymous piece published in the *Economist,* entitled "Roosevelt and America." The author of this piece lamented the defeat of the court-"packing" plan and the executive reorganization act, arguing that "the American political system can only meet the needs of the changing times if it is dominated by a powerful President, who is the nearest thing in Washington to a direct representative of the people." Sachs rejected this constitutional diagnosis, claiming it misapprehended the meaning of democracy in the United States. "The major elements . . . constituting what I have called the Third New Deal," Sachs wrote, including "control of the Court, reduction of Congress to a resonator and ratifier of the executive, and supplanting the Cabinet by a personal secretariat," threatened not only the independence of the branches of government, but the "democratic concept of government" in the United States. That understanding of democracy—rooted in Jeffersonian principles and institutionalized by a decentralized party system—abhorred bureaucracy. See "Roosevelt and America," *The Economist,* July 31, 1937, 242; and Memorandum, Alexander Sachs to Foxy and Co., August 17, 1937, Box 107, *Alexander Sachs Papers,* Franklin D. Roosevelt Library, Hyde Park, New York.

12. Hawley, "The New Deal State and the Anti-Bureaucratic Tradition," 88.

13. James Piereson, "Party Government," *The Political Science Reviewer* 12 (Fall, 1982), 51–52.

14. Statement of Franklin D. Roosevelt before the Select Committee on the Budget of the House of Representatives, October 1, 1919, transcript found in the Papers of the President's Committee on Administrative Management, Box 5, Roosevelt Library.

15. Lindsay Rogers, "Reorganization: Post-Mortem Notes." *Political Science Quarterly* 53 (June, 1938), 162.

16. For example, Senator Burton Wheeler wrote to Roosevelt on January 39, 1935, complaining of the difficulty caused by relief being administered by several different agencies. Wheeler to Roosevelt, January 30, 1935, President's Official File 285-C (Government Reorganization), Roosevelt Papers.

17. High Diary, October 20, 1936, *Stanley High Papers,* Roosevelt Library. In a note written in 1941 for Volume 7 (1938) of his *Public Papers and Addresses,* Roosevelt indi-

cates that he had become convinced by 1935 "that it would take an overhauling of the entire administrative mechanism in order to make it run more efficiently and economically." Roosevelt, *Public Papers and Addresses,* ed. Samuel I. Rosenman, 13 volumes (New York: Random House, 1938–1950), Vol. 7, 183–84.

18. Louis Brownlow, *A Passion for Anonymity* (Chicago, Illinois: University of Chicago Press, 1958), 392.

19. Roosevelt, *Public Papers and Addresses,* Vol. 7, 182–83.

20. Peri E. Arnold, *Making the Managerial Presidency: Comprehensive Reorganization Planning, 1905–1980* (Princeton, New Jersey: Princeton University Press, 1986).

21. Brownlow, *A Passion for Anonymity,* 382.

22. Roosevelt expressed his concern regarding the independence of the committee with Charles Merriam on February 2, 1936. Merriam wrote to Brownlow: "The President seemed apprehensive that recommendations might be brought in of a kind which might embarrass him in the development of some plan of his own." Of the meeting, Merriam summarized: "We had quite a discussion but believe it will be all right." Merriam to Brownlow, February 20, 1936, Papers of the President's Committee on Administrative Management, Franklin D. Roosevelt Library, Hyde Park, New York.

23. Barry D. Karl, *Executive Reorganization and Reform in the New Deal: The Genesis of Administrative Management* (Cambridge: Harvard University Press, 1963), 206.

24. Rogers, "Reorganization: Post-Mortem Notes," 168.

25. Karl, *Executive Reorganization and Reform in the New Deal,* 258.

26. Hawley, "The New Deal State and the Anti-Bureaucratic Tradition," 87.

27. Daniels to FDR, March 29, 1938, President's Personal File 86, Roosevelt Papers.

28. Daniels to FDR, March 6, 1937, ibid.

29. Barry D. Karl, *Charles E. Merriam and the Study of Politics* (Chicago: University of Chicago Press, 1974), 256.

30. Luther Gulick, "Politics, Administration, and the New Deal," *The Annals,* Vol. 169 (September, 1933): 64–66.

31. Ibid., 64.

32. Ibid., 65.

33. For a full discussion of the individual backgrounds and political views of the committee, see Karl, *Executive Reorganization and Reform in the New Deal,* Chapters 2–4.

34. Louis Brownlow, Final Edited Manuscript, Vol. II, Chapter 30 ("We Report to the President"), 20, Louis Brownlow Papers, John F. Kennedy Library, Boston, MA. For a discussion of the constitutional significance of the Brownlow Report that offers a different interpretation than the one offered here, see John A. Rohr, "Constitutional Legitimacy and the Administrative State: A Reading of the Brownlow Commission Report," in Eden, *The New Deal and Its Legacy.*

35. Roosevelt's rationale for taking this route in the court-"packing" plan was candidly put forth in a letter to Felix Frankfurter, written on February 9, 1937. An excerpt from this letter, marked "privatissimo," reveals his concern to circumvent rather than challenge directly the political opposition to constitutional change: "The reason for the elimination of the amendment process was to me entirely sufficient: to get two-thirds of both houses of this session to agree on the language of an amendment which would cover all of the social and economic legislation, but at the same time, not go too far would have

been most difficult. In fact, the chance of a two-thirds vote in this session was about fifty–fifty.'' FDR to Frankfurter, February 9, 1937, *The Felix Frankfurter Papers,* Microfilm Reel 60, Manuscript Department, Library of Congress, Washington, D.C.

36. Roosevelt's orientation to political change led him to seek ground between radicalism and conservatism—a key element of this middle ground was the concern to build a commitment to rational discourse and planning into constitutional democracy. FDR's confidence in the superiority of a program of practical reform enabled him to take delight in characterizing various political ideologies according to their positions on change. For example, FDR wrote Felix Frankfurter in October, 1939:

> Here is my latest. I send it to you for correction or editing.
>
> A radical is a man with both feet firmly planted—in the air.
>
> A conservative is a man with two good legs who has never learned to walk.
>
> A reactionary is a somnambulist walking backwards.
>
> A liberal is a man who uses his legs and hands at the command of his intelligence.

FDR, Memorandum for Felix Frankfurter, October 5, 1939, ibid.

37. *Report of the President's Committee on Administrative Management* (Washington: Government Printing Office, 1937), 38, 53 (hereafter cited as *PCAM Report*).

38. Joseph P. Harris, ''Outline for the New York Conference,'' April 28, 1936, 18–19. Papers of the President's Committee on Administrative Management.

39. Ibid.

40. Theodore Lowi, *The End of Liberalism,* 2nd edition (New York: W. W. Norton, 1979), 270; see also Lowi, ''The Roosevelt Revolution and the New American State,'' 203.

41. *Humphrey's Executor v. United States* 295 U.S. 602 (1935); *Schechter Poultry Corp. v. United States,* 295 U.S. 495 (1935).

42. 272 U.S. 53 (1926). On the significance of the *Myers* case, see Sidney M. Milkis and Michael Nelson, *The American Presidency: Origins and Development* (Washington, D.C.: Congressional Quarterly, 1990), 245–46.

43. Karl, ''Constitution and Central Planning: The Third New Deal Revisited,'' 197.

44. High Diary Notations, March 28, 1936, *Stanley High Papers,* Roosevelt Library.

45. Frank Freidel, *Franklin D. Roosevelt: A Rendezvous With Destiny* (Boston: Little, Brown, 1990), 162.

46. Roosevelt, *Public Papers and Addresses,* Vol. 4, 205.

47. Ibid., 218–21.

48. William E. Leuchtenburg, ''Franklin D. Roosevelt's Supreme 'Court-Packing' Plan,'' in *Essays on the New Deal,* eds. Harold M. Hollingsworth and William F. Holmes (Austin: University of Texas Press, 1969), 115; for an analysis of the court-''packing'' plan that suggests FDR may have, in fact, lost the war, see Michael Nelson, ''The President and the Court: Reinterpreting the Court-Packing Episode of 1937,'' *Political Science Quarterly* **103** (Summer 1988): 267–93.

49. Lowi, *The End of Liberalism,* 300–1.

50. Rather than calling for a ''responsible two-party system,'' which political scientists have advocated since the end of the nineteenth century, Lowi advocates the formation of a multiparty system. ''A ''three-party system,'' he believes, could be the only reasonable

way to make "real parties" possible. See Lowi, *The Personal President: Power Invested and Promise Unfulfilled* (Ithaca: Cornell University Press, 1985), 208–12. The desirability of such a proposal aside, it is not likely, as Lowi himself grants, that the American political system can support an ongoing multiparty system.

51. Brownlow, *A Passion For Anonymity,* 356; Don K. Price, *America's Unwritten Constitution: Science, Religion, and Political Responsibility* (Cambridge: Harvard University Press, 1985), 121. Elliot's manuscript, entitled "The President's Role in Administrative Management," can be found in the *Papers of the President's Committee on Administrative Management* in the Roosevelt Library. It departs from the Brownlow Committee report both in advocating mechanisms to link the executive and legislature, such as giving the president the right to dissolve a refractory Congress, and in putting more emphasis on staffing the modern presidency with political appointees rather than career staff.

52. Roosevelt apparently conveyed the concern about the long-term prospects for liberal reform quite early in his presidency. See Turner Catledge, "Will the New Deal Make Peace With Business," October 16, 1938, *New York Times,* Section 4, 3.

53. Brownlow, *A Passion for Anonymity,* 329.

54. Roosevelt, *Public Papers and Addresses,* Vol. 5, 670.

55. Ibid., 671–72.

56. See, for example, Luther Gulick to Herbert Hoover, February 1, 1937, Papers of the President's Committee on Administrative Management.

57. "Hearings before the Joint Committee on Government Organization," Congress of the United States, 75th Congress, 3d Session, February 24, 1937, 105.

58. Herbert Emmerich and G. L. Belsley, "The Merit System, Its Reorganization and Extension," 17–18, Papers of the President's Committee on Administrative Management. Much of this report found its way into the final commission document. See *PCAM Report,* 11.

59. *PCAM Report,* 40.

60. Croly, *Progressive Democracy,* 364.

61. Ibid., 365.

62. James Landis, *The Administrative Process,* (New Haven: Yale University Press, 1938), 4, 46.

63. Brownlow, *A Passion for Anonymity,* 391.

64. George Creel, "Byrd Song," *Collier's Magazine,* August 21, 1937, 31.

65. While the PCAM called for a thorough revamping of the General Accounting Office, Brownlow stressed that, at least, McCarl should be replaced by an individual more sympathetic to New Deal policy. He wrote Roosevelt, "If immediate action is not taken here, there is grave danger that any spending and recovery program that you initiate may be quite effectively sabotaged by the present inimical regime in this office." Brownlow to Roosevelt, March 11, 1938, Official File 285–C (Government Reorganization), Roosevelt Papers. Interestingly, Roosevelt and the PCAM members had a few run-ins with McCarl over the allocation of funds to the Committee itself. Before releasing these funds, McCarl demanded strict authorization from Congress, an action that did not endear him to the Brownlow Committee. See Brownlow, *A Passion for Anonymity,* 343–51.

66. Ernest Cuneo, "Tommy the Cork: A Secret Chapter of American History: Of Recession, Roosevelt and Corcoran." Unpublished manuscript found in *James Rowe Pa-*

pers, Roosevelt Library. Alexander Sachs considered this departure in fiscal policy an integral part of FDR's political program to strengthen executive administration. A significant part of the Third New Deal, he wrote, was "the perpetuation of lump sum appropriations to be spent at the discretion of the Executive for relief and other needs of the dependent elements in the body politics." Sachs to Foxy and Co., August 17, 1937, Sachs Papers.

67. *New York Times,* January 17, 1937, 7.

68. Eugene S. Legget, Memorandum for Roosevelt, December 29, 1936, Official File 285–C (Government Reorganization), Roosevelt Papers.

69. Gulick to Roosevelt, September 30, 1937, ibid.

70. *Time* magazine, April 4, 1938, 10. It was at Senator Wagner's insistence that the National Labor Relations Board was set up as an independent agency. Roosevelt and Secretary of Labor Francis Perkins wanted the Board placed in the Department of Labor, but Wagner held firmly to his view that it should be established as an independent regulatory commission. See Frances Perkins, *The Roosevelt I Knew* (New York: The Viking Press, 1946), 242–43.

71. *Time,* April 18, 1938, 16.

72. Roosevelt, *Public Papers and Addresses,* Vol. 7, 179–81.

73. Alexander Hamilton, James Madison, and John Jay, *The Federalist Papers* (New York: New American Library, 1961), #70, 35.

74. Roosevelt to Frankfurter, April 4, 1938, Frankfurter Papers, Microfilm Reel 60, Folder: 1938 (16).

75. Richard Polenberg, *Reorganizing Roosevelt's Government* (Cambridge: Harvard University Press, 1966), 159–60.

76. Cushman to Brownlow, March 24, 1937, Papers of the President's Committee on Administrative Management. Several members of the President's Committee urged some modification of the sweeping authority the bill conferred to the president over regulatory commissions. In late January, 1937, for example, Luther Gulick urged that the executive reorganization bill more explicitly define the modifications to be undertaken regarding these government bodies. Gulick to Brownlow, January 26, 1937, ibid. In spite of this advice and considerable congressional pressure, however, Roosevelt maintained his stand on independent regulatory commissions. On February 2, 1937, James Roosevelt indicated to a member of the Committee that it had been decided not to weaken the bill in regard to the independent regulatory commission's unless they were insisted upon later. See the "Journal" of the Committee staff member John Miller, February 2, 1937, ibid. Despite FDR's reluctance to compromise on reorganization power, both the House and Senate bills as they emerged in Congress spared to some degree the independent regulatory commissions.

77. According to Title I of the bill, the president would not only have the authority to transfer agencies but also abolish and create them. In fact, the functions of any agency could be prescribed or abolished. Homer Cummings to Roosevelt, January 4, 1937, Official File 285-C (Government Reorganization), Roosevelt Papers.

78. Carter Glass to Ernest Stack, August 31, 1937, Box 380, Carter Glass Papers, Accession #2913, University of Virginia Library.

79. John Miller, "Journal," May, 1938, Papers of the President's Committee on Administrative Management.

80. Not only the members of the PCAM but some of the more perspicacious opponents of the executive reorganization plan recognized the relationship between the proposals of

administrative reform and the American party system. During debate on the executive reorganization bill in Congress, Republican Senator James J. Davis of Pennsylvania suggested to his colleagues that the objective of FDR's administrative reform was to free the president from the limits of constitutional government, as set by Jeffersonian principles and the American party system. Like the members of the Brownlow Committee, Davis realized that the president, although the tacit leader of his party and government, was under normal circumstances the prisoner of the American political process. As he told the Senate: ". . . the political system under which we live was not made by any one man or any one party. The President of the United States may most earnestly seek to escape the system that has grown up around him. More often than not he will be captured by it." *Congressional Record,* 75th Congress, 3rd Session, Vol. 83, 3931.

81. Felix Belair, Jr., "Roosevelt Drives for Completion of the New Deal," *New York Times,* August 16, 1938, Section 4, 3.

82. *Congressional Record,* 75th Congress, 3rd Session, 5121.

83. Ibid., 4610.

84. Printed in *Congressional Record,* 75th Congress, 3rd Session, Appendix, 1454.

85. Lindsay Rogers took this position in criticizing those who interpreted the defeat of the reorganization bill as a vote of no confidence. See "Reorganization: Post-Mortem Notes," 172.

86. Lewis to Roosevelt, April 11, 1938, *President's Secretary File* 140, Roosevelt Papers.

87. Polenberg, *Reorganizing Roosevelt's Government,* 183.

Chapter 6

1. FDR to Lindsay Warren, November 16, 1938, President's Secretary File, 140, *Franklin D. Roosevelt Papers,* Hyde Park, New York. Warren was appointed by FDR as Comptroller General in 1940; while serving in that office, he carried out most of the reforms of the General Accounting Office called for by the 1937 administrative reform proposal, but never formally enacted into law. As a result, the executive office was no longer exposed to the kind of rigid control J. Raymond McCarl had exercised over agency spending decisions. See Herbert Emmerich, *Federal Organization and Administrative Management* (Birmingham: University of Alabama Press, 1971), 22–23, 116–17; and Frederick C. Mosher, *The GAO: The Quest for Accountability in American Government* (Boulder, Colorado: Westview Press, 1979), Chapters 3 and 4. Warren's accomplishments as Comptroller General suggest how the half-loaf legislation passed in 1939 grew in time to something far more substantial.

2. The so-called "legislative veto" was first used in the Executive Reorganization Act of 1932. At first, legislative veto provisions were confined to executive reorganization bills but eventually became a widely used and controversial means to check executive administration. The Supreme Court declared the legislative veto unconstitutional in *Immigration and Naturalization Service v. Chadha,* 103 U.S. 2764 (1983). This condition on the delegation of executive authority proved to be a rather weak and ad hoc check on administrative power; indeed, in that its inclusion in legislation assuaged congressional concern about delegating its legislative power to the president and administrative agencies, the veto may have contributed to the expansion of executive administration. See Stanley C. Brubaker,

"Slouching Toward Constitutional Duty: The Legislative Veto and the Delegation of Authority," *Constitutional Commentary,* Vol. 1, no. 1 (Winter, 1984): 81–105. Congress's intervention in the details of administration, which became more prevalent and controversial during the 1970s, is discussed in Chapter 9.

3. Emmerich, *Federal Organization and Administrative Management,* 134.

4. Harold Ickes, *The Secret Diary of Harold L. Ickes,* Vol. 2 (New York: Simon and Schuster, 1954), 602–3. "Probably promises were made to Chavez," Ickes wrote in his Diary, "because he is that kind of statesman." In fact, Roosevelt had won the support of Chavez, as well as Nevada Senator Key Pittman, by promising them that he would not transfer the national forests to the Department of Interior. The Forestry Service had long been coveted by Interior, and Ickes fought hard to get it under his juridiction. But FDR, although sympathetic to Interior's claim that the national forests should be part of the federal department charged with regulating natural resources, sacrificed administrative "rationality" to practical necessity. He needed the votes of Pittman and Chavez, both of whom came from states with large cattle interests; Western cattlemen were adamant that the Forestry Service stay in the Department of Agriculture. Ibid., 604; see also Frank Friedel, *Franklin D. Roosevelt: A Rendezvouz With Destiny* (Boston: Little, Brown, 1990), 278.

5. *New York Times,* March 23, 1939, 1.

6. Bailey to Miller, February 4, 1939, *Josiah Bailey Papers,* Senatorial Series, Political National Papers, Box 474, William R. Perkins Library, Duke University, Durham, North Carolina.

7. Gulick, as cited in Clinton Rossiter, *The American Presidency,* 2nd edition (New York: Harcourt, Brace and World, 1960), 129.

8. *PCAM Report,* 5. The phrase "passion for anonymity" caused much merriment in the press and Congress. Roosevelt, too, burst out laughing upon reading this part of the report. This language revealed the Committee's interest in equipping the presidency with an institution similar to the British Cabinet secretariat. The term was suggested by Tom Jones, private secretary to three Prime Ministers, who said the president needed a secretariat headed by a selfless administrative assistant like Maurice Hankey, the first Chief of the British Cabinet secretariat when it was set up at the end of the First World War. "Tell the President," said Jones, "that the way to solve his problem is to find that one man who would turn out to be another Maurice Hankey, a man possessed of high competence, great physical vigor, and a passion for anonymity." Later, when the committee rejected the one-man idea and proposed six administrative assistants, they used Tom Jones's language to describe their qualifications. Louis Brownlow, *A Passion For Anonymity* (Chicago: University of Chicago Press, 1958), 356–57.

9. *Time,* September 12, 1938, 24.

10. Fred I. Greenstein, "Nine Presidents In Search of A Modern Presidency," in *Leadership In the Modern Presidency,* ed. Greenstein, (Cambridge, MA: Harvard University Press, 1988), 300 (Greenstein's emphasis).

11. *PCAM Report,* 5.

12. *New York Times,* January 17, 1937, 7.

13. Blair Moody, "Mr. Smith Doubles For Roosevelt," *Saturday Evening Post,* March 27, 1943, 24–25, 54–56, 58–59, 61.

14. Barry Karl, "The Constitution and Central Planning: The Third New Deal Revisited," 181–88, in *The Supreme Court Review,* eds. Philip B. Kurland, Gerhard Casper,

and Daniel Hutchinson (Chicago and London: The University of Chicago Press, 1989); see also Ellis Hawley, "The New Deal State and the Anti-Bureaucratic Tradition," in the *New Deal and Its Legacy: Critique and Reappraisal*, ed. Robert Eden (Westport, Connecticut: Greenwood Press, 1989), 88.

15. According to Harold Smith, Merriam's view of the NRPB was that it "should deal only with the long swing of national planning and should not become involved in any way in the solution of immediate problems. Otherwise, the National Resource Planning Board would not survive from administration to administration in order that it might deal with the basic and fundamental problems of a long term nature, an approach which tends to keep complicated social and economic inter-relationships in proper perspective." Daily memoranda, July 6, 1939, *Harold Smith Papers,* Roosevelt Library.

16. Such an objective was outlined by FDR when the National Resources Board was first created in 1934. It was important for the Board to formulate "a long range program," he believed, with "a plan strong enough to withstand Congressional pressure." Notes of the Meeting of June 25, 1934 with the President, *Papers of the National Resources Planning Board,* Central Office Correspondence, 1933–34, Box 195, Folder: National Planning Board Minutes, 16th Meeting. National Archives, Washington, D.C.

17. National Resources Planning Board, *National Resources Development Report for 1943: Post-War Plan and Program* (Washington, D.C.: U.S. Government Printing Office, 1943). The economic bill of rights was actually first pronounced in the NRPB's 1942 report; however, it was the reaffirmation of these programmatic rights in the 1943 report that FDR decided to publicize. In defending the need for a new understanding of rights, the 1942 NRPB report followed closely the arguments of Roosevelt's Commonwealth Club address. "Their problem," the report claimed with respect to the founding generation, "was freedom and the production of wealth, the building of this continent with its farms, industries, transportation and power; ours is freedom and the distribution of abundance, so that there may be no unemployment while there are adequate resources and men ready to work and in need of food, clothing, and shelter." National Resources Planning Board, *National Resources Development Report for 1942* (Washington, D.C.: United States Government Printing Office, 1942), 4.

18. *New York Times,* March 11, 1943, 1. The Beveridge Report, the British "cradle to grave" social security plan, was submitted to the British parliament about the same time Roosevelt issued the NRPB report to Congress. For an insightful comparison of the ideas and politics that shaped the welfare state in Britain, France, and the United States after World War II, see James T. Kloppenberg, "Elusive Consensus: Shaping the Welfare State in Britain, France and the United States Since World War II," paper presented at the 1989 Annual Meeting of the American Historical Association, San Francisco, California, December.

19. National Resources Planning Board, *Security, Work and Relief Policies* (Washington, D.C.: Government Printing Office, 1943). This report was submitted to the president on December 4, 1941, although not published until 1943, along with the NRPB report of that year.

20. Marion Clawson, *New Deal Planning: The National Resources Planning Board* (Baltimore and London: The Johns Hopkins University Press, 1981), 258; see also Kloppenberg, "Elusive Consensus: Shaping the Welfare States in Britain, France and the United States."

21. Daily Memoranda, April 9, 1943, *Smith Papers*; and *New York Times,* March 11, 1943, 1:8.

22. Daily Memoranda, June 3, 1943, *Smith Papers.*

23. Roosevelt to Wallace, January 10, 1944, President's Personal File 41, *Roosevelt Papers*; Franklin D. Roosevelt, *Public Papers and Addresses,* 13 volumes (New York: Random House, 1938–1950), Vol. 13, 40–41. The "economic bill of rights" was made part of the 1944 campaign with FDR's October 28 address at Soldiers Field in Chicago, ibid., 369–78.

24. Bowles to Rosenman, and attached "Outline of A Suggested Home Front Speech," *Samuel Rosenman Papers,* Box 1, Folder: Bowles, Chester (Bowles's emphasis), Roosevelt Library. See also John W. Jeffries, "The 'New' New Deal: FDR and American Liberalism, 1937–1945," *Political Science Quarterly* **105** (3) (Fall, 1990), 415–16.

25. Daily Memoranda, August 31, 1943, *Smith Papers.*

26. Smith anticipated and advocated a more systematic commitment by the Roosevelt administration to Keynesian policies from the start of his tenure at the budget bureau. As his June 12, 1939 diary notes about a meeting with Charles Merriam and Beardsley Ruml on Federal fiscal policy reads: "During the discussion I indicated that it was my feeling that the New Deal was an expression of economic and social forces that had been gathering momentum at least since the 1920s, if not before, and that actually the Federal government had embarked upon a radically different fiscal policy than that employed in this country heretofore, but that there had been no effort to define or to limit that fiscal policy, or to describe it in a manner that would make it clear generally. It seemed to me that the President essentially was a budget-balancer, and an adherent to old fiscal schemes, but that gradually he had come to a realization that something had to be done and slowly was being pushed into a new conception of the role of the Federal financing in the national economy. . . . The experimentation that has been going on is very desirable, but the time has come in my judgment to judge the results of such experimentation as a basis for shaping a coherent, unified national fiscal policy." Daily Memoranda, June 12, 1939, *Smith Papers.*

27. Memorandum, Harold Smith to Samuel Rosenman, December 23, 1944, and attached draft of remarks on full employment, *Smith Papers*; Roosevelt, *Public Papers and Addresses,* Vol. 13, 503–6.

28. Leonard D. White, "Franklin Roosevelt and the Public Service," *Public Personnel Review,* Vol. 6 (July, 1945), 142; and FDR to David Jennings, October 13, 1939, President's Personal File 4080, *Roosevelt Papers.*

29. Memorandum, Herbert Emmerich to Louis Brownlow, June 29, 1938, on "Extending the Competitive Classified Civil Service"; and Civil Service Commission, Statement regarding executive order of June 24, 1938, extending the merit system; both in Papers of the *President's Committee on Administrative Management,* Roosevelt Library; see also Richard Polenberg, *Reorganizing Roosevelt's Government* (Cambridge, MA: Harvard University Press, 1966), 23, 184.

30. White, "Franklin D. Roosevelt and the Public Service," 142.

31. Brownlow, *A Passion For Anonymity,* 417.

32. A. J. Wann, *The President As Chief Administrator* (Washington, D.C.: Public Affairs Press, 1968), 187–88.

33. Joseph Pika, "White House Public Liaison: The Early Years," presented at the 1984 Annual Meeting of the Midwest Political Science Association, April, Chicago, Illinois.

34. See Chapter 4.

35. Memorandum, FDR to Marvin McIntyre, June 7, 1941, Official File 391, Folder: Marches on Washington, 1937–1945, *Roosevelt Papers*; and Memorandum, Wayne Coy to Steven Early, June 12, 1941, and attached correspondence, ibid.

36. John B. Kirby, *Black Americans in the Roosevelt Era: Liberalism and Race* (Knoxville: The University of Tennessee Press, 1980), 170–75; and Gunnar Myrdal, with the assistance of Richard Sterner and Arnold Rose, *An American Dilemma: The Negro Problem and Modern Democracy* (New York: Harper and Brothers, 1944), 414–19.

37. Kirby, *Black Americans in the Roosevelt Era*, 119.

38. Eleanor Roosevelt is often miscast, at least in popular lore, as the "moral conscience" of the administration, who stood above party politics. Mrs. Roosevelt may have been an influential source of moralism, especially in race relations, but she was hardly apolitical. As Rowe related in his oral history: "One thing I can remember, which people don't quite understand about Mrs. Roosevelt: she came up through the regular political organization in New York. In fact, Farley and Flynn had pushed her into politics to help the president, and she got active in it, and in that sense was sort of a professional, regular politician. I remember on a number of appointments I used to have fights with Farley and Flynn. . . . And they complained about me to the president through her. . . . It always interested me that that was the vehicle that the Democratic chairmen used: Mrs. Roosevelt." James Rowe, Jr., Oral History Interview, by Thomas F. Soapes, July 12, 1978, 26, Roosevelt Library.

39. Memorandum, Rowe to FDR, October 20, 1941, *James Rowe Papers*, Roosevelt Library; see also Memorandum, Rowe to Flynn, September 17, 1941; James T. Mathews to Rowe, September 26, 1941; Memorandum, Rowe to Mathews, September 29, 1941; and Rowe to Flynn, October 23, 1941, ibid.

40. In March, 1942, Smith assumed the responsibility of fending off Flynn's efforts to establish a partisan wedge within the growing presidential institution. He persuaded FDR to reject a Flynn proposal to designate a liaison for each department who would look out for the party organization's interests in personnel policy. Daily Memoranda, March 14, 1942, *Smith Papers*.

41. *New York Times*, August 6, 1939, Section 4, 2.

42. *New York Times*, July 30, 1939, Section 4, 7; *Time*, July 30, 1939, 7–11.

43. Charles H. Shreve to Thomas Corcoran, and attached letter to FDR, July 24, 1939, Box 253, *Corcoran Papers*.

44. Joseph Alsop and Robert Kintner, *Men Around The President* (New York: Doubleday, Moran, 1939), 196.

45. Norris to FDR, July 26, 1939, President's Secretary File 152, *Roosevelt Papers*.

46. FDR to Norris, July 28, 1939, ibid.

47. Corcoran to FDR, July 30, and attached "Draft Speech on Returning the Hatch Bill," dated July 29, 1939, ibid.

48. "Draft Speech on Returning Hatch Bill," ibid.

49. "Message to the Congress on the Signing of the Hatch Bill," August 2, 1939, President's Secretary File 152, *Roosevelt Papers*.

50. Norris to Pepper, August 28, 1939, Box 208, *Corcoran Papers*.

51. Roosevelt, *Public Papers and Addresses*, Vol. 9, 28.

52. Cuneo, "Tommy the Cork: A Secret Chapter of American History," 3.

53. Ibid., 4; *New York Times,* July 25, 1938, 3.

54. Memorandum, Rowe to FDR, February 8, 1940, *Rowe Papers.*

55. *Time,* July 25, 1940, 11.

56. Cuneo, "Tommy the Cork: A Secret Chapter in American History," 7.

57. Thomas Corcoran, "Rendezvous with Democracy: The Memoirs of Tommy the Cork," unpublished manuscript written with Philip Kooper, Box 586a, Chapter 5, (Trouble Shooting at the RFC), 38, Corcoran Papers. That the 1940 campaign centered on legislation like the Ramspeck Bill further ensured that it represented a triumph of "enlightened administration."

58. Samuel Lubell, "Post-Mortem: Who Elected Roosevelt?" *The Saturday Evening Post,* January 25, 1941, 9–10.

59. Roosevelt, *Public Papers and Addresses,* Vol. 7, XXXII.

60. To some degree, Roosevelt's interest in reshaping the Democratic party continued to the end of his life. In contemplating a fourth run for the presidency, FDR made overtures to Wendell Wilkie, the liberal Republican who ran for office in 1940, and was rejected by conservatives in his own party in favor of Thomas Dewey in 1944, about the possibility of forming a new liberal party after the election. The project was never pursued very far, however, because by election day Wilkie was dead, and 5 months after election day Roosevelt was dead also. For an account of the collaboration between Roosevelt and Wilkie, see Samuel Rosenman, *Working With Roosevelt* (New York: Harper and Row, 1952), 463–70; see also FDR to Wilkie, July 13, 1944, President's Personal File 7023, *Roosevelt Papers.*

61. In the 5 years before 1939, five new independent commissions were established; in the three decades after, the only major commission to be created was the Atomic Energy Commission, which was only partly regulatory and was not independent of the executive. See Emmerich, *Federal Organization and Administrative Management,* 11–13.

62. Robert Leon Lester, "Developments in Presidential–Congressional Relationships: FDR–JFK," unpublished Ph.D. dissertation, University of Virginia, 1968, 134.

63. Alexander Hamilton, James Madison, and John Jay, *The Federalist Papers* (New York: New American Library, 1961), 423.

64. Commission on Organization of the Executive Branch, a report to the Congress, February, 1949 (Washington, D.C.: U.S. Government Printing Office).

65. Roosevelt, *Public Papers and Addresses,* Vol. 9, 618–19.

66. Martha Derthick, *Policymaking for Social Security* (Washington, D.C.: The Brookings Institution, 1983), 17–37.

67. FDR as quoted in ibid., 230.

68. Ibid., 417.

69. Theda Skocpol and John Ikenberry, "The Political Formation of the American Welfare State: In Historical and Comparative Perspective," *Comparative Social Research* **6** (1983), 140.

70. It is likewise misleading to portray social security as simply an earned pension, based on an actuarial system, where contributions are calculated according to payroll tax contributions. In fact, social security has a progressive benefit schedule, one that provides for low-income earners to get proportionately more for their payroll taxes than high-income earners. Derthick, *Policymaking for Social Security,* 255–56. David Stockman's charge

that social security constituted a "closet socialism" is certainly histrionic. But he is correct in characterizing the social security program as a "hybrid" of welfare benefits and earned pension annuities. David Stockman, *The Triumph of Politics: Why the Reagan Revolution Failed* (New York: Harper and Row, 1986), 181–83.

71. Hugo Black to James Farley, June 19, 1934, The *James Farley Papers,* Folder: Roosevelt, Franklin D., 1934, Manuscript Division, Library of Congress, Washington, D.C.

Chapter 7

1. Samuel Rosenman, *Working With Roosevelt* (New York: Harper and Row, 1952), 439; and Edward J. Flynn, *You're the Boss* (New York: The Viking Press, 1947), 180.

2. *Newsweek,* March 6, 1944, 34. Once the tax issue was settled, Barkley, as FDR himself proposed in a letter, was soon re-elected as majority leader. But the relationship between the two was never the same. Frank Friedel, *Franklin D. Roosevelt: A Rendezvous With Destiny* (Boston: Little, Brown, 1990), 502.

3. Rosenman, *Working With Roosevelt,* 439.

4. Prior to the convention, FDR gave a letter to Democratic National Committee chair Robert Hannegan, indicating that he would "be very glad to run with either [Harry Truman or William Douglas] and believ[ed] that either one of them would bring real strength to the ticket." FDR to Hannagan, July 19, 1944, President's Secretary File 143, *Roosevelt Papers.* Douglas was the only front-runner for the Vice Presidency who took himself out of contention. As the Democrats convened in Chicago, he empowered a friend to withdraw his name and then went on a "pack trip" into the Wallowa Mountains of Oregon, where he was unreachable. "He had miscalculated," historian Frank Fridel has suggested, "feeling it was more important to sit on the Supreme Court than to be an impotent vice president, and his backers were aiming him for the presidency in 1948." Douglas to FDR, July 27, 1944, Ibid.; Friedel, *Franklin D. Roosevelt: A Rendezvous With Destiny,* 535.

5. Ibid., 534.

6. Harry Truman, *Memoirs,* 2 vols. (Garden City, New York: Doubleday, 1955), 1:4–5; and William E. Leuchtenburg, *In the Shadow of FDR: From Harry Truman to Ronald Reagan,* rev. ed. (Ithaca and London: Cornell University Press, 1985), 1.

7. William S. White, "A Plain Politician From Missouri," Harry Truman," *The New Republic,* November 7, 1955, 16.

8. Truman, *Memoirs,* 1:483.

9. White, "A Plain Politician From Missouri," 15.

10. Truman, *Memoirs,* 1:485–86.

11. *Public Papers of the Presidents: Harry S. Truman,* 14 vols. (Washington, D.C.: Government Printing Office, 1961–1966), Vol. 1, September 6, 1945, 263–308.

12. Leuchtenburg, *In the Shadow of FDR . . . ,* 23.

13. Truman, as cited in Alonzo L. Hamby, *Beyond the New Deal: Harry S. Truman and American Liberlism* (New York and London: Columbia University Press, 1973), 180.

14. Hamby, *Beyond the New Deal,* 180.

15. Rowe incorrectly attributes the Hamilton quote to *Federalist* 70. The correct citation is Alexander Hamilton, James Madison, and John Jay, *The Federalist Papers* (New York: New American Library, 1961), No. 71, 432–33.

16. James Rowe, "Cooperation—or Conflict?" December, 1946, 19, 22–3, *James Rowe Papers,* Franklin D. Roosevelt Library, Hyde Park, New York. The statement that the "White House was a powerhouse without transmission lines" was apparently first made by Thomas Corcoran.

17. Hamby, Beyond the New Deal . . . , 181.

18. Fred I. Greenstein, "Nine Presidents in Search of a Modern Presidency," in *Leadership in the Modern Presidency,* ed. Greenstein (Cambridge, MA: Harvard University Press, 1988), 306.

19. The Taft–Hartley Act allowed the closed shop, made unions liable for damages by breach of contract, enabled the president to declare a "cooling-off period" before a strike, forbade unions to make political contributions or exact excessive dues, and required elected union officials to take an oath that they were not communists.

20. *Public Papers of the Presidents: Harry S. Truman,* June 27, 1947, 299.

21. *The Nation,* June 20, 1947, 755.

22. Angus Campbell et al., *The American Voter* (Chicago and London: The University of Chicago Press, 1980, first published in 1960 by John Wiley), especially Chapter 10.

23. James Rowe, "The Politics of 1948," September 18, 1947, *Rowe Papers,* 4–5.

24. Mathew Josephson, *Sidney Hillman: Statesman of American Labor* (Garden City, New York: Doubleday, 1952), 598. Rowe's memo made note of the PAC and its relationship to the party: "Those alert party machines, which, beginning in 1932, turned out such huge majorities in the big cities for the Democratic ticket have all through the years of their victories been steadily deteriorating underneath—until in 1944 the Democratic organization found itself rivaled, in terms of money and workers, and exceeded in alertness and enthusiasm by the PAC." Rowe, "The Politics of 1948," 13.

25. Ibid., 5.

26. Ibid., 7.

27. Hamby, *Beyond the New Deal,* 211–12; and Richard S. Kirkendall, "Election of 1948," in *History of American Presidential Elections,* eds. Arthur M. Schlesinger and Fred L. Israel (New York: Chelsea House, 1971), vol. 4, 3106–26. Rowe believed that the memo would be delivered to Truman in his own name. For many years afterwards, in fact, Rowe incorrectly thought the president had received and read his original memorandum. According to Clifford, Truman disliked Thomas Corcoran and, by association, his law partner, Rowe. The president would have "dismissed it if it was associated with Rowe," Clifford would write many years later, "so I did not mention Rowe's role in its drafting." Clifford's legerdemain is understandable, given the uneasy relationship between Truman and the New Dealers—it is curious, however, that Clifford never told Rowe that his memo went to the White House under a different name. See James Rowe, Jr., *Oral History Interview,* September 30, 1969, by Jerry N. Hess, 26–31, Harry S. Truman Library; and Clark Clifford with Richard Holbrooke, *Counsel to the President—A Memoir* (New York: Random House, 1991), 189–94.

28. *Public Papers of the President's of the United States: Harry S. Truman,* 1948, 1–10.

29. Seymour Scher, "Regulatory Agency Control through Appointments: The Case of the Eisenhower Administration and the NLRB," *The Journal of Politics* 23 (1961), 667–

69; Terry Moe, "Interests, Institutions, and Positive Theory: The Politics of the NLRB," *Studies in American Political Development,* Vol. 2 (New Haven: Yale University Press, 1987), 236–43. The administrative shelter the Truman presidency gave to labor reform was made possible by the discretion Congess and the Courts accorded to regulatory bodies. No statutory requirements governed the procedures of federal administrative agencies until the enactment of the Administrative Procedures Act (APA) in 1946. This legislation, largely based on the Report of the Attorney General's Committee on Administrative Procedure of 1941, was, in effect, the Roosevelt administration's answer to the restrictive Walter–Logan Act. It imposed some constraints on administrative agencies, especially where specific statutes required "on the record" proceedings. On the whole, however, the APA left agencies considerable autonomy from both judicial and legislative interference. "New Deal lawyers," Martin Shapiro has written, "created a body of administrative law that rationalized and legitimized the administrative state the New Deal created and that the New Deal ideology defended." Shapiro, "APA: Past, Present, Future," *Virginia Law Review* **72** (1986), 449.

30. President Harry Truman, "Executive Order 9808 Establishing the President's Committee on Civil Rights," December 5, 1946. Printed in *To Secure These Rights: The Report of the President's Committee on Civil Rights* (New York: Simon and Schuster, 1947), VIII–IX.

31. *To Secure These Rights,* 151–73; and President Harry S. Truman, "Special Message to Congress on Civil Rights," February 2, 1948, printed in *The Growth of Presidential Power,* ed. William B. Goldsmith (New York: Chelsea House, 1974), Vol. 3, 1586–92. The Fair Employment Practices Committee, as noted in Chapter 5, was first set up by FDR on June 25, 1941, partly to avoid a threatened march on Washington, D.C. The Committee, which was created to prevent discrimination in the national defense program, continued until June 30, 1946, under the National War Agency Appropriations Act, when it was terminated against Truman's wishes.

32. John Hope Franklin, "Civil Rights and the Truman Administration," Public Address at the University of Chicago, April 5, 1968, in *Conference of Scholars on the Truman Administration and Civil Rights,* eds. Donald McCoy, Richard T. Reutten, and J. R. Fuchs (Independence, Missouri: Harry S. Truman Library Institute, 1968), 134. On Truman's view of party and civil rights, see the comments by Richard Kirkendall, "First Session," ibid., 33.

33. Alonzo L. Hamby, "Harry S. Truman: Insecurity and Responsibility." In ed. Greenstein, *Leadership In the Modern Presidency,* 42.

34. Ibid., 42–43.

35. Louis Brownlow, "Perfect Union," President's Official File 101 and 101b, *Roosevelt Papers.*

36. FDR to Delano, February 22, 1943, ibid.

37. Daily Memoranda, May 4, 1945, *Harold Smith Papers,* Roosevelt Library.

38. Ibid., August 10, 1945.

39. Greenstein, "Nine Presidents In Search of A Modern Presidency," 304.

40. The analogy of the powerhouse, first made by Thomas Corcoran, and discussed in Rowe's 1946 memo on Truman's relations with Congress, was also mentioned to the President in a conversation with Harold Smith. See Daily Memoranda, May 4, 1945, *Smith Papers.*

41. Peri E. Arnold, *Making the Managerial Presidency: Comprehensive Reorganiza-*

tion Planning, 1905–1980 (Princeton, New Jersey: Princeton University Press, 1986), 126–30.

42. The Commission on Organization of the Executive Branch, *Concluding Report* (Washington, D.C.: Government Printing Office, 1949).

43. Martha Derthick and Paul J. Quirk, *The Politics of Deregulation* (Washington, D.C.: The Brookings Institution, 1985), 61–74.

44. Truman's budget director James Webb, as quoted in Arnold, *Making the Managerial Presidency,* 142.

45. Hamby, *Beyond the New Deal . . .* , 225–29, 238–39, and 242–43.

46. Richard Neustadt, *Presidential Power: The Politics of Leadership From FDR to Carter,* 3rd edition (New York: Wiley, 1980), 120–21.

47. Marquis Child, *Eisenhower: Captive Hero* (New York: Harcourt, Brace, 1958), 179.

48. Joseph C. Harsch, "Eisenhower's First Hundred Days," *Reporter,* May 12, 1953, 9.

49. Fred I. Greenstein, *The Hidden-Hand Presidency: Eisenhower As Leader* (New York: Basic Books, 1982).

50. Quoted in Leuchtenburg, *The Shadow of FDR,* 68.

51. For a detailed study of Eisenhower's party leadership, see Cornelius P. Cotter, "Eisenhower As Party Leader," *Political Science Quarterly* **98** (2) (Summer, 1983): 255–83.

52. As Lubell wrote, "it would be difficult to cite any president, including both Roosevelts, who has been more adept in 'giving the people what they want,' or has been more of a 'party' man in patronage matters and in building a party organization. . ." Samuel Lubell, *Revolt of the Moderates* (New York: Harper and Brothers, 1956), 25.

53. Theodore Lowi, *The Personal President: Power Invested, Promise Unfulfilled* (Ithaca, New York: Cornell University Press, 1985), 73–79; and Broder, *The Party's Over: The Failure of Politics in America,* (New York: Harper and Row, 1972), 1–15.

54. Cotter, "Eisenhower as Party Leader," 268–69.

55. Ibid., 260, 266, 268–69; Paul Van Riper, *History of the United States Civil Service* (Evanston, Illinois: Row, Peterson, 1958), 493–94.

56. *Public Papers of the Presidents of the United States: Dwight D. Eisenhower,* 1956 (Washington, D.C., Government Printing Office, 1956), 298.

57. Cotter, "Eisenhower As Party Leader," 260.

58. Scher, "Regulatory Agency Control Through Appointment: The Case of the Eisenhower Administration and the NLRB," 670–75.

59. Ibid., 677.

60. Cited in ibid., 687.

61. Moe, "Interests, Institutions, and Positive Theory," 256–57.

62. Phillip G. Henderson, *Managing the Presidency: The Eisenhower Legacy—From Kennedy to Reagan* (Boulder, CO: Westview Press, 1988), 17–24. A second Hoover Commission was created by Congress in 1953. Republican leaders in the House and Senate hoped for a replay of the first Hoover Commission, this time with the assurance that it would not be sidetracked from its mission to reduce the size of government. These hopes

were realized. Although the first Hoover Commission had become interested primarily in improving the administrative management of the new executive branch, the second concentrated on issues of policy and function. At the heart of the second Hoover Commission's recommendations was the idea that many Roosevelt-era programs and agencies had been counterproductive. But the second Hoover study had far less influence than the first on the Eisenhower presidency; in fact, the second Hoover Commission's conservative ideological approach guaranteed that it would have little influence on the Eisenhower administration, which accepted most of the changes brought by the New Deal. See Arnold, *Making the Managerial Presidency,* 166–227.

63. Henderson, *Managing the Presidency,* 29–32; and Greenstein, "Nine Presidents In Search of A Modern Presidency," 307–11.

64. Henderson, *Managing the Presidency,* 18–19.

65. See Chapter 6, p. 346, n.8.

66. "Politics Without Patronage," *Time,* June 7, 1954, 23.

67. Ibid.

68. Van Riper, *History of the United States Civil Service,* 495–99.

69. Elmo Richardson, *The Presidency of Dwight D. Eisenhower* (Lawrence: University of Kansas Press, 1979), 14.

70. Ibid., 51.

71. Cited in Henderson, *Managing the Presidency,* 45.

72. Quoted in Gary W. Reichard, *The Reaffirmation of Republicanism: Eisenhower and the Eighty-Third Congress* (Knoxville: The University of Tennessee Press, 1975), 67.

73. John F. Kennedy, speech to the National Press Club, Washington, D.C., January 14, 1960, in *"Let the Word Go Forth": The Speeches, Statements, and Writing of John F. Kennedy,* ed. Theodore C. Sorenson (New York: Bantam Doubleday Dell Publishing Group, 1988), 17–23.

74. "The President's Call on Justice Frankfurter," July 26, 1962, contained in Oral History Interview, Felix Frankfurter, June 19, 1964, by Charles McLaughlin, John F. Kennedy Library, Boston, Massachusetts, 67–68.

75. James MacGregor Burns, *Deadlock of Democracy: Four Party Politics in America* (Englewood Cliffs, New Jersey: Prentice Hall, 1963).

76. Kennedy's effective use of the media—the fact that he was the first television president—was only one part of this development. All of Kennedy's campaigns for office, including the presidency, were highly personal undertakings; indeed, they were run by members of his own family, especially his brother Robert. Eisenhower's campaign for the presidency in 1952 was the first to be run separately from the regular party apparatus. But John Kennedy's organization, the "Kennedy Machine," as it was called, was much more vigorous and elaborate than that of Eisenhower. The Kennedy organization also made its mark on government. Most of the personnel from the Kennedy campaign staff were relocated in parallel or compatible positions in the White House Office, contributing to a significant personalization of the presidential staff. This development was reinforced by the concentration of more policy responsibility in the executive office during Kennedy's presidency when compared to past administrations. For a discussion of Kennedy's influence on the modern presidency, see Sidney M. Milkis and Michael Nelson, *The American Presidency: Origins and Development, 1776–1990* (Washington, D.C.: Congressional Quarterly Press, 1990), 295–302.

77. Lyndon Baines Johnson, *The Vantage Point: Perspective on the Presdiency, 1963–1969* (New York: Holt, Rinehart and Winston, 1971), 18.

78. Jeffrey Tulis, *The Rhetorical Presidency* (Princeton, New Jersey: Princeton University Press, 1987), 162.

79. Leuchtenburg, *In the Shadow of FDR,* 142.

An account of Leuchtenburg's interview with Johnson is given in Leuchtenburg, "A Visit With LBJ," *American Heritage,* May/June 1990, 47–64.

80. Thomas Corcoran to LBJ, April 21, 1964, Box 1, White House Central File, PL (Political Affairs), Executive File, Lyndon Baines Johnson Library, Austin, Texas.

81. James MacGregor Burns, *John Kennedy: A Political Profile* (New York: Harcourt Brace, 1960), 266. The Johnson Administration viewed Kennedy as seeking a departure from FDR's political program and, to a point, considered this effort to move beyond the New Deal a sound strategy. As Johnson aide Horace Busby wrote in a 1964 memo, "Since November there has been a natural but unrealistic tendency to equate Kennedy's politics—as well as his stature—with FDR. This is not valid. . . . Subsequent to his election, Kennedy's political thrusts were in many sectors directed toward disassociation—rather than closer association—with the FDR political image. . . . In essence, his concept seemed to treat the 1960 ticket as a holding maneuver, meant to restore the Democrats to the White House—from which the party image could be reshaped and modernized." Horace Busby, "The Democratic Party and the Presidency in the Twentieth Century, 1900–1960: A Closer Look at Reality." July 13, 1964, Office Files of Horace Busby, Box 52, Folder: July, 1964, Johnson Library.

82. William S. White, *The Professional: Lyndon B. Johnson* (Boston, Massachusetts: Houghton, Mifflin, 1964), 260.

83. Lyndon B. Johnson, Radio Address Over KNOW: "Eight in the Dark," March 18, 1937, Johnson Library.

84. Richard A. Rovere, "A Man For This Age Too," *New York Times Magazine,* April 11, 1965, 118.

85. Horace Busby interview with the author, June 25, 1987. Busby's memory of this event is accurate. FDR dedicated the Robert E. Lee Memorial Statue in Dallas, Texas on June 12, 1936, offering the following words to the occasion: "We recognize Robert E. Lee as one of our greatest American Christians and one of our greatest American gentlemen." Franklin Delano Roosevelt, *Public Papers and Addresses,* 13 volumes (New York: Random House, 1938), Vol. 5, 214.

86. Johnson, *The Vantage Point,* 323.

87. *Public Papers of the Presidents: Lyndon B. Johnson,* 1963–1964, Vol. 2, 1179.

88. Tom Wicker, "The Campaign Ahead: Major Issues and Goldwater's Strategy," *New York Times,* July 19, 1964, E3.

89. Anthony Lewis, "Convention Mood Reflects a Historic Change," *New York Times,* July 19, 1964, E4.

90. Tom Wicker, "Johnson Plurality Sets Record; Many Democrats Gain By Sweep," *New York Times,* November 5, 1964, 1, 21. On election night, Johnson was intensely interested in how he was doing compared to FDR in 1936. Unable to take joy from his landslide victory over Goldwater alone, LBJ remained cranky until the morning after the election, when it finally became clear that his plurality had broken Roosevelt's record,

though his proportion of the popular vote was not so great, nor was his tally in the Electoral College so impressive. See Leuchtenburg, *In the Shadow of FDR*, 145.

91. *New York Times,* August 28, 1964, 12.

92. Leuchtenburg, "A Visit With LBJ," 54.

93. Henry Ford II to LBJ, August 7, 1964, Office Files of Horace Busby, Box 52, Folder: Memos to Mr. Johnson, August, 1964, Johnson Library. "Let's Do This," LBJ wrote on Ford's letter.

94. James Rowe to Harry Middleton, June 20, 1969, *James Rowe Papers,* Box 100, File: LBJ, 1969–1976, Franklin D. Roosevelt Library, Hyde Park, New York. For a detailed and carefully argued discussion of Johnson's efforts to form ties with business, see Cathie Jo Martin, "Business and the New Economic Activism: The Growth of Corporate Lobbies in the Sixties," September, 1992 (mimeo copy provided by the author).

95. Jerald Terhorst and James Welch, "The Business Role in the Great Society," *The Reporter,* December 25, 1965, 26; see also Herbert S. Parmet, *The Democrats: The Years After FDR* (New York: MacMillan Publishing Co., 1976), 242–43.

96. Memorandum: Henry H. Wilson, Jr., to Lawrene O'Brien, July 8, 1964, *Henry H. Wilson Papers,* Box 1, Folder: Campaign, 1964, Johnson Library. Wilson's concern was deepened by Governor George Wallace's surprising showing in Northern Democratic primaries in 1964. There white backlash had first shown up, especially among heavy industrial workers, many of them Catholics of East European origin. Wallace carried such areas as Gary, Indiana, and Baltimore.

97. Busby to LBJ, July 13, 1964, and attached memorandum, "The Democratic Party and the Presidency in the Twentieth Century, 1900–1960." *Office Files of Horace Busby,* Box 54, Memos to Mr. Johnson, July, 1964.

98. Memorandum, Horace Busby to LBJ, no date, *Office Files of Horace Busby,* Box 52, Folder: Memos to Mr. Johnson, June, 1964.

99. LBJ describes the legislative maneuvering that led to the enactment of the civil rights bill in his memoirs. See Johnson, *The Vantage Point*, 159–60. LBJ's ardent support for civil rights as president was not as radical a shift as it might have seemed to those who remembered only his opposition to federal lynching laws as a member of the House and his steadfast support for the filibuster while in the Senate. As majority leader, Johnson steered the 1957 and 1960 voting laws through the Senate. These were weak laws, designed as compromises that would pacify Northern liberals while preserving Southern patience. But LBJ saw these statutes as significant steps—the best that could be hoped for at the time. Taking umbrage at Eleanor Roosevelt's criticism of the 1957 bill for not overriding the laws of the states, but merely affecting the administration of these unjust laws, LBJ wrote: "No one touched upon the point that voters will have to qualify under the laws of the individual states simply because that could be effected only by changing the Constitution itself and the facts are that no Constitutional amendment on that question could be attempted at this time." Johnson to Eleanor Roosevelt, August 22, 1957, *White House Famous Names,* Box 7, Folder: Mrs. Franklin D. Roosevelt, Johnson Library. Johnson's militant liberalism with respect to Civil Rights first came into view when he was Vice President. Against the advice of James Rowe, who warned LBJ he was becoming involved in an explosive situation, the Vice President accepted the role of Chairman of the President's Committee on Equal Employment Opportunity, where he began a quiet and unpublicized campaign for a strong civil rights program. Having received a favorable report from Gladys Duncan of the Urban League about LBJ's activities as Chairman, Rowe wrote the

Vice President on March 6, 1962: "She told me that as a member of the District of Columbia Delegation at the [1960 Democratic] Convention she had been extremely opposed to
your nomination as Vice President. . . . She said she has changed her attitude about you
completely because of all you have done for her people as Chairman of the Equal Employment Committee. . . . So perhaps you were right about taking the Chairmanship and I
was wrong (although I am not yet fully convinced!)," Memos, Rowe to Johnson, December 22, 1960; and March 6, 1962. *James Rowe Papers,* Box 100, Folders: LBJ (1960–
1961) and LBJ (1962–1963). See also Parmet, *The Democrats,* 221–22.

100. White, *The Professional: Lyndon B. Johnson,* 261.

101. Telephone conversation between Lyndon Johnson and Ted Sorenson, June 3,
1963, *George Reedy Office Files,* Box 1, Johnson Library.

102. Johnson often spoke of FDR's habit of not consulting Congressional leadership as
unfortunate, and of his own intention to do better as legislative leader. LBJ had especially
strong recollections of an episode in 1941, when Sam Rayburn, who served as House
majority leader during Roosevelt's presidency, was humiliated by the administration sending a message to the Congress about which he had no knowledge. Johnson reflected on this
incident in a 1972 interview with Walter Cronkite: "Mr. Rayburn said to me, 'I just wish
that he'd [FDR] give me five minutes' notice before he sends those messages. . . . How
can I explain something I never heard of? . . . He makes it awful hard to help him.' Well
that's what caused me to have so many legislative conferences with the Democrats and
Republicans all the time I was President, so I wouldn't catch them off guard." Transcript,
CBS–Cronkite Interviews with Lyndon B. Johnson, Number 4, January 27, 1972, "Lyndon Johnson Talks Politics," 10. Johnson Library.

103. James H. Rowe, Jr., Oral History, interviewed by Joe B. Frantz, interview #2,
September 16, 1969, 45, Johnson Library.

104. Theodore White, *The Making of A President, 1968* (New York: Atheneum Publishers, 1969), 107. Johnson's hostility to the Democratic National Committee had its roots
in the conflicts he had as Senate majority leader with national party chairman Paul Butler.
Butler was Adlai Stevenson's choice for the DNC chair; Stevenson hoped that Butler's
militant partisanship would compensate for, indeed challenge, the tendency of Johnson and
Speaker of the House Sam Rayburn to establish cooperative relations with the Eisenhower
administration. Stevenson and Butler, along with many other liberals, argued that the Democratic leaders in Congress were undermining their efforts to unite the party for a spirited
challenge to the Republican administration in the 1956 presidential campaign. Johnson
considered Butler's advice to pursue a militantly partisan legislative program irresponsible,
and his disinclination to follow Butler's strategy was confirmed by his first major legislative
floor fight as majority leader. In March, 1955, he reluctantly took a populist tax reduction
proposal favored by Butler and Rayburn before the Senate, only to suffer a humiliating
defeat. The loss was a watershed. Thereafter, Johnson would eschew militant partisanship,
and when he became president, he was determined that the national party headquarters
would not again challenge or undermine his leadership. See Wiliam S. White, "Democrats
Rush New Tax Cut Bill in Senate Battle," *New York Times,* March 10, 1955, 1, 17; White,
"Humphrey Calls Cut in Tax 'Silly,' " ibid., March 11, 1955, 1, 7; White, "Senate
Defeats Tax Cut Moves; President Wins," ibid., March 16, 1955; and Roland Evans and
Robert Novak, *Lyndon B. Johnson: The Exercise of Power* (New York: The New American
Library, 1966), 145–48.

105. Meg Greenfield, "LBJ and the Democrats," *The Reporter,* May 22, 1966, 9.

106. Roland Evans and Robert Novak, Too Late For LBJ," *Boston Globe,* December
21, 1966, 27.

107. David Broder, "Consensus Politics: End of an Experiment," *Atlantic Monthly,* October, 1966, 62.

108. Personal interview with John P. Roche, June 11, 1986.

109. Doris Kearns, *Lyndon Johnson and the American Dream* (New York: New American Library, 1976), 256.

110. Johnson, *The Vantage Point,* 160. Henry Wilson, a member of Larry O'Brien's congressional liaison team, gives an interesting report on one of the early strategy sessions that led to the Great Society in a November, 1964, memo, which expresses concern about the acute political problems he anticipated would result from LBJ's large programmatic ambitions. Memorandum, Henry Wilson to Larry O'Brien, November 25, 1964, *Henry Wilson Papers,* Box 4, Folder: Larry O'Brien.

111. Black riots erupted within days of Goldwater's nomination in July—1964 was the first of the "long hot summers" that revealed the previously unsuspected depths of black discontent. As the rioting spread, and civil rights demonstrations continued after the passage of the Civil Rights Act, the administration feared that racial unrest would turn white voters against a president identified with the black cause. The White House sought to halt the demonstrations and riots by quietly persuading civil rights leaders to call for a moratorium on black unrest. Direct evidence of LBJ's efforts to influence the Civil Rights leadership thus is lacking, but leaders of the major black organizations convened on July 29, and issued public statements that comported with LBJ's immediate political objectives. See *New York Times,* July 30, 1964, 12; and Bruce Miroff, "Presidential Leverage Over Social Movements: The Johnson White House and Civil Rights," *Journal of Politics* **43** (February, 1981), 10–11. Johnson's efforts to "manage" the civil rights situation, as revealed in Chapter 8, would not be so successful in 1965 and the remaining years of his presidency.

112. *Public Papers of the Presidents of the United States: Lyndon Baines Johnson,* 1963–1964, Vol. 1, 704.

113. Memorandum, Moyers to LBJ, September 21, 1965, *Office Files of Bill Moyers,* Box 11, Johnson Library.

114. Richard Goodwin, *Remembering America* (Boston: Little, Brown, 1988), 275.

115. Ibid.

116. Students for a Democratic Society, "Port Huron Statement," Printed in *The New Left: A Documentary History,* ed. Missimo Teodori (Indianapolis, Indiana: Bobbs–Merril, 1969), 165. See also Goodwin, *Remembering America,* 276.

117. Ibid., 274.

118. Johnson, *The Vantage Point,* 73. As we will see in Chapter 8, LBJ's NYA experience was especially relevant to his support of the community action programs. See Chapter 5 for a detailed discussion of the National Resources Planning Board. The discussion of the NYA comes in the second part of the 1943 NRPB report: "Wartime Planning for War and Post War," in *National Resources Development Report for 1943* (Washington, D.C.: U.S. Government Printing Office, January 1943), 394–95.

119. Miroff, "Presidential Leverage Over Social Movements," 11.

120. Paul Conkin, *Big Daddy from the Pedernales: Lyndon B. Johnson* (Boston, MA: Twayne, 1986), 209.

121. Memorandum, Larry O'Brien to LBJ, January 10, 1964, *Henry H. Wilson Papers,* Box 5.

122. Busby interview, June 25, 1987.

Chapter 8

1. Theodore White, *America in Search of Itself: The Making of the President, 1956–1980* (New York: Harper and Row, 1982), 124.

2. Doris Kearns, *Lyndon Johnson and the American Dream* (New York: New American Library, 1976), 359.

3. Tom Wicker paints such a picture of LBJ's fall. See Wicker, *JFK and LBJ: The Influence of Personality Upon Politics* (New York: Penguin Books, 1968), 235, 276.

4. Harry McPherson, Personal Interview, July 30, 1985.

5. Samuel Beer, "In Search of A New Public Philosophy," *The New American Political System,* ed. Anthony King (Washington, D.C.: American Enterprise Institute, 1978), 26.

6. *Public Papers of the Presidents: Lyndon Baines Johnson,* 1966, Vol. 1, 3–7.

7. *Public Papers of the Presidents, Lyndon B. Johnson,* 1966, Vol. 1, 6.

8. Donald L. Horowitz, "Is the Presidency Failing? " *Public Interest,* Vol. 88 (Summer, 1987), 25.

9. Fred I. Greenstein, "Nine Presidents in Search of A Modern Presidency," in ed. Greenstein, *Leadership in the Modern Presidency,* 329.

10. Leuchtenburg, "The Genesis of the Great Society," *Reporter,* April 21, 1966, 38; and James Gaither, Oral History, interviewed by Dorothy Pierce, November 19, 1968–March 24, 1970, Tape 1, p. 24 and Tape 4, pp. 1–2, Lyndon Baines Johnson Library, Austin, Texas.

11. Memorandum: Hayes Redmon to Bill Moyers, May 5, 1966, *Office Files of Bill Moyers,* Box 12, Johnson Library. For a solid book-length account of Lyndon Johnson's personnel policy, see Richard L. Schott and Dagmar S. Hamilton, *People, Positions and Power: The Political Appointments of Lyndon Johnson* (Chicago and London: The University of Chicago Press, 1983). Although Macy's authority was considerable, it certainly did not mean that Johnson himself was not active in personnel matters. Johnson used Macy's visibity to his advantage by telling job seekers and their patrons that, as much as he'd like to appoint them, he couldn't do so because Macy insisted that appointments be based on merit and had come up with a sterling candidate of his own. In this way, Macy's role helped the president protect the position of his personnel staff from patronage claims, thus strengthening the reforming impulse of his administration. See John W. Macy, Bruce Adams, and J. Jackson Walter, *America's Unelected Government,* Senior Consultant: G. Calvin MacKenzie (Cambridge, MA: Ballinger, 1983), 31.

12. Memorandum, James Rowe to John Macy, September 26, 1967, *John Macy Papers,* Box 504, Johnson Library.

13. See Chapter 6.

14. Memorandum, James Rowe to John Macy, April 28, 1965, *John Macy Papers,* Box 504; and James H. Rowe, Oral History, interviewed by Joe B. Frantz, Interview 2, September 16, 1969, 46–47, Johnson Library.

15. Memorandum: John Roche to LBJ, September 8, 1967, *Marvin Watson Files,* Box 29, File: John Roche Memos, Johnson Library.

16. Personal interview with John P. Roche, June 11, 1986.

17. Bliss, cited in David W. Reinhard, *The Republican Right Since 1945* (Lexington: University Press of Kentucky, 1983), 217.

18. Paul Hope, "Tuesday Vote Recasts the Picture for 1968," *The Washington Star,* November 13, 1966, A-4; Gerald Griffin, "A Shell of a Party," December 19, 1966, *The Baltimore Sun*; and Marianne Means, "Precinct Chiefs Link President to Party's Fall," *Philadelphia Inquirer,* November 16, 1966.

19. Memorandum, James Rowe to LBJ, January 6, 1967, and attached report, "Elections 1966 and 1968," January 1, 1967, *Marvin Watson Files,* Box 23, Folder: Election Results, 1966 (emphasis in original).

20. Ibid.

21. Minutes of the Meeting with the president and Chairman Bailey, January 7, 1967, Diary Backup, Box 52, Johnson Library.

22. Roche interview, June 11, 1986.

23. The task force charged with the design of the administration's reorganization, the so-called Price Commission, recommended that the president have the authority to make political appointments to a percentage of super-grade positions, and that he have authority to move super-grade civil servants among agencies. See *Report of the President's Task Force on Government Reorganization,* November 6, 1964, Task Forces, Box 1, Johnson Library.

24. For a description of the Executive Assignment system, see John Macy, L. J. Andolsek, and Robert E. Hampton (Civil Service Commissioners) to LBJ, November 11, 1967, *White House Central Files,* Box 13 (Ex PE 2), Folder: PE 2 (9/2/67–12/1/67). Some 4000 positions were included in the Executive Assignment System. The Civil Service Reform Act created a 7,000 member corps of senior civil servants—the Senior Executive Service—and permitted even greater flexibility than did Johnson's executive order in the assignment of executives within and among agencies.

25. Memorandum, Horace Busby to the president, April 21, 1965, and attached letter from John Macy, April 17, 1965, Box 51, *Office Files of Horace Busby*; Joseph Young, "Johnson Boost to Career People Called Strongest by a President," *Washington Post,* May 16, 1965. Eugene Patterson, "The Johnson Brand," *Atlanta Constitution,* April 30, 1965; and Raymond P. Brandt, "Johnson Inspires the Civil Service by Appointing His Top Aides from among Career Officials," *St. Louis Dispatch,* May 2, 1965. For a sound secondary treatment of Johnson's management of the bureaucracy, see James A. Anderson, "Presidential Management of the Bureaucracy and the Johnson Presidency: A Preliminary Exploration," *Congress and the President* 1 (August, 1984): 137–63.

26. Memorandum, Bill Moyers to LBJ, December 11, 1965, *Office Files of Bill Moyers,* Box 11.

27. Leuchtenburg, "The Genesis of the Great Society," 37–38. The task force approach originated with the Kennedy administration, but it was extended and refined by the Johnson administration, which made a greater effort to prepare the task force reports for careful political consideration. See Hugh Davis Graham, "The Transformation of Federal Education Policy," in *Exploring the Johnson Years,* ed. Robert A. Devine (Austin: University of Texas Press, 1981), 163–69.

28. Broder, "Consensus Politics: An End of An Experiment," *Atlantic Monthly,* October, 1966, 62.

29. Thomas Corcoran to Lady Bird and Lyndon Johnson, November 10, 1955, *Thomas*

Corcoran Papers, Box 66, Folder: Johnson, Lyndon B., 1945–1959, Library of Congress, Manuscript Division, Washington, D.C.

30. Harvey C. Mansfield, Jr., *Taming the Prince: The Ambivalence of Modern Executive Power* (New York: The Free Press, 1989).

31. Walter Lippman, "The Peculiar Weakness of Mr. Hoover," *Harper's Magazine,* 161, June 1930, 5.

32. *CBS Cronkite Interview with Lyndon Johnson,* no. 1, December 27, 1969, "Why I Chose Not to Run," 5. Johnson Library.

33. In opposing re-eligibility, Johnson outdid even the twenty-second amendment in rejecting Alexander Hamilton's argument in favor of allowing presidents to serve for an unlimited number of terms. Alexander Hamilton, James Madison, and John Jay, *The Federalist Papers,* no. 72 (New York: New American Library, 1961), 437; for a rewarding discussion of Johnson's proposal for constitutional reform, see Wilson Carey McWiliams, "Lyndon B. Johnson: The Last of the Great Presidents," in *Modern Presidents and the Presidency,* ed. Marc Landy (Lexington, MA: D. C. Heath, 1985), 169–70.

34. Memorandum, Hayes Redmon to Bill Moyers, June 9, 1966, *Office Files of Bill Moyers,* Box 12.

35. Herbert S. Parmet, *The Democrats: The Years After FDR* (New York: MacMillan, 1976), 248.

36. Jack Newfield, "A Man For This Season," *Commonweal,* December 29, 1967, 400–1.

37. "Moment of Truth," editorial, *Washington Post,* October 8, 1966. The openly segregationist campaigns in Arkansas and Maryland did not succeed, as pro-civil-rights majorities formed behind the moderate Republican candidacies of Winthrop Rockefeller, Nelson's brother, and Spiro Agnew, a big Nelson supporter, respectively. See Paul Hope, "New Faces Mark Victory of Republicans," *Washington Star,* November 9, 1966. Agnew's identity as a Rockefeller-type Republican was short-lived, of course. He got tough on "race" and "law and order" after the April, 1968 riots in Baltimore. Soon thereafter, he was selected as Richard Nixon's running mate; in his campaign for and tenure as Vice President he made "Agnewism" synonymous with a conservative stance on the social issues that broke apart the Democratic party. See Richard M. Scammon and Ben J. Wattenberg, *The Real Majority* (New York: Coward–McCann, 1970), 29, 209–10.

38. Telephone conversation between Lyndon Johnson and Ted Sorenson, June 3, 1963, *George Reedy Office Files,* Box 1, Johnson Library, 6, 10.

39. *Public Papers of the Presidents,* Lyndon B. Johnson, 1965, Vol. 1, 284.

40. Paul Conkin, *Lyndon Baines Johnson: Big Daddy from the Pedernales* (Boston, MA: Twayne Publishers, 1986), 334.

41. McPherson interview, July 30, 1985.

42. Richard Goodwin, *Remembering America* (Boston: Little, Brown, 1988), 316.

43. Memorandum, Ervin Duggan to Douglas Cater, November 9, 1966, *Henry Wilson Papers,* Box 15, Folder: Staff Contacts, 1967, Johnson Library.

44. Memorandum, Henry Wilson to Douglas Cater, January 19, 1967, *Henry Wilson Papers,* Box 15, Folder: Staff Contacts, 1967.

45. Memorandum, Marvin Watson to LBJ, January 23, 1968, and attached memo from Billie Farnum to John Criswell, no date, *Marvin Watson Files,* Box 7, Folder: Louisiana,

Johnson Library. In April, 1967, Marvin Watson passed on to Johnson the remarks of Wiley A. Branton, Special Assistant to the Attorney General, before the Special Equal Rights Committee of the DNC. Branton reported on the ever-increasing black voter registration in the eleven Old Confederacy states between 1964 and 1967 as a result of the gains made following the passage of the 1965 Voting Rights Act. See Memorandum, Watson to LBJ, April 19, 1967, *Marvin Watson Files,* Box 18, File: Civil Rights/Negroes (2), Johnson Library.

46. J. Harvie Wilkinson III, *Harry Byrd and the Changing Face of Virginia Politics* (Charlottesville: University of Virginia Press, 1968), Chapter 12; see also Parmet, *The Democrats . . . ,* 266–67.

47. Memoranda, Hayes Redmon to Bill Moyers, November 27, 1965 and November 30, 1965, *Files of Bill Moyers,* Box 11.

48. Memorandum, Harry McPherson to LBJ, September 12, 1966, *Office Files of Harry McPherson,* Box 22, File: Civil Rights (2), Johnson Library.

49. Memorandum, Nicholas de B. Katzenbach to Harry McPherson, September 17, 1966, ibid.

50. An interesting account of the ghetto visits is given in the oral history of Sherwin Markman, the most enthusiastic and influential of the White House aides who participated in this project. Markman notes that one of the biggest tactical problems Johnson aides faced is how they would "go about living in the ghetto without getting [their heads] cut off." The solution was that every white, middle-class Johnson man had to find a black official in the administraiton who could serve as their guide and protector during their visits to the ghetto. See Oral History of Sherwin, J. Markman, Tape 1, May 21, 1969, interviewed by Dorothy Pierce McSweeney, 24–36, Johnson Library.

51. Memorandum, Harry McPherson to LBJ, August 14, 1967, *Office Files of Harry McPherson,* Box 53, File: Memoranda for the President, 1967; and Oral History of Sherwin Markman, Tape 1, 33–34.

52. McPherson reported after a visit to Harlem and Beford–Stuyvesant in mid-August, 1967 that HARYOU [Harlem Community Action Agency], a New York anti-poverty office, and a number of neighborhood youth groups were "making gains with a great number of young people." Memorandum, Harry McPherson to LBJ, August 14, 1967, as cited in note 51.

53. Economic Opportunity Act of 1964, Title 2, Part A, Section 202(a).

54. Samuel H. Beer, "In Search of a New Public Philosophy," in *The New American Political System,* ed. Anthony King (Washington, D.C.: American Enterprise Institute, 1979), 16.

55. Daniel P. Moynihan, *Maximum Feasible Misunderstanding: Community Action in the War on Poverty* (New York: The Free Press, 1970), 139.

56. The Heineman group was the second task force to report on government organization during the Johnson presidency; the first, chaired by Don K. Price, issued its study in 1964. The Johnson administration's embarrassment at the criticism of the Office of Economic Opportunity placed the management of the war on poverty program at the top of the Heineman task force's agenda. Its recommendations appear in two lengthy memoranda: Task Force on Government Organization, Memorandum to the President, December 15, 1966, *White House Central File,* Box 43, Folder: Heineman Task Force; and "A Final Report By the President's Task Force on Government Organization," June 15, 1967, 18–20, *Outside Task Forces,* Box 4, Folder: Task Force on Government Organization, both in

Johnson Library. See also, Peri Arnold, *Making the Managerial Presidency* (Princeton, New Jersey: Princeton University Press, 1986), 250–53.

57. Nicolau as cited in Moynihan, *Maximum Feasible Misunderstanding*, 139.

58. Ibid., Chapter 5; James A. Morone, *The Democratic Wish: Popular Participation and the Limits of American Government* (New York: Basic Books, 1990), 226.

59. Lyndon Johnson, *The Vantage Point: Perspectives on the Presidency, 1963–1969* (New York: Holt, Rinehart, and Winston, 1971), 74. Moynihan claims that Johnson hoped to help the poor, while visionary reformers in the Office of Economic Opportunity "wished to arouse them." See Moynihan, *Maximum Feasible Misunderstanding*, 96. In fact, a careful study of the record suggests that LBJ believed that "arousing" the poor, through political participation in the administration of programs, was central to helping them. Attention to community action, no matter how poorly conceived, was a central, and not ancillary, part of the philosophy underlying the Great Society. The unintended consequences of this attention to democratic administration are explored in Chapter 9.

60. *National Resources Development Report for 1943*, Part II: "Security, Work, and Relief Policies." (Washington, D.C.: Government Printing Office, 1943), 486.

61. Ibid., 394–95.

62. Johnson, *The Vantage Point*, 73.

63. *Task Force Report on Intergovernmental Program Coordination*, December 22, 1965, i, Outside Task Forces, Box 3, Johnson Library. See also the evaluation of the Heineman task force reports as cited in note 56; and the 1969 retrospective on the public administration of the poverty program by James Sundquist, who served on Johnson task forces in 1964 and 1965 that influenced the planning and operation of the war on poverty. James L. Sundquist, "Co-ordinating the War on Poverty," *The Annals*, vol. 385 (September, 1969): 41–49.

64. Johnson gave expression to such a view in his memoirs. "I heard bitter complaints from the mayors of several cities," he wrote. "Some funds were used to finance questionable activities. Some were badly mismanaged. That was all part of the risk. We created new bureaus and consolidated old ones. We altered priorities. We learned from mistakes. But as I used to tell our critics: 'We have to pull the drowning man out of the water and talk about it later.' " Johnson, *The Vantage Point*, 81. David Welborn and Jesse Burkhead reveal that Johnson stuck with the war on poverty, and was deeply involved in the fight over its reauthorization in 1967, although he feared that it was unduly influenced by "Kooks and Sociologists." See *Intergovernmental Relations in the American Administrative State* (Austin: University of Texas Press, 1989), 56–76.

65. Lillian B. Rubin, "Maximum Feasible Participation: The Origins, Implications, and Present Status," *The Annals*, Vol. 385, September, 1969, 17.

66. *Examination of the War on Poverty*, prepared for the Subcommittee on Employment, Manpower, and Poverty of the Committee on Labor and Public Welfare, United States Senate (Washington, D.C.: Government Printing Office, 1967), V, 1238, 1241–42. For this quote and many of the ideas expressed in the discussion of the Community Action Program, I am indebted to Morone, *The Democratic Wish . . .* , Chapter 6.

67. Douglas Ireland, "McCarthy in Chicago: Ready, Willing and Able," *Commonweal*, December 22, 1967, 375–76.

68. Memorandum, Roche to LBJ, February 9, 1967, *Marvin Watson Files*, Box 26, File: Labor Block (emphasis in original). About a year later, Reuther did, in fact, formally

break with the AFL–CIO. See Joseph C. Goulden, *Meany* (New York: Antheneum, 1972), Chapter 16.

69. In 1984, John Roche wrote that liberal internationalists committed their greatest error—in a clinical, if not moral sense—by getting involved in a war "at the end of the world for an abstraction. Vietnam had little to do with a calculation of national interest," he insisted. "The war in fact was fought to protect the freedom of 16 million Asians—'not our kind of people, Lyndon Johnson,' as Senator Fullbright told the President." See Roche, "The Passing of 'the Class of 1941' " *National Review,* October 19, 1984, 24–28. See also Harry McPherson, *A Political Education* (Boston: Little, Brown, 1972), 383.

70. Memorandum, Bill Moyers to LBJ, June 21, 1965, *Office Files of Bill Moyers,* Box 11.

71. Johnson's faith in liberal internationalism was tempered by his view that many New Deal liberals, following in the tradition of Henry Wallace, believed that the commitment to domestic reform was compromised, even desecrated, by military adventures abroad. Thus, Johnson believed that the war was worth fighting—in order to resist aggression and to maintain American integrity—but that victory in Vietnam was not worth total war. This position, in the end, alienated doves and hawks alike, leaving Johnson without the liberal consensus he had worked so hard to establish.

72. Parmet, *The Democrats . . . ,* 250.

73. Remarks by John M. Bailey, Chairman, Democratic National Committee, at Democratic National Committee Meeting, Chicago, January 8, 1968. *Records of the Democratic National Committee,* Box 100, Johnson Library.

74. Memorandum, Ralph Huitt to Marvin Watson, December 14, 1967, *Marvin Watson Files,* Box 17, Folder: Wisconsin-A.

75. David Broder, "Democrats Enter Campaign with Organization Badly Split," *The Washington Post,* September 26, 1967. By March, 1968, Johnson had even lost his deft touch with members of Congress. Consequently, members of the President's Congressional liaison team were greeted with criticism about the lack of consultation when they sought to shore up support in response to the McCarthy–Kennedy challenge. As Indiana Congressman John Brademas, a strong and influential supporter of party organization, told Johnson aide Barefoot Sanders on March 20: "I wish he [LBJ] would talk more with those of us who have influence in the House. When we 'consult' with him we often have the feeling that his mind is already made up—particularly in the past few months. For this reason, he hasn't established personal loyalties among Northern liberals which would have served him well in this time of trial. The problem is that he isn't comfortable in the politics of the industrial states. He doesn't put the same stress on organization—that's why the DNC has deteriorated so badly. All of this gives Bobby his best—and only chance." Memorandum, Barefoot Sanders to the President, March 20, 1968, *Barefoot Sanders Papers,* Box 27, Folder: Political Canvas—1968, Johnson Library.

76. *The Wall Street Journal* reported on December 28, 1967 that the Johnson administration's disregard of party greatly "accelerated the breakdown of state and local Democratic party machinery," placing organizations in "acute distress in nearly every large state." Allan Otten, "The Incumbent's Edge," *The Wall Street Journal,* December 28, 1967.

77. Goulden, *Meany,* 358–60; *Philadelphia Inquirer,* February 22, 1968.

78. Memorandum, Cliff Carter to the President, July 20, 1966, *Office Files of the President,* Dorothy Territo, Box 2, Folder: Cliff Carter, Johnson Library.

79. Barken was also upset by the DNC's termination of support for the National Council of Senior Citizens, a party auxiliary, which had been jointly subsidized by the party and labor; and the firing, with the 1965 cutbacks at the national committee, of the labor liaison. Ibid.; see also Paul Hope, "The Democrats: Debts and Discontent," *Washington Star,* August 19, 1966.

80. Memorandum, Billie S. Farnum to John B. Crisswell, April 23, 1967, *Marvin Watson Files,* Box 26, Folder: Labor bloc.

81. Goulden, *Meany,* 359.

82. Memorandum, Harry McPherson to LBJ, March 18, 1968, *Harry McPherson Files,* Box 53, Folder: Memoranda for the President (1968).

83. Memorandum, John Criswell to Marvin Watson, March 13, 1968, *Marvin Watson Files,* Box 18, Folder: Wisconsin-B—Primary.

84. Memorandum, Richard Cudahy to LBJ, March 19, 1968, *Official Files of the President,* Dorothy Territo, Box 10, Folder: Politics—General. LBJ was, understandably, distressed by Cudahy's memo. He had the source of the memo removed, and distributed it among his top political advisors. This terrible news from Wisconsin, one suspects, pushed LBJ towards a decision not to run. The announcement of March 31, at any rate, was not the result of a sudden impulse.

85. Memorandum, John Bailey to James Rowe, February 29, 1968, *Marvin Watson Files,* Box 4, Folder: Connecticut.

86. Memorandum, John Roche, to LBJ, December 4, 1967, White House Central Files, Confidential File, Folder: PL (Political Affairs), Johnson Library.

87. Memorandum, Harry McPherson to LBJ, March 18, 1968, as cited in note 82.

88. The plan for LBJ's re-election campaign was prepared by Larry O'Brien—it conceived of an elaborate Johnson campaign organization that would leave very little for the DNC to do. See Lawrence F. O'Brien, "A White Paper for the President on the 1968 Presidential Campaign," September 29, 1967. *Marvin Watson Files,* Box 20, Folder: DNC—Rowe–O'Brien–Crooker–Criswell Operation.

89. Notes of Meeting—Rowe, Cater, Friedman, Criswell, Burney, March 15, 1968, ibid.

90. Memorandum, Neal Peterson to Marvin Watson, no date (passed through William Connel on December 12, 1967), *Marvin Watson Files,* Box 24, Folder: Johnson–Humphrey.

91. James Rowe, "Notes and Comments on 'A White Paper for the President on the 1968 Presidential Campaign,' " no date, *Marvin Watson Files,* Box 20, Folder: DNC—Rowe–O'Brien–Criswell–Crooker Operation.

92. Ibid. (Rowe's emphasis). Interestingly, Rowe's proposal for a 1948 White House task force was at the time viewed by him and the Truman advisor who carried the proposal out, Clark Clifford, as an institutional step required by the Roosevelt revolution—by the increasing importance the New Deal legacy had bestowed upon the executive office and independent issue activists to the detriment of party. The further playing out of that legacy, and LBJ's zealous attachment to it, meant that Rowe's concern for party renewal would be viewed skeptically, if not with hostility, in 1968.

93. Peter Lisagor, "FDR Formula Called Risky for Johnson," *Chicago Daily News,* March 19, 1968, 6.

94. Memorandum, Douglas Cater to LBJ, November 17, 1967, *Office Files of the President,* Dorothy Territo, Box 10, Folder: Political, DNC.

95. George E. Reedy, *The Twilight of the Presidency* (New York: New American Library, 1970), XV.

96. Greenstein, "Nine Presidents in Search of a Modern Presidency," 330.

97. Conkin, *Big Daddy From the Pedernales,* 239.

98. Samuel P. Huntington, "The Democratic Distemper," in *The American Commonwealth: The Promise of Disharmony,* eds. Nathan Glazer and Irving Kristol (Cambridge, MA: Harvard University Press, 1981), 167–220.

99. On the Mississippi seating controversy, see Mark Stern, "Lyndon Johnson and the Democratization of the Democratic National Delegate Selection Process," paper delivered at the 1990 Annual Meeting of the American Political Science Association, San Francisco, California, August 29–September 1, 1990; and Hal F. Bass, Jr., "Presidential Party Leadership and Party Reform: Lyndon B. Johnson and the MFDP Controversy," paper delivered at the 1987 Annual of the Southwestern Political Science Association Meeting, March 18–21, Dallas.

100. For an example of the view that LBJ did not anticipate the long-term consequences of the MFDP compromise, see Stern, "Lyndon Johnson and the Democratization of the Democrats' National Convention Delegate Selection Process." It is true, of course, that Johnson did not anticipate the use that reformers would make of this rule. As we have noted, LBJ took seriously the concept of "participatory democracy," but he did not expect that it would eventually be used against him and the institution of the modern presidency.

101. Johnson was kept apprised of the DNC's activites that carried out the 1964 Convention's call for greater voter participation; given the tight reins the White House kept on the committee, these activities certainly could not have gone on without the president's approval. See Memorandum, Marvin Watson to LBJ, April 19, 1967, *Marvin Watson Files,* Box 18, Folder: Civil Rights/Negroes (2).

102. Max Frankel, "Democrats to Seat Mississippi Rebels," *New York Times,* August 21, 1968, 1, 32.

103. "Mississippi Wins," editorial, *New York Times,* August 23, 1968, 38.

104. "Disputed Delegates," editorial, *New York Times,* August 18, 1968, Section 4, 14; and Max Frankel, "Democratic Unit Lays Racial Bias to Mississippians," *New York Times,* August 19, 1968, 1, 31.

105. *Report of the Commission on the Democratic Selection of Presidential Nominees,* reprinted in *The Congressional Record,* Vol. 114, 90th Congress, 2nd Session, 1968, 31544.

106. "Floor Fight Due on Delegate Rule," August 26, 1968, *New York Times,* 23; and Tom Wicker, "Unit Rule Ended," *New York Times,* August 27, 1968, 1, 24.

107. Report of the Commission on the Democratic Selection of Presidential Nominees, 31546.

108. Austin Ranney, *Curing the Mischiefs of Faction: Party Reform in America* (Berkeley: University of California Press, 1975), 184.

109. Memorandum, James R. Jones to Marvin Watson, September 15, 1967, *Marvin Watson Files,* Box 5, Folder: Illinois–A. Daley not only impressed the Johnson adminis-

tration with his organizational abilities, but with his unflinching support for LBJ's Indo-China policy. Adlai Stevenson III was passed over by the Daley organization in his bid for the Democratic nomination for the United States Senate in 1968 when he declined to give advance approval of any action the president might take in Vietnam. Stevenson vowed his support of Johnson for re-election, but that was not enough. Stevenson was also prevented from joining Daley's slate for the Chicago convention for failing to meet the loyalty oath applied to each delegate. The Mayor required all candidates for the Illinois delegation to pledge their support for the Johnson administration's Vietnam policy. The *Washington Evening Star,* March 8, 1968; and Parmet, *The Democrats,* 251.

110. Roche interview, June 11, 1986.

111. Byron E. Shafer, *Quiet Revolution: The Struggle for the Democratic Party and the Shaping of Post-Reform Politics* (New York: Russell Sage Foundation, 1983).

112. David Truman, "Party Reform, Party Atrophy and Constitutional Change," *Political Science Quarterly* 99 (Winter 1984–1985), 639.

113. A special problem was presented by the so-called "force primary" laws of Oregon, Wisconsin, and Nebraska, where an undeclared candidate was forced to run unless he submitted an affidavidt of noncandidacy. In such states, there could be no "stand-ins" who could run for the president and protect him in case of a bad vote; consequently, as Wattenberg noted, "the old idea of an incumbent President being able to stand aloof from primaries is a good deal less valid than before." These "force primaries," moreover, made it less likely that incumbents would use "stand-ins" in other states, especially in those states considered favorable turf. Interestingly, it was the fear of doing badly in Wisconsin that encouraged the Administration to organize a write-in campaign, rather than use a stand-in, for the New Hampshire primary. "New Hampshire is the only primary before Wisconsin," Wattenberg wrote, and "you're likely to run stronger there than in Wisconsin." Memorandum, Ben Wattenberg to LBJ, December 13, 1967, *Marvin Watson Files,* Box 10, folder: Nebraska-B.

114. Ben Wattenberg to LBJ, March 13, 1968, *Marvin Watson Files,* Box 11, Folder: New Hampshire-B–Primary.

115. W. W. Rostow, Memorandum of Conversation, Participants: The President; the Vice President; Charles Murphey; W.W. Rostow, April 5, 1968, *White House Famous Names,* Box 6, Folder: Robert F. Kennedy, 1968 Campaign, Johnson Library.

116. Busby interview, June 25, 1987.

117. William S. White, "Johnson Shifts Political Burden Chiefly to His Second Term," *The Washington Post,* February 19, 1968.

118. James Ceaser, *Presidential Selection: Theory and Development* (Princeton, New Jersey: Princeton University Press, 1979), 283.

119. W. W. Rostow, Memorandum of Conversation, as cited in note 115.

120. Richard Goodwin, "Sources of the Public Unhappiness," January 4, 1969, *The New Yorker,* p. 40.

Chapter 9

1. Denis W. Brogan, "Omen for the Democrats: Tide is Beginning to Ebb," *World Journal Tribune,* November 13, 1966.

2. Theodore H. White, "The Making of the President—1972," in *Watergate and the American Political Process,* ed. Ronald E. Pynn (New York: Praeger, 1975), 109.

3. "Election Marked by Split Tickets," *The New York Times,* November 20, 1966.

4. Memorandum, George Reedy to LBJ, November 11, 1968, White House Central Files, Political Affairs (PL-2), Box 90, Folder: PL-2, 11/3/68, Lyndon Baines Johnson Library, Austin, Texas.

5. Reedy to Johnson, November 7, 1968, and attached memorandum, White House Central Files, Political Affairs (PL-2), Folder: PL-2, 11/3/68.

6. Ibid.

7. Richard Nixon, *RN: The Memoirs of Richard Nixon* (New York: Grosset and Dunlap, 1978), 352.

8. Erlichman, quoted in Richard Nathan, *The Administrative Presidency* (New York: Wiley, 1983), 30.

9. Joel D. Aberbach and Bert A. Rockman, "Clashing Beliefs within the Executive Branch," *The American Political Science Review* **LXX** (2) (June, 1976), 467.

10. Memorandum, Patrick J. Buchanan to Nixon, November 10, 1972, printed in *From: The President—Richard Nixon's Secret Files,* ed. Bruce Oudes (New York: Harper and Row, 1989), 558–59.

11. Memorandum, Roche to LBJ, July 6, 1967, *Marvin Watson Files,* Box 29, Folder: John Roche memos, Johnson Library.

12. James Gaither Oral History, interviewed by Dorothy Pierce, Tape 4, January 17, 1969, 27, Johnson Library.

13. Oudes, *From the President,* lxvi; Nixon, *Memoirs,* 681, 768. The quote was lifted exactly as it appears in Blake's book; see Robert Blake, *Disraeli* (New York: St. Martin's Press, 1967), 764. The very next sentence of the text provides a delicious description of Disraeli's flexible conservatism that penetrates to the heart of Nixon's world view: "They [politicians] know how much the art of politics lies in concealing behind a facade of rigid adherence to immutable principles those deviations or reversals which events and responsibility so often force upon government," ibid.

14. John Adams Wettergreen, "Origins of Affirmative Action," paper presented at the 1987 annual meeting of the American Political Science Association, September, Chicago, Illinois; and Herman Belz, *Affirmative Action From Kennedy to Reagan: Redefining American Equality* (Washington, D.C.: Washington Legal Foundation, 1984), 5.

15. *Public Papers of the Presidents of the United States,* Richard Nixon, 1972, 852.

16. Wettergreen, "The Origins of Affirmative Action."

17. Blake, *Disraeli,* 477. Blake attributes this saying to Lord Beavorbrook, who made it in reference to Lloyd George.

18. Barry D. Karl, *The Uneasy State* (Chicago, Illinois: University of Chicago Press, 1983), 226.

19. Richard Nixon, Television Address on the New Federalism, August 8, 1969, printed in Richard Nathan, *The Plot That Failed: Nixon and the Administrative Presidency* (New York: Wiley, 1975), 102.

20. For a summary of Nixon's New Federalism program, see Nathan, *The Plot That Failed,* Chapter 2.

21. *Public Papers of the Presidents,* Richard Nixon, 1971, 55; see also Nathan, *The Plot That Failed,* 26–29.

22. *Pubic Papers of the Presidents,* Richard Nixon, 1971, 53, 56; see also A. James Reichley, *Conservatives in an Age of Change* (Washington, D.C.: Brookings Institution, 1985), 257–59.

23. Garment quoted in Reichley, *Conservatives in an Age of Change,* 259; Nixon quoted in Joan Hoff-Wilson, "Richard M. Nixon: The Corporate Presidency," in *Leadership in the Modern Presidency,* ed. Fred I. Greenstein (Cambridge, MA: Harvard University Press, 1988), 177.

24. Louis W. Koenig, *The Chief Executive* (New York: Harcourt, Brace, Jovanovich, 1975), 3rd edition, 115.

25. Howard L. Reiter, "Purging the GOP," *Commonweal,* October 23, 1970, 71–74.

26. Ibid., 71.

27. Ibid., 72; and *New York Times,* October 7, 1970, 1.

28. *New York Times,* September 26, 1970.

29. *New York Times,* October 14, 1970, 35.

30. *New York Times,* November 13, 1970, 41.

31. "Despite the uncertainty over the president's position on Senator Goodell," the *Times* reported on October 14, "300 members of the Republican elite—including Senator Hugh Scott, the GOP leader, and Senator Robert P. Griffin, the whip, and Senator Gordon Abbott, the Chairman of the Republican policy committee—attended a fund-raising party for the Senator Monday evening at Governor Rockefeller's Washington estate." *New York Times,* October 14, 1970, 1. Vice President Agnew backed gingerly away from a direct confrontation with the moderate Scott. Senator Goodell was too strange a bedfellow for the White House, he announced, while Senator Scott was a fairly regular fellow. *New York Times,* October 7, 1970, 1.

32. *Public Papers of the Presidents,* Richard Nixon, 1970, 1107.

33. David W. Reinhard, *The Republican Right Since 1945* (Lexington: University Press of Kentucky, 1983), 221–22.

34. Clifford W. Brown, Jr. and The Ripon Society, *Jaws of Victory* (Boston: Little, Brown, 1974), 230.

35. Ibid., 231.

36. *New York Times,* March 27, 1973, 27.

37. Nixon, *Memoirs,* 415.

38. Nathan, *The Administrative Presidency,* 45.

39. Memorandum, Nixon to Erlichman, April 9, 1972, printed in Oudes, *Richard Nixon's Secret Files,* 410–11.

40. Nixon, cited in George C. Herring, *America's Longest War: The United States and Vietnam* (New York: John Wiley, 1979), 19.

41. Nixon and his national secruity advisor, Henry Kissinger, envisioned at least a limited accommodation with the Soviet Union and China. Yet he wanted to shape a policy of "detente" that would continue the United States's role as the principal power among the non-Communist nations. Nixon and Kissinger thereby believed that they had to extricate the United States from the war in a manner that would demonstrate firmness of purpose

and certainty of action, so as to earn the respect of friend and foe alike. "Ending the war, honorably," Kissinger argued, "is essential for the peace of the world. Any other solution may unloose forces that would complicate the prospects of international order." Henry A. Kissinger, "The Vietnam Negotiations," *Foreign Affairs* **47** (2) (January, 1969), 234.

42. Fred I. Greenstein, "Nine Presidents in Search of a Modern Presidency," 322. For a balanced account of Nixon's "administrative presidency," see Nathan, *The Administrative Presidency,* 43–56; on Kissinger's NSC, see John D. Leecacos, "Kissinger's Apparat," *Foreign Policy* (5) (Winter, 1971–1972): 3–27.

43. Eisenhower, cited in Stephen E. Ambrose, *Eisenhower: The President* (New York: Simon and Schuster, 1984), 673.

44. Haldeman, cited in Reichley, *Conservatives in an Age of Change,* 242.

45. Nixon, *Memoirs,* 768.

46. *Public Papers of the Presidents,* Richard Nixon, 1971, 56.

47. *New York Times,* January 6, 1973, 1; see also Nathan, *The Plot That Failed,* 68–69; and Peri Arnold, *Making the Managerial Presidency: Comprehensive Reorganization Planning, 1905–1980* (Princeton, New Jersey: Princeton University Press, 1986), 299.

48. Task Force on Government Organization, "The Organization and Management of the Great Society Programs," June 15, 1967; and "A Recommendation for the Future Organization of the Executive Branch," September 15, 1967, both reports located in *Outside Task Forces,* Box 4 Folder: Task Force on Government Organization, Johnson Library. See also, Peri Arnold, *Making the Managerial Presidency,* 268.

49. The Johnson administration was not anxious to make this report, which was not published, available to a conservative Republican administration. Since the report had not been made public, Ash, through the Nixon transition team in Washington, asked the Johnson White House for a copy; LBJ vetoed this idea, and his office denied that such a report existed. Ash, nevertheless, obtained a copy from one of the members of the Commission. See Reichley, *Conservatives in an Age of Change,* 72.

50. Koenig, *The Chief Executive,* 145.

51. "A Conversation with the President," interview with Howard K. Smith of ABC, March 22, 1971, *Public Papers of the Presidents,* Richard Nixon, 1971, 460–61.

52. Memorandum, Patrick J. Buchanan to the President, November 10, 1972, Printed in Oudes, *Richard Nixon's Secret Files,* 558–68.

53. Memorandum, Nixon to H. R. Haldeman, November 15, 1972, Printed in Oudes, *Richard Nixon's Secret Files,* 569–71.

54. Malek cited in Reichley, *Conservatives in an Age of Change,* 244–45.

55. *New York Times,* March 27, 1973, 27.

56. Ibid.; see also the Ripon Society and Clifford Brown, Jr., *The Jaws of Victory,* 231.

57. Ibid.

58. Memorandum, L. Higby to H. R. Haldeman, November 21, 1972; and "Talking Paper," H. R. Haldeman to Colson, November 22, 1972. Both printed in Oudes, *Richard Nixon's Secret Files,* 572.

59. Memorandum, Nixon to H. R. Haldeman, November 15, 1972, Printed in Oudes, *Richard Nixon's Secret Files,* 569–71.

60. Irving Louis Horowitz, "The Europeanization of American Politics," in Pynn, *Watergate and the American Political Process*, 98–99.

61. Walter Dean Burnham, *Critical Elections and the Mainsprings of American Politics* (New York: W. W. Norton, 1970); Everitt Carll Ladd, *Transformations of the American Party System* (with Charles D. Hadley), 2nd edition (New York: W. W. Norton, 1978).

62. Arthur M. Schlesinger, Jr., *The Imperial Presidency* (New York: Popular Library, 1973), 10.

63. Arnold, *Making the Managerial Presidency*, 274.

64. Samuel P. Huntington, "The Democratic Distemper," in *The American Commonwealth*, eds. Nathan Glazer and Irving Kristol (New York: Basic Books, 1976), 24.

65. Huntington develops this point most fully in his *American Politics: The Promise of Disharmony* (Cambridge, Massachusetts: Harvard University Press, 1981), 167–220.

66. R. Shep Melnick, "The Politics of Partnership," *Public Administration Review* **45** (November, 1985): 653–60.

67. For my understanding of the institutional arrangements that defined liberalism after 1968, I am indebted to R. Shep Melnick. For an especially rich and perceptive account of this development, see his "Judicial Activism Meets the New Congress: The Growth of Programmatic Rights," Paper presented for the Conference on the American Constitutional Experiment, Harvard University, March, 1987.

68. On the Democratic Study Group, see Mark F. Ferber, "The Formation of the Democratic Study Group," in *Congressional Behavior*, ed. Nelson W. Polsby (New York: Random House, 1971).

69. R. Shep Melnick, "The New Politics of Poverty: The Food Stamp Program in Congress and the Courts," paper presented at the 1990 Annual Meeting of the American Political Science Association, San Francisco, September.

70. Ibid.

71. *U.S. v. Nixon*, 418 U.S. 683 (1974).

72. Greenstein, "Nine Presidents in Search of A Modern Presidency," 334.

73. Benjamin Ginsberg and Martin Shefter, *Politics by Other Means* (New York: Basic Books, 1990), 16.

74. Reichley, *Conservatives in an Age of Change*, 259.

75. R. Shep Melnick, "The Politics of Partnership," 655.

76. On "procedural rights," see R. Shep Melnick, "The Court, Congress, and Programmatic Rights," in *Remaking American Politics*, eds. Richard A. Harris and Sidney M. Milkis (Boulder, Colorado: Westview Press, 1989), 195–98.

77. Walter A. Rosenbaum, "Public Involvement as Reform and Ritual: The Development of Federal Participation Programs," in *Citizen Participation in America: Essays on the State of the Art*, ed. Stuart Langton (Lexington, MA and Toronto: Lexington Books, 1978).

78. For a more detailed discussion of the meaning and political significance of social regulation, see Richard A. Harris and Sidney M. Milkis, *The Politics of Regulatory Change: A Tale of Two Agencies* (New York: Oxford University Press, 1989), especially Chapters 1 and 3.

79. Falk, cited in Jeffrey M. Berry, *The Interest Group Society* (Boston: Little, Brown, 1984), 36.

80. Ralph Nader, "The Case for Federal Chartering," in *The Consumer and Corporate Accountability*, ed. Nader (New York: Harcourt Brace Jovanovich, 1973), 365.

81. Michael W. McCann, "Public Interest Liberalism and the Modern Regulatory State," *Polity* **21** (2) (Winter, 1988), 389, 394.

82. Samuel Beer, "In Search of A New Public Philosophy, in *The New American Political System*, ed. Anthony King (Washington, D.C.: The American Enterprise Institute, 1979), 27–28.

83. Joseph Sax, *Defending the Environment* (New York: Vintage, 1970), 64; and McCann, "Public Interest Liberalism and the Modern State," 389.

84. The discussion of the Federal Trade Commission is drawn from a much longer account in Harris and Milkis, *The Politics of Regulatory Change,* Chapter 5.

85. An interesting description of the "entrepreneurial coalition" that gave impetus to the expansion of consumer protection is given by Michael Pertschuk. See his *Revolt Against Regulation: The Rise and Pause of the Consumer Movement* (Berkeley: University of California Press, 1982), 13–36.

86. *National Petroleum Refiners Association vs. FTC* (482 F 2d, 672, D.C. Cir., 1973).

87. Personal interview with Terry Latanich, former Assistant Director for Service Industry Practice, Bureau of Consumer Protection, Federal Trade Commission, December 17, 1982; see also Timothy J. Muris, "Statutory Powers," in *The Federal Trade Commission Since 1970: Economic Regulation and Bureaucratic Behavior,* eds. Kenneth Clarkson and Timothy J. Muris (Cambridge: Cambridge University Press, 1981), 14–15.

88. American Bar Association, *Report on the Federal Trade Commission,* 1969, 3.

89. For a list of grants made under the FTC public-intervenor program, see Hearings, Subcommittee for Consumers, Committee on Commerce, Ninety-Sixth Congress, First Session, "Oversight to Examine the Enforcement and Administrative Authority of the FTC to Regulate Unfair and Deceptive Trade Practices," September 18, 19, 27, 28; October 4, 5, 10, 1979, 158–60.

90. Barry B. Boyer, "Funding Public Participation in Agency Proceedings: The Federal Trade Commission Experience," *Georgetown Law Journal* **70** (Number 1, 1980), 71.

91. For example, in a 1972 decision involving alleged illegal trade practices by the company issuing S & H stamps, the Supreme Court ruled that "unfairness" for all intents and purposes meant what the Commission said it did (*Federal Trade Commission vs. Sperry & Hutchinson,* 405 U.S. 233).

92. See Chapter 7, note 29.

93. The discussion of the 1964 Civil Rights Act here owes to Melnick, "Judicial Activism Meets the New Congress: The Growth of Programmatic Rights."

94. Alexander Bickel, "The Civil Rights Act of 1964," *Commentary,* August, 1964, 33. As Gary Bryner has said with respect to enforcement of Title VII, "While nondiscrimination is clearly an issue within the purview of constitutional law, preferential treatment through government-imposed goals and timetables on private employers goes beyond anything provided for in the Constitution and thus should be evaluated as a political choice." Bryner, "Congress, Courts, and Agencies: Equal Employment and the Limits of Policy Implementation," *Political Science Quarterly* **93** (3) (Fall, 1981), 429.

95. See, for example, Jeremy Rabkin, *Judicial Compulsions* (New York: Basic Books, 1989).

96. Martin Shapiro, "APA: Past, Present, and Future," *Virginia Law Review* **72,** 1986, 461–62.

97. Richard B. Stewart, "The Reformation of American Administrative Law," *Harvard Law Review* **88** (8) (June, 1975), 1712. See also Melnick, "Judicial Activism Meets the New Congress: The Growth of Programmatic Rights," 20–27.

98. James Q. Wilson, "The Politics of Regulation," in ed. James Q. Wilson, *The Politics of Regulation* (New York: Basic Books, 1980), 370–71.

99. Pertschuk, *Revolt Against Regulation . . . ,* 130.

100. Allen Schick, "Congress and the 'Details of Administration,' " *Public Administration Review* **36** (September/October, 1976): 516–28; and Rabkin, *Judicial Compulsions.*

101. The legislative veto was declared unconstitutional in the case of *Immigration and Naturalization vs. Chadha,* 103 S Ct., 2764 (1983). Nevertheless, this court decision, which ostensibly represented a sweeping challenge to the current structure of the administrative state, was largely ignored by both the Congress and the Reagan administration. For example, during the ninety-eighth Congress (1983–1985), 53 legislative vetoes were added to the books. See Louis Fisher, *The Politics of Shared Power: Congress and the Executive* (Washington, D.C.: Congressional Quarterly, 1987), 2nd edition, 102. Notwithstanding this modus operandi with respect to certain policies, as Chapter 10 will show, much of the Reagan "revolution" involved a continuation of the Nixon presidency's project to seize the levers of administrative power from the liberal "establishment."

102. Jeremy Rabkin, "The Judiciary in the Administrative State," *The Public Interest,* number 71 (Spring, 1983), 63.

103. E. Donald Elliot, "INS v. Chadha: The Administrative Constitution, the Constitution, and the Legislative Veto," *Supreme Court Review,* 1983, 167.

104. Hugh Heclo, "Issue Networks and the Executive Establishment," in ed. King, *The New American Political System,* 124.

105. Franklin D. Roosevelt, *Public Papers and Addresses,* 13 volumes (New York: Random House, 1938–1950), Vol. 1, 753.

106. Ralph Nader, "A Citizens's Guide to the American Economy," in ed. Nader, *The Consumer and Corporate Accountability,* 4. It is important to recognize, of course, that not all of those active in the consumer movement endorse Nader's ardent criticism of the American political economy. For example, influential organizations such as the Consumers Union have a primary interest in testing products and informing the consumer, which, from Nader's point of view, is too limited an agenda for the consumer movement.

107. See, for example, Donald R. Brand, "Reformers of the Sixties and Seventies: Modern Anti-Federalists?," in eds. Harris and Milkis, *Remaking American Politics.*

108. Personal interview with Harry McPherson, July 30, 1985.

109. Alexis de Tocqueville, *Democracy in America* (Garden City, New York: Doubleday, 1969), 263.

110. Thus, although the expansion of administrative power has occurred in other Western democracies, one would not necessarily expect this development to affect political parties in other countries in the same way. The relationship between national and administrative power and party politics is exceptionally problematic in the United States, due both to the origins and organizing principles of political parties in the United States and to the tendency for Americans to convert all policy questions into constitutional and legal

ones. In this study, comparison is confined to historical change in elections and national governing institutions within the United States. How similar developments actually are elsewhere, and whether these developments point to similar causes, cannot be determined in this book. It is my expectation, however, that the changes analyzed herein will apply elsewhere only to the extent that political doctrines and institutional arrangements are truly similar. For a useful comparative discussion of the sort of causal factors and evidence that account for party decline in Western industrialized nations, see Howard L. Reiter, "Party Decline in the West," *Journal of Theoretical Politics* 1 (July, 1989): 325–48.

111. R. Shep Melnick, "The Politics of Partnership: Institutional Coalitions and Statutory Rights," Occasional Paper No. 84–3, Center for American Political Studies, Harvard University, 8.

112. Nixon established in the executive office of the president a "quality of life" review of regulations pertaining to environmental controls, consumer protection, and occupational and public health and safety. For certain categories of regulation, agencies were instructed to provide the OMB a summary description indicating the principal objectives of programs, as well as evidence that some consideration was given to the costs of, and alternatives to, the proposed actions. The Ford administration, in turn, required agencies to prepare, and the OMB to review, "inflation and impact" statements for major agency rules. This process was mandated by Executive Order 11821, issued on November 27, 1974, which initiated for the first time a cost–benefit policy evaluation program. Carter continued this emphasis on systematically comparing the cost and benefits of regulatory programs, requiring detailed analysis of regulatory actions and review by the executive office of the president. In early 1978, he established the Regulatory Analysis and Review Group (RARG) to manage the policy analysis mandated by Executive Order 12044. As was the case with the Nixon and Ford administrations, the focus of executive oversight was on social regulations, especially those issued by the Environmental Protection Agency and the Occupational Safety and Health Administration. Thus, during the 1970s, presidents established elaborate administrative mechanisms to control the expansion of government interference in the marketplace, with special emphasis on reducing the heavy costs generated by social regulation. For a review of these institutional developments, and how they were modified during the Reagan years, see Harris and Milkis, *The Politics of Regulatory Change*, Chapter 4.

113. Charles O. Jones, *The Trusteeship Presidency* (Baton Rouge and London: Louisiana State University Press, 1988).

114. Jimmy Carter, *Keeping Faith: Memoirs of a President* (New York: Bantam Books, 1982), 80.

115. Quoted in Jones, *The Trusteeship Presidency*, 7.

116. Erwin Hargrove, *Jimmy Carter as President: Leadership and the Politics of the Public Good* (Baton Rouge and London: Louisiana State University Press, 1988), 192.

117. The United States, Tocqueville observed, combined a due attention to national unity with a wide distribution of power. It achieved *governmental* centralization, which involved the federal government "only with a small number of matters important enough to attract its attention . . . , such as the enactment of general laws and the nation's relations with foreigners." But *administrative* centralization, involving the national authority in the details of the application of these general principles of government, was "almost unknown." Thus, in the United States "the majority, though ever increasingly absolute, [had] not enlarged the prerogatives of the central authority; it [had] only made it omnipotent

within its own sphere.'' Tocqueville, *Democracy in America*, 262. For a more detailed discussion of the distinction between governmental and administrative centralization, as well as the role of political parties in ''enforcing'' this distinction, see Chapter 2.

118. This point is made persuasively by John Marini. See his ''Bureaucracy and Constitutionalism,'' in *Constitutionalism in Perspective: The United States Constitution in Twentieth Century American Politics,* ed. Sarah Baumgartner Thurow (Lantham, Maryland: University Press of America, 1988).

119. Alonzo L. Hamby, *Liberalism and Its Challengers: FDR to Reagan* (New York: Oxford University Press, 1985), especially Chapter 6, epilogue.

Chapter 10

1. Gerald Ford, ''Imperiled, Not Imperial,'' *Time,* November 10, 1980, 30.

2. As a 1967 report on the Western Governor's Conference, prepared by the Assistant Director of the Office of Emergency Planning, informed LBJ, ''The Conference was free from partisanship with one or two exceptions. Governor Reagan in a discussion on the water issue, stated, 'Unless we decide the issue ourselves someone 3,000 miles away is going to do it.' '' Memorandum, Endicott Peabody to LBJ, July 5, 1967, *Marvin Watson Files,* Box 28, Folder: Ronald Reagan, Lyndon Johnson Library, Austin, Texas.

3. Ronald Reagan, ''A Time for Choosing,'' October 27, 1964. Printed in *Ronald Reagan Talks to America,* ed. Richard M. Scaife (Old Greenwich, Connecticut: Devin Adair, 1983), 4–5. On Reagan's rhetoric, see William K. Muir, Jr., ''Ronald Reagan: The Primacy of Rhetoric,'' in *Leadership in the Modern Presidency,* ed. Fred I. Greenstein (Cambridge, MA: Harvard University Press, 1988).

4. ''Inaugural Address of Ronald Reagan,'' January 20, 1981. Printed in Richard Nathan, *The Administrative Presidency* (New York: Wiley, 1983), 159.

5. *New York Times,* July 20, 1980, E20.

6. William E. Leuchtenburg, *In the Shadow of FDR: From Harry Truman to Ronald Reagan,* revised edition (Ithaca and London: Cornell University Press, 1985), 210.

7. Personal interview with Congressman Dana Rohrabacher, former speech writer, Reagan administration, July 31, 1989. On Coolidge's presidency, see Sidney M. Milkis and Michael Nelson, *The American Presidency: Origins and Development, 1776–1990* (Washington, D.C.: Congressional Quarterly, 1990), 247–51.

8. *Public Papers of the Presidents of the United States: Ronald Reagan,* 1983, Vol. 1 (Washington, D.C.: Government Printing Office, 1984), 364; see also Muir, ''Ronald Reagan: The Primacy of Rhetoric,'' 273–78.

9. Personal interview with Philip Kawior, Director of Research Division, Republican National Committee, June 3, 1986.

10. Ibid.; Thomas E. Cavanaugh and James L. Sundquist, ''The New Two Party System,'' in *The New Direction in American Politics,* eds. John E. Chubb and Paul E. Peterson (Washington, D.C.: Brookings Institution, 1985), 43–48.

11. Ronald Reagan, ''Remarks of the President to the 12th Annual Conservative Political Action Conference,'' March 1, 1985, mimeocopy provided to the author by the White House. The Research Director of the Republican National Committee noted in 1986 that in considering Reagan's impact on the party, it was useful to compare his triumph in 1984

with Nixon's in 1972. "In both years," he suggested, "the Democratic ticket was flawed. . . . But in 1984, unlike 1972, the message of the Republican party prevailed. . . . I would stress that it was not the messenger but the message that triumphed. The election of 1984 was not a matter of personality." Kawior interview, June 3, 1986.

12. Ronald Reagan, State of the Union Address, February 6, 1985, Transcript in *New York Times,* February 7, 1985, B8.

13. A. James Reichley, "The Rise of National Parties," in eds. Chubb and Peterson, *The New Direction in American Politics,* 191–95.

14. Ibid., 195–200; Cornelius P. Cotter and John F. Bibby, "Institutionalization of Parties and the Thesis of Party Decline," *Political Science Quarterly* **95** (Spring, 1980): 1–27; Joseph A. Schlesinger, "The New American Party System," *American Political Science Review* **79** (December, 1985): 1152–69; Michael Nelson, "The Case for the Current Nominating Process," in *Before Nomination,* ed. George Grassmuck (Washington, D.C.: American Enterprise Institute, 1985); Larry Sabato, *The Party's Just Begun* (Glenview, IL: Scott, Foresman, 1988); and Paul S. Herrnson, *Party Campaigns in the 1980s* (Cambridge, MA: Harvard University Press, 1988).

15. For a detailed look at Reagan's programs of New Federalism and Regulatory Relief, see Richard A. Harris and Sidney M. Milkis, *The Politics of Regulatory Change: A Tale of Two Agencies* (New York: Oxford University Press, 1989), especially Chapters 1, 4, and 7.

16. Rhodes Cook, "Reagan Nurtures His Adopted Party to Strength," *Congressional Quarterly Weekly Report,* September 28, 1985, 1927–30.

17. Reichley, "The Rise of National Parties," 181, 189.

18. Howell Raines, "Laxalt and Political Ally Chosen For G.O.P. Posts," *New York Times,* January 9, 1983, 10; Steven V. Roberts, "Packwood Loses Party Job in the Senate," *New York Times,* December 3, 1982, 19.

19. Personal interview with Frank Fahrenkopf, July 27, 1987.

20. David S. Broder, "A Party Leader Who Works At It, *Boston Globe,* October 21, 1985, 14. Personal interview with Mitchell E. Daniels, Assistant to the President for Political and Governmental Affairs, June 5, 1986.

21. Brock considered it significant that Reagan had "converted" to the Republican party. "There is something about that act," he observed, "that leads to strong party loyalty." Personal interview with Secretary William Brock, Department of Labor, August 12, 1987. Brock, himself, was a convert, having switched from the Democratic to Republican party in 1960.

22. Cotter and Bibby, "Institutional Development of Parties . . . ," 25.

23. *New York Times,* June 14, 1980, A1.

24. Brock interview, August 12, 1987.

25. Leon D. Epstein, *Political Parties in the American Mold* (Madison: The University of Wisconsin Press, 1986), 225.

26. Personal interview with William I. Greener III, June 4, 1986.

27. Personal interview with Congressman Newt Gingrich, July 26, 1988.

28. Personal interview with Congressman Connie Mack, June 23, 1987.

29. *Washington Post,* December 2, 1984, D8. On the Conservative Opportunity Society and the Republican party, see John J. Pitney, Jr., "The Conservative Opportunity

Society,'' unpublished manuscript, Department of Government, Claremont McKenna College.

30. The Reagan re-election campaign, relying on soft-focus issues—"It's Morning Again"—rather than sharp issue stands disappointed many conservatives. But the COS, through its White House liaison Newt Gingrich, managed some victories. For example, it defended the president's stand against raising taxes in the face of opposition from people such as Kansas Senator Robert Dole and Chief of Staff James Baker. The result was a Republican platform plank that opposed "any attempts to increase taxes, which would harm the recovery." An earlier draft had ommitted the comma, thereby implying that some new taxes could be acceptable. Gingrich interview, July 26, 1988; personal interview with Congressman Vin Weber, June 26, 1987. See also Douglas A. Jeffre and Dennis Teti, "A Political Party in Search of Itself," in *The 1984 Election and the Future of American Politics,* eds. Peter W. Schramm and Dennis Mahoney (Durham, NC: Carolina Academic Press, 1987), 59–60.

31. Alan Ehrenhalt, "Changing South Perils Conservative Coalition," *Congressional Quarterly Weekly Report,* August 1, 1987, 1704.

32. Richard B. Stewart, "The Reformation of American Administrative Law," *Harvard Law Review* 88 (June, 1975): 1669–813.

33. Wilson Carey McWilliams, "Parties as Civic Associations," in *Party Renewal in America,* ed. Gerald Pomper (New York: Praeger, 1980), 52.

34. Reichley, "The Rise of National Parties," 199. By the end of the 1980s, Reichley was much less hopeful that the emergent national parties were well suited to perform the parties' historic function of mobilizing public support for political values and substantive governmental approaches and policies. See his richly detailed study, *The Life of the Parties: A History of American Political Parties* (New York: The Free Press, 1992), especially Chapters 18–21.

35. Fahrenkopf interview, July 27, 1987.

36. Robert Kuttner, *The Life of the Party: Democratic Prospects in 1988 and Beyond* (New York: The Viking Press, 1987), 72–88.

37. Representative Price, as quoted in Rhodes Cook, "Pressed by Jackson Demands, Dukakis Yields on Party Rules," *Congressional Quarterly Weekly Report,* July 2, 1988, 179. In September, 1989 the Democratic National Committee voted to rescind the part of the Jackson–Dukakis agreement concerning the cutback in "superdelegate" seats, but the proportional requirement was retained. See Rhodes Cook, "Democratic Party Rules Changes Readied for '92 Campaign." *Congressional Quarterly Weekly Report,* March 17, 1990, 847–49. For scholarly treatments of the relationship between the candidate-centered presidential selection process and "dealignment" in the electorate, see Stephen A. Salmore and Barbara G. Salmore, "Candidate Centered Parties: Politics without Intermediaries," in *Remaking American Politics,* eds. Richard A. Harris and Sidney M. Milkis (Boulder, CO: Westview Press, 1989); and Martin Wattenberg, "From a Partisan to a Candidate-Centered Electorate," in *The New American Political System,* second version, ed. Anthony King (Washington, D.C.: The AEI Press, 1990).

38. See, for example, Walter Dean Burnham, "Elections As Democratic Institutions," in *Elections in America,* ed. Kay Schlozman (Boston: Allen and Unwin, 1987), 58–60; and Robert Kuttner, "Fat and Sassy," *The New Republic,* February 3, 1987, 21–23.

39. Personal interview with Loren Smith, June 23, 1987.

40. Brock interview, August 12, 1987.

41. Fahrenkopf interview, July 27, 1987; and Fahrenkopf, Statement on the 1991 Plan, Republican National Committee, 1987.

42. Personal interview with Joseph Gaylord, June 3, 1986.

43. "[N]o countries need associations more . . . than those with a democratic social state," wrote Tocqueville. "In aristocratic nation's secondary bodies form *natural* associations which hold abuses in check. In countries, where such associations do not exist, if private people do not *artificially* and temporarily create something like them, I see no other dyke to hold back tyranny of any sort, and a great nation might with impunity be oppressed by some tiny faction or by a single man." Alexis de Tocqueville, *Democracy in America,* ed. by J. P. Mayer, translated by George Lawrence (Garden City, NY: Doubleday and Co., 1969), 192 (my emphasis).

44. On the continuing importance of state parties within a more national party system, see John F. Bibby, "Party Organization at the State Level," in *The Parties Respond,* ed. L. Sandy Maisel (Boulder, CO: Westview Press, 1990). A considerably less optimistic note about state and local parties is sounded by Reichley, *The Life of the Party: A History of American Political Parties,* Chapters 19 and 20.

45. James W. Ceaser, "The Reagan Presidency and American Public Opinion," In *The Reagan Legacy,* ed. Charles Jones (Chatham, NJ: Chatham House Publishers, 1989), 201.

46. *Report of the Congressional Committees Investigating the Iran–Contra Affair,* with supplemental, minority, and additional views, House Report No. 100–433, Senate Report No. 100–216, 100th Congress, 1st Session, November 13, 1987, 501.

47. *Report of the Congressional Committees Investigating the Iran–Contra Affair,* 515. The split among those who served on the House and Senate select committees was highly partisan, albeit not completely so. Three Republican Senators lent their signatures to the majority document, which was far more condemning of the administration's actions: Senator Warren Rudman, New Hampshire; Senator William S. Cohen, Maine; and Senator Paul Tribble of Virginia. The House committee divided strictly along party lines.

48. Benjamin Ginsberg and Martin Shefter, *Politics by Other Means: The Declining Importance of Elections in America* (New York: Basic Books, 1990), Chapter 5.

49. Bert A. Rockman, "The Style and Organization of the Reagan Presidency," in Jones, *The Reagan Legacy,* 10.

50. For an examination of Reagan's regulatory program that addresses the question of realignment, see Harris and Milkis, *The Politics of Regulatory Change. . . .*

51. Dick Kirschten, "Administration Using Carter-Era Reform to Manipulate the Levers of Government," *National Journal,* April 9, 1983, 732–36; Richard Nathan, *The Administrative Presidency* (New York: Wiley, 1983), 76, 77–78; Joel D. Aberbach and Bert A. Rockman, with Robert Copeland, "From Nixon's Problem to Reagan's Achievement: The Federal Executive Reexamined," in *Looking Back on the Reagan Presidency,* ed. Larry Berman (Baltimore and London: Johns Hopkins University Press, 1990).

52. Kirschten, "Administration Using Carter-Era Reform to Manipulate the Levers of Government," 733.

53. For a detailed discussion of Reagan's personnel policies, see Harris and Milkis, *The Politics of Regulatory Change,* Chapter 4. See also The Report of the National Commission of the Public Service and the Task Force Reports to the National Commission on the Public Service (Paul A. Volker, Chairman), *Leadership For America* (Lexington, MA: D. C. Heath, 1989), especially 213–42.

54. Sidney Blumenthal, *The Rise of the Counterestablishment: From Conservative Ideology to Political Power* (New York: Times Books, 1986), 9.

55. Brock interview, August 12, 1987.

56. Alan Ehrenhalt, "Failed Campaign Cost Republicans the Senate," *Congressional Quarterly Weekly Report,* November 8, 1986, 2803.

57. Background information for the discussion of the 1986 campaign was obtained through a number of interviews with RNC staff, as well as GOP members of Congress. Many of those interviewed requested anonymity.

58. Personal interview with Vin Weber, July 28, 1987. Weber's disgruntlement about the 1986 campaign cannot be dismissed as the dissent of an ideological conservative. A similar sentiment was lodged by more pragmatic Republicans, including Bill Brock, who said of the midterm campaign effort: "In the 1986 election we may have snatched defeat from the jaws of victory. The White House was part of a conscious decision that we would not run as a party in 1986. This is an old story—when Republicans run as individuals, we lose. There is a potential Republican majority in this country, and its time these 'experts' [in the White House] understood this." Brock interview, August 12, 1987.

59. Ronald Reagan, "Remarks at a Rally for Senator James T. Broyhill," October 28, 1986, *Weekly Compilation of Presidential Documents,* November 3, 1986, 1476. "When a house is messy, its residents welcome a cleanup crew," Ehrenhalt observed about the president's campaign speeches. "When the place is clean again, they thank the crew, pay them, and let them leave. If a crew wants to stay, it has to offer reasons why it is still needed." Ehrenhalt, "Failed Campaign Cost the Republicans the Senate," 2803, 2871.

60. House of Representatives, Committee on Appropriations, *Views and Estimates on the Budget Proposed for Fiscal Year 1983,* 97th Congress, 2nd session (Committee Print, 1982), 12.

61. David Stockman, *The Triumph of Politics: Why the Reagan Revolution Failed* (New York: Harper and Row, 1986), 159.

62. Jeffrey Tulis, *The Rhetorical Presidency* (Princeton, NJ: Princeton University Press, 1983), 197.

63. James P. Pfiffner, *The President and Economic Policy* (Philadelphia: Institute for the Study of Human Issues, 1986), 122.

64. William Greider, *The Education of David Stockman and Other Americans* (New York: Dutton, 1982), 23. See also Stockman, *The Triumph of Politics,* 79–99.

65. James M. Perry and David Shribman, "Reagan Era Restored Faith in Government Until Recent Slippage," *Wall Street Journal,* November 30, 1987, 1, 13; see also William Schneider, "The Political Legacy of the Reagan Years," in *The Reagan Legacy,* eds. Sidney Blumenthal and Thomas Byrne Edsall (New York: Pantheon Books, 1988); Walter Dean Burnham, "The Reagan Heritage," in *The Election of 1988: Reports and Interpretations,* ed. Gerald M. Pomper (Chatham, NJ: Chatham House, 1989).

66. Ronald Reagan, "Remarks to Administration Officials on Domestic Policy," December 13, 1988, *Weekly Compilation of Presidential Documents,* Vol. 24, no. 50, 1619. The phrase *iron triangle* had been used by practitioners and scholars since the advent of the New Deal to describe the vitiation of representative government by particular interests. Reagan's use of the term was the first to elevate the press to full triangularity. Hitherto the triangle of institutions denounced in political science texts and popular lore had been described as an alliance of executive bureaus, congressional committees, and interest groups,

all linked together in a sort of closed-door conspiracy to maintain and expand particular programs. The importance of the media's role in Reagan's analysis testifies both to the reformation of administrative politics in the late 1960s and 1970s and the president's failure to come to terms with this change.

67. Harris and Milkis, *The Politics of Regulatory Change,* especially Chapter 7; Merrick B. Garland, "Deregulation and Judicial Review," *Harvard Law Review* (January, 1985): 507–91.

Chapter 11

1. Morris Fiorina, *Congress: Keystone of the Washington Establishment,* 2nd edition (New Haven: Yale University Press, 1989), 164, no. 27; see also Benjamin Ginsberg and Martin Shefter, *Politics by Other Means* (New York: Basic Books, 1990), Chapter 1.

2. See, for example, Sundquist, "The New Era of Coalition Government in the United States"; and Committee on the Constitutional System, *A Bicentennial Analysis of the American Political Structure* (Washington, D.C.: Committee on the Constitutional System, 1987).

3. James Sterling Young and Russel L. Riley, "Party Government and Political Culture," paper presented at the American Political Science Association Meeting, San Francisco, California, September 1990, 6.

4. Personal interview, comments not for attribution.

5. Young and Riley, "Party Government and Political Culture," 39.

6. *Weekly Compilation of Presidential Documents,* July 6, 1987, Vol. 23, no. 26, 764–68.

7. Phone conversation with Martin Anderson, Senior Fellow, the Hoover Institution, former Special Assistant to the President for Policy Development (1981–1982), August 9, 1987. Interestingly, Anderson was not aware that Roosevelt had called for an economic bill of rights. It fell to Dana Rohrabacher, the White House speech writer who drafted the Economic Bill of Rights address, to make this connection in 1987, when he was given the responsibility to write the bicentennial address. One might say, therefore, that for much of its tenure, the Reagan administration did not know what it was up against. Personal interviews with Congressman Dana Rohrabacher, former speech writer for the Reagan White House, August 11, 1987 and July 31, 1989.

8. David M. O'Brien, "The Reagan Judges: His Most Enduring Legacy?" *The Reagan Legacy,* ed. Charles Jones (Chatham, NJ: Chatham House Publishers, 1989).

9. John Marini, "The Political Conditions of Legislative–Bureaucratic Supremacy," *The Claremont Review of Books,* Spring, 1988. There was also disagreement among conservatives concerning the role of the courts. While Bork defended a position of judicial restraint, other conservatives favored an activist court that would protect property rights, and a few advocated the renewal of a concept of natural rights that could clearly be distinguished from interests. See, for example, Stephen Macedo, *The New Right v. The Constitution* (Washington, D.C.: The Cato Institute, 1987). Thus, just as New Dealers were divided about whether to limit the power of the court or remake it, conservatives have disagreed about whether to enlist judicial support for their program. The condition of divided political realms in the 1980s, however, made the issue a more immediate problem for those seeking a right turn than it was for New Dealers during the 1930s. As the judicial

scholar Walter Murphy has observed, Reagan's hope to reshape the long-term course of public policy depended partly upon his judicial appointees' willingness to disregard his legal philosophy of judicial restraint: "It is shrewd for a president who brings about an electoral realignment to select judges who will defer to his new majority. If, however, a president fails to carry out such a realignment—and in this respect, Reagan failed badly— then his substantive policy goals might well be better served by judges who share those goals but are less than pure in their commitment to judicial deference to legislative decisions." Walter Murphy, "Reagan's Judicial Strategy," in *Looking Back on the Reagan Presidency,* ed. Larry Berman (Baltimore and London: Johns Hopkins University Press, 1990), 230.

10. In *Grove City* the Court ruled 6–3 that when an institution receives federal aid, only the "program or activity" actually getting the aid—not the entire institution—was covered by the laws. The civil rights restoration law passed over President Reagan's veto stated that federal anti-discrimination statutes apply to an institution in its entirety if it accepts federal aid for as little as one program. *Grove City College v. Bell,* 79 L. Ed. 2d 516, 1984; Mark Willen, "Congress Overrides Reagan's Grove City Veto," *Congressional Quarterly Weekly Report,* March 26, 1988, 774–76. The congressional vote did not fall strictly along party lines. Twenty-one Republican Senators joined 52 Democrats to override the president's veto, reflecting the sensitivity of the civil rights issue. The vote in the House was much more partisan, however, with 240 Democrats and 52 Republicans voting to override the veto, while 123 Republicans and 10 Democrats voted to sustain it. As has been the case with other conflicts over the proper definition of "new" rights, partisanship was stoked by extensive lobbying by liberal and conservative public advocacy groups. See Irvin Molotsky, "House and Senate Vote to Override Reagan on Rights," *New York Times,* March 23, 1988, 1.

11. Harvey C. Mansfield, Jr., "The 1984 American Election: Entitlements Versus Opportunity," *Government and Opposition,* Vol. 20 (Winter, 1985), 17.

12. *New York Times,* March 4, 1988, A1, B8.

13. Michael Nelson, "Constitutional Aspects of the Elections," in *The Elections of 1988,* ed. Nelson (Washington, D.C.: Congressional Quarterly Press, 1989), 192.

14. Ibid., 191–92.

15. The Democrats gained three seats in the House, one in the Senate, one governorship, and more than a dozen seats in the state legislatures.

16. Walter Dean Burnham, "The Reagan Heritage." in *The Election of 1988: Reports and Interpretations,* ed. Gerald M. Pomper (Chatham, NJ: Chatham Publishing Company, 1989), 27–28.

17. Interview with Kenneth Duberstein, August 3, 1989.

18. Interview with Newt Gingrich, July 26, 1988.

19. "Inaugural address of George Walker Herbert Bush," printed in Pomper, *The Election of 1988,* 209–10.

20. Eisenach, as quoted in Burt Solomon, "Bush's Zeal for Partisan Duties Tempered by His Bipartisan Style," *National Journal,* October 28, 1989, 2651.

21. Solomon, "Bush's Zeal," 2651.

22. Interview with Mary Matalin, Chief of Staff for Lee Atwater, August 4, 1989; and Solomon, "Bush's Zeal for Partisan Duties . . . ," 2651.

23. Philip Kawior, head of the Research Division, Republican National Committee,

"The State of the GOP: A Review of Recent Polling Data," February, 1990. Mimeo copy provided to the author by the Republican National Committee.

24. On the budget battles of 1990, see Barbara Sinclair, "Bush and the 101st Congress," in *The Bush Presidency: First Appraisals,* eds. Colin Campbell, S. J. and Bert Rockman (Chatham, NJ: Chatham House, 1991), 174–83.

25. Harold F. Bass, "George Bush: Party Leader," paper delivered at the 1991 Annual Meeting of the American Political Science Association, Washington, D.C., 10–11.

26. Burt Solomon, "In Atwater's Absence, Sununu Is Bush's Top Political Advisor," *National Journal,* June 23, 1990, 1554–55.

27. Jack Pitney, letter to the author, August 12, 1991.

28. Bass, "George Bush: Party Leader," 13–14.

29. Interview with Frank Fahrenkopf, former head of the Republican National Committee, July 26, 1991; James A. Barnes, "Back to Square One," November 10, 1990, *National Journal,* 2704–09.

30. Edwin J. Feulner, "Building the New Establishment," interview by Adam Meyerson, printed in *Policy Review,* Fall, 1990, 10.

31. George C. Edwards III, "George Bush and the Public Presidency: The Politics of Inclusion," in Campbell and Rockman, *The Bush Presidency,* 138.

32. Richard M. Pious, "Prerogative Power and the Reagan Presidency: A Review Essay," *Political Science Quarterly* **106** (3) (Fall, 1991), 510.

33. Clarence Thomas, "Toward a 'Plain Reading' of the Constitution—the Declaration of Independence in Constitutional Interpretation," *Howard Law Journal* **30,** 1987, 691–703.

34. Joan Biskupic, "Thomas' Victory Puts Icing on Reagan–Bush Court," *Congressional Quarterly Weekly Report,* October 19, 1991, 3033.

35. Ibid., 3026.

36. *Willie S. Griggs v. Duke Power Company,* 401 U.S. 424 (1971); *Wards Cove Packing Company v. Frank Atonio,* 490 U.S. 642 (1989).

37. Pamela Fessler, with Joan Biskupic, "Rights Bill Rises from the Ashes of the Senate's Thomas Fight," *Congressional Quarterly Weekly Report,* October 26, 1991, 3125.

38. Jonathan Rauch, "The Regulatory President," *National Journal,* November 30, 1991, 2902–06.

39. Joan Biskupic, "Bush Signs Anti-Job Bias Bill amid Furor over Preferences," *Congressional Quarterly Weekly Report,* November 23, 1991, 3463.

40. "Statement on the Signing of the Civil Rights Act of 1991," November 21, 1991, *Weekly Compilation of Presidential Documents,* November 25, 1991, Vol. 27, Number 47, 1702.

41. Biskupic, "Bush Signs Anti-Job Bias Bill Amid Furor over Preferences," 3463.

42. OMB Watch, "President Bush's Regulatory Moratorium," *OMB Watch Alert,* January 24, 1992.

43. Interview with Newt Gingrich, July 25, 1991.

44. Although reiterating his own formal opposition to abortion, Bush pledged his active support to several Republican candidates in the 1990 elections who were supporters of

abortion rights. Robin Toner, "GOP Blurs Abortion Focus, Dismaying Some in the Party," *New York Times,* January 18, 1990, A1, B6.

45. *Rust v. Sullivan,* No. 89-1391; Linda Greenhouse, "5 Justices Uphold U.S. Rule Curbing Abortion Advice," *New York Times,* May 24, 1991, A1, A18–A19.

Chapter 12

1. Walter Dean Burnham, *Critical Elections and the Mainsprings of American Politics* (New York: W. W. Norton, 1970), 188–89.

2. James Piereson, "Party Government," *The Political Science Reviewer* **12** (Fall, 1982), 46.

3. Charles Edward Merriam, "The Written Constitution and Unwritten Attitude," in *The Party Battle* (New York: Arno Press, 1974), 85.

4. Barry D. Karl, *The Uneasy State* (Chicago: Chicago University Press, 1983), 223.

5. Barry D. Karl, "The Constitution and Central Planning Revisited," *The Supreme Court Review, 1988,* eds. Philip Kurland, Gerhard Casper, and Dennis J. Hutchinson (Chicago and London: The University of Chicago Press, 1989).

6. Robert Eden, "Introduction: A Legacy of Questions," in *The New Deal and Its Legacy: Critique and Reappraisal,* ed. Eden (New York: Greenwood Press, 1989), 20.

7. Robert K. Murray and Tim H. Blessing, "The Presidential Performance Study: A Progress Report," *The Journal of American History* **70** (3) (December, 1983), 539–41; Alonzo L. Hamby, "Harry S. Truman: Insecurity and Responsibility," in *Leadership in the Modern Presidency,* ed. Fred I. Greenstein (Cambridge, MA: Harvard University Press, 1988), 41.

8. Hugh Heclo, "Issue Networks and the Executive Establishment," in *The New American Political System,* ed. Anthony King (Washington, D.C.: American Enterprise Institute, 1978).

9. Alexis de Tocqueville, *Democracy in America,* ed. J. P. Mayer (New York: Doubleday, 1969), 638.

10. Marvin Myers, *The Jacksonian Persuasion* (Stanford, CA: Stanford University Press, 1957), Chapter 3.

11. Lincoln's use of this phrase appears in " 'Secession' or 'Rebellion,' " Message to Special Session of Congress, July 4, 1861, *The Political Thought of Abraham Lincoln,* ed. Richard N. Current (Indianapolis: Bobbs–Merrill, 1967), 187–88.

12. Morton Keller, *Affairs of State: Public Life in Late Nineteenth Century America* (Cambridge, MA: Harvard University Press, 1977), 258.

13. Samuel P. Huntington, *American Politics: The Promise of Disharmony* (Cambridge, MA: Harvard University Press, 1981), Chapter 5.

14. John Dewey, "A Liberal Speaks Out," *The New York Times Magazine,* February 23, 1936, 3, 24.

15. Some scholars claim that "critical realignment theory" has not been able to account for what has happened over the past generation in American politics. See, for example, *The End of Realignment?—Interpreting American Electoral Eras,* ed. Byron E. Shafer (Madison, WI: University of Wisconsin Press, 1991). But none of them identifies

the New Deal as a critical event in bringing secular changes that would make future realignments unlikely—a realignment to end realignments.

16. Robert Eden, "Partisanship and Constitutional Revolution: The Framers' View Is Newly Problematic," in *Constitutionalism in Perspective: The United States Constitution in Twentieth Century Politics,* ed. Sarah Baumgartner Thurow (Lanham, NY, and London: University Press of America, 1988).

17. Alexander Hamilton, James Madison, and John Jay, *The Federalist Papers* (New York: New American Library, 1961), 426–27.

18. Thomas Jefferson to James Madison, September 6, 1789, Printed in *The Portable Thomas Jefferson,* ed. Merril D. Peterson (New York: The Viking Press, 1975), 444–51.

Postscript

1. See, for example, Theodore J. Lowi, "The Part Crasher," *The New York Times Magazine,* August 23, 1992, 28, 33.

2. Paul Starobin, "President Perot?" *National Journal,* July 4, 1992, 1567–1572.

3. William Schneider, "A Loud Vote for Change," *National Journal,* November 7, 1992, 2544.

4. Ibid.

5. Gary Wills, "Can Clinton Close the Vision Gap? " *New York Times,* November 8, 1992, Section 4, 17.

6. Schneider, "A Loud Vote for Change," 2542, and James A. Barnes, "Tainted Triumph?" *Ibid.* 2537–2541.

7. Bill Clinton, "The New Covenant: Responsibility and Rebuilding the American Community," speech delivered at Georgetown University, October 23, 1991. For a detailed discussion of the Commonwealth Club Address, see Chapter 2.

8. These ideas, and attendant policy proposals, are spelled out in detail in Will Marshall and Martin Schram, eds., *Mandate for Change* (New York: Berkley Books, 1993).

9. For an analysis of this political crisis that focuses on policy, see Marc Landy and Martin Levin, eds., *The New Politics of Public Policy Making* (Baltimore: Johns Hopkins University Press, forthcoming).

Index